WHAT'S COOKING

Mexican

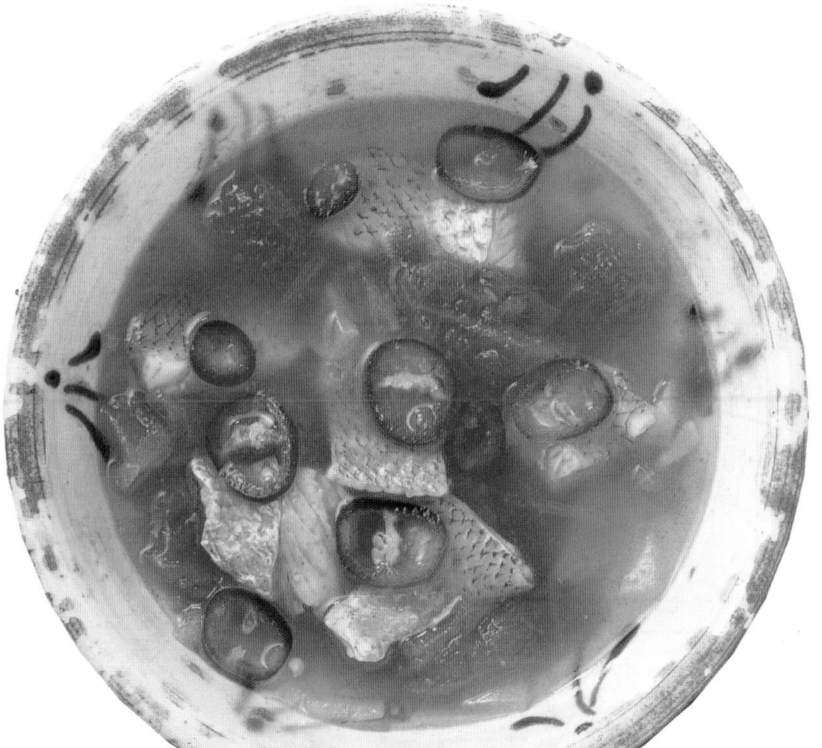

Marlena Spieler

p

This is a Parragon Book
First published in 2000

Parragon
Queen Street House
4 Queen Street
Bath BA1 1HE, UK

ISBN: 0-75253-520-X (Hardback)
ISBN: 0-75254-036-X (Paperback)

Printed in Singapore

ACKNOWLEDGEMENTS

Editorial Consultant: Felicity Jackson
Photography: Colin Bowling, Paul Forrester and Stephen Brayne
Home Economist and Stylist: Vicki Smallwood

All props supplied by Barbara Stewart at Surfaces.

NOTE

Cup measurements in this book are for American cups. All-purpose flour is measured in scooped cups. Tablespoons are assumed to be 15ml. Unless otherwise stated, milk is assumed to be full fat, eggs are medium and pepper is freshly ground black pepper.

Recipes using uncooked eggs should be avoided by infants, the elderly, pregnant women and anyone suffering from an illness.

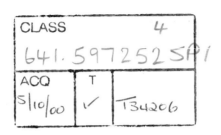

Contents

Introduction

The cuisine of Mexico is a diverse and extraordinary cuisine, a complex layering of cultures, starting with the ancient Indian civilizations and built upon by the Spanish conquest as well as other European rulers and influences.

The soul of Mexican food lies in its ancient roots: Aztec, Toltec, Zapotec, Ohnec and Mayan. Deeply coloured, complex, rich sauces made of mild and hot chillies, seeds, herbs and vegetables are as ancient as the cultures from which they come. Long-stewed meats, such as the Spanish contribution of pork, figure prominently in the Mexican kitchen; the broth that comes about through the cooking makes soups that fuel everyday life and add flavour and depth to dishes of beans, rice and stews. Fish from the coastlines that cover thousands of miles and define the shape of the country, are eaten cloaked with spicy pastes, splashed with chillies, wrapped in tortillas or fragrant leaves.

Over this ancient cuisine of indigenous foods and techniques lies a veneer of Spanish propriety and European tradition, as well as the imports from Spain: wheat (for those flour tortillas and the crusty bread rolls, bolillos), domesticated animals whose milk added cheese to the menu, and the pig! With the abundant fat provided by the pig, frying became possible, adding a new dimension to the cooking methods.

TORTILLAS

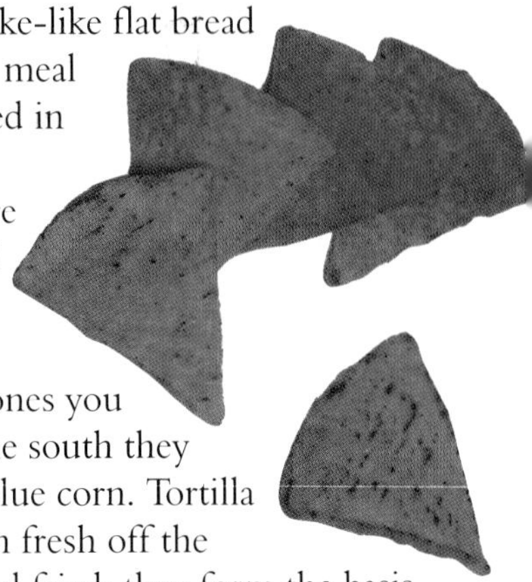

The tortilla – a thin pancake-like flat bread – is eaten for nearly every meal throughout Mexico. Served in the same way as bread to accompany dishes, they are also wrapped around food as an eating utensil.

In the north, wheat or flour tortillas will be the ones you will find most often; in the south they will be corn, sometimes blue corn. Tortilla may be tiny or huge, eaten fresh off the griddle (*comal*) or filled and fried; they form the basis of the foods of Mexico.

Wrapped around any filling, a corn tortilla becomes a taco, a flour tortilla a burrito. Fresh and warm, a corn tortilla is a soft taco, fried to a crisp it is a crisp taco. A flat crisply fried tortilla is a tostada – top them with a layer of warm refried beans, cheese, pickled chillies or salsa, salad and morsels of meat or vegetables.

Stale corn tortillas are never thrown away in the frugal Mexican kitchen, and the cuisine is all the better for it: dipped into spicy sauces then rolled around various fillings they make the wonderful casserole that is called enchiladas, or fried and layered with sauce they are called chilaquiles.

Most of us are familiar with tortilla chips – at their best when freshly made from stale corn tortillas, but also widely available in packets.

BEANS

Beans, too, are basic, with rice and chillies. In every marketplace café (*fonda*) and home kitchen, you'll find pots and *cazuelas* of simmering beans, ready to be eaten in all of their guises, or just from a bowl with a few tortillas to roll around them to satisfy hunger.

Throughout Mexico, the types of beans vary delightfully, from the tender pale pink beans of the north, such as pinto, to the inky black beans of the south. Beans that are puréed and cooked in fat and spices are called refried beans, though they are not really fried at all, merely cooked down to an intense paste in a puddle of (traditional) lard or (contemporary) vegetable oil.

CHILLIES

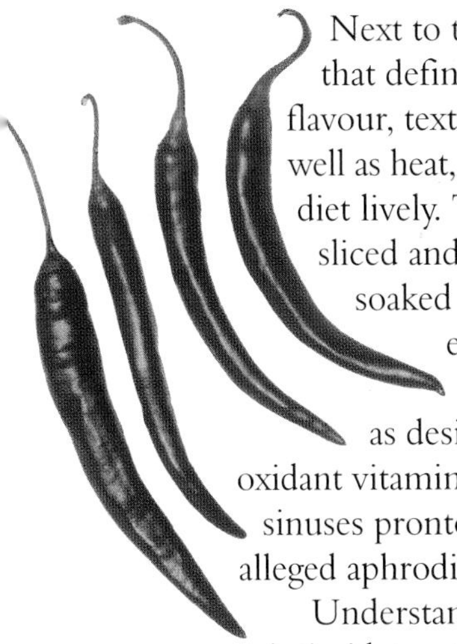

Next to tortillas and beans, it is chillies that define Mexican food. They offer flavour, textures, colours and aromas as well as heat, and keep the often monotonous diet lively. They are eaten raw and cooked, sliced and stewed, stuffed and puréed, soaked and fried, and are eaten at every meal, usually in the form of a salsa to spoon on as desired. They are rich in anti-oxidant vitamins and will clear your sinuses pronto, not to mention their alleged aphrodisiac qualities.

Understandably, chillies can intimidate – they can be searingly hot, and should be added a little at a time.

Mild chillies are usually eaten red and dried, though Mexicans also dote on crushed hot red chillies – usually a dried cayenne. Mild chillies, such as pasilla, ancho, mulatto and negro, make up the distinctive flavourful mixture sold simply on our spice shelf as 'mild chilli powder'.

Most fresh chillies are hot and hotter. Jalapeño are probably most often eaten, a good all purpose little chilli with a nice fiery heat and delicious flavour. Serrano is another popular fresh chilli. In the Caribbean region habanero and Scotch bonnet peppers add their distinctive fire.

Two milder chillies, the anaheim and poblano are utterly delicious eaten stuffed, as you would a pepper; if unavailable, use ordinary green peppers, roasted and marinated with a chopped fresh hot chilli or two to enliven them.

Bottled hot seasonings are ubiquitous, too; you'll find one on practically every table as well as kitchen shelf: a nice jolt of tangy fire for those who dare.

OTHER FLAVOURINGS

Mexican spicing, however, is not limited to chillies: cinnamon, cloves, black pepper, cocoa powder and especially cumin are used with enthusiasm, as are the herbs of oregano, marjoram, mint, epazote and fresh coriander (cilantro). Roasted onion and whole garlic cloves are often crushed to form the basis of a sauce, and wedges of lime or lemon are served with soups, meats, fish, almost everything, Mediterranean–style.

MEXICAN STYLE

Meals in Mexico are a never ending fiesta. The main meal, the *comida corrida*, is served Spanish style, in the afternoon. Breakfast may either be a light one of hot chocolate or coffee with sweet rolls or *churros* to dip in, or a hearty late breakfast *almuerzo*, often consisting of the exquisite egg dishes which Mexico is well known for. The markets and their *fondas*, *cantinas* and *taquerias*, beckon with their irresistible aromas, convincing you that you are indeed hungry, and an endless parade of tacos, tostadas, enchiladas, burritos, soups, shellfish, grilled fish tantalise the palate.

And if your appetite is jaded from the sultry heat and feasting, and you don't have room for even one more burrito, persuade yourself to nibble a reviving snack – fresh fruit, such as pineapple, oranges and mango – sprinkled with hot red pepper and served with a squeeze of lime juice. After that you will be ready for anything.

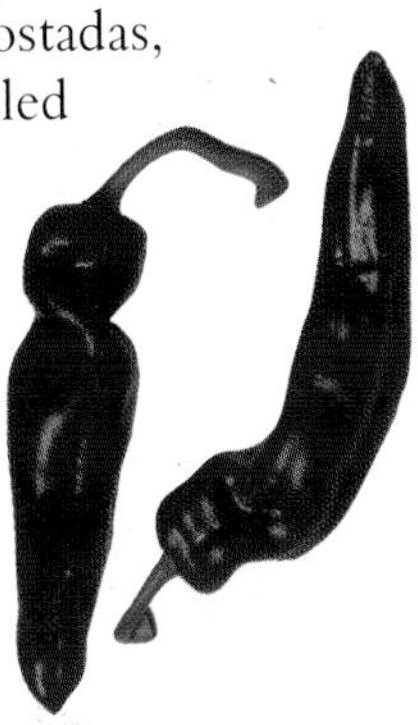

Soups & Starters

Start your meal in authentic Mexican style with a bowl of homemade soup. Mexican soups are distinctive and varied, ranging from light soups of plain stock served with a spoonful of salsa and a little lime, to hearty one-bowl meals such as Pozole. Whatever your soup, expect to find it served with a wedge of lime, lemon or orange, a sprinkling of pungent fresh coriander and a hint of hot chilli.

Little niblles, to, are an important part of any Mexican meal. The world-famous Guacamole, mashed avocado with seasonings and spices, makes the most perfect appetizer I know – delicious with crunchy tortilla chips and a killing Mexican beer or a shot of Tequila. Spicy-sweet Meat Empanadas, filled with savoury meat, aromatic spices and nuts, are as moreish as they are unusual, and you can keep them in your freezer ready to take out for an impromptu party, anytime.

With its thousands of miles of coastline, seafood cocktails and marinated fish make cooling, refreshing and utterly light appetizers, to start a Mexican feast. Alternatively, you could serve tiny tacos, rolls of tortillas filled with tantalising Mexican mixtures, or a salad of crunchy raw vegetables spiced with chillies. Whatever your taste, you will surely be enticed by the recipes in this chapter.

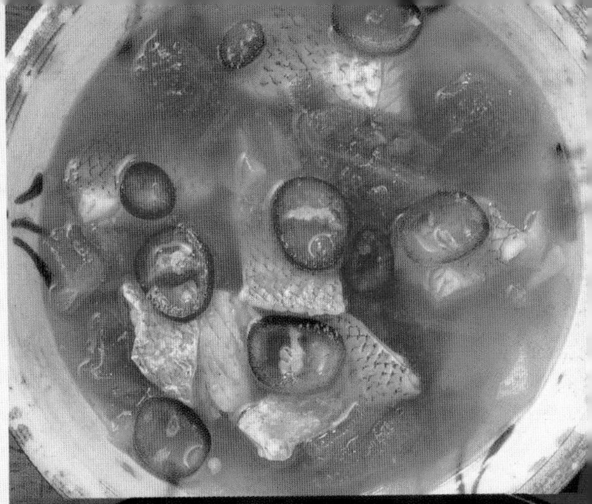

Yucatecan Citrus Soup

Roasted onion and garlic are combined with tangy citrus flavours to create a soup full of tantalising tastes.

Serves 4

INGREDIENTS

2 onions
15 large garlic cloves, unpeeled
1 tbsp extra-virgin olive oil
1.3 litres/2¼ pints/6 cups vegetable, chicken or fish stock
225 ml/8 fl oz/1 cup water
8 ripe tomatoes, diced
pinch of dried oregano
1 fresh green chilli, such as jalapeño or serrano, deseeded and chopped
pinch of ground cumin
½ tsp finely grated grapefruit rind
½ tsp finely grated lime rind
½ tsp finely grated orange rind
juice and diced flesh of 2 limes
juice of 1 orange
juice of 1 grapefruit
salt and pepper

TO GARNISH:
tortilla chips, or sliced tortilla strips fried until crisp
2 tbsp chopped fresh coriander (cilantro)

1 Half one unpeeled onion. Peel and finely chop the other.

2 Heat a large heavy-based frying pan (skillet), add the unpeeled onion halves and garlic and cook over a medium-high heat until the skins char and the onions are caramelized on their cut sides; the garlic should be soft on the inside. Remove from the pan and allow to cool slightly.

3 Meanwhile, heat the oil in a pan and lightly sauté the remaining onion until softened. Add the stock and water and bring to the boil. Reduce the heat and simmer for a few minutes.

4 Peel the charred onion and garlic, then chop coarsely and add to the simmering soup, together with the tomatoes, oregano, chilli and cumin. Cook for about 15 minutes, stirring the soup occasionally.

5 Add the citrus rind, season with salt and pepper, then simmer for a further 2 minutes. Remove from the heat and stir in the lime flesh and citrus juices.

6 Ladle into soup bowls, garnish with tortilla chips and fresh coriander (cilantro) and serve .

2

4

5

Spicy Gazpacho

This classic Spanish cold soup is given a Mexican twist by adding chillies and fresh coriander (cilantro). Serve with chunks of bread for a refreshing start to a meal.

Serves 4–6

INGREDIENTS

1 cucumber
2 green (bell) peppers
6 ripe flavourful tomatoes
½ fresh hot chilli
½–1 onion, finely chopped
3–4 garlic cloves, chopped
4 tbsp extra-virgin olive oil
¼ –½ tsp ground cumin
2–4 tsp sherry vinegar, or a combination of balsamic vinegar and wine vinegar
4 tbsp chopped fresh coriander (cilantro)
2 tbsp chopped fresh parsley
300 ml/10 fl oz/1¼ cups vegetable or chicken stock
600 ml/1 pint/2½ cups tomato juice or canned crushed tomatoes
salt and pepper
ice cubes, to serve

1 Cut the cucumber in half lengthways, cut into quarters. Remove the seeds with a teaspoon, then dice the flesh. Cut the (bell) peppers in half, remove the cores and seeds, then dice the flesh.

2 If you prefer to skin the tomatoes, place in a heatproof bowl, pour boiling water over to cover and stand for 30 seconds. Drain and plunge into cold water. The skins will then slide off easily. Cut the tomatoes in half, deseed if wished, then chop the flesh. Deseed and chop the chilli.

3 Combine half the cucumber, green (bell) pepper, tomatoes and onion in a blender or food processor with all the chilli, garlic, olive oil, cumin, vinegar, coriander (cilantro) and parsley. Process with enough stock for a smooth purée.

4 Pour the puréed soup into a bowl and stir in the remaining stock and tomato juice. Add the remaining green (bell) pepper, cucumber, tomatoes and onion, stirring well. Season with salt and pepper to taste, then cover and chill for a few hours.

5 Ladle into bowls and serve with ice cubes in each bowl.

VARIATION

Freeze tomato juice ice cubes as a delicious alternative.

Spicy Courgette (Zucchini) Soup with Rice & Lime

Mild red chilli powder and pan-browned garlic give flavour to this simple, homely soup. Quick to make, it's ideal for a light lunch.

Serves 4

INGREDIENTS

2 tbsp oil
4 garlic cloves, thinly sliced
1–2 tbsp mild red chilli powder
¼–½ tsp ground cumin
1.5 litres/2¾ pints/6¼ cups chicken, vegetable or beef stock
2 courgettes (zucchini), cut into bite-sized chunks
4 tbsp long-grain rice
salt and pepper
fresh oregano sprigs, to garnish
lime wedges, to serve (optional)

1 Heat the oil in a heavy-based pan, add the garlic and fry for about 2 minutes until softened and just beginning to change colour. Add the chilli powder and cumin and cook over a medium-low heat for a minute.

2 Stir in the stock, courgettes (zucchini) and rice, then cook over a medium-high heat for about 10 minutes until the courgettes (zucchini) are just tender and the rice is cooked through. Season the soup with salt and pepper.

3 Ladle into soup bowls, garnish with oregano and serve with lime wedges.

VARIATION

Instead of rice, use rice-shaped pasta, such as orzo or semone de melone, or very thin pasta known as fideo. Use yellow summer squash instead of the courgettes (zucchini) and add cooked pinto beans in place of the rice. Diced tomatoes also make a tasty addition.

COOK'S TIP

Choose courgettes (zucchini) which are firm to the touch and have shiny skin. They should not be too large.

Mexican Vegetable Soup with Tortilla Chips

Crisp tortilla chips act as croûtons in this hearty vegetable soup which is found throughout Mexico. Add cheese to melt in, if you wish, and make the soup as hot tasting as you like!

Serves 4–6

INGREDIENTS

2 tbsp vegetable or extra-virgin olive oil
1 onion, finely chopped
4 garlic cloves, finely chopped
1/4–1/2 tsp ground cumin
2–3 tsp mild chilli powder, such as ancho or New Mexico
1 carrot, sliced
1 waxy potato, diced
350 g/12 oz/1 1/2 cups diced fresh or canned tomatoes
1 courgette (zucchini), diced
1/4 small cabbage, shredded
1 litre/1 3/4 pints/4 cups vegetable or chicken stock or water
1 corn-on-the-cob, the kernels cut off the cob, or canned sweetcorn
about 10 green or runner beans, topped and tailed, then cut into bite-sized lengths
salt and pepper

TO SERVE:
4–6 tbsp chopped fresh coriander (cilantro)
salsa of your choice, or chopped fresh chilli, to taste
tortilla chips

1 Heat the oil in a heavy-based pan. Add the onion and garlic and cook for a few minutes until softened, then sprinkle in the cumin and chilli powder. Stir in the carrot, potato, tomatoes, courgettes (zucchini) and cabbage and cook for 2 minutes, stirring the mixture occasionally.

2 Pour in the stock. Cover and cook over a medium heat for about 20 minutes until the vegetables are tender.

3 Add extra water if necessary, then stir in the sweetcorn and green beans and cook for a further 5–10 minutes or until the beans are tender. Season with salt and pepper to taste, bearing in mind that the tortilla chips may be salty.

4 Ladle the soup into soup bowls and sprinkle each portion with fresh coriander (cilantro). Top with a dab of salsa, then add a handful of tortilla chips.

Crab & Cabbage Soup

From the Vera Cruz region, this delicious soup uses fresh crab meat to add a rich flavour to a mildly spicy vegetable and fish broth.

Serves 4

INGREDIENTS

1/4 cabbage
450 g/1 lb ripe tomatoes
1 litre/1 3/4 pints/4 cups fish stock or water mixed with 1–2 fish stock cubes
1 onion, thinly sliced
1 small carrot, diced
4 garlic cloves, finely chopped
6 tbsp chopped fresh coriander (cilantro)
1 tsp mild chilli powder, such as New Mexico
1 whole cooked crab or 175–225 g/6–8 oz crab meat
1 tbsp torn fresh oregano leaves
salt and pepper

TO SERVE:
1–2 limes, cut into wedges
salsa of your choice

1 Cut out any thick stalk from the cabbage, then shred finely using a large knife.

2 To skin the tomatoes, place in a heatproof bowl, pour boiling water over to cover and stand for 30 seconds. Drain and plunge into cold water. The skins will then slide off easily. Next, chop the skinned tomatoes.

3 Place the tomatoes and stock in a pan with the onion, carrot, cabbage, garlic, fresh coriander (cilantro) and chilli powder. Bring to the boil, then reduce the heat and simmer for about 20 minutes until the vegetables are just tender.

4 Remove the crab meat from the whole crab, if using. Twist off the legs and claws and crack with a heavy knife. Remove the flesh from the legs with a skewer; leave the cracked claws intact, if wished. Remove the body section from the main crab shell and remove the meat, discarding the stomach bag and feathery gills.

5 Add the oregano and crab meat to the pan and simmer for 10–15 minutes to combine the flavours. Season the mixture with salt and pepper.

6 Ladle into deep soup bowls and serve with 1–2 wedges of lime. Hand round the salsa separately.

3

4
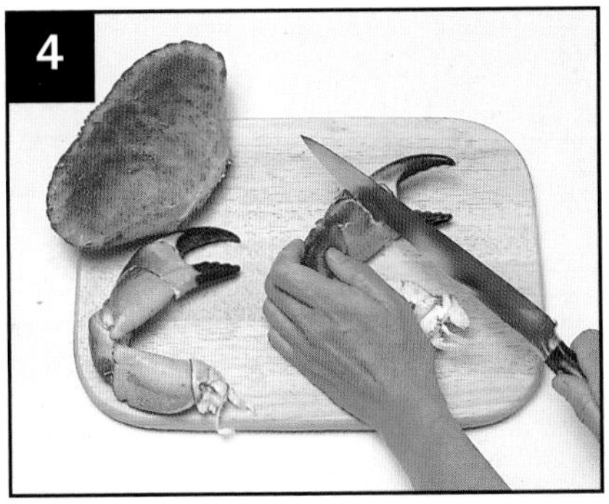

5

Mexican Fish & Roasted Tomato Soup

Mexico's long shoreline yields an abundance of fish and shellfish, which are often turned into spicy, satisfying soups.

Serves 4

INGREDIENTS

5 ripe tomatoes
5 garlic cloves, unpeeled
500 g/1 lb 2 oz snapper, cut into chunks
1 litre/1¾ pints/4 cups fish stock, or water plus a fish stock cube or two
2–3 tbsp olive oil
1 onion, chopped
2 fresh chillies, such as serrano, deseeded and thinly sliced
lime wedges, to serve

1 Heat an ungreased heavy-based frying pan (skillet), add the whole tomatoes and garlic and char over a high heat or under a preheated grill (broiler). The skins of the vegetables should blacken and char, and the flesh inside should be tender. Alternatively, place the tomatoes and garlic cloves in a roasting tin (pan) and bake in a preheated oven at 190–200°C/375–400°F/ Gas Mark 5–6 for about 40 minutes.

2 Leave the tomatoes and garlic to cool, then remove the skins and chop coarsely, combining them with any juices from the pan. Set aside.

3 Poach the snapper in the stock over medium just until it is opaque and firmish. Remove from the heat and set aside.

4 Heat the oil in a pan and cook the chopped onion until softened. Strain in the cooking liquid from the fish, then add the coarsley chopped tomatoes and garlic, and stir.

5 Bring to the boil, then reduce the heat and simmer for about 5 minutes to combine the flavours. Add the serrano chillies.

6 Divide chunks of the poached fish between soup bowls, ladle over the hot soup and serve with lime wedges for squeezing over the top.

1

3

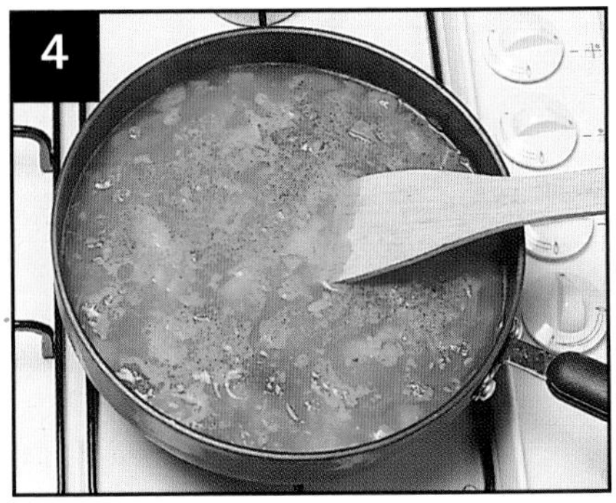
4

Chicken, Avocado & Chipotle Soup

This soup evolved from the foodstalls that line the streets of Tlalpan, a suburb of Mexico City: rich avocado, shreds of chicken and the smoky hit of chipotle make it special.

Serves 4

INGREDIENTS

1.5 litres/2¾ pints/6¼ cups chicken stock
2–3 garlic cloves, finely chopped
1–2 chipotle chillies, cut into very thin strips (see Cook's Tip)
1 avocado
lime or lemon juice, for tossing
3–5 spring onions (scallions), thinly sliced
350–400 g/12–14 oz cooked chicken breast meat, torn or cut into shreds or thin strips
2 tbsp chopped fresh coriander (cilantro)

TO SERVE:
1 lime, cut into wedges
handful of tortilla chips (optional)

1 Place the stock in a pan with the garlic and chipotle chillies and bring to the boil.

2 Meanwhile, cut the avocado in half around the stone (pit). Twist apart, then remove the stone (pit) with a knife. Carefully peel off the skin, dice the flesh and toss in lime or lemon juice to prevent discoloration.

3 Arrange the spring onions (scallions), chicken, avocado and fresh coriander (cilantro) in the base of 4 soup bowls or in a large serving bowl.

4 Ladle hot stock over, and serve with lime and a handful of tortilla chips if using.

VARIATION

Add a drained 400 g/14 oz can chick-peas (garbanzo beans) to the bowls in Step 3.

COOK'S TIP

Chipotle chillies are smoked and dried jalapeño chillies and are available canned or dried from specialist stores. They add a distinctive smoky flavour to dishes and are very hot. Use chipotles canned in adobo marinade for this recipe, if possible. Drain the canned version before using. Dried chipotles need to be reconstituted before using (see page 100).

1

3

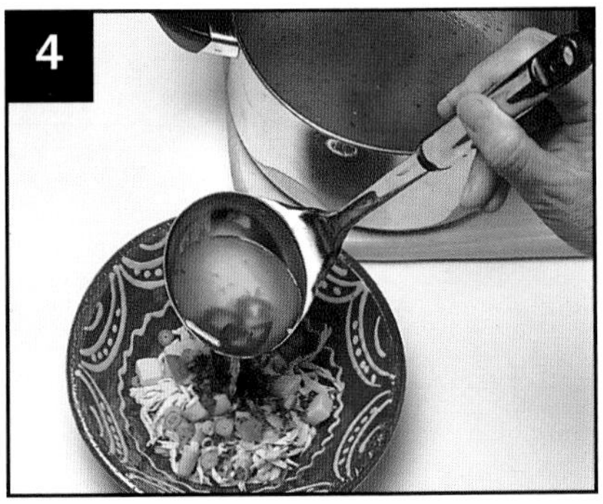
4

Big Pot of Simmered Meat

The Mexican kitchen traditionally simmers big chunks of meat, which gives two meals in one: tender boiled meat for tacos or enchiladas, as well as a hearty rich stock for soups and rice.

Serves 6

INGREDIENTS

- 2 kg/4 lb 8 oz beef, pork, chicken for stewing – any combination or just one type
- 2 onions, chopped
- 1 whole garlic bulb, divided into cloves and peeled
- several sprigs of fresh herbs, such as parsley, oregano, coriander (cilantro)
- 1 carrot, sliced
- 1–2 stock cubes
- salt and pepper
- cooked macaroni or thin noodles, to serve
- finely sliced spring onions (scallions), to garnish

1 Place the meat in a large pan and cover with cold water. Bring to the boil and skim off the scum that forms on the surface. Reduce the heat and add the onions, garlic, herbs and carrot. Simmer, covered, for 1 hour.

2 Add the stock cubes and salt and pepper to taste. (If using a combination of meat and chicken, cook the meat first for 1 hour, then add the chicken.) Continue to simmer over a very low heat for about 2 hours until the meat is very tender.

3 Remove from the heat and allow the meat to cool in the stock. Using a slotted spoon, transfer the meat to a board and shred; set aside. Skim the fat from the stock, or leave to chill then remove the fat by simply lifting it off. Strain the soup for a clearer soup. Reheat before serving.

4 To serve, spoon the hot macaroni or noodles into soup bowls, then top with the shredded meat and ladle over the soup. Garnish with spring onions (scallions) and serve.

VARIATION

For a simple soup to make from the strained stock, cook diced courgettes (zucchini) in the stock with a cinnamon stick; remove and discard the cinnamon stick, then serve the soup with a wedge of lime, a dash of salsa to taste and a sprinkling of fresh coriander (cilantro).

Beef & Vegetable Soup

A wonderful meal-in-a-bowl, this soup is ideal for a winter supper or lunch. The beefy flavour, enhanced with spices, is very warming.

Serves 4–6

INGREDIENTS

225 g/8 oz tomatoes
2 corn-on-the-cobs
1 litre/1¾ pints/4 cups beef soup or stock, following the recipe on page 22, or use a chilled ready-made stock
1 carrot, thinly sliced
1 onion, chopped
1–2 small waxy potatoes, diced
¼ cabbage, thinly sliced
¼ tsp ground cumin
¼ tsp mild chilli powder
¼ tsp paprika
225 g/8 oz cooked beef (preferably from the recipe on page 22), cut into bite-sized pieces
3–4 tbsp chopped fresh coriander (cilantro) (optional)
hot salsa, such as Scorched Chilli Salsa (see page 102), to serve

1 To skin the tomatoes, place in a heatproof bowl, pour boiling water over to cover and stand for 30 seconds. Drain and plunge into cold water. The skins will then slide off easily. Chop the tomatoes.

2 Using a large knife, cut the corn-on-the-cobs into 2.5 cm/1 inch pieces.

3 Place the stock in a pan with the tomatoes, carrot, onion, potatoes and cabbage. Bring to the boil, then reduce the heat and simmer for 10–15 minutes or until the vegetables are tender.

4 Add the corn-on-the-cob pieces, the cumin, chilli powder, paprika and beef pieces. Bring back to the boil over a medium heat.

5 Ladle into soup bowls and serve sprinkled with fresh coriander (cilantro), if using, with salsa handed round separately.

COOK'S TIP

To thicken the soup and give it a flavour of the popular Mexican steamed dumplings, known as a tamale, add a few tablespoons of masa harina, mixed into a thinnish paste with a little water, at Step 4. Stir well, then continue cooking until thickened.

Pozole

The dish of hulled maize kernels – hominy – simmered in rich stock is eaten all over Mexico, and is served with lots of fresh garnishes: shredded cabbage, onion, fried tortilla or crisp fried pork skin (chicharrones), and of course, chillies and lime wedges.

Serves 4

INGREDIENTS

450 g/1 lb pork for stewing, such as lean belly
½ small chicken
about 2 litres/3½ pints/8 cups water
1 chicken stock cube
1 whole garlic bulb, divided into cloves but not peeled
1 onion, chopped
2 bay leaves
450 g/1 lb canned or cooked hominy or chick-peas (garbanzo beans)
¼–½ tsp ground cumin
salt and pepper

TO SERVE:
½ small cabbage, thinly shredded
fried pork skin
dried oregano leaves
dried chilli flakes
tortilla chips
lime wedges

1 Place the pork and chicken in a large pan. Add enough water to fill the pan. (Do not worry about having too much stock – it is wonderful for the rest of the week, and freezes well.)

2 Bring to the boil, then skim off the scum that rises to the surface. Reduce the heat and add the stock cube, garlic, onion and bay leaves. Simmer, covered, over a medium-low heat until the pork and chicken are both tender and cooked through.

3 Using a slotted spoon, remove the pork and chicken from the soup and leave to cool. When cool enough to handle, remove the chicken flesh from the bones and cut into small pieces. Then, cut the pork into bite-sized pieces. Set aside.

4 Skim the fat off the soup and discard the bay leaves. Add the hominy or chick-peas (garbanzo beans) and cumin, salt and pepper to taste. Bring to the boil.

5 To serve, place a little pork and chicken in soup bowls. Top with cabbage, fried pork skin, oregano and chilli flakes, then spoon in the hot soup. Serve with tortilla chips and lime as wished.

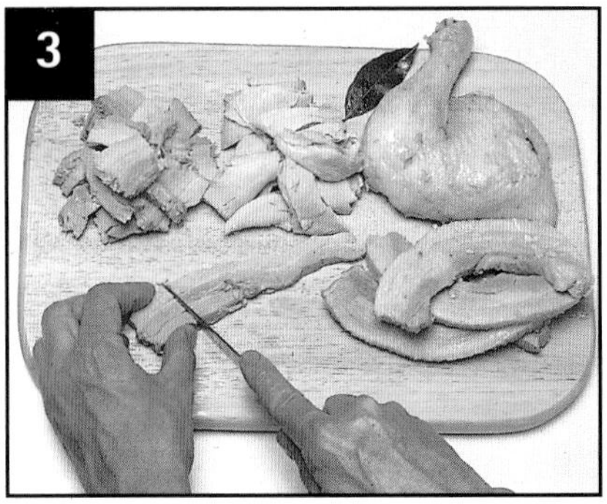

Authentic Guacamole

Guacamole is at its best when freshly made, with enough texture to really taste the avocado. Serve as a sauce for anything Mexican, or dip into it with vegetable sticks or tortilla chips.

Serves 4

INGREDIENTS

1 ripe tomato
2 limes
2–3 ripe small to medium avocados, or 1–2 large ones
1/4–1/2 onion, finely chopped
pinch of ground cumin
pinch of mild chilli powder
1/2–1 fresh green chillies, such as jalapeño or serrano, deseeded and finely chopped
1 tbsp finely chopped fresh coriander (cilantro) leaves, plus extra for garnishing
salt (optional)
tortilla chips, to serve (optional)

1 To skin the tomato, place in a heatproof bowl, pour boiling water over to cover and stand for 30 seconds. Drain and plunge into cold water. The skin will then slide off easily. Cut in half, deseed and chop the flesh.

2 Squeeze the juice from the limes into a small bowl. Cut one avocado in half around the stone (pit). Twist apart, then remove the stone (pit) with a knife. Carefully peel off the skin, dice the flesh and toss in the bowl of lime juice to prevent them from discolouring. Repeat with the remaining avocados. Mash the avocados coarsely.

3 Add the onion, tomato, cumin, chilli powder, chillies and fresh coriander (cilantro) to the avocados. If using as a dip for tortilla chips do not add salt. If using as a sauce, add salt to taste.

4 To serve the Guacamole as a dip, transfer to a serving dish, garnish with finely chopped fresh coriander (cilantro) and serve with tortilla chips.

COOK'S TIP

Avocados grow in abundance in Mexico, and Guacamole is used to add richness and flavour to all manner of dishes. Try spooning it into soups, especially chicken or seafood, or spreading it into sandwiches on thick crusty rolls (tortas). Spoon Guacamole over refried beans and melted cheese, then dig into it with salsa and crisp tortilla chips. Try Guacamole with roast chicken, or stir it into the pan juices for a rich avocado sauce.

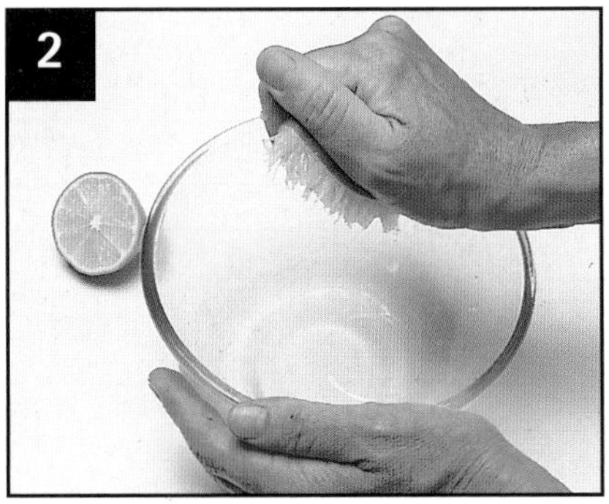

Roasted Cheese with Salsa

The combination of melting cheese and hot salsa is completely irresistible! Called oueso fundito *in Mexico, it is often prepared on the barbecue (grill) to nibble on while you wait for the rest of the meal to cook.*

Serves 4

INGREDIENTS

225 g/8 oz mozzarella, fresh pecorino or Mexican queso oaxaca

175 ml/6 fl oz/$\frac{3}{4}$ cup Salsa Cruda (see page 96), or other good salsa

$\frac{1}{2}$–1 onion, finely chopped

8 tortillas, to serve

1 To warm the tortillas ready for serving, heat a non-stick frying pan (skillet), add a tortilla and heat through, sprinkling with a few drops of water as it heats. Wrap in kitchen foil to keep warm. Repeat with the other tortillas.

2 Cut chunks or slabs of cheese and arrange them in a shallow ovenproof dish or in individual dishes.

3 Spoon the salsa over the cheese to cover and place in either a preheated oven at 200°C/400°F/Gas Mark 6 or under a preheated grill (broiler). Cook until the cheese melts and bubbles, lightly browning in spots.

4 Sprinkle with chopped onion to taste and serve with the warmed tortillas for dipping. Serve immediately as the melted cheese turns stringy when cold and becomes difficult to eat.

COOK'S TIP

Queso oaxaca is the authentic cheese to use, but mozzarella or pecorino make excellent substitutes, since they produce the right effect when melted.

VARIATION

Use Salsa Verde (see page 102) in place of the red tomato salsa, and serve tortilla chips for dipping rather than soft corn tortillas.

2

3

4

Seafood Cocktail à la Veracruz

'Mariscos!' cry the signs in brightly painted colours along Mexico's beaches and sea fronts, wherever fresh seafood is served. This is a typical salad dish you will find on offer, full of spicy flavours.

Serves 6

INGREDIENTS

- 1 litre/1¾ pints/4 cups fish stock or water mixed with 1 fish stock cube
- 2 bay leaves
- 1 onion, chopped
- 3–5 garlic cloves, cut into big chunks
- 650 g/1 lb 8 oz mixed seafood, such as prawns (shrimp) in their shells, scallops, squid rings, pieces of squid tentacles, etc
- 175 ml/6 fl oz/¾ cup tomato ketchup (catsup)
- 50 ml/2 fl oz/¼ cup Mexican hot sauce
- generous pinch of ground cumin
- 6–8 tbsp chopped fresh coriander (cilantro)
- 4 tbsp lime juice, plus extra for tossing
- salt
- 1 avocado, to garnish

1 Place stock in a pan and add the bay leaves, half the onion and all of the garlic. Bring to the boil, then simmer for about 10 minutes or until the onion and garlic are soft and the stock tastes flavourful.

2 Add the seafood in the order of the amount of cooking time required. Most small pieces of shellfish take a very short time to cook, and can be added together. Cook for 1 minute, then remove the pan from the heat and allow the seafood to finish cooking by standing in the cooling stock.

3 When the stock has cooled, remove the seafood from the stock with a slotted spoon. Shell the prawns (shrimp) and any other shellfish. Reserve the stock.

4 Combine the ketchup (catsup), hot sauce and cumin in a bowl, reserve a quarter of the sauce mixture for serving. Add the seafood to the bowl with the remaining onion, fresh coriander (cilantro), lime juice and about 225 ml/8 fl oz/1 cup of the reserved cooled fish stock. Stir carefully to mix and season with salt to taste.

5 Peel and stone the avocado, then dice or slice the flesh. Toss gently in lime juice to prevent discoloration.

6 Serve the seafood cocktail in individual bowls, garnished with the avocado, and topped with a spoonful of the reserved sauce.

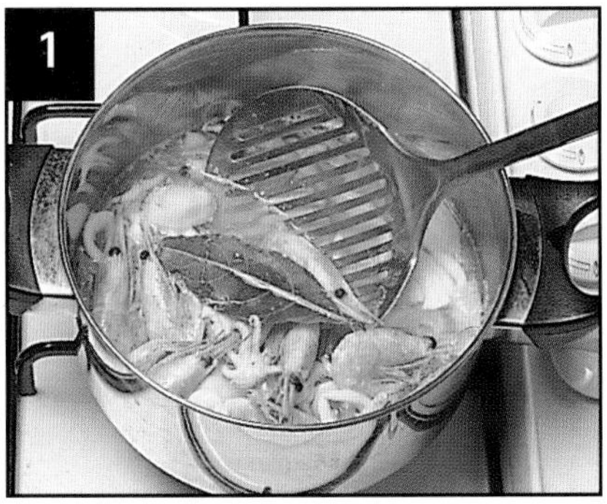

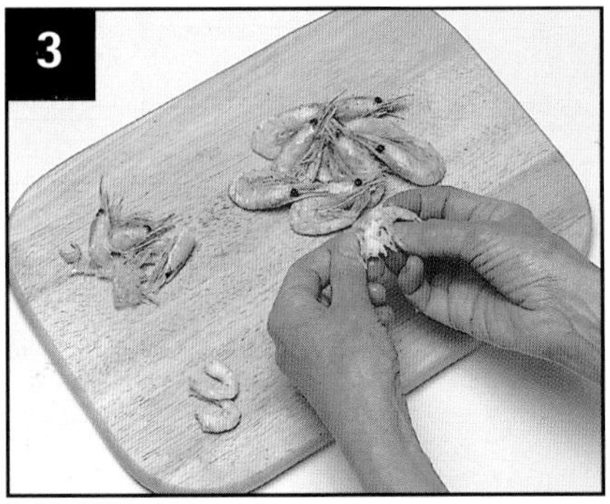

Citrus-marinated Fish

Ceviche, as it is called in Mexican, is one of Mexico's classic dishes: raw fish, cured in a bath of citrus juices, chillies and aromatics. It must be made with the freshest fish to be sublime.

Serves 4

INGREDIENTS

450 g/1 lb white-fleshed fish fillets, cut into bite-sized chunks
juice of 6–8 limes
2–3 ripe flavourful tomatoes, diced
3 fresh green chillies, such as jalapeño or serrano, deseeded and thinly sliced
½ tsp dried oregano
80 ml/3 fl oz/1/3 cup extra-virgin olive oil
1 small onion, finely chopped
salt and pepper
2 tbsp chopped fresh coriander (cilantro)

1 Place the fish in a non-metallic dish, add the lime juice and mix well. Marinate in the refrigerator for 5 hours, or until the mixture looks opaque. Turn from time to time so that the lime juice permeates the fish.

2 An hour before serving, add the tomatoes, chillies, oregano, olive oil and onion, and then season with salt and pepper to taste.

3 About 15 minutes before serving, remove from the refrigerator so that the olive oil comes to room temperature. Serve the dish sprinkled with fresh coriander (cilantro).

COOK'S TIP

This dish makes an elegant starter served layered with rounds of crisp tortillas, like a stacked tostada. Or it makes a refreshing lunch, served piled up in halved avocados, surrounded by sliced mango, papaya or grapefruit.

COOK'S TIP

In this salad the fish is 'cooked' by the lime juice – do not leave too long otherwise the texture will spoil.

VARIATION

Serve garnished with cooked marinated artichoke hearts, or drained artichokes from a can or jar.

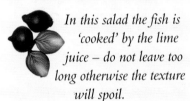

Salpicon of Crab

This lightly spiced crab salad is a cooling treat for a hot day. Eat it with crisp tortilla chips, or wrapped in a tender warm corn tortilla.

Serves 4

INGREDIENTS

¼ red onion, chopped
½–1 fresh green chilli, deseeded and chopped
juice of ½ lime
1 tbsp cider or other fruit vinegar, such as raspberry
1 tbsp chopped fresh coriander (cilantro)
1 tbsp extra-virgin olive oil
225–350 g/8–12 oz fresh crab meat
lettuce leaves, to serve

TO GARNISH:
1 avocado
lime juice, for tossing
1–2 ripe tomatoes
3–5 radishes

1 Combine the onion, with the chilli, lime juice, vinegar, fresh coriander (cilantro) and olive oil. Add the crab meat and the ingredients toss lightly together.

2 To make the garnish, cut each avocado in half around the stone (pit). Twist apart, then remove the stone (pit) with a knife. Carefully peel off the skin and slice the flesh. Toss the avocado gently in lime juice to prevent discoloration.

3 Halve the tomatoes, then remove the cores and seeds. Dice the flesh. Slice the radishes thinly.

4 Arrange the crab salad on a bed of lettuce leaves, garnish with the avocado, tomatoes and radishes and serve at once.

VARIATION

For a toasted crab salad sandwich, split open a long roll or baguette and heap on crab salad. Top with a generous layer of cheese. Place the open roll under the grill (broiler) to melt the cheese. Spread the toasted plain side with a little mayonnaise and close the sandwich up. Cut and serve with salsa.

1

2

5

Pickled Cauliflower, Carrots & Chillies

In Mexican cantinas, these pickled vegetables are munched alongside a stack of warm buttered tortillas and washed down with glasses of chilled lager, or maybe a little shot of tequila and a wedge of lime.

Serves 6

INGREDIENTS

- 3 tbsp vegetable oil
- 1 onion, thinly sliced
- 5 garlic cloves, cut into slivers
- 3 carrots, thinly sliced
- 2 fresh green chillies, such as jalapeño or serrano, deseeded and cut into strips
- 1 small cauliflower, broken into florets or cut into bite-sized chunks
- ½ red (bell) pepper, cored, deseeded and diced or cut into strips
- 1 stalk celery, cut into bite-sized pieces
- ½ tsp oregano leaves
- 1 bay leaf
- ¼ tsp ground cumin
- 80 ml/3 fl oz/⅓ cup cider vinegar
- salt and pepper

1 Heat the oil in a heavy-based frying pan (skillet) and lightly sauté the onion, garlic, carrots, chillies, cauliflower, red (bell) pepper and celery for about a minute until soft.

2 Add the oregano, bay leaf, cumin, cider vinegar and salt and pepper to taste. Add enough water to just cover the vegetables. Cook for a further 5–10 minutes or just long enough for the vegetables to be tender but still firm to the bite.

3 Adjust the seasoning, adding more vinegar if needed. Leave to cool and serve as a relish. The mixture will keep for up to 2 weeks, if covered and stored in the refrigerator.

COOK'S TIP

Wear rubber gloves when slicing and deseeding fresh chillies and do not touch your eyes during preparation.

Cheese & Bean Quesadillas

These bite-sized rolls are made from flour tortillas filled with a scrumptious mixture of refried beans, melted cheese, fresh coriander (cilantro) and salsa.

Serves 4–6

INGREDIENTS

8 flour tortillas
½ quantity Mexican Refried Beans (see page 146) or refried beans (see page 144)
200 g/7 oz Cheddar cheese, grated
1 onion, chopped
½ bunch fresh coriander (cilantro) leaves, chopped
1 quantity Salsa Cruda (see page 96)

1 First make the tortillas pliable, by warming them gently in a lightly greased non-stick frying pan (skillet).

2 Remove the tortillas from the pan and quickly spread with a layer of warm beans. Top each tortilla with grated cheese, onion, fresh coriander (cilantro) and a spoonful of salsa. Roll up tightly.

3 Just before serving, heat the non-stick frying pan (skillet) over a medium heat, sprinkling lightly with a drop or two of water. Add the tortilla rolls, cover the pan and heat through until the cheese melts. Allow to lightly brown, if wished.

4 Remove from the pan and slice each roll, on the diagonal, into about 4 bite-sized pieces. Serve the dish at once.

VARIATION

Top each tortilla with florets of lightly cooked broccoli or sautéed sliced wild mushrooms instead of the beans, for a more lightweight filling if you wish.

VARIATION

Cooked drained black beans can also be substituted for the refried beans – use with Chipotle Salsa (see page 98) instead of the Salsa Cruda for a subtle change of flavour.

COOK'S TIP

Flour tortillas can also be warmed in the microwave, but take care not to heat them for too long as they can become leathery.

2
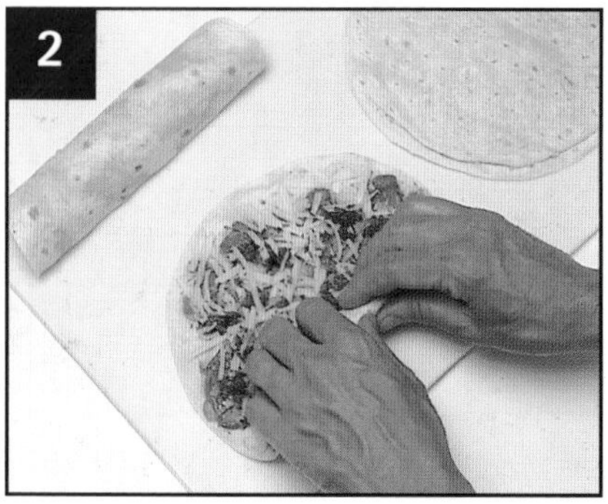

3

4
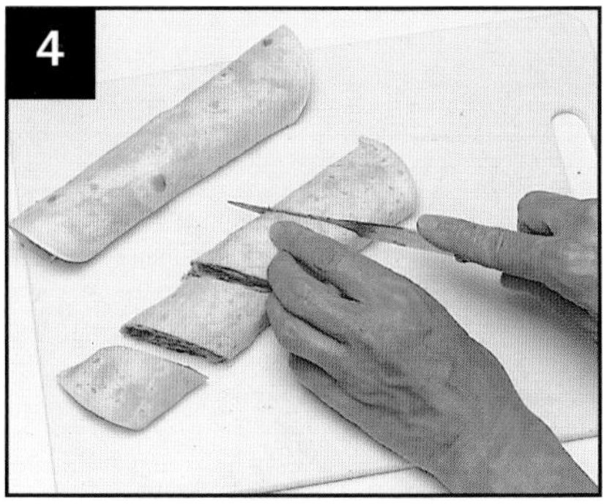

Chorizo & Artichoke Heart Quesadillas

Ideal to serve with drinks, these bites are incredibly easy to make – simply top flat tortillas with a delicious filling, pop them under the grill (broiler), then serve in wedges.

Serves 4–6

INGREDIENTS

1 chorizo
1 large mild green chilli or green (bell) pepper (optional)
8–10 marinated artichoke hearts or canned artichoke hearts, drained and diced
4 corn tortillas, warmed
2 garlic cloves, finely chopped
350 g/12 oz cheese, grated
1 tomato, diced
2 spring onions (scallions), thinly sliced
1 tbsp chopped fresh coriander (cilantro)

1 Dice the chorizo sausage. Heat a heavy-based frying pan (skillet); add the chorizo and fry until it browns in places.

2 If using the mild chilli or (bell) pepper, place under a preheated hot grill (broiler) and grill (broil) for about 10 minutes, or until the skins are charred and the flesh softened. Place in a plastic bag, twist to seal and set aside for about 20 minutes. Carefully, remove the skins from the chilli or (bell) pepper with a knife, then deseed and chop.

3 Arrange the browned chorizo and artichoke hearts on the corn tortillas, then transfer half to a baking (cookie) sheet.

4 Sprinkle with the garlic, then the grated cheese. Place under a preheated hot grill (broiler) and grill (broil) until the cheese melts and sizzles. Repeat with the remaining tortillas.

5 Sprinkle the warm tortillas with the diced tomato, sliced spring onions (scallions), green chilli or (bell) pepper, if using, and chopped fresh coriander (cilantro). Cut into wedges and serve immediately.

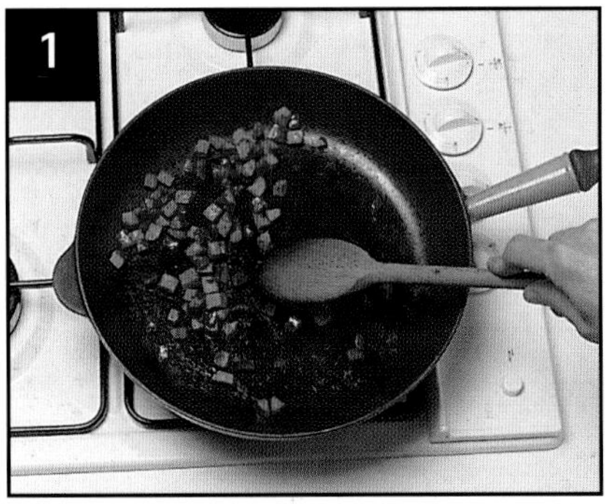

1

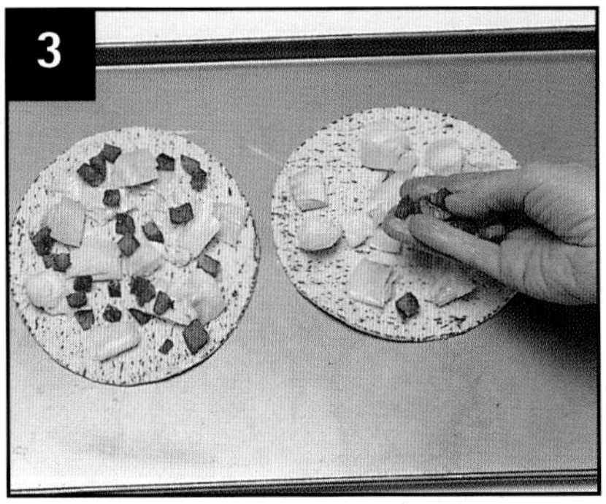

3

5

Spicy Prawns (Shrimp) & Avocado on Crisp Tortilla Wedges

A winning combination of textures and flavours, spiced prawns (shrimp) and creamy avocado are served on crisply fried tortilla wedges to make an irresistible appetizer.

Serves 8–10

INGREDIENTS

500 g /1 2 oz lb cooked prawns (shrimp)
4 garlic cloves, finely chopped
1/2 tsp mild chilli powder
1/2 tsp ground cumin
juice of 1 lime
1 ripe tomato, diced
salt
6 corn tortillas
vegetable oil, for frying
2 avocados
200 ml/7 fl oz 3/4 cup soured cream
mild chilli powder, to garnish

1 Place the prawns (shrimp) in a bowl with the garlic, chilli powder, cumin, lime juice and tomato. Add salt to taste and stir gently to mix. Chill for at least 4 hours or overnight to allow the flavours to mingle.

2 Cut the tortillas into wedges. Heat a little oil in a non-stick frying pan (skillet), add a batch of tortilla wedges and fry over a medium heat until crisp. Repeat with the remaining wedges and transfer to a serving platter.

3 Cut each avocado in half around the stone (pit). Twist apart, then remove the stone (pit) with a knife. Carefully peel off the skin and dice the flesh. Gently stir the avocado into the prawn (shrimp) mixture.

4 Top each tortilla wedge with a small mound of the prawn (shrimp) and avocado mixture. Finish with a dab of soured cream, garnish with a light sprinkling of chilli powder and serve at once while hot and crisp.

COOK'S TIP

For speed, you can use crisp corn tortillas (tostadas) or nacho chips (not too salty) instead of the corn tortillas.

VARIATION

Substitute diced mozzarella or mild fresh pecorino for the prawns and marinate for a few hours.

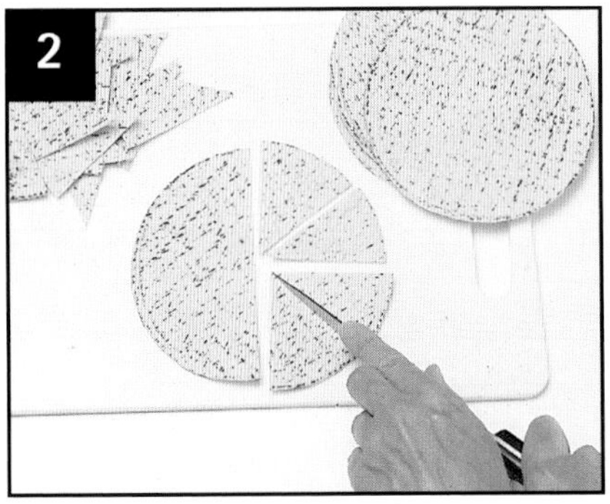

Black Bean Nachos

Packed with authentic Mexican flavours, this tasty black bean and cheese dip is fun to eat and will get any meal off to a good start! As an added bonus, it takes mere minutes to put together.

Serves 4

INGREDIENTS

225 g/8 oz/1 cup dried black beans, or canned black beans, drained
175–225 g/6–8 oz grated cheese, such as Cheddar, Fontina, pecorino, asiago, or a combination
about 1/4 tsp cumin seeds or ground cumin
about 4 tbsp soured cream
thinly sliced pickled jalapeños (optional)
1 tbsp chopped fresh coriander (cilantro)
handful of shredded lettuce
tortilla chips, to serve

1 If using dried black beans, soak the beans overnight, then drain. Put in a pan, cover with water and bring to the boil. Boil for 10 minutes, then reduce the heat and simmer for about 1½ hours until tender. Drain well.

2 Spread the beans in a shallow ovenproof dish, then scatter the cheese over the top. Sprinkle with cumin, to taste.

3 Bake in a preheated oven at 190°C/375°F/Gas Mark 5 for 10–15 minutes or until the beans are cooked through and the cheese is bubbly and melted.

4 Remove the beans and cheese from the oven and spoon the soured cream on top. Add the jalapeños, if using, and sprinkle with fresh coriander (cilantro) and lettuce.

5 Arrange the tortilla chips around the beans, sticking them into the mixture. Serve the nachos at once.

VARIATION

To add a meaty flavour, spoon chopped and browned chorizo on top of the beans, before sprinkling over the cheese, and cook as in Step 3 – the combination is excellent. Finely chopped leftover cooked meat can also be added in this way.

2

4

5

Refried Bean Nachos

A Mexican classic, refried beans and tortilla crisps are topped with luscious melted cheese, salsa, and assorted toppings, to make an irresistible dip. Perfect for an informal gathering!

Serves 6–8

INGREDIENTS

- 400 g/14 oz refried beans
- 400 g/14 oz can pinto beans, drained
- large pinch of ground cumin
- large pinch of mild chilli powder
- 175 g/6 oz bag tortilla chips
- 225 g/8 oz grated cheese, such as Cheddar
- salsa of your choice
- 1 avocado, stoned (pitted), diced and tossed with lime juice
- ½ small onion or 3–5 spring onions (scallions), chopped
- 2 ripe tomatoes, diced
- handful of shredded lettuce
- 3–4 tbsp chopped fresh coriander (cilantro)
- soured cream, to serve

1 Place the refried beans in a pan with the pinto beans, cumin and chilli powder. Add enough water to make a thick soup-like consistency, stirring gently so that the beans do not lose their texture.

2 Heat the bean mixture over a medium heat until hot, then reduce the heat and keep the mixture warm while you prepare the rest of the dish.

3 Arrange half the tortilla chips in the bottom of a flameproof casserole or gratin dish and cover with the bean mixture. Sprinkle with the cheese and bake in a preheated oven at 200°C/400°F/ Gas Mark 6 until the cheese melts.

4 Alternatively, place the casserole under the grill (broiler) and grill (broil) for 5–7 minutes or until the cheese melts and lightly sizzles in places.

5 Arrange on top of the melted cheese the salsa, avocado, onion, tomato, lettuce and fresh coriander (cilantro). Surround with the remaining tortilla chips and serve immediately with with soured cream.

VARIATION

Replace the soured cream with Greek yogurt as an alternative.

Sincronizadas

Once you've tried this Mexican version of a toasted ham and cheese sandwich, you'll never look back! Serve with a tangy salsa and Mexican beer to complete the snack.

Serves 6

INGREDIENTS

vegetable oil, for greasing
about 10 flour tortillas
about 500 g/1 lb 2 oz grated cheese
225 g/8 oz cooked ham, diced
salsa of your choice
soured cream with herbs, to serve

1 Lightly grease a non-stick frying pan (skillet). Off the heat, place 1 tortilla in the pan and top with a layer of cheese and ham. Generously spread salsa over another tortilla and place, salsa-side down, on top of the cheese and ham tortilla in the pan.

2 Place over a medium heat and cook until the cheese is melted and the base of the tortilla is golden brown.

3 Place a heatproof plate, upside-down, on top of the pan. Taking care to protect your hands, hold the plate firmly in place and carefully invert the pan to turn the 'sandwich' out on to the plate.

4 Slide the 'sandwich' back into the frying pan (skillet) and cook until the underside of the tortilla is golden brown.

5 Remove from the pan and serve cut into wedges, accompanied with soured cream sprinkled with herbs.

VARIATIONS

For a vegetarian version, sauté 225 g/8 oz thinly sliced mushrooms in a little olive oil with a crushed garlic clove and use instead of the ham. Alternatively, lightly fry finely chopped garlic in a little oil, then add rinsed spinach leaves and cook until wilted; chop and substitute for the ham.

COOK'S TIP

Protect your hands with oven gloves (pot holders) when turning the tortillas on to the plate.

Tortas

Throughout Mexico you will find street vendors selling these substantial Mexican rolls. Filled with all sorts of ingredients, they are 'Muy Delicioso'! Make your own and vary the filling as you wish.

Serves 4

INGREDIENTS

4 crusty rolls, such as French rolls or bocadillos
melted butter or olive oil, for brushing
225 g/8 oz/1 cup refried beans (see page 144)
350 g/12 oz/1½ cups shredded cooked chicken, browned chorizo pieces, sliced ham and cheese or any leftover cooked meat you have to hand
1 ripe tomato, sliced or diced
1 small onion, finely chopped
2 tbsp chopped fresh coriander (cilantro)
1 avocado, stoned (pitted), sliced and tossed with lime juice
4–6 tbsp soured cream or Greek yogurt
salsa of your choice
handful of shredded lettuce

1 Cut the rolls in half and remove a little of the crumb to make space for the filling.

2 Brush the outside and inside of the rolls with butter or oil and toast, on both sides, on a hot griddle or frying pan (skillet) for a few minutes until crisp. Alternatively, place in a preheated oven at 200°C/400°F/Gas Mark 6 until lightly toasted.

3 Meanwhile, place the beans in a pan with a tiny amount of water and heat through gently.

4 When the rolls are heated, spread one half of each roll generously with the beans, then top with a layer of cooked meat. Top with tomato, onion, fresh coriander (cilantro) and avocado.

5 Generously spread soured cream or yogurt on to the other side of each roll. Drizzle the salsa over the filling, add a little shredded lettuce, then sandwich the two sides of each roll together; press tightly. Serve immediately.

VARIATION

Add any Mexican sauce, such as Chile Verde (see page 204), to the meat filling to vary the flavour.

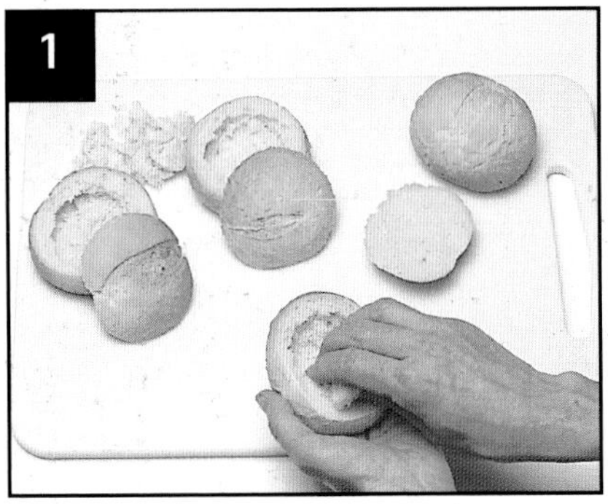
1

4

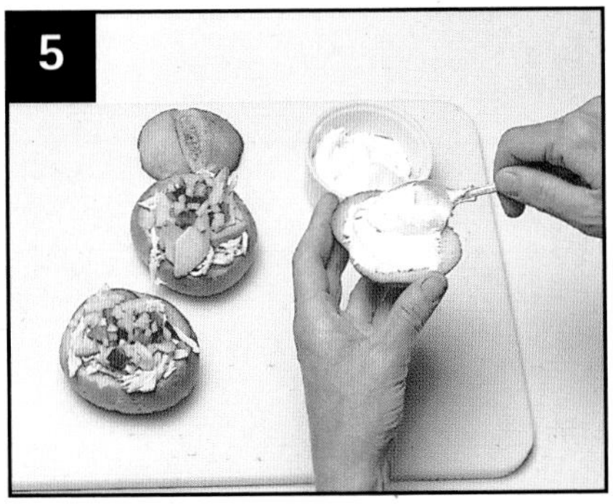
5

Molletes

Molletes are crusty rolls stuffed with hot melted beans and cheese, then garnished with a tangy hot salsa. In this version, a spicy shredded cabbage salad adds extra crunch to the snacks.

Serves 4

INGREDIENTS

4 bread rolls
1 tbsp vegetable oil, plus extra for brushing
400 g/14 oz can refried beans
1 onion, chopped
3 garlic cloves, chopped
3 slices bacon, cut into small pieces, or about 80 g/3 oz spicy chorizo, diced
225 g/8 oz diced fresh or canned tomatoes
¼–½ tsp ground cumin
250 g/9 oz grated cheese

CABBAGE SALAD:
½ cabbage, thinly sliced
2 tbsp sliced pickled jalapeños
1 tbsp extra-virgin olive oil
3 tbsp cider vinegar
¼ tsp dried oregano
salt and pepper

1 Cut the rolls in half and remove a little of the crumb to make space for the filling.

2 To make the cabbage salad, combine the cabbage with the jalapeños, olive oil and vinegar. Season with salt, pepper and oregano. Set aside.

3 Brush the rolls all over with oil. Arrange on a baking (cookie) sheet and toast in a preheated oven at 200°C/400°F/Gas Mark 6 oven for 10–15 minutes until the rolls are crisp and light golden.

4 Meanwhile, place the beans in a pan and heat through gently with enough water to thin them to a smooth paste.

5 Heat 1 tablespoon of the oil in a frying pan (skillet). Add the onion, garlic and bacon or chorizo and cook until the bacon or chorizo is browned and the onion softened. Add the tomatoes and simmer, stirring, until they break down to form a thick sauce.

6 Add the beans to the frying pan (skillet) and stir to combine with the onion mixture. Stir in the cumin, to taste. Set aside.

7 Remove the rolls from the oven: keep the oven on. Fill the rolls with the warm bean mixture, then top with the cheese and close up tightly. Return to the baking (cookie) sheet and heat through in the oven until the cheese melts.

8 Open the rolls up and spoon in a little cabbage salad. Serve.

Spicy-sweet Meat Empanadas

This is a great make-ahead appetizer as it can be frozen for a month, then just popped into the oven at the last moment – will still taste marvellous!

Serves 4–6

INGREDIENTS

350 g/12 oz puff pastry
plain (all-purpose) flour, for dusting
1 quantity Spicy Beef Filling (see page 198)
1 egg yolk, beaten with 1–2 tbsp water

TO SERVE:
green olives
mixed chillies

1 Roll out the puff pastry into a thin layer on a lightly floured surface. Using a 15 cm/6 inch cutter, cut the pastry into 8 rounded shapes.

2 Place a tablespoon or two of the filling in the middle of one round.

3 Brush the edge of the pastry with beaten egg, then fold in half and press the edges together to seal.

4 Press the tines of a fork along the sealed edges of the pastry to make the seal more secure. Prick the top of the empanada with the fork, then place on a baking (cookie) sheet. Brush with beaten egg. Repeat this process with the remaining pastry rounds and filling.

5 Bake the empanadas in a preheated oven at 190°C/375°F/Gas Mark 5 for 15–25 minutes or until a light golden brown on the outside and hot in the middle.

6 Serve immediately, hot and sizzling from the oven, accompanied by a bowl of olives and chillies.

VARIATION

For chicken empanadas, replace the Spicy Beef Filling with diced cooked chicken, flavoured with some mild chilli sauce.

VARIATION

For vegetarian empanadas, replace the filling with a mixture of diced Gouda or Cheddar cheese, chopped onion, fresh coriander (cilantro), cumin seeds and sliced pimiento-stuffed green olives. Fill and bake as described.

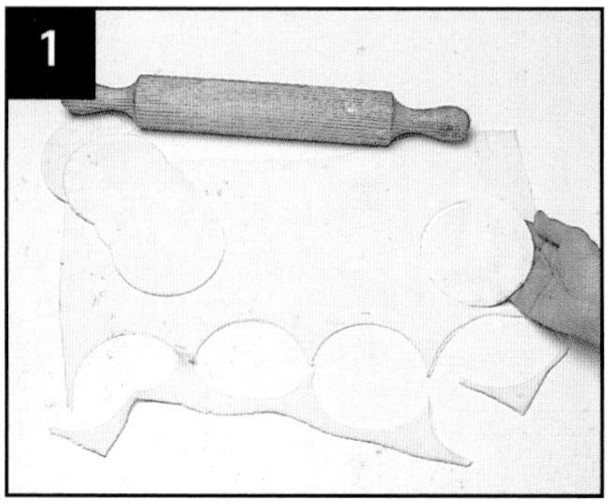

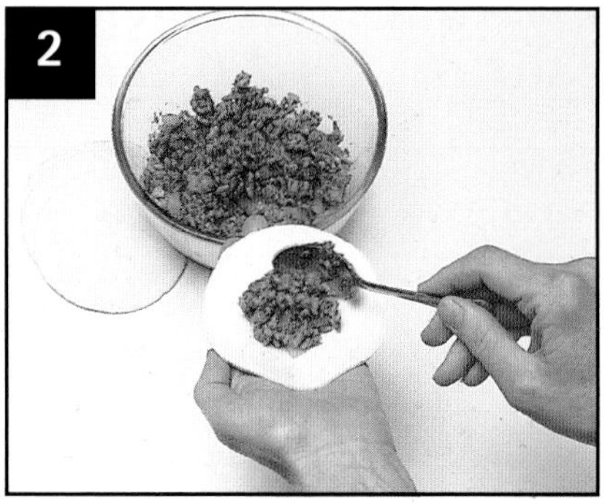

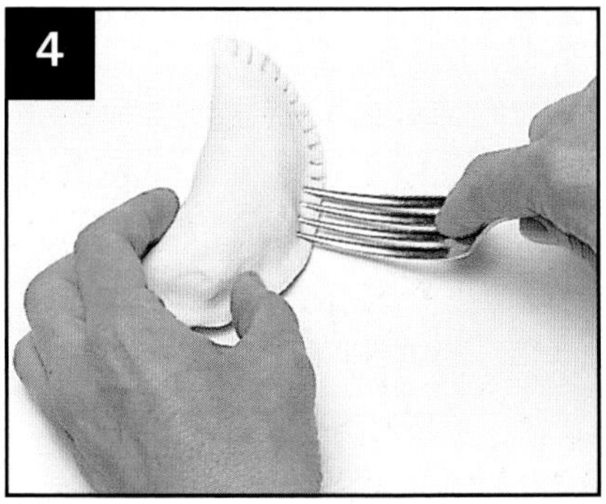

Masa Tartlets with Beans & Avocado

Packed with Mexican flavours, these little golden tartlets make a colourful start to a meal or a tasty light lunch, when served with mixed salad leaves.

Serves 4

INGREDIENTS

8–10 tbsp masa harina
3 tbsp plain (all-purpose) flour
pinch of baking powder
about 225 ml/8 fl oz/1 cup warm water
vegetable oil, for frying
225 g/8 oz/1 cup pinto beans or refried beans, heated through
1 avocado, stoned (pitted), sliced and tossed with lime juice
80 g/3 oz queso fresco or fresh cream cheese or crumbled feta
salsa of your choice
2 spring onions, thinly sliced

TO GARNISH:
fresh flat-leaf parsley sprigs
lemon wedges

1 Mix the masa harina with the plain (all-purpose) flour and baking powder in a bowl, then mix in enough warm water to make a firm yet moist dough.

2 Pinch off about a walnut-sized piece of dough and, using your fingers, shape into a tiny tartlet shape, pressing and pinching to make it as thin as possible without falling apart. Repeat with the remaining dough.

3 Heat a layer of oil in a deep frying pan (skillet) until it is smoking. Add a batch of tartlets to the hot oil and fry, spooning the hot fat into the centre of the tartlets and turning once, until golden on all sides.

4 Using a slotted spoon, remove the tartlets from the hot oil and drain on paper towels. Place on a baking (cookie) sheet and keep warm in the oven on a low temperature, while cooking the remaining tartlets.

5 To serve, fill each tartlet shell with the warmed beans, avocado, cheese, salsa and spring onions (scallions). Garnish with parsley and lemon wedges and serve at once.

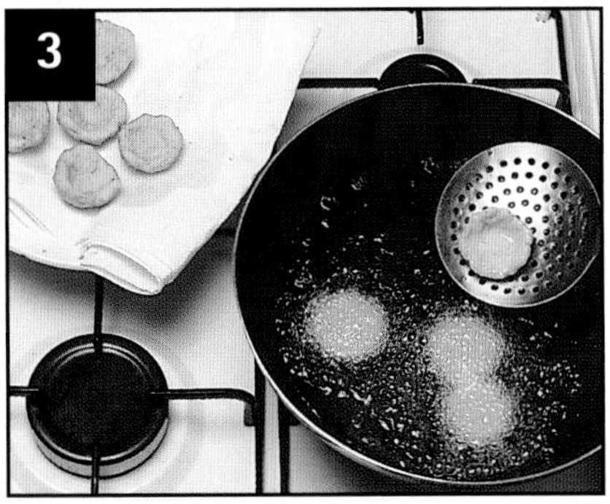

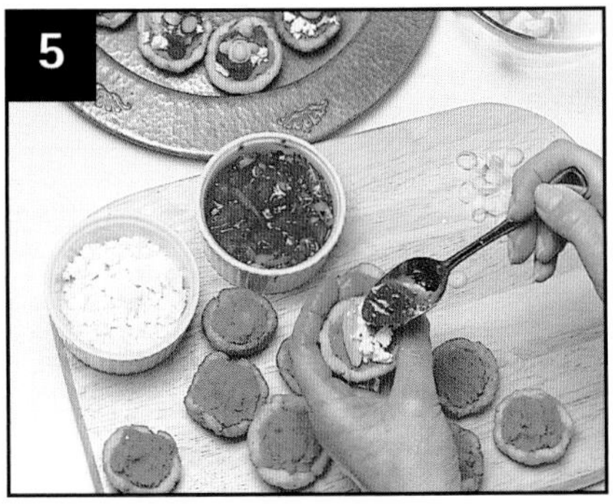

Salads, Side Dishes & Sauces

Salads of crisp raw vegetables and fruits, often eaten piled on top of richer savoury cooked dishes, such as enchiladas or barbecued (grilled) food, are full of strong fresh flavour and rich with vitamins, too. Pomegranate, papaya and tangy citrus fruits are combined with avocado or red (bell) peppers to stunning effect.

For heartier salads, Steak, Avocado Bean Salad is a substantial dish, while summer squash and chorizo, two popular ingredients in Mexico, make the basis for a great lunch-time snack.

For a delicious side dish, try a gratin of potatoes lavished with mild red chilli sauce, layered with goats' cheese and baked until lightly crusty. Or try fragrant Roasted Green Chillies in Cumin-garlic Cream – a classic accompaniment to all sorts of main courses.

Sauces for topping meat and fish or for filling tortillas are on offer in this chapter, too – the Quick Tomato Sauce can be used for all manner of dishes, while Hot Sauce of Dried Chillies will add a hotnesss that is the very essence of Mexican cuisine. Mole Poblano, the classic sauce of chillies and chocolate, is not to be missed.

Papaya, Avocado & Red (Bell) Pepper Salad

This colourful and refreshing salad, with its sweet and spicy flavours, is the perfect foil to a meaty main dish, and is particularly good with barbecued (grilled) food.

Serves 4–6

INGREDIENTS

200 g/7 oz mixed green salad leaves
2–3 spring onions (scallions), chopped
3–4 tbsp chopped fresh coriander (cilantro)
1 small papaya
2 red (bell) peppers
1 avocado
1 tbsp lime juice
3–4 tbsp pumpkin seeds, preferably toasted (optional)

DRESSING:
juice of 1 lime
large pinch of paprika
large pinch of ground cumin
large pinch of sugar
1 garlic clove, finely chopped
4 tbsp extra-virgin olive oil
dash of white wine vinegar (optional)
salt

1 Combinethe salad leaves with the spring onions (scallions) and coriander (cilantro). Mix well, then transfer the salad to a large serving dish.

2 Cut the papaya in half and scoop out the seeds with a spoon. Cut into quarters, remove the peel and slice the flesh. Arrange on top of the salad leaves. Cut the (bell) peppers in half, remove the cores and seeds, then slice thinly. Add the peppers to the salad leaves.

3 Cut the avocado in half around the stone (pit). Twist apart, then remove the stone (pit) with a knife. Carefully peel off the skin, dice the flesh and toss in lime juice to prevent the avocado from discolouring. Add to the other salad ingredients.

4 To make the dressing, whisk together the lime juice, paprika, ground cumin, sugar, garlic and olive oil. Add salt to suit your taste.

5 Pour the dressing over the salad and toss lightly, adding a dash of wine vinegar if a flavour with more 'bite' is preferred. Sprinkle with the toasted pumpkin seeds, if using.

1

3

5

Aceite

Green Bean Salad with Feta Cheese

This fresh-tasting salad is flavoured with fresh coriander (cilantro), a herb used widely in Mexican cooking.

Serves 4

INGREDIENTS

- 350 g/12 oz green beans, topped and tailed
- 1 red onion, chopped
- 3–4 tbsp chopped fresh coriander (cilantro)
- 2 radishes, thinly sliced
- 75 g/2 ¾ oz feta cheese, crumbled
- 1 tsp chopped fresh oregano or ½ tsp dried
- 2 tbsp red wine or fruit vinegar
- 80 ml/3 fl oz/⅓ cup extra-virgin olive oil
- 3 ripe tomatoes, cut into wedges
- pepper

1 Bring about 5 cm/2 inches water to the boil in the bottom of a steamer. Add the beans to the top part of the steamer, cover and steam for about 5 minutes until just tender.

2 Put the beans in a bowl and add the onion, coriander (cilantro), radishes and feta cheese.

3 Sprinkle the oregano over the salad, then grind pepper over to taste. Mix the vinegar and olive oil together and pour over the salad. Toss gently to mix well.

4 Transfer to a serving platter, surround with the tomato wedges and serve at once, or chill until ready to serve.

VARIATION

This recipe is also delicious made with nopales, or edible cactus, which is used as a vegetable in Mexican cooking. It is available in specialist stores in cans or jars. Simply drain the cactus, then slice and use instead of the green beans, missing out Step 1. When using cactus, replace the feta cheese with 1–2 chopped hard-boiled (hard-cooked) eggs.

Citrus Salad with Pomegranate & Avocado

A salad like this reminds one of how much Mexico and the Mediterranean share in terms of sunny flavours and ingredients.

Serves 4

INGREDIENTS

1 large pomegranate
1 grapefruit
2 sweet oranges
finely grated rind of ½ lime
1–2 garlic cloves, finely chopped
3 tbsp red wine vinegar
juice of 2 limes
½ tsp sugar
¼ tsp dry mustard
4–5 tbsp extra-virgin olive oil
1 head red leafy lettuce, such as oakleaf, washed and dried
1 avocado, stoned (pitted), diced and tossed with a little lime juice
salt and pepper
½ red onion, thinly sliced, to garnish

1 Cut the pomegranate into quarters, then press back the outer skin to push out the seeds into a bowl.

2 Using a sharp knife, cut a slice off the top and bottom of the grapefruit, then remove the peel and pith, cutting downwards. Cut out the segments from between the membranes, then add to the pomegranate.

3 Finely grate the rind of half an orange and set aside. Using a sharp knife, cut a slice off the top and bottom of both oranges, then remove the peel and pith, cutting downwards and taking care to retain the shape of the oranges. Slice horizontally into slices, then cut into quarters. Add the oranges to the pomegranate and grapefruit and stir to mix well.

4 Combine the reserved orange rind with the lime rind, garlic, vinegar, lime juice, sugar and mustard. Season with salt and pepper, then whisk in the olive oil.

5 Place the lettuce leaves in a serving bowl, then top with the citrus mixture and the avocado. Pour over the dressing and toss gently. Garnish with the onion rings and serve at once.

Courgettes (Zucchini) & Tomatoes with Green Chilli Vinaigrette

Lightly cooked courgettes (zucchini) are mixed with ripe, juicy tomatoes and dressed with a chilli vinaigrette to create a perfect side salad for a summer lunch or supper.

Serves 4–6

INGREDIENTS

1 large fresh mild green chilli, or a combination of 1 green (bell) pepper and ½–1 fresh green chilli
4 courgettes (zucchini), sliced
2–3 garlic cloves, finely chopped
pinch sugar
¼ tsp ground cumin
2 tbsp white wine vinegar
4 tbsp extra-virgin olive oil
2–3 tbsp coriander (cilantro)
4 ripe tomatoes, diced or sliced
salt and pepper

1 Roast the mild chilli, or the combination of the green (bell) pepper and chilli, in a heavy-based ungreased frying pan (skillet) or under a preheated grill (broiler) until the skin is charred. Place in a plastic bag, twist to seal well and leave the mixture to stand for 20 minutes.

2 Peel the skin from the chilli and (bell) pepper, if using, then remove the seeds and slice the flesh. Set aside.

3 Bring about 5 cm/2 inches water to the boil in the bottom of a steamer. Add the courgettes (zucchini) to the top part of the steamer, cover and steam for about 5 minutes until just tender.

4 Meanwhile, thoroughly combine the garlic, sugar, cumin, vinegar, olive oil and coriander (cilantro) in a bowl. Stir in the chilli and (bell) pepper, if using, then season with salt and pepper to taste.

5 Arrange the courgettes (zucchini) and tomatoes in a serving bowl or on a platter and spoon over the chilli dressing. Toss gently, if wished, and serve.

VARIATION

Add 225 g/8oz cooked peeled prawns (shrimp) to the courgettes (zucchini) and tomatoes, then coat with the dressing as in Step 5.

Steak, Avocado & Bean Salad

The Californian influence on Mexican food is evident in this big, hearty salad. Packed with delicious ingredients, this fantastic dish is a meal in itself.

Serves 4

INGREDIENTS

- 350 g/12 oz tender steak, such as sirloin or filet
- 4 garlic cloves, chopped
- juice of 1 lime
- 4 tbsp extra-virgin olive oil
- 1 tbsp white or red wine vinegar
- 1/4 tsp mild chilli powder
- 1/4 tsp ground cumin
- 1/2 tsp paprika
- pinch of sugar (optional)
- 5 spring onions (scallions), thinly sliced
- about 200 g/7 oz crisp lettuce leaves, such as cos (romaine), or mixed herb leaves
- 400 g/14 oz can pinto, black or red kidney beans, drained
- 1 avocado, stoned (pitted), sliced and tossed with a little lime juice
- 2 ripe tomatoes, diced
- 1/4 fresh green or red chilli, chopped
- 3 tbsp chopped fresh coriander (cilantro)
- 225 g/8 oz can sweetcorn, drained
- generous handful of crisp tortilla chips, broken into pieces
- salt and pepper

1 Place the steak in a non-metallic dish with the garlic and half the lime and olive oil. Season with salt and pepper, then leave to marinate.

2 To make the dressing, combine the remaining lime juice and olive oil with the vinegar, chilli powder, cumin and paprika. Add a pinch of sugar to taste. Set aside.

3 Pan fry the steak, or cook under a preheated grill (broiler), until browned on the outside and cooked to your liking in the middle. Remove from the pan, cut into strips and reserve; keep warm or allow to cool.

4 Toss the spring onions (scallions) with the lettuce and arrange on a serving platter. Pour about half the dressing over the leaves, then arrange the sweetcorn, beans, avocado and tomatoes over the top. Sprinkle with the chilli and coriander (cilantro).

5 Arrange the steak and the tortilla chips on top, pour over the rest of the dressing, and serve at once.

Courgettes (Zucchini) & Summer Squash with Chorizo

The spicy richness of chorizo marries well with courgettes (zucchini) and squash, giving them a real flavour lift.

Serves 4

INGREDIENTS

- 2 courgettes (zucchini), thinly sliced
- 2 yellow summer squash, thinly sliced
- 2 fresh chorizo sausages, diced or sliced
- 3 garlic cloves, finely chopped
- juice of ½–1 lime
- 1–2 tbsp chopped fresh coriander (cilantro)
- salt and pepper

1 Cook the courgettes (zucchini) and summer squash in boiling salted water for 3–4 minutes until they are just tender, then drain well.

2 Brown the chorizo in a heavy-based frying pan (skillet), stirring with a spoon to break up into pieces. Pour off any excess fat from the browned chorizo, then add the garlic and blanched courgettes (zucchini) and summer squash. Cook for a few minutes, stirring gently, to combine the flavours.

3 Stir in the lime juice, to taste. Season with salt and pepper and serve at once sprinkled with chopped coriander (cilantro).

COOK'S TIP

Mild in flavour and ideal for combining with spicy meats, squash is a favourite Mexican vegetable. If wished, this dish can be prepared with squash only – yellow pattypans would be ideal.

VARIATION

For variety, why not use the rather more exotic squash known as chayote or cho-cho, which is indigenous to Mexico. This is pear-shaped and is usually pale green, with a corrugated skin. To prepare, simply peel and slice, then blanch as in Step 1, cooking for a few minutes longer. Use with yellow-coloured courgettes (zucchini) for visual appeal.

Summer Squash with Green Chillies, Tomatoes & Sweetcorn

Garlicky butter and a hint of chilli flavour this summertime vegetable pot of squash and sweetcorn. Serve alongside almost any meaty main course, especially a roasted chicken; good, too with Fajitas.

Serves 4–6

INGREDIENTS

- 2 corn-on-the-cobs
- 2 small courgettes (zucchini) or other green summer squash, such as pattypan, cubed or sliced
- 2 small yellow summer squash, cubed or sliced
- 2 tbsp butter
- 3 garlic cloves, finely chopped
- 3–4 large, ripe flavourful tomatoes, diced
- several pinches of mild chilli powder
- several pinches of ground cumin
- ½ fresh green chilli, such as jalapeño, deseeded and chopped
- pinch of sugar
- salt and pepper

1 Bring about 5 cm/2 inches water to the boil in the bottom of a steamer. Add the corn-on-the-cobs, courgettes (zucchini) and summer squash to the top part of the steamer, cover and steam for about 3 minutes depending on their maturity and freshness. Alternatively, blanch in boiling salted water for about 3 minutes, then drain. Set aside until cool enough to handle.

2 Using a large knife, slice the corn kernels off the cobs and set aside.

3 Melt the butter in a heavy-based frying pan (skillet). Add the garlic and cook for 1 minute to soften. Add the tomatoes, chilli powder, ground cumin, green chilli and sugar to taste. Season with salt and pepper to taste and cook for a few minutes or until the flavours have mingled.

4 Add the corn kernels, courgettes (zucchini) and squash. Cook for 2 minutes, stirring, to warm through. Serve at once.

VARIATION

Any leftovers will make a good base for a lovely summer soup. Simply thin with lots of stock and freshen up with chopped herbs.

1

3

4

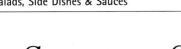

Potatoes in Green Sauce

Earthy potatoes, served in the tangy spicy tomatillo sauce and topped with spring onions (scallions) and soured cream, are delicious either as a side dish with simmered or braised meat, or as a vegetarian main course.

Serves 6

INGREDIENTS

- 1 kg/2 lb 4 oz small waxy potatoes, peeled
- 1 onion, halved and unpeeled
- 8 garlic cloves, unpeeled
- 1 fresh green chilli
- 8 tomatillos, outer husks removed, or small tart tomatoes
- 225 ml/8 fl oz/1 cup chicken, meat or vegetable stock, preferably homemade
- ½ tsp ground cumin
- 1 sprig fresh thyme or generous pinch dried
- 1 sprig fresh oregano or generous pinch dried
- 2 tbsp vegetable or extra-virgin olive oil
- 1 bunch fresh coriander (cilantro), chopped
- 1 courgette (zucchini), roughly chopped
- salt

1 Put the potatoes in a pan of salted water. Bring to the boil and cook for about 15 minutes or until almost tender. Do not overcook them. Drain and set aside.

2 Lightly char the onion, garlic, chilli and tomatillos or tomatoes in a heavy-based ungreased frying pan (skillet). Set aside, and when cool enough to handle, peel and chop the onion, garlic and chilli; chop the tomatillos or tomatoes. Put in a blender or food processor with half the stock and process to form a purée. Add the cumin, thyme and oregano.

3 Heat the oil in the heavy-based frying pan (skillet). Add the purée and cook for 5 minutes, stirring, to reduce slightly and concentrate the flavours.

4 Add the potatoes and courgette (zucchini) to the purée and pour in the rest of the stock. Add about half the coriander (cilantro) and cook for a further 5 minutes or until the courgettes (zucchini) tender.

5 Transfer to a serving bowl and serve sprinkled with the remaining chopped coriander (cilantro) to garnish.

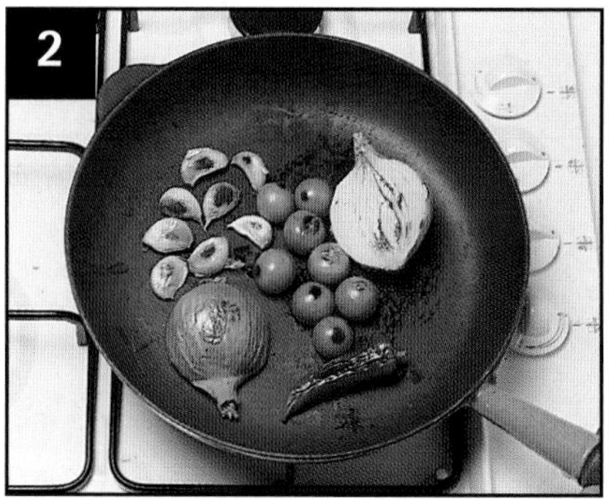

Potatoes with Goat's Cheese & Chipotle Cream

This makes a luscious side dish to serve with meat, or a satisfying vegetarian main course. Goat's cheese is a traditional food of Mexico, and is enjoying great renewed popularity.

Serves 4

INGREDIENTS

- 1.25 kg/2 lb 12 oz baking potatoes, peeled and cut into chunks
- pinch of salt
- pinch of sugar
- 200 ml/7 fl oz/¾ cup crème fraîche
- 120 ml/4 fl oz/½ cup vegetable or chicken stock
- 3 garlic cloves, finely chopped
- a few shakes of bottled chipotle salsa, or ½ dried chipotle, reconstituted (see page 100), deseeded and thinly sliced
- 225 g/8 oz goat's cheese, sliced
- 175 g/6 oz mozzarella or Cheddar cheese, grated
- 50 g/¾ oz Parmesan or pecorino cheese, grated
- salt

1 Put the potatoes in a pan of water with the salt and sugar. Bring to the boil and cook for about 10 minutes until they are half cooked.

2 Combine the crème fraîche with the stock, garlic and the chipotle salsa.

3 Arrange half the potatoes in a casserole. Pour half the crème fraîche sauce over the potatoes and cover with the goat's cheese. Top with the remaining potatoes and the sauce.

4 Sprinkle with the grated mozzarella or Cheddar cheese, then with either the grated Parmesan or pecorino.

5 Bake in a preheated oven at 180°C/350°F/Gas Mark 4 until the potatoes are tender and the cheese topping is lightly golden and crisped in places. Serve at once.

2

3

4

Roasted Green Chillies in Cumin-garlic Cream

Roasted mild green chillies are delicious simmered with cumin-scented cream. It's important not to make this too hot, otherwise the fragrant aromas will be overpowered.

Serves 4–6

INGREDIENTS

4 large fresh mild green chillies, such as anaheim or poblano, or a combination of 4 green (bell) peppers and 2 jalapeños
2 tbsp butter
1 onion, finely chopped
3 garlic cloves, finely chopped
1/4 tsp ground cumin
225 ml/8 fl oz/1 cup single (light) cream
225 ml/8 fl oz/1 cup chicken or vegetable stock
salt and pepper
1 lime, halved, to serve

1 Roast the mild chillies, or the combination of (bell) peppers and jalapeños, in a heavy-based ungreased frying pan (skillet) or under a preheated grill (broiler) until the skins are charred. Place in a plastic bag, twist to seal well and leave to stand for 20 minutes to allow the skins to loosen.

2 Remove the seeds from the chillies and (bell) peppers, if using, and peel off the skins. Slice the flesh. Set aside.

3 Melt the butter in a large frying pan (skillet), add the onion and garlic and sauté for about 3 minutes until softened. Sprinkle with the cumin and season with salt and pepper to your taste.

4 Stir in the sliced chillies and pour in the cream and stock. Cook over a medium heat, stirring, until the liquid reduces in volume and forms a richly flavoured sauce.

5 Transfer to a serving dish and serve warm, squeezing over lime juice at the last minute.

VARIATION

Add an equal amount of sweetcorn with the chillies – they add a delicious sweetness to the dish.

2

5

4

Quick Tomato Sauce

Simple to make, this versatile sauce is not only a great accompaniment for barbecued (grilled) meat and fish, but also invaluable for baked tortilla dishes and taco fillings.

Serves 4–6

INGREDIENTS

- 2 tbsp vegetable or olive oil
- 1 onion, thinly sliced
- 5 garlic cloves, thinly sliced
- 400 g/14 oz can tomatoes, diced, plus their juices, or 600 g/1 lb 5 oz fresh diced tomatoes
- several shakes of mild chilli powder
- 350 ml/12 fl oz/1½ cups vegetable or chicken stock
- salt and pepper
- pinch of sugar (optional)

1 Heat the oil in a large frying pan (skillet). Add the onion and garlic and cook, stirring, until just softened.

2 Add the tomatoes, chilli powder to taste and the vegetable or chicken stock. Cook over a medium-high heat for about 10 minutes or until the tomatoes have reduced slightly and the flavour of the sauce is more concentrated.

3 Season the sauce with salt, pepper and sugar to taste and serve the dish warm.

COOK'S TIP

The sauce will keep covered in the refrigerator for up to 3 days.

COOK'S TIP

If using fresh tomatoes for this sauce, make sure they are very ripe and flavourful. Skin and deseed fresh tomatoes before dicing.

VARIATION

For a hotter kick, add a ½ teaspoon of finely chopped fresh chilli with the onion.

Hot Tomato Sauce

This tangy sauce is excellent with crispy tortillas and tostadas, or with grilled (broiled) or fried fish. Try it with fish and chips for a change!

Serves 4

INGREDIENTS

- 2–3 fresh green chillies, such as jalapeño or serrano
- 225 g/8 oz canned chopped tomatoes
- 1 spring onion (scallion), thinly sliced
- 2 garlic cloves, chopped
- 2–3 tbsp cider vinegar
- 50–80 ml/2–3 fl oz/$\frac{1}{4}$–$\frac{1}{3}$ cup water
- large pinch of dried oregano
- large pinch of ground cumin
- large pinch of sugar
- large pinch of salt

1 Slice the chillies open, remove the seeds if wished, then chop the chillies.

2 Put the chillies in a blender or food processor together with the tomatoes, spring onion (scallion), garlic, vinegar, water, oregano, cumin, sugar and salt. Process until smooth.

3 Adjust the seasoning and chill until ready to serve. The sauce will keep for up to a week, covered, in the refrigerator.

COOK'S TIP

If you have sensitive skin, it may be advisable to wear rubber gloves when preparing chillies, as the oil in the seeds and flesh can cause irritation. Make sure that you do not touch your eyes when handling cut chillies.

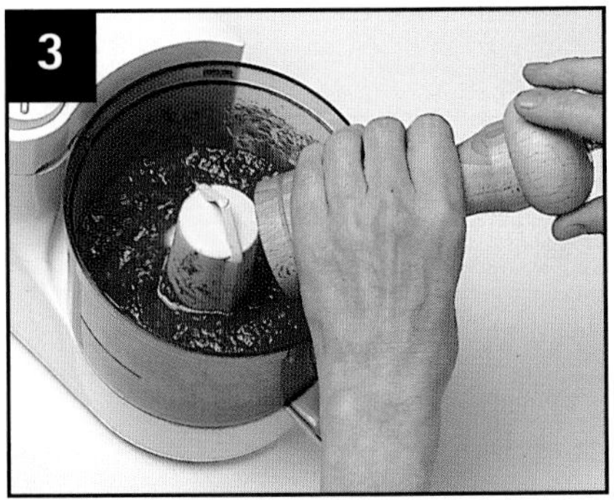

Mild Red Chilli Sauce

This milder sauce is ideal for enchiladas and stewed meat. Keep some stashed in your freezer at all times, for an instant hit of Mexico!

Makes about 350 ml/12 fl oz/1½ cups

INGREDIENTS

5 large fresh mild chillies, such as New Mexico or ancho
450 ml/16 fl oz /2 cups vegetable or chicken stock
1 tbsp masa harina or 1 crumbled corn tortilla, puréed with enough water to make a thin paste
large pinch of ground cumin
1–2 garlic cloves, finely chopped
juice of 1 lime
salt

1 Using metal tongs, roast each chilli over an open flame until the colour darkens on all sides. Alternatively, place the chillies under a preheated grill (broiler), turning them frequently.

2 Put the chillies in a bowl and pour boiling water over them. Cover and leave the chillies to cool.

3 Meanwhile, put the stock in a pan and bring to a simmer.

4 When the chillies have cooled and are swelled up and softened, remove from the water with a slotted spoon. Remove the seeds from the chillies, then cut or tear the flesh into pieces and place in a blender or food processor. Process to form a purée, then mix in the hot stock.

5 Put the chilli and stock mixture in a pan. Add the masa harina or puréed tortilla, cumin, garlic and lime juice. Bring to the boil and cook for a few minutes, stirring, until the sauce has thickened. Adjust the seasoning and serve.

Hot Sauce of Dried Chillies

Perfect for adding a splash of authentic hot Mexican flavour to a dish, this sauce will prove to be a handy standby.

Makes about 225 ml/8 fl oz/1 cup

INGREDIENTS

10 dried arbol chillies, stems removed (see Cook's Tip)
225 ml/8 fl oz/1 cup cider or white wine vinegar
½ tsp salt

1 Place the dried arbol chillies in a mortar and crush finely with a pestle.

2 Put the cider or white wine vinegar in a pan and add the crushed chillies and salt. Stir to combine, then bring the liquid to the boil.

3 Remove from the heat and leave to cool completely to allow the flavours to infuse. Pour into a bowl and serve. The sauce will keep for up to a month, if covered and kept in the refrigerator.

COOK'S TIP

Hot sauce can be bottled by pouring into sterilized jars and treating it as you would any long-keeping jam, jelly or preserve.

COOK'S TIP

Arbol are dried long hot red chillies, with a dusty heat that is reminiscent of the Mexican desert. If arbol chillies are not available, use any hot dried chilli, or chilli flakes, such as cayenne.

Mole Poblano

This great Mexican celebration dish, ladled out at village fiestas, birthday parties, baptisms and weddings, is known for its unusual combination of chillies and chocolate.

Serves 8–10

INGREDIENTS

- 3 mulato chillies
- 3 mild ancho chillies
- 5–6 New Mexico or California chillies
- 1 onion, chopped
- 5 garlic cloves, chopped
- 450 g/1 lb ripe tomatoes
- 2 tortillas, preferably stale, cut into small pieces
- pinch of cloves
- pinch of fennel seeds
- 1/8 tsp each ground cinnamon, coriander and cumin
- 3 tbsp lightly toasted sesame seeds or tahini
- 3 tbsp flaked or coarsely ground blanched almonds
- 2 tbsp raisins
- 1 tbsp peanut butter (optional)
- 450 ml/16 fl oz/2 cups chicken stock
- 3–4 tbsp grated semi-sweet chocolate, plus extra for garnishing
- 2 tbsp mild chilli powder
- 3 tbsp vegetable oil
- about 1 tbsp lime juice
- salt and pepper

1 Using metal tongs, toast each chilli over an open flame for a few seconds until the colour darkens. Alternatively, roast in an ungreased frying pan (skillet) over a medium heat, turning constantly, for about 30 seconds.

2 Place the toasted chillies in a bowl or a pan and pour boiling water over to cover. Cover with a lid and leave to soften for at least one hour or overnight. Once or twice lift the lid and rearrange the chillies so that they soak evenly.

3 Remove the softened chillies with a slotted spoon. Discard the stems and seeds and cut the flesh into pieces. Place in a blender.

4 Add the onion, garlic, tomatoes, tortillas, cloves, fennel seeds, cinnamon, coriander, cumin, sesame seeds, almonds, raisins and peanut butter if using, then process to combine. With the motor running, add enough stock through the feed tube to make a smooth paste. Stir in the remaining stock, chocolate and chilli powder.

5 Heat the oil in a heavy-based pan until it is smoking, then pour in the mole mixture. It will splatter and pop as it hits the hot oil. Cook for about 10 minutes, stirring occasionally to prevent it from burning.

6 Season with salt, pepper and lime juice, garnish with grated chocolate and serve.

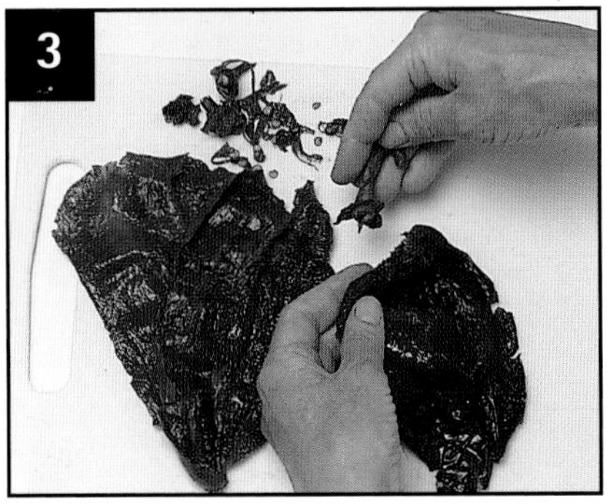

Mole Verde

Moles are purées and, depending on the ingredients, they vary in colour from yellow and green to chocolate brown. This green mole is a speciality of Jalisco. Serve with either warm corn tortillas or unfilled tamales.

Serves 4–6

INGREDIENTS

- 250 g/9 oz toasted pumpkin seeds
- 1 litre/1¾ pints/4 cups chicken stock
- several pinches of ground cloves
- 8–10 tomatillos, diced or use 225ml/8 fl oz/1 cup mild tomatillo salsa
- ½ onion, chopped
- ½ fresh green chilli, deseeded and diced
- 3 garlic cloves, chopped
- ½ tsp fresh thyme leaves
- ½ tsp fresh marjoram leaves
- 3 tbsp lard or vegetable oil
- 3 bay leaves
- 4 tbsp chopped fresh coriander (cilantro)
- salt and pepper
- fresh green chilli slices, to garnish

1 Grind the toasted pumpkin seeds in a food processor. Add half the chicken stock, the cloves, tomatillos, onion, chilli, garlic, thyme and marjoram and blend to a purée.

2 Heat the lard or oil in a heavy-based frying pan and add the puréed pumpkin seed mixture and the bay leaves. Cook over a medium-high heat for about 5 minutes until the mixture has began to thicken.

3 Remove from the heat and add the rest of the stock and the coriander (cilantro). Return the pan to the heat and cook until the sauce thickens, then remove from the heat.

4 Remove the bay leaves and process the sauce until completley smooth again. Add salt and pepper to taste.

5 Transfer to a bowl, garnish with chilli and serve.

VARIATION

Make a tamale dough (see page 138) and poach in the mole as dumplings, making a filling snack.

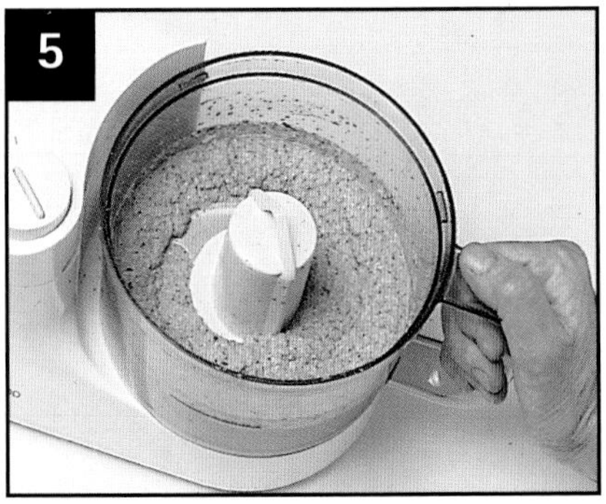

Salsa, Tortillas, Beans & Rice

Salsas appear on every table of every corner of Mexico, raw, cooked, chopped, chunky, smooth, spicy, mild or fiery. They are what adds interest to often simple fare. What's more, they are delicious and good for you too, as long as you don't burn your tongue. In this recipe you'll find the full range from sizzling Salsa Verde to powerful and smoky Chipotle Salsa and cooling Fresh Pineapple Salsa.

Tortillas are not only the bread of Mexico, they are also its knives and forks: break off a piece of tortilla, wrap it up in whatever you are eating, and you have an instant taco, no eating utensils needed. The variety of dishes made with tortillas in this chapter, range from fish-filled tacos and tostadas topped with chicken and green salsa, to burritos filled with lamb and black beans.

In Mexico, beans and rice are eaten every day, for nearly every meal: a pot of beans is almost always simmering on the back of nearly every stove in the land, and great pots of rice are cooked using the stock of simmering meats. Discover how to make Mexico's famous dish of refried beans, and learn the secret of Green Rice – a delicious dish, flavoured with roasted onions, garlic, chilli and plenty of coriander (cilantro).

If you ate nothing but salsas, dishes of tortillas, beans and rice, you would be eating the very soul of Mexico.

Two Classic Salsas

A Mexican meal is not complete without an accompanying salsa. These two traditional salsas are ideal for seasoning any dish, from filled tortillas to grilled (broiled) meat – they add a spicy hotness that is the very essence of Mexican cooking.

Serves 4–6

INGREDIENTS

JALAPEÑO SALSA:
- 1 onion, finely chopped
- 2-3 garlic cloves, finely chopped
- 4-6 tbsp coarsely chopped pickled jalapeño chillies
- juice of ½ lemon
- about ¼ tsp ground cumin
- salt

SALSA CRUDA:
- 6–8 ripe tomatoes, finely chopped
- about 100 ml/3½ fl oz/scant ½ cup tomato juice
- 3–4 garlic cloves, finely chopped
- ½–1 bunch fresh coriander (cilantro) leaves, coarsely chopped
- pinch of sugar
- 3–4 fresh green chillies, such as jalapeño or serrano, deseeded and finely chopped
- ½–1 tsp ground cumin
- 3–4 spring onions (scallions), finely chopped
- salt

1 To make the jalapeño salsa, put the onion in a bowl with the garlic, jalapeños, lemon juice and cumin. Season with salt and stir together. Cover and chill until required.

2 To make a chunky-textured salsa cruda, stir all the ingredients together in a bowl, adding salt to taste. Cover and chill until required.

3 To make a smoother-textured salsa, process the ingredients in a blender or food processor. Cover and chill until required.

VARIATION

For the salsa cruda, substitute finely chopped orange segments and deseeded diced cucumber for the tomatoes to add a fresh, fruity taste.

COOK'S TIP

You can vary the amount of garlic, chillies and ground spices according to taste, but make sure the salsa has quite a 'kick', otherwise it will not be effective.

Chipotle Salsa

Chipotles are the smoked jalapeño chilli sold either dried or in cans, packed in a spicy flavourful marinade called adobo. Here the marinade from the canned version is used to perk up a simple fresh tomato salsa.

Makes about 450 ml/16 fl oz/2 cups

INGREDIENTS

450 g/1 lb ripe juicy tomatoes, diced
3–5 garlic cloves, finely chopped
½ bunch fresh coriander (cilantro) leaves, coarsely chopped
1 small onion, chopped
1–2 tsp adobo marinade from canned chipotle chillies
½–1 tsp sugar
lime juice, to taste
salt
pinch of cinnamon (optional)
pinch of ground allspice (optional)
pinch of ground cumin (optional)

1 Put the tomatoes, garlic and coriander (cilantro) in a blender or food processor.

2 Process the mixture until it is smooth, then add the onion, adobo marinade, sugar.

3 Squeeze in lime juice to taste. Season with salt to taste, then add the cinnamon, allspice or cumin, if wished.

4 Serve at once, or cover and chill until ready to serve, although the salsa is at its best when served freshly made.

COOK'S TIP

To simplify preparation, the fresh tomatoes can be replaced with a 400 g/14 oz can chopped tomatoes.

COOK'S TIP

Canned chipotle chillies are available from specialist Mexican stores.

1

2

3

Cooked Chipotle Salsa

This rich, tomato-red chipotle salsa is sweet and tangy, delicious with anything barbecued (grilled), or dabbed into a taco or burrito.

Makes about 450 ml/16 fl oz/2 cups

INGREDIENTS

3 dried chipotle chillies
1 onion, finely chopped
400 g/14 oz can tomatoes, including their juices
2–3 tbsp dark brown (molasses) sugar
2–3 garlic cloves, finely chopped
pinch of ground cinnamon
pinch of ground cloves or allspice
large pinch of ground cumin
juice of ½ lemon
1 tbsp extra-virgin olive oil
lemon rind strips, to garnish

1 Place the chillies in a pan with enough water to cover. Protecting your face against fumes and making sure the kitchen is well ventilated, bring the chillies and water to the boil. Cook for about 5 minutes, then remove from heat, cover and leave to stand until softened.

2 Remove the chillies from the water with a slotted spoon. Cut away and discard the stem and seeds, then either scrape the flesh from the skins or chop up the whole chillies.

3 Put the onion in a pan with the tomatoes and sugar and cook over a medium heat, stirring, until thickened.

4 Remove from the heat and add the garlic, cinnamon, cloves, cumin, lemon juice, olive oil and prepared chipotle chillies. Season with salt to taste and leave to cool. Serve garnished with lemon rind.

COOK'S TIP

Do not inhale the fumes given off during the boiling process as they can irritate your lungs.

COOK'S TIP

This salsa freezes extremely well. Freeze in an ice-cube tray, then pop the cubes out and store in a plastic bag, ready to use for individual portions.

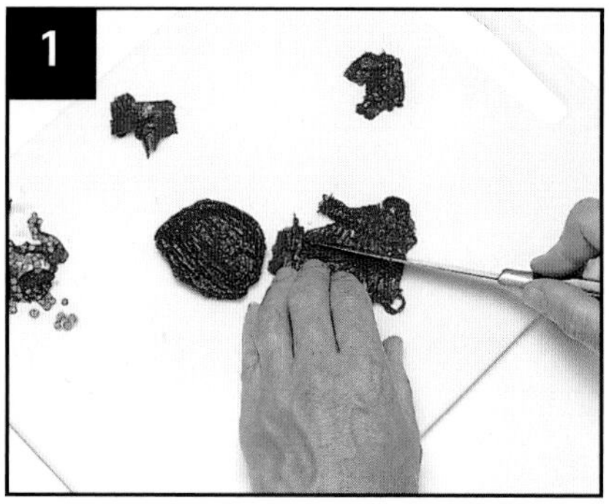

Hot Mexican Salsas

These salsas capture the inimitable tangy, spicy flavour of Mexico. Choose from a fresh minty fruit salsa, charred chilli salsa or a spicy 'green' salsa.

Serves 4–6

INGREDIENTS

TROPICAL FRUIT SALSA:
½ sweet ripe pineapple, peeled, cored and diced
1 mango or papaya, peeled, deseeded and diced
½–1 fresh green chilli, such as jalapeño or serrano, deseeded and chopped
½–1 fresh red chilli, chopped
½ red onion, chopped
1 tbsp sugar
juice of 1 lime
3 tbsp chopped fresh mint
salt

SCORCHED CHILLI SALSA:
1 green (bell) pepper
2–3 fresh green chillies, such as jalapeño or serrano
2 garlic cloves, finely chopped
juice of ½ lime
1 tsp salt
large pinch of dried oregano
large pinch of ground cumin
2–3 tbsp extra-virgin olive oil or vegetable oil

SALSA VERDE:
450 g/1 lb oz canned tomatillos, drained and chopped, or tart tomatoes, chopped
1–2 fresh green chillies, such as jalapeño or serrano, deseeded and finely chopped
1 green (bell) pepper or large mild green chilli, such as anaheim or poblano, deseeded and chopped
1 small onion, chopped
1 bunch fresh coriander (cilantro) leaves, finely chopped
½ tsp ground cumin
salt

1 To make the tropical fruit salsa, combine all the ingredients in a large bowl, adding salt to taste. Cover the bowl and chill in the refrigerator until required.

2 For scorched chilli salsa, char the chillies and (bell) pepper in an ungreased frying pan (skillet). Cool, deseed, skin and chop. Mix with the garlic, lime juice, salt and oil. Top with oregano and cumin.

3 For salsa verde, combine the ingredients in a bowl, adding salt to taste. If a smoother sauce is preferred, blend the ingredients in a food processor. Spoon into a bowl to serve.

Salsa of Marinated Chipotle Chillies

Dried chipotle chillies make a spicy-sweet smoky relish, good for adding to tostadas, tacos and any other tortilla dish.

Serves 4–6

INGREDIENTS

6 dried chipotle chillies
6 tbsp tomato ketchup (catsup)
350 g/12 oz ripe tomatoes, diced
1 large onion, chopped
5 garlic cloves, chopped
2 tbsp cider vinegar
300 ml/10 fl oz/1¼ cups water
1 tbsp extra-virgin olive oil
2 tbsp sugar, preferably molasses sugar
pinch of salt
¼ tsp ground allspice
¼ tsp ground cloves
¼ tsp ground cinnamon
¼ tsp ground cumin
3–4 tbsp lime juice or combination of pineapple and lemon juice
pepper

1 Place the chipotles in a pan with enough water to cover. Bring to the boil, taking care not to inhale the fumes given off as they can irritate your lungs. Simmer, covered, for about 20 minutes, then remove from the heat and leave to cool.

2 Remove the chillies from the water. Cut away and discard the stem and seeds, then either scrape the flesh from the skins or chop up the whole chillies.

3 Place the tomato ketchup (catsup) and tomatoes in a pan with the onion, chillies, garlic, vinegar, water, olive oil, sugar, salt, allspice, cloves, cinnamon and cumin. Bring to the boil. Reduce the heat and simmer for about 15 minutes until the mixture has thickened.

4 Season with salt and pepper to taste, then stir in the fruit juice and use as required.

1

3

4

Fresh Pineapple Salsa

This sweet fruity salsa is fresh and fragrant, a wonderful foil to spicy food from the barbecue (grill).

Serves 4

INGREDIENTS

- ½ ripe pineapple
- juice of 1 lime or lemon
- 1 garlic clove, finely chopped
- 1 spring onion (scallion), thinly sliced
- ½–1 fresh green or red chilli, deseeded and finely chopped
- ½ red (bell) pepper, deseeded and chopped
- 3 tbsp chopped fresh mint
- 3 tbsp chopped fresh coriander (cilantro)
- pinch of salt
- pinch of sugar

1 Using a sharp knife, cut off the top and bottom of the pineapple. Place upright on a board, then slice off the skin, cutting downwards. Cut the flesh into slices, halve the slices and remove the cores, if wished. Dice the flesh. Reserve any juice that accumulates as you cut the pineapple.

2 Place the pineapple in a bowl and stir in the lime juice, garlic, spring onion (scallion), chopped chilli and red (bell) pepper.

3 Stir in the chopped fresh mint and coriander (cilantro). Add the salt and sugar and stir well to combine all the ingredients. Chill until ready to serve.

COOK'S TIP

A fresh pineapple is ripe if it has a sweet aroma. The flesh will still be fairly firm to touch. Still, fresh-looking leaves are a sign of good condition.

VARIATION

Replace the pineapple with 3 juicy oranges, peeled and divided into segments.

Crab & Avocado Soft Tacos

Crab meat and avocado make an elegant yet very authentic filling for tacos. Eat one and you will be transported to a beach somewhere south of Acapulo!

Serves 4

INGREDIENTS

8 corn tortillas
1 avocado
lime or lemon juice, for tossing
4–6 tbsp soured cream
250–275 g/9–10 oz cooked crab meat
½ lime
½ fresh green chilli, such as jalapeño or serrano, deseeded and chopped or thinly sliced
1 ripe tomato, deseeded and diced
½ small onion, finely chopped
2 tbsp chopped fresh coriander (cilantro)
salsa of your choice, to serve (optional)

1 Heat the tortillas in an ungreased non-stick frying pan (skillet), sprinkling them with a few drops of water as they heat; wrap in a clean tea towel (dish cloth) as you work to keep them warm.

2 Cut the avocado in half around the stone (pit). Twist apart, then remove the stone (pit) with a knife. Carefully peel off the skin from the avocado, slice the flesh and toss in lime or lemon juice to prevent any discoloration.

3 Spread one tortilla with soured cream. Top with crab meat, a squeeze of lime and a sprinkling of chilli, tomato, onion, coriander (cilantro) and avocado, adding a splash of salsa if desired. Repeat the procedure with the remaining tortillas and serve immediately.

VARIATION

To transform into tostadas, fry the tortillas in a small amount of oil in a non-stick pan until crisp. Top one crisp tortilla with the filling, as in Step 3. Prepare a second tortilla with the filling and place on top of the first filled tortilla. Repeat once more, to make a small tower, top with shredded lettuce and serve.

1

3

5

Fish Tacos Ensenada Style

These tacos of fried fish chunks and red cabbage salad are served up in the cantinas and fondas of the coastal town of Ensenada, in Mexico's Baja California.

Serves 4

INGREDIENTS

about 450 g/1 lb firm-fleshed white fish, such as red snapper or cod
1/4 tsp dried oregano
1/4 tsp ground cumin
1 tsp mild chilli powder
2 garlic cloves, finely chopped
3 tbsp plain (all-purpose) flour
vegetable oil, for frying
1/4 red cabbage, thinly sliced or shredded
juice of 2 limes
hot pepper sauce or salsa to taste
8 corn tortillas
1 tbsp chopped fresh coriander (cilantro)
1/2 onion, chopped (optional)
salt and pepper
salsa of your choice

1 Place the fish on a plate and sprinkle with half the oregano, cumin, chilli powder and garlic and salt and pepper, then dust with the flour.

2 Heat the oil in a frying pan (skillet) until it is smoking, then fry the fish in several batches until it is golden on the outside, and just tender in the middle. Remove from the pan and place on paper towels to drain.

3 Combine the cabbage with the remaining oregano, cumin, chilli and garlic, then stir in the lime juice, salt and hot pepper sauce to taste. Set aside.

4 Heat the tortillas in an ungreased non-stick frying pan (skillet), sprinkling with a few drops of water as they heat; wrap the tortillas in a clean tea towel (dish cloth) as you work to keep them warm. Alternatively, heat through in a stack in the pan, alternating the tortillas from the top to the bottom so that they warm evenly.

5 Place some of the warm fried fish in each tortilla, along with a large spoonful of the hot cabbage salad. Sprinkle with chopped fresh coriander (cilantro) and onion, if desired. Add the salsa to taste and serve immediately.

Fish & Refried Bean Tostadas with Green Salsa

Crisp tostadas are topped with spiced fish, refried beans and crunchy lettuce – perfect for a well-balanced lunch.

Serves 4

INGREDIENTS

about 450 g/1 lb firm-fleshed white fish, such as red snapper or cod
120 ml/4 fl oz/½ cup fish stock, or water mixed with a fish stock cube
¼ tsp ground cumin
¼ tsp mild chilli powder
pinch of dried oregano
4 garlic cloves, finely chopped
juice of ½ lemon or lime
8 soft corn tortillas
vegetable oil, for frying
400 g/14 oz can refried beans, warmed with 2 tbsp water to thin
salsa of your choice
2–3 leaves cos (romaine) lettuce, shredded
3 tbsp chopped fresh coriander (cilantro)
2 tbsp chopped onion
salt and pepper

TO GARNISH:
soured cream
chopped fresh herbs

1 Put the fish in a pan with the fish stock, cumin, chilli, oregano, garlic and salt and pepper. Gently bring to the boil, then immediately remove from the heat and leave the fish to cool in the cooking liquid.

2 When cool enough to handle, remove from the liquid with a slotted spoon; reserve the cooking liquid. Break the fish up into bite-sized pieces, put in a bowl, sprinkle with the lemon or lime juice and set aside.

3 To make tostadas, fry the tortillas in a small amount of oil in a non-stick frying pan (skillet) until crisp. Spread the tostadas evenly with the warm refried beans.

4 Gently reheat the fish with a little of the reserved cooking liquid, then spoon the fish on top of the beans. Top each tostada with some of the salsa, lettuce, chopped fresh coriander (cilantro) and onion. Garnish each one with a dollop of soured cream and a sprinkling of chopped fresh herbs. Serve immediately.

2
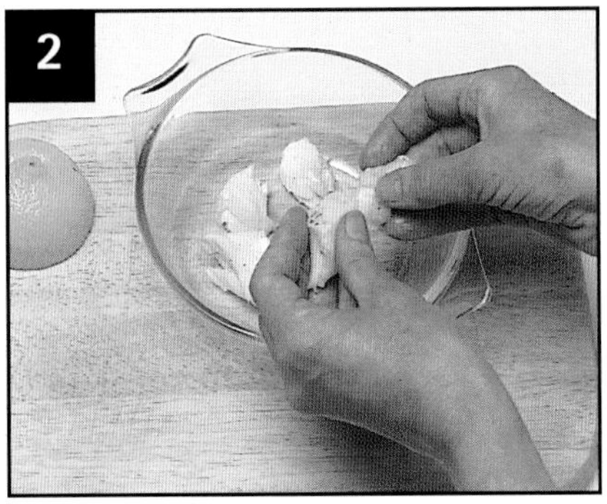

3

4

Fish Burritos

You can use any seafood you like in this tasty Mexican snack. Tacos are eaten in the hand, like sandwiches.

Serves 4–6

INGREDIENTS

- about 450 g/1 lb firm-fleshed white fish, such as red snapper or cod
- 1/4 tsp ground cumin
- pinch of dried oregano
- 4 garlic finely cloves, chopped
- 120 ml/4 fl oz fish stock, or water mixed with a fish stock cube
- juice of 1/2 lemon or lime
- 8 flour tortillas
- 2 ripe tomatoes, diced
- 1 quantity Salsa Cruda (see page 96)
- 2–3 leaves cos (romaine) lettuce, shredded
- salt and pepper
- lemon slices, to serve

1 Season the fish with salt and pepper, then put in a pan with the cumin, oregano, garlic and enough fish stock to cover.

2 Bring to the boil, then cook for about a minute. Remove the pan from the heat and leave the fish to cool in the cooking liquid for about 30 minutes.

3 Remove the fish from the stock and break up into bite-sized pieces. Sprinkle with the lemon or lime juice and set aside.

4 Heat the tortillas in an ungreased non-stick frying pan (skillet), sprinkling them with a few drops of water as they heat; wrap in a clean tea towel (dish cloth) as you work to keep them warm.

5 Arrange shredded lettuce in the middle of one tortilla, spoon on a few big chunks of the fish, then sprinkle with the tomato. Add salsa cruda. Repeat with the other tortillas and serve at once with lemon slices.

VARIATION

Cook several peeled waxy potatoes in the fish stock, then dice and serve wrapped up in the warm tortillas along with the lettuce, fish, tomato and salsa. Or add sliced lime-dressed avocado with the filling.

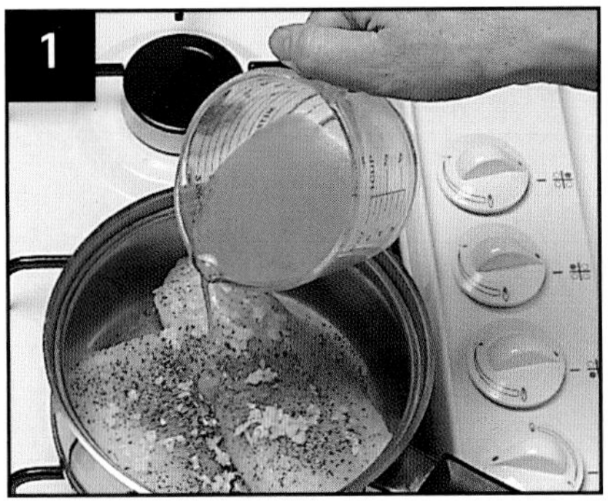

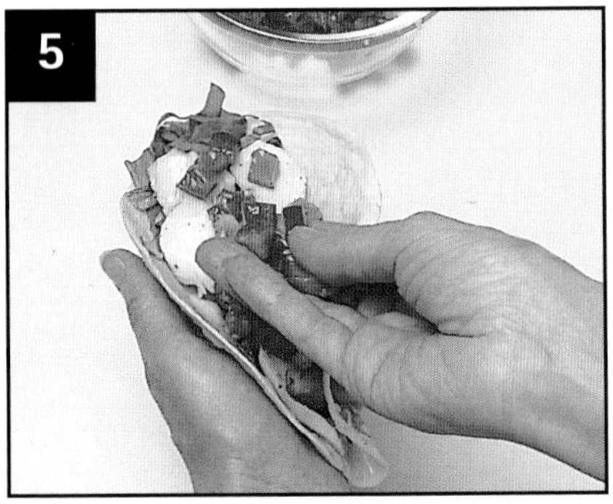

Chicken Tacos from Puebla

Seasoned chicken fills these soft tacos, along with creamy refried beans, avocado, smoky chipotle and soured cream. A feast of tastes!

Serves 4

INGREDIENTS

8 corn tortillas
2 tsp vegetable oil
225–350 g/8–12 oz leftover cooked chicken, diced or shredded
225 g/8 oz can refried beans, warmed with a 2 tbsp water to thin
¼ tsp ground cumin
¼ tsp dried oregano
1 avocado, stoned (pitted), sliced and tossed with lime juice
Salsa Verde (see page 102) or salsa of your choice
1 canned chipotle chilli in adobo marinade, chopped, or bottled chipotle salsa
175 ml/6 fl oz/¾ cup soured cream
½ onion, chopped
handful of lettuce leaves
5 radishes, diced
salt and pepper

1 Heat the tortillas in an ungreased non-stick frying pan (skillet) in a stack, alternating the top and bottom tortillas so that the tortillas heat evenly. Wrap in kitchen foil or a clean tea towel (dish cloth) to keep warm.

2 Heat the oil in a frying pan (skillet), add the chicken and heat through. Season with salt and pepper to taste.

3 Combine the refried beans with the cumin and oregano.

4 Spread one tortilla with warm refried beans, then top with a spoonful of the chicken, a slice or two of avocado, a dab of salsa, chipotle to taste, a dollop of soured cream and a sprinkling of onion, lettuce and radishes. Season with salt and pepper to taste, then roll up, as tightly as you can.

Repeat with the remaining tortillas and serve at once.

VARIATION

Replace the chicken with 450 g/1 lb minced (ground) beef browned with a seasoning of chopped onion, mild chilli powder and ground cumin to taste.

Chile Verde Tacos with Pinto Beans

This is also an ideal way of using up any leftover spicy stewed meat – use in place of the Chile Verde and you have an almost instant meal!

Serves 4

INGREDIENTS

8 corn tortillas
vegetable oil, for greasing
400 g/14 oz can pinto beans
1/3 quantity Chile Verde (see page 204)
3 ripe tomatoes, diced
1/2 onion, chopped
2 tbsp finely chopped fresh coriander (cilantro)

TO GARNISH:
soured cream
mild chilli powder

TO SERVE:
salsa of your choice
shredded lettuce

1 Heat the tortillas in a lightly greased non-stick frying pan (skillet); wrap the tortillas in a tea towel (dish cloth) as you work to keep them warm.

2 Drain the beans, reserving a few tablespoons of the liquid. Heat the beans in a pan with the reserved canned liquid.

3 Heat through the Chile Verde in a pan until just boiling.

4 Spoon some of the drained beans on to a warm tortilla. Top with warm Chile Verde, then sprinkle with tomatoes, onion and fresh coriander (cilantro). Roll up and repeat with the remaining tortillas. Garnish with a spoonful of soured cream and a sprinkling of chilli powder, then serve at once with salsa and shredded lettuce.

VARIATION

For a tostada version, heat tostadas (crisp tortillas) under the grill (broiler), then spread with warmed slightly thinned refried beans and top with the Chile Verde, shredded lettuce, a little grated pecorino cheese, salsa, onion, fresh coriander (cilantro) and soured cream. Serve at once.

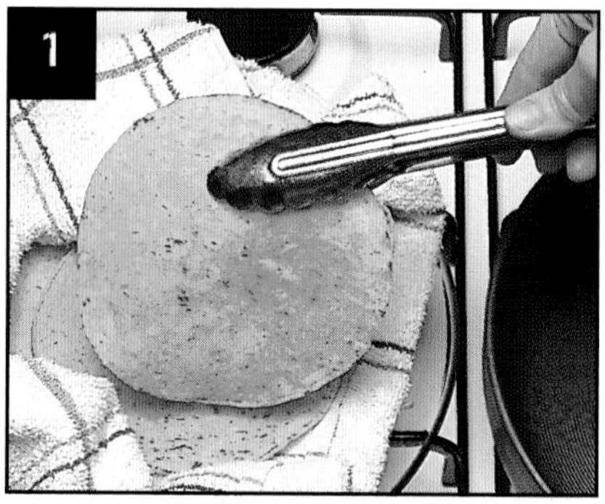

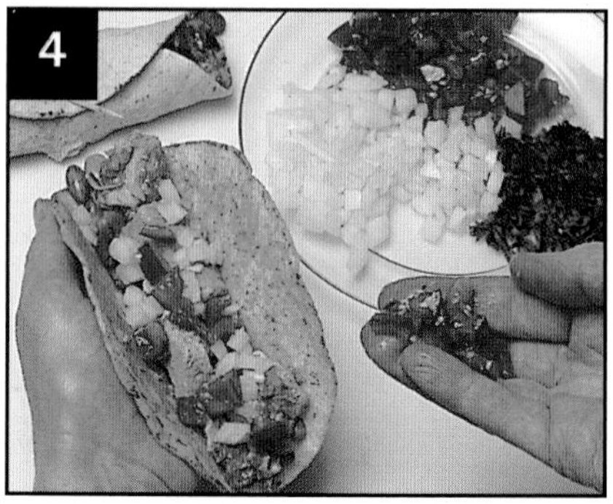

Chicken Tostadas with Green Salsa & Chipotle

Chicken makes a delicate yet satisfying topping for crisp tostadas. You do not need to prepare chicken especially for this recipe: any leftover chicken is equally delicious.

Serves 4–6

INGREDIENTS

6 corn tortillas
vegetable oil, for frying
450 g/1 lb skinned boned chicken breast or thigh, cut into strips or small pieces
225 ml/8 fl oz/1 cup chicken stock
2 garlic cloves, finely chopped
400 g/14 oz refried beans (see page 144) or canned
large pinch of ground cumin
225 g/8 oz grated cheese
1 tbsp chopped fresh coriander (cilantro)
2 ripe tomatoes, diced
handful of crisp lettuce leaves, such as cos (romaine) or iceberg, shredded
4–6 radishes, diced
3 spring onions (scallions), thinly sliced
1 ripe avocado, stoned (pitted), diced or sliced and tossed with lime juice
soured cream to taste
1–2 canned chipotle chillies in adobo marinade, or dried chipotle reconstituted (see page 100), cut into thin strips

1 To make tostadas, fry the tortillas in a small amount of oil in a non-stick pan until crisp.

2 Put the chicken in a pan with the stock and garlic. Bring to the boil, then reduce the heat and cook for 1–2 minutes until the chicken begins to turn opaque.

3 Remove the chicken from the heat and leave to steep in its hot liquid to cook through.

4 Heat the beans with enough water to form a smooth purée. Add the cumin and keep warm.

5 Reheat the tostadas under a preheated grill (broiler), if necessary. Spread the hot beans on the tostadas, then sprinkle with the grated cheese. Lift the cooked chicken from the liquid and divide between the tostadas. Top with the coriander (cilantro), tomatoes, lettuce, radishes, spring onions (scallions), avocado, soured cream and a few strips of chipotle. Serve immediately.

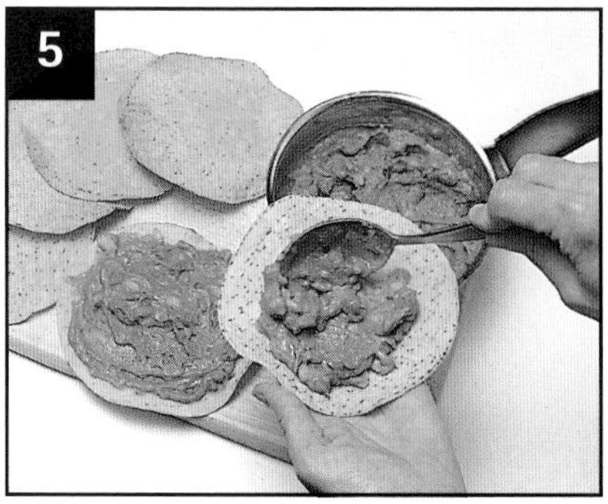

Vegetable Tostadas

Top a crisp tostada (fried tortilla) with spicy vegetables and you have a vegetarian feast!

Serves 4

INGREDIENTS

4 corn tortillas
vegetable oil, for frying
2–3 tbsp extra-virgin olive oil or vegetable oil
2 potatoes, diced
1 carrot, diced
3 garlic cloves, finely chopped
1 red (bell) pepper, deseeded and diced
1 tsp mild chilli powder
1 tsp paprika
½ tsp ground cumin
3–4 ripe tomatoes, diced
115 g/4 oz green beans, blanched and cut into bite-sized lengths
several large pinches dried oregano
400 g/14 oz cooked black beans, drained
225 g/8 oz crumbled feta cheese
3–4 leaves cos (romaine) lettuce, shredded
3–4 spring onions (scallions), thinly sliced

1 To make tostadas, fry the tortillas in a small amount of oil in a non-stick pan until crisp.

2 Heat the olive oil in a frying pan (skillet), add the potatoes and carrot and cook until softened. Add the garlic, red (bell) pepper, chilli powder, paprika and cumin. Cook for 2–3 minutes until the peppers have softened.

3 Add the tomatoes, green beans and oregano. Cook for 8–10 minutes until the vegetables are tender and form a sauce-like mixture. The mixture should not be too dry; add a little water if necessary, to keep it moist.

4 Heat the black beans in a pan with a tiny amount of water, and keep warm. Reheat the tostadas under the grill (broiler).

5 Layer the beans over the hot tostadas, then sprinkle with the cheese and top with a few spoonfuls of the hot vegetables in sauce. Serve at once, each tostada sprinkled with the lettuce and spring onions (scallions).

Broccoli Enchiladas in Mild Chilli Salsa

This is reminiscent of a sort of Mexican spiced cannelloni, with flour tortillas taking the place of the pasta tubes.

Serves 4

INGREDIENTS

- 450 g/1 lb broccoli florets
- 225 g/8 oz ricotta cheese
- 1 garlic clove, chopped
- ½ tsp ground cumin
- 175–200 g/6–8 oz Cheddar cheese, grated
- 6–8 tbsp freshly grated Parmesan cheese
- 1 egg, lightly beaten
- 4–6 flour tortillas
- vegetable oil, for greasing
- 1 quantity Mild Red Chilli Sauce (see page 86)
- 225 ml/8 fl oz/1 cup chicken or vegetable stock
- ½ onion, finely chopped
- 3–4 tbsp chopped fresh coriander (cilantro)
- 3 ripe tomatoes, diced
- salt and pepper
- hot salsa, to serve

1 Bring a pan of salted water to the boil, add the broccoli, bring back to the boil and blanch for 1 minute. Drain, refresh under cold running water, then drain again. Cut off the stems, peel and chop. Dice the heads.

2 Mix the broccoli with the ricotta cheese, garlic, cumin, half the Cheddar and Parmesan in a bowl. Mix in the egg and season with salt and pepper.

3 Heat the tortillas in a lightly greased non-stick frying pan (skillet); then wrap in kitchen foil. Fill the tortillas with the broccoli mixture, rolling them up.

4 Arrange the tortilla rolls in an ovenproof dish, then pour the mild chilli sauce over the top. Pour over the stock.

5 Top with the remaining Cheddar and Parmesan cheeses and bake in a preheated oven at 190°C/375°F/Gas Mark 5 for about 30 minutes. Serve sprinkled with the onion, fresh coriander (cilantro) and tomatoes. Serve with a hot salsa.

Cheese Enchiladas with Mole Flavours

Mole sauce makes a delicious enchilada – a good reason to make yourself a big pot of Mole Poblano (see page 90). But if you are short of time, you can always use bottled mole paste instead.

Serves 4–6

INGREDIENTS

8 corn tortillas
vegetable oil, for greasing
450 ml/16 fl oz/2 cups mole sauce
about 225 g/8 oz grated cheese, such as Cheddar, mozzarella, asiago or Mexican queso oaxaco, one type or a mixture
225 ml/8 fl oz/1 cup chicken or vegetable stock
5 spring onions (scallions), thinly sliced
2–3 tbsp chopped fresh coriander (cilantro)
handful of cos (romaine) lettuce leaves, shredded
1 avocado, stoned (pitted), diced and tossed in lime juice
4 tbsp soured cream
salsa of your choice

1 Heat the tortillas in a lightly greased non-stick frying pan (skillet); wrap the tortillas in kitchen foil as you work to keep them warm.

2 Dip the tortillas into the mole sauce, and pile up on a plate. Fill the inside of the top sauced tortilla with a few spoonfuls of cheese. Roll up and arrange in a shallow ovenproof dish. Repeat this process with the remaining tortillas, reserving a handful of the cheese to sprinkle over the top

3 Pour the rest of the mole sauce over the rolled tortillas, then pour the stock over the top. Sprinkle with the reserved cheese and cover with kitchen foil.

4 Bake in a preheated oven at 190°C/375°F/Gas Mark 5 until the tortillas are piping hot and the cheese filling melts.

5 Arrange the spring onions (scallions), fresh coriander (cilantro), lettuce, avocado and soured cream on top. Add salsa to taste. Serve at once.

Santa Fe Red Chilli Enchiladas

These enchiladas are served stacked, in the traditional New Mexican style, but you can always roll them up with the filling if you prefer.

Serves 4

INGREDIENTS

- 2-3 tbsp masa harina or 1 corn tortilla, crushed or crumbled
- 4 tbsp mild chilli powder, such as New Mexico
- 2 tbsp paprika
- 2 garlic cloves, finely chopped
- 1/4 tsp ground cumin
- pinch of ground cinnamon
- pinch of ground allspice
- pinch of dried oregano
- 1 tbsp lime juice
- 1 litre/1 3/4 pints/4 cups vegetable, chicken or beef stock, simmering
- 8 flour tortillas
- about 450 g/1 lb cooked chicken or pork, cut into pieces
- 80 g/3 oz grated cheese
- 1 tbsp extra-virgin olive oil
- 4-6 eggs

TO SERVE:

- 1/2 onion, finely chopped
- 1 tbsp finely chopped fresh coriander (cilantro)
- salsa of your choice

1 Mix the masa harina with the chilli powder, paprika, garlic, cumin, cinnamon, allspice, oregano and enough water to make a thin paste. Process in a blender or food processor until smooth.

2 Stir the paste into the simmering stock, reduce the heat and cook until it thickens slightly, then remove the sauce from the heat and stir in the lime juice.

3 Dip the tortillas into the warm sauce. Cover one tortilla with some of the cooked meat. Top with a second dipped tortilla and more meat filling. Make 3 more towers in this way, then transfer to an ovenproof dish.

4 Pour the remaining sauce over the tortillas, then sprinkle with the grated cheese. Bake in a preheated oven at 180°C/ 35O°F/ Gas Mark 4 for 15-20 minutes or until the cheese has melted.

5 Meanwhile, heat the olive oil in a non-stick frying pan (skillet) and cook the eggs until the whites are set and the yolks are still soft.

6 To serve the enchiladas, top each with a fried egg. Serve with the onion mixed with fresh coriander (cilantro) and salsa.

1

3

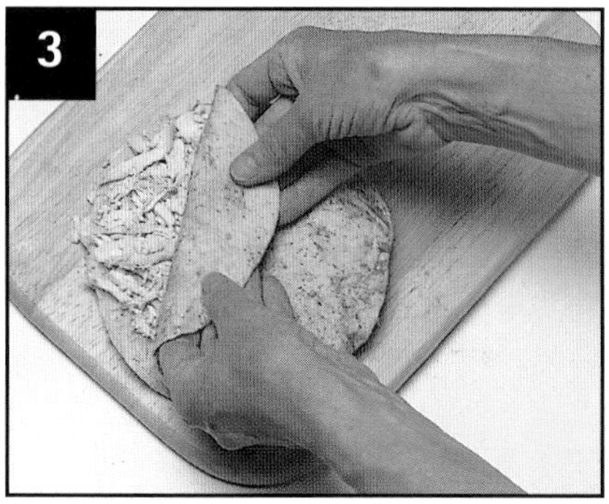

Chicken Tortilla Flutes with Guacamole

These crisply fried, rolled tortillas are known as flauta, *meaning 'flutes' in Mexican, because of their delicate, long shape.*

Serves 4

INGREDIENTS

8 corn tortillas
350 g/12 oz cooked chicken, diced
1 tsp mild chilli powder
1 onion, chopped
1–2 tbsp crème fraîche
vegetable oil, for frying
2 tbsp finely chopped fresh coriander (cilantro)
1 quantity of Guacamole (see page 28)
salsa of your choice
salt

1 Heat the tortillas in an ungreased non-stick frying pan (skillet) in a stack, alternating the top and bottom tortillas so that all of the tortillas warm evenly. Wrap in kitchen foil or a clean tea towel (dish cloth) to keep warm

2 Place the chicken in a bowl with the chilli powder, half the onion, half the coriander (cilantro) and salt to taste. Add enough crème fraîche to hold the mixture together.

3 Arrange 2 corn tortillas on the work surface so that they are overlapping, then spoon some of the filling along the centre. Roll up very tightly and secure in place with a toothpick or two. Repeat with the remaining tortillas and filling.

4 Heat oil in a deep frying pan (skillet) until hot and fry the rolls until golden and crisp. Carefully remove from the oil and drain on paper towels.

5 Serve immediately, garnishing with the guacamole, salsa, diced tomato and the remaining onion and fresh coriander (cilantro).

VARIATION

Replace the chicken with seafood, such as cooked prawns (shrimp) or crab meat, and serve the rolls with lemon wedges.

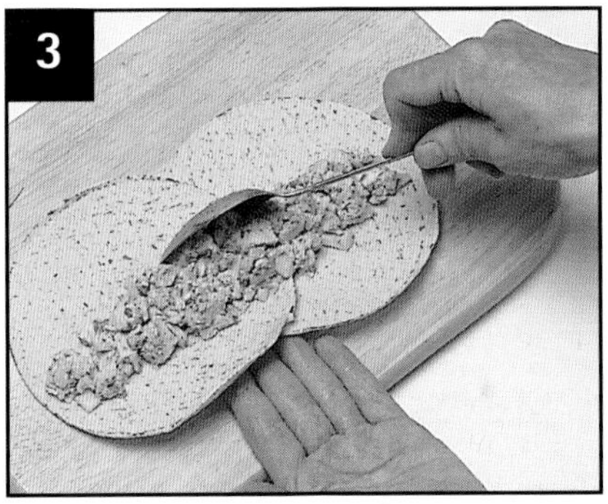

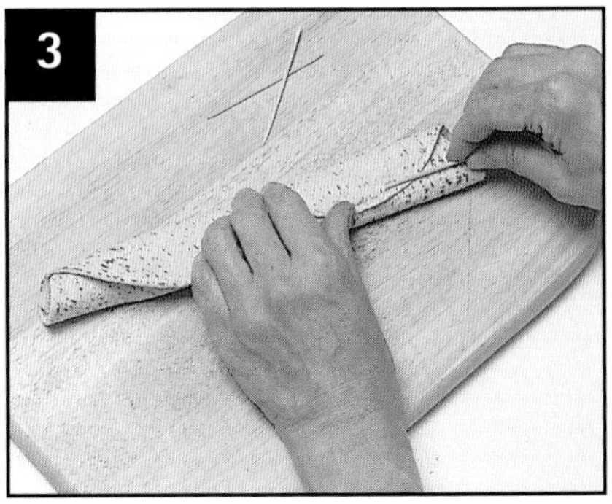

Pork Quesadilla with Pinto Beans

These melt-in-the-mouth tortilla parcels have a lovely pork, bean and melted cheese filling. Any leftover cooked meat may be used instead of the Carnitas.

Serves 4

INGREDIENTS

1 quantity of Carnitas (see page 208) or about 100 g/3½ oz cooked pork strips per person
1 ripe tomato, deseeded and diced
½ onion, chopped
3 tbsp chopped fresh coriander (cilantro)
4 large flour tortillas
350 g/12 oz grated or thinly sliced cheese, such as mozzarella or gouda
about 375 g/13½ oz cooked drained pinto beans
hot salsa of your choice or bottled hot sauce, to taste
pickled jalapeño chillies, cut into thin rings, to taste
vegetable oil, for frying

TO SERVE:
pickled chillies
mixed salad

1 Heat the Carnitas in a pan and keep hot over a low heat.

2 Combine the tomato, onion and coriander (cilantro) in a bowl and set aside.

3 Heat a tortilla in an ungreased non-stick frying pan (skillet). Sprinkle the tortilla with cheese, then top with some of the meat, beans and reserved tomato mixture. Add salsa and pickled jalapeños to taste. Fold over the sides to make a parcel.

4 Heat the parcels gently on each side in the frying pan (skillet), adding a few drops of oil to keep it all supple and succulent, until the tortilla is golden and the cheese inside has melted. Keep warm. Repeat with the remaining tortillas and filling.

5 Transfer the quesadillas to a plate and serve at once, with pickled chillies and salad.

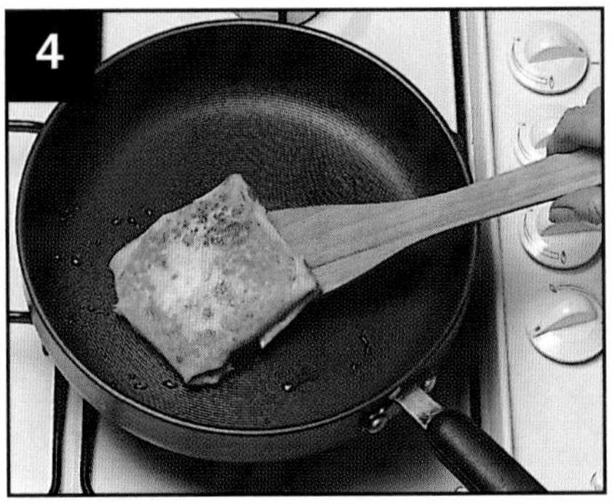

Casserole of Tortilla Chips & Chorizo

Called chilaquiles *in Mexican, this dish turns everyday leftovers into something quite special! Excellent served for brunch, topped with an egg.*

Serves 6–8

INGREDIENTS

12 stale tortillas, cut into strips
1 tbsp vegetable oil
2–3 chorizo sausages, thinly sliced or diced
2 garlic cloves, finely chopped
225 g/8 oz chopped canned tomatoes
3 tbsp chopped fresh coriander (cilantro)
450 ml/16 fl oz/2 cups chicken or vegetable stock
225 g/8 oz grated cheese
1 onion, finely chopped
salt and pepper

1 Place the tortilla strips in a roasting tin (pan), toss with the oil and bake in a preheated oven at 190°C/375°F/Gas Mark 5 for about 30 minutes until they are crisp and golden.

2 Brown the chorizo with the garlic in a frying pan (skillet) until the meat is cooked; pour away any excess fat. Add the tomatoes and the coriander (cilantro) and season with salt and pepper to taste. Set aside.

3 In an ovenproof dish, about 30 cm/12 inches square, layer the tortilla chips and chorizo mixture, finishing with the tortilla chips.

4 Pour the stock over the top of the dish, then sprinkle with the cheese. Bake in a preheated oven at 190°C/375°F/Gas Mark 5 for about 40 minutes until the tortilla chips are fairly soft.

5 Serve immediately, sprinkled with the chopped onion.

VARIATION

Serve with a fried egg or two alongside. The soft yolk tastes wonderful with the spicy casserole – offer a bowl of spicy salsa for those who want it hotter.

2

3

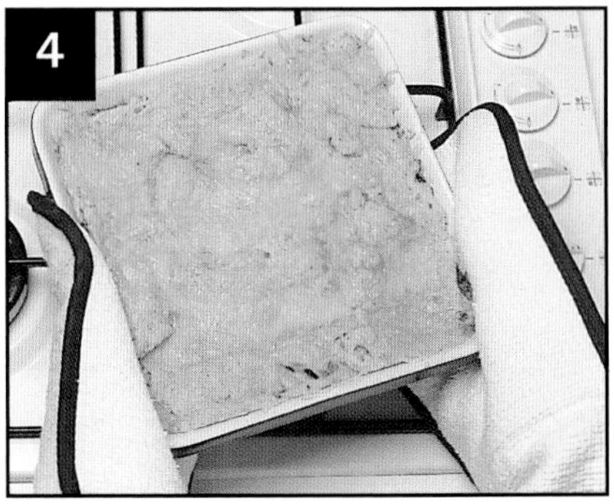
4

Green Chilli & Chicken Chilaquiles

Easy to put together, this dish makes a perfect mid-week supper. Use tortilla chips instead of baking the tortillas, if you prefer.

Serves 4–6

INGREDIENTS

- 12 stale tortillas, cut into strips
- 1 tbsp vegetable oil
- 1 small cooked chicken, meat removed from the bones and cut into bite-sized pieces
- Salsa Verde (see page 102)
- 3 tbsp chopped fresh coriander (cilantro)
- 1 tsp finely chopped fresh oregano or thyme
- 4 garlic cloves, finely chopped
- $1/4$ tsp ground cumin
- 350 g/12 oz grated cheese, such as Cheddar, manchego or mozzarella
- 450 ml/16 fl oz/2 cups chicken stock
- about 115 g/4 oz/$1\,1/3$ cups freshly grated Parmesan cheese

TO SERVE:

- 350 ml/12 fl oz/$1\,1/2$ cups crème fraîche or soured cream
- 3–5 spring onions (scallions), thinly sliced
- pickled chillies

1 Place the tortilla strips in a roasting tin (pan), toss with the oil and bake in a preheated oven at 190°C/375°F/Gas Mark 5 for about 30 minutes until they are crisp and golden.

2 Arrange the chicken in a 23 x 33 cm/9 x 13 inch casserole, then sprinkle with half the salsa, coriander (cilantro), oregano, garlic, cumin and some of the soft cheese. Repeat these layers and top with the tortilla strips.

3 Pour the stock over the top, then sprinkle with the remaining cheeses.

4 Bake in a preheated oven at 190°C/375°F/Gas Mark 5 for about 30 minutes until heated through and the cheese is lightly golden in areas.

5 Serve garnished with the crème fraîche, sliced spring onions (scallions) and pickled chillies to taste.

VARIATION

For a vegetarian Mexicana filling, add diced sautéed tofu and sweetcorn kernels in place of the cooked chicken.

2

3

4

Tamales

Traditional Mexican fare, tamales are large dumplings of corn flour, stuffed with a moist filling, then wrapped in either banana leaves or husks of corn. They make attractive party food.

Serves 4–6

INGREDIENTS

6 tbsp lard or vegetable shortening
½ tsp salt
pinch of sugar
pinch of ground cumin
225 g/8 oz masa harina
½ tsp baking powder
about 225 ml/8 fl oz/1 cup beef, chicken or vegetable stock

8–10 corn husks or several banana leaves, cut into 30 cm/12 inch squares

TO SERVE:
shredded lettuce
salsa of your choice

FILLING:
115 g/4 oz cooked sweetcorn, mixed with a little grated cheese and chopped green chilli, or simmered pork in a mild chilli sauce

1 If using corn husks, soak in hot water to cover for at least 3 hours or overnight. If using banana leaves, warm them by placing over an open flame for just a few seconds, to make them pliable.

2 To make the tamale dough, beat the lard or shortening until fluffy, then beat in the salt, sugar, cumin, masa harina and baking powder until the mixture resembles tiny crumbs.

3 Add the stock very gradually, in several batches, beating until mixture becomes fluffy and resembles whipped cream

4 Spread 1–2 tablespoons of the tamale mixture on either a soaked and drained corn husk or a piece of pliable heated banana leaf.

5 Spoon in the filling. Fold the sides of the husks or leaves over the filling to enclose. Wrap each parcel in a square of kitchen foil, and arrange in a steamer.

6 Pour hot water in the bottom of the steamer, cover, and boil. Cook for 40–60 minutes, topping up the water in the bottom of the steamer when needed. Remove the tamales and serve.

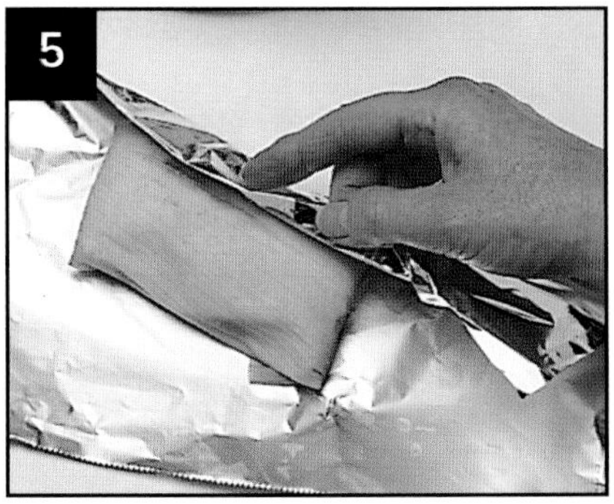

Burritos of Lamb & Black Beans

Stir-fried marinated lamb strips are paired with earthy black beans in these tasty burritos.

Serves 4

INGREDIENTS

- 650 g/1 lb 5 oz lean lamb
- 3 garlic cloves, finely chopped
- juice of ½ lime
- ½ tsp mild chilli powder
- ½ tsp ground cumin
- large pinch of dried oregano leaves, crushed
- 1–2 tbsp extra-virgin olive oil
- 400 g/14 oz cooked black beans, seasoned with a little cumin, salt and pepper
- 4 large flour tortillas
- 2–3 tbsp chopped fresh coriander (cilantro)
- salsa, preferably Chipotle Salsa (see page 98)
- salt and pepper

1 Slice the lamb into thin strips, then combine with the garlic, lime juice, chilli powder, cumin, oregano and olive oil. Season with salt and pepper. Leave to marinate in the refrigerator for 4 hours.

2 Warm the black beans with a little water in a pan.

3 Heat the tortillas in an ungreased non-stick frying pan (skillet), sprinkling them with a few drops of water as they heat; wrap the tortillas in a clean tea towel (dish cloth) as you work to keep them warm. Alternatively, heat through in a stack in the pan, alternating the top and bottom tortillas so that they warm evenly. Wrap to keep warm.

4 Stir-fry the lamb in a heavy-based non-stick frying pan over high heat until browned on all sides. Remove from the heat.

5 Spoon some of the beans and browned meat into a tortilla, sprinkle with coriander (cilantro), then dab with salsa and roll up. Repeat with the remaining tortillas and serve at once.

VARIATION

Add a spoonful or two of cooked rice to each burrito.

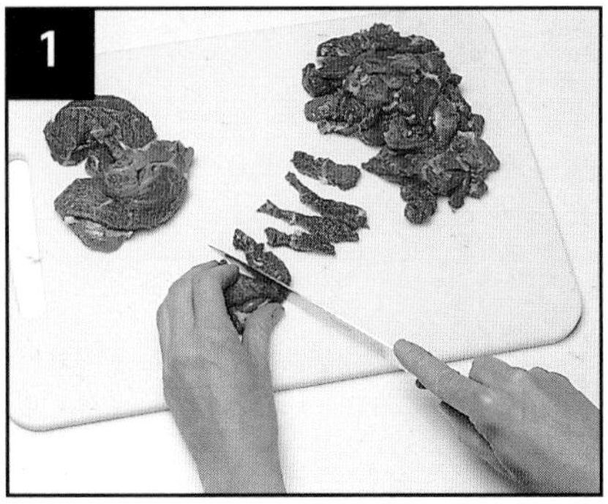

Mexican Beans

A pot of beans, bubbling away on the stove, is the basic everyday food of Mexico – delicious and healthy!

Serves 4–6

INGREDIENTS

500 g/1 lb 2 oz dried pinto or borlotti beans
sprig of fresh mint
sprig of fresh thyme
sprig of fresh flat-leaf parsley
1 onion, cut into chunks
salt

TO SERVE:
shreds of spring onion (scallion)
warmed flour or corn tortillas

1 Pick through the beans and remove any bits of grit or stone. Cover the beans with cold water and leave to soak overnight. If you want to cut down on soaking time, bring the beans to the boil, cook for 5 minutes, then remove from the heat and leave to stand, covered, for 2 hours.

2 Drain the beans, place in a pan and cover with fresh water and the mint, thyme and parsley. Bring to the boil, then reduce the heat to very low and cook gently, covered, for about 2 hours until the beans are tender. The best way to check that they are done is to sample a bean or two every so often, after 1¾ hours cooking time.

3 Add the onion and continue to cook until the onion and beans are very tender.

4 To serve as a side dish, drain, season with salt and serve in a bowl lined with warmed corn or flour tortillas, garnished with spring onion (scallion) shreds (see Cook's Tip).

COOK'S TIP

If using the beans for Refried Beans (see page 144), do not drain as the liquid is required for the recipe.

COOK'S TIP

The length of time the beans take to cook will depend on the age of the beans – old beans take longer than younger beans; the mineral content of the water matters, too.

Refried Beans

One of Mexico's most famous dishes, refried beans, or frijoles refritos, *is incredibly versatile. Serve them piled on to crisp tostadas or crusty rolls, spooned beside rice or rolled into a tortilla.*

Serves 4–6

INGREDIENTS

- 1 quantity Mexican Beans, with their cooking liquid (see page 142)
- 1–2 onions, chopped
- 120 ml/4 fl oz/½ cup vegetable oil or 125 g/4½ oz lard or dripping
- ½ tsp ground cumin
- salt
- 250 g/9 oz grated Cheddar cheese (optional)

1 Put two-thirds of the cooked beans, with their cooking liquid, in a food processor and process to a purée. Stir in the remaining whole beans. Set aside.

2 Heat the oil or fat in a heavy-based frying pan (skillet). Add the onions and cook until they are very soft. Sprinkle with cumin and salt to taste.

3 Ladle in a cupful of the bean mixture, and cook, stirring, until the beans reduce down to a thick mixture; the beans will darken slightly as they cook.

4 Continue adding the bean mixture, a ladleful at a time, stirring and reducing down the liquid before adding the next ladleful. You should end up with a thick, chunky purée.

5 If using cheese, sprinkle it over the beans and cover tightly until the heat in the pan melts the cheese. Alternatively, place under a preheated grill (broiler) to melt the cheese. Serve immediately.

VARIATION

Add several browned, broken-up chorizo sausages to the beans, along with a small tin of sardines, mashed to a paste. Serve stuffed into crusty rolls for a classic mollete, or as a party dip. Good spread on to crisp tostadas for an afternoon pick-me-up.

Mexican Refried Beans 'With Everything'

These are refried beans fit for a fiesta, rich with everything – bacon, fried onions, tomatoes, even a bit of beer! As delicious as it sounds!

Serves 4

INGREDIENTS

- 1–2 tbsp vegetable oil
- 1–1½ large onions, chopped
- 125 g/4½ oz bacon lardons or bacon cut into small pieces
- 3–4 garlic cloves, finely chopped
- about 1 tsp ground cumin
- ½ tsp mild chilli powder
- 400 g/14 oz can tomatoes, diced and drained, reserving about 150–175 ml/5–6 fl oz/¾–¾ cup of their juices
- 400 g/14 oz can refried beans, broken up into pieces
- 100 ml/3½ fl oz/scant ½ cup beer
- 400 g/14 oz can pinto beans, drained
- salt and pepper

TO SERVE:

- warmed flour tortillas
- soured cream
- sliced pickled chillies

1 Heat the oil in a frying pan (skillet). Add the onion and bacon and fry for about 5 minutes until they are just turning brown. Stir in the garlic, cumin and chilli powder and continue to cook for a minute. Add the tomatoes and cook over a medium-high heat until the liquid has evaporated.

2 Add the refried beans and mash lightly in the pan with the tomato mixture, adding beer as needed to thin out the beans and make them smoother. Lower the heat and cook, stirring, until the mixture is smooth and creamy.

3 Add the pinto beans and stir well to combine; if the mixture is too thick, add a little of the reserved tomato juice. Adjust the spicing to taste. Season with salt and pepper and serve with warmed tortillas, soured cream and sliced chillies.

VARIATION

Top the dish with grated cheese, then pop under a preheated grill (broiler) to melt and sizzle. Serve at once. This makes a luscious filling for warm flour tortillas.

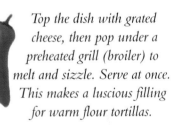

Spicy Fragrant Black Bean Chilli

Black beans are fragrant and flavourful; enjoy this chillied bean stew Mexican style with soft tortillas, or Californian style in a bowl with crisp tortillas chips crumbled in.

Serves 4

INGREDIENTS

- 400 g/14 oz dried black beans
- 2 tbsp olive oil
- 1 onion, chopped
- 5 garlic cloves, coarsely chopped
- 2 slices bacon, diced (optional)
- ½–1 tsp ground cumin
- ½–1 tsp mild red chilli powder
- 1 red (bell) pepper, diced
- 1 carrot, diced
- 400 g/14 oz fresh tomatoes, diced, or chopped canned
- 1 bunch fresh coriander (cilantro), coarsely chopped
- salt and pepper

1 Soak the beans overnight, then drain. Put in a pan, cover with water and bring to the boil. Boil for 10 minutes, then reduce the heat and simmer for about 1½ hours until tender. Drain well, reserving 225 ml/8 fl oz/1 cup of the cooking liquid.

2 Heat the oil in a frying pan (skillet). Add the onion and garlic and fry for 2 minutes, stirring. Stir in the bacon, if using, and cook, stirring occasionally, until the bacon is cooked and the onion is soften.

3 Stir in the cumin and red chilli powder and continue to cook for a moment or two. Add the red (bell) pepper, carrot and tomatoes. Cook over a medium heat for about 5 minutes.

4 Add half the coriander (cilantro) and the beans and their reserved liquid. Season with salt and pepper. Simmer for 30–45 minutes or until very flavourful and thickened.

5 Stir through the remaining coriander (cilantro), adjust the seasoning and serve at once.

COOK'S TIP

You can use canned beans, if wished: drain and use 225 ml/ 8 fl oz/1 cup water for the liquid added in Step 4.

Rice with Lime

The tangy citrus taste of lime is marvellous with all sorts of rice dishes. Although not typically Mexican, you could add wild rice to this dish, if liked.

Serves 4

INGREDIENTS

- 2 tbsp vegetable oil
- 1 small onion, finely chopped
- 3 garlic cloves, finely chopped
- 175 g/6 oz long-grain rice
- 450 ml/16 fl oz/2 cups chicken or vegetable stock
- juice of 1 lime
- 1 tbsp chopped fresh coriander (cilantro)

1 Heat the oil in a heavy-based pan or flameproof casserole. Add the onion and garlic and cook gently, stirring occasionally, for 2 minutes. Add the rice and cook for a further minute, stirring. Pour in the stock, increase the heat and bring the rice to the boil. Reduce the heat to a very low simmer.

2 Cover and cook the rice for about 10 minutes or until the rice is just tender and the liquid is absorbed.

3 Sprinkle in the lime juice and fork the rice to fluff up and to mix the juice in. Sprinkle with the coriander (cilantro) and serve.

COOK'S TIP

Garnish the rice with sautéed plantains: slice a ripe peeled plantain, preferably on the diagonal, then fry in a heavy-based pan in a small amount of oil until they have browned in spots and are tender. Arrange in the bowl of rice.

VARIATION

Fork about 225 g/8 oz cooked sweetcorn into the rice when it is almost but not quite cooked, then allow the sweetcorn to warm through as the rice finishes cooking. Sprinkle with diced cucumber and a squeeze of lime juice to add a fresh tang.

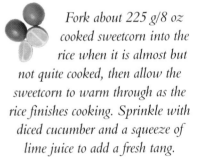

Cumin Rice with Sweet (Bell) Peppers

Cumin seeds add a distinctive flavour to this colourful rice dish. Serve as a side dish for any roasted or barbecued (grilled) meat.

Serves 4

INGREDIENTS

2 tbsp butter
1 tbsp vegetable oil
1 green (bell) pepper, deseeded and sliced
1 red (bell) pepper, deseeded and sliced
3 spring onions (scallions), thinly sliced
3–4 garlic cloves, finely chopped
175 g/6 oz/scant 1 cup long-grain rice
1½ tsp cumin seeds
½ tsp dried oregano or marjoram, crushed
450 ml/16 fl oz/2 cups chicken or vegetable stock

1 Heat the butter and oil in a heavy-based pan or flameproof casserole. Add the (bell) peppers and cook until softened.

2 Add the spring onions (scallions), garlic, rice and cumin seeds. Cook for about 5 minutes or until the rice turns slightly golden.

3 Add the oregano and stock to the pan or casserole, bring to the boil, then reduce the heat and cook for about 5 minutes.

4 Cover with a clean tea towel (dish cloth) and remove from the heat. Leave to steam for about 10 minutes, depending upon the age and maturity of the rice. If the rice is pretty mature, extend the initial cooking time to 10 minutes.

5 Fluff up the rice with a fork and serve at once.

VARIATION

Serve folded through a portion or two of black beans, and serve as a side dish with hearty roasted meat or poultry.

Green Rice

A paste of roasted onions, garlic and chillies, puréed with lots of green coriander (cilantro) leaves gives this rice a lovely fresh colour and stunning taste.

Serves 4

INGREDIENTS

- 1–2 onions, halved and unpeeled
- 6–8 large garlic cloves, unpeeled
- 1 large mild chilli, or 1 green (bell) pepper and 1 small green chilli
- 1 bunch fresh coriander (cilantro) leaves, chopped
- 225 ml/8 fl oz/1 cup chicken or vegetable stock
- 175 g/6 oz/scant 1 cup long-grain rice
- 80 ml/3 fl oz/$^1/_3$ cup vegetable or olive oil
- salt and pepper
- fresh coriander sprig, to garnish

1 Heat a heavy-based ungreased frying pan (skillet) and cook the onion, garlic, chilli and (bell) pepper, if using, until lightly charred on all sides, including the cut sides of the onions. Cover and leave to cool.

2 When cool enough to handle, remove the seeds and skin from the chilli and (bell) pepper, if using. Chop the flesh.

3 Remove the skins from the cooled onion and garlic and chop finely.

4 Place the vegetables in a food processor with the coriander (cilantro) leaves and stock, then process to a smooth thin purée.

5 Heat the oil in a heavy-based pan and fry the rice until it is glistening and lightly browned in places, stirring to prevent it from burning. Add the purée, cover and cook over a medium-low heat for 10–15 minutes until the rice is just tender.

6 Fluff up the rice with a fork, then cover and stand for about 5 minutes. Adjust the seasoning, garnish with a sprig of coriander (cilantro) and serve.

COOK'S TIP

Leftover green rice is delicious mixed with minced (ground) beef and/or pork for savoury meatballs, or as a filling for (bell) peppers.

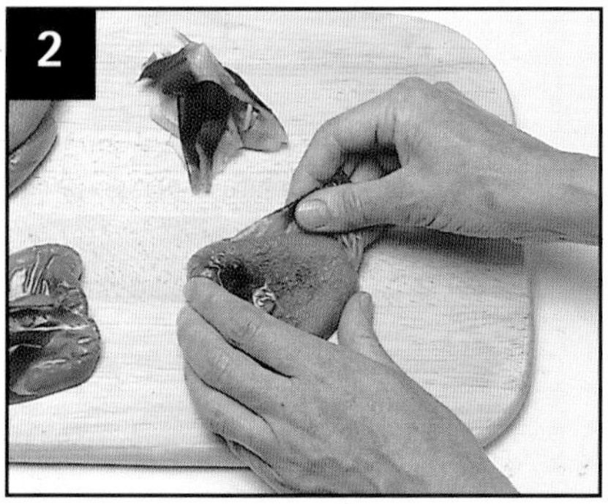

2

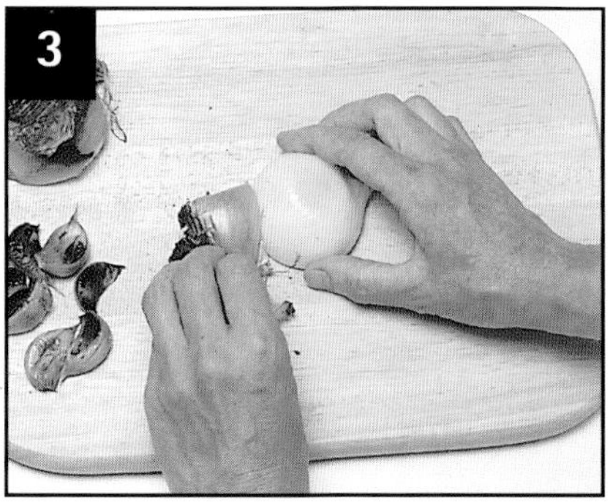

3

5

Rice with Black Beans

Any kind of bean cooking liquid is delicious for cooking rice – black beans are particularly good for their startling grey colour and earthy flavour.

Serves 4

INGREDIENTS

1 onion, chopped
5 garlic cloves, chopped
225 ml/8 fl oz/1 cup chicken or vegetable stock
2 tbsp vegetable oil
175 g/ 6 oz long-grain rice
½ tsp ground cumin
225 ml/8 fl oz/1 cup liquid from cooking black beans (including some black beans, too)
salt and pepper

TO GARNISH:
3–5 spring onions (scallions), thinly sliced
2 tbsp chopped fresh coriander (cilantro) leaves

1 Put the onion in a blender with the garlic and stock and blend until the consistency of a chunky sauce.

2 Heat the oil in a heavy-based pan and cook the rice until it is golden. Add the onion mixture, with the cooking liquid from the black beans (and any beans, too). Add the cumin, with salt and pepper to taste

3 Cover the pan and cook over a medium-low heat for about 10 minutes or until the rice is just tender. The rice should be a greyish colour and taste delicious.

4 Fluff up the rice with a fork, and leave to rest for about 5 minutes, covered. Serve sprinkled with thinly sliced spring onions (scallions) and chopped coriander (cilantro).

VARIATION

Instead of black beans, use pinto beans or chick-peas (garbanzo beans). Proceed as above and serve with any savoury spicy sauce, or as an accompaniment to roasted meat.

Lentils Simmered with Fruit

Although this might seem an unusual combination, when you spoon up this traditional dish you'll see how the fruit lightens the earthy lentils, to create a delicious side dish.

Serves 4

INGREDIENTS

125 g/4½ oz brown or green lentils
about 1 litre/1¾ pints/4 cups water
2 tbsp vegetable oil
3 small to medium onions, chopped
4 garlic cloves, coarsely chopped
1 large tart apple, roughly chopped
about ¼ ripe pineapple, skin removed and roughly chopped
2 tomatoes, deseeded and diced
1 almost ripe banana, cut into bite-sized pieces
salt
cayenne pepper, to taste
fresh parsley sprig, to garnish

1 Combine the lentils with the water in a pan, then bring to the boil. Reduce the heat and simmer over a low heat for about 40 minutes until the lentils are tender. Do not let them get mushy.

2 Meanwhile, heat the oil in a frying pan (skillet) and fry the onions and garlic until lightly browned and softened. Add the apple and continue to cook until golden. Add the pineapple, heat through, stirring, then add the tomatoes. Cook over a medium heat until thickened, stirring occasionally

3 Drain the lentils, reserving 120 ml/4 fl oz/1 cup of the cooking liquid. Add the drained lentils to the sauce, stirring in the reserved liquid if necessary. Heat through for a minute to mingle the flavours.

4 Add the banana to the pan, then season with salt and cayenne pepper. Serve garnished with parsley.

VARIATION

Instead of lentils, prepare the dish using cooked pinto or borlotti beans.

Dry Soup of Thin Noodles

This curiously named baked dish is made with pasta, tortillas or rice, and has an appetising dense texture. It often has a cheesy topping, and is served either as a first course, such as an Italian might, or as a comforting supper dish.

Serves 4

INGREDIENTS

- 350 g/12 very thin pasta, such as fideo or capellini
- 2–3 bay leaves
- 2–3 chorizo sausages
- 1 onion, chopped
- 1 green (bell) pepper or mild green chilli, such as anaheim or poblano, deseeded and chopped
- 4–5 garlic cloves, finely chopped
- 350 ml/12 fl oz/1½ cups tomato passata
- 350 ml/12 fl oz/1½ cups hot chicken, meat or vegetable stock
- ¼ tsp ground cumin
- ½ tsp mild red chilli powder
- pinch of dried oregano leaves
- 350 g/12 oz grated sharp cheese
- 2 tbsp chopped fresh coriander (cilantro)

1 Boil the pasta in boiling salted water with the bay leaves. Drain and discard the bay leaves. Rinse the noodles to rid them of excess starch. Leave to drain.

2 Fry the chorizo in a frying pan (skillet). When it begins to brown, add the onion, (bell) pepper and garlic, then continue to cook, stirring occasionally, until the vegetables are softened.

3 Add the tomato passata, stock, cumin, chilli and oregano and remove from the heat.

4 Toss the pasta with the hot sauce, then transfer to an ovenproof dish. Level the surface with a spoon, then cover with a layer of the grated cheese.

5 Bake in a preheated oven at 200°C/400°F/Gas Mark 6 for about 15 minutes until the top is lightly browned and the pasta is heated through. Serve at once, sprinkled with the chopped fresh coriander (cilantro).

2

3

4

Main Courses

In Mexico the main meal is traditionally served at midday, a gloriously relaxed affair, with usually a fish or meat dish for the central course. Using a wonderful mix of flavours and cooking methods, a result of Mexico's complex and colourful past, the cuisine offers some delicious main dishes, full of spicy tastes.

Eggs are cooked with spices, tangy herbs, garlic and tomatoes to make an appetizing topping to tortillas, while fish is given a lift with subtle spicy marinades – salmon grilled with a smoky chilli dressing or snapper baked with lime and coriander (cilantro) is a feast of Mexican flavours.

Sizzling strips of beef rolled up with crunchy vegetables in a tortilla is classic Mexican fare, as is pork stewed with mild chillies, sweet plantains and potatoes – an inspiring marriage of flavours and textures. Or try the classic Mexican way of simmering pork until meltingly tender, then frying it until crisp and golden. Cook chicken with Mexican flair by stewing it with vegetables and fruit, or marinate chicken wings in tequila, to tenderise and add flavour for barbecuing.

Serve any of the dishes in this chapter to bring a touch of sunny Mexico to your meals, whether it is a family lunch or a dinner with friends.

Jalisco-style Eggs

This hearty breakfast dish from Jalisco is a classic Mexican way of serving eggs – a feast of flavours!

Serves 4

INGREDIENTS

- 4 corn tortillas
- 1 avocado
- lime or lemon juice, for tossing
- 175 g/6 oz chorizo sausage, sliced or diced
- 2 tbsp butter or water, for cooking
- 4 eggs
- 4 tbsp feta or Wensleydale cheese, crumbled
- salsa of your choice
- 1 tbsp chopped fresh coriander (cilantro)
- 1 tbsp finely chopped spring onions (scallions)

1 Heat the tortillas in an ungreased non-stick frying pan (skillet), sprinkling them with a few drops of water as they heat; wrap the tortillas in a clean tea towel (dish cloth) as you work to keep them warm. Alternatively, heat through in a stack in the pan, alternating the top and bottom tortillas so that they warm evenly. Wrap to keep warm.

2 Cut the avocado in half around the stone (pit). Twist apart, then remove the stone (pit) with a knife. Carefully peel off the skin, dice the flesh and toss in lime or lemon juice to prevent discoloration.

3 Brown the chorizo sausage in a pan, then arrange on each warmed tortilla. Keep warm.

4 Meanwhile, heat the butter or water in the non-stick frying pan (skillet), break in an egg and cook until the white is set but the yolk still soft. Remove from the pan and place on top of one tortilla. Keep warm.

5 Cook the remaining eggs in the same way, adding to the tortillas.

6 Arrange the avocado, cheese and a spoonful of salsa on each tortilla. Add the fresh coriander (cilantro) and spring onions (scallions) and serve.

Migas

A wonderful brunch or late-night supper dish, this is made by scrambling egg with chillies, tomatoes and crisp tortilla chips.

Serves 4

INGREDIENTS

- 2 tbsp butter
- 6 garlic cloves, finely chopped
- 1 fresh green chilli, such as jalapeño or serrano, deseeded and diced
- 1½ tsp ground cumin
- 6 ripe tomatoes, coarsely chopped
- 8 eggs, lightly beaten
- 8–10 corn tortillas, cut into strips and fried until crisp, or an equal amount of not too salty tortilla chips
- 4 tbsp chopped fresh coriander (cilantro)
- 3–4 spring onions (scallions), thinly sliced
- mild chilli powder, to garnish

1 Melt half the butter in a pan. Add the garlic and chilli and cook until softened, but not browned. Add the cumin and cook for 30 seconds, stirring, then add the tomatoes and cook over a medium heat for a further 3–4 minutes, or until the tomato juices have evaporated. Remove from the pan and set aside.

2 Melt the remaining butter in a frying pan (skillet) over a low heat and pour in the beaten eggs. Cook, stirring, until the eggs begin to set.

3 Add the reserved chilli tomato mixture, stirring gently to mix into the eggs.

4 Carefully add the tortilla strips or chips and continue cooking, stirring once or twice, until the eggs are the consistency you wish. The tortillas should be pliable and chewy.

5 Transfer to a serving plate and surround with the fresh coriander (cilantro) and spring onions. Garnish with a sprinkling of mild chilli powder and serve.

COOK'S TIP

Serve the migas with soured cream or crème fraîche on top, to melt seductively into the spicy eggs.

VARIATION

Add browned minced (ground) beef or pork to the softly scrambling egg mixture at Step 3. A bunch of cooked, chopped, spinach or chard can be stirred in as well, to add fresh colour.

Eggs Oaxaca Style

Cooking eggs in a flat omelette, then cutting them into strips and simmering them in a spicy sauce makes an unusual dish for brunch or dinner.

Serves 4

INGREDIENTS

1 kg/2 lb 4 oz ripe tomatoes
about 12 small button onions, halved
8 garlic cloves, whole and unpeeled
2 fresh mild green chillies
pinch of ground cumin
pinch of dried oregano,
pinch of sugar, if needed
2–3 tsp vegetable oil
8 eggs, lightly beaten
1–2 tbsp tomato purée (paste)
salt and pepper
1–2 tbsp chopped fresh coriander (cilantro), to garnish

1 Heat an ungreased heavy-based frying pan (skillet), add the tomatoes and char lightly, turning them once or twice. Allow to cool.

2 Meanwhile lightly char the onions, garlic and chillies in the pan. Allow to cool slightly.

3 Cut the cooled tomatoes into pieces and place in a blender or food processor, with their charred skins. Remove the stems and seeds from the chillies, then peel and chop. Remove the skins from the garlic, then chop. Roughly chop the onions. Add the chillies, garlic and onions to the tomatoes.

4 Process to make a rough purée, then add the cumin and oregano. Season with salt and pepper to taste, and add sugar if needed.

5 Heat the oil in a non-stick frying pan (skillet), add a ladleful of egg and cook to make a thin omelette. Continue to make omelettes, stacking them on a plate as they are cooked. Slice into noodle-like ribbons.

6 Bring the sauce to the boil, adjust the seasoning, adding tomato purée (paste) to taste. Add the omelette strips, warm through and serve at once, garnished with a sprinkling of fresh coriander (cilantro).

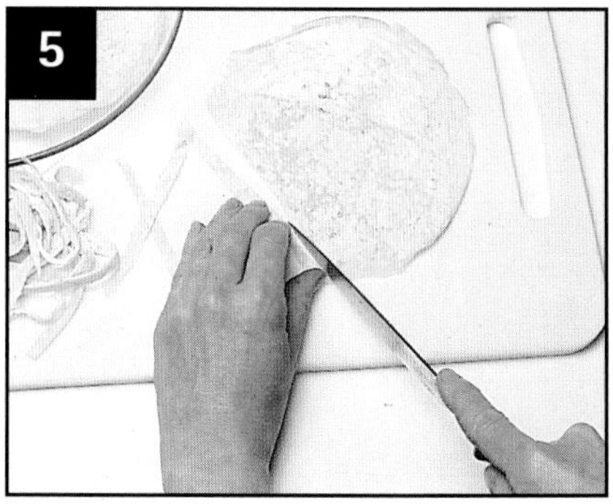

Eggs with Refried Beans

In the Yucatan, this classic dish would be sandwiched between two crisp tortillas, but layering it all on top of one tortilla looks much more festive.

Serves 4

INGREDIENTS

- 400 g/14 oz tomatoes, skinned and chopped
- 1 onion, chopped
- 1 garlic clove, finely chopped
- ½ fresh green chilli, such as jalapeño or serrano, deseeded and chopped
- ¼ tsp ground cumin
- 2 tbsp extra-virgin olive oil
- 1 plantain, peeled and diced
- 1 tbsp butter
- 4 corn tortillas, warmed or fried crisply into a tostada
- about 400 g/14 oz can refried beans, warmed with 2 tbsp of water
- 2 tbsp water or butter
- 8 eggs
- 1 red (bell) pepper, grilled (broiled), peeled, deseeded and cut into strips
- 3–4 tbsp cooked green peas, at room temperature
- 4–6 tbsp diced cooked or smoked ham
- 50–75 g/2–3 oz crumbled feta cheese
- 3 spring onions (scallions), thinly sliced
- salt and pepper

1 Process the tomatoes in a blender or food processor with the onion, garlic, chilli, cumin, salt and pepper to a purée.

2 Heat the oil in a heavy-based frying pan (skillet), then ladle in a little of the sauce and cook until it reduces in volume and becomes almost paste-like. Continue adding and reducing the sauce in this way. Keep warm.

3 Brown the plantain in the butter in a heavy-based non-stick frying pan (skillet). Remove and set aside. Spread the tortillas with the refried beans and keep warm in a low oven.

4 Heat the water or butter in the frying pan (skillet), break in an egg and cook until the white is set but the yolk still soft. Remove from the pan and place on top of one tortilla. Cook the remaining eggs in the same way, adding to the tortillas.

5 To serve, spoon the warm sauce around the eggs on each tortilla. Sprinkle over the diced plantain, (bell) pepper, peas, ham, feta cheese and spring onions (scallions). Season with salt and pepper to taste and serve immediately.

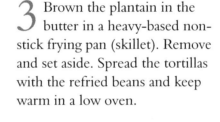

Fish with Yucatecan Flavours

Annatto seeds are rock hard little red seeds that need to be soaked overnight before you can grind them. They have a distinctive lemony flavour and impart a dark orange colour to the dish.

Serves 8

INGREDIENTS

4 tbsp annatto seeds, soaked in water overnight
3 garlic cloves, finely chopped
1 tbsp mild chilli powder
1 tbsp paprika
1 tsp ground cumin
½ tsp dried oregano
2 tbsp beer or tequila
juice of 1 lime and l orange or 3 tbsp pineapple juice
2 tbsp olive oil
2 tbsp chopped fresh coriander (cilantro)
¼ tsp ground cinnamon
¼ tsp ground cloves
1 kg/2 lb 4 oz swordfish steaks
banana leaves, for wrapping (optional)
fresh coriander (cilantro) leaves, to garnish
orange wedges, to serve

1 Drain the annatto, then crush them to a paste with a pestle and mortar. Work in the garlic, chilli powder, paprika, cumin, oregano, beer or tequila, fruit juice, olive oil, fresh coriander (cilantro), cinnamon and cloves.

2 Smear the paste on to the fish and marinate in the refrigerator for at least 3 hours or overnight.

3 Wrap the fish steaks in banana leaves, tying with string to make parcels. Bring water to the boil in a steamer, then add a batch of parcels to the top part of the steamer and cook for about 15 minutes or until the fish is cooked through.

4 Alternatively, cook the fish without wrapping in the banana leaves. To cook on the barbecue (grill), place in a hinged basket, or on a rack, and cook over the hot coals for 5–6 minutes on each side until cooked through. Or cook the fish under a preheated grill (broiler) for 5–6 minutes on each side until cooked through.

5 Garnish with coriander (cilantro) and serve with orange wedges for squeezing over the fish.

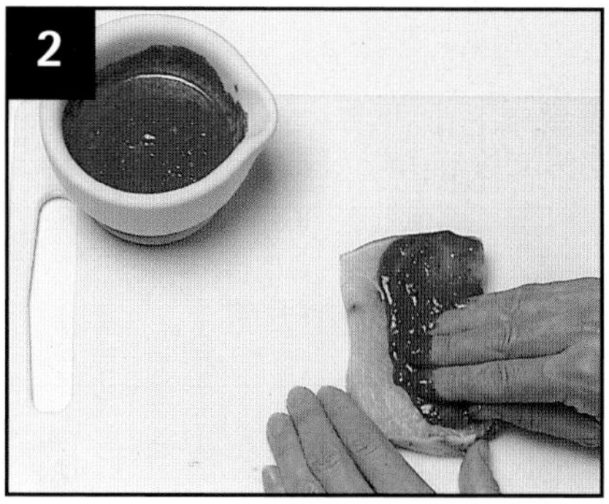

Prawns (Shrimp) in Green Bean Sauce

The sweet briny flesh of prawns (shrimp) is wonderful paired with the smoky scent of chipotle chilli.

Serves 4

INGREDIENTS

3 onions, chopped
5 garlic cloves, chopped
2 tbsp vegetable oil
5–7 ripe tomatoes, diced
175–225 g/6–8 oz green beans, cut into 5 cm/2 inch pieces and blanched for 1 minute
1/4 tsp ground cumin
pinch of ground allspice
pinch of ground cinnamon
1/2–1 canned chipotle chilli in adobo marinade, with some of the marinade
450 ml/16 fl oz/2 cups fish stock or water mixed with a fish stock cube
450 g/1 lb raw prawns (shrimp), peeled
fresh coriander (cilantro) sprigs
1 lime, cut into wedges

1 Lightly fry the onions and garlic in the oil over a low heat for 5–10 minutes until softened. Add the tomatoes and cook for a further 2 minutes.

2 Add the green beans, cumin, allspice, cinnamon, the chipotle chilli and marinade and fish stock. Bring to the boil, then reduce the heat and simmer for a few minutes to combine the flavours.

3 Add the prawns (shrimp) and cook for 1–2 minutes only, then remove the pan from the heat and leave the prawns (shrimp) to steep in the hot liquid to finish cooking. They are cooked when they have turned a bright pink colour.

4 Serve the prawns (shrimp) immediately, garnished with the fresh coriander (cilantro) and accompanied by the lime wedges.

VARIATION

If you can find them, use bottled nopales (edible cactus), cut into strips, to add an exotic touch to the dish.

Mussels Cooked with Lager

Mussels cooked in beer, tomatoes and Mexican spices are great summertime fare.

Serves 4

INGREDIENTS

1.5 kg/3 lb 5 oz live mussels
450 ml/16 fl oz/2 cups lager
2 onions, chopped
5 garlic cloves, chopped coarsely
1 fresh green chilli, such as jalapeño or serrano, deseeded and thinly sliced
175 g/6 oz/$^{2}/_{3}$ cup fresh tomatoes, diced, or canned chopped
2–3 tbsp chopped fresh coriander (cilantro)

1 Scrub the mussels under cold running water to remove any mud. Using a sharp knife, cut away the feathery 'beards' from the shells. Discard any open mussels that do not shut when tapped sharply with a knife. Rinse again in cold water.

2 Place the lager, onions, garlic, chilli and tomatoes in a heavy-based pan. Bring to the boil.

3 Add the mussels and cook, covered, over a medium-high heat for about 10 minutes until the shells open. Discard any mussels that do not open.

4 Ladle into individual bowls and serve sprinkled with fresh coriander.

VARIATION

Add the kernels of 2 corn-on-the-cobs to the lager mixture in Step 2. A pinch of sugar might be needed to bring out the sweetness of the corn.

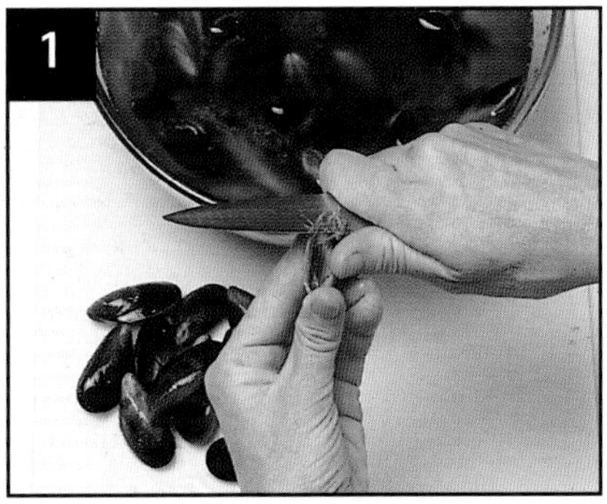

Barbecued (Grilled) Clams with Sweetcorn Salsa

Cook with Mexican flair, and serve up clams from the barbecue (grill), topped with a spicy sweetcorn salsa.

Serves 4

INGREDIENTS

- 2 kg/4 lb 8 oz clams in their shells
- 5 ripe tomatoes
- 2 garlic cloves, finely chopped
- 225 g/8 oz can sweetcorn, drained
- 3 tbsp finely chopped fresh coriander (cilantro)
- 3 spring onions (scallions), thinly sliced
- 1/4 tsp ground cumin
- juice of 1/2 lime
- 1/2–1 fresh green chilli, deseeded and finely chopped
- salt
- lime wedges, to serve

1 Place the clams in a large bowl. Cover with cold water and add a handful of salt. Leave to soak for 30 minutes to rinse out the sand and grit.

2 Meanwhile, skin the tomatoes. Place in a heatproof bowl, pour boiling water over to cover and stand for 30 seconds. Drain and plunge into cold water. The skins will then slide off easily. Cut the tomatoes in half, deseed, then chop the flesh.

3 To make the salsa, combine the tomatoes, garlic, sweetcorn, coriander (cilantro), spring onions (scallions), cumin, lime juice and chilli in a bowl. Season with salt to taste.

4 Drain the clams, discarding any that are open. Place the clams on the hot coals of a barbecue (grill), allowing about 5 minutes per side. They will pop open when they are ready. Discard any that do not open.

5 Immediately remove from the barbecue (grill), top with the salsa and serve with lime wedges for squeezing over the clams.

VARIATION

Mussels can be used in place of the clams very successfully.

Chilli-marinated Prawns (Shrimp) with Avocado Sauce

Avocado salsa is delicious spooned on to anything spicy from the grill (broiler) or barbecue (grill), especially seafood.

Serves 4

INGREDIENTS

650 g/1 lb 5 oz large prawns (shrimp), shelled
½ tsp ground cumin
½ tsp mild chilli powder
½ tsp paprika
2 tbsp orange juice
grated rind of 1 orange
2 tbsp extra-virgin olive oil
2 tbsp chopped fresh coriander (cilantro), plus extra for garnishing
2 ripe avocados
½ onion, finely chopped
¼ fresh green or red chilli, deseeded and chopped
juice of ½ lime
salt and pepper

1 Combine the prawns (shrimp) with the cumin, chilli powder, paprika, orange juice and rind, olive oil and half the coriander (cilantro). Season to taste.

2 Thread the prawns (shrimp) on to metal skewers, or bamboo skewers that have been soaked in cold water for 30 minutes.

3 Cut the avocados in half around the stone (pit). Twist apart, then remove the stone (pit) with a knife. Carefully peel off the skin, then dice the flesh. Immediately combine the avocados with the remaining coriander (cilantro), onion, chilli and lime juice. Season with salt and pepper and set aside.

4 Place the prawns (shrimp) on a hot barbecue (grill) and cook for only a few minutes on each side.

5 Serve the prawns (shrimp), garnished with coriander (cilantro) and accompanied by the avocado sauce.

VARIATION

For luscious sandwiches, toast crusty rolls, cut in half and buttered, over the hot coals and fill them with the cooked prawns (shrimp) and avocado sauce.

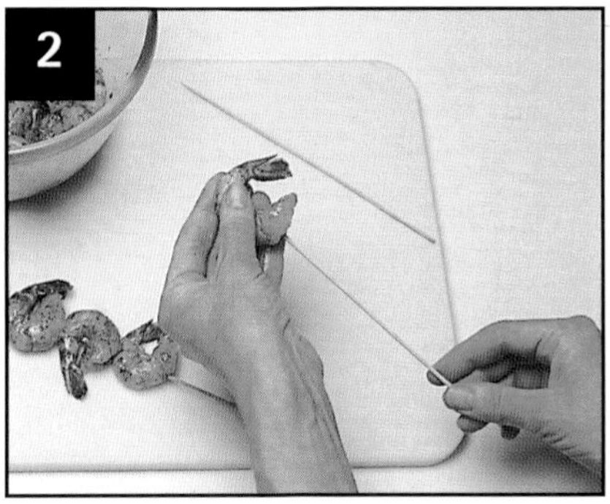

Squid Simmered with Tomatoes, Olives & Capers

This flavourful squid dish from Vera Cruz would be good with warmed flour tortillas, for do-it-yourself tacos.

Serves 4

INGREDIENTS

3 tbsp extra-virgin olive oil
900 g/2 lb cleaned squid, cut into rings and tentacles
1 onion, chopped
3 garlic cloves, chopped
400 g/14 oz can chopped tomatoes
½–1 fresh mildish green chilli, deseeded and chopped
1 tbsp finely chopped fresh parsley
¼ tsp chopped fresh thyme
¼ tsp chopped fresh oregano
¼ tsp chopped fresh marjoram
large pinch of ground cinnamon
large pinch of ground allspice
large pinch of sugar
15–20 pimiento-stuffed green olives, sliced
1 tbsp capers
salt and pepper
1 tbsp chopped fresh coriander (cilantro), to garnish

1 Heat the oil in a pan and lightly fry the squid until it turns opaque. Season with salt and pepper and remove from the pan with a slotted spoon.

2 Add the onion and garlic to the remaining oil in the pan and fry until softened. Stir in the tomatoes, chilli, herbs, cinnamon, allspice, sugar and olives. Cover and cook over a medium-low heat for 5–10 minutes until the mixture thickens slightly. Uncover the pan and cook for a further 5 minutes to concentrate the flavours.

3 Stir in the reserved squid and any of the juices that have gathered. Add the capers and heat through.

4 Adjust the seasoning, then serve immediately, garnished with fresh coriander (citantro).

Pan-fried Scallops Mexicana

Scallops, with their sweet flesh, are delicious with the rindy flavours of Mexico. Often they are prepared just this simply, served with wedges of lime to squeeze over as desired, and a stack of warm corn tortillas.

Serves 4–6

INGREDIENTS

2 tbsp butter
2 tbsp extra-virgin olive oil
650 g/1 lb 6 oz scallops, shelled
4–5 spring onions (scallions), thinly sliced
3–4 garlic cloves, finely chopped
½ fresh green chilli, deseeded and finely chopped
2 tbsp finely chopped fresh coriander (cilantro)
juice of ½ lime
salt and pepper
lime wedges, to serve

1 Heat half the butter and olive oil in a heavy-based frying pan (skillet) until the butter foams.

2 Add the scallops and cook quickly until just turning opaque; do not overcook. Remove from the pan with a slotted spoon and keep warm.

3 Add the remaining butter and oil to the pan, then toss in the spring onions (scallions) and garlic and cook over a medium heat until the spring onions (scallions) are wilted. Return the scallops to the pan.

4 Remove the pan from the heat and add the chopped chilli and coriander (cilantro). Squeeze in the juice from half a lime. Season with salt and pepper to taste and stir to mix well.

5 Serve immediately with lime wedges for squeezing over the scallops.

VARIATION

Mix leftover scallops with a little aioli or mayonnaise mixed with garlic and a little olive oil. Serve with roasted (bell) peppers on a bed of greens, with a handful of salty black olives for a taste of the Mediterranean, Mexico style.

Spicy Grilled (Broiled) Salmon

The woody smoked flavours of the chipotle chilli are delicious brushed on to salmon for grilling (broiling).

Serves 4

INGREDIENTS

4 salmon steaks, about 175–225 g/6–8 oz each
lime slices, to garnish

MARINADE:
4 garlic cloves
2 tbsp extra-virgin olive oil
pinch of ground allspice
pinch of ground cinnamon
juice of 2 limes
1–2 tsp marinade from canned chipotle chillies or bottled chipotle chilli salsa
1/4 tsp ground cumin
pinch of sugar
salt and pepper

TO SERVE:
tomato wedges
3 spring onions (scallions) finely chopped
shredded lettuce

1 To make the marinade, finely chop the garlic and place in a bowl with the olive oil, allspice, cinnamon, lime juice, chipotle marinade, cumin and sugar. Add salt and pepper and stir to combine.

2 Coat the salmon with the garlic mixture, then place in a non-metallic dish. Leave to marinate for at least an hour or overnight in the refrigerator.

3 Transfer to a grill (broiler) pan and cook under a preheated grill (broiler) for 3–4 minutes on each side. Alternatively, cook the salmon over hot coals on a barbecue (grill) until cooked through.

4 To serve, mix the tomato wedges with the spring onions (scallions). Place the salmon on individual plates and arrange the tomato salad and shredded lettuce alongside. Garnish with lime slices and serve immediately.

VARIATION

The marinade also goes well with fresh tuna steaks.

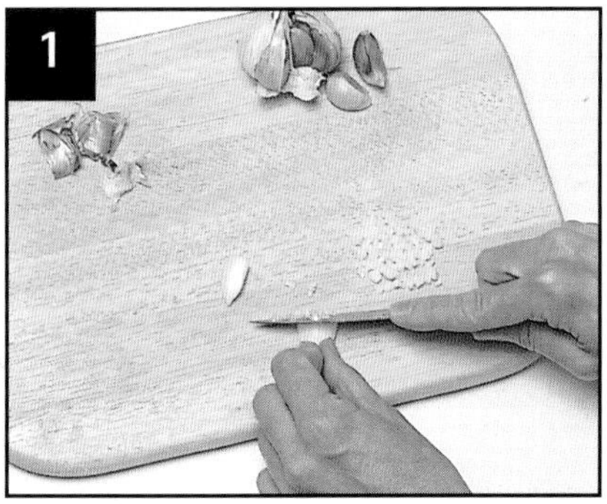
1

1

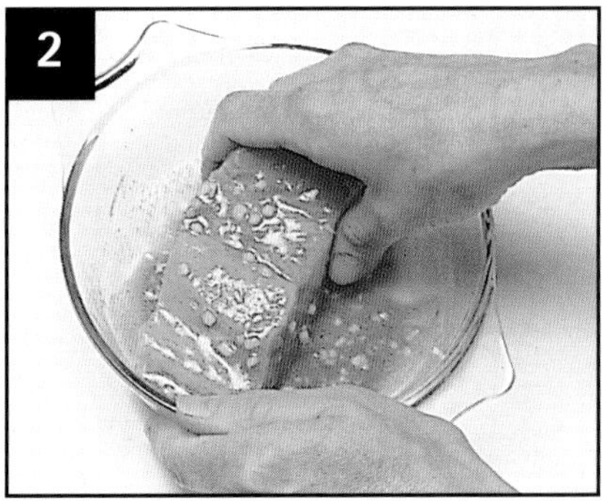
2

Fish Baked with Lime

Tangy and simple to prepare, this is excellent served with rice and beans for an easy lunch. Follow up with coffee ice cream topped with espresso beans and chocolate sauce.

Serves 4

INGREDIENTS

- 1 kg/2 lb 4 oz white fish fillets, such as bass, plaice or cod
- 1 lime, halved
- 3 tbsp extra-virgin olive oil
- 1 large onion, finely chopped
- 3 garlic cloves, finely chopped
- 2–3 pickled jalapeño chillies (see Cook's Tip), chopped
- 6–8 tbsp chopped fresh coriander (cilantro)
- salt and pepper
- lemon and lime wedges, to serve

1 Place the fish fillets in a bowl and sprinkle with salt and pepper. Squeeze the juice from the lime over the fish.

2 Heat the olive oil in a frying pan (skillet). Add the onion and garlic and fry for about 2 minutes, stirring frequently, until softened. Remove from the heat.

3 Place a third of the onion mixture and a little of the chillies and coriander (cilantro) in the bottom of a shallow baking dish or roasting tin (pan). Arrange the fish on top. Top with the remaining onion mixture, chillies and coriander (cilantro).

4 Bake in a preheated oven at 180°C/350°F/Gas Mark 4 for about 15–20 minutes or until the fish has become slightly opaque and firm to the touch. Serve at once, with lemon and lime wedges for squeezing over the fish.

COOK'S TIP

Pickled jalapeños are called jalapeños en escabeche *and are available from specialist stores.*

VARIATION

Add sliced flavourful fresh tomatoes, or canned chopped tomatoes, to the onion mixture at the end of Step 2.

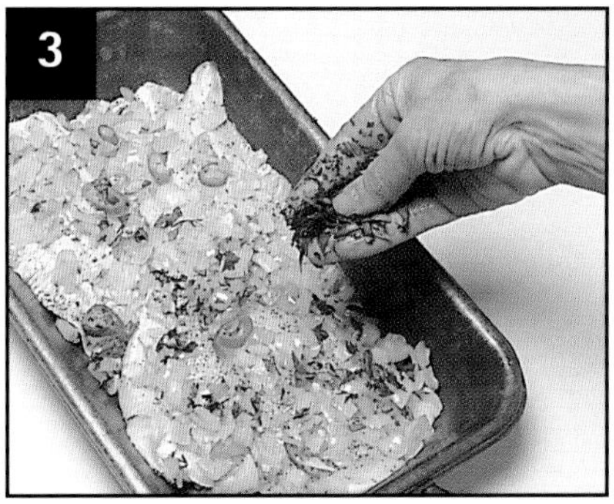

Lobster Cooked Rosarita Beach Style

Barbecuing (grilling) gives lobsters a lovely smoky scent that is enhanced by spicy red chilli. Serve with creamy refried beans and a stack of warm corn tortillas and pretend you're on Rosarita Beach in Baja California!

Serves 4

INGREDIENTS

2–4 cooked lobsters, depending on their size, cut through the middle into two halves, or 4 lobster tails, the meat loosened slightly from its shell

CHILLI BUTTER:
115 g/4 oz unsalted butter, softened
3–4 tbsp chopped fresh coriander (cilantro)
about 5 garlic cloves, chopped
2–3 tbsp mild chilli powder
juice of ½ lime
salt and pepper

TO SERVE:
400 g/14 oz refried beans, warmed with 2 tbsp water
chopped spring onions (scallions)
lime wedges
salsa of your choice

1 To make the chilli butter, put the butter in a bowl and mix in the coriander (cilantro), garlic, chilli powder and lime juice. Add salt and pepper.

2 Rub the chilli butter into the cut side of the lobster or the lobster tails, working it into all the lobsters cracks and crevices.

3 Wrap loosely in kitchen foil and place, cut-side up, on a rack over the hot coals of a barbecue (grill). Cook for 15 minutes or until heated through.

4 Serve with warm refried beans, topped with chopped spring onions (scallions), plus lime wedges and salsa.

COOK'S TIP

The flavoured butter is also delicious with grilled (broiled) fish steaks and large prawns (shrimp).

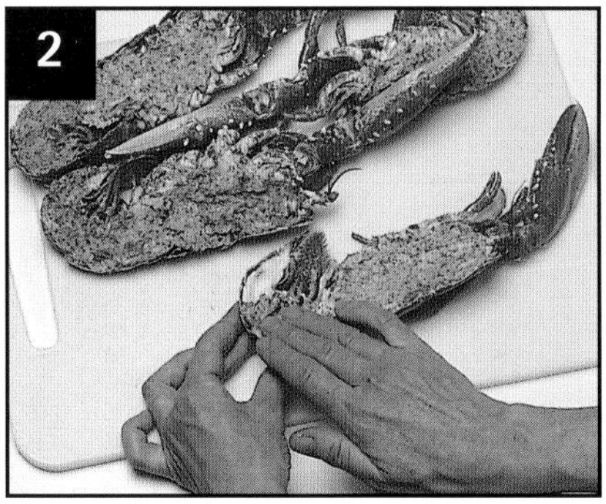

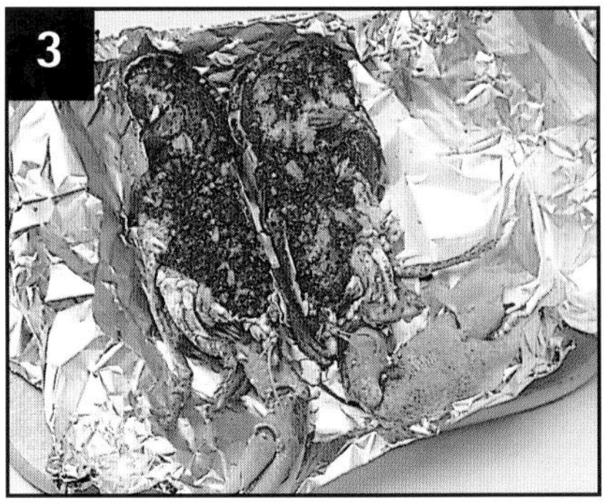

Ropa Vieja

Fill warmed tortillas with this tender, browned beef and a selection of crisp vegetables to make wonderful tacos

Serves 6

INGREDIENTS

1.5 kg/3 lb 5 oz flank beef steak or other stewing meat
beef stock
1 carrot, sliced
10 garlic cloves, sliced
2 tbsp vegetable oil
2 onions, thinly sliced
3–4 mild fresh green chillies, such as anaheim or poblano, deseeded and sliced
warmed flour tortillas, to serve

SALAD GARNISHES:
3 ripe tomatoes, diced
8–10 radishes, diced
3–4 tbsp chopped fresh coriander (cilantro)
4–5 spring onions (scallions), chopped
1–2 limes, cut into wedges

1 Put the meat in a large pan and cover with a mixture of stock and water. Add the carrot and half the garlic with salt and pepper to taste. Cover and bring to the boil, then reduce the heat to low. Skim the scum from the surface, then re-cover the pan and cook the meat gently for about 2 hours until very tender.

2 Remove the pan from the heat and leave the meat to cool in the liquid. When cool enough to handle, remove from the liquid and shred with your fingers and a fork.

3 Heat the oil in a large frying pan (skillet), add the remaining garlic, onions and chillies and fry until lightly coloured. Remove from the pan and set aside.

4 Add the meat to the pan and cook over a medium-high heat until browned and crisp. Transfer to a serving dish. Top with the onion mixture and surround with the tomatoes, radishes, coriander (cilantro), spring onions (scallions) and lime wedges. Serve with warmed tortillas.

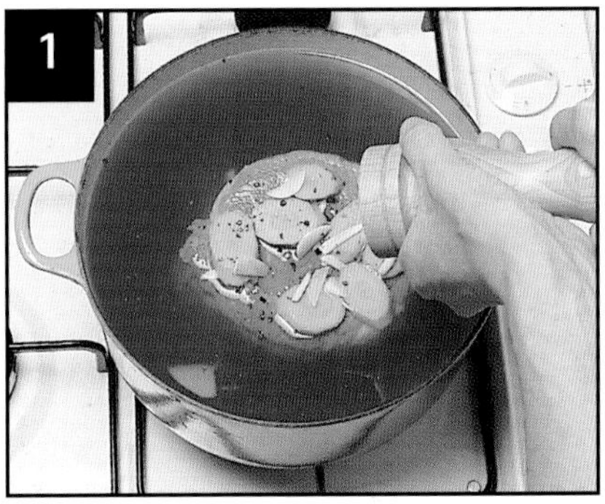

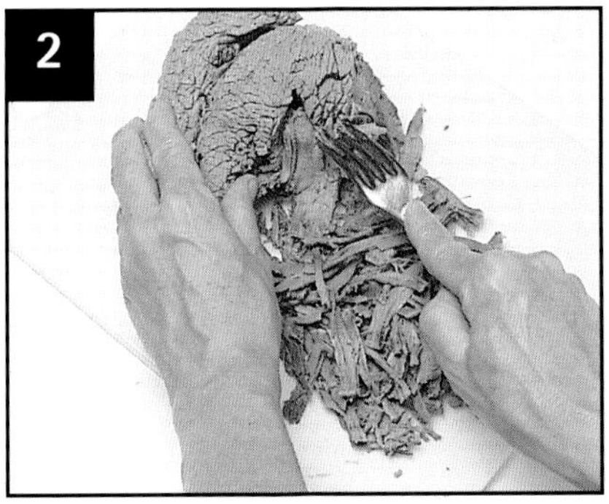

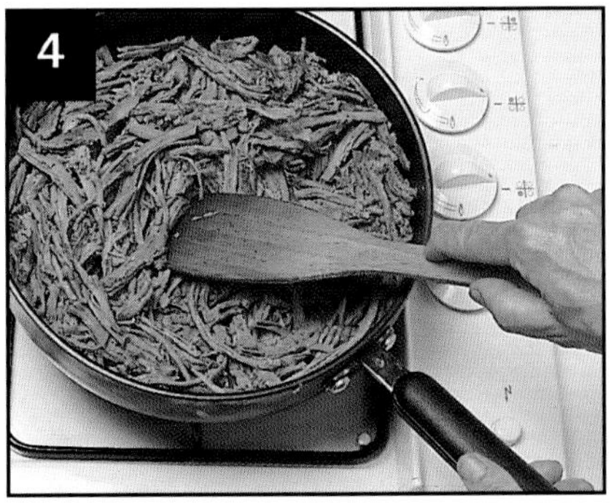

Classic Beef Fajitas

Sizzling marinated strips of meat rolled up in soft flour tortillas with a tangy salsa is a real Mexican treat, perfect for relaxed entertaining.

Serves 4–6

INGREDIENTS

700 g/1 lb 9 oz beef skirt steak or other tender steak, cut into strips
6 garlic cloves, chopped
juice of 1 lime
large pinch of mild chilli powder
large pinch of paprika
large pinch of ground cumin
1–2 tbsp extra-virgin olive oil
12 flour tortillas
vegetable oil, for frying
1–2 avocados, stoned (pitted), sliced and tossed with lime juice
120 ml/4 fl oz/½ cup soured cream
salt and pepper

PICO DE GALLO SALSA:
8 ripe tomatoes, diced
3 spring onions (scallions), sliced
1–2 fresh green chillies, such as jalapeño or serrano, deseeded and chopped
3–4 tbsp chopped fresh coriander (cilantro)
5–8 radishes, diced
ground cumin

1 Combine the beef with half the garlic, half the lime juice, the chilli powder, paprika, cumin and olive oil. Add salt and pepper, mix well and leave to marinate for at least 30 minutes at room temperature, or up to overnight in the refrigerator.

2 To make the pico de gallo salsa, put the tomatoes in a bowl with the spring onions (scallions), green chilli, coriander and radishes. Season to taste with cumin, salt and pepper. Set aside.

3 Heat the tortillas in a lightly greased non-stick frying pan (skillet); wrap in kitchen foil as you work, to keep them warm.

4 Stir-fry the meat in a little oil over a high heat until browned and just cooked through.

5 Serve the sizzling hot meat with the warm tortillas, the pico de gallo salsa, avocado and soured cream for each person to make his or her own rolled up fajitas.

COOK'S TIP

A lettuce and orange salad makes a refreshing accompaniment.

Michoacan Beef

This rich smoky flavoured stew is delicious; leftovers make a great filling for tacos, too!

Serves 4–6

INGREDIENTS

about 3 tbsp plain (all-purpose) flour
1 kg/2 lb 4 oz stewing beef, cut into large bite-sized pieces
2 tbsp vegetable oil
2 onions, chopped
5 garlic cloves, chopped
400 g/14 oz tomatoes, diced
1$\frac{1}{2}$ dried chipotle chillies, reconstituted (see page 100), deseeded and cut into thin strips, or a few shakes of bottled chipotle salsa
1.5 litres/2$\frac{3}{4}$ pints/6$\frac{1}{4}$ cups beef stock
350 g/12 oz green beans, topped and tailed
a pinch of sugar
salt and pepper

TO SERVE:
simmered beans
cooked rice

1 Place the flour in a large bowl and season with salt and pepper. Add the beef and toss to coat well. Remove from the bowl, shaking off the excess flour.

2 Heat the oil in a frying pan (skillet) and brown the meat briefly over a high heat. Reduce the heat to medium, add the onions and garlic and cook for a further 2 minutes.

3 Add the tomatoes, chillies and stock, then cover and simmer over a low heat for 1$\frac{1}{2}$ hours or until the meat is very tender, adding the green beans 15 minutes before the end of the cooking time. Skim off any fat that rises to the surface, every now and again.

4 Transfer to individual bowls and serve with simmered beans and rice.

COOK'S TIP

This is traditionally made with nopales, edible cactus, which gives the dish a distinctive flavour. Look out for them in specialist stores. For this recipe you need 350–400 g/12–14 oz can nopales, or fresh nopales, peeled, sliced and blanched. Add them with the tomatoes at Step 3.

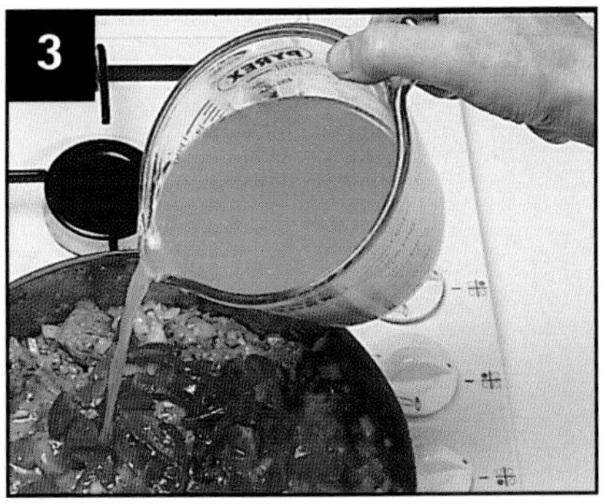

Chillies Stuffed with Spicy Beef

Large mildish-tasting green chillies are roasted, peeled and stuffed with a succulent meat mixture that is sweet, spicy and punctuated with nuts.

Serves 4

INGREDIENTS

4 large fresh poblano chillies
flour for dusting
vegetable oil, for frying
Quick Tomato Sauce (see page 82), to serve

SPICY BEEF FILLING:
500 g/1 lb 2 oz minced (ground) beef
1 onion, finely chopped
2–3 garlic cloves, finely chopped
50 ml/2 fl oz/¼ cup dry or sweet sherry
pinch of ground cinnamon
pinch of ground cloves
pinch of ground cumin
400 g/14 oz can chopped tomatoes
1–3 tsp sugar
1 tbsp vinegar
3 tbsp chopped fresh coriander (cilantro)
2–3 tbsp coarsely chopped toasted almonds
salt and pepper

BATTER:
6–8 Tbsp plain (all purpose) flour
3 eggs, separated
120 ml/4 fl oz/½ cup water

1 Roast the chillies under a preheated grill (broiler) until the skin is charred. Place in a plastic bag, seal well and leave to stand for 20 minutes. Make a slit in the side of each chilli and remove the seeds, leaving the stems intact. Set aside.

2 Brown the meat and onion together in a heavy-based frying pan (skillet) over a medium heat. Pour off any extra fat, then add the garlic and sherry and boil down until the liquid has nearly evaporated.

3 Season with salt, pepper, cinnamon, cloves and cumin, then add the tomatoes, sugar and vinegar and cook over a medium heat until the tomatoes have reduced to a thick, strongly flavoured sauce.

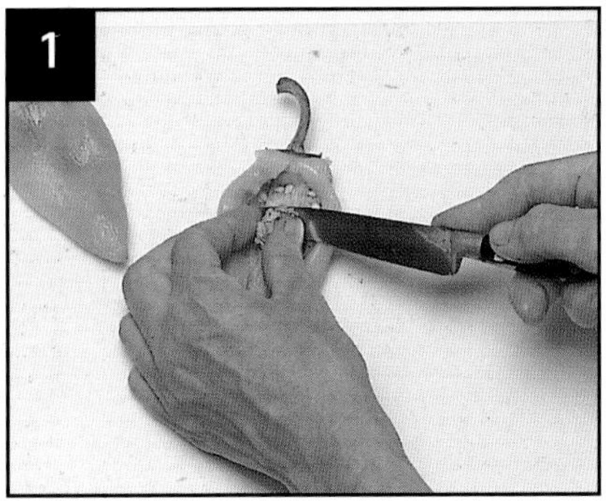
1

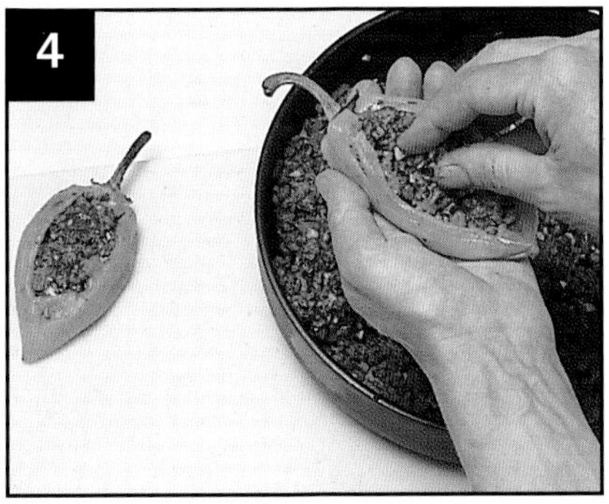
4

4 Stir in the chopped fresh coriander (cilantro) and almonds and heat through. Stuff as much of this filling into the chillies as will fit, then dust each with flour. Set aside.

5 Lightly beat the yolks with the flour, a pinch of salt and enough water to make a thick batter. Whisk the egg whites until they form stiff peaks. Fold the egg whites into the batter mixture, then gently dip each stuffed chilli into the batter.

6 Heat the oil in a deep frying pan (skillet) until very hot and just smoking. Gently fry the chillies until they are golden brown. Serve hot, topped with the tomato sauce.

Spicy Pork with Prunes

Prunes add an earthy, wine flavour to this spicy stew. Serve with tortillas or crusty bread to dip into the rich sauce.

Serves 4–6

INGREDIENTS

- 1.5 kg/3 lb 5 oz pork joint, such as leg or shoulder
- juice of 2–3 limes
- 10 garlic cloves, chopped
- 3–4 tbsp mild chilli powder, such as ancho or New Mexico
- 4 tbsp vegetable oil
- 2 onions, chopped
- 500 ml/18 fl oz/2¼ cups chicken stock
- 25 small tart tomatoes, roughly chopped
- 25 prunes, stoned (pitted)
- 1–2 tsp sugar
- about a pinch of ground cinnamon
- about a pinch of ground allspice
- about a pinch of ground cumin
- salt
- warmed corn tortillas, to serve

1 Combine the pork with the lime juice, garlic, chilli powder, 2 tablespoons of oil and salt. Leave to marinate in the refrigerator overnight.

2 Remove the pork from the marinade. Wipe the pork dry with paper towels and reserve the marinade. Heat the remaining oil in a flameproof casserole and brown the pork evenly until just golden. Add the onions, the reserved marinade and stock. Cover and cook in a preheated oven at 180°C/350°F/Gas Mark 4 for about 2–3 hours until tender.

3 Spoon off fat from the surface of the cooking liquid and add the tomatoes. Continue to cook for about 20 minutes until the tomatoes are tender. Mash the tomatoes into a coarse purée. Add the prunes and sugar, then adjust the seasoning, adding cinnamon, allspice and cumin to taste, as well as extra chilli powder, if wished.

4 Increase the oven temperature to 200°C/400°F/Gas Mark 6 and return the meat and sauce to the oven for a further 20–30 minutes or until the meat has browned on top and the juices have thickened.

5 Remove the meat from the pan and let it stand for a few minutes. Carefully carve it into thin slices and spoon the sauce over the top. Serve warm, with corn tortillas.

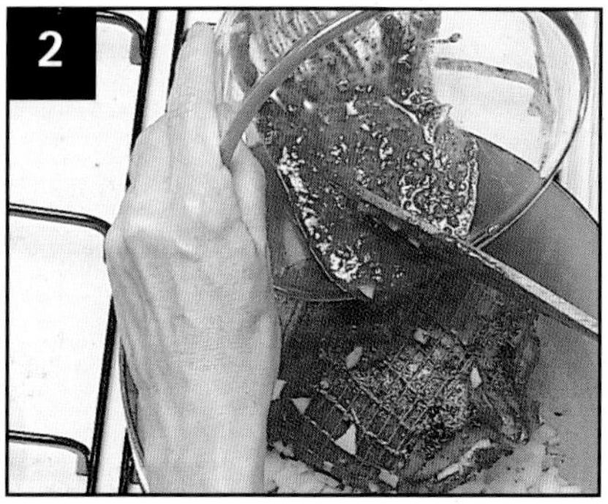

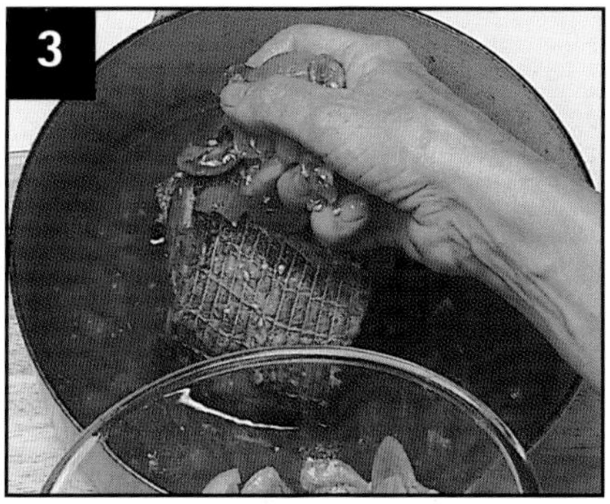

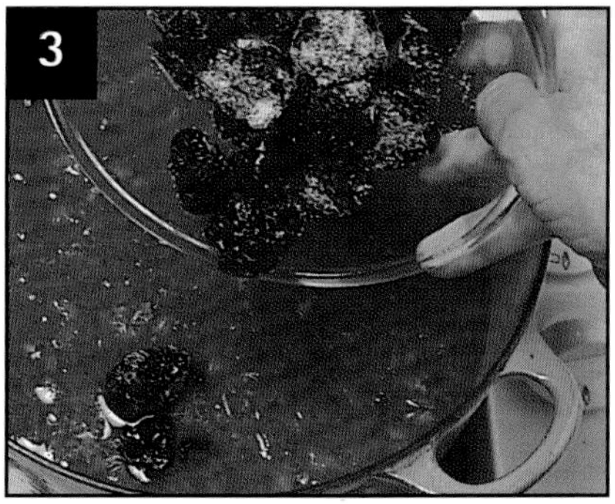

Red Mole of Pork & Red Chillies

Plantain and sesame seeds add a delicious hint of sweetness to this fragrant stew of pork and mild chillies, while potatoes add a satisfying chunky texture.

Serves 6

INGREDIENTS

1.25 kg/2 lb 12 oz pork shoulder or lean belly, cut into bite-sized pieces
1 onion, chopped
1 whole garlic bulb
2 bay leaves
1–2 stock cubes
6 dried ancho chillies
6 guajillo chillies
3–5 ripe big flavourful tomatoes
¼ tsp ground cloves
¼ tsp ground allspice
80 g/3 oz sesame seeds, toasted
1 large ripe plantain or banana, peeled and diced
3 tbsp vegetable oil
6–8 waxy potatoes, cut into chunks
3 tbsp yerba santa, or a combination of chopped fresh mint, oregano and coriander (cilantro)
1 cinnamon stick
salt and pepper

1 Place the pork in a large pan with the onion, the garlic, bay leaves and salt and pepper. Fill with cold water to the top.

2 Bring to the boil, then reduce the heat to a slow simmer. Skim off the scum, then stir in the stock cubes and cook the meat, covered, for about 3 hours until very tender.

3 Meanwhile, lightly roast the chillies in an ungreased heavy-based frying pan (skillet) until they just change colour. Put them in a bowl and cover with boiling water. Cover and leave to soften for 20–30 minutes.

4 Roast the tomatoes in the frying pan (skillet), to brown the bases, then char the tops under a hot grill (broiler). Leave to cool.

5 When the chillies are softened, remove the stems and seeds, then purée them with enough liquid to make a paste. Add the roasted tomatoes, cloves and allspice, with two-thirds of the sesame seeds and the plantain. Purée until smooth.

6 Remove the meat from the pan and reserve. Skim the fat from the surface of the stock.

7 Heat the oil in a pan, add the tomato purée mixture and cook for about 10 minutes until thickened. Do not let it burn. Add the potatoes and the herbs, with enough of the stock to keep the potatoes covered in sauce. Add the cinnamon stick.

8 Cook, covered, until the potatoes are tender, then add the reserved meat and heat through. Serve in bowls, sprinkled with the reserved sesame seeds.

Chile Verde

If tomatillos are not available, use fresh tomatoes and bottled green salsa instead, and add a good hit of lime juice at the end.

Serves 4

INGREDIENTS

1 kg/2 lb 4 oz pork, cut into bite-sized chunks
1 onion, chopped
2 bay leaves
1 whole garlic bulb, cut in half
1 stock cube
2 garlic cloves, chopped
450 g/1 lb oz fresh tomatillos, husks removed, cooked in a small amount of water until just tender, then chopped, or canned
2 large fresh mild green chillies, such as anaheim, or a combination of 1 green (bell) pepper and 2 jalapeño chillies, deseeded and chopped
3 tbsp vegetable oil
225 ml/8 fl oz/1 cup pork or chicken stock
½ tsp mild chilli powder, such as ancho or New Mexico
½ tsp cumin
4–6 tbsp chopped fresh coriander (cilantro), to garnish

TO SERVE:
warmed flour tortillas
lime wedges

1 Place the pork in a large pan with the onion, bay leaves and garlic bulb. Add water to cover and bring to the boil. Skim off the scum from the surface, reduce the heat to very low and simmer gently for about 1½ hours or until the meat is very tender.

2 Meanwhile, put the chopped garlic in a blender or food processor with the tomatillos and green chillies and (bell) pepper, if using. Process to a purée.

3 Heat the oil in a pan, add the tomatillo mixture and cook over a medium-high heat for about 10 minutes or until thickened. Add the stock, chilli powder and cumin.

4 When the meat is tender, remove from the pan and add to the sauce. Simmer gently to combine the flavours.

5 Garnish with the chopped coriander (cilantro) and serve with warmed tortillas and lime wedges.

1

3

4

Meatballs in Spicy-sweet Sauce

Called albondigas in Mexican, these tasty meatballs are set off brilliantly against the rich sauce and golden sweet potatoes.

Serves 4

INGREDIENTS

225 g/8 oz minced (ground) pork
225 g/8 oz minced (ground) beef or lamb
6 tbsp cooked rice or finely crushed tortilla chips
1 egg, lightly beaten
1½ onions, finely chopped
5 garlic cloves, finely chopped
½ tsp ground cumin
large pinch of ground cinnamon
2 tbsp raisins
1 tbsp molasses sugar
1–2 tbsp cider or wine vinegar
400 g/14 oz can tomatoes, drained and chopped
350 ml/12 fl oz/1½ cups beef stock
1–2 tbsp mild chilli or ancho chilli powder
1 tbsp paprika
1 tbsp chopped fresh coriander (cilantro)
1 tbsp chopped fresh parsley or mint
2 tbsp vegetable oil
2 sweet potatoes, peeled and cut into small bite-sized chunks
salt and pepper
grated cheese, to serve

1 Mix thoroughly the meat with the rice or crushed tortilla chips, the egg, half the onion, half the garlic, the cumin, cinnamon and raisins.

2 Divide the mixture into even-sized pieces and roll into balls. Fry the balls in a non-stick frying pan (skillet) over a medium heat, adding a tiny bit of oil, if necessary, to help them brown. Remove the balls from the pan and set aside. Wipe the frying pan (skillet) clean.

3 Place the molasses sugar in a blender or food processor, with the vinegar, tomatoes, stock, chilli powder, paprika and remaining onion and garlic. Process together until blended, then stir in the chopped fresh herbs. Set aside.

4 Heat the oil in the cleaned frying pan (skillet), add the sweet potatoes and cook until tender and golden brown. Pour in the blended sauce and add the meatballs to the pan. Cook for about 10 minutes until the meatballs are heated through and the flavours have completletely combined. Season with salt and pepper. Serve accompanied with grated cheese.

1

2

4

Carnitas

In this classic Mexican dish, pieces of pork are first simmered to make them meltingly tender, then browned until irresistibly crisp.

Serves 4–6

INGREDIENTS

1 kg/2 lb 4 oz pork, such as lean belly
1 onion, chopped
1 whole garlic bulb, cut in half
½ tsp ground cumin
2 meat stock cubes
2 bay leaves
vegetable oil, for frying
salt and pepper
fresh chilli strips, to garnish

TO SERVE:
cooked rice
refried beans (see page 144)
salsa of your choice

1 Place the pork in a heavy-based pan with the onion, garlic, cumin, stock cubes and bay leaves. Add water to cover. Bring to the boil, then reduce the heat to very low. Skim off the foam and scum that has formed on the surface of the liquid.

2 Continue to cook very gently for about 2 hours or until the meat is tender. Remove from the heat and leave the meat to cool in the liquid.

3 Remove the meat from the pan with a slotted spoon. Cut off any rind (roast separately to make crackling). Cut the meat into bite-sized pieces and sprinkle with salt and pepper. Reserve 300 ml/10 fl oz/1¼ cups of the cooking liquid.

4 Brown the meat in a heavy-based frying pan (skillet) for about 15 minutes, to cook out the fat. Add the reserved meat cooking liquid and allow to reduce down. Continue to cook the meat for 15 minutes, covering the pan to avoid splattering. Turn the meat every now and again.

5 Transfer the meat to a serving dish, garnish with chilli strips and serve with rice, refried beans and salsa.

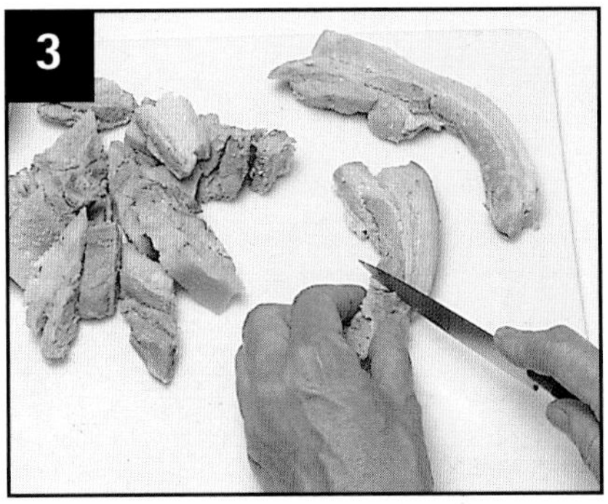

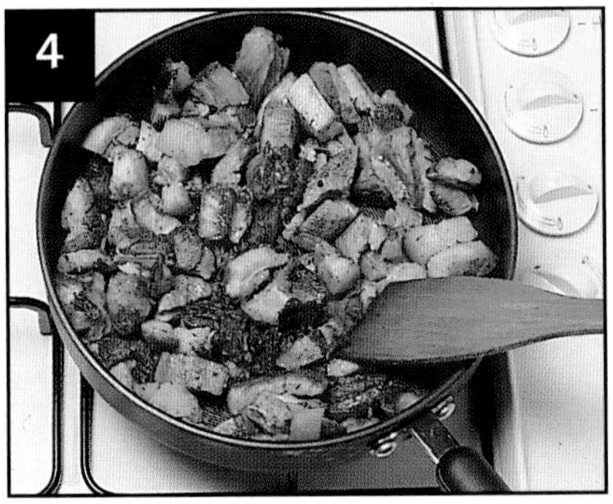

Spicy Meat & Chipotle Hash

This speciality from the town of Puebla in Mexico makes divine soft tacos: simply serve with a stack of warm soft corn tortillas and let everyone roll their own, fajita-style.

Serves 6

INGREDIENTS

- 1 tbsp vegetable oil
- 1 onion, finely chopped
- 450 g/1 lb leftover meat, such as simmered pork or beef, cooled and cut into thin strips
- 1 tbsp mild chilli powder
- 2 ripe tomatoes, deseeded and diced
- about 225 ml/8 fl oz/1 cup meat stock
- ½–1 canned chipotle chillies, mashed, plus a little of the marinade, or a few shakes bottled chipotle salsa
- 120 ml/4 fl oz/½ cup soured cream
- 4–6 tbsp chopped fresh coriander
- 4–6 tbsp chopped radishes
- 3–4 leaves crisp lettuce, such as cos (romaine), shredded

1 Heat the oil in a frying pan (skillet), add the onion and cook until softened, stirring occasionally. Add the meat and sauté for about 3 minutes, stirring, until lightly browned.

2 Add the chilli powder, tomatoes and stock and cook until the tomatoes reduce to a sauce; mash the meat a bit as it cooks.

3 Add the chipotle chillies and continue to cook and mash until the sauce and meat are nearly blended.

4 Serve the dish with a stack of warmed corn tortillas so that people can fill them with the meaty mixture to make tacos. Also serve soured cream, fresh coriander, radishes and lettuce for each person to add to the meat.

COOK'S TIP

Avocados add an interesting texture contrast to the spicy meat – serve with 2 sliced avocados, tossed with lime juice. Try serving on top of tostada, crisply fried tortillas, instead of wrapping taco-style.

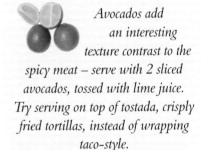

Simmered Stew of Meat, Chicken, Vegetables & Fruit

A big pot of cocido is warming on a cold day, great for a family meal. Serve with a selection of several salsas, a stack of corn tortillas and a bowl of rice.

Serves 6–8

INGREDIENTS

- 900 g/2 lb boneless pork, either in one joint or in pieces
- 2 bay leaves
- 1 onion, chopped
- 8 garlic cloves, finely chopped
- 2 tbsp chopped fresh coriander (cilantro)
- 1 carrot, thinly sliced
- 2 celery sticks, diced
- 2 chicken stock cubes
- ½ chicken, cut into portions
- 4–5 ripe tomatoes, diced
- ½ tsp mild chilli powder
- grated rind of ¼ orange
- ¼ tsp ground cumin
- juice of 3 oranges
- 1 courgette (zucchini), cut into bite-sized pieces
- ¼ cabbage, thinly sliced and blanched
- 1 apple, cut into bite-sized pieces
- about 10 prunes, stoned (pitted)
- ¼ tsp ground cinnamon
- pinch of dried ginger
- 2 hard chorizo sausages, about 350 g/12 oz in total, cut into bite-sized pieces
- salt and pepper

1 Combine the pork, bay leaves, onion, garlic, coriander (cilantro), carrot and celery in a large pan and fill with cold water. Bring to the boil, skim off the scum on the surface. Reduce heat and simmer gently for an hour.

2 Add the stock cubes to the pan, along with the chicken, tomatoes, chilli powder, orange rind and cumin. Continue to cook for a further 45 minutes or until the chicken is tender. Spoon off the fat that forms on the top of the liquid.

3 Add the orange juice, courgette (zucchini), cabbage, apple, prunes, cinnamon, ginger and chorizo. Continue to simmer for a further 20 minutes or until the courgette (zucchini) is soft and tender and the chorizo cooked through.

4 Season the stew with salt and pepper to taste. Serve immediately with rice, tortillas and salsa.

Chicken Breasts in Green Salsa with Soured Cream

Chicken breasts bathed in a fragrant sauce make a delicate dish, perfect for dinner parties. Serve with rice to complete the meal.

Serves 4

INGREDIENTS

4 chicken breast fillets
flour, for dredging
2–3 tbsp butter or combination butter and oil
450 g/1 lb mild green salsa or puréed tomatillos
225 ml/8 fl oz /1 cup chicken stock
1–2 garlic cloves, finely chopped
3–5 tbsp chopped fresh coriander (cilantro)
½ fresh green chilli, deseeded and chopped
½ tsp ground cumin
salt and pepper

TO SERVE:
225 ml/8 fl oz/1 cup soured cream
several leaves cos (romaine) lettuce, shredded
3–5 spring onions (scallions), thinly sliced
coarsely chopped fresh coriander (cilantro)

1 Sprinkle the chicken with salt and pepper, then dredge in flour. Shake off the excess.

2 Melt the butter in a frying pan (skillet), add the chicken and cook over a medium-high heat, turning once, until they are golden but not cooked through – they will continue to cook slightly in the sauce. Remove from pan and set aside.

3 Place the salsa, chicken stock, garlic, coriander (cilantro), chilli and cumin in a pan and bring to the boil. Reduce the heat to a low simmer. Add the chicken breasts to the sauce, spooning the sauce over the chicken. Continue to cook until the chicken is cooked through.

4 Remove the chicken from the pan and season with salt and pepper to taste. Serve with the soured cream, shredded lettuce, sliced spring onions (scallions) and chopped fresh coriander leaves.

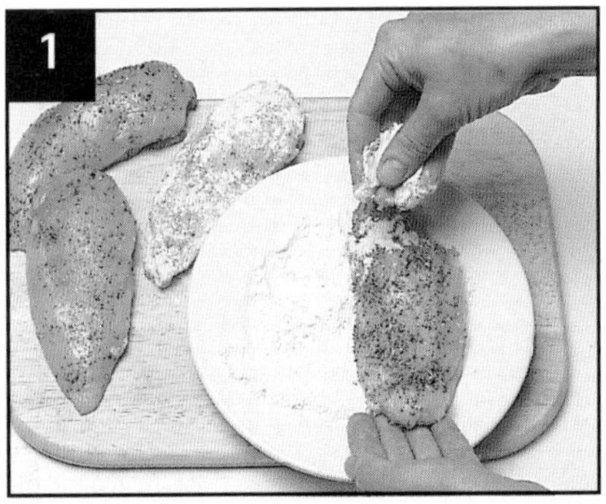

Chicken with Yucatecan Vinegar Sauce

A paste of roasted garlic and mixed spices gives its evocative flavour to this tangy dish of simmered chicken, a speciality of Valladolid in the Yucatan peninsula.

Serves 4–6

INGREDIENTS

8 small boned chicken thighs
chicken stock
15–20 garlic cloves, unpeeled
1 tsp cumin seeds, lightly toasted
1 tsp coarsely ground black pepper
½ tsp ground cloves
2 tsp crumbled dried oregano or ½ tsp crushed or powdered bay leaves
about ½ tsp salt
1 tbsp lime juice
1 tbsp flour, plus extra for dredging the chicken
3–4 onions, thinly sliced
2 fresh chillies, preferably mildish yellow ones, such as Mexican Guero or similar Turkish or Greek chillies, deseeded and sliced
120 ml/4 fl oz /1 cup vegetable oil
100 ml/3½ fl oz/scant ½ cup cider or sherry vinegar

1 Place the chicken in a pan with enough stock to cover. Bring to the boil, then reduce the heat and simmer for 5 minutes. Remove from the heat and allow the chicken to cool in the stock; the chicken will continue to cook as it cools in the hot stock.

2 Meanwhile, roast the garlic cloves in an ungreased heavy-based non-stick frying pan (skillet) until they are lightly browned on all sides and tender inside. Remove from the heat. When cool enough to handle, squeeze the flesh from the skins and place in a bowl.

3 Grind the garlic with the pepper, cloves, oregano, salt, lime juice and three-quarters of the cumin seeds. Mix with the flour.

4 When the chicken is cool, remove from the stock and pat dry. Reserve the stock. Rub the chicken with about two-thirds of the garlic-spice paste and stand at room temperature for at least 30 minutes or up to overnight in the refrigerator.

5 Fry the onions and chillies in a tiny bit of the oil until golden brown and softened. Pour in the vinegar and remaining cumin seeds, cook for a few minutes, then add the reserved stock and remaining spice paste. Boil, stirring, for about 10 minutes until reduced in volume.

6 Dredge the chicken in flour. Heat the remaining oil in a heavy-based frying pan (skillet). Fry the chicken until lightly browned, then remove from the pan and serve immediately, each portion topped with the onion and vinegar sauce.

Tequila-marinated Crisp Chicken Wings

The tequila tenderises these tasty chicken wings and gives them a delicious flavour. Serve as part of a barbecue, accompanied by corn tortillas, refried beans, salsa and lots of chilled lager.

Serves 4

INGREDIENTS

900 g/2 lb chicken wings
11 garlic cloves, finely chopped
juice of 2 limes
juice of 1 orange
2 tbsp tequila
1 tbsp mild chilli powder
2 tsp Chipotle Salsa (see page 98) or 2 dried chipotle chillies, reconstituted (see page 100) and puréed
2 tbsp vegetable oil
1 tsp sugar
1/4 tsp ground allspice
pinch of ground cinnamon
pinch of ground cumin
pinch of dried oregano

1 Cut the chicken wings into two pieces at the joint.

2 Place the chicken wing in a non-metallic dish and add the remaining ingredients. Toss well to coat, then leave to marinate for at least 3 hours or overnight in the refrigerator.

3 Cook over the hot coals of a barbecue (grill) for about 15–20 minutes or until the wings are crisply browned, turning occasionally. To test whether the chicken is cooked, pierce a thick part with a skewer – the juices should run clear. Serve at once.

COOK'S TIP

Made from the agave plant, tequila is Mexico's famous alcoholic drink.

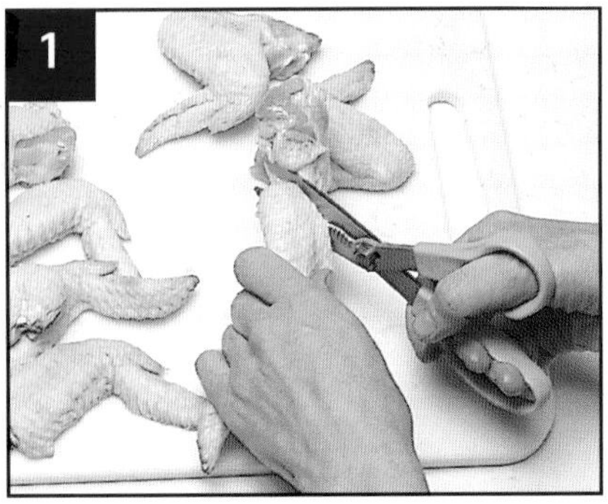

Citrus-marinated Chicken

This is a great dish for a summer meal. The marinade gives the chicken an appetizing flavour and helps keeps it succulent and moist during cooking.

Serves 4

INGREDIENTS

1 chicken, cut into 4 pieces
1 tbsp mild chilli powder
1 tbsp paprika
2 tsp ground cumin
juice and rind of 1 orange
juice of 3 limes
pinch of sugar
8–10 garlic cloves, finely chopped
1 bunch fresh coriander (cilantro), coarsely chopped
2–3 tbsp extra-virgin olive oil
50 ml/2 fl oz/¼ cup beer, tequila, or pineapple juice (optional)
salt and pepper

TO SERVE:
lime wedges
tomato, (bell) pepper and spring onion (scallion) salad
fresh coriander (cilantro) sprigs

1 Place the chicken in a non-metallic dish. To make the marinade, mix the remaining ingredients together in a bowl, seasoning with salt and pepper.

2 Pour the marinade over the chicken, turn to coat well, then leave to marinate for at least an hour at room temperature. If possible leave for 24 hours in the refrigerator to marinate.

3 Remove the chicken from the marinade and pat dry with paper towels.

4 Put the chicken on a grill (broiler) pan and place under a preheated grill (broiler) for 20–25 minutes, turning once, until the chicken is cooked through. Alternatively cook in a ridged pan. Brush with the marinade occasionally. To test whether it is cooked, pierce a thick part with a skewer – the juices should run clear.

5 Garnish with coriander (cilantro) and serve with lime wedges and a refreshing side salad.

2

3

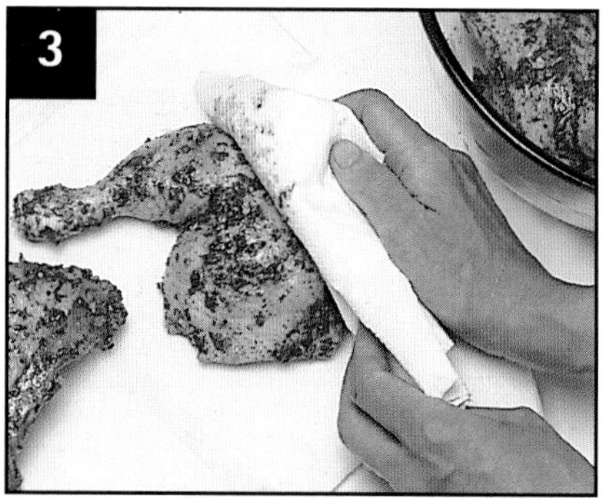

4

Poussins in Green Marinade

Flavoured with a green herb marinade, these elegant poussins are packed with lively Mexican flavours.

Serves 4

INGREDIENTS

10 garlic cloves, chopped
juice of 1 lime
1 bunch fresh coriander (cilantro), finely chopped
½ fresh green chilli, deseeded and chopped
1 tsp ground cumin
4 poussins
350 g/12 oz/1½ cups crème fraîche
1 red (bell) pepper, roasted, peeled, deseeded and diced
¼–1 tsp marinade from chipotle canned in adobo, or chipotle salsa
3–5 spring onions (scallions), thinly sliced
handful of toasted pumpkin seeds
salt and pepper

1 Combine about 9 garlic cloves with the lime juice, about three-quarters of the fresh coriander (cilantro), the green chilli and half the cumin in a bowl. Press the mixture on to the poussins and leave to marinate for at least 3 hours in the refrigerator or preferably overnight.

2 Place the poussins in a roasting tin (pan) and cook in a preheated oven at 200°C/400°F/ Gas Mark 5 for 15 minutes. Remove one from the oven at this point, to check whether it is cooked – pierce the thigh with a knife and if the juices run clear, the poussin is cooked. If necessary, return to the oven and continue to roast until cooked through.

3 Meanwhile, mix the crème fraîche with the (bell) pepper, chipotle marinade and remaining garlic and cumin. Season.

4 Serve each poussin with a spoonful of the pepper sauce and a sprinkling of the remaining coriander, the spring onions (scallions) and pumpkin seeds. Serve right away.

VARIATION

For barbecued (grilled) lamb, skewer lamb chunks, such as shoulder or leg, on to metal or soaked bamboo skewers. Marinate in the green herbed marinade as in Step 1, then cook over the hot coals of a barbecue (grill) until the lamb is cooked to your liking.

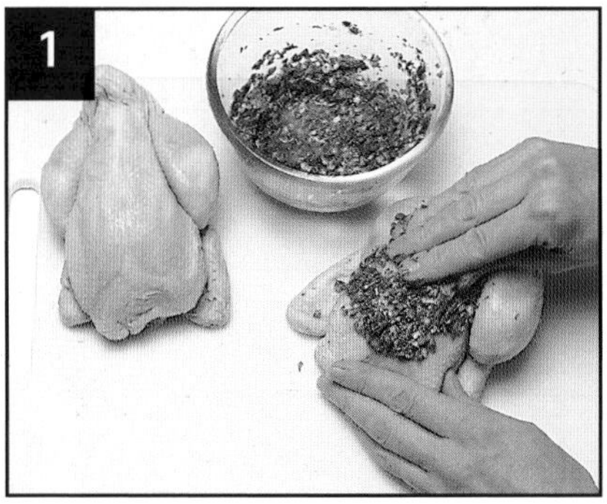

Chicken with Purslane & Chilli

Purslane is terribly fashionable, due to its unique flavour and healthy dose of omega-3 fatty acids. It is a weed, and beloved by the Mexicans, who stew it as well as eat it raw.

Serves 4

INGREDIENTS

juice of 1 lime
6 garlic cloves, finely chopped
1/4 tsp dried oregano
1/4 tsp dried marjoram
1/4 tsp dried thyme
1/2 tsp ground cumin
1 chicken, cut into 4 pieces
about 10 large dried mild chillies, such as pasilla, toasted
450 ml/16 fl oz/2 cups boiling water
450 ml/16 fl oz/2 cups chicken stock
3 tbsp extra-virgin olive oil
700 g/1 lb 9 oz tomatoes, charred under the grill (broiler), skinned and deseeded
handful of corn tortilla chips, crushed
several large handfuls of purslane, cut into bite-sized lengths
1/2 lime
salt and pepper
lime wedges, to serve

1 Combine the lime juice, half the garlic, the oregano, marjoram, thyme, cumin and salt to taste. Rub the mixture over the chicken and leave to marinate for at least an hour, or overnight in the refrigerator.

2 Place the chillies in a pan and pour the boiling water over them. Cover and leave for 30 minutes until softened. Remove the stems and seeds. Purée the chillies in a food processor or blender, adding just enough of the stock to make a smooth paste. Add the rest of the stock and mix well.

3 Heat a tablespoon of oil in a heavy-based frying pan (skillet). Add the chilli purée with the tomatoes and remaining garlic. Cook over a medium heat, stirring, until it has thickened and reduced by about half. Set aside.

4 Remove the chicken from the marinade, reserving any marinade juices. Brown the chicken in the remaining oil, then place in flameproof casserole. Add any reserved marinade juices and the reduced chilli sauce. Cover and simmer over a low heat for about 30 minutes until the chicken is tender.

5 Stir the crushed tortillas into the sauce and cook for a few minutes. Return to the casserole and add the purslane. Season with salt, pepper and a squeeze of lime. Heat and serve with lime wedges.

Duck with Mole Sauce & Pineapple

A wonderful combination of sweet and spicy flavours, this dish is bursting with Mexican flavours. Serve with a mixture of long-grain and wild rice for a sophisticated touch.

Serves 4

INGREDIENTS

1 duck, cut into 4 pieces
juice of 2 limes
120 ml/ 4 fl oz/½ cup pineapple juice
5–8 garlic cloves, sliced or chopped
a few shakes of mild red chilli powder, such as ancho
2 tbsp sugar
salt
½ pineapple, peeled and cut into slices
450 ml/16 fl oz/2 cups mole sauce (see page 90)
salt
fresh chilli strips, to garnish

1 Combine the duck with the lime juice, pineapple juice, garlic, chilli powder, salt and half the sugar. Leave to marinate for at least 2 hours, preferably overnight in the refrigerator.

2 Remove the duck from the marinade and pat dry with paper towels. Arrange the dark meat in a roasting tin (pan) and roast in a preheated oven at 160°C/325°F/Gas Mark 3 for about 20 minutes. Pour off the fat as it renders from the duck.

3 Add the breast pieces and continue to roast slowly for about 20 more minutes. Pour off the fat. Increase the temperature to 200–220°C/400–425°F/Gas Mark 6–7 for 5–10 minutes or until crisp and brown the duck.

4 Warm the mole sauce with enough water to prevent it from sticking and burning. Set aside and keep warm.

5 Sprinkle the pineapple with the remaining sugar and grill (broil) on both sides until the pineapple is lightly browned.

6 Serve the duck portions accompanied by the pineapple slices and topped with the mole sauce. Garnish with chilli and serve.

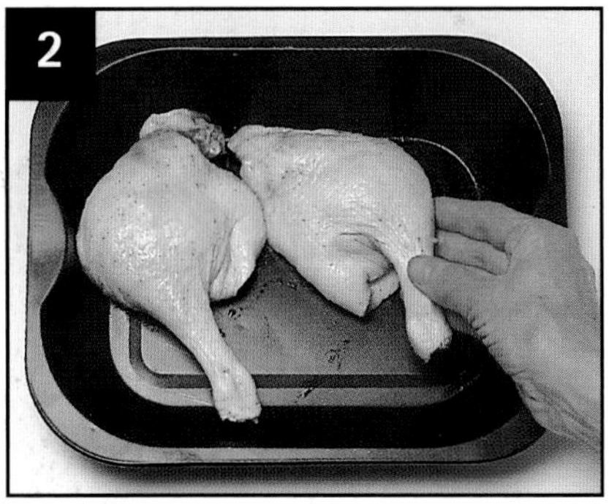

Turkey with Mole

In Mexican groceries you can buy a jar of mole paste – useful for when you don't have a stash of leftover mole in your refrigerator or freezer.

Serves 4

INGREDIENTS

4 turkey portions, cut into 4 pieces
about 450 ml/16 fl oz/2 cups chicken stock
about 225 ml/8 fl oz/ 1 cup water
1 onion, chopped
1 whole garlic bulb, divided into cloves and peeled
1 celery stick, chopped
1 bay leaf
1 bunch coriander (cilantro), finely chopped
500 ml/18 fl oz/2¼ cups mole sauce (see page 90) or use ready-made mole, thinned as instructed on the container

TO GARNISH:
4–5 tbsp sesame seeds
4–5 tbsp chopped fresh coriander (cilantro)

1 Arrange the turkey in a large flameproof casserole. Pour the stock and water around the turkey, then add the onion, garlic, celery, bay leaf and half the coriander (cilantro).

2 Cover and bake in a preheated oven at 190°C/ 375°F/Gas Mark 5 for about 1–½ hours; the turkey should be very tender. Add extra liquid if needed.

3 Warm the mole in a pan with enough stock to make it the consistency of thin cream.

4 To toast the sesame seeds for the garnish, put the seeds in an ungreased frying pan (skillet) and fry, shaking the pan, until lightly golden.

5 Arrange the turkey pieces on a serving plate and spoon the warmed mole over the top. Sprinkle with the toasted sesame seeds and chopped fresh coriander (cilantro) and serve.

Desserts & Beverages

Mexico is a land that swelters in the heat of the sun, and living there one needs constant refreshment and rehydration. The cuisine offers a wealth of drinks to slake this thirst, to refresh, to replenish: drinks based on juices or fruits mixed with milk. For a drink with a bit more punch, try tequila-based Margarita, and on the soothing side, relax with a traditional Mexican hot chocolate.

For dessert, fresh fruit, the amazing fragrant and sweet fresh fruit of Mexico, is often all you'll want, especially after the hearty and satisfying fare of this land. If you yearn for something rich however, try Churros, cinnamon-scented doughnut-like fritters, or little meringues named after the sigh of a nun.

Aztec Oranges

Simplicity itself, this refreshing orange dessert is hard to beat and is the perfect follow up to a hearty, spiced main course dish.

Serves 4–6

INGREDIENTS

6 oranges
1 lime
2 tbsp tequila
2 tbsp orange-flavoured liqueur
dark soft brown sugar, to taste
fine lime rind strips, to decorate (see Cook's Tip)

1 Using a sharp knife, cut a slice off the top and bottom of the oranges, then remove the peel and pith, cutting downwards and taking care to retain the shape of the oranges.

2 Holding the oranges on their side, cut them horizontally into slices.

3 Place the oranges in a bowl. Cut the lime in half and squeeze over the oranges. Sprinkle with the tequila and liqueur, then sprinkle over sugar to taste.

4 Chill until ready to serve, then transfer to a serving dish and garnish with lime strips.

COOK'S TIP

To make the decoration, finely pare the rind from a lime using a vegetable peeler, then cut into thin strips. Add to boiling water and blanch for 2 minutes. Drain in a sieve (strainer) and rinse under cold running water. Drain again and pat dry with paper towels. Use this method for orange and lemon decorative strips as well.

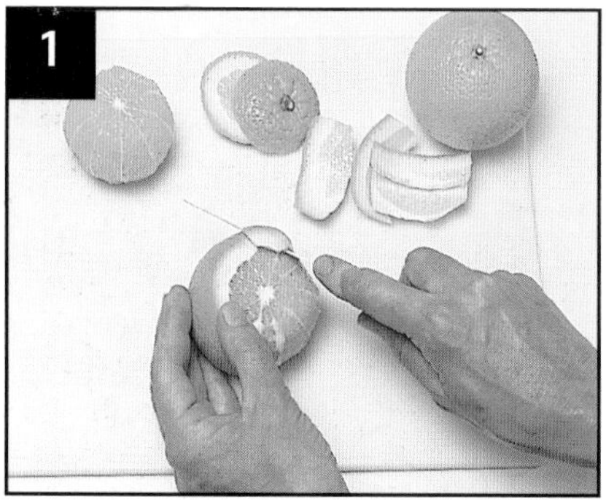

Pineapple Compote with Tequila & Mint

This light, chilled dessert is a refreshing way to finish a Mexican spread. For a more elaborate dish, accompany the pineapple with a scoop of good-quality pineapple sorbet.

Serves 4–6

INGREDIENTS

1 ripe pineapple
sugar, to taste
juice of 1 lemon
2–3 tbsp tequila or a few drops of vanilla essence (extract)
several sprigs of fresh mint, leaves removed and cut into thin strips
fresh mint sprig, to decorate

1 Using a sharp knife, cut off the top and bottom of the pineapple. Place upright on a board, then slice off the skin, cutting downwards. Cut in half, remove the core if wished, then cut the flesh into slices. Cut into the fruit chunks.

2 Put the pineapple in a bowl and sprinkle with the sugar, lemon juice, tequila or vanilla essence (extract).

3 Toss the pineapple to coat well, then chill until ready to serve.

4 To serve, arrange on a serving plate and sprinkle with the mint strips. Decorate the dish with a mint sprig.

COOK'S TIP

Make sure you slice off the 'eyes' when removing the skin from the pineapple.

VARIATION

Substitute 3 peeled sliced mangoes for the pineapple. To prepare mango, slice of a large piece of flesh on either side of the stone, peel and cut into chunks. Slice off the remaining flesh attached to the stone.

1

2

3

Oranges & Strawberries with Lime

Ideal as a summery dessert, this dish can also be served as a fresh fruit dish with brunch. The oranges enhance the delicate flavour of the berries.

Serves 4

INGREDIENTS

- 3 sweet oranges
- 225 g/8 oz strawberries
- grated rind and juice of 1 lime
- 1–2 tbsp caster (superfine) sugar
- fresh mint sprig, to decorate

1 Using a sharp knife, cut a slice off the top and bottom of the oranges, then remove the peel and pith, cutting downwards and taking care to retain the shape of the oranges.

2 Using a small sharp knife, cut down between the membranes of the oranges to remove the segments. Discard the membranes.

3 Hull the strawberries, pulling the leaves off with a pinching action. Cut into slices, along the length of the strawberries.

4 Put the oranges and strawberries in a bowl, then sprinkle with the lime rind, lime juice and sugar. Chill until ready to serve.

5 To serve, transfer to a serving bowl and decorate the dish with a mint sprig.

COOK'S TIP

An optional hit of orange-flavoured liqueur is delicious on this – reduce or omit the sugar.

VARIATION

Replace the oranges with mangoes, and the strawberries with blackberries, for a dramatically coloured dessert.

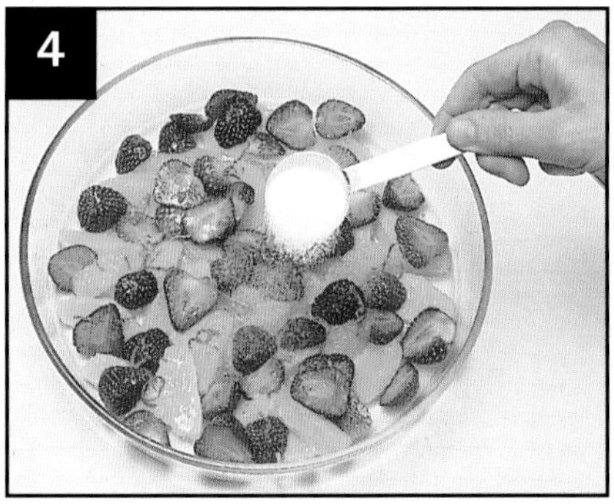

Icy Fruit Blizzard

Keep a store of prepared fruit in the freezer, then whirl it up into this refreshing dessert, which is as light and healthy as it is satisfying. You can vary the fruit as you like.

Serves 4

INGREDIENTS

- 1 pineapple
- 1 large piece deseeded watermelon, peeled and cut into small pieces
- 225 g/8 oz strawberries or other berries, hulled and whole or sliced
- 1 mango, peach or nectarine, peeled and sliced
- 1 banana, peeled and sliced
- orange juice
- caster (superfine) sugar, to taste

1 Cover 2 non-stick baking (cookie) sheets or ordinary baking (cookie) sheets with a sheet of cling film (plastic wrap). Arrange the fruit on top and freeze for at least 2 hours or until firm and icy.

2 Place one type of fruit in a food processor and process until it is all broken up into small pieces.

3 Add a little orange juice and sugar, to taste, and continue to process until it forms a granular mixture. Repeat with the remaining fruit. Arrange in chilled bowls and serve immediately.

COOK'S TIP

The fruit can be processed all together, if preferred, or use just one type of fruit – match the juice to the fruit.

VARIATION

For an icy fruit yogurt shake, omit the pineapple and watermelon and process the remaining fruit together, replacing the juice with a half and half mix of milk and fruit yogurt.

Bunuelo Stars

Cutting the flour tortillas into star shapes makes a whimsical treat, and the points of the stars get deliciously crisp.

Serves 4

INGREDIENTS

4 flour tortillas
3 tbsp ground cinnamon
6–8 tbsp caster (superfine) sugar
vegetable oil, for frying
chocolate ice cream, to serve
fine orange rind strips, to decorate

1 Using a sharp knife or kitchen scissors cut each tortilla into star shapes.

2 Mix the cinnamon and sugar together and set aside.

3 Heat the oil in a shallow wide frying pan (skillet) until it is hot enough to brown a cube of bread in 30 seconds. Working one at a time, fry the star-shaped tortillas until one side is golden, then turn and cook until golden on the other side. Remove from the hot oil with a slotted spoon and drain on paper towels.

4 Sprinkle generously with the cinnamon and sugar mixture. Serve with chocolate ice cream, sprinkled with orange rind strips.

COOK'S TIP

These star-shaped bunuelos make an attractive decoration for an ice cream sundae with Mexican flavours, caramel, cinnamon, coffee, chocolate.

VARIATION

Drench the bunuelos in a simple syrup, flavoured with a little cinnamon or aniseed.

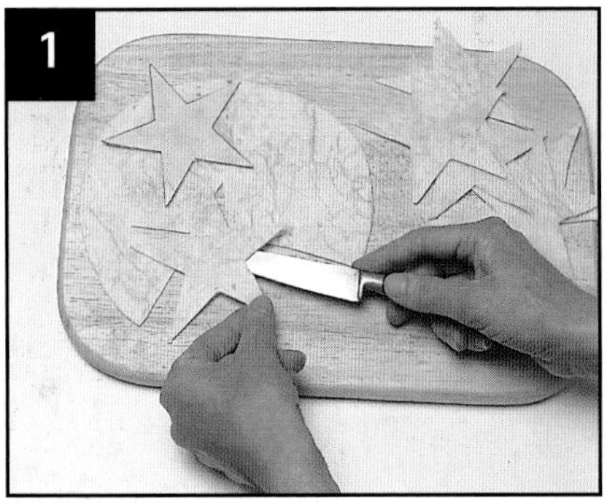
1

3

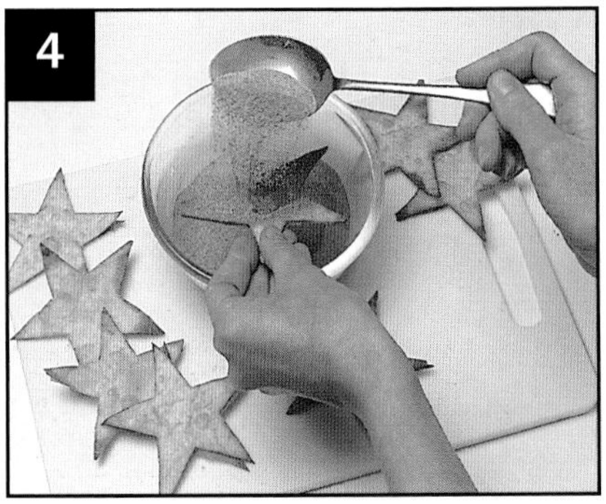
4

Empanadas of Banana & Chocolate

Using filo pastry makes these empanadas light and crisp on the outside, while the filling of diced banana and pieces of chocolate melt into a scrumptious hot banana-chocolate goo.

Serves 4–6

INGREDIENTS

- about 8 sheets of filo pastry, cut into half lengthways
- melted butter or vegetable oil, for brushing
- 2 ripe sweet bananas
- 1–2 tsp sugar
- juice of 1/4 lemon
- 175–200 g/6–7 oz dark chocolate, broken into small pieces
- icing (confectioners') sugar, for dusting
- ground cinnamon, for dusting

1 Working one at a time, lay a long rectangular sheet of filo out in front of you and brush it with butter or oil.

2 Peel and dice and bananas and place in a bowl. Add the sugar and lemon juice and stir well to combine. Stir in the chocolate.

3 Place a couple of teaspoons of the banana and chocolate mixture in one corner of the pastry, then fold over into a triangle shape to enclose the filling. Continue to fold in a triangular shape, until the filo is completely wrapped around the filling.

4 Dust the parcels with icing (confectioners') sugar and cinnamon. Place on a baking (cookie) sheet and continue the process with the remaining filo and filling.

5 Bake in a preheated oven at 190°C/375°F/Gas Mark 5 for about 15 minutes or until the little pastries are golden. Remove from the oven and serve hot – warn people that the filling is very hot.

COOK'S TIP

You could use ready-made puff pastry instead of filo for a more puffed-up effect.

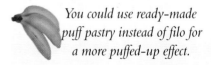

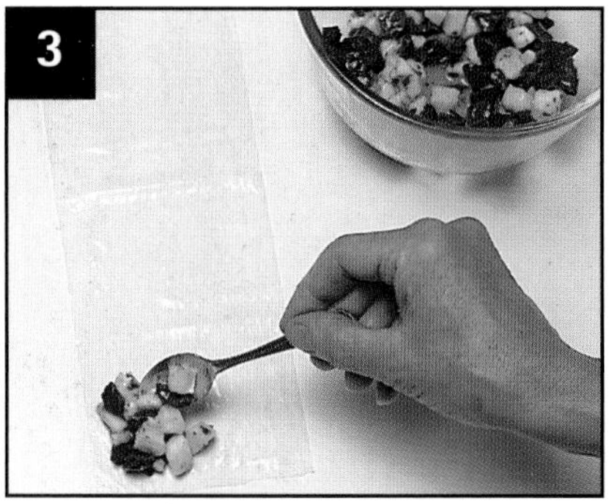

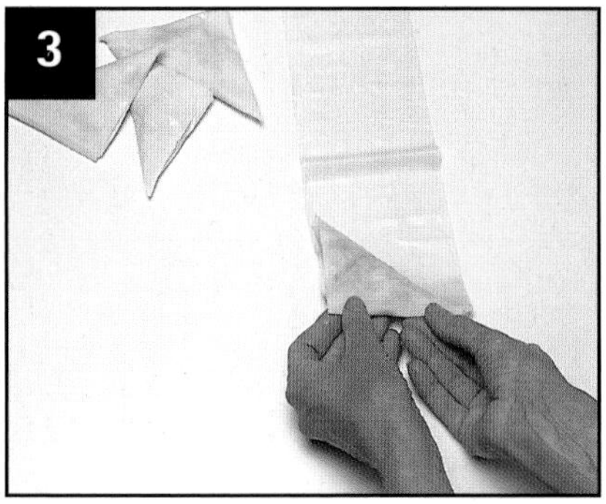

Churros

Sold on the streets of Mexico, these tempting treats can be enjoyed at any time of the day – dip them into a cup of hot chocolate for breakfast, nibble them as a mid-day snack with coffee, or serve them as part of a late-night supper.

Serves 4

INGREDIENTS

225 ml/8 fl oz/1 cup water
rind of 1 lemon
6 tbsp butter
1/8 tsp salt
125 g/4 oz/1 cup plain (all-purpose) flour
1/4 tsp ground cinnamon, plus extra for dusting
1/2–1 tsp vanilla essence (extract)
3 eggs
vegetable oil, for frying
caster (superfine) sugar, for dusting

1 Place the water with the lemon rind in a heavy-based saucepan. Bring to the boil, add the butter and salt and cook the mixture for a few moments until the butter melts.

2 Add the flour all at once, with the cinnamon and vanilla, then remove the pan from the heat and stir rapidly until it forms the consistency of mashed potatoes.

3 Beat in the eggs, one at a time, using a wooden spoon; if you have difficulty incorporating the eggs to a smooth mixture, use a potato masher, then when it is mixed, return to a wooden spoon and mix until smooth.

4 Heat 2.5 cm/1 inch oil in a deep frying pan (skillet) until it is hot enough to brown a cube of bread in 30 seconds.

5 Place the batter in a pastry tube with a wide nozzle, then squeeze out 12 cm/5 inch lengths directly into the hot oil, making sure that the churros are about 7.5–10 cm/3–4 inches apart, as they will puff up as they cook. You may need to fry them in 2 or 3 batches.

6 Cook the churros in the hot oil for about 2 minutes on each side, until they are golden brown. Remove with a slotted spoon and drain on paper towels.

7 Dust generously with sugar and sprinkle with cinnamon to taste. Serve the dish either hot or at room temperature.

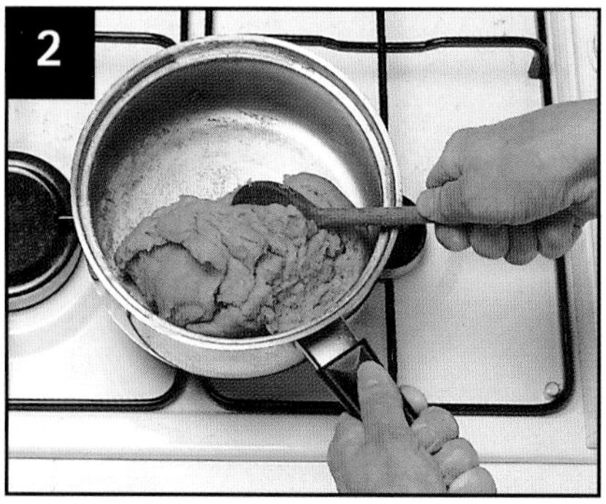
2

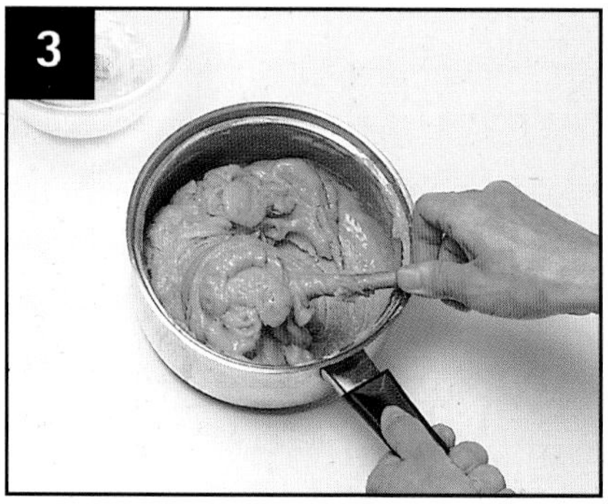
3

6

Torta de Cielo

This flat almond-flavoured sponge cake has a dense, moist texture which melts in the mouth. The perfect accompaniment to a good strong cup of coffee for either brunch or afternoon tea.

Serves 4–6

INGREDIENTS

175 g/6 oz raw almonds, in their skins
225 g/8 oz unsalted butter, at room temperature
225 g/8 oz/1 cup plus 2 tbsp sugar
3 eggs, lightly beaten
1 tsp almond essence (extract)
1 tsp vanilla essence (extract)
9 tbsp plain (all-purpose) flour
a pinch of salt
butter, for greasing

TO SERVE:
icing (confectioners') sugar, for dusting
flaked (slivered) almonds, toasted

1 Lightly butter a 20 cm/8 inch round or square cake tin (pan) and line the tin with baking parchment.

2 Put the almonds in a food processor to form a 'mealy' mixture. Set aside.

3 Beat together the butter and sugar in a bowl until smooth and fluffy. Beat in the eggs, almonds and both the almond and vanilla essences (extracts) until well blended.

4 Stir in the flour and salt and mix briefly, until the flour is just incorporated.

5 Pour or spoon the batter into the greased tin (pan) and smooth the surface. Bake in a preheated oven at 180°C/350°F/ Gas Mark 4 for 40–50 minutes or until the cake feels spongy when gently pressed.

6 Remove from the oven, and leave to stand on a wire rack to cool. To serve, dust with icing (confectioners') sugar and decorate with toasted almonds.

3

4

5

Mexican Chocolate Meringues

The Mexican name for these delicate meringues is suspiros, *meaning 'sighs' – supposedly the contented sighs of the nuns who created them. They are lightly crisp on the outside, with a deliciously chewy texture centre.*

Makes about 25 meringues

INGREDIENTS

4–5 egg whites, at room temperature
a pinch of salt
1/4 tsp cream of tartar
1/4–1/2 tsp vanilla essence (extract)
175–200 g/6–7 oz/3/4–1 cup caster (superfine) sugar
1/8–1/4 tsp ground cinnamon
115 g/4 oz dark or semi-sweet chocolate, grated

TO SERVE:
ground cinnamon
115 g/4 oz strawberries
chocolate-flavoured cream (see Cook's Tip)

1 Whisk the egg whites until they are foamy, then add the salt and cream of tartar and beat until very stiff. Whisk in the vanilla, then slowly whisk in the sugar, a small amount at a time, until the meringue is shiny and stiff. This should take about 3 minutes by hand, and under a minute with an electric beater.

2 Whisk in the cinnamon and grated chocolate. Spoon mounds, about 2 tablespoonfuls, on to an ungreased non-stick baking (cookie) sheet. Space the mounds well.

3 Place in a preheated oven at 150°C/300°F/Gas Mark 2 and cook for 2 hours until set.

4 Carefully remove from the baking (cookie) sheet. If the meringues are too moist and soft, return them to the oven to firm up and dry out more. Allow to cool completely.

5 Serve the meringues dusted with cinnamon and accompanied by strawberries and chocolate-flavoured cream.

COOK'S TIP

To make the flavoured cream, simply stir half-melted chocolate pieces into stiffly whipped cream, then chill until solid.

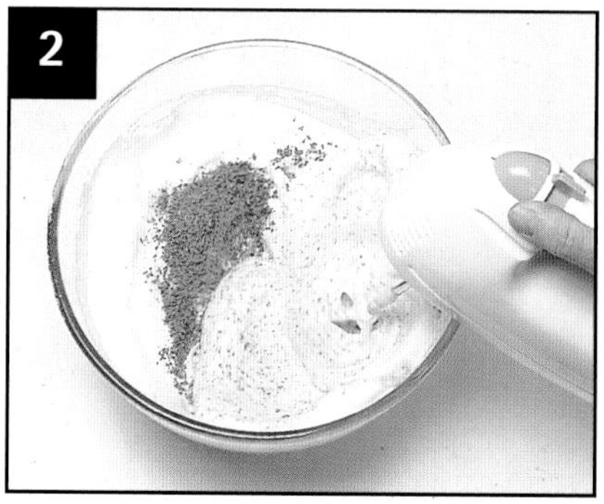

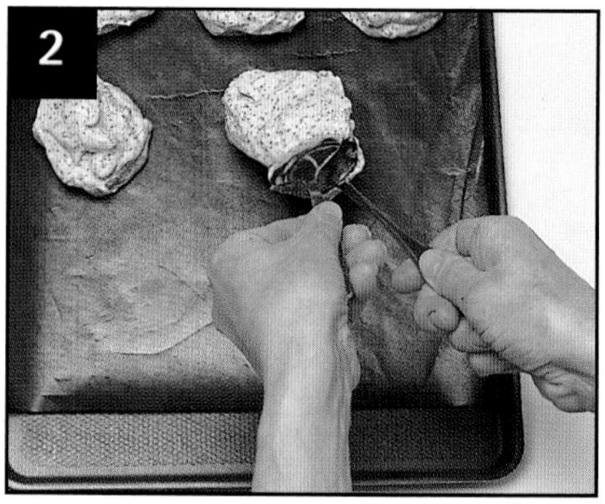

Soothing Mexican Drinks

Two milky drinks, packed with authentic Mexican flavours – choose a cooling strawberry milkshake for a hot summer's day, or a rich hot chocolate drink, with spicy aromas, as a winter warmer.

Serves 4

INGREDIENTS

STRAWBERRY MILKSHAKE:
450 g/1 lb strawberries
700 ml/1¼ pints/3 cups milk
225 ml/8 fl oz/1 cup strawberry yogurt (optional)
sugar, to taste
2 handfuls of ice cubes

MEXICAN HOT CHOCOLATE:
115–175 g/4–6 oz plain chocolate, broken into small pieces
½ tsp ground cinnamon
1 litre/1¾ pints/4 cups milk
dash of almond essence (extract)
dash of vanilla essence (extract)
just a few grains of salt (to bring out the flavour of the chocolate)
caster (superfine) sugar, to taste
2 tbsp grated chocolate
4 cinnamon sticks, to serve (optional)

1 To make the strawberry milkshake, place half the strawberries in a blender or food processor, reserving 4 for decoration. Add half milk and yogurt, if using, to the blender and process to a purée.

2 Add sugar, to taste, and ice cubes, then blend again until the ice is crushed and the drink is thick and icy. Pour into tall glasses, decorate with the reserved strawberries and serve at once. Repeat with the rest.

3 To make the Mexican hot chocolate, gently heat the chocolate with the cinnamon and milk in a saucepan.

4 When the chocolate has melted, add the almond and vanilla essences (extracts) with the salt and sugar. Whisk together until well blended and heated through.

5 Pour into cups, sprinkle with grated chocolate and serve each cup with a cinnamon stick for stirring, if wished.

VARIATION

To vary the flavour of the milkshake, substitute raspberries, bananas or mango for the strawberries and use a yogurt of your choice.

1

3

4

Fruity Refreshers

These fragrant, utterly refreshing drinks are full of the tropical flavours of Mexico. They cool and revive with each sip...

Serves 4–6

INGREDIENTS

COCONUT-LIME DRINK:
- 450 ml/16 fl oz/2 cups coconut milk (unsweetened)
- 120 ml/4 fl oz/1 cup freshly squeezed lime juice
- 1 litre/1¾ pints/4 cups tropical fruit juice, such as mango, papaya, guava or passion fruit
- sugar, to taste
- crushed ice
- fresh mint sprigs, to decorate

SANGRIA:
- 1 bottle dry full-bodied red wine
- 50 ml/2 fl oz orange-flavoured liqueur
- 50 ml/2 fl oz ¼ cup brandy
- 225 ml/8 fl oz/1 cup orange juice
- sugar, to taste
- 1 orange, washed
- 1 lime, washed
- 1 peach or nectarine
- ½ cucumber, thinly sliced
- ice cubes
- bubbly mineral water, for topping up

1 To make the coconut-lime fruit drink, combine the coconut milk with the lime juice, tropical fruit juice and sugar, to taste. Add the ice and whisk until well mixed. Alternatively, place the ingredients in a food processor and process until well mixed. Serve immediately, decorated with mint leaves.

2 To make the sangria, pour the wine into a punch bowl and mix in the liqueur, brandy, orange juice and sugar, to taste. Cover and leave to infuse in the refrigerator for a few hours.

3 Just before serving, slice the orange and lime widthways. Cut the peach in half, remove the stone and slice the flesh.

4 Add the prepared fruit, cucumber and ice cubes to the punch bowl and top up with mineral water. Serve at once.

COOK'S TIP

To turn the coconut-lime drink into an alcoholic cocktail, add 2 tablespoons white rum per person. Add an extra decoration of tropical fruit pieces, threaded on to bamboo skewers.

Classic Margaritas

Margaritas are what makes a hot and sultry Mexican afternoon not only tolerable, but something to look forward to. A tropical holiday in a glass.

Serves 2

INGREDIENTS

CLASSIC MARGARITAS:
pared lime or lemon peel
salt, for dipping
3 tbsp tequila
3 tbsp orange-flavoured liqueur
3 tbsp freshly squeezed lime juice
handful of cracked ice
fine strips of lime rind, to decorate

MELON MARGARITAS:
1 small flavourful cantaloupe melon peeled, deseeded, and diced
several large handfuls of ice
juice of 1 lime
100 ml/3½ fl oz/scant ½ cup tequila
sugar, to taste

FROZEN PEACH MARGARITAS:
1 peach, sliced and frozen, or an equal amount of purchased frozen peaches
50 ml/2 fl oz ¼ cup tequila
50 ml/2 fl oz ¼ cup peach or orange-flavoured liqueur
juice of ½ lime
diced fresh peach or 1–2 tbsp orange juice, if needed

1 To make the classic margaritas, moisten the rim of two shallow, stemmed glasses with the lime or lemon peel, then dip the edge of the glasses in salt. Shake off the excess.

2 Put the tequila in a blender or food processor with the liqueur, lime juice and cracked ice. Process to blend well.

3 Pour the drink into the prepared glasses, taking care not to disturb the salt-coated rim. If preferred, strain the drink before pouring into the glass. Decorate with lime rind and serve.

4 To make the melon margaritas, put the melon in a food processor and process to form a purée. Add the ice, lime juice, tequila and sugar to taste and process until smooth. Pour into chilled shallow glasses.

5 To make the frozen peach margaritas, blend the frozen fruit, tequila, liqueur and lime juice in a food processor until a thick purée. If too thick, add diced peach or orange juice to thin. Pour into chilled glasses and serve.

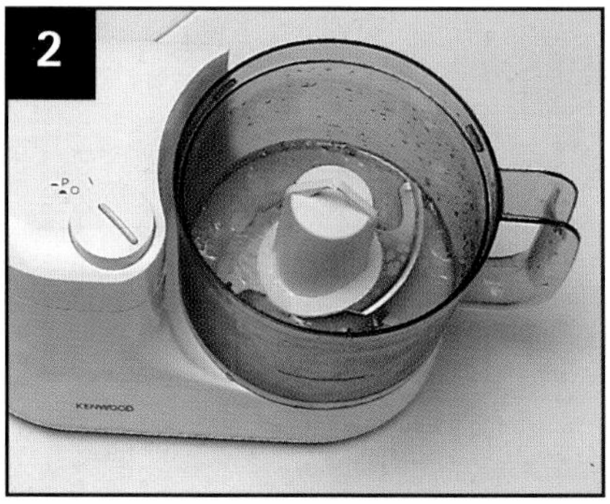

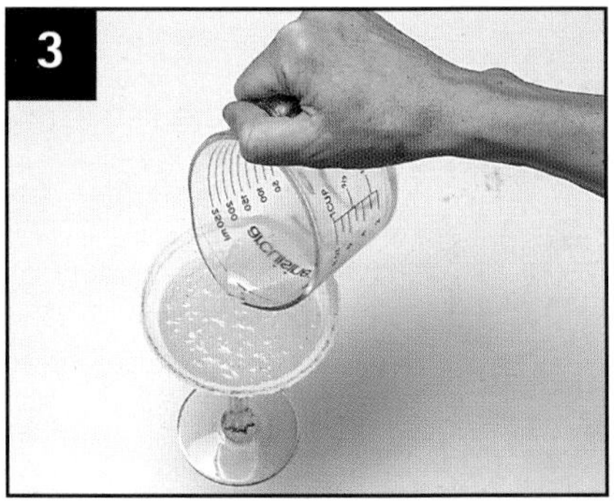

Index

THE EXPERIENCE OF WORLD WAR I

J·M·WINTER

PAPERMAC

Volume editor Robert Peberdy
Art editor Ayala Kingsley
Cartographic editor Olive Pearson
Designers Nicholas Rous, Janet MacCallum, Gill Mouqué, Tony de Saulles
Picture research Charlotte Ward-Perkins, Linda Proud, Rebecca Hirsh (USA)
Editorial assistant Monica Byles
Typesetting Anita Rokins

Project editor Peter Furtado
Art direction John Ridgeway
Production Clive Sparling

AN EQUINOX BOOK

Planned and produced by Equinox (Oxford) Ltd, Musterlin House, Jordan Hill Road, Oxford, England, OX2 8DP

First published 1988 by Macmillan London Limited

First published in paperback 1989 by PAPERMAC
a division of
Macmillan Publishers Limited
4 Little Essex Street London
WC2R 3LF and Basingstoke

Associated companies in Auckland, Delhi, Dublin, Gaborone, Hamburg, Harare, Hong Kong, Johannesburg, Kuala Lumpur, Lagos, Manzini, Melbourne, Mexico City, Nairobi, New York, Singapore and Tokyo

British Library Cataloguing in Publication Data

Winter, J.M. (Jay Murray), 1945–
The experience of World War I
1. World War I
I. Title
940.3
ISBN 0–333–4461–3

Color origination by Scantrans, Singapore

Printed in Yugoslavia

ADVISORY EDITORS

Alan Borg
Imperial War Museum, London

Hartmut Pogge von Strandmann
University College, Oxford

Philip Waller
Merton College, Oxford

CONTRIBUTORS

Ian Beckett 95
Simon Boughey 149
Gail Braybon 176
Jane Carmichael 184
Malcolm Cooper 78–79, 86–87, 108–09, 190–91
Robert Dare 117
David Fletcher 100–01
Brian Foss 235
Nathaniel Harris 28, 31, 34, 36, 39, 45
Ghislaine Lawrence 152–53
Peter Martland 80, 103, 120, 128, 156, 158, 167, 186, 195, 205
David Penn 122–23
Catherine Reilly 228
T.H.E. Travers 84, 93
S.B. Whitmore 138–39

CARTOGRAPHIC ADVISORS

Colin Bruce
John Pimlott

CONTENTS

PREFACE

World War I dominates the history of the 20th century. The shock waves it set off were felt long after the Allied–German Armistice of November 1918, and its uneasy outcome prepared the way for a second and even more terrible conflict.

The central theme of this account is the gigantic scale of the military effort waged by perhaps 70 million men in uniform, of whom about 9 million were killed. It is organized in such a way as to suggest that the upheaval of war was felt by different levels of society in different ways. The book follows four groups – politicians, generals, soldiers and civilians – through four phases of the war: first, the war of illusions of 1914; second, the war of stalemate and stagnation of 1915; third, the war of the great slaughter of 1916–17; and fourth, the reemergence of social conflict and revolution in 1917–18, which precipitated the Armistice on 11 November 1918.

One way to understand the experience of war is to see it as a man-made earthquake, moving outward from an epicenter to the periphery through a series of concentric circles. Distance from the epicenter is defined in terms of access to control over the instruments of physical force in society: the army, the police, the law courts. Thus the politicians, who were ultimately responsible for decisions of war and peace, formed the innermost circle; the generals, who controlled the armed forces and whose requirements of men and materiel required a reorganization of industry and society, were in the second circle. The soldiers and sailors, who bore the brunt of the fighting and whose enthusiasm or disillusionment could make or break a country's war effort, were the third circle, and the civilians, engaged in war work or families of frontline soldiers, formed the outermost circle.

Some qualifications must be made. First, the social categories overlapped considerably. Other than the small number of regular soldiers, the vast majority of men in uniform were civilians, and did not cease to be so when they put on their uniforms. Similarly, where the military world stopped and the political world began was unclear in Germany and, to a lesser extent, in all combatant countries.

Second, the reality of the war was much more fluid than may appear here. None of the four phases of the war can be regarded as watertight. In some minds, the illusions of 1914 lasted well into the later years of the war. Despite all kinds of evidence, some people continued to believe that the war was an agent of renewal and rejuvenation; the capacity for self-delusion is, of course, unlimited. Again, it is obviously improper to suggest that the stalemate which set in by early 1915 was absolute. In some places in the west and virtually throughout the Eastern Front, there was also a war of movement going on. Likewise, to see 1916–17 as the period of the great slaughter is not to belittle the enormous waste of life in other years. And finally, social conflicts of various kinds clearly emerged well before the spring of 1917; it did not take the first Russian Revolution to bring home to many ordinary people that the conflict was destroying much of the political and social order, in defense of which the war ostensibly had been launched. The war was so vast that all attempts to contain it in any single or simple explanatory framework are bound to fail. The hope is that the approach of this book will highlight the salient features of a conflict which has moved from reality to myth.

J.M. Winter   Pembroke College, Cambridge

1914	1915	1916

POLITICIANS

- ▲ June 28: Assassination of Franz Ferdinand at Sarajevo
- ▲ July 28: Austria-Hungary declares war on Serbia
- ▲ Aug. 1: Germany declares war on Russia
- ▲ Aug. 3: Germany declares war on France
- ▲ Aug. 4: UK declares war on Germany
- ▲ Aug. 4: Germany declares war on Belgium
- ▲ Nov. 2: Russia declares war on Turkey
- ▲ Nov. 6: UK and France declare war on Turkey
- ▲ April 26: Italy and Allies agree Treaty of London
- ▲ May 23: Italy declares war on Austria-Hungary
- ▲ Aug. 25: Italy declares war on Turkey
- ▲ Aug. 26: Italy declares war on Germany
- ▲ Oct. 14: Bulgaria joins Central Powers
- ▲ Nov. 30: France, UK, Russia and Japan sign Pact of London
- Nov. 7: Woodrow Wilson is reelected president of the USA ▲
- Dec. 7: Lloyd George becomes prime minister of the UK ▲
- ▲ April 24–29: Easter Rising in Dublin, Ireland
- ▲ April 26: Berlin agreement, to transfer sick prisoners to Switzerland
- ▲ June 5: UK minister of war, Kitchener, dies when HMS *Hampshire* is sunk
- Nov. 21: Death of Austro-Hungarian emperor, Franz Josef ▲

WESTERN FRONT

- ▲ Aug. 4: Germans invade Belgium
- ▲ Aug. 7-16: British Expeditionary Force lands in France
- ▲ Aug. 23: Battle of Mons
- ▲ Aug. 24: Main German armies enter France
- ▲ Sept. 5–10: First Battle of the Marne - German invasion halted
- ▲ Sept. 15: First trenches are dug
- Sept. 17–Oct. 18: Race to the Sea
- Oct. 12–Nov. 11: First Battle of Ypres
- ▲ March 10–13: Battle of Neuve Chapelle
- May 4–June 18: Second Battle of Artois
- ▲ May 9–10: Battle of Aubers Ridge
- April 22–May 27: Second Battle of Ypres
- ▲ May 15–25: Battle of Festubert
- Sept. 25–Nov. 4: Battle of Loos
- Sept. 25–Oct. 14: Third Battle of Artois
- Sept. 25–Oct. 6: French offensive in Champagne
- Feb. 21–Dec. 18: Battle of Verdun
- July 1–Nov. 19: Battle of the Somme

EASTERN FRONT

- ▲ Aug. 26–30: Battle of Tannenberg
- ▲ Sept. 6–15: Battle of the Masurian Lakes
- Nov. 11–early Dec: Germans push Russians further east
- ▲ Jan. 3: Germans make first use of gas-filled shells
- ▲ Feb. 8–22: Winter Battle of Masuria
- ▲ May 2–4: Battle of Gorlice-Tarnow
- June 4–Oct. 10: Brusilov offensive

OTHER CONFLICTS

Balkan conflicts

- ▲ Sept. 8–12: Battle of Lemberg
- ▲ Dec. 2: Austro-Hungarians capture Belgrade
- ▲ Dec. 11: Serbians recapture Belgrade
- Oct. 7–Nov. 20: Austro-Hungarians invade Serbia
- ▲ Oct. 5: Allied troops begin disembarking at Salonika
- Sept.–Dec.: Central Powers invade Romania

Anti-Turkish campaigns

- ▲ Feb: Allies bombard Turkish forts at entrance of Dardanelles
- ▲ March 18: Allies attempt naval attack on Dardanelles
- April 25–Jan. 9: Allied land operations at Gallipoli
- Feb.-Nov: Allied campaign along R. Tigris, Mesopotamia
- Dec. 5–April 29: Siege of Kut
- ▲ June 6: Start of Arab revolt in the Hejaz

Italian front

- June 23–July 7: Battle of the Isonzo
- ▲ Aug. 6–17: Sixth Battle of the

African campaigns

- Aug.–Nov.: First campaign in East Africa
- ▲ Oct.: Allied conquest of German Southwest Africa
- June–Jan.: Main Allied campaign in Cameroon
- ▲ Sept. 4: Allies capture Dar Es Salaam in German East Africa

War at sea

- ▲ Nov. 1: Battle of Coronel
- ▲ Dec. 8: Battle of the Falkland Islands
- ▲ Jan. 24: Battle of Dogger Bank
- ▲ May 7: Sinking of the *Lusitania*
- Feb.–Sept.: First period of intensive German submarine warfare
- ▲ May 31–June 1: Battle of Jutland
- March–April: Second period of German submarine warfare

GENERALS

- ▲ Aug. 2: Moltke appointed commander of German field armies
- ▲ Aug. 4: French appointed commander of the British Expeditionary Force
- ▲ Sept. 14: Moltke resigns; succeeded by Falkenhayn
- ▲ Aug. 21: Ludendorff appointed chief of staff of German Eighth Army
- ▲ Aug. 22: Hindenburg appointed commander of German Eighth Army
- ▲ June 15: Pétain appointed commander of French armies
- ▲ Sept. 5: Czar Nicholas II takes command of Russian armies
- ▲ Dec. 3: Joffre appointed commander of French armies
- ▲ Dec. 19: Haig becomes commander of British Expeditionary Force
- ▲ April 4: Brusilov appointed commander of Russian southern armies
- Dec. 12: Nivelle is appointed commander of ▲ French northern and northeastern armies
- ▲ Aug. 29: Hindenburg commander of German fie armies with Ludendorff as quartermaster general

1917

1918

1919

▲ April 6: USA enters the war on the side of the Allies

▲ Jan. 8: Woodrow Wilson, US president, publishes 14 Points as basis for peace

▲ Nov. 16: Clemenceau becomes prime minister of France

▲ Nov. 9: German kaiser abdicates

▲ May 7: Romania and Central Powers sign the Peace of Bucharest

Jan. 18: Peace conference begins at Versailles near Paris ▲

▲ June 28: Versailles Treaty signed

Oct. 3–4: Germany offers peace based on Wilson's Fourteen Points ▲

▲ Nov. 11: Armistice between Allies and Germany takes effect

▲ March 15: Czar Nicholas II of Russia abdicates; provisional government is formed

▲ Nov. 7: In Russia Bolsheviks overthrow the provisional government

▲ Jan. 5–11: Spartacist revolt in Germany

▲ Dec. 3: Bolshevik government in Russia signs armistice with Germany

▲ March 3: Russia and Central Powers sign the Treaty of Brest-Litovsk

▲ Oct. 27: Austria-Hungary asks Italy for an armistice

▲ Sept. 30: Armistice concluded between Allies and Bulgaria

▲ April 16–29: Chemin des Dames offensive

March 21–July 18: German Spring offensive

July 31–Nov. 10: Third Battle of Ypres

March 23–Aug. 15: Germans shell Paris

▲ Nov. 20–Dec. 8: Battle of Cambrai

▲ April 2: US troops enter war on Western Front

July 18–Nov. 10: Allied counteroffensive

▲ June 18–July 13: Kerensky offensive

▲ September 3: Germans capture Riga

.–Feb: Sporadic fighting in the Carpathians

May-Oct. 1919: Allies intervene in Russian civil war

Sept. 14-29: Allied offensive makes gains from Bulgaria

· April 24–May 22: Battle of Doiran

▲ Dec. 11: British capture Jerusalem

Sept. 19–Oct. 25: British capture Damascus, Beirut and Aleppo

Feb. 24–March 11: British retake Kut and capture Baghdad

Oct. 24–Nov. 10: Battle of Caporetto

▲ Oct. 24–Nov. 2: Battle of Vittorio Veneto

Dec.–Nov. 25: Lettow-Vorbeck's long retreat

▲ October 28: Mutiny of German sailors at Kiel

▲ June 21: German fleet scuppered at Scapa Flow

▲ Feb. 1: Germans recommence unrestricted submarine warfare

▲ April 29: Pétain appointed chief of French general staff

▲ May 10: Pershing appointed commander of American Expeditionary Forces

▲ Oct. 27: Ludendorff resigns command

▲ May 15: Foch appointed chief of French general staff

▲ April 14: Foch appointed commander of most Allied forces

▲ Nov. 5: Foch given responsibility for Allied strategy

▲ June 4: Brusilov appointed commander of Russian armies

▲ Jan. 28: Bolsheviks found the Red Army in soviet Russia

INTRODUCTION

First let us consider the politicians' war. At the center of power in 1914 were the political leaders of the major European states. Since their words and deeds set off the catastrophe of World War I, a history of the war must begin with them. To do so is to address these questions: first, why did war break out in 1914? Second, what did the political leaders of Europe understand was happening when they went to war? And third, how did they react when the war itself took control of their lives and fortunes?

To understand the decisions made in 1914, we must bear in mind the situation, aims and aspirations of the major political leaders of the time. They operated within both an international power system, dominated by alliances, and domestic political structures of equal or even greater complexity. In 1882 Germany, Austria-Hungary and Italy had formed a Triple Alliance, according to which the parties would be defended by the others, if attacked. This agreement was renewed at regular intervals until 1914. On the other side, Russia and France had concluded a pact in 1892 to resist any aggression by the Triple Alliance. In 1904 an Anglo-French understanding (the so-called Entente Cordiale) added another plane to the circle of alliance and hostility in which diplomatic events were determined.

The divisions within European domestic politics were as deep and at times seemed to be as threatening as those in the international sphere. Partly this was a result of the basically undemocratic character of all major regimes of the pre-1914 period. In 1914 both the nature of the franchise and the rules of political power were very remote from those of the late 20th century. Modern parliamentary systems now taken as the norm, in which the executive is responsible to a legislature elected by universal suffrage, existed nowhere in Europe in 1914. That this should have been the case in autocratic Russia, even after the 1905 revolution, should cause no surprise. But few realize that the "mother of parliaments" – the center of the British political system – was in no sense a democratic institution in 1914. There were only two countries which did not have universal manhood suffrage in Europe in 1914. One was the United Kingdom; the other, Hungary. Other states had introduced manhood suffrage in parliamentary elections earlier – Austria in 1907, Italy in 1912, and states in Germany as early as 1867. But such measures were often more symbolic than real, especially in light of the limitations on parliamentary power in the Habsburg (Austro-Hungarian) and Hohenzollern (German) monarchies. Furthermore, while New Zealand and Australia had introduced votes for women in 1893 and 1902 respectively, no European state had done so before 1914. Indeed women were disenfranchised in the UK until after World War I; in France, until after World War II.

The British system had the advantage of making the government of the day answerable to an elected legislature, which could dismiss it, should a vote of confidence fail in the House of Commons. The German system operated on different assumptions. The Kaiser appointed the chancellor, who was answerable to him and not to the German parliament or Reichstag. It was said that the only major requirement for the chancellorship in pre-1914 Germany was that the candidate should have no party political experience at all. In addition, the Kaiser appointed the chief of the imperial general staff. Should his choice be eccentric, there was no constitutional way to change it.

The best way to characterize pre-1914 political life in Europe is to suggest that political power was exercised by a small circle of men drawn from the upper-middle class and the aristocracy. Some were appointed; others were elected; but most acted without the constraint of a system of checks and balances between the executive and legislative arms of government. Politicians and the civil servants who staffed their offices and ministries were also recruited from a tiny minority of the populations they ostensibly served. Their knowledge of the conditions and hopes of their people varied considerably; their desire to preserve power in the hands of their nationality or class did not.

On both grounds – nationality and class – political leaders in prewar Europe were under threat. It is important to note that every major European country was a mix of nationalities. The British had the Irish problem (see p.57): Ireland became independent only in 1922. The Germans and Russians both had a Polish problem: Polish independence dated from 1919. The Russian and Austro-Hungarian monarchies were kaleidoscopes of nationalities. Even in France it was difficult to speak of a national identity before 1914: a majority of recruits to the army did not speak French in the generation before the war.

The challenge to established political power on grounds of social class was equally problematic. The emergence of an industrial proletariat, a central feature of 19th-century industrialization, led inevitably to the appearance of a mass labor movement dedicated to securing economic, political and social rights for ordinary working people. Different national labor movements adopted different forms of political action. In Germany the political struggle overshadowed the industrial struggle. The key institution was the Marxist German social democratic party. In France industrial power predominated, through the general federation of labour (*CGT*) though the socialist party (*SFIO*) had substantial working-class support.

These groups acted internationally too. In the 1860s and then again in the 1880s an international association of socialist groups was formed, known as the First and Second Internationals. They encompassed a wide array of political parties, some reformist, some revolutionary, but all were dedicated to the transformation of capitalism into a more just and equitable social order. The European socialist movement threw up leaders of outstanding ability and integrity, men and women of deep humanistic convictions. Jean Jaurès in France and August Bebel in Germany stood for a future in which inequality and poverty would be but memories of a distant past.

The issues of nationality and class deeply divided European society after 1918, but in ways very different from those of 1914. First, the war broke up the Austro-Hungarian Empire, and created the states of Austria, Hungary, Czechoslovakia and Yugoslavia. Secondly, Poland regained its independence, after a century of domination by Russia, Austria and Germany. Thirdly, nationalist politics within the defeated powers as well as in the victorious powers intensified after the war, as was evident in the postwar rise of fascism first in Italy and then in

▶ The socialist challenge to European regimes: Jean Jaurès in 1913.

Germany. World War I reordered but did not resolve the nationalities problem.

Similarly the problem of class conflict deepened after the war. At first, there was collaboration across class lines in war production and in the ranks of the armies. But after the onset of war weariness in 1916–17, class conflict recurred in new and more ominous forms. This was due in part to the overthrow of the Russian czar, and the seizure of power in 1917 first by a provisional government of liberals and moderate socialists, and then by the Bolsheviks under Lenin (see p.60). But internal pressures within each combatant country also made the challenge of labor in 1917–18 more powerful than it had ever been before. That it could be contained was not at all clear when the Armistice was signed in November 1918. World War I first blunted and then sharpened class conflict in Europe, and presented an ominous threat to the capitalist system at the end of the war. By 1919 the overlap between war and revolution was clear to all who had eyes to see. Inflation bred strikes, and revolutionary groups attempted to seize power in many cities in central Europe. In most places they failed completely; occasionally they succeeded for a brief period, before being swept away by a counterrevolutionary tide, which grew in the interwar years. By the 1930s millions had succumbed to the temptation of fascism.

By 1919 a new generation of socialist leaders had emerged. Bebel died peacefully in 1913. Jaurès was murdered in July 1914. Gone too were Rosa Luxemburg and Karl Liebknecht, murdered in 1919. In their places stood the men of the Bolshevik revolution, above all Lenin and Trotsky. They took part of the socialist movement into a communist international organization. The remainder retained their commitment to democratic socialism.

◀ **Technology of the future? Cavalry watch the first British "flypast", 1913.**

The German general Paul von Hindenburg came from the Prussian Junker class of large landowners; his French opponent in 1918, Philippe Pétain, came from a farming family in the north of France; John J. Pershing, who led the American Expeditionary Forces, came from a small town in Missouri. A military career was the natural choice of sons of such families, whose contact with the complexities of urban and industrial life was at times tenuous or nonexistent. Many passed through the high military academies of their countries – Sandhurst in the UK, Saint-Cyr in France, West Point in the USA – and progressed through the chain of command in the relatively peaceful decades before 1914. Some saw service in colonial wars, and were schooled in the arts of maneuver in which cavalry had traditionally played an important part.

The very expansion of armies in the prewar period necessitated a change in the social composition of the officer corps. More and more men were required to process the annual crop of recruits, leading to an infiltration of middle-class men into the army as professional soldiers. Between 1860 and 1913 the nobles' share in the German officer corps had dropped from 60 to 30 percent.

This "democratization" of the officer corps was accompanied by a deepening of the significance of the military in the political and social life of the nation. As imperial power grew in the late 19th century, nation and army had grown closer together. This was not true in all countries – witness the turmoil over the Dreyfus affair (1896–1905) and the evidence it disclosed of incompetence, corruption, and worse in the higher reaches of the French high command (see p. 32). But even under these difficult circumstances, the prestige of the army survived the disgrace of a few of its most senior men.

Many of those in positions of command in European armies in 1914 were wedded by temperament and training to a belief, first, in military action as the solution to political problems and, second, in the offensive as the answer to all military problems. In many way, an emphasis on the offensive suited the needs of military planners in the prewar period. First, political support could be secured more easily for creating weapons of attack rather than defense. Secondly, if these weapons were seen as the cutting edge of a short, decisive war, then offensive strategies appeared cheaper than defensive ones. Thirdly, offensive strategies were intellectually more attractive. They could be worked out on drawing boards and in war games with some degree of precision; defensive strategies were clouded in uncertainty, and thereby threatened the organizational unity of armies. In effect, developments in strategy helped to weaken the hand of diplomats who wanted to threaten the use of force rather than to resort to it, and thereby made war more likely in the years before 1914.

The shadow of World War I fell over military planning long after the Armistice in 1918. The failure of a short, sharp, decisive offensive, in which the infantry was the key element, led in two contradictory directions: first, toward new theories of armored warfare, pioneered by those who knew the ghastliness of trench warfare, such as Basil Liddell Hart or Charles de Gaulle; secondly, toward defensive strategies, such as the ill-fated Maginot line, a series of concrete fortifications built by the French in the interwar years, which were easily overcome by the Germans in 1940. Ironically, the failure of the war of movement in 1914 prepared the way for a more successful war of movement 25 years later, in which tanks, artillery and air power produced the decisive breakthrough which had eluded the generals of World War I until the very end of the conflict.

Generals

The second concentric circle of power in World War I was composed of the men who directed military and naval affairs. The boundaries between this circle and that of the political elites was never clear and occasionally nonexistent. "The Generals' War" follows the failure of the original strategy of the German general staff, and considers the various attempts made by the generals of all armies to break the stalemate in the following four years. Here we also explore the protracted struggle between generals and politicians for control of strategy. By and large the generals won.

The social composition of the general staffs of the major European armies was remarkably similar. Most men who made the army their career and who rose to the top were raised in the country among the titled or untitled gentry.

Soldiers

In discussing the soldiers of World War I there are two central questions to be answered. Why did they go to war? Why did they stay once they knew the war they had expected was not the war they had to fight?

An answer to the first question requires some consideration of the history of the draft. In most continental countries (but not in the UK or the USA) conscription was established in law in 1914. The origins of conscription can be located in the Revolutionary and Napoleonic Wars (1793–1815), when the success of French mass recruitment led the defeated powers to emulate the methods of the victors. Austria and Prussia adopted conscription after defeats at the hands of the French at Austerlitz in 1805 and at Jena in 1806 respectively. In the 19th century the French army largely reverted to a professional corps, due to a provision in the law whereby citizens could buy themselves out of military service. Prussia's victories against Austria-Hungary in 1866 and against France in 1870 reset the model just as Napoleon's had done 60 years earlier. In 1872 "buying out" was abolished in France, as it was in Italy and Russia in 1873 and 1874. But some privileges remained: Frenchmen with higher education retained the right to a reduction in length of military service until 1905.

For those of more modest means, the major method of avoiding military service before 1914 was emigration. In Italy conscription was adopted in 1873, but in the following years, young men preferred to seek a new life overseas rather than to join the army. A law was passed in 1888 with the intention of preventing men below age 32 from leaving the country, but the outflow of young potential recruits continued unabated in the following decades. The same happened in the Austro-Hungarian and Russian Empires.

If emigration reduced military manpower in one way, poverty did so in another. It was simply impossible for the bulk of the urban proletariat to pass the usually lax medical examinations of the major armies. Peasants did better, and thereby constituted the majority of land armies in 1914.

In absolute terms, Russia had most men under uniform among the great powers in 1914. Its 1.3 million-man standing contingent exceeded the military and naval personnel of France and Germany by about 400,000 men. In turn these dwarfed the smaller armies of Britain, Italy, and Austria-Hungary, numbering between 250,000 and 500,000 men. Further afield, the Japanese boasted 300,000 men under arms; the USA around 160,000. Of course, quantity and quality were by no means identical, among both professional soldiers and the reserve forces of former conscripts which theoretically stood ready to serve in the event of a national emergency.

The vast expansion of regular forces when that emergency came is a story told later in this book. The fact that mass armies were already in existence in 1914 and that millions of Europeans – however reluctantly – had already spent a part of their youth in them may help to account for the relative ease with which manpower was mobilized after the outbreak of war.

Civilians

Behind the armies were the home fronts, the concentric circle of widest dimensions, from which soldiers and sailors were drawn and supplied. Again, this account will chart the progressive disturbance of civilian life in wartime, from the period of illusions in 1914 to the disillusionment, anger, defiance and despair of 1917–18. Questions of propaganda, women's work, strikes, and food dominate the discussion, as they did that of contemporaries. These issues also suggest that the outcome of the war was not solely a function of the bravery and tenacity of fighting men. Victory in war arose out of the economic resources and social cohesion of one side and the progressively more damaging shortages and social divisions within the other. This was true in Russia in 1917, and to a certain extent in Italy and Austria-Hungary in the last year of the war. But the decisive fact was that Germany cracked in 1918, both at home and in the field of battle, and lost the war.

Some believe that, given the economic potential of the two sides, what was remarkable was not Germany's defeat, but that it held out for so long. Together Germany and Austria-Hungary constituted a bloc representing about 19 percent of world manufacturing production in 1913. France, Russia and Britain represented a bigger industrial base, about 28 percent of world manufacture. This advantage became more important the longer the war dragged on. The displacement of Russia by the USA on the Allied side in 1917 only made matters worse for Germany. The British-French-US manufacturing bloc occupied over 50 percent of world production in 1913.

It is true that the German economy was strong in areas essential for munitions production. This gave it an advantage in the first year of the war. But the imbalance in overall industrial power and in financial resources, as well as the greater sophistication of the Allied system of civilian supply, ultimately gave the Allies a decisive superiority, which Germany could not resist in the last year of the war.

The four phases of World War I

World War I was not one continuous struggle but consisted of four separate phases, each with its own character and distinguishing features. Each phase presents major issues, which will be summarized here.

1914: the war of illusions

World War I erupted at the beginning of August 1914, when the two major power-blocs in Europe – Germany and Austria-Hungary on one side (the Central Powers), and the UK, France, and Russia (the Entente Powers), on the other – declared war on each other. This was the first general war to break out for a century, and its initial phase was dominated by a series of illusions as to its likely duration and character. There had been wars between *industrializing* states before: witness the Crimean War of 1853–56, the Franco-German War of 1870–71 and the Russo-Japanese War of 1904–05, as well as the real prototype of the bloodbath of 1914–18, the American Civil War. But never before had there been a conflict between all the *industrialized* nations of Europe. It is perhaps understandable that most political and military leaders, as well as the populations they led, grossly underestimated the time and the exertions necessary to win such a war.

1915: stalemate and stagnation

The invasion of France by the German army in 1914 was the first of four military gambles which determined the course of the war. By late autumn 1914 it was apparent that the first gamble had failed, and that the kind of lightning military victory won by the Prussian army in the early stages of the Franco-Prussian War had eluded the Germans. Consequently battle lines hardened in the west to produce a series of linked fortifications across southern Belgium and northern France from the English Channel to the Swiss border – the Western Front. In the east a war of movement continued, but soldiers became entrenched in most theaters of operation in the second year of the war, as shown by the fighting in Gallipoli in Turkey

▶ **German strength in munitions: a Krupp factory in the early 20th century.**

Nr. 827.
Tragf.
75000 Kg
25000 Kg

The Western Front 1914

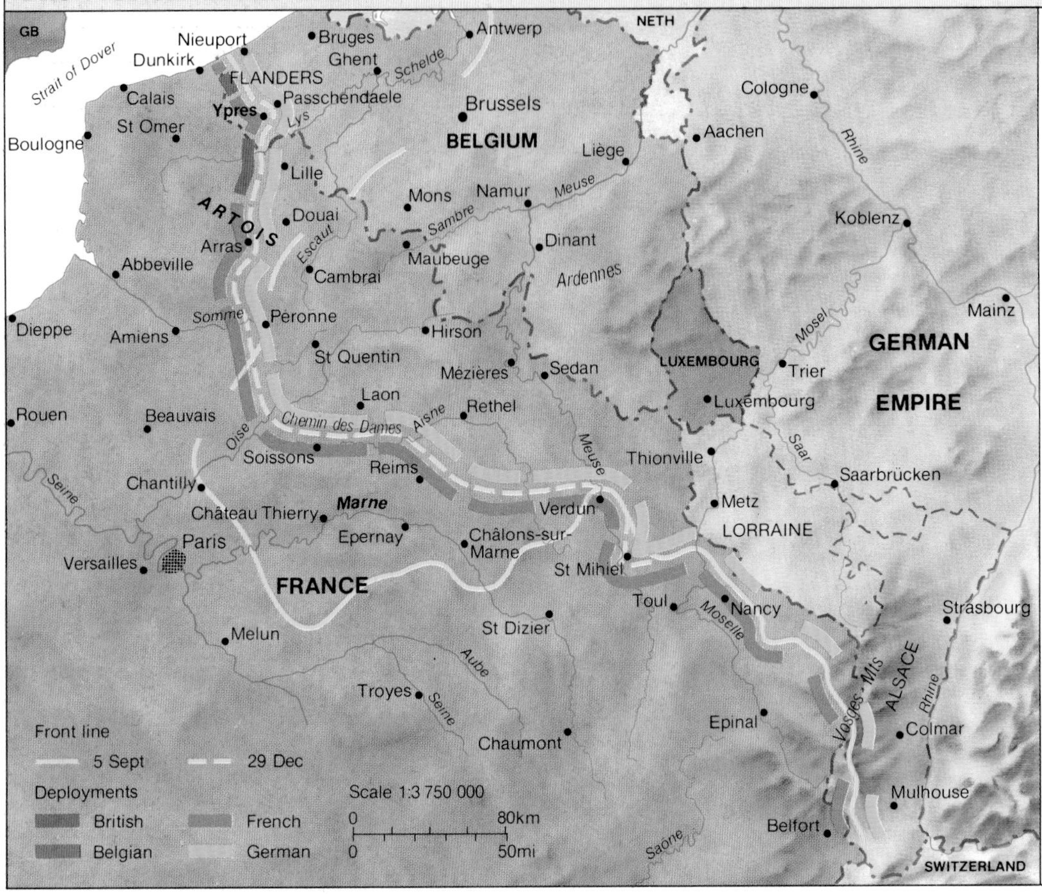

August 4
(to Sept. 4) Main weight of the German army swings through Belgium and into France, pushing back the small Allied force in front of it. Meanwhile the main weight of the French army is being thrown (unsuccessfully) against German positions in Lorraine.

September 5–10
Battle of the Marne. French Fifth and Ninth Armies and the British Expeditionary Force stop the German invasion along the River Marne.

September 13
(to Oct. 18) With deadlock on the newly established front along the River Aisne, the Allies try to turn the Germans' northern flank. The Germans, however, have exactly the same idea and the moves of each side merely extend the front (and the deadlock) all the way to the sea.

October 18
(to Nov. 22) Battle of Ypres. The Germans attempt to bludgeon their way through the new Allied line so as to reestablish a war of movement, but find it impossible.

December 17–29
Battle of Artois. The French try to break the German line, and fail.

The Western Front 1915

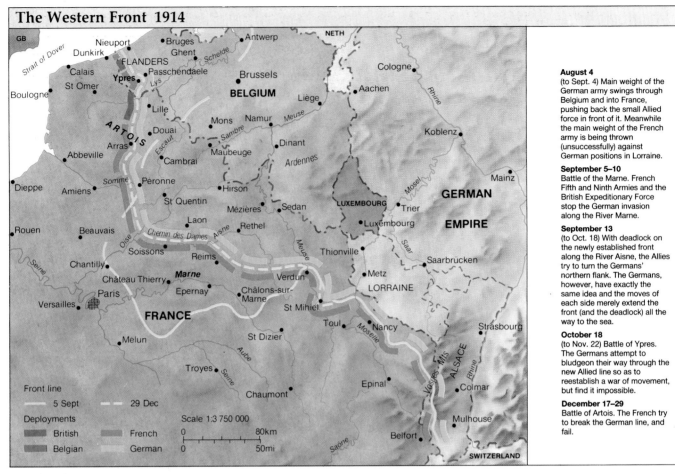

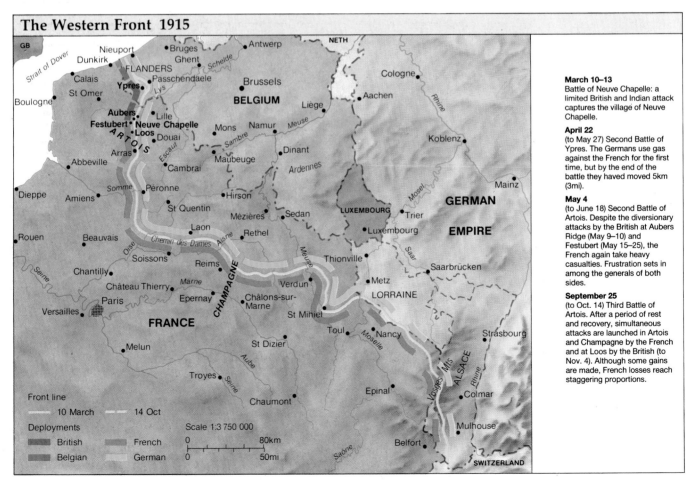

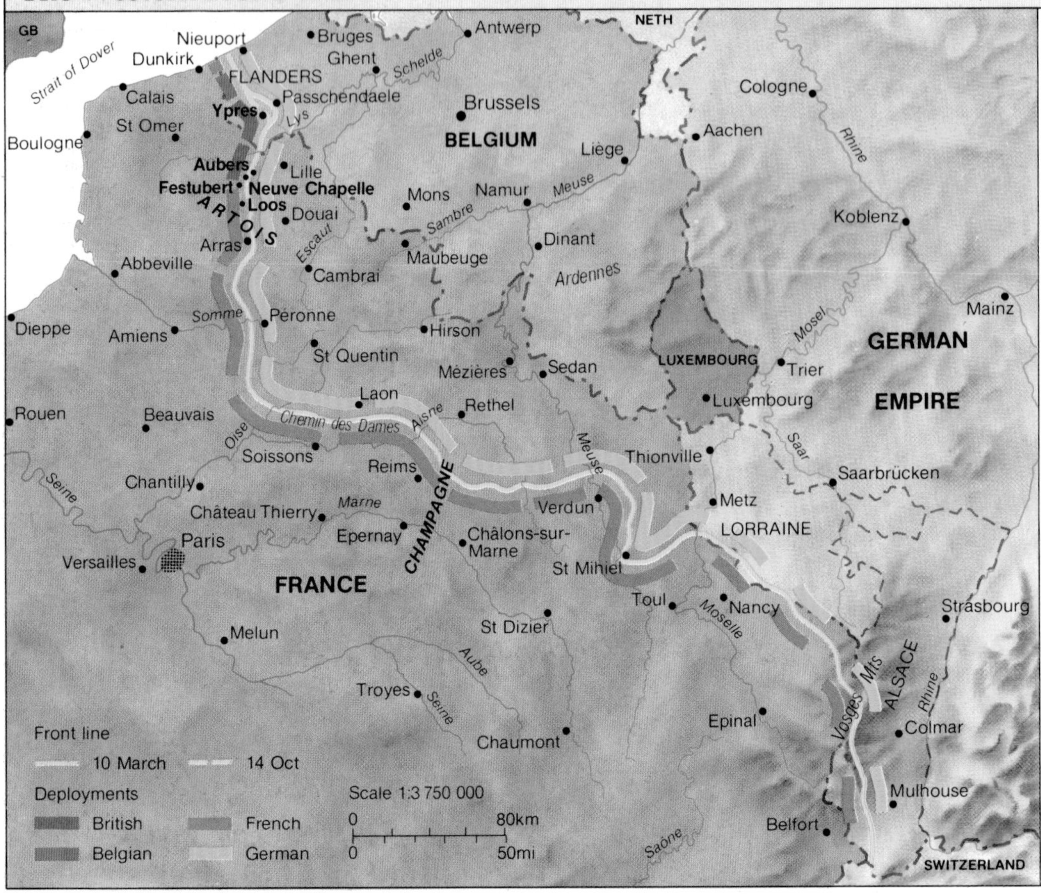

March 10–13
Battle of Neuve Chapelle: a limited British and Indian attack captures the village of Neuve Chapelle.

April 22
(to May 27) Second Battle of Ypres. The Germans use gas against the French for the first time, but by the end of the battle they haved moved 5km (3mi).

May 4
(to June 18) Second Battle of Artois. Despite the diversionary attacks by the British at Aubers Ridge (May 9–10) and Festubert (May 15–25), the French again take heavy casualties. Frustration sets in among the generals of both sides.

September 25
(to Oct. 14) Third Battle of Artois. After a period of rest and recovery, simultaneous attacks are launched in Artois and Champagne by the French and at Loos by the British (to Nov. 4). Although some gains are made, French losses reach staggering proportions.

The Western Front 1916–17

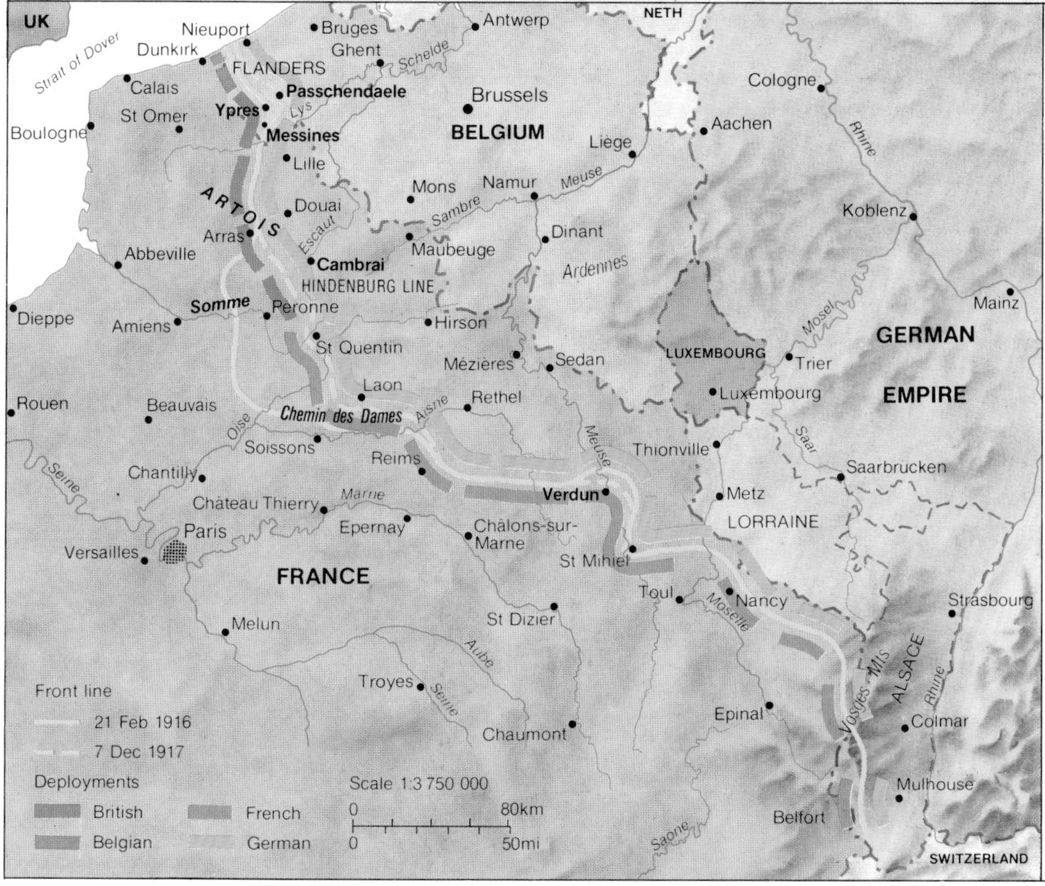

1916

February 21
(to Dec. 18) Battle of Verdun. Germans attack Verdun.

July 1
(to Nov. 19) Battle of the Somme. British and French infantry mount assaults on the German lines. Eight km (5mi) are gained.

1917

March 16
A section of German line is moved back to the Hindenburg Line.

April 9–14
British and Canadians attack at Arras. Canadians take Vimy Ridge.

April 19–29
Nivelle's Chemin des Dames offensive against the German lines. French gains are negligible; mutinies follow.

June 7–14
Battle of Messines Ridge. After a great mine explosion, British forces clear ground for the next major offensive.

July 31
(to Nov. 10) Third Battle of Ypres. The British, Australians and Canadians grind forward to the village of Passchendaele.

November 20
(to Dec. 7) Battle of Cambrai. British tanks break the German line, but soon lose captured territory.

The Western Front 1917–18

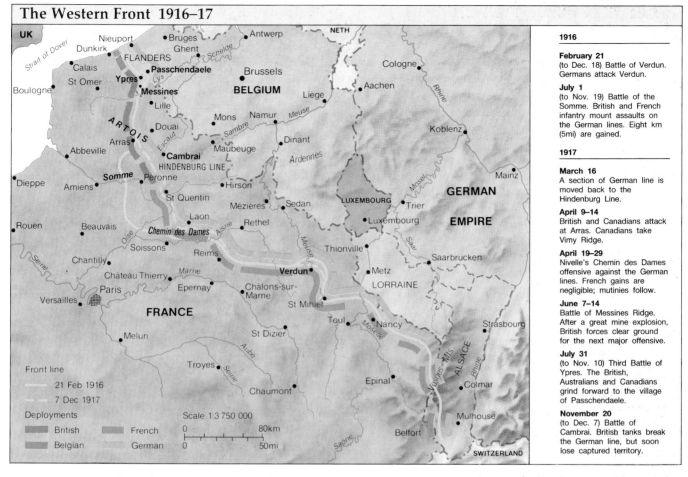

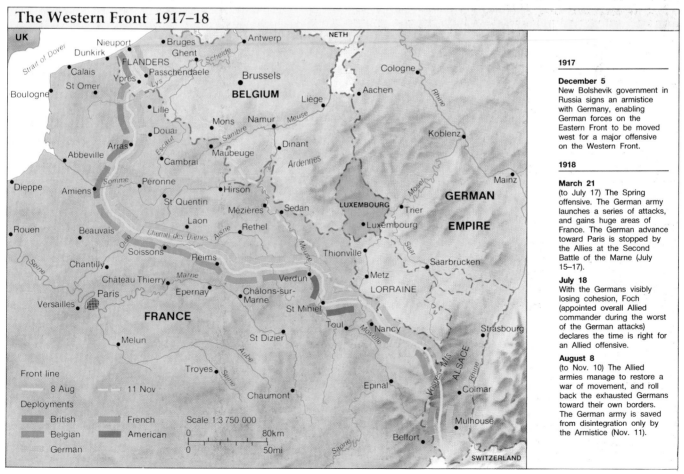

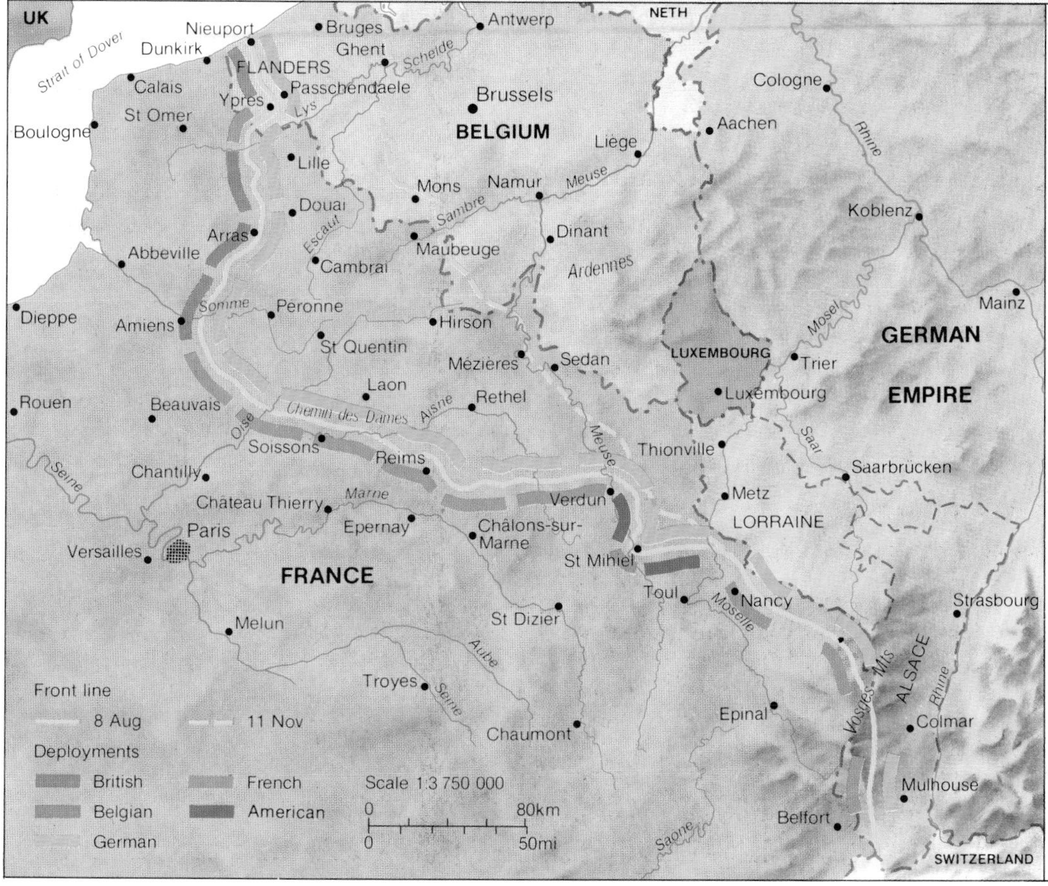

1917

December 5
New Bolshevik government in Russia signs an armistice with Germany, enabling German forces on the Eastern Front to be moved west for a major offensive on the Western Front.

1918

March 21
(to July 17) The Spring offensive. The German army launches a series of attacks, and gains huge areas of France. The German advance toward Paris is stopped by the Allies at the Second Battle of the Marne (July 15–17).

July 18
With the Germans visibly losing cohesion, Foch (appointed overall Allied commander during the worst of the German attacks) declares the time is right for an Allied offensive.

August 8
(to Nov. 10) The Allied armies manage to restore a war of movement, and roll back the exhausted Germans toward their own borders. The German army is saved from disintegration only by the Armistice (Nov. 11).

and in Italy, which had entered the war in late 1914 and early 1915 respectively.

1916–17: the great slaughter

The scale of the war on the Eastern Front was monumental, but it was never at the heart of the war. Whatever happened in the vast operations in Poland and the Balkans, the conflict would be won and lost on the Western Front. The effort to do so dominated events in 1916–17.

If the first military gamble made by Germany in the war was the invasion of France in 1914, the second was the Battle of Verdun. The first was an attempt to win a war of annihilation; the second, a war of attrition. Starting on 21 February 1916 the German army tried to "bleed the French army white", by an assault on the salient of Verdun in eastern France. This battle turned into a ten-month bloodbath for both sides.

While the fighting around Verdun raged, the British opened a major offensive further west in France, near the River Somme. This gigantic assault, launched on 1 July 1916, was renewed periodically throughout the following six months, but without any success in its primary objective, which was to break through the German lines in order to fight the war of movement everyone had been waiting for since October 1914.

In late July 1917 the British tried again, this time in southern Belgium, near the city of Ypres. This cluster of offensive operations, which dragged on remorselessly until November, is called the Third Battle of Ypres, or simply Passchendaele. It was a complete failure. In the three major military operations of this phase of the war – Verdun, the Somme, and Passchendaele – the defensive positions held out, but at a cost to both sides of approximately two million casualties.

There were other major military and political events in 1916: for instance, the Russian army achieved a major military victory in the Brusilov offensive and in the Battle of Jutland, despite its inconclusive outcome the British navy kept control over the North Sea. This meant that the blockade of German ports continued, putting a strain on the German economy which was deepened by a series of poor harvests leading to the "turnip winter" of 1916–17. These difficulties forced the Germans to press home a submarine war – their third major gamble of the war. This aimed to cut essential supplies and force the UK to the conference table, but at the risk of widening the conflict by killing neutral citizens.

1917–18: revolution and peace

In April 1917 the United States responded to the German U-boat campaign by delcaring war on the Central Powers. This was one of the two major events which fundamentally changed the character of the war. The other was the Russian Revolution of March 1917, which toppled the czar's imperial regime and placed a Provisional government in its place. The new regime was made up of liberals and moderate socialists who were still committed to throwing the German army off Russian soil. But the failure of their offensive undermined the basis of popular support for the new government. In November power was seized by Lenin and the revolutionary Bolshevik socialists – the only group that had been committed to taking Russia out of the war at whatever the price.

The price was high, but the Russians had no alternative. At the Treaty of Brest-Litovsk, signed on 3 March 1918, the Russians handed over a vast territory, including Poland, the Ukraine, the Baltic states and Finland, thereby creating a huge satellite empire for Germany in the east. The price for the Allies was heavy too. The defeat of Russia meant that Germany could concentrate its efforts on the Western Front and reinforce its position in Belgium and France in order to launch an offensive to win the war before the weight of American manpower and materiel would be felt. This offensive came on 21 March 1918, and very nearly achieved its objective. Within a few weeks the German army was within 80 km (50 mi) of Paris, but could not capitalize on its initial gains.

But that was the end of Germany's fourth and last gamble of the war. It ran out of reserves of manpower and materiel just as the United States was beginning to play a major role in the conflict. By the summer of 1918, the tide had turned. The German army started to retreat, and the high command began to see that the war was lost. All of Germany's allies collapsed, and to prevent further slaughter and the invasion of their country – by this time torn by dissension and incipient revolt – the German high command informed the Kaiser that Germany could not win an outright victory. In effect they had to accept the bitter fact that the war was lost. The Kaiser abdicated, and an armistice took effect on 11 November 1918.

The first "people's war"

This description of the four phases of the war presents only the outlines of the conflict. But it does suggest a number of points which help to account for its outcome. Again it may be useful to encapsulate this argument.

It is possible to see World War I as a series of gambles taken by Germany: the Schlieffen Plan, Verdun, the U-boat campaign, and the March 1918 offensive. Each nearly brought victory; each ultimately failed. The reasons for failure are complex. But one important part of the story is social and economic. In other words, military Front and home front stood together and collapsed together during World War I, as the hungry populations of German and Austria recognized by 1918. The Allies won the war primarily because they were able to field their armies without starving their civilian populations. In this respect, the first "people's war" was won by the "people's democracies" in more than just the obvious sense. This is the appropriate context in which to place America's contribution to the war. Both before 1917 and after, the United States helped the Allies win the "people's war".

The aftermath of the war

This account will present an image of the war as a man-made shock wave spreading out from an epicenter to various peripheries. This is a useful way of describing the war, as it moved from the centers of political power, to the general staffs, to the armies they led, and to the populations they defended, with varying degrees of success. But this approach has one serious drawback; it neglects the factors that made people call it the "Great War": first, its gigantic scale; and second, the deep and indelible mark it left on the cultural life of the 20th century. In the final chapters we attend to aspects of the aftermath of World War I.

The aftermath of the war was a time of reckoning and a time of mourning for millions of people throughout the world. This indeed is another way of seeing the conflict as a "people's war". They paid the price. The casualty lists which grew and grew as the war continued preclude any conclusion other than that the war was one of the most miserable chapters in human history. The fact that much bravery and some good came out of it is beside the point; the war was an abomination. Being so many, the victims of the war became one: the Lost Generation. Their shadow is cast wherever one looks in Europe. If this book succeeds in suggesting some of the dimensions of the catastrophe, and some of its enduring consequences, then it will have achieved its purpose.

The Eastern Front 1914–15

1914

August 17–26
Russians launch a two-pronged offensive into lightly-held East Prussia and beat off an initial German counterattack at Gumbinnen (Aug. 20).

August 26–30
Battle of Tannenberg. Germans crush the southern prong of the Russian advance.

September 5–9
Battle of the Masurian Lakes. Germans turn back the eastern prong of the Russian advance.

September 28
(to Oct. 27) First Battle of Warsaw. The Germans and Austro-Hungarians attack the huge concentrations of Russian troops in Poland, south of Warsaw, head on. The Russians stop the opposing armies and force them back.

November 11–25
Second Battle of Warsaw. The Germans and Austro-Hungarians renew their attack on the Russians; this time to the west of Warsaw. The Russians are caught off guard and the Germans and Austro-Hungarians advance as far as Lodz.

November 16–29
The Austro-Hungarians attack in the Krakow sector. The attack is blunted by the Russians. In the Carpathians, denuded of Austro-Hungarian troops for the Krakow battles, the Russians make substantial gains.

December 3–15
Battle of Limanowa. The Russians attack Krakow, which is successfully defended by the Germans and Austro-Hungarians.

1915

January 23
(to mid April) Both sides launch attacks in the Carpathians. Since 11 November 1914 the Russians have besieged the city of Przemysl. Austro-Hungarian attempts to relieve the city fail with heavy losses. Przemysl falls to the Russians on March 22.

February 8–22
Winter Battle of Masuria (to the east of the Masurian Lakes). The Germans and Austro-Hungarians force the Russians to retreat but they fail to break through.

May 2
(to Sept. 30) Central Powers' Summer offensive. The Germans lead a breakthrough at Gorlice which throws the Russians back from the Carpathians. Further north, under strong German and Austro-Hungarian pressure, the Russians retreat to shorten their line and abandon the vast "bulge" of Russian Poland.

The Eastern Front 1916–17

1916

June 4
(to Aug. 10) Brusilov offensive. The Russians attack on the relatively open ground between the Pripet Marshes and the Carpathians and roll back the Austro-Hungarian line. The Germans stabilize the situation by sending reinforcements to the Austro-Hungarians.

July 19
(to Aug. 4) The Germans launch a counteroffensive and push the Russian line further east. The effort stalls for want of reserves and supplies.

September 1–5
After intensive training of their assault units, the Germans capture the Russian port of Riga (at the extreme northern end of the Front), but fail to trap the defending Russian army, which escapes.

1917

January-February
Sporadic fighting in the Carpathians.

June 18
(to July 13) The Kerensky offensive. The Russians launch a series of weak offensives along the Eastern Front, which are easily repulsed.

December 5
Armistice is signed on the Eastern Front between the Germans and the new Bolshevik government of Russia.

FROM BALKAN CONFLICT TO WORLD WAR

Why did armed conflict in southeastern Europe engulf the world? The first reason is that the European alliance system converted a localized conflict into a general European war. In 1879 Germany and Austria-Hungary had formed the Dual Alliance; in 1893–94 France and Russia had become allies. Thus an Austro-Russian military conflict was bound to become a Russo–German one, which in turn touched off Franco–German conflict, leading to the invasion of Belgium, which ensured Britain's entry into the war. Thus once war was declared between Austria and Serbia on 28 July, and Russia mobilized its armies, a general war broke out. An alliance system conceived as a deterrent to European war helped precipitate one.

Secondly, a European war became a world war because it was waged between imperial powers, able to summon the manpower and resources of colonies and dependencies throughout the world. The Senegalese joined the French; an Indian army supplemented the British in Mesopotamia and on the Western Front. In German East Africa German troops led British and African soldiers on a wild goose chase for four years. Portugal joined the Allies in part to defend or extend its African empire. In August 1914 Japan seized former German possessions in China. The Allies put pressure on China formally to enter the war, which it did on 14 August 1917. After the USA joined the Allies in April 1917 (see page 59) American diplomacy brought Central American satellite states into the conflict: within 24 hours of the US declaration of war, Panama and Cuba followed suit. Brazil, Guatemala, Nicaragua, Costa Rica, Haiti and Honduras joined in later. In addition, extra-European colonies and dependencies were populated by European immigrants. Many Canadians, Australians and New Zealanders who joined up in 1914 were indeed defending their country – Britain. Anglo–American family ties were also strong.

Thirdly, the conflict became worldwide because the economic intrerests of the major powers were spread throughout the globe. Britain had built a vast international trading network in the late 19th century. This was both its strength, and its vulnerable point, at which Germany's U-boats struck. They failed in every respect. The UK blockade of Germany was more successful in stripping it of vital supplies.

The economic side of the war touched neutrals in many ways. All were affected by wartime inflation. Some, like Denmark or Holland, had to consent to trading arrangements with Germany which were distinctly unfavorable. To feed German families, Danes went without milk. Sweden introduced food rationing to deal with severe shortages. Other economic effects of the war were less deleterious. Many countries were starved of European finished goods, and had to produce their own. The economies of Brazil, Argentina, Japan, China and India "took off" during a war which was both the apogee and the end of European dominance of the world.

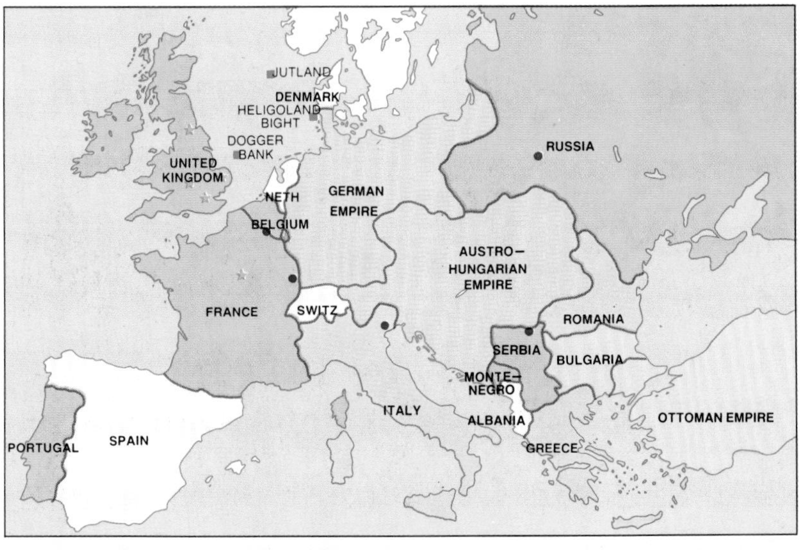

◀ No Japanese troops fought in Europe during the war, but Japanese warships protected Allied troop carriers and supply ships in both the Mediterranean and the Pacific. In light of the Japanese attack on Pearl Harbor in 1941, it may come as a surprise to note that in the 1914–18 war Japanese warships helped protect the Pacific coast of the United States.

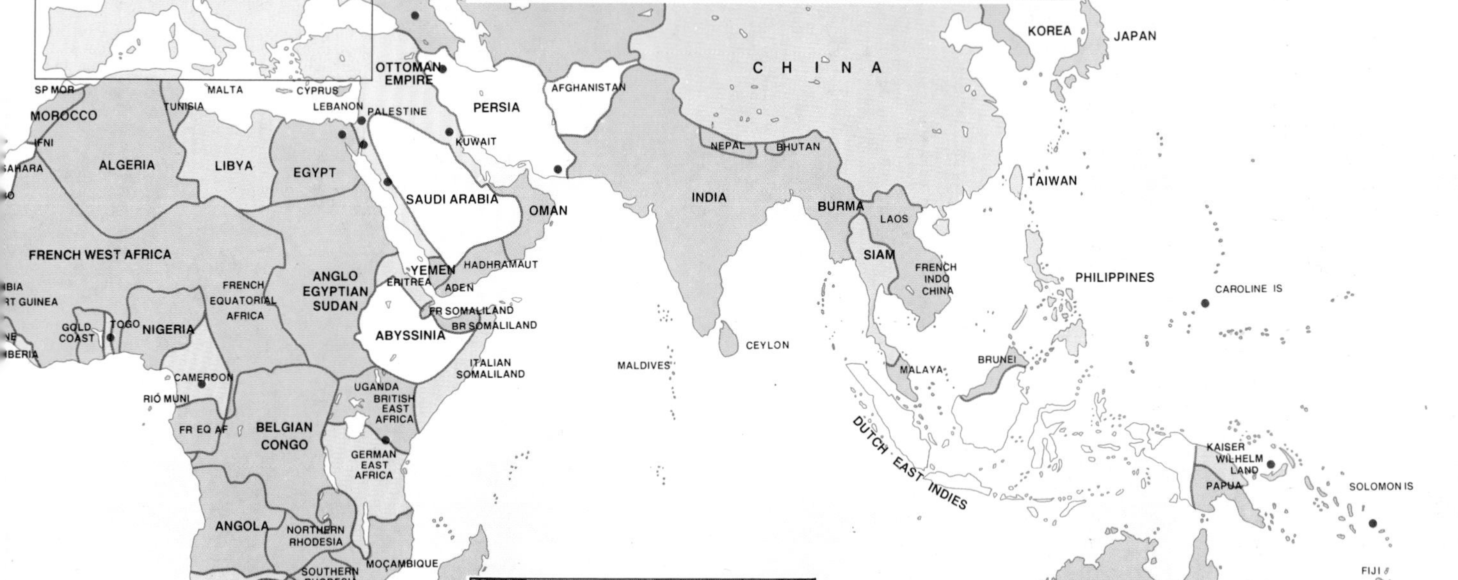

▼ The war against Germany took place wherever German colonies were located. In Africa troops from South Africa (below) and Portugal (below right) fought a protracted bush war with German and native soldiers.

◀ The war against Turkey was fought from Gallipoli to the Persian gulf. These Indian sappers are building a bridge over the Tigris river in present-day Iraq.

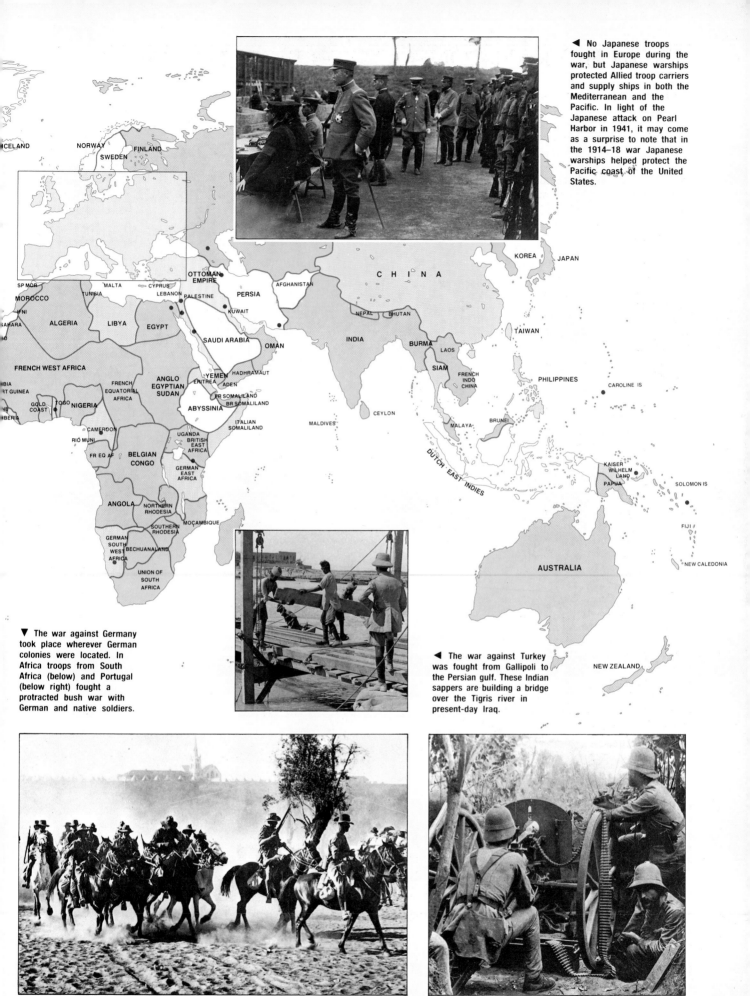

PART 1

THE POLITICIANS' WAR

WARTIME POLITICIANS AND GLOSSARY

AUSTRALIA

Governor General

Ronald Craufurd Munro-Ferguson	1914–20

Prime Minister

Joseph Cook	1913–14
Andrew Fisher	1914–15
William Morris Hughes	1915–23

Foreign Minister

Patrick McMahon Glynn	1913–14
John Andrew Arthur	1914
Hugh Mahon	1914–16

Minister of Defense

Edward Davis Millen	1913–14
George Foster Pearce	1914–18

AUSTRO-HUNGARIAN EMPIRE

Head of State

Franz Josef I, Emperor	1848–1916
Charles I, Emperor	1916–18

Lord Chamberlain and Foreign Minister

Count Leopold Berchtold	1912–15
Baron István Burián	1915–16
Count Ottokar Czernin	1916–18
Count István Burián	1918
Count Andrássy Gyula	1918
Baron Ludwig Flotow	1918

Minister of War

General Alexander, Baron Krobatin	1912–17
General Rudolf Stöger-Steiner von Steinstätten	1917–18

Navy Minister

Anton Haus	1913–17
Karl Kailer von Kagenfels	1917
Maximilian Njegovan	1917
Franz von Holub	1918–19

BELGIUM

Head of State

Albert, King	1909–34

Prime Minister

Baron Charles de Broqueville	1911–18
Gerhard Cooreman	1918

Foreign Minister

Julien Davignon	1912–16
Baron Eugène van Beyens	1916–17
Baron Charles de Broqueville	1918
Paul Hymans	1918–20

Minister of War

Baron Charles de Broqueville	1912–16
Emile Vandervelde	1916–17
Lieutenant-General A. de Cennynck	1917–18
Paul Emile Janson	1918–19

BULGARIA

Head of State

Ferdinand, King	1908–18
Boris III, King	1918–43

Prime Minister

Dr Vasil Radoslavov	1913–18
Aleksandŭr Malinov	1918

Foreign Minister

Dr Vasil Radoslavov	1914–15
General Fefov	1915–18
T. Todoraff	1918

Minister of War

General Boyadjīev	1914–16
General Naidenov	1916–17
A. Liaptchev	1917–18
General Savov	1918

CANADA

Governor General

Arthur, Duke of Connaught	1911–16
Victor Cavendish, Duke of Devonshire	1916–21

Prime Minister and Foreign Minister

Sir Robert Laird Borden	1911–20

Minister of Defense and Munitions

Sir Samuel Hughes	1911–16
Sir Albert Edward Kemp	1916–17
Sidney Chilton Mewburn	1917–20

CHINA

Head of State

Yüan Shih-K'ai, President	1912–16
Li Yuan-hung, President	1916–17
Feng Kuo-chang, President	1917
Hsüan-T'ung (P'u-i), Emperor	1917
Feng Kuo cheng, President	1917–18
Hsü Shih-ch'ang, President	1918–22

Prime Minister

No appointment	1913–16
Tuan Ch'i-jui	1916–17
Chang-hsün	1917
Tuan Ch'i-jui	1917–18
Ch'ien Neng-hsün	1918–19

FRANCE

Head of State

Raymond Poincaré, President	1913–20

Prime Minister

Gaston Doumergue	1913–14
René Viviani	1914–15
Aristide Briand	1915-17
Alexandre Felix Joseph Ribot	1917
Paul Painlevé	1917
Georges Clemenceau	1917–20

Foreign Minister

Léon Bourgeois	1914
Théophile Delcassé	1914
Gaston Doumergue	1914
Théophile Delcassé	1914–15
René Viviani	1915
Aristide Briand	1915–17
Alexandre Felix Joseph Ribot	1917
Louis Hubert Lyautey	1917
Marie Jean Lucien Lacaze	1917
Alexandre Felix Joseph Ribot	1917
Stéphan Pichon	1917–20

War Minister

Joseph Noulens	1913–14
Edouard, Vicomte Castelnau-de-Curières	1914
Alexandre Millerand	1914–15
Joseph Gallieni	1915–16
Pierre Auguste Roques	1916
Louis Hubert Lyautey	1916–17
Marie Jean Lucien Lacaze	1917
Paul Painlevé	1917
Georges Clemenceau	1917–20

Munitions and War Materials

Albert Thomas	1916-17
Louis Loucheur	1917–18

GERMANY

Head of State

William II, Emperor	1888–1918

Chancellor

Theobald von Bethmann-Hollweg	1909–17
Georg Michaelis	1917
Count Georg von Hertling	1917–18
Prince Max of Baden	1918
Friedrich Ebert	1918–19

Foreign Minister

Gottlieb von Jagow	1913–16
Arthur Zimmermann	1916–17
Richard von Kühlmann	1917–18
Paul von Hintze	1918
Wilhelm Solf	1918
Count Ulrich von Brockdorff-Rantzau	1918-19

Minister of War/Admiralty

Admiral Alfred von Tirpitz	1897–16
Admiral Eduard von Capelle	1916–18
Paul von Behnke	1918
Ernest von Mann	1918–19

INDIA

Viceroys

Charles Hardinge, Baron Hardinge of Penshurst	1910–16
Frederick John Napier Thesiger	1916–1921

ITALY

Head of State

Victor Emmanuel III, King	1900–46

Prime Minister

Antonio Salandra	1914–16
Paolo Boselli	1916–17
Vittorio Emanuele Orlando	1917–19

Foreign Minister

Marquis Antonio Paternò Castello di San Giuliano	1911–14
Baron Sidney Sonnino	1914–18

Minister of War

General Domenico Grandi	1914
General Vittorio Zupelli	1914–16
General Paolo Morone	1916–17
Gaetano Ettore Giardino	1917
General Vittorio Alfieri	1917–18
General Vittorio Zupelli	1918–19

JAPAN

Head of State

Yoshihito (Taisho), Emperor	1912–26

Prime Minister

Marquis Shigenobu Okuma	1914–16
Count Musatake Terauchi	1916–18
Takashi Hara	1918–21

Foreign Minister

Count Yasuya Uchida	1918–23

NEW ZEALAND

Governor (after 1917, Governor General)

Arthur William de Brito Savile Foljambe, 5th Earl of Liverpool	1912–20

Prime Minister

William Ferguson Massey	1912–25

OTTOMAN EMPIRE

Head of State

Mehmed V, Sultan	1909–18

Prime Minister

Prince Said Halim Pasha,	1913–17
Mehmed Talât Pasha	1917–18
Ahmed Izzed Pasha	1918
Ahmed Tevfik Pasha	1918–19

Foreign Minister

Prince Said Halim Pasha	1914–16
Halil Bey	1916–17
Ahmed Nessimy Bey	1917–18
Naby Bey	1918

Minister of War

General of Brigade Enver Pasha	1914–22

PORTUGAL

Head of State

Manoel d'Arriaga, President	1911–15
Bernardino Machado Guimarães, President	1915–18
Sidónio Pais, President	1918

Prime Minister

Bernardino Machado Guimarães	1914
Vitor Hugo de Azevedo Coutinho	1914–15
General Pimenta de Castro	1915
Joās Pinheiro Chagas	1915
Dr Afonso Costa	1915
José de Castro	1915
Dr Afonso Costa	1915
Dr António José d'Almeīda	1916–17
Dr Afonso Costa	1917
Sidónio Pais	1917–18

Foreign Minister

Bernardino Machado Guimarães	1914–15
General Pimenta de Castro	1915–16
Augusto Soares	1916–18

Minister of War

General Periera Eca	1914–15
General Pimenta de Castro	1915–16
Norton de Mattos	1916–18
Amilcar Motta	1918
Major Bernardino Ferreira	1918

ROMANIA

Head of State

Carol I, King	1881–1914
Ferdinand I, King	1914–27

Prime Minister

Ion I.C. Brătianu	1914–18
Alexandru Averescu	1918
Alexandru Marghiloman	1918
Constantin Coandă	1918

RUSSIAN EMPIRE

Head of State

Nicholas II, Emperor	1894–17
Lev Borisovich Kamenev, President	1917
Yakov Mikhailovich Sverdlov, President	1917–19

Chairman of the Council of People's Commissars

Lenin (Vladimir Ilyich Ulyanov)	1917–24

Prime Minister

Ivan Longinovich Goremykin	1914–16
Boris Vladimirovich Stürmer	1916
Aleksandr Fyodorovich Trepov	1916–17
Prince Nikolai Golitsyn	1917
Prince Georgy Evgenyevich Lvov	1917
Alexandr Fedorovich Kerensky	1917

Foreign Minister

Sergyei Dmitrievich Sazonov	1914–16
Nikolai Nikolaevich Pokrovsky	1916–17
Pavel Nikolaevich Milyukov	1917
Mikhail Ivanovich Tereshchenko	1917
Leon Trotsky (Lev Davidovich Bronstein)	1917–18
Adolf Abramovich Joffe	1918
Karl Berngardovich Radek (Sobelsohn)	1918

SERBIA

Head of State

Peter I, King	1903–27

Prime Minister

Nikola Pašić	1912–18

Foreign Minister

Nikola Pašić	1912–18
M. Gavilovitch	1918

Minister of War

Colonel Dusham Stephanovitch	1912–14
Colonel Boyanovitch	1914–17
General Bozidav Terzitch	1917–18

UK OF GREAT BRITAIN & IRELAND

Head of State

George V, King	1910–36

Prime Minister

Herbert Henry Asquith	1908–16
David Lloyd George	1916–22

Foreign Minister

Sir Edward Grey	1905–16
Arthur Balfour	1916-22

Minister of War

Herbert Henry Asquith	1914
Earl Kitchener of Khartoum	1914–16
David Lloyd George	1916–18
Viscount Milner	1918–19

UNION OF SOUTH AFRICA

Governor General

Sidney, 1st Earl of Boxton	1914–20

Prime Minister

Louis Botha	1912–19

Minister of Defense

Jan Christian Smuts	1912–19

UNITED STATES OF AMERICA

Head of State

Thomas Woodrow Wilson, President	1913-21

Vice-President

Thomas Riley Marshall	1913–21

Secretary of State

William Jennings Bryan	1913–15
Robert Lansing	1915–21

Secretary of War

Lindley Miller Garrison	1913–16
Newton Diehl Baker	1916–21
Josephus Daniels	1913–21

Allies
France, Russia, the British Empire, Serbia and Belgium, later joined by Italy, Japan, China, the USA (as an Associated Power) and other countries.

Armistice
Agreement between belligerents to suspend hostilities, especially the Allied–German Armistice of 11 November 1918.

Army bill
Legislation to increase the size of the army by broadening the terms of military service.

Bolshevik
Supporter of the radical wing of the Russian social democratic party, led by Lenin. Also a foreign sympathizer with Bolshevik policies.

Blockade
Cutting, especially by naval means, of the enemy's overseas communications to disrupt the domestic economy.

Central Powers
The German and Austro-Hungarian Empires in alliance; later joined by Turkey and Bulgaria.

Consortium system
French system of managing the wartime economy through governmental control of supplies to industry.

Contraband
Goods that neutrals are forbidden, by international law, to supply to belligerents.

Dictatorship
The concentration of absolute power in the hands of a single individual.

Dilution of labor
Easing or abandonment of trade-union restrictive practices, to allow quick introduction of newcomers to established work forces.

Dual monarchy
The kingdoms of Austria and Hungary, ruled by the Habsburg emperor but separated by imperial decree in 1867. (The Austro- Hungarian Empire, ruled by the Habsburg Emperor as king of Austria and Hungary.)

Easterner
One who believed that the war could be won if military effort included serious attention to the Eastern Front or Turkey.

Entente
(Fr: understanding) The alliance of the UK, France and Russia, named for the Triple Entente of 1907 among these nations.

Entente powers
The UK, France and Russia; later joined by Italy, Japan, China and the United States (the latter as an Associated Power).

Executive
The branch of government responsible for putting policies into effect.

Flanking operation
Indirect assault on an army or an ally of a belligerent.

Franchise
The right to vote for members of an elected representative body.

Hindenburg Plan
Plan to increase German munitions production, by placing control of the economy in the hands of industrial magnates acting under the authority of the army high command.

Home Rule
The cause of seeking self-government for Ireland, spearheaded by the Irish Nationalist Party and supported by the Liberals.

Imperialist
A supporter of foreign rule over overseas territories.

Labour Party
British political party representing the interests of organized labor.

Liberal Party
British political party, in power on the outbreak of war, committed to Free trade, social legislation and Home Rule for Ireland.

Materiel
The military equipment of an army.

mobilization
The calling up of reserves to bring units of a standing army up to war strength.

Monarchical system
Rule by an hereditary monarch; prevalent in central and eastern Europe.

Munitions
Military equipment, particularly bullets, shells and explosives but including transport, clothing etc.

Patriotic league
An association of nationalistic supporters of the war effort.

Political truce
An agreement between opposing political parties to suspend domestic political differences in time of war.

Quartermaster general
The officer responsible for the logistical support of an army through the provision of men and military supplies.

Reichstag
The elective legislative assembly of the German Empire.

Reparations
Financial and material payments extracted from a defeated nation by the victors as compensation for the cost of a war.

Republican
One who believes that supreme power should be derived from the people rather than a monarch, and expressed through their elected representative.

Restrictive practices
Regulations governing use of labor imposed by organized labor.

Revolutionary defensism
Strategy of the Kerensky government in Russia in 1917, with the object of driving the Germans from occupied Russian territory.

Social Democratic Party
Title of socialist opposition parties in Russia and Germany.

Socialist International
International association of national parties representing labor and socialist principles.

Soviet
Elected workers' and soldiers' councils formed in 1917 in revolutionary Russia.

Strategy
The planning and general conduct of war.

Tirpitz Plan
Plan to turn Germany into a major naval power. Initiated by Admiral Tirpitz with the German navy laws of 1898 and 1900.

Total war
The subordination of the whole national economy and its resources to the war effort.

War credits
Extraordinary parliamentary vote of credit, without gold backing, to meet the cost of war.

Westerner
One who believed that the war could only be won by a decisive military victory on the Western Front.

Datafile

War broke out in 1914 after a decade of international tension. The decision to go to war was taken by a handful of men. Their understanding of the strategic situation and of the underlying power relationships was flawed. The outcome was a series of miscalculations which converted a local incident in the Balkans into a world war. Some leaders greeted war enthusiastically; but some saw they had opened a Pandora's box.

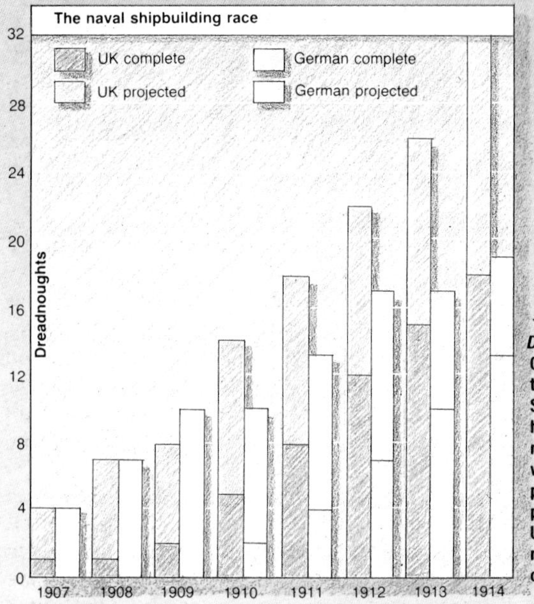

◀ The British ship HMS *Dreadnought*, launched in October 1906, gave her name to a new class of battleships. She displaced 22,000 tonnes, had 12in guns and was the most powerful prewar warship. Its appearance provoked ship-building programs in Germany and the UK. The German program was not to match the UK but to create a deterrent to war.

▲ German fears of encirclement grew out of an alliance system which developed in the period 1890–1910. First a Franco–Russian rapprochement in the 1890s, and secondly growing Anglo–German tensions over Admiral Tirpitz's naval program, left Germany allied with the weakest of the great powers: Austria-Hungary.

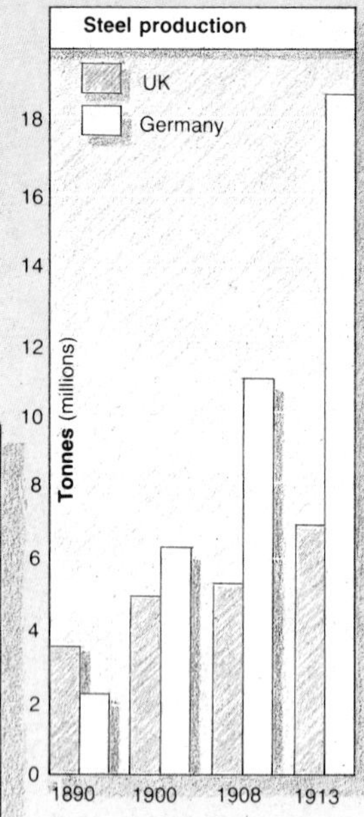

◀ After 1900 Germany outstripped the UK in steel production. Germany had emerged as a major economic power.

▼ The two phases of the July war crisis present sharp contrasts: an early phase with relatively little activity; a later phase, from 23 July – very rapid, occasionally frantic, and irreversible.

Chronology

June 28
Assassination of Austro-Hungarian Archduke Franz Ferdinand in Sarajevo

July 23
(to Aug. 4) War crisis in Europe

August 3
German invasion of Belgium begins

August 4
UK: First meeting of War Council

August 11
Goeben and *Breslau* enter the Black Sea

August 23
JAP: Japan declares war on Germany

August 24
Main German armies enter France

August 26
FR: General Galliéni appointed governor of Paris

August 26–30
Battle of Tannenberg: German victory in East Prussia

September 2
FR: Government transferred from Paris to Bordeaux

September 3
New pope elected: Benedict XV

September 5
Pact of London: French British and Russian governments agree not to make separate peace

September 5–10
First Battle of the Marne: German advance halted

September 6–15
Battle of the Masurian Lakes: German victory in East Prussia

September 8–12
Battle of Lemberg: Russians capture Austria–Hungary's fourth-largest city

September 15
First trenches of the war are dug

September 17
(to Oct. 18) "Race to the Sea": front in the west is extended to the Channel coast

October 7
BELG: Government transferred from Antwerp to Ostend

October 12
(to Nov. 11) First Battle of Ypres: inconsequential conflict between Germans and Allies

November 1
Russia declares war on Turkey. Battle of Coronel: German Pacific Squadron defeats British naval force off coast of Chile

November 11
(to early Dec.) Germans force Eastern Front further to the east

November 18
FR: Retransfer of government from Bordeaux to Paris begins

December 2
Austro-Hungarians capture Belgrade (capital of Serbia)

December 8
Battle of the Falkland Islands: British fleet defeats the German Pacific Squadron

December 11
Serbians recapture Belgrade

December 26
GER: Government places food supplies and allocations under government control

UK: Government declares all foodstuffs on the high seas destined for enemy ports as contraband

Chronology of outbreak of war

June
28 Assassination of Crown Prince Franz Ferdinand at Sarajevo

July
5 Germany promises Austria-Hungary support for conflict with Serbia

20 President Poincaré of France visits Russia
21
22
23 Austro-Hungarian ultimatum to Serbia
24
25 Serbia mobilizes army; Germany encourages Austria-Hungary to declare war on Serbia
26 Austria-Hungary mobilizes army on Russian frontier
27
28 Austria-Hungary declares war on Serbia
29
30 Russia orders mobilization of army
31 Germany demands end to Russian mobilization; Germany refuses British request to respect neutrality of Belgium; France, Austria-Hungary and Germany mobilize

August
1 Germany declares war on Russia
2 Germany invades Luxemburg
3 Germany declares war on France
4 Germany invades Belgium; Britain declares war on Germany
5
6 Austria-Hungary declares war on Russia

1914 THE WAR OF ILLUSIONS

How did a local crisis turn into World War I?

Who was responsible for the escalation?

Three schools of thought and their answers

Was the war the culmination of German expansionist ambitions?

Or did Germany risk war to support Austria-Hungary?

Or should European countries collectively be blamed for failure to maintain peace?

One of the most controversial questions of 20th-century history is how did the war crisis of 1914 turn into World War I? The basic chronology is not in dispute. The crown prince of the Austro-Hungarian Empire, the Archduke Franz Ferdinand, chose to visit Sarajevo in Bosnia with his wife on 28 June 1914. Bosnia was an imperial province, but one that had only been incorporated in the Empire in 1908 (after annexation from the Turkish Empire). Most of its inhabitants were Serbs, many of whom felt more affinity with the neighboring kingdom of Serbia. The day of the crown prince's visit was St Vitus' Day: the great Serbian festival that marked the end of medieval Serbia's independence. That day in Sarajevo a handful of students, who were members of a fanatical Serbian nationalist organization, the Black Hand, tried to assassinate the couple. They missed on the first attempt, but succeeded on the second. The Austro-Hungarian response was to label the assassins puppets of Serbian intelligence, whose aim was to challenge Austro-Hungarian sovereignty over all its south-Slavic lands (which today largely form Yugoslavia). After consultations with its German allies on 5–6 July, Austria-Hungary presented Serbia with a set of political demands – an ultimatum deliberately designed so Serbia would reject it.

Balkan conflict to international confrontation

The ultimatum was sent on 23 July. It was perceived as a challenge to the status quo in the Balkans by Russia, the protector and promoter of Slav nationalism in the region and the enemy of Austria-Hungary. With Russian backing Serbia met most of the demands, but refused to give in completely. Russia reacted quickly, and ordered a partial mobilization for 29 July.

This changed an Austro–Russian quarrel into a Russo–German one, because Russian mobilization threatened Germany. It also presented Germany with the real possibility of a two-front war, because a conflict with Russia would trigger the intervention of Russia's ally, France. German military planning had anticipated this and took for granted that, in any war against Russia, Germany would have to attack France first.

Even though the Sarajevo crisis did not concern any issue of dispute between Germany and France, German mobilization on 31 July – which was in fact decided upon before the news of the Russian mobilization reached Berlin – was linked

▼ Gavrilo Princip, an 18-year-old Bosnian Serb student, was easily apprehended after firing the shots that killed the Archduke Franz Ferdinand and his wife in Sarajevo. Princip was too young to face the death sentence; he received a 20-year prison term but died of tuberculosis in an Austrian fortress near Prague in 1918.

to a military plan that would turn a Russo-German conflict into a pan-European conflict. In this plan Germany would preempt a possible protracted war on two fronts by knocking the French army out of the conflict before Russia was able to occupy the whole of Eastern Germany. This was to be accomplished by a huge operation – based on a modified version of the famous Schlieffen Plan of 1905 – in which the German army would pass through Belgium and northern France in an enormous arc. The aims were to outflank French forces on the German–French border, sweep up the French army near Paris and then take the capital itself, or encircle it, as had been done in 1870.

◀ The "Eastern Question" in the eyes of the cartoonist of the Parisian *Petit Journal*. The reference is to 5–6 October 1908, when Bulgaria declared its independence from Turkey and Austria annexed Bosnia and Herzegovina. The first step led the following year to military conflict between Bulgaria and Turkey. The second step set up a collision course between Austria and Serbia, which vigorously opposed the annexations.

Austria-Hungary and The Balkans

On account of its explosive mixture of peoples and the interest of the great powers in the region, the Balkans was the most volatile area of prewar Europe. The great power most directly concerned was the Austro-Hungarian Empire, because its territory extended into the Balkans and many of its subject peoples belonged to ethnic groups (such as the Serbs and Romanians) who had also set up Balkan kingdoms of their own. Sprawling over a vast area of central and eastern Europe, the Austro-Hungarian Empire was a multinational entity with a population of some 50 million. The only thing that united its various nationalities was that they were subjects of the Habsburgs, one of the great European dynasties, whose chief representative in 1914 was the Emperor Franz Josef.

During his reign, from 1848, defeats by France (1859) and Prussia (1866) had virtually ended Habsburg influence in Italy and Germany, turning Austria into an east European power. However, these reverses proved a less serious threat to the integrity of the Empire than the growing national consciousness of its various peoples. Of these the magyars (Hungarians) had been the strongest and most restive. The Habsburg solution to the Magyar problem, implemented in 1867, was to convert the Austrian Empire into the dual monarchy of Austria-Hungary. In effect the Hungarians were taken into partnership with the "Austrian" (German) element, and the Empire was divided.

This situation remained unchanged down to 1914, despite its manifest dangers. Some foresaw the eventual collapse of the Empire, but prophecies of Austria's doom were not new, and the Habsburgs had an impressive record for adaptation and survival. Some security was also provided by the alliance with Germany, signed in 1879.

The rulers of Austria-Hungary were naturally afraid that the existence of new nations such as Serbia would cause unrest among minority groups of the same language and culture who lived within the borders of the Empire. But they also entertained ambitious schemes for expansion into the Balkans, possibly in collaboration with Russia. In 1908 a mixture of expansionist and defensive motives impelled Austria-Hungary to annex Bosnia and Herzegovina, Turkish provinces which the Austrians had administered since 1878. Most of the population were Serbs, and the annexation was denounced by Serbia, with the backing of Russia; but both were forced to climb down when Germany supported Austria.

The Austrians were not the only disturbers of the Balkan status quo. Bulgaria, Serbia, Greece and Montenegro coveted the remaining Turkish territory in Europe. They joined forces and secured their various aims. But Austria and Italy intervened to prevent the establishment of an enlarged Serbia on the Adriatic; instead, Albania was created. Differences between Serbia and Bulgaria then led to a second Balkan War (June–July 1913), when an alliance of states stripped Bulgaria of territory won in the first war.

In 1914 Austro-Serbian hostility persisted and Bulgaria nursed grievances. The Balkans were already tension-ridden when, on 28 June 1914, the Archduke Franz Ferdinand was assassinated at Sarajevo in Bosnia.

▼ In Europe only Switzerland was able to create political unity out of linguistic diversity. Lacking the unifying features of geography or tradition, the Austro-Hungarian Empire presented a collage of linguistic cultures, in which nationalist aspirations were expressed. Omitted from the map is the Yiddish language, spoken by millions of Eastern European Jews.

Language Groups 1914

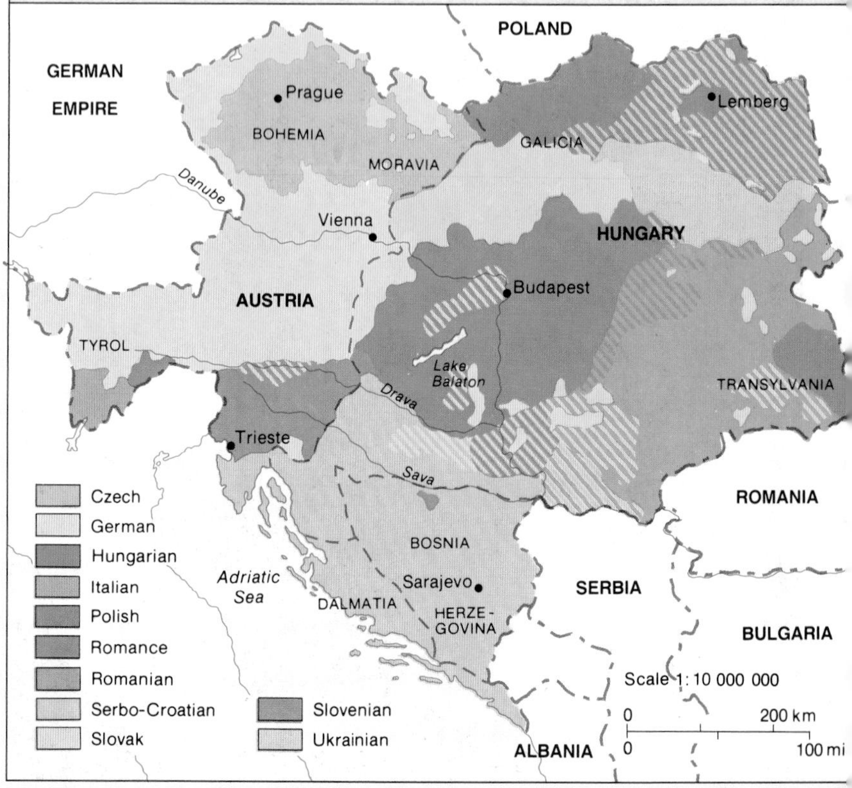

Whatever the military implications of this plan, its political costs were profound. Schlieffen violated the central tenet of Karl von Clausewitz, that war was politics by other means. The Schlieffen Plan was based upon the assumption that German troops would cross Belgium to attack France. But the sovereignty of Belgian territory had been guaranteed by all the major powers, including Britain, in 1839. The swing through Belgium risked bringing the UK into the war. This is precisely what happened. On 4 August Britain declared war on Germany and its allies. The ensuing spiral of conflict, which had started with the murder of two Austrian nobles, ended with the deaths of 9 million men.

Why war in 1914?

By and large historians know what happened in 1914. But since virtually the end of the war they have argued about who was responsible for the escalation of a Balkan quarrel into a world war. Basically there are three schools of thought: first, the "primacy of German responsibility" approach; second, the "calculated risk" approach; and third, the "collective guilt" approach.

The primacy of German responsibility

In order to understand this argument, vigorously promoted by the Hamburg historian Fritz Fischer during the 1960s, one of the basic factors in the political equation of 1914 must first be considered.

Franz Josef 1830–1916

Franz Josef I, emperor of Austria and king of Hungary, came to the throne during the turmoil of one revolution and died on the eve of another. His early days were spent in a rigorous clerical environment, and military service in Italy during the 1848 revolution prepared him for his life-long work: the maintenance of monarchical power and the extirpation of revolution. But eventually, economic difficulties and military and diplomatic setbacks forced him to come to terms with the warring factions within the Empire, in particular Magyar nobles, but also Germans, Czechs, Poles and Slavs. In 1866–67, he recognized these claims by becoming king of Hungary and by instituting a limited constitutional system in Austria. His personal life was equally unfulfilled. His son Rudolf committed suicide in 1889, his wife was assassinated in 1897, and his heir Franz Ferdinand was of a different cast of mind.

Franz Ferdinand 1863–1914

Two untimely deaths made Franz Ferdinand, the nephew of Franz Josef I, heir to the Austro-Hungarian Empire: Crown Prince Rudolf's suicide in 1889 and the death of his father, Archduke Charles Louis, in 1896. Over the next 18 years he was given a wider role in domestic and military affairs, and took a more flexible line in considering reform than the emperor. His commitment to the monarchy was unequivocal, and he spent years in opposition to the Magyar nobles, whose aspirations, he believed, were inconsistent with the stability of the dynasty and of the Empire itself. In foreign affairs he balanced warmth toward Britain with coolness toward Italy and France. His sympathies were with the czar as a bulwark against revolution but he was an uncompromising enemy of Serbian nationalism. His visit to Sarajevo in Bosnia on the anniversary of the end of the medieval independence of Serbia was as a sworn enemy of the Serbian cause. His assassination on 28 June 1914 brought that conflict to a head, and destroyed everything for which Franz Ferdinand had worked throughout his life.

◀ The heir apparent of the Austro-Hungarian Empire, Archduke Franz Ferdinand, and his wife Sophia Chotek with their three children – the first orphans of the 1914–18 war.

In the late 19th and early 20th century no one had worked out a stable solution to the problems posed by the growth of the German Empire, problems both economic and political. When the German Empire was formed in 1871, its industrial revolution was well under way. Forty years later it was an economic and political power of the first order. But this was not enough; prodigious industrial growth had not been accompanied by a commensurate expansion in its sphere of influence in world affairs. There was thus an imbalance between the distribution of the economic and international political power of European states.

By 1900 Germany's leaders and many influential political groups refused to tolerate this situation indefinitely. It also was an important source of the growing antagonism between Germany and Britain in the prewar period as well as a key to German policy in the July 1914 crisis itself.

This is the context in which to place three sets of critical events that weigh heavily in the accounts of those who emphasize German responsibility for the war. The first is a plan fostered by Admiral Alfred von Tirpitz to strengthen the German high seas fleet to a level that would enable it to challenge British naval supremacy. The second is the increasing strength of the German army, underwritten by two smaller army bills in 1911 and 1912 and a third large one in 1913. The third is the evidence of belligerence and the acceptance of the likelihood of war among Germany's military elite at a "war council" summoned by Kaiser Wilhelm II on 8 December 1912. There is controversy over the importance of this last event in the road to war. Fischer places great weight on it; others do not. But in fairness to all opinions, the issues involved will be presented and then assessed.

▲ **Otto von Bismarck, architect of the German Empire, founded in 1871. After he resigned as chancellor in 1890, lesser men failed to control the system of power relations which in large part had been Bismarck's legacy.**

Theobald von Bethmann-Hollweg 1856–1921

Descended from prosperous Frankfurt bankers, Bethmann-Hollweg became chancellor of Germany in 1909. He was only moderately successful in mediating between competing factions in domestic policy in the prewar period, but more adroit in convincing the German nation that it was fighting a defensive war in 1914. He adopted a fatalistic pose in the war crisis, but played a crucial part in presenting the military with the best possible political conditions for the waging of war. He tried to float several peace initiatives during the war, but the German high command never let them get out of hand. By 1917 he had lost the support of all political groups, and his dismissal was demanded by Hindenburg and Ludendorff. The Kaiser concurred and he retired in July 1917.

▲ The Krupp family dynasty created an industrial empire based on the production of steel and armaments. Founded in the early 19th century, the Krupp works employed 10,000 men in the 1860s, and owned coal and iron mines. In 1902 the firm acquired the "Germania" shipbuilding yards in Kiel, and provided steel plate for the German navy. During the war, it produced artillery, including "Big Bertha", the heavy gun that bombarded Paris.

◄▼ The German fleet created under Admiral Alfred von Tirpitz (left) was intended to deter any of Germany's rivals from goint to war with it. The fleet was, therefore, a monumental failure.

The Rise of Germany

On the eve of World War I the German Empire was the youngest as well as the strongest of the great European powers. Its creator was Otto von Bismarck, chief minister of Prussia from 1862, whose foreign policy culminated in a double triumph: Prussia's victory over France in the war of 1870–71 and the proclamation of the king of Prussia as emperor or Kaiser of a united Germany (1871). Twenty-five German states came together to form the new *Reich*, which was designed as a federation; but Prussia was easily the largest and most powerful of the states.

Between 1870 and 1914 Germany underwent a rapid industrial revolution and its population soared to almost 65 million. As early as the 1880s its iron and steel industries were challenging Britain's, and new chemical and electrical industries were growing. Under Bismarck's guidance the state intervened to protect and encourage German industries, and set up a system of technical education that gave Germans a deserved reputation for workmanship and expertise.

The two faces of Prussian paternalism were in evidence during Bismarck's regime. He made protracted and ultimately unsuccessful efforts to control the Catholic Church and, later, to suppress the socialists (social democrats); but he also introduced "state socialism" – old age pensions and schemes for sickness and accident insurance. They were bold steps for a conservative regime. Even so, by 1914 the social democrats were the largest single party in the Reichstag.

After 1871 Bismarck made security rather than expansion his objective. In particular he aimed to keep France diplomatically isolated so that it would be in no position to fight a war to avenge the defeat of 1870–71 and recover the lost provinces of Alsace and Lorraine. Bismarck chose Austria-Hungary as Germany's principal ally (1879); later (1882) Italy was brought in to form the Triple Alliance. But Bismarck also cultivated Russia, seeking to smooth over Russo-Austrian differences and maintain a "Three Emperors' League" based on a common conservatism. German relations with Britain were more uncertain, since in the 1880s Germany began to take part in "the scramble for Africa", acquiring an empire there and in the Pacific. Ironically, in colonial affairs Bismarck and his successors found themselves collaborating with the French in opposition to Britain.

Significant changes followed the accession of Wilhelm II as German emperor in 1888. Wilful and impulsive, the Kaiser forced Bismarck to resign (1890) and took a prominent role in policy-making; he also made frequent statements that offended public opinion in other countries and reinforced the impression that Germany was an aggressive, warlike power. Russia became steadily alienated from Germany; and the great program of German naval building inaugurated in 1898 was seen as a threat by Britain. Inept German diplomacy was largely responsible for the formation of a French-Russian-British "Triple Entente", which intensified German fears of "encirclement". The decision to go to war was in part taken to end that encirclement and bring Germany the geopolitical power it deserved.

Wilhelm II 1859–1941

Wilhelm II ascended to the Hohenzollern throne in 1888. The young Kaiser had had a liberal education, as well as the requisite years of discipline in the regiment of guards and among the Prussian officer corps in Potsdam. He shared with them the view that Germany's place in world affairs required a strengthened military and naval arm, and an authoritarian regime to run domestic affairs. The strength of his personality and emotional temperament made it inevitable that he would find it difficult to work with Otto von Bismarck, the architect of his power and prestige. In dismissing Bismarck in 1890, Wilhelm opened the field to politicians who could not control the international system Bismarck had created. The "war council" called by the Kaiser with his military advisers in December 1912 shows that he was not averse to a general European war; his attitude in the war crisis itself was more equivocal. His chief influence after 1914 was in his choice of the men who would run the war effort. Their failure required his abdication as a condition of the Armistice. He fled to Holland, and was interned there at Doorn.

The Tirpitz Plan, sketched out between 1898 and 1900, formed the basis of an ambitious program of shipbuilding in the subsequent decade and a half. Its aim was political: to provide the German Empire with a weapon to wrest its fair share of imperial power from the hands of the British. Precisely what territorial gains Tirpitz and his followers had in mind is unclear, but there is no doubt about their determination to increase Germany's armaments and thereby to provide the German Empire with greater leverage in world affairs.

According to this interpretation, the German high command precipitated countermeasures – in particular, the arms race between Britain and Germany – for which Tirpitz and his circle, backed by a large number of nonsocialist Germans, were primarily responsible. The British reacted by effectively joining the Franco-Russian military alliance in 1904, which was interpreted in Germany as an act of encirclement. Thus Germany was not forced into a defensive war but acted throughout the prewar period in an aggressive manner, intending to break out of the "containment" of her empire.

It has been argued that this set of political objectives was made explicit in an extraordinary meeting called by the Kaiser on 8 December 1912, in response to a conversation between the German ambassador in London and the British minister of war, Lord Haldane. Haldane was reported to have said that, in the event of war, his government would not tolerate a French military defeat by Germany and would not stand idly by if Austria-Hungary attacked Serbia. The Kaiser's response was to call a meeting of his military – but not his political – advisers. This meeting debated the merits of going to war then and there, which was apparently favored by the chief of the imperial general staff, Helmuth von Moltke. Instead, it was agreed to play a waiting game, as advocated by Tirpitz, and put off any decision for a further 18 months, until military and naval preparations would be completed, in particular the widening of the Kiel Canal which would enable Germany's biggest ships to move from the Baltic to the North Sea.

Eighteen months from December 1912 brings us to the summer of 1914. In the light of German ambitions, Fritz Fischer and his supporters have concluded that well before the war Germany deliberately set out on a collision course with Russia and France, and was thereafter preparing for a major war.

All it required was an auspicious opportunity to utilize its military power. That occasion was presented by the Sarajevo murders of 28 June 1914. Far from defusing the situation, the Kaiser and his advisors decided to exploit it as part of their own carefully constructed long-term military and political strategy. For these reasons they must bear primary responsibility for the outbreak of the 1914 war. The events between the war council of December 1912 and the summer of 1914 had merely made them all the more determined to use the July crisis as the golden opportunity to achieve a major breakthrough, by military means, to world power status.

The "calculated risk" interpretation

Fischer's interpretation has been challenged. One set of qualifications can be summarized under the heading of the "calculated risk". According to this argument a distinction must be made between German policy in early July, when it was a matter of providing political support for Austria-Hungary in its quarrel with Serbia, and German policy in late July and early August, when the Balkan crisis turned into the world war. Most historians agree with Fischer and his school about the last days of peace: at this point the German military pressed for war and resisted all suggestions that they might pull back from the brink. But in early July, Fischer's critics believe, the German strategy was indeed to pursue the conflict, but to *contain* it within the Balkans. Germany's hope was to give Austria the opportunity to punish Serbia swiftly and thereby to present Russia, Britain and France with a resolved problem, which they would not challenge by going to war for Serbia. Austria-Hungary and its ally Germany, finding themselves increasingly isolated and with their international position deteriorating, would have won a major diplomatic victory. The ramshackle Habsburg Empire would have been propped up.

This argument holds, therefore, that Germany's political and military leaders tried to play a dangerous – but calculated – game, which simply got out of hand. They miscalculated the responses of each of their potential adversaries abroad and underestimated the momentum toward a general war that the Balkan crisis provided. The war was not an outcome of long-term strategy; it was a monumental failure of foreign policy.

Fischer would be fundamentally skeptical of this interpretation. There is controversy too over whether the outlook of the German military elite differed from that of its political leadership. Fischer believes that it is impossible to distinguish between the two. But those who subscribe to the "calculated risk" school think otherwise. They reject any suggestion of a *concerted* design by the German military and political elite to precipitate a major European war. Instead they suggest that when, by 25 July, it became clear that the limited strategy had failed and the war crisis had got out of hand, the German chancellor, Theobald von Bethmann-Hollweg, was defeated by the German military who now pushed for a major war. He now merely saw it as his purpose to provide Germany with the best possible political conditions in which to wage war. This *required* that Russian mobilization should be seen to be the cause of German mobilization, and that consequently Germany's decision to go to war should be considered a *defensive* one. Such an argument was, he believed, essential to ensure the support of the mass of the German population – including the large socialist party – for the decision to go to war.

In the light of all the documentation available today, we can dismiss the claim that Germany was pushed by Russia into a defensive war in 1914. But this is not to say – as Fischer and his camp argue – that there is a clear and long-term line in German foreign policy leading to a general

▶ The signatures of Palmerston for Britain and Bülow for Germany on the 1839 Treaty guaranteeing Belgian independence were visible proof for British propaganda and public alike that the war against Germany was a just one.

▼▶ Europe's civil war in 1914–18 was also a war within European royal families, which were related through marriage. The interlocking of European royalty in the late 19th century is captured in this photograph which includes Wilhelm II and Nicholas II (numbers 2 and 3 in the key) in the family party surrounding Queen Victoria of the UK (1) at Baden-Baden in Germany.

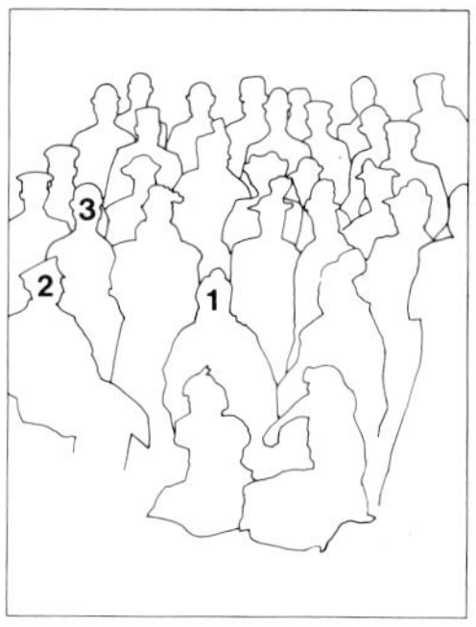

European war. The bywords of this interpretation of the war crisis are incompetence and mismanagement rather than deliberate design.

This second line of argument has been extended in recent years by what may be termed the "primacy of domestic politics" approach. The key to this view is that the men who made foreign policy were also acutely aware of the threat to the existing monarchical system posed by a growing socialist movement, especially (but not only) in Germany. Some leaders may therefore have felt that a victorious war would unify the nation and close the increasingly ominous gap between the classes. This provides further information as to why certain leaders were willing to take the calculated risk and, when pushed, to go to the brink of war and beyond.

As might be expected, this revised view provoked fresh controversy, with its critics arguing that it presents too simple and conspiratorial a vision of foreign policy as being no more than a diversionary tactic. Of course political leaders were conscious of domestic tensions and of the possible effect of their actions on them. But the links between foreign policy and domestic policy are rarely clear or direct.

Those who emphasize the domestic origins of foreign policy have provided a real service in broadening the study of the origins of the war from a purely diplomatic level. It is important to place foreign policy in a wider political framework and to look at its interaction with domestic affairs. The difficulty is in moving from a general background of events to the specific links between one sphere of politics and another: the domestic origins approach is a useful addition to other interpretations, not an alternative to them.

Collective guilt

One way of interpreting the different schools of thought on the origins of World War I is to see them as asking different kinds of questions and therefore as emphasizing different kinds of evidence. Fischer's school uses primarily diplomatic and military evidence to trace the evolution of German imperialist ambitions. The "calculated risk" school exploits similar sources, but also explores questions of social history and class conflict. A third line of argument stresses the usefulness of understanding intellectual history and the climate of opinion in the analysis of both the war crisis of 1914 and the first phase of the conflict – the war of illusions. This approach has been pioneered by the British historian James Joll, who has pointed out the "unspoken assumptions" of both leaders and masses in 1914. Thus some scholars have moved beyond the field of German foreign policy to suggest that a more universal set of miscalculations and mistakes contributed to both the atmosphere in which the war crisis developed and its ultimate resolution in war. In this school of thought German belligerence is not excused, but rather it assumes an integral part in a wider European failure to keep the peace.

This interpretation rests upon a substantial body of evidence as to the pervasive unreality of perceptions, expectations and predictions that

▲ **These wreath-layers are mourning the assassination of Jean Jaurès, the French socialist leader, on 31 July 1914 in Paris, a murder which robbed France and the international socialist movement, of their most eloquent leader. The voice of Jaurès was that of a moralist, denouncing capitalism as an outrage against human decency and fraternity. The founder-editor of the socialist newspaper *L'Humanité*, Jaurès spoke out fervently in a language which was both patriotic and internationalist. He was the author of a study of popular defense, *The New Army*, and the central figure in futile attempts to mobilize the socialist Second International against war in 1914.**

characterized the judgment of *all* the major political leaders of the European powers and of public opinion, both during the growing crisis of 1912–14 and in the first six months of war.

Those who advance this argument accept that the growth of German power made international politics inherently unstable in the prewar period. But they assert that structures do not go to war; individual states do so on the advice of their leaders, who, in turn, are pushed on by nationalist and militaristic lobbies. Hence they base their view of the crisis on an analysis of how international affairs were perceived by key political figures in all the major powers of Europe.

Scholars who believe in collective responsibility for the outbreak of war stress the limitations of the argument (endorsed by the Versailles peace treaty) that Germany was exclusively to blame for the outbreak of war. They admit that German support for Austria was crucial in the escalation of hostilities described above. But the other actors in this drama, they assert, also bear a degree of responsibility for the growing tensions and ultimately the transformation of a Balkan conflict into a world war, largely because so many of the key decisions they made in 1914 were based on misperceptions, miscalculations and illusions as well as on power-politics and imperialism.

Illusions about war

Such illusions were of many kinds and were shared by many politicians and other people in all the warring nations. Of all the illusions of 1914, five stand out: first, the illusion that since war involved domestic risks, both political and economic, relatively unstable regimes would avoid it; second, the illusion of the fail-safe and rational character of diplomacy; third, the illusion that any war would not be long; fourth, the illusion that war could be controlled and limited; fifth, the illusion that war could be a means of rebirth and rejuvenation.

Thus it comes that all nations attempting to live by conquest end by being themselves the victims of a military tyranny precisely similar to that which they hope to inflict; or, in other terms, that the attempt to impose by force of arms a disadvantageous commercial situation to the advantage of the conqueror ends in the conqueror's falling a victim to the very disadvantages from which he hoped by a process of spoilation to profit.

NORMAN ANGELL, 1910

The Third Republic in France

By 1914 the French Third Republic had been in existence for 43 years – far longer than any previous system of government in France since the Revolution of 1789. For much of its history there had been bitter political strife; yet, against all odds, the Republic had survived. And as a result of its unexpected durability, France had been able to recover from the defeat by Prussia in 1870–71 and to become a great power again. By the standards of the period, republican France was an advanced democracy in which all adult males were entitled to vote. But no political party ever won a majority of seats in the chamber of deputies, so that each new government had to be based on a fragile coalition, and prime ministers rarely held office for more than a few months.

The Republic faced its greatest internal crisis over the Dreyfus affair, which began in 1894 with the conviction for treason of a Jewish army officer. Attempts to prove Dreyfus innocent were frustrated by the army's general staff. Heightened by antisemitism, "the Affair" developed into a political confrontation between the parties committed to the Republic and the reactionary forces hostile to it – the army, the Church and the royalists. Dreyfus was eventually rehabilitated in 1906. It was a triumph for republicanism, but the Affair left bitter memories.

The early years of the 20th century brought new dissensions. Animosity between Church and State culminated in complete separation between the two. As gradual industrialization swelled the ranks of the working class, the Left became a force in French politics, and militant trade unionism challenged the established social order. But from about 1905 there was also a striking revival of right-wing and extreme nationalist feeling.

Meanwhile, French governments had worked since 1871 to improve the country's international standing. France followed the German example by introducing universal education and mass conscription. Frenchmen continued to resent the defeat of 1870 and the loss of Alsace-Lorraine to Germany, but dreams of a war of revenge faded as Germany forged ahead in industrial development and population. Partly in compensation, France turned to colonial expansion, mainly in Africa and Indo-China. In quest of security in Europe, France made an alliance with Russia (1894) and, formed an understanding, or "Entente", with the UK (1904).

In the last years of peace the French took a firmer line against Germany. Internal antagonisms persisted, however, and in 1913 a bill to extend military service to three years was fiercely resisted by the antimilitarist Left. But antimilitarism evaporated as soon as war was declared, and a united France prepared to face the enemy. In doing so, the population of France became fully Republican for the first time. The war had indeed created a political culture which was to last until 1940 and be reborn in 1944.

▶ **The trial of Captain Dreyfus, 1894.**

Raymond Poincaré 1850–1934

President of France throughout the 1914–18 war, Poincaré had a long and varied political career behind him. He served in various ministries in the 1890s, and became prime minister and minister of foreign affairs in 1912. During this period he introduced proportional representation and guided France through the Agadir crisis with Germany. The following year he was elected president, a post he held for seven years. In 1914 he learned of the Austrian ultimatum to Serbia while travelling home after a state visit to Russia. During the war he stood back while others ran the war. In the peace negotiations after the Armistice, Poincaré counted for little. He retired from the presidency in 1920, but reentered politics as a senator from the Department of the Meuse, where he had been born and raised. In January 1922 he once more became prime minister, and presided over the French occupation of the Ruhr, following Germany's failure to pay reparations. He formed three more coalition governments in the 1920s and died in 1934.

René Viviani 1863–1925

Algerian-born, Viviani was first elected as a socialist deputy for Paris in 1893. In 1906 he became minister of labor in Clemenceau's ministry, but created more of a stir by the clear enunciation of his nonreligious beliefs. By 1914 he had also served as minister of foreign affairs. In June 1914 he became premier. On the outbreak of war his oratory lifted the nation. He accompanied the government to Bordeaux in September 1914, and returned in December. In 1915 he made way as premier for Aristide Briand, and served as minister of justice. He shared the fate of all French politicians – with the exception of Clemenceau – of acting more as a figurehead than a formulator of policy during the war.

The first illusion was that a general European war would not break out since it was not worth the risk to the fragile political cohesion of several regimes. This belief may have prevented some politicians from acting to stop the spread of the conflict until it was too late. In economic terms, many people argued that the idea of war between the great powers was an absurdity, since no one in power stood the slightest chance of making any gain worth the required risk. Before the war, others had stated that a general European war had become an economic impossibility. Many of the world's bankers concurred; to them war would lead to international financial collapse and for Britain bankruptcy, as, in a way, it did. In 1911 the English author Norman Angell had published *The Great Illusion,* which argued that no one profited from war. In the midst of the war crisis Sir Edward Grey, British foreign secretary, predicted that bread queues would form in Britain by Christmas. To many people, then, a decision to go to war on a grand scale was economically irrational and out of the question.

Equally it seemed to make no political sense. The argument was raised that the so-called "Eastern Question" – what to do about the chronic instability of the region contested by Turkey, Austria and Russia – was a perennial political headache rather than a real threat to the peace of Europe; after all, numerous crises – in the Balkans and elsewhere – had come and gone in the two decades before 1914. Why should the assassination in Sarajevo lead to trouble when other explosive incidents had been defused? Furthermore, they pointed out that most of the crowned heads of Europe were related to each other and shared certain clearly conservative aspirations that could be compromised by war. Few monarchists needed a reminder that at the Stuttgart conference of 1907 the socialist parties affiliated to the Socialist International had committed themselves to taking all necessary steps to stop the outbreak of war. This would not rule out a general strike which could lead to revolution. Armed conflict therefore involved real internal risks for all European powers. In Germany the social democratic party, since 1912 the largest single party in the Reichstag (the German parliament), was committed to the eventual takeover of the state; who in his right mind would present them with the chance to achieve their ambition? The threat of industrial unrest was seen in Italy in May 1914, when some of the worst strikes in history took place. Armies might be infected with dissent: who was rash enough to believe in the loyalty of the many nationalities who served in the armies of the Austro-Hungarian and Russian Empires? Some regimes were thought to be particularly vulnerable. After 1905 the Russian monarchy was regarded as most unstable.

In France and Britain it was doubted that there would be sufficient popular support for a decision to go to war. In France memories of the Dreyfus affair (1894–1906) were still very fresh. This controversy, over the false imprisonment of a Jewish officer on trumped-up charges of espionage, and the subsequent military cover-up had split the French nation. Supporters of the army and supporters of "justice and the people" had grown dangerously apart, at a time of growing socialist agitation. For many reasons, therefore, lists were prepared of troublemakers to be arrested in the event of war (known as the *Carnet B*). In Britain realistic doubts about the army's willingness to enforce Home Rule in Ireland (demonstrated in the so-called Curragh mutiny) implied questions about its general loyalty.

If this first set of opinions – that cautious people would avoid war because it was a Pandora's box – was clearly mistaken, then scholars who argue for collective responsibility for the outbreak of the 1914 war suggest that we must look elsewhere for the true reasons for the outbreak of war. Effectively they pose two questions. Why did all the Great Powers take the risk of war in the summer of 1914? And why, when their individual and collective bluff was called, did they actually go to war? Many clues, they note, may be found in other illusions of the men in power in 1914, as they operated against the background of years of nationalist and militarist agitation.

The Russian Empire

In 1914 Czar Nicholas II reigned over a vast, backward, multinational empire that stretched from Poland to the Caucasus, Central Asia and Siberia. Nicholas was an autocrat whose regime relied on a brutal if inefficient system of repression. Prison, exile and death were meted out to dissidents. Intense efforts were made to impose the Russian language and culture on all the czar's subjects, and from the 1880s, as opposition mounted, popular antisemitism was encouraged as a safety valve for discontent; widespread pogroms shocked the civilized world and persuaded hundreds of thousands of Russian Jews to emigrate, mainly to the USA. Inevitably, liberal-minded people everywhere looked on czarist Russia with distaste – yet the two most progressive great powers, France and the UK, made alliances with the czar.

The czar's subjects numbered about 150 million, of whom the overwhelming majority were peasants. Nevertheless, great changes were taking place in Russia. Industrialization had made rapid headway and there had been a dramatic increase in the reach of the railway network. Above all the growth of an industrial, urban working class transformed the political situation. Densely concentrated, badly paid and badly treated, it promised to become a highly effective force in the struggle against the autocracy. Trade unionism gathered strength and socialist ideas exercised a wide influence, even though most of the socialist leaders were imprisoned or living in exile abroad.

The autocracy remained unmoved until 1904–05, when Russian expansion in the Far East led to a war against the rising power of Japan. Humiliating reverses on land and sea discredited the regime, and "Bloody Sunday" – a massacre of peaceful demonstrators bound for the Winter Palace – dealt the czar's reputation as the "Little Father" of his people a blow from which it never recovered. Strikes, mutinies and disorders in town and country paralyzed the government, and Nicholas had to grant a constitution and set up a "parliament", the Duma. However, these concessions enabled the czar to ride out and eventually destroy the 1905 Revolution: nothing survived but an emasculated Duma.

For a few years the autocracy seemed to be in the ascendant. But from 1912 strikes and disturbances became ever more frequent, while the rural order became destabilized by an ambitious attempt to create a new class of capitalist farmers. War came into this threatening situation when the long Balkan rivalry between Austria-Hungary and Russia, exacerbated by Russian disquiet at German influence in Turkey, produced a crisis that found neither side ready to back down. Yet Russia in 1914 was ill-prepared for war and industrially far behind its allies and enemies.

Military reversals in Galicia led to the entry of civilians, including representatives of the Duma, into the administration of the war economy. But the czar resisted calls for a coalition government, along British and French lines, to control munitions production and rally public support for the war. In September 1915 he prorogued the Duma and dismissed all liberal cabinet members in favor of coalition government. While the czar took up his post of commander in chief of his armies, the czarina commanded the court, filled with sycophants, charlatans, and religious fanatics, and stood in the path of any political reform, any hint of which was drowned out by a thunder of reactionary piety. Even the assassination of Rasputin did not deflect the czarina from placing every obstacle in the path of change. The meeting of the Duma was postponed again and again; when it was finally convened in February 1917, disturbances broke out in Petrograd, and soldiers refused to put them down. This was the beginning of the revolution which would put an end to the monarchy and to a war which brought Russia nothing but disaster.

◀ The symbol of the corruption of the Romanov court was Gregory Rasputin, pictured here with a group of female admirers. His name means "the debauched one", and despite a poor background and no education, he managed to live up to it in the highest circles in the land. "Sin in order that you may obtain forgiveness" was Rasputin's message, proclaimed with a passion which converted lechery into a pietistic act. In 1907 he was presented at court, and made a deep impression on the czar and czarina, and became a power in church and court circles in the next decade. He was murdered in 1916 by his court enemies, but the empress built a chapel to his memory and worshiped at his grave.

The volatility of international politics

This is the place to consider the second illusion: that war could be avoided by traditional diplomatic gambits, which were based on rational and cool assessment of national interest. This illusion suffered from two flaws. The first was that the international political system in the years before 1914 was more volatile than anyone had realized. In the hands of a man like Otto von Bismarck, the founder and first chancellor of the German Empire, diplomacy was a game of chess played by a grandmaster. His aim had been to isolate France and never to allow Germany to be isolated from three of the Great Powers, with the support of only one other major nation. Since gaming images abound in studies of international relations, it may not be too fanciful to suggest that after Bismarck left the scene in 1890, world politics moved from the realm of chess to that of roulette or poker. The stakes were higher, the skill and intelligence of the players were less important than their nerve and their luck, and the outcome of events was far less predictable.

Any system of international affairs that relied on the skill of one major figure to keep it from falling apart was bound to collapse sooner or later. But the fact that it did so in 1914 is related to another feature of the war crisis, which is an area of much controversy. Some historians believe that the diplomats of 1914 saw perfectly well what they were doing. But others state that they failed to see until it was too late how dangerous a game they were playing. Furthermore – and this is the second flaw in the argument for "rational" diplomancy as a bulwark against war – they shared a tendency to miscalculate the intentions of both allies and adversaries. It is true, scholars in this tradition note, that some politicians in Vienna saw a short Balkan war as part of a wider scheme, and on 5 July Germany did offer its ally support for action against Serbia. But they also argue that, whatever was in the minds of the German military or of their political supporters, a general European war was not the objective of the diplomatic maneuvering of the major powers in 1914. That this happened anyway was because those in power did not adequately understand their adversaries' minds or likely responses.

This argument has already appeared in considering the approach of the "calculated risk" interpretation of the war crisis. But what the "collective guilt" school of thought suggests is that the failure of crisis management was general rather than specifically or primarily German. For example, there was insufficient appreciation in several European capitals of the dynamic potential of public opinion. As a result of the formation of a wide array of political groups working for imperial glory or increased armaments expenditure or the "mission" of the nation, the pressures on the international system had grown ominously in the prewar decades. Patriotic leagues were manipulated by politicians, but public opinion once aroused was difficult to ignore. It could be "turned on" – but not so easily "turned off". Consequently "rational" games in international politics had become more difficult to manage, as those in power in 1914 recognized belatedly.

The "collective guilt" school suggests a powerful image of international affairs: that of an outmoded but still intact roulette table at which a handful of old men staked empires and literally millions of lives. This indicates something of the character of the war crisis of 1914. But once the "game" was over, and war had begun, new illusions began to crowd out the old.

Belief in swift and decisive warfare

The third illusion was that any war would be short: in 1914 men went to war believing it would be over by Christmas. This illusion was a consequence of the military training of conscript armies in the prewar period. All had been versed in a war of movement which would lead to decisive victory. Something resembling this kind of warfare occurred in the east, but nothing of the kind occurred on the Western Front. Without a quick victory on the Western Front, the dream of a short war evaporated.

With it went the fourth illusion of the first months of war: that conflict was a kind of local

◀ Nicholas II was the perfect illustration of the central defect of absolute monarchies: their tendency, through the accident of birth, to place men without the ability or the desire to lead in a position of authority they neither sought nor could spurn. The czar of Russia, shown here with his second daughter Tatiana, the young czarevitch (heir to the throne) Alexei, and Prince Nikita in 1916, was a shy and awkward man, who longed for the peace of family life which he would never know. His son Alexei was a hemophiliac, whose perilous situation turned the czar (and even more emphatically, the czarina) to the help of "holy men" like Rasputin. The czar's natural tendency was to look back to the remote and religious past for guidance in his attitude to contemporary developments. The temperaments of the czar and czarina thus presented reactionaries with a splendid weapon to foil reform. After revolution and abdication, Nicholas and his family were murdered by revolutionaries in July 1918.

surgery – painful, no doubt, to those at the cutting edge of war, but unlikely to disturb the health or life of the nation as a whole. Indeed there were many who argued precisely the opposite, along the lines of the fifth illusion: that war was a redemptive event, able to tear millions from their petty preoccupations, and give a new sense of direction to the nation.

In 1914 this did seem to have occurred. The so-called "subversives" on the French police lists could not be arrested in August 1914 because most had joined the army. The rhetoric of the Socialist International vanished in a puff of smoke, with socialist deputies in the German Reichstag voting for war credits. Protestant and Catholic Irishmen volunteered by the thousand.

But this remarkable moment of social solidarity was also partly an illusion. Class collaboration did not destroy class conflict in 1914. It masked it for a time, but only for a time, and when it returned it showed that perhaps the most profound illusion of the early days of the 1914–18 conflict was the belief in the unifying effects of war.

Toward a synthesis

One of the least satisfying aspects of the acrimonious debate over the war crisis of 1914 is that historians refuse to see that there are merits in all three interpretations. In a sense they must be combined to get a full sense of the causes of the war. Fischer is indisputably correct in asserting the imperialist ambitions of the German leadership in the prewar period. The "calculated risk" school is also justified in distinguishing the different phases of the war crisis. And the "collective guilt" argument presents powerful reasons to indict the leaders of other countries for a general failure to protect the peace of Europe. Perhaps the best way to fuse these arguments is to speak of levels of responsibility.

At the heart of the war crisis was the political and military leadership of Germany, and in its wake, that of Austria-Hungary. Given the structure of the German political system, the chancellor, Bethmann-Hollweg, was under great pressure from the military. He tried to appear to be a peacemaker while helping to create favorable conditions for a German declaration of war. What Bethmann-Hollweg did was to present Germany's case in the best possible light, as a defensive war not of making. The fact that this is not corroborated by the documents that are now available means that primary responsibility for war must rest in Berlin and nowhere else.

Recently published research on all major European countries has established that the war was not planned nor fostered in any countries other than Germany and Austria-Hungary. Without German ambitions and without the joint German-Austrian handling of the July crisis, war would not have broken out.

But to argue that responsibility for the war crisis and war ends there is short-sighted and misleading, for it acquits the leaders of the other European countries of secondary responsibility for war. On the one hand, somebody had to pull the trigger. That was Germany. But on the other hand, its actions exposed the weaknesses and confusions of both its allies and its adversaries. Their collective illusions about war may help to explain why greater and more effective efforts were not made to defuse the conflict.

The other European states must bear some responsibility for the war, first, because of their false and incomplete appreciation of the nature of international affairs in an age of imperialist designs and mass politics; and secondly, because of their fateful miscalculations of the likely responses of their adversaries to their own policy initiatives. If Germany may be said to have brought about World War I, it did so as part of a political community which collectively let the peace of Europe slip through its fingers.

Sir Edward Grey 1862–1933

Educated at Winchester and Oxford, Sir Edward Grey entered the House of Commons as a Liberal at the age of 23. he served as a junior minister in Liberal ministries in 1892–95, and became a foreign minister in 1905. His real test came in the war crisis of 1914. He saw immediately in the Austrian ultimatum to Serbia the potential for a general war, and tried various schemes of conciliation and mediation. All failed. What troubled his conscience in later years was whether he had made British policy sufficiently clear. The nagging doubt remained that caution and diplomatic language had been the wrong choice; bluntness and threats were the only way to derail the war party in Germany. Grey's education and temperament suited him to uphold the principles of honor and decency, exemplified by the defense of Belgium, but they did not enable him to prevent a war waged by more ruthless men. He resigned in 1916 due to failing eyesight. His departure from the foreign office after 11 years as foreign minister symbolized the end of an era, and perhaps the end of Liberalism itself.

◀ George V began the war as head of the House of Saxe-Coburg-Gotha, or the house of Hannover or Brunswick, and ended it as head of the House of Windsor. The severing of symbolic ties with German royalty was one way to support the war effort. Another was as confidant of General Haig, commander in chief of the British Expeditionary Force in France.

▲ After two elections in 1910, a Home Rule bill for Ireland was introduced by the ruling Liberal government. The bill was passed twice by the House of Commons and rejected by the House of Lords. In 1914 the Liberals introduced a compromise whereby the six provinces in the north of Ireland with a Protestant majority had the right to opt out of home rule for six years. The Home Rule bill passed for the third time on 26 May 1914, and under the Parliament Act of 1911 it was no longer subject to veto by the Lords. The measure became law on 18 September 1914, but its operation was suspended for the duration of the war. In fact it was a casualty of the war.

The United Kingdom

In 1914 the United Kingdom of Great Britain and Ireland appeared to be at the height of its power. A worldwide empire covered a fifth of the land surface of the globe. A vast network of imperial trade and comunications was sustained by a supremely powerful navy and merchant marine. Economically Britain continued to be highly productive, although its industrial structure was beginning to look a little old-fashioned by comparison with the dynamic economies of the USA and Germany. But its position in international trade was second to none; the City of London was the world's greatest money market; and Britain's prosperity seemed further assured by the immense volume of its investments abroad in both its imperial possessions and the USA.

Most Britons were proud of their institutions, including the "Mother of Parliaments" at Westminster, despite the fact that most men and all women were still without the right to vote. The two main parties were the Liberals and Conservatives, not yet seriously threatened by the Labour Party, which had been represented in Parliament only since 1906. By 1914 the Liberals had been in office for eight years; the period had been one of significant social reforms, including the introduction of old age pensions and, for some groups of workers, of national insurance against sickness and unemployment.

Yet early 20th-century Britain was beset by social conflict. In 1909 the House of Lords rejected Lloyd George's "People's Budget", mainly because it included a capital gains tax on landed property; after two bitter elections, the Lords were forced to consent to the Parliament Act of 1911, abolishing their absolute veto on legislation. Social unrest threatened for a time when an epidemic of strikes broke out in 1910–12, but ideas of direct union action to overthrow capitalism were never put to the test. By contrast, a determined suffragette campaign to win votes for women went over to often sensational militant action, and British society was shocked by the sight of respectable ladies being sent to prison and, when they went on hunger strike, forcibly fed.

The most serious problem concerned Ireland. Since 1885 the Liberals had been pledged to meet the demands of the majority of Irishmen by introducing a Home Rule Bill. This was fiercely opposed by the Conservatives, who encouraged the Protestant Ulstermen to arm and, if necessary, resist by force any attempt to incorporate them into a self-governing Ireland with a Catholic majority. In 1914, when the Home Rule Act finally reached the statute book, civil war in Ireland seemed possible. It even looked as if senior army officers might be unwilling to enforce the Act. But the war crisis buried the Act before it came into force.

In foreign affairs the UK had formed the "*entente cordiale*" with France in 1904 and had resolved many differences with Russia in 1907. By 1914 military and naval cooperation with France had become routine. The British fleet was concentrated in the Atlantic, leaving the French to guard the Mediterranean; and army reforms had created a highly trained force ready for service on the continent.

But in 1914 war was not seen as imminent. Relations with Germany were better than they had been for some time, and even after the Sarajevo assassinations the British foreign secretary, Sir Edward Grey, believed that the Austro–Serbian dispute could be settled by an international conference in London. The German invasion of Belgium ended British neutrality, and opened a war which, even in victory, impoverished the UK and marked the beginning of its decline to a second-rank power.

Herbert Henry Asquith 1852–1928

The son of a Yorkshire cloth manufacturer, H.H. Asquith moved south after his father's death and had a brilliant career at Oxford University. He was an accomplished barrister, who easily moved from the courtroom to the cabinet room. His first post was home secretary in W.E. Gladstone's government in 1892. In the following decade he championed first Liberal imperialism and then free trade. The latter issue brought the Liberals to power in 1906, and made Asquith chancellor of the exchequer. Two years later he succeeded Henry Campbell-Bannerman as prime minister. He presided over the most spectacular program of social reform in 20th-century British history.

His cabinet ran the war until May 1915, when, after serious problems of munitions supply and disputes over the Gallipoli invasion, he formed a coalition government. This arrangement undermined Asquith's position: he received all the criticism for mistakes and his chancellor of the exchequer, Lloyd George, all the credit for successes. In December 1916 Lloyd George ousted Asquith, who led the Liberal Party into the political wilderness.

THE CENTRAL POWERS: THE COST OF WAR

The paradox of World War I was that Germany fought a war to gain an empire, but needed an empire in order to win the war. In other words, the economic strength of the Allies derived from their extra-European reserves of manpower, materiel and money. Germany and Austria-Hungary lacked this second line of supply, support and finance. The longer the war went on, the greater was the economic gap between the two sides. To try to bridge that gap, Germany launched unrestricted submarine warfare. This policy failed. In contrast the Allied blockade of central Europe was a major source of the greater cost of war to the Central Powers. Bureaucratic inefficiency, harvest failures, labor shortages and the Allied squeeze formed a recipe for black-marketeering, which flourished during the war. Official rations simply could not feed the German population; economic policy therefore made everybody break the law, and provided the opportunity for thousands of petty crooks and swindlers to make their fortunes.

Worsening inflation in the Central Powers was another sign of economic difficulties. While retail prices doubled in wartime Britain and France, they trebled or quadrupled in Germany and Austria-Hungary. Market prices were higher still. The driving force was military expenditure. To pay for it, the government simply printed money. Bills in circulation in wartime Germany rose by over 1,000 percent.

The German war economy was totally unbalanced. Germany spent 83 percent of total public expenditure on military items; 2 percent on the civilian sector. The figures in Britain were 62 percent and 16 percent respectively. The needs of the army and heavy industry came first. While this may appear to be common sense in wartime, it was an invitation to disaster. The strength of a war economy is its efficiency in distributing scarce goods and services between competing groups. The Allies succeeded here, because they had greater resources, and because they never starved home populations to keep armies well provisioned.

Some groups prospered in wartime. War contractors did not go poor, and for workers in war industries, pay was good, though hours were interminable. Unemployment vanished and wages rose, especially those of unskilled workers, but for most people in Vienna, Prague, Budapest or Berlin, the war was a time of severe deprivation. People generally accepted these difficult conditions in order to win the war. This explains the extraordinary disparity between the remarkable feats of wartime industrial production and the impoverishment of the population. Heavy industry boomed while ordinary people went hungry. This bifurcated world of industrial power and material deprivation was the breeding ground both for mass protest and for imperialist designs to create a vast economic empire in the east, the wealth of which would help compensate the German people for the hardships endured during the war. Such plans, like the German economy itself, never stood a chance of success.

▼ These captured German weapons represent one tiny fragment of the vast outpouring of human and material capital that went into armaments manufacture before and during the war. The Central Powers placed arms production before every other economic priority. The resulting imbalances and strains ultimately brought about their defeat.

▼ Austro-Hungarian and German agriculture should have made the Central Powers self-sufficient in food. But shortages of labor and nitrates, exacerbated by mismanagement, led inexorably to a steep decline in agricultural production (bottom). By 1917 prewar levels of food supply had been halved. This was the economics of the soup kitchen.

► **Army, bureaucracy and industry in Germany combined to create a vast industrial complex to produce materiel. Manufacturers set their own price and profit levels, and passed on the bill to the state. The state printed paper money to pay for the war, setting off the worst inflationary spiral in European history.**

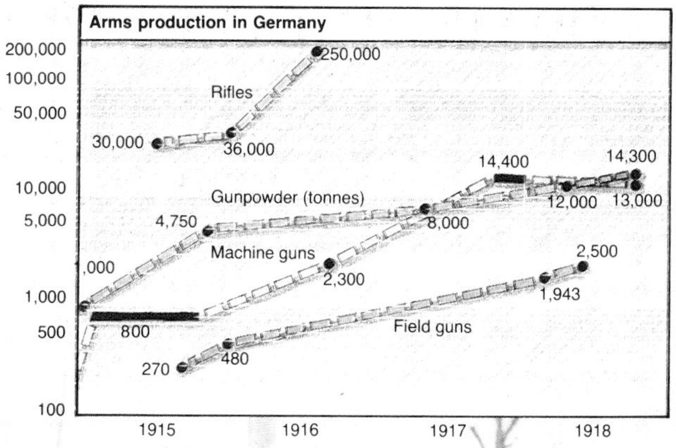

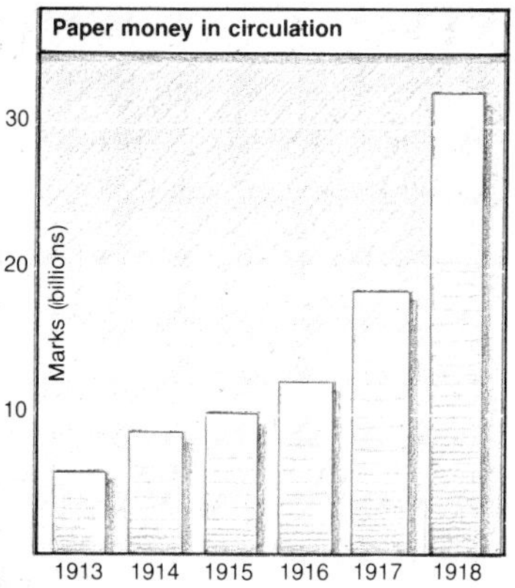

Datafile

In 1914 Germany had the economic advantage. It had internal lines of supply and a highly professional army logistical corps. But the balance of economic power shifted to the Allies after 1915; thanks to their blockade and economic management. Domestically and internationally, the Allies succeeded with a vast program of economic mobilization, on which military victory ultimately rested.

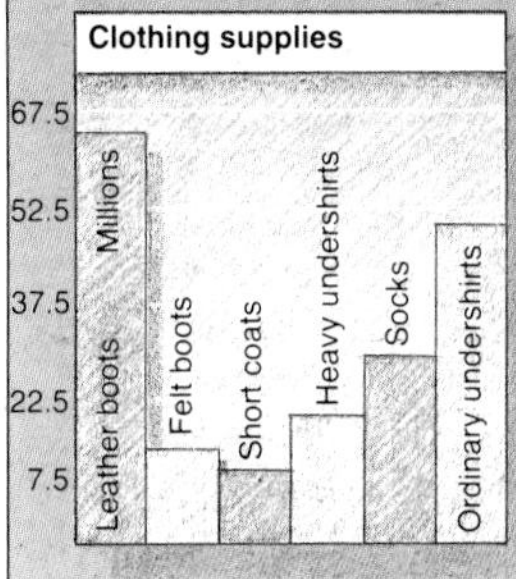

◄ The materiel supplied by domestic industry to the Russian army testifies to both the scale of operations on the Eastern Front and the strength of Russian production. Economic power in wartime was less a question of output than of management and control, which eventually collapsed in Russia.

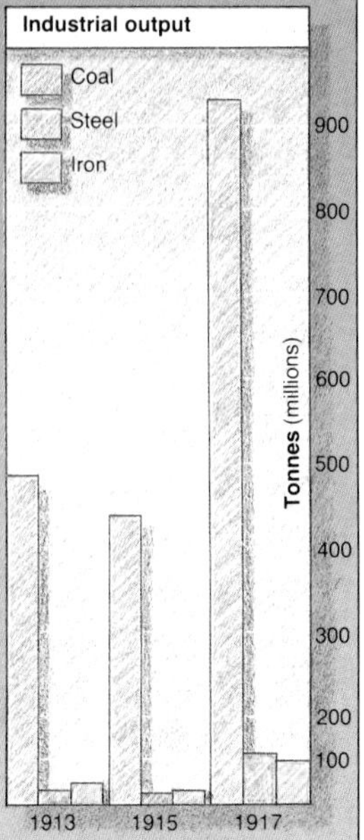

▲ The loss of the industrial northeast of France after the German invasion of 1914 was a severe blow to the Allies' economies. In addition the mobilization of manpower for the Allied armies was bound to reduce output, until American production doubled or trebled Allied resources in the last year of the war.

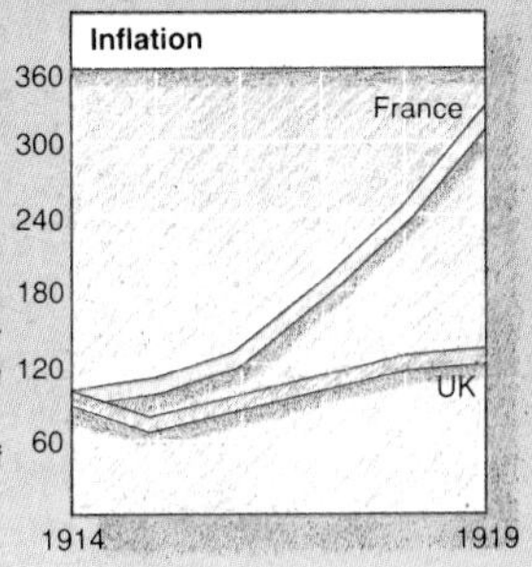

► Between 1914 and 1918 prices roughly doubled in both France and Britain. Inflation impoverished those on fixed rents or incomes, salaried workers and some manual workers. Those working in the munitions sector – over 70 percent of all workers by 1917 – had real wages equal to or above those of 1914.

Chronology

1915

February 8–22
Winter Battle of Masuria: Germans and Austro-Hungarians force Russians to retreat

February 15
Entente governments support Greek aid to Serbia and offer military support at Salonika

March 10–13
Battle of Neuve Chapelle: British and Indian offensive on Western Front captures village of Neuve Chapelle

April 22
(to May 27) Second Battle of Ypres: German offensive on Western Front against Ypres fails to capture the town

April 25
(to Jan. 9 1916) Allied land campaign against Turks on Gallipoli peninsula

April 26
IT: Treaty of London commits Italy to war on the side of the Entente Powers

May 2–4
Battle of Gorlice-Tarnow: Central Powers break Russian line

May 4
(to 18 June) Second Battle of Artois: French make small gain on Western Front

May 7
German submarine sinks passenger liner *Lusitania*

May 9–10
Battle of Aubers ridge: unsuccessful British offensive on Western Front against Germans

May 15–25
Battle of Festubert: unsuccessful British and Canadian offensive on Western Front against Germans

May 23
Italy declares war on Austria-Hungary

May 25
UK: Asquith forms coalition government

China and Japan sign treaty concerning South Manchuria and Inner Mongolia

May 26
IT: Italian government announces blockade of Austro-Hungarian coast

July 2
UK: Ministry of munitions formed with David Lloyd George as minister

July 30
Pope Benedict XV appeals to belligerent governments for peace

August 25
IT: Italy declares war on Turkey

August 26
IT: Italy declares war on Germany

September 25
(to Oct. 6) French offensive in Champagne: small amount of territory gained from Germans

September 25
(to Oct. 14) Third Battle of Artois: French offensive on Western Front brings small gain of territory from the Germans

September 25
(to Nov. 4) Battle of Loos: British offensive on the Western Front captures the town of Loos

October 14
Bulgaria enters war on side of Central Powers

October 30
FR: Briand replaces Viviani as premier and foreign minister

November 10
UK: order in (privy) council authorizes requisition of ships for carriage of foodstuffs

November 30
France, UK, Russia, Japan sign Pact of London

On the outbreak of hostilities the illusion of a short war was shared by most political and military leaders. Six months later, by the beginning of 1915, it began to dawn on all but those still intoxicated by their own propaganda that victory had receded over the horizon. The central preoccupation of those in authority on both sides now became what to do next. Their responses were similar. They tried to protect their political position both internationally and internally by concluding alliances or tacit agreements to strengthen the platform from which decisive military action could be launched, either in France and Flanders or on the Eastern Front.

In addition they further extended the war to the economic realm. This took many forms, but the most important was through blockade. Naval interdiction of supplies was a mutual act. Starting in August 1914, Germany mined the English Channel and within a few months the UK declared that consignments destined for Germany on neutral ships would be treated as contraband unless proven otherwise. Both measures were bound to raise the political stakes of the war, since they touched neutral – and in particular, American – shipping and ultimately took the lives of hundreds of noncombatants as well.

The geographic expansion of the war had another implication. The failure of the German offensive to achieve an early victory meant that the war would drag on, and that it would be fought on many fronts and in many countries. This occasioned a fierce political debate in all combatant countries over where the major emphasis on military action should be placed. The shorthand for this intense and protracted argument is to describe it as a difference between "Easterners" and "Westerners". This is much too simple a distinction. Both the political and the military leadership of the UK and France were united about the purpose of the war: to destroy German militarism and remove the German army from all of France and Belgium. The disputes were about how to achieve these aims. In 1915 a joint approach was tried: to keep up pressure in the west while launching a daring operation in the east to knock Germany's new ally, Turkey, out of the war. The failure of this campaign (on the Gallipoli Peninsula) gave the upper hand to the "Westerners" in future strategic debates.

New belligerents

That Turkey fought on the side of the Central Powers in World War I was one of the major German political triumphs of the early years of the conflict. Turkish inclinations were seen as early as 11 August 1914 when the German warships *Goeben* and *Breslau* passed through the Dardanelles, the Turkish straits between the

1915 STALEMATE AND STAGNATION

Political leaders react to the failure to achieve a quick victory

The blockades begin

The search for new alliances

Turkey supports the Central Powers

Germany lands Bulgaria

Italy supports the Allies

Wartime politics: military dictatorship supported by civilian coalitions

In central and eastern Europe the war divides the socialist movement

Aegean Sea and the Sea of Marmara, eluding British warships in the Mediterranean. The Turkish government officially purchased the cruisers to replace two that had been on order in British shipyards, but which had been commandeered by the British government on the outbreak of war, damaging Britain's standing in Istanbul.

This clear political sign of the attitude of the Turkish government was a worrying development. Numerous British diplomatic gestures were made to secure at least Turkish neutrality, but to no avail. Here was a major German diplomatic victory. In drawing Turkey into the Central Powers, Germany demonstrated that it could outbid Britain and spread the war to a point where British interests in the Middle East were threatened. Even more alarming for the Allies was the menace to the southern reaches of Russia. On 29 October the two cruisers shelled the Russian Black Sea ports of Odessa, Sevastopol and Theodosia. Russia declared war on Turkey three days later; Britain followed on 5 November.

With Turkey on the side of the Central Powers, the position of Bulgaria became of great strategic importance. Once again the bargaining for an alliance produced counteroffers aimed at satisfying Bulgarian territorial ambitions. What Bulgaria wanted was territory claimed or occupied by Serbia, Greece and Romania. This put Germany in an unassailable position. To satisfy Bulgaria the

The Ottoman Empire

In 1914 the Ottoman or Turkish Empire stretched from the Bulgarian and Russian coasts of the Black Sea to the Arabian peninsula as far south as present-day Bahrain on the Persian Gulf and South Yemen on the Red Sea. It was an Islamic sultanate. In the early 19th century Constantinople had controlled the Balkans, all of North Africa and the Middle East as far as Iran. A century later the centrifugal forces of nationalism and imperialism had stripped the Empire of substantial areas. Serbia, Albania, Bulgaria and Romania had all been Ottoman provinces, but by 1914 they were independent states. By then predatory imperial powers had taken indirect or direct control of all of North Africa and much of the Middle East. European bankers and merchants came by the thousands, and created the transportation networks and infrastructure necessary for linking this huge region to the European and world economies. The classic pattern of exchange of raw materials and primary products for finished European goods entered a new phase, and older hierarchical social structures began to give way to the rudiments of "modernity". The political echoes of these changes may be heard in the slogans of the "Young Turk" movement, many of whose members were liberals exiled in Europe, and who brought back to Turkey a new and strident nationalism. Their influence in the army grew, and lay behind the successful revolt of 1908 against the dictatorship of Sultan Abdul Hamid, who was deposed the following year. His brother Mohammed became Sultan but had no power. The Young Turk leader, Enver Pasha, became minister of war. He admired German military strength, and sponsored the appointment of Liman von Sanders as inspector general of the Turkish army. On 30 July 1914 Turkey concluded a treaty with Germany, and entered the war three months later, on the German side.

▶ Territorial losses of the Ottoman Empire.

The Ottoman Empire

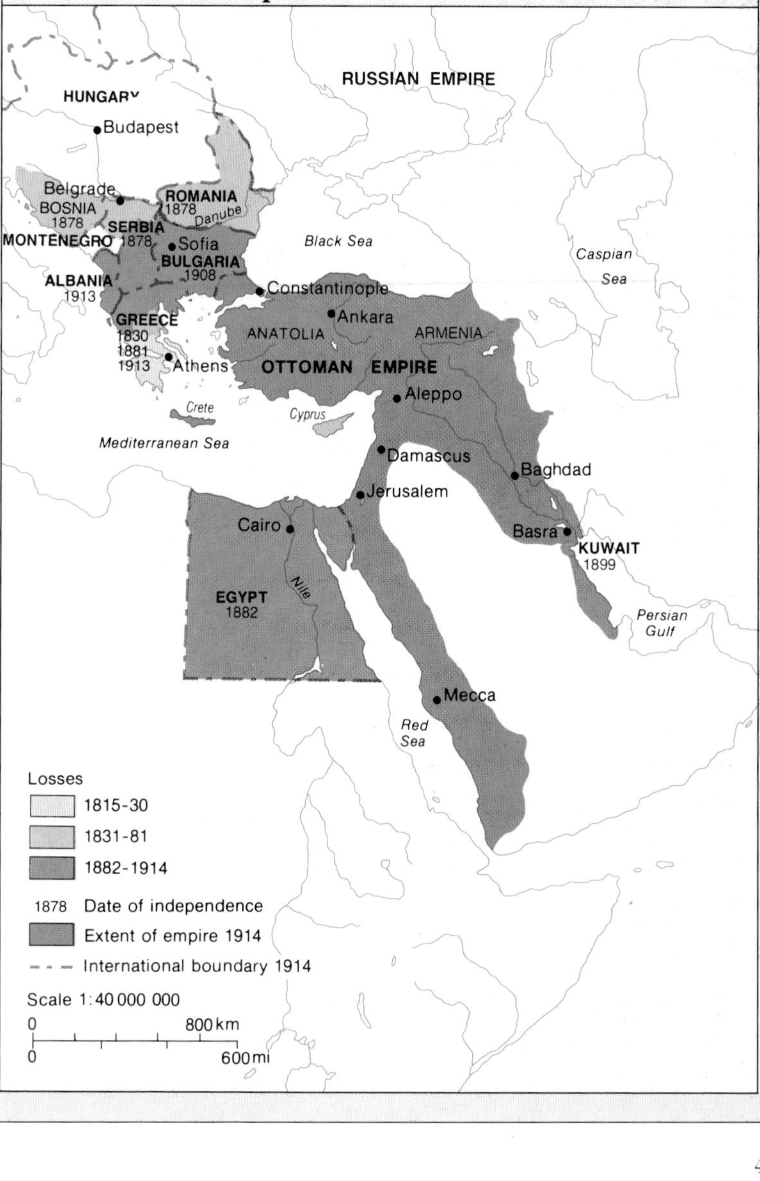

Allies would have to promise to raid one set of countries which were either already on their side, or which were being courted to join the Allied cause, in order to obtain the assistance of another set. Allied diplomats were not above doing this: it was rather that their promises lacked credibility. Consequently in September 1915 Bulgaria concluded an alliance (planned in 1913) with Germany and Austria-Hungary, received substantial financial credits, and mobilized for war against Serbia. As a result Serbia appealed to Greece for assistance, to which it was entitled under a treaty of May 1913. This was given in the form of Greek secret approval (and public disapproval) for an Allied landing in Greece at Salonika, which was intended to provide assistance for Serbia. (It took place in October – see p. 76.)

The German coup of landing Bulgaria as an ally counterbalanced to some extent the intervention of Italy on the Allied side a few months earlier in 1915. Italy had been allied to Germany and Austria-Hungary before the war, but took the attack on Serbia as an excuse to declare neutrality. Now the shoe was on the other foot: what had hampered Allied approaches to Bulgaria now stymied German pleas to Italy, since Italian territorial ambitions (to acquire Italian-speaking areas of Austria) collided with Austrian interests. Under German pressure Austria-Hungary granted concessions, but not enough to satisfy the Italians, who pressed for more than any Austrian government could politically afford to make. The Germans pressed the Austrians for more, to which Vienna reluctantly and belatedly agreed.

The delay coincided with the growth of a popular movement within Italy to bring it into the war on the side of the Allies. This brought together strange bedfellows: conservative nationalists and the king on the one hand, Futurist artists and socialists on the other. The Italian socialist Mussolini, who had originally opposed the war on socialist grounds, reversed his position within a few months and founded a newspaper, *Il Popolo d'Italia*, to put forward the interventionist case.

There is still some dispute about the extent to which all this was paid for by French subsidies; there is less argument about its effect. The campaign increased the pressure on the Italian government to jump off the tightrope of neutrality. It was prepared to do so, but of course only

◀ Kaiser Wilhelm II inspecting Bulgarian troops in the Serbian city of Nish, on the vital rail link between the Serbian capital of Belgrade and the Bulgarian capital of Sofia. Nish fell to the Bulgarians during combined operations with the German and Austrian armies on 5 November 1915.

◀ The accession to the throne of Romania in October 1914 of Ferdinand on the death of his uncle Carol – an ardent supporter of Austria – opened the way for Romanian entry into the war on the Allied side. This took place in August 1916 with disastrous results for Romania.

▼ The German cruiser *Breslau* in Constantinople harbor in August 1914. After eluding the British Royal Navy, the warship was purchased by the Turks.

Italy in 1915

Italy was not a great power in prewar Europe. Yet the rivalries between the true European great powers enabled Italy's leaders to fish in troubled waters, neglecting pressing problems at home in pursuit of an elusive and insubstantial greatness.

Like the German Empire, Italy was a recent arrival among European states. The Kingdom of Italy had been founded in 1860, uniting most of the peninsula. Its largely ineffective participation in the Austro-Prussian War of 1866 had gained her the Venetia, the last major province held by Austria. In 1870 the occupation of Rome, which became the capital, completed prewar Italy. The displaced ruler of Rome, the Pope, refused to accept his loss of political power or to recognize the new state. He became the voluntary "prisoner of the Vatican". For 20 years Catholics were forbidden to take part in Italian politics, and the breach between Church and State remained a serious difficulty in 1915.

The new Italy had an increasing population (36 million by 1914), but was economically backward and beset by problems such as widespread rural poverty and mass illiteracy. Against this background the parliamentary system functioned badly; political parties were poorly disciplined and engaged in the most unlikely alliances in order to gain power. Social reforms tended to be shelved or implemented with staggering inefficiency. Italian prime ministers generally occupied themselves with political intrigues or foreign affairs.

After 1870 many Italians hoped to claim *Italia irredenta* – "unredeemed Italy", territories with large Italian populations that were still under Austrian rule, notably Trentino in the north and the great Adriatic port of Trieste. But "irredentism" was not practical politics once Germany and Austria-Hungary had become allies, and Italy's leaders turned to colonial expansion. Italian designs on Tunis were frustrated by French action, and Franco-Italian hostility persisted into the mid-1890s; it was the principal reason for Italy's adhesion to the Triple Alliance of 1882, which brought it into partnership with Germany and Austria-Hungary.

Italian imperialism scored a modest success in 1885, when its outposts on the Red Sea were organized into the colony of Eritrea. But an Italian attempt to conquer Ethiopia turned into a disaster: the Italian army was crushed at the Battle of Adowa (1896) and Italy was forced to recognize Ethiopian independence. This unparalleled humiliation by a "native" people led to a suspension of Italian colonial ambitions, although Italian governments prepared for a takeover of Tripoli (present-day Libya), which was part of the Turkish Empire, by making a number of separate – and secret – agreements with each of the great powers. Finally, in 1911 Italy waged a successful war on Turkey; confronted with a looming Balkan War the Turks ceded Tripoli.

The Libyan war split the socialists and led to the expulsion of those who supported the government's African policy. The revolutionary left gained a majority at the 1912 party convention. Mussolini proclaimed the revolutionary line as editor of the party newspaper *Avanti*.

In 1914 Italy remained neutral, but the prime minister, Antonio Salandra, favored intervention, and during the winter of 1914–15 irredentist and interventionist sentiment gathered force. In effect, Italy sold itself to the highest bidder. In spite of intense German pressure, the Austrians yielded only slowly to Italian demands for the Trentino, Trieste and substantial territories in Dalmatia. By the time they agreed, it was too late. The Triple Entente had promised Italy everything it wanted, and in April 1915 it agreed to undertake hostilities against Austria-Hungary. Italians, like other peoples, entered the war in a blaze of enthusiasm.

Antonio Salandra 1853–1931

Salandra was an authoritarian conservative who presided over both Italy's decis ion to adopt a neutral stance in August 1914 and its decision to go to war ten months later in May 1915. He entered politics after training as a barrister and a career as a professor of public administration at the University of Rome. He adopted what in Italy were called "liberal" politics (for which in his case read conservative), served in several prewar cabinets, and became premier on Giovanni Giolitti's resignation in March 1914. The stormy days of the "Red week" of socialist and anarchist demonstrations and violence in May 1914 were the first major challenges he had to meet. The second was the war crisis of the summer. Salandra's initial line was a cautious one. Italy was an ally of Germany and Austria-Hungary, but Salandra wisely concluded that the quarrel with Serbia was not one which required Italian entry into the war on the side of the Central Powers. Over the following months, wisdom vanished and instead Italy conducted a diplomatic auction, promising its services in war to the highest bidder. The Allies won, and Salandra the neutralist became Salandra the war leader. He was forced to resign after military reversals in 1916. In the postwar years he smiled benignly on the aims of the Fascist movement.

for a price, specified in secret in the Treaty of London of 26 April 1915. At the end of the war Italy was to get what it wanted in the areas disputed with Austria, as well as financial reparations and chunks of German colonies in Africa. Four weeks after the secret treaty had been concluded, Italy declared war on Austria, and entered a disastrous phase of its history.

New allies

The way in which Italy entered the conflict reflected one of the most important political changes of the war: the eclipse of parliamentary power. The Treaty of London only came to light years later, when the Bolsheviks began to read the archives of the czar's foreign office and let foreign journalists into the secrets of Allied diplomacy. Similarly, Italian legislators only learned of their government's initial war policy in 1915 through a Swedish newspaperman's Russian sources.

Perhaps this kind of executive fiat is inevitable in wartime, when time is short and secrecy a necessity. But in all major combatant countries, the assumption of untrammeled power by the executive had two important results: it gave a small number of men virtually unheard-of powers, and it created new political alliances which would have been impossible before the war.

Wartime politics can be described as varying types and degrees of military dictatorship, supported by a wide range of civilian coalitions. In France, in the first three years of the war, dictatorship and coalition largely went hand in hand. Some attempts to revive parliamentary authority occurred from time to time, but it was only in 1918 that Georges Clemenceau reasserted the right of the prime minister to have the final say over military policy.

▲ The Serbian general staff, with the 71-year-old King Peter seated among his officers, crossing the River Drina in what is now Yugoslavia in late 1915. The ordeal of the Serbian army in the winter of 1915 was one of the tragedies of the war. General von Mackensen's joint Central Powers operation against Serbia began in October 1915 and successfully swept the Serbian army to the Albanian mountains in the west. They and the thousands of prisoners and refugees with them endured appalling conditions in the mountains of Albania. How many died before reaching the sea will never be known.

General Joseph Gallieni 1849–1916

Gallieni was military governor of Paris during the German advance on the capital in August and September 1914. He was a veteran of the Franco-Prussian war in which he had been wounded and taken prisoner. In 1914 he was a 65-year old professional soldier, recently retired, and a veteran colonial administrator. He was in line for the post of commander in chief of the armies, but deferred to Joffre on grounds of age and health. Gallieni energetically mobilized the Paris garrison and was the first to see the opportunity to counterattack the flank of the advancing German army. He played a significant part in launching the decisive French attack on the line of the Ourcq north of the Marne (6–10 September).

Recognition of his achievement followed when Briand brought him into the cabinet as minister of war. His military and administrative experience in the colonies gave his voice authority, which he used to defend Joffre and the high command. The crisis of Verdun showed the need for further reorganization of French command, but by then Gallieni had resigned on grounds of ill health. He died on 27 May 1916, was given a state funeral and the posthumous rank of marshal.

In the early months of the conflict the French government almost ceased to exist. It fled to Bordeaux to avoid the embarrassment of being trapped in Paris, as had happened in 1870–71, and granted Generals Gallieni and Joffre full authority to run the city of Paris and the war. But once the first crisis had passed, and the lines had stabilized on the Marne, an attempt was made to restore some semblance of civilian control. In December 1914 most ministers returned to Paris, but the important ministries of war, the navy and justice stayed in the south. At this stage there was little politicians could do to reassert their right to run the war. Instead they declared a political truce and supported the creation of a coalition government of all the talents to provide whatever the army decided it had to have.

This brought socialists into government early in the war. The most important of these was Albert Thomas, who in 1915 became undersecretary in charge of artillery and military equipment at the French ministry of war. Thomas was instrumental in giving the French trade union movement a chance to help run the war.

In the UK the same suspension of the normal political game occurred. The Liberal prime minister Herbert Asquith appointed Lord Kitchener as minister of war soon after hostilities began. At this stage his word was final, among both politicians and generals. Later in the war it was not so easy to tell who was running the war, but for a time it was Kitchener.

The British parliament passed the Defence of the Realm Act, or DORA as it was universally known, which gave the government powers to do what it liked during the war. Initially many prominent men were reluctant to accept the argument that Britain had a moral obligation to

Albert Thomas 1878–1932

Like his mentor Jean Jaurès, Thomas was an intellectual who espoused socialist internationalism and French patriotism. He was the quintessential reformist socialist, a leader of moderate opinion both within the French trade union movement and in the socialist party. The son of a baker, Thomas's family still managed to send him to the *Ecole Normale Supérieure* in Paris, the breeding ground for France's intellectual and political elite. His brilliance brought him to the attention of Jaurès. In 1904 Thomas became assistant editor on the new socialist newspaper, *L'Humanité*. In 1910 he was elected to the French chamber of deputies.

On the outbreak of war Thomas, now 36, adopted a patriotic stance and joined his regiment. He was soon recalled to organize the railways. In May 1915 he joined the French cabinet as under-secretary (and later minister) of munitions and served in successive administrations. In the accompanying photograph he is addressing workers at the opening of a canteen in the Citroën factory in Paris in 1917.

After the war he became the guiding force behind the International Labor Organization (ILO) of the League of Nations. This organization remains his most enduring memorial.

join in the conflict. Within the Liberal camp and in Labour Party circles individual voices were raised against intervention, but such doubts and anxieties did not inform a wider political movement against the war. A characteristic attitude was that of J.A. Pease, the Quaker president of the British Peace Society, who was also a cabinet minister. In August 1914 he wavered, he worried, but he did not resign. J. Ramsay MacDonald, a prominent Labour leader, gave up his chairmanship of the Parliamentary Labour Party, but he did not try to convince his colleagues to vote against war credits. Some artists and writers turned their backs emphatically against the war, but elsewhere unanimity reigned. The war had to be won. Even the Irish Nationalist Party – which participated in the Westminster parliament simply to legislate itself out of existence by bringing Home Rule to Ireland – did its bit for the war effort. The party encouraged its supporters to join up and thus reinforce claims for Home Rule, which was still to be won by constitutional means. The Liberal government had already sponsored legislation to this effect, but it had been shelved on account of the war.

Soon after the invasion of Belgium the British trade union movement declared its unequivocal support for the war. In the first months of the conflict so many workingmen joined up that supplies of essential war materiel were scarce. Something had to be done to rationalize labor. The result was the Treasury Agreement of 1915: the trade unions accepted restrictions for the duration of the war in return for recognition as a partner in the management of the war economy.

What they gave up were the right to strike and the restrictive practices that determined the skill composition of the labor force in any munitions factory. These concessions assured continuous production and the injection of workers into jobs previously only done by skilled men – in a word, dilution. In return they received recognition – no

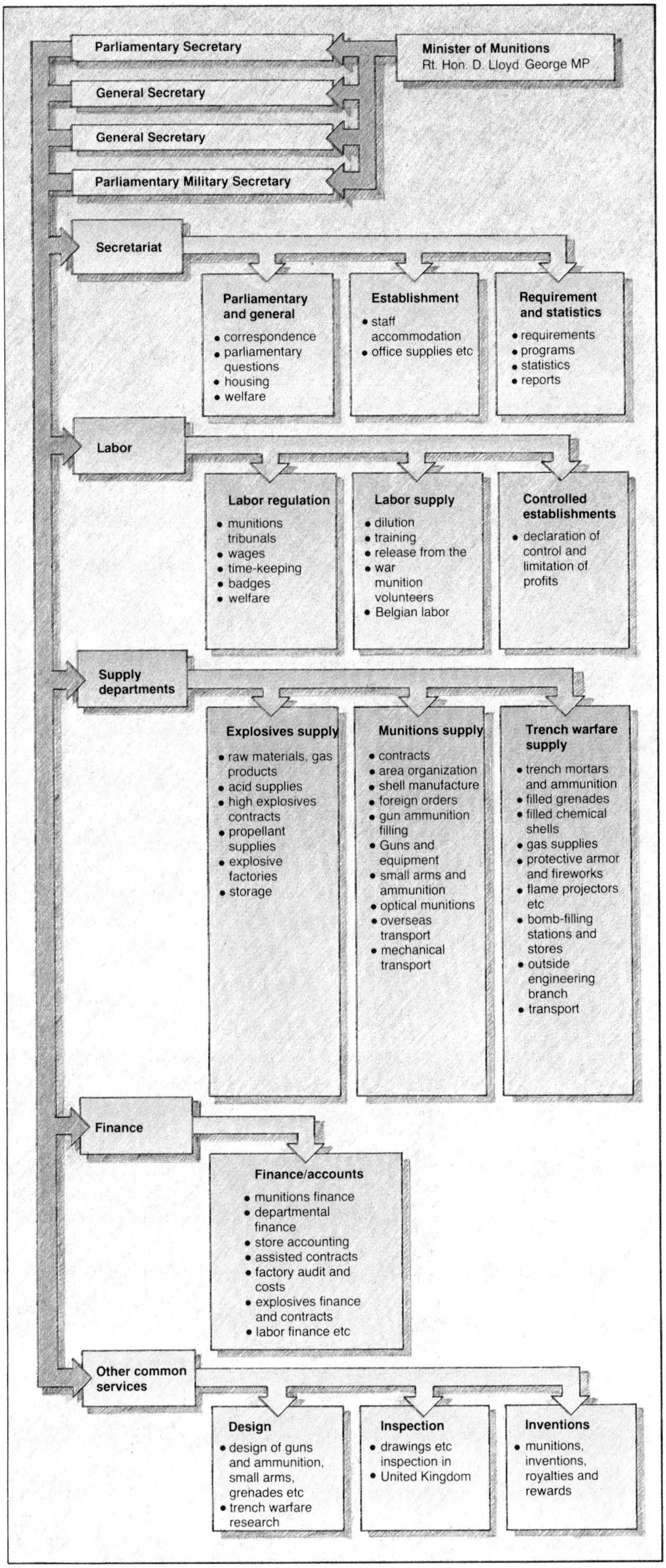

Arthur Henderson 1863–1935

Henderson was the single most powerful Labour leader in wartime Britain. In 1914 he was aged 55 and was a member of parliament for a mining district in the Northeast of England as well as a veteran of the trade union movement. He believed in the rise of labor rather than in any specific socialist doctrine. In May 1915 Henderson became the first Labour member of parliament to sit in a British cabinet, as president of the board of education. In reality his role was as a trouble-shooter and mediator with organized labor. When Lloyd George came to power in 1916, Henderson served in his inner cabinet. After a visit Petrograd, to convince Russia to stay in a war during which his own son had been killed, Henderson began to adopt a wider political vision. He spoke out for British attendance at a socialist meeting at Stockholm, and for his independence he was sacked from the cabinet. He returned to rebuild the Labour Party as a national party. In later years he served as a cabinet minister and won the Nobel Peace Prize for his work for disarmament.

◀ The cartoon from the English magazine *Punch* shows the British chancellor of the exchequer David Lloyd George harnessing capital and labor to produce the weapons needed to win the war. The cartoon appeared shortly after the Treasury Agreement of 1915, whereby trade unionists abrogated both restrictive practices and the right to strike in return for a recognized place in the management of the war economy. This they duly received, and participated at all levels of the new ministry of munitions, whose structure in August 1916 is sketched left. The ministry was staffed by civil servants and businessmen who put together a successfyl industrial empire efficient enough to keep the allied armies supplied for the next three years.

mean achievement at a time when strikes were often held to gain union recognition.

This arrangement was given legal force in the Munitions of War Act of July 1915. It also created a ministry of munitions to oversee war production. At its head was David Lloyd George, previously Liberal chancellor of the exchequer, who used his reputation as a man of "push and go" to improve both war production and his chances of becoming prime minister. By then the Liberal government had agreed to invite leaders of opposition parties into a coalition to run the war. Thus Arthur Henderson, a moderate trade unionist, became the first member of the Labour Party to sit in a British cabinet.

The coalition occurred in the light of the second major military crisis of the war: that of the Dardanelles (for which, see p. 82). The major political casualty of this disastrous episode was the first lord of the admiralty, Winston Churchill. He was replaced by the former Conservative prime minister, Arthur Balfour.

Political effects

In the UK and France the war's political effects were twofold: to displace power from elected leaders to generals, and to blur prewar political lines. In Germany and Austria-Hungary the situation was more stable, due to the accepted limits of parliamentary power. Legislators had the right to vote war credits – and then, to keep their doubts to themselves. This was, of course, the rule in Russia too.

But in Central and Eastern Europe the war brought about one fundamental political change, which in 1915 was still simmering under the surface. This was the divide within the international socialist movement between those who supported the war and those who, whatever their initial positions, were beginning to ask questions about its direction, its costs and even its justification.

Lord Kitchener of Khartoum 1850–1916

One of the best-known images of World War I is the British recruiting poster with Kitchener's face and pointing finger, calling on British men to join up (see p. 119). In 1914 Kitchener was Britain's most famous soldier and prime minister Asquith's natural choice as secretary of state for war. Kitchener had made his reputation in Britain's imperial wars from Egypt to South Africa and was aged 64 in 1914. He saw quickly that the war could last at least three years, an opinion contrary to the popular illusion of a short war. It was his decision to create a mass army of volunteers to bolster Britain's small standing army and territorial force. The popular response to his call was far beyond his (or anyone else's) expectations. One million men joined up voluntarily in 1914 alone. These men formed what became known as the "Kitchener armies". The first trained units were despatched to France in 1915, and formed the heart of the force which led the disastrous attacks on the Somme in July–November 1916.

Initially Kitchener ran the war virtually single-handed. He was closer to his French colleagues than to many British politicians, and helped to build up the necessary liaison to secure the Western Front. By mid-1915 the task of provisioning the armies was entrusted to the ministry of munitions, under Lloyd George. The inevitable political intrigues and maneuvers which the war bred hampered Kitchener's leadership on questions of strategy to the point that he considered resigning in late 1915. He stayed on, in part because he knew he was an indispensable symbol of the nation's will.

In June 1916 Kitchener embarked on a mission to Russia. He never reached his destination. He and all hands drowned when HMS *Hampshire* was sunk by a mine in the Baltic Sea.

BRITAIN'S SECOND LINE: EMPIRE & DOMINIONS

One reason why Britain won the war was that it was able to call on men, money and resources in its overseas dominions and dependencies. Canada, Australia, New Zealand, India and South Africa put more men into the field than did the United States. These British allies lost over 200,000 killed and 600,000 wounded, or twice the casualties suffered by the American Expeditionary Forces.

Economic power reinforced military power. Total war expenditure for the five countries listed above reached one billion pounds sterling. Complex negotiations governed the maintenance of Dominions forces abroad. Initially Britain paid for their upkeep, but the sums expended were kept as debts owed to Britain payable after the war. In turn, Britain bought Dominion goods to provide the income needed to pay for the war effort.

Other kinds of material support were also organized. Munitions factories opened in Australia, which also sent 3,000 skilled and unskilled workers to British war factories. The Australian government paid the costs of their transport to Britain, and since Australian wages were significantly higher than British wages, a government subsidy was paid to top up their pay packets in England. In Newfoundland a war loan of 6 million dollars was raised, which paid for the 6,326 men in the Royal Newfoundland Regiment. India helped in other ways too. Over 100,000 animals were sent from India to Mesopotamia to help in transport.Indeed, over 50,000 Indian animals (including elephants) were brought to France.

In financial terms, the Dominions provided Britain with only a fraction of the support which came from the USA, but without the Empire and Dominions, Britain's dependency on America and its overall economic position would have been substantially worse. Indeed, it is arguable that with its overseas dependencies and assets, Britain was unbeatable. In geopolitical and economic terms, once the stalemate of 1915 had begun, Germany had already lost the war.

The contribution of Britain's second line of defense was acknowledged by the new and important role played by Canadian, Australian and South African politicians in war policy and peace negotiations. In London an imperial war cabinet sat alongside the British war cabinet, both chaired by the British prime minister. The Australian prime minister Billy Hughes and the South African soldier and statesman Jan Christiaan Smuts took an active part in forming imperial war policy and in shaping the peace treaty. Hughes in particular pressed for harsh terms for Germany.

During Smuts' visit to London in 1917 he spoke openly of his idea of a British Commonwealth of Nations, which was duly recognized at the imperial conference of 1926 and enacted by the Statute of Westminster of 1931. In a sense, this family of nations, joined by history and kinship to Britain, was born during and because of the 1914–18 war.

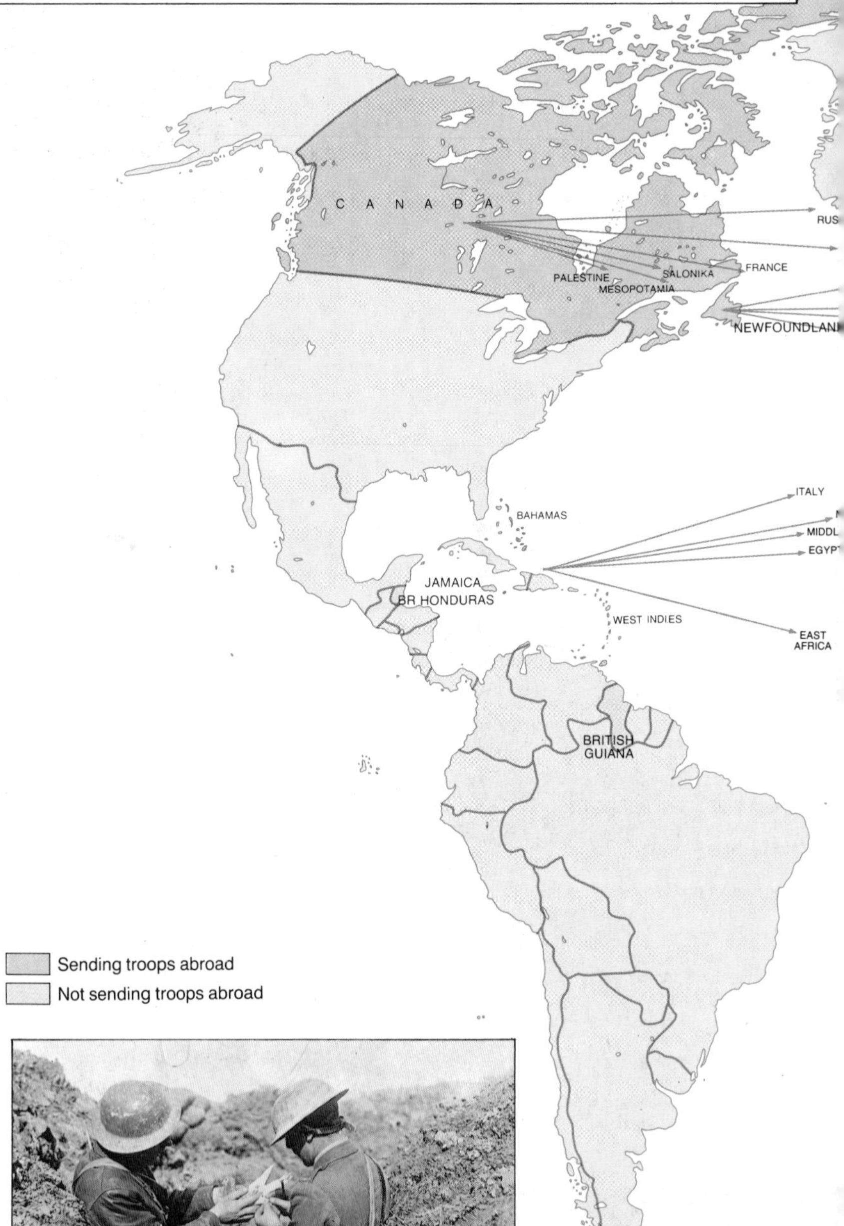

▲ **Members of the Canadian Signal Service, fixing a message to the foot of a homing pigeon on the Western Front, October 1917. The Canadians' greatest victory was the capture at Vimy Ridge early that year.**

► **Black men served in the British, French and American armies during the war. Here men of the British West Indies Regiment clean their guns on the Albert–Amiens road in September 1916, at the half-way point of the Battle of the Somme.**

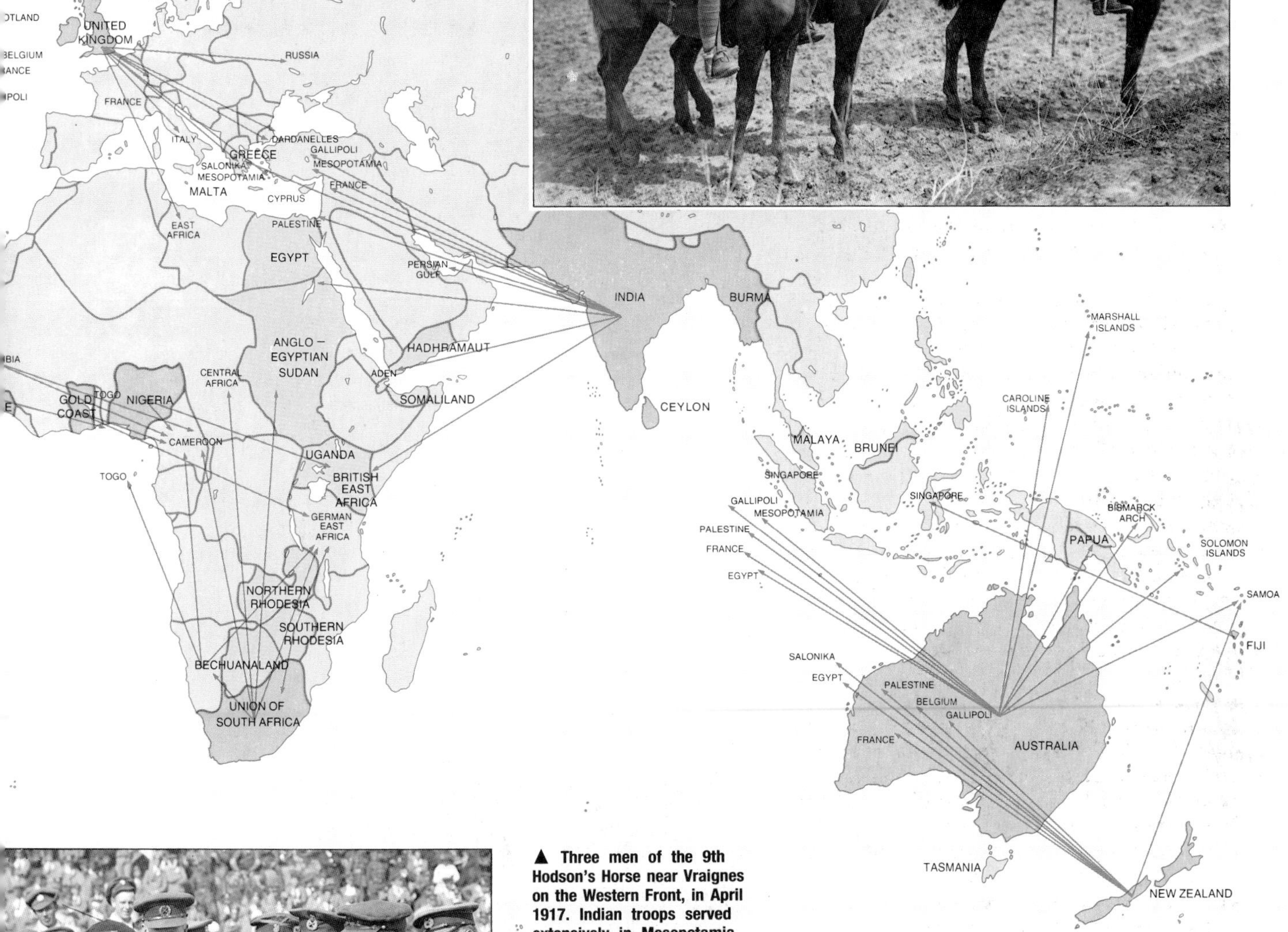

▲ Three men of the 9th Hodson's Horse near Vraignes on the Western Front, in April 1917. Indian troops served extensively in Mesopotamia and France, where lie the graves of thousands of Sikh, Moslem and Hindu soldiers.

◄ Men of the South African Native Labour Corps at a war dance and sports day in France in June 1917. Here a Zulu warrior is presented to General Maxwell. Black soldiers also fought in the King's African Rifles against German units in East Africa.

► Australian troops at tea in the first support trench at Westholk ridge near Ypres on 19 September 1917. They went over the top the next day; whether they survived is not recorded.

Datafile

In the 1914–18 war German war production succeeded but the German war economy failed. This was because the key to victory was the maintenance of a balance between civilian and military needs. In Germany that balance was never struck, in part because of the Allied blockade and in part because of the way the war economy was run. The result was rampant inflation, a black market and the impoverishment of the population.

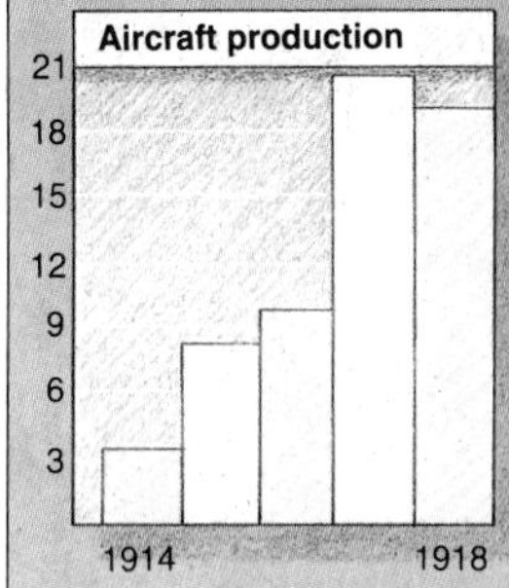

◀ The German economy produced prodigious feats during the 1914–18 war. One was the expansion of the aircraft industry. The Albatros factory in Berlin was a typical example. Between 1914 and 1918 output of aircraft rose by over 600 percent and the quality of the machines improved equally dramatically.

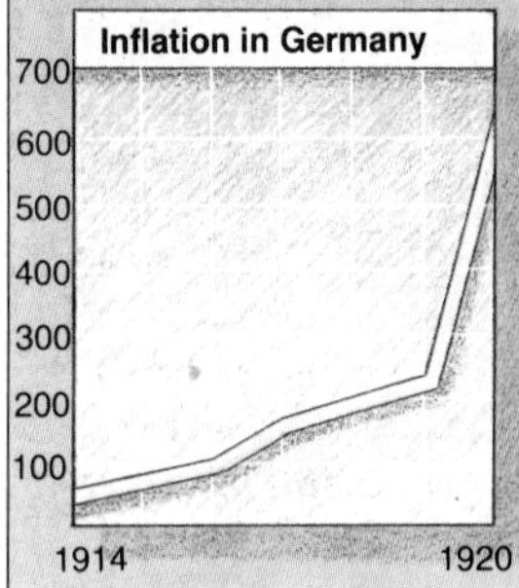

◀ The official rise in German retail prices was only the tip of the iceberg of inflation. The black market provided perhaps half of the essential items of daily consumption for ordinary Germans by 1917. A realistic graph of price rises would show inflation in the Germany in the last year of the war at perhaps 400 percent of 1914 figures.

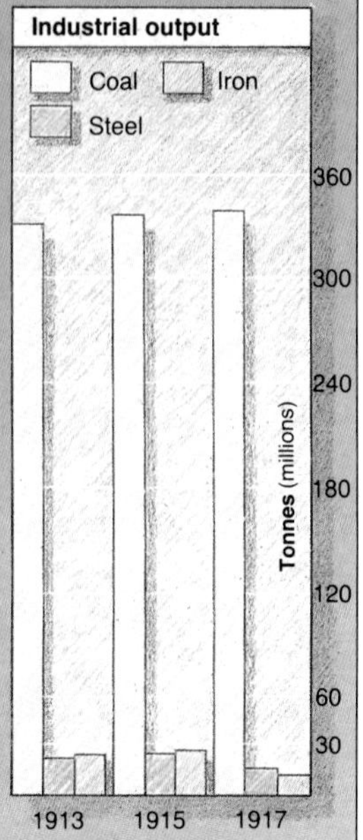

▲ Until 1917 the Central Powers roughly matched or exceeded Allied levels of industrial output of coal, iron and steel. But from 1917 the disparity between the two camps grew wider. US output alone equalled that of the Central Powers in basic producers' goods, and US finance provided the foundation for the entire Allied war effort.

Chronology

1916

February 21
(to Dec. 18) Battle of Verdun: unsuccessful German attack on French city of Verdun

March 1
GER: Extended submarine campaign started

April 24–29
Easter Rising in Irish Republican Brotherhood against the British in Dublin, Ireland

April 29
In Mesopotamia, Turks capture Kut and the remnants of the British invasion force

May 31
(to June 1) Battle of Jutland: major naval battle of war between UK and Germany

June 4
(to Oct. 10) Brusilov offensive: Russians push back the Austro-Hungarian line north of the Carpathians

June 5
UK: British minister for war, Lord Kitchener, is drowned when HMS *Hampshire* is sunk

June 6
Start of Arab revolt against the Turks in the Hejaz

June 15
IT: Boselli replaces Salandra as premier

July 1
(to Nov. 19) Battle of the Somme: unsuccessful Allied attack on German lines in the Somme Valley, France

August 8
Portuguese government decides to offer military support to Entente Powers

November 7
Woodrow Wilson is reelected president of the USA

November 21
AH: Death of Emperor Franz Joseph; succeeded by Archduke Karl

December 7
UK: Lloyd George becomes prime minister

December 31
RUSS: Murder of influential faith-healer Rasputin

1917

March 15
RUSS: Czar Nicholas II of Russia abdicates. Provisional Government assumes power.

March 20
FR: Ribot replaces Briand as premier and foreign minister

April 6
The USA enters the war fighting on the side of the Allies

April 16–29
Chemin des Dames offensive: a large-scale French offensive on the Aisne fails to break the German line

July 14
GER: Chancellor Bethmann-Hollweg resigns: succeeded by Michaelis

July 31
(to Nov. 10) Third Battle of Ypres: unsuccessful British offensive against the German forces in Flanders

August 1
Pope Benedict XV appeals to belligerents for peace

If 1915 was the time during World War I when the conflict was broadened to include new alliances both among the warring parties and within them, 1916 was the time when the war was deepened, invading every facet of economic, social and political life: when total war was born. In the Central Powers this happened later than in the Entente Powers, but the general tendency was the same on both sides.

For the state to become the center of virtually all social affairs involved major political risks, for it raised the stakes of the war considerably. A ruling elite that took over most of the key tasks of social organization, and demanded unprecedented sacrifices, could not afford to lose the war. Total war exposed the weaknesses of policies and politicians, and placed in the balance the very legitimacy of the regimes that waged it.

This is at least partly why the ferocity of the war increased as it went on. Furthermore the political stakes rose as the casualty lists lengthened, for the reason advanced in one of Abraham Lincoln's phrases, that the dead could not be seen to have died in vain.

But as the war killed literally millions of men, it both brought the men and women of nations and empires together and began to tear them apart. On the one hand, social bonds had been created in wartime that enabled the war to expand to unprecedented heights. In all countries labor and capital worked together. After a few months' work, recruits to the war factories were doing jobs that were supposed to require years of training. Furthermore, huge armies of a dozen nationalities had been forged in Austria-Hungary and in France, where alongside indigenous French forces stood Algerians and Senegalese as well as laborers brought from Vietnam and China, such as Ho Chi Minh and Zhou Enlai.

Shrill patriots, who had shouted down the few who dared to dissent in 1914, grew more and more shrill two years later. Everything for the nation; no sacrifice is too great for the state, they declared from Preston to Prague to Petrograd. The flag-wavers and chauvinists failed to see that the longer the war went on, the less likely it was that some of the combatant countries would carry the struggle through to a decisive conclusion.

That this should have been the case with Russia is not surprising, given the inherent instability of the regime. But it was also a truth that the rulers of Germany ignored, to their cost. The reason is simple. The deeper those in power dug, as it were, to lay the foundations of the war effort, the more they exposed the fissures which threatened to bring down the scaffolding on their heads. Those fissures were clearly visible in 1914, reflecting all the hatreds and animosities that made going to war such a risk in the first place.

1916–17 THE GREAT SLAUGHTER

As the war deepens, the state assumes the key tasks of social organization

In Germany military leaders assume command of the economy

Production increases but at considerable cost

In France and Britain the government controls supplies to industry

1916 sees protests against the war in Germany

Britain supports the Arab revolt agains the Turks

Germany supports an Irish insurrection against Britain

By the end of 1916 they were visible again, and widened further, given the onset of war weariness and wartime shortages, presenting a real and growing threat to the authoritarian regimes that ran the war.

The political economy of total war

Economic warfare was an integral part of the war. As was noted earlier, blockade was used as an instrument of war from virtually the beginning of the conflict. It put a strain on both sides, and together with the ever-growing demand for munitions production, necessitated major adjustments in economic organization and management. These changes evolved everywhere in piecemeal fashion in 1915.

A year later, even greater efforts at industrial rationalization were required. The Allies' industrial strength was brought home forcibly to the Central Powers by the great battles of 1916 on the Western Front. Allied firepower, more than anything else, convinced Germany's military and industrial leaders that only by a massive effort of industrial mobilization could it win the war. In 1914 industrialists carried little weight in German politics. Two years later the situation was entirely different. Working closely with the high command, German industrialists planned a new approach to the war effort. This was known as the Hindenburg Plan.

► Kaiser Wilhelm, flanked by Hindenburg (left) and Ludendorff (right).

▼ Albert Thomas and Lloyd George (left and right) with Haig and Joffre (center).

To understand it we must look back at the early stages of the formation of the German war economy. Early in the war Walther Rathenau, head of the General Electric Company (*AEG*), went to Falkenhayn, then Prussian minister of war, and sketched out a plan for the organization of raw materials production. Consequently Rathenau became head of the *Kriegsrohstoffabteilung* (*KRA*), or war raw materials department, and produced results by setting up war corporations to handle problems of supply. Rathenau was one of many men of industry who helped harness the benefits of German science – in particular the Haber-Bosch process of nitrate synthesis – to the needs of war.

Given the Allied blockade and the consequent shortages of imported saltpeter, essential for the production of explosives for the army and navy, this contribution was of the highest importance to the German war effort.

As the war went on, though, it became apparent that scientific ingenuity alone would not win the war. Increasing criticism was directed by army and industry at the responsible agencies – the Prussian war ministry and the ministry of the interior – which had clearly been unable to provide adequate supplies of guns and butter. The outcome was a price spiral and, even more ominously, the emergence in the shadows of a black market on which virtually anything could be bought.

The quarrel was as much about political power as about economic policy. Its outcome was the creation of what some scholars term "the silent dictatorship" of the two most powerful men in Germany, Paul von Hindenburg, chief of the imperial staff of the German army, and Erich Ludendorff, first quartermaster general. According to one school of historians, in all important respects these two men – together with their allies in industry and politics – ran the German war effort between 1916 and 1918. Again this is an area of historical controversy: other scholars see German wartime politics and administration in much more complicated terms.

But all agree that the new leadership's solution to the supply problem was to give army and industry full control over the economy. An important aspect of the authority of the Prussian war ministry was vested in a new war office, run by General Groener, the man in charge of military railways in 1914. This created the framework for the working out of the Hindenburg Plan, derived from a letter the chief of staff wrote to the minister of war on 31 August 1916. Hindenburg demanded, among other things, a doubling of the output of machine guns and a trebling of the output of artillery by the spring of 1917.

This gigantic program was planned and run by industrialists. Any worries they may have had about state dominance in economic affairs were allayed by the fact that pricing and profit margins remained their responsibility. Labor too was given incentives to increase productivity: under the Auxiliary Service Law of 5 December 1916 a new framework of industrial bargaining was promulgated – no mean achievement in a country in which trade unions were regarded by many military men and industrialists with suspicion or contempt. Labor mobility was curtailed, but works councils were created to arbitrate disputes over permission to leave work.

This gives in outline what has been termed the "corporatist" solution to Germany's wartime economic difficulties. It left the management of the economy to particular interest groups – the large firms, working under the aegis of the army. The result was total chaos. Labor shortages remained chronic, in part due to the demand for more and more men for the Front. The big firms benefited from the scheme, at the expense of prewar competitors and of the state. War production did increase, and by 1918 Germany produced more ammunition than at any time during World War II. But profits soared, with the costs passed on to the army and then to the consumer, thus ensuring the acceleration of the inflationary spiral of the war years, as well as producing a subsistence crisis that undermined the regime itself.

The contrast with Germany's two most important adversaries, the UK and France, tells us much about why Germany lost the war. The French abjured a military solution to economic difficulties, and found a way to increase production without giving in to particular interest groups. It was the consortium system, created in 1916 under the leadership of Etienne Clémentel, the minister of commerce. This apparatus of controls grew out of the international character of the Allied war effort. Given the disastrous loss of men, materiel and industrial potential suffered by France in the first months of the war, there was no alternative to a growing reliance on British economic support. The British insisted upon the coordination of Allied supply policy, and set up international commissions to oversee wheat, coal, credit and shipping. This structure gave Britain virtual control of the essential supplies required by French industry.

What the Allies were forced to do on the international level, Clémentel succeeded in doing within the French economy. He used French dependence on Britain to justify his control of supply to individual firms, undermining their autonomy and room for maneuver. It worked. Through the consortium system the rapacity of individual firms was checked, and an essential balance was maintained: production and profits were secured without undue pressure on prices and thus on wages and living standards.

The same was true in the UK. Even though Lloyd George saw it as an imperative task to bring in the best business talent available to run the war economy, the edifice over which he presided as minister of munitions, and after December 1916 as prime minister, never became either a "business state" or the economic equivalent of the internal war of rapacious self-interest that evolved in Germany. Output of war materiel in the UK was assured within a framework which managed – not without difficulty – to place national interests above employers' interests.

It is therefore one of the paradoxes of the war that the most authoritarian war economy was probably the least efficient. This was because the waging of war – in economic matters as much as

Walther Rathenau 1867–1922

The son of an industrialist, Rathenau was one of the most powerful leaders of German industry before World War I. He was a man of philosophical as well as scientific and industrial interests. In 1899 he became director of *AEG*, the General Electric Company founded by his father. His managerial talent, scientific training, energy and vision made him an indispensable adviser to the German ministry of war in 1914. He created the war raw materials department (*KRA*), and helped ease the transition from a war of annihilation to a war of attrition. After the Armistice he was active in centrist politics, both within industry and in parliamentary affairs. In 1921–22, as minister of reconstruction and later as foreign minister, he helped to ease the burdens of reparations and to fashion a rapprochement with the Soviet Union, expressed in the Rapallo Treaty of 1922. He was a magnet for right-wing and antisemitic malice, and was assassinated on 24 June 1922.

Wilhelm Groener 1867–1939

Groener was a maverick among the German military: a highly efficient administrator with moderate political views. In 1914 he headed the railway section of the German general staff and was responsible for the timetabling of mobilization. His record of success made him the ideal choice as head of the new war office set up in 1916 to reorganize German industry. His fairness and honesty made him enemies among industrialists and the military, and he was fired in 1917. He then served on the Eastern Front, and succeeded Ludendorff as quartermaster general at the end of the war. He came to an understanding with Ebert that the army would support the new regime, and later served in various governments as minister of communications, defense, and the interior.

The *KRA* and German Industry

Germany had many disadvantages in the economic war. The Allied blockade made it impossible for Germany to secure an uninterrupted flow of essential raw materials. In 1915 Walther Rathenau, director of *AEG*, offered to help deal with the crisis of supply. His plea was for the establishment of the *Kriegsrohstoffabteiling* (*KRA*), or war raw materials department. This office set up war corporations to oversee supply to domestic industry. All raw materials were categorized as "emergency materials", and procurement strategies were fixed. A constant search for primary and secondary product substitutes was undertaken. Then priorities were set, by which different industrial claimants for supply were placed in order of importance to the war effort. By late 1915 over 100 war materials companies controlled supplies of basic commodities, with which German industry provided munitions of war. This system worked and provided a temporary solution to Germany's economic problems which, the longer the war dragged on, proved ultimately insurmountable.

◀ **German barbed wire destined for the Western Front.**

▲ **One of the most prominent dissenters in Germany was Karl Liebknecht, shown here imprisoned, pushing a wheelbarrow while working in a munitions factory in occupied France in 1915. Prisoners of conscience in Britain included the prominent philosopher Bertrand Russell, who also lost his post at Trinity College, Cambridge. Only in Russia did antiwar sentiment become a popular force; in the west, pacifism was unable to shorten the war by one day.**

in other spheres – is essentially a political matter. However much they juggled the bureaucratic forms, Germany's leaders never established effective political control over the war economy – neither in industry nor in agriculture. They therefore could not hope to balance the claims of competing sectors for scarce commodities. The result was a free-for-all, despite the strenuous efforts of the military authorities. As the American historian Gerald Feldman has demonstrated, under the pressure of industrial war the German state dissolved and competing interest groups grabbed what they could.

The worsening economic outlook at home is also the context in which to set Germany's increasingly aggressive campaign of submarine warfare, as well as the exploitation of both occupied Belgium and a new adversary, Romania, which entered the war on the Allies' side in August 1916 and was subdued six months later. But all of these compensatory steps were ultimately futile, since they could do little other than postpone the demise of a regime that collapsed from within.

Dissent and dissenters

On the evening of 1 May 1916 a small demonstration occurred in the center of Berlin. It was led by Karl Liebknecht, the son of one of the founders of the German social democratic party who had opposed Germany's war effort in 1870–71. In 1916 it took perhaps even more courage for his son to stand up within sight of passing soldiers, and shout "Down with the war! Down with the government!" The outcome was predictable. Liebknecht was arrested, charged with treason, and sentenced by a military court to two and a half years in jail, raised to four years and one month on appeal. But the affair led to the first major political strike of the war. On the day of the trial about 50,000 workers in over 40 Berlin munitions factories downed tools in solidarity with Liebknecht. Similar protests took place in other German towns.

None of this posed a direct threat to the war effort, but such vocal opposition signaled that the

It should have been understood that each new form of production or increase in industrial activity needs a starting period dependent on a whole series of requirements: availability of working space, machines, raw materials and so forth. This was constantly overlooked in the high command and stemming from this, the first sense of disappointment arose.... and so the Hindenburg Plan suffered from the suddenness with which it was issued like a bullet from the barrel, and this at a time when food shortages were growing at a catastrophic rate following the poor harvest of 1916.

WILHELM GROENER

▼ Etienne Clémentel, French minister of commerce, succeeded in converting the economic weakness of France into a domestic political weapon. The UK controlled French imports; hence the careful distribution of supply in France was a key to economic survival. Clémentel's consortium system succeeded in subordinating the interests of individual firms to the needs of the economy as a whole.

days of the social truce were over. This was the precondition for the reemergence of the international socialist movement, which had unceremoniously collapsed in 1914.

Several attempts had been made to revive it in the ensuing months. Two international conferences of socialists opposed to the war were held in the Swiss hamlets of Zimmerwald in September 1915 and Kienthal in April 1916. There the Russian socialist Lenin met other socialists, whose views on the war and how to end it varied considerably. They agreed that this war was not their war, but few were prepared to accept Lenin's view that the old international movement was dead and that a new one, based on new principles, had to take its place.

In the course of 1916 other dissenters came to public prominence too. In Britain the introduction of compulsory military service created its share of political prisoners, men like the young socialist activists Clifford Allen and Fenner Brockway, who refused even alternative noncombative service which would free someone else to carry a gun. A conspicuous voice among the "No Conscription Fellowship" was the philosopher Bertrand Russell, who helped defend war resisters facing military tribunals, and as a result, later in the war, found that his lectureship at Trinity College, Cambridge, would not be renewed. He also spent a brief period in prison for suggesting in print that American troops would more likely be used to intimidate British workers than attack German soldiers.

It was easier for a government to tolerate dissent when it came from a soldier, which accounts for the extraordinary success of one of the most powerful novels of the war, Henri Barbusse's *Under Fire*, which won the French Goncourt literary prize in 1916 and subsequently became a bestseller. It is a mystery how this book got past the censors, for it broadcast all kinds of subversive ideas. On the eve of his own death, one of the most attractive figures in the book, a young French officer, tells the narrator that only one name will emerge with any honor at the end of the war: the name of Liebknecht. In a final scene, mud-encrusted soldiers on both sides cry out that the war is a crime, which those who had fought it would never allow to happen again. Strong words for 1916, and an indication that the certainties of the war's early days were gone.

Further afield other cracks appeared in both opposition camps. In the spring of 1916 an Arab revolt against Turkish rule began, and was carefully nurtured by the British. But subversion was a game both sides could play. The Germans took a keen interest in Irish nationalism, and helped provide the means for an insurrection in Dublin against British rule planned for Easter 1916. The rising was a military disaster, but a political victory. The rebels were easily overpowered, but the execution of their leaders turned them into martyrs.

Repression in the aftermath of the Easter Rising did no good to the efforts of the British to bring the USA into the war. The Irish vote mattered in American urban politics; and the Irish revolt occurred in the run-up to the 1916 election, fought by both major candidates (Woodrow Wilson for the Democrats and Charles Evans Hughes for the Republicans) on a ticket pledging them to stay out of the war.

David Lloyd George 1863–1945

David Lloyd George was the son of a schoolmaster turned farmer, and grew up in impoverished circumstances in North Wales. He trained as a solicitor and entered parliament as a Liberal in 1890. He built a reputation as a fiery orator, and staunchly opposed British policy in the Anglo-Boer War (1899–1902). In 1906 he became president of the board of trade, and from 1908–1914 he served as chancellor of the exchequer. In these years he piloted through parliament a series of bills which laid the foundation of the welfare state. To pay for them, he incurred the wrath of the propertied classes and the Conservative Party. The House of Lords rejected his Finance Bill. Two general elections followed, leaving Lloyd George and the Liberals in power, determined to restrict the veto power of the House of Lords. This they did through the Parliament Act of 1911. During the war Lloyd George served as minister of munitions (1915–16) and then as prime minister (1916–18). He conducted a long and ultimately unsuccessful guerrilla campaign against Haig and the general staff to wrest from them control of war policy. He was more successful in domestic affairs. He brought men from outside politics to run the home front, and symbolized British determination to see the war through. He was reelected prime minister in 1918 and served until 1922.

World War I and Ireland

The "Irish question" has been a perennial headache in British politics. It is more accurately called the "British problem", since the occupation of Catholic Ireland in the 17th century first by Presbyterian settlers from Scotland and then by Oliver Cromwell's armies, never succeeded in merging the political cultures of Britain and Ireland. In the years following the potato famine of 1846, which reduced the population of Ireland by 2 million within five years, separatist and nationalist movements grew. In 1858 the Irish Republican Brotherhood was founded. In 1870 the Home Rule Association was created to work for self-government for Ireland. Irish members of parliament, led by Charles Stewart Parnell, fought for home rule and assistance to the rural poor.

The Liberal-dominated House of Commons passed a Home Rule bill in 1893, but it was blocked by the House of Lords. In 1900 a new party, Sinn Fein ("Ourselves Alone"), was founded, and tapped a surge of Irish nationalism among a new generation of militants. When the Liberals once more passed a Home Rule bill in 1912, it could no longer be vetoed by the Lords. Protestants then insisted on the exclusion of the six northern counties with a Protestant majority, and on armed resistance. German arms were landed at Larne for the Protestant "Ulster volunteers", and a number of British officers stated that they would not enforce Home Rule. Catholics formed the "Irish volunteers", and shots were fired when troops attempted to block their arms shipments.

Civil war seemed likely, when in 1914 the world war overtook it. Catholic leaders joined Protestants in rallying to the cause. Over 200,000 Irishmen volunteered, with the full support of the Irish Nationalist Party. Irish nationalism, though, grew as the war went on.

A small group of nationalists in the Irish Republican Brotherhood decided to seize the moment and fight for independence. Their plan to smuggle in German arms went hopelessly wrong on 21 April 1916, two days before their planned insurrection. The mobilization order was cancelled, but 2,000 men took over the Central Post Office and other key buildings in Dublin anyway. The rebels had no hope of victory, and after a week of fighting, they surrendered. The leaders were executed, shocking Irish opinion and boosting Sinn Fein support. Their "martydom" inspired the Irish Republican Army in its nasty guerrilla war against British troops and Irish "collaborators", which was partially resolved in 1921 by the creation of the Irish Free State, without the six counties of Ulster.

▲ The burnt-out shell of the central Post Office in Dublin announced the end of the "Easter Rising" of 1916. This seizure of key points in Dublin by lightly-armed members of the Irish Republican Brotherhood had no hope of military success. The insurgents were outnumbered and probably under few illusions about their chances of sparking off a general uprising. But their quixotic action succeeded politically, when the British decided to execute the leaders of the uprising. Their martyrdom fuelled Irish resistance to continued British occupation, which ended in the south of Ireland in 1922. The six northern provinces of "Ulster" remain British to this day.

Datafile

The entry of the United States into the war and the two Russian revolutions of 1917 changed the character of World War I. Initially American involvement strengthened the Allies' claim to be fighting a war for democratic principles. In military terms, these parallel developments presented both a serious threat to and a fundamental reinforcement of the Allied position. With Russia out of the war from December 1917, the question was how rapidly could American military power be brought to bear on the Central Powers. In political terms, these changes were momentous. What had begun as a war between Europe's great multinational and imperial powers threatened to turn into a revolutionary war. Wilson and Lenin thought in terms very different from those of the men of 1914. In 1918 each offered a different vision of the future. When it became clear in 1918 that the German cause was lost, the question became which vision would guide the future of Europe and the world?

▼ Wilson's 14 points had three foundations: self-determination of peoples, free trade, and the desirability of a League of Nations. The difficulty was that in recognizing nationalism, he undermined the second and the third propositions. Wilson's political failure arose from this dilemma.

► The Treaty of Brest-Litovsk exposed the full imperialist objectives of the German war effort. The Treaty created a system of satellite states between Germany and Russia, remarkably similar to that which the Soviet Union established after 1945. Had the Germans won the war in the west, a similar settlement was likely.

The Treaty of Brest-Litovsk 3 March 1918

1. Territories previously belonging to Russia west of the agreed line will no longer be subject to Russian sovereignty. Germany and Austria-Hungary will determine the future status of these regions in agreement with their populations.

2. Russia to demobilize its army and bring its warships to port; mines to be removed from the Black Sea.

3. Russia to conclude peace with the Ukrainian People's Republic and recognize the treaty of 9 February 1918 between the Republic and the Central Powers.

4. Estonia and Livonia to be cleared of Russian troops and occupied by a German police force until national institutions can ensure their security. Finland to be cleared of Russian troops and ships.

5. The contracting parties renounce compensation for war expenses and war losses.

6. Independence of Persia and Afghanistan to be maintained.

President Wilson's 14 Points

1. Open covenants of peace, openly arrived at
2. Freedom of navigation upon the seas in peace or war
3. The removal of all economic barriers and the establishment of an equality of trade conditions among all nations
4. Adequate safeguards given and taken that national armaments will be reduced to the lowest point consistent with domestic safety
5. A free, open-minded and impartial adjustment of all colonial claims, based on the principle that the interests of the populations concerned have equal weight with the equitable claims of the government whose title is to be determined
6. The evacuation of all Russian territory
7. Belgium must be evacuated and restored
8. All French territory should be freed and the invaded portions restored, and the loss of Alsace-Lorraine in 1871 righted
9. Readjustment of the frontiers of Italy should be effected along clearly recognizable lines of nationality
10. The peoples of Austria-Hungary should be accorded the freest opportunity of autonomous development
11. Rumania, Serbia and Montenegro should be evacuated; occupied territory restored; and the relations of the several Balkan states to one another determined by friendly counsel along lines of allegiance and nationality
12. The Turkish portions of the Ottoman empire should be assured secure sovereignty, but the other nationalities now under Turkish rule should be assured an undoubted security of life and unmolested opportunity of autonomous development
13. An independent Polish state should be erected, including territories inhabited by indisputably Polish populations, which should be assured a free and secure access to the sea
14. A general association of nations must be formed under specific covenants for the purpose of affording mutual guarantees of political independence and territorial integrity to great and small states alike.

Chronology

1917

August 6
Kerensky appointed prime minister of Russia

September 3
Germans capture Riga on the Baltic coast

November 7
Bolshevik socialists in Russia overthrow the provisional government

November 16
FR: Clemenceau becomes premier and minister for war

December 3
The Bolshevik government in Russia signs an armistice with Germany

December 6
Finland declares independence from Russia

December 7
USA: Declares war on Austro-Hungarian Empire

1918

January 8
US president Woodrow Wilson publishes his 14 points as a basis for peace

March 3
Russia signs the Treaty of Brest-Litovsk

March 21
The Germans launch their Spring Offensive on the Western Front and push back the Allied forces

April 14
Foch appointed commander in chief of Allied forces (except for Belgian army)

May
(to Oct. 1919) Allied forces intervene in the Russian civil war

May 7
The Central Powers and Rumania sign the Peace of Bucharest

July 16
RUSS: Ex-czar Nicholas II and family murdered

July 18
(to Nov. 10) Allied counteroffensive on the Western Front: German forces are pushed back toward the German border

September 30
The Allies and Bulgaria conclude an armistice

October 3–4
The German government offers peace based on President Wilson's 14 points

GER: Max von Baden replaces Hertling as chancellor

October 4
British and Arab forces occupy Damascus

October 14
Turkey sends note to Wilson proposing an armistice

October 16
AH: Government declares AH as federal state based on nationalities (except for kingdom of Hungary)

October 27
AH/IT: Austro-Hungarian government asks Italian government for an armistice

October 28
German sailors mutiny at Kiel

November 3
Austria–Hungary sues for peace with the Allies

November 4–5
Antiwar and pro-Bolshevik risings in Germany

November 7
GER: A republic is proclaimed in Bavaria

November 9
Kaiser Wilhelm II abdicates

November 11
The Allies and Germany sign the Armistice: fighting ends on the Western Front at 11 a.m.

1917–18 REVOLUTION AND PEACE

The German U-boat campaign brings America into the war

Strikes, riots and mutiny topple Russia's imperial regime

The new Russian government fails on both military and diplomatic fronts

Bolsheviks seize power and take Russia out of the war

Germany launches another western offensive

But under the strain of counterattacks the German army retreats

Within a few months of his victory in the presidential election of 1916, Woodrow Wilson brought the USA into the war. That he could do so with his country behind him was almost certainly due to the impact of unrestricted submarine campaign waged by Germany from 1 February 1917.

Even before that date, German–American relations had been damaged by the interception by British naval intelligence of a message from the German foreign secretary Arthur Zimmerman – to Heinrich von Eckhardt, the German minister in Mexico. The message (now known as the Zimmermann Telegram) spoke of two matters: the need to offer Mexico an alliance with Germany in the event that the United States would go to war, and the possibility of German assistance for Mexico "to regain by conquest its lost territories in Texas, Arizona, and New Mexico". The cable, dated 17 January 1917 and was passed on to President Wilson on 24 February. He was furious, and a week later released the text to the press. Astoundingly, Zimmermann confimed its authenticity and thereby under mined the noninterventionist argument completely.

Long before this episode, though, Germany and the United States were on a collision course, so to speak, over the sinking of neutral ships or of ships with neutrals aboard, like the British liner *Lusitania,* on which over 100 Americans died when she went down on 7 May 1915. American protests brought some German assurances that it would not adopt a sink-without-warning submarine policy. But the assurances were worthless,

▼ "Wake Up America Day" parade in New York, 19 April 1917.

as the German sinking of the British steamship *Sussex* showed on 24 March 1916. This time Wilson issued an ultimatum to Germany about its U-boat campaign, and again Germany appeared to back off.

But only for a brief interval. By early 1917 it was the hope in Berlin that Britain – cut off at sea and with an increasingly exhausted French ally in tow – would sue for peace. The submarine campaign was thus an effort to restrict the flow of essential supplies to the UK and force it to its knees. It was a disastrous gamble. Not only did it fail to throttle the UK's war effort, it also provided Wilson with the pretext for war he needed. The United States declared war on Germany on 6 April 1917.

This was an outcome that Bethmann-Hollweg, the German chancellor, had tried to forestall. His own views on the U-boat campaign were not unequivocal, but his strictures were ignored by the military, who believed that the United States was already effectively on the side of the Allies. Bethmann-Hollweg had antagonized the military even more by his advocacy of the reform of the Prussian franchise. Ludendorff and Hindenburg were so incensed that they hurried to Berlin and threatened to resign if these "radical" measures were adopted. The Kaiser consulted the crown prince, well known for his reactionary views. More remarkably the crown prince consulted a number of political leaders. This was an unprecedented step, which yielded a surprisingly broad consensus against the chancellor. On 14 July 1917, in face of opposition from all sides, Bethmann-Hollweg resigned, and was replaced by the Prussian food controller, Georg Michaelis, a figure who dutifully carried out the orders of the ruling military junta.

Five days later the Reichstag passed a resolution calling for a negotiated peace on the basis of no annexations. This measure reflected the political mood in Germany after most people had come to see that the U-boat campaign would not bring about a decisive victory. But the Reichstag peace resolution was a dead letter from the start. This was partly due to the vague wording, which could be (and was) interpreted to mean everything and nothing at the same time. But it was also because the very notion of giving up territory after three years of war was completely unacceptable to the German high command and its political suporters.

Similarly stillborn was a papal peace initiative launched in August 1917. This attempt at mediation ran aground over the question of the future of Belgium. Whatever the Reichstag had said, the high command of the German army was simply not prepared to agree to the unconditional restoration of the prewar situation. And without such assurances, there was no hope of finding a basis for a negotiated settlement between the Entente and Central Powers.

Later in the summer of 1917 and beyond, those conservative and reactionary elements opposed to a compromise peace rallied around a new political formation, the Fatherland Party. This grew into a mass organization of the right, and drew support from heavy industry, farmers' organizations, middle-class groups, and extreme nationalist

▼ The neutral stance of the Roman Catholic Church in the war offended patriotic communicants in several combatant countries, each convinced of the holy mission of their fighting men. Pope Benedict XV condemned both the sinking of the *Lusitania* and the blockade of Germany, and thereby outraged French Catholics in particular. The pope made a peace overture in 1917, but it got nowhere, since it suggested a return to the prewar situation which to the Allies was simply out of the question.

Russia in 1917

In 1917 the war on the Russian sector of the Eastern Front came to an end. The army at the front lost any belief in victory; the army in the rear joined rebellious masses no longer prepared to fight for the czar. When riots broke out in Petrograd on 8 March soldiers refused to put them down. On 15 March the Duma appointed a Provisional government, which persuaded the czar to abdicate. Alongside this new executive body, a series of workers' and soldiers' councils (soviets) were set up to defend the revolution. These groups appeared spontaneously in cities, towns and villages. Soldiers' councils abolished much of the degrading routine of military life; if officers wanted to keep their units intact, they worked with the soviets.

The Provisional government was destroyed by the war, which it refused to abandon. To continue the fight, it had to keep much of the old regime intact. The generals, the bankers, the industrialists were still there. But while bureaucratic power was held by the provisional government, popular power – in particular among soldiers and urban workers – shifted to the Petrograd soviet. The new government effectively lost control of the peasantry and then of the army. The first was unavoidable. Peasants simply seized land and tried to survive the chaos of 1917. The second arose out of the impossibility of continuing the war.

The central problem was that Russia could not continue the war, but that all political

groups, save the Bolsheviks, ruled out the idea of a separate peace. This was a recipe for political paralysis, visible in the countless mass demonstrations held daily on the streets of Moscow and Petrograd. A sense of these extraordinary days may be gained from Boris Pasternak's *Dr Zhivago*. The choice was between the Provisional government and its leader Kerensky, who upheld "revolutionary defensism", throwing the invader off the soil of the new regime, and "revolutionary defeatism", the conversion of war into class war and the overthrow of the Provisional government. This was the position of Lenin and his Bolshevik supporters, whose ideas were captured in two slogans: "All power to the soviets" and "Bread, peace, and land."

The moderates launched a peace offensive, aimed at European socialist movements, who could put pressure on Western governments to end the war. This policy got nowhere. Without peace, and without an army, which dissolved after the military defeats incurred during the Kerensky offensive of June and July 1917, the provisional government simply held on. This presented the Bolsheviks with ideal conditions to increase their support. An attempt to suppress them in September failed. Equally unsuccessful was an abortive right-wing coup, led by General Kornilov. On 6 November 1917 the moment to strike had come. Bolshevik red guards captured the Winter Palace and other key points in Petrograd. Kerensky fled. The Bolshevik Revolution had begun.

Alexander Feodorovich Kerensky 1881–1971

Kerensky was born at Simbirsk and trained as a lawyer. He was a powerful orator and joined the Duma as a member of the labor group. He served as minister of justice in the first Provisional government of February 1917. Later on he became minister of war, and prime minister of the doomed regime. His commitment to carrying on the war, announced in powerful speeches, ensured his political failure. By July 1917 the middle ground on which he stood had crumbled. After the Bolshevik coup he fled Petrograd, and after failing to rally forces loyal to the regime, began a life of exile in the West. He died in 1971.

Lenin (Vladimir Ilyich Ulyanov) 1870–1924

In 1917 Lenin was a 44-year-old exile in Switzerland. After the February revolution he returned to Russia, with German assistance, and through his theoretical writings and daily leadership, prepared the ground for the Bolshevik revolution. He blocked moves toward an insurrection in July, and then led the seizure of power in November. In 1918 he took Russia out of the war, ratified peasant seizures of land, and with Trotsky led the struggle against counterrevolutionary armies. Lenin was the only man in Russia with the political insight and iron determination both to seize power and to hold it. He died in 1924.

Leon Trotsky 1879–1940

Trotsky was raised in the Ukraine and took an active part in the 1905 revolution. In February 1917 he was a 38-year-old exile in America. He returned to Russia, joined the Bolsheviks and after the November revolution became people's commissar for war. He forged the Red Army and must be credited with having saved the revolution. After Lenin's death he lost the succession struggle to Stalin, was expelled from the party (1927), and resumed his earlier life as an emigre. He was murdered in Mexico in 1940 by one of Stalin's agents. A spell-binding orator, Trotsky embodied the spirit of the revolution before it was deformed by Stalinism.

◀ The Russian army sealed the fate of the Provisional government of Kerensky by its disintegration after the July 1917 offensive. Soldiers simply had had enough. They streamed home, and joined peace demonstrations in the major cities. Power slipped from the hands of the Kerensky regime into those of the Bolsheviks, the one political group unequivocally committed to ending Russian participation in the war.

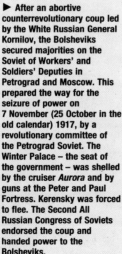

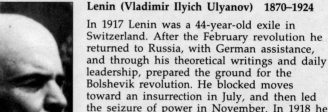

► After an abortive counterrevolutionary coup led by the White Russian General Kornilov, the Bolsheviks secured majorities on the Soviet of Workers' and Soldiers' Deputies in Petrograd and Moscow. This prepared the way for the seizure of power on 7 November (25 October in the old calendar) 1917, by a revolutionary committee of the Petrograd Soviet. The Winter Palace – the seat of the government – was shelled by the cruiser *Aurora* and by guns at the Peter and Paul Fortress. Kerensky was forced to flee. The Second All Russian Congress of Soviets endorsed the coup and handed power to the Bolsheviks.

associations. The party's program was unashamedly imperialistic, and advocated control of the Belgian and Dutch coasts and expansion into Russia and Turkey. Elements in the high command smiled benignly on this mad vision of Germany's future greatness. It was apparent, therefore, that the question of war aims further deepened the perilous social and political divisions within the Wilhelmine empire.

The Bolshevik road to peace

In the last year of the war, diplomacy moved both west and east. The Pope attempted to act as a middleman in diplomatic moves toward a compromise peace, but failed. Perhaps the high-minded Presbyterian in the White House could find a way to break the deadlock. Long before the United States entered the war, President Wilson had publicly pressed the belligerents for a declaration of war aims that could form the basis of a negotiated settlement. In January 1917 he had told the United States Senate of his commitment to "peace without victory". But initially his efforts were an insufficient force in and of themselves to get the combatants to consider realistically an alternative to the continuation of the war.

What concentrated their minds wonderfully was the first Russian revolution of March 1917. Strikes, riots and a general mutiny toppled the Russian imperial regime and a Provisional government was installed. But the new government, headed by Prince Lvov and later Alexander Kerensky, was committed to driving the German invaders off Russian land. This policy was termed "revolutionary defensism" – and ensured a collision with those who, like Lenin and his radical or Bolshevik followers, proclaimed the need to end the war, no matter what the cost.

The Germans were fully aware of the potentially disruptive effects of Bolshevik ideas on the course of the Russian war effort. They therefore had no difficulty in arranging passage for the exiled Lenin from Switzerland through the German and Austrian lines back to the Finland Station in Petrograd in April 1917.

Lenin proceeded to fuse the disparate factions within the Russian revolutionary movement into a powerful antiwar force. Many of these oppositional elements clustered around the councils of workers' and soldiers' deputies, or soviets. The most important such council sat in Petrograd, and in the chaotic conditions of early 1917 it assumed a position of power rivaling that of the provisional government itself.

At this time the radical (or Bolshevik) wing of the Russian social democratic party did not have anything like a majority in the soviets, but the decision to continue the war ultimately gave it to them. The new Russian regime was trying to keep open both diplomatic and military options. It therefore looked favorably on attempts by the Petrograd soviet to convene an international conference of socialists at Stockholm in the summer of 1917. The hope was that delegates from both sides would reach agreement on the basis of a negotiated settlement, and then return to lobby their respective governments to find an end to the war.

◄ Trotsky signed an armistice on 5 December 1917 in Brest-Litovsk. But peace negotiations dragged on for three months, while Trotsky (seen here on the right, arriving at Brest-Litovsk) tried to avoid the harsh terms set by the Germans.

► The German response to the Bolshevik tactic of "No war, no peace" was simply to move forward on a broad front in the Ukraine. Here German troops enter Minsk.

▼ Red Army soldiers choosing delegates in Petrograd for the first post-revolutionary congress of soviets.

Even though delegations were formed from all European belligerents, the full conference never took place. The reason was that, to increase its standing with the Allies, the Russian government authorized an offensive. It opened on 1 July 1917, and soon turned into a fiasco. Consequently Britain and France saw little military advantage in supporting the Kerensky government politically, by going along with the Stockholm idea. The French government withheld passports from its delegates, British seamen refused to transport the British delegation and so the initiative sank, along with the chances of survival of those still advocating "revolutionary defensism".

A few months later, in November, Lenin and the Bolsheviks seized power, and proceeded to act on their commitment to end the war. The price was the humiliating Treaty of Brest-Litovsk, signed on 3 March 1918, giving Germany a huge satellite empire in the east. But Lenin (and the Germans who had organized his return to Russia) judged correctly that bad as these terms were most Russians preferred them to the continuation of the war.

This "betrayal" of the Allied cause, not Bolshevik Marxism (which the Western leaders did not understand anyway), led Britain and France to sponsor the domestic enemies of the new regime. In 1918–19 British, French and American troops arrived in Russia, to try to hold down German troops and prevent their acquisition of Allied supplies, and then, if possible, to topple the regime. This intervention was half-hearted and futile. It did not possess the strength to influence Russian events one way or the other, and it betrayed a phenomenal ignorance of Russian conditions. The only outcome of Allied intervention was to create in the new regime a suspicion of Western motives which to some extent exists to this day.

Peace or revolution

German victory on the Eastern Front presented the Allies with the specter of increased military pressure in the west producing a decisive German thrust in France and Flanders before the American army could take the field. This is *almost* what happened, following the last German gamble of the war, the offensive launched on 21 March 1918. Within a few days the Germans had achieved what had eluded everyone else since 1914: a dislodgement of the enemy and an advance of about 65km (40mi). Further gains were made south of Ypres in April, and in Champagne in late May, and as far as the Marne on 30 May, at a point only 60km (37mi) from Paris.

But, though it was unclear at the time, that was the end of the offensive. The German army had staged a remarkable coup, but like every other major offensive of the war on the Western Front it could not produce a *decisive* breakthrough. The German army did not have the means to exploit its initial successes and rout the French or British armies completely. Faced with considerable logistical difficulties, and with few reserves on which to call, the German army could not stop the Allied counterattacks of August 1918.

Ludendorff later wrote that the "black day" of the German army was 8 August 1918. On the ground Canadian, Australian and British troops succeeded in pushing the Germans back from Amiens. In fact little in these developments was earth-shattering. Much more ominous than the outcome of this particular engagement were reports reaching the German high command of demoralization among their troops, leading to mass surrenders. This is what gave the 8th of August its real significance. It is not that the German army collapsed; it is rather that, from that moment, it ceased to believe it could achieve victory. Ludendorff was presented with increasing and undeniable evidence of a soldiers' strike among his men in the late summer and early autumn of 1918. After four years of believing their own claims of invincibility and propaganda about a pending victory, the recognition that they could not win came suddenly and bitterly to the German army.

This collapse of military morale was rapidly conveyed to the home front, which by the summer of 1918, had its own reasons for believing that the game was up. In March 1918 the nation had united once again, and great hopes had been placed on the one final push needed for victory. But when this proved chimerical, disillusionment spread like wildfire. Shortages of essential supplies became intolerable, and the situation was made worse by the onset of the worst epidemic of influenza the world had ever seen.

In military terms the disintegration of the Eastern Front and the loss of Bulgaria in September – which stripped Germany of essential petroleum reserves – were probably the last straws. The German high command simply could not carry on for more than a few weeks with what had become an increasingly mechanized war. Under the circumstances Ludendorff bitterly recognized that an outright victory had eluded him, and that the only alternatives to a military collapse in the west and an Allied invasion of Bohemia and southern Germany were an armistice and a negotiated peace. To seek an end to hostilities was also imperative for another, domestic, reason: it was to Ludendorff the only alternative to chaos – by which he meant the spread of revolution.

It is therefore ironic that Ludendorff turned to Woodrow Wilson as the man who could save Germany from catastrophe, both military and political. Ludendorff knew that Wilson would not deal with the old regime. Consequently he and his allies proceeded to hand over to his arch enemies in the Reichstag the political power the high command had exercised with such disastrous results over the previous two years.

In October 1918 the political scene was transformed. With the blessings of the high command, a major set of constitutional reforms was implemented. These steps virtually introduced parliamentary government, as a means of saving the Hohenzollern monarchy and of forestalling more radical developments. A new government under Prince Max of Baden was formed on 1 October, supported by a party political majority in the

Georges Benjamin Clemenceau 1841–1929

The son of a Vendée physician, Clemenceau received a medical education, and then entered political life. He was mayor of Montmartre at the time of the Paris commune. In the 1870s he became the leader of the radical party. He championed Zola and Dreyfus in his newspaper *L'Aurore*, and became minister of the interior in 1906, and premier from 1906 to 1909. His second ministry was during the war, when in 1917, at the age of 76, he became premier and minister of war, and reasserted parliamentary control over military affairs. He served until 1920, and died nine year later.

The Armistice of 11 November

The collapse of the Central Powers began on the Eastern Front. In September 1918 a major Allied offensive broke the German-Bulgarian line. On 30 September the Bulgarian government signed an armistice at Salonika. This convinced the German high command to force the government to enter into negotiations for an immediate general armistice, understood by Hindenburg and Ludendorff as creating a breathing space for regrouping their forces rather than as surrender. On 3 October Prince Max von Baden sent a note to President Wilson asking him to arrange an armistice. This was an admission of defeat, on which there was no going back. In the next three weeks the Allies pressed their offensive in bitter fighting on the Western Front, but the German line, in full retreat, did not break. Worse news for the Germans came from the Italian Front, where the Austro-Hungarian army was split into two in an Italian drive towards Vittorio Veneto. On 3 November Austria-Hungary capitulated. This followed by a few days the surrender of Turkey, on 30 October, after they had suffered a major defeat at the hands of British forces under Allenby. By early November, Germany was stripped of oil supplies, had run out of allies, men and essential materiel, faced revolution at home, and an Allied invasion of Germany from the south and east. The only option was to sue for peace. On 6 November a German armistice commission, led by the centrist deputy Mathias Erzberger, met General Foch in a railway carriage in Compiègne. They negotiated an armistice to come into effect at 11am on 11 November, to last 30 days. It was periodically renewed. The terms agreed were the immediate German evacuation of occupied territory behind the Western Front, the renunciation of the Treaty of Brest-Litovsk, the withdrawal of German troops in the east, and the surrender of certain war materiel, including 10 battleships, 6 cruisers, 8 light cruisers, 50 destroyers and 160 submarines. The U-boat fleet sailed into Harwich on 20 November. France was evacuated by the German army on 18 November; the Germans finally left Belgium eight days later. An Allied occupation of Germany began on 1 December. The naval blockade continued, to prevent any renewal of hostilities.

▶ Foch and German delegates outside Foch's carriage.

Reichstag. Within two days the new regime sent a note to President Wilson asking him personally "to take steps for the restoration of peace". This note and later exchanges were published, and made it apparent that the price of peace was to be high. The negotiations dragged on, and given the publicity that surrounded them, they contributed to a sense of despair and confusion in the population at large as to why the war was continuing.

The collapse of the Austro-Hungarian Empire in October 1918 placed in unmistakably high relief the hopelessness of the German cause. Consequently the pressure to conclude a peace at virtually any price grew apace. The process of political reform was accelerated simply to bring about an armistice. This helps account for the fact that on the same day, 26 October, Ludendorff resigned as quartermaster general, and the Reichstag completed its deliberations on the shape of a future parliamentary government. Ludendorff's replacement was Groener.

Thus the decision to end the war and to accept political reform – the "revolution from above" was taken by the German high command and their allies well before the outbreak of widespread revolutionary activity among workers and sailors from 28 October – "the revolution from below".

What in the eyes of the masses seemed to make peace all the more urgent was the treasonous activities of the admirals. Concerned to secure a future for the navy in postwar Germany, they ordered a sortie of the battle fleet for a heroic do-or-die encounter with the more powerful Royal Navy. They did so in the knowledge that this was bound to discredit the armistice negotiations of their political superiors. But the "honor" of the navy, as they understood it, was more important to them than an end to the war or the lives of the men they led. The sailors, learning of the suicide mission, took a different view and disobeyed orders. This time mutiny merged with revolution; the sailors had won the day. Demonstrations broke out, first in the port cities and then in other urban centers. By 7–8 November the situation had got completely out of hand. The "revolution from below" was underway.

Prince Max announced the abdication of the Kaiser before the latter had given his consent. His generals persuaded the monarch that he had no choice but to go; they arranged for him to slip across the Dutch border near his headquarters at Spa in Belgium. Prince Max also resigned, and the Hohenzollern monarchy simply collapsed. Power was lying in the streets of Berlin, as it did in other capitals of Central Europe.

On 11 November 1918 the Armistice was signed. In Germany the old order had put an end to the military conflict and had managed to transfer responsibility for the mess they had created to the new democratic regime. At last the politicians' war was over.

We know, too, that the object of the war is attained; the object upon which all free men had set their hearts; and attained with a sweeping completeness which even now we do not realize. Armed imperialism such as the men conceived who were but yesterday the masters of Germany is at an end, its illicit ambitions engulfed in black disaster. Who will now seek to revive it?

WOODROW WILSON
11 NOVEMBER 1918

Thomas Woodrow Wilson 1856–1924

The son of a Presbyterian minister from Virginia, Wilson was an academic, a moralist and a Democratic politician. In 1910 he was elected governor of New Jersey, and two years later, president of the United States. He was reelected in 1916, in the midst of a war toward which he had maintained a neutral stance. Wilson tried to act as an honest broker between the sides, but gradually saw war with Germany as inevitable, given German unrestricted submarine warfare and approaches to Mexico. He led his country into war in April 1917. After the Armistice he played a central part in the creation of the League of Nations. The rejection of its covenant by the US senate was the worst reversal of Wilson's career. He was not reelected in 1920, and died four years later.

PART 2

THE GENERALS' WAR

MILITARY COMMANDERS AND GLOSSARY

AUSTRO-HUNGARIAN EMPIRE

Commander-in-Chief

Field Marshal Franz Conrad von Hötzendorf 1914–17
General Artur Arz von Straussenberg 1917–18

Principal Army Commanders

First Army
General Baron Viktor Dankl von Krasnik 1914–15
General Puhallo 1915–16
General Artur Arz von Straussenberg 1916–17
General Rohr 1917

Second Army
General Oskar Potiorek 1914
Field Marshal Baron Eduard von Böhm-Ermolli 1914–17

Third Army
General Rudolf Brudermann 1914
Field Marshal Baron Svetozar von Boroević von Bojna 1914–16
General Baron Hermann Kovess von Kovesshaza 1916–17
General von Terszytyansky 1917

Fourth Army
General Moritz Auffenberg von Komarow 1914
General Archduke Josef 1914–16
General von Terszytyansky 1916–17
General von Kirchbach 1917

Fifth Army
General Frank 1914–16
Field Marshal Baron Svetozar von Boroević von Bojna 1916–17

Sixth Army
General Oskar Potiorek 1914–15
General Archduke Josef 1918

Seventh Army
General Karl Pflanzer-Baltin 1915–17
General Baron Hermann Kovess von Kovesshaza 1917

Tenth Army
General Rohr 1916
Field Marshal Baron von Krobatin 1916–18

Eleventh Army
General Baron Viktor Dankl von Krasnik 1916
General Rohr 1916–17
General Count Sheuchenstuel 1917–18

BELGIUM

Principal Army Commander
King Albert I 1914–18

BULGARIA

Commander-in-Chief
King Ferdinand I 1915–18

Principal Army Commanders

1st Army
General Boyadzhiyev 1915–16
General Gesov 1916–18
General Nerezov 1918

Second Army
General Todorov 1915–18
General Lukov 1918

Third Army
General Toshev 1915–17
General Nerezov 1917–18

Fourth Army
General Toshev 1917–18

FRANCE

Commander-in-Chief
Marshal Joseph Joffre 1914–16
General Robert Nivelle 1916–17
Marshal Philippe Pétain 1917–18

Supreme Commander of all Allied armies on Western Front
Marshal Ferdinand Foch 1918

Principal Army Commanders

First Army
General Augustin Dubail 1914–15
General Pierre Roques 1915–16
General Mazel 1916
General Gerard 1916
Marshal Emile Fayolle 1916–17
General Joseph Micheler 1917
General Henri Gouraud 1917
General François Anthoine 1917
General Marie Debeney 1917–18

Second Army
General Eduard de Curières de Castelnau 1914–15
Marshal Philippe Petain 1915–16
General Robert Nivelle 1916
General Louis Guillaumat 1916–17
General Hirschauer 1917–18

Third Army
General Pierce Ruffey 1914
General Maurice Sarrail 1915–15
General Georges Humbert 1915–18

Fourth Army
General Fernand de Langle de Cary 1914–15
General Henri Gouraud 1915–16
Marshal Emile Fayolle 1916
General Pierre Roques 1916–17
General François Anthoine 1917
General Henri Gouraud 1917–18

Fifth Army
General Charles Lanrezac 1914
Marshal Louis Franchet d'Esperey 1914–16
General Mazel 1916–17
General Joseph Micheler 1917–18
General Edmond Buat 1918
General Henri Berthelot 1918
General Louis Guillaumat 1918

Sixth Army
General Manoury 1914–15
General Pierre Dubois 1915–16
Marshal Emile Fayolle 1916
General Charles Mangin 1916–17
General Paul Maistre 1917
General Denis Duchène 1917–18
General Jean Degoutte 1918

Seventh Army
General Putz 1914–15
General Louis de Maud'huy 1915
General de Villaret 1917–18
General Marie Debeney 1916–17
General Baucheron de Boissoudy 1917–18
General Georges Humbert 1918
General. M. Henri de Mitry 1918

Eighth Army
General Victor d'Urbal 1914–15
General Putz 1915
General Gerard 1917–18

Ninth Army
Marshal Ferdinand Foch 1914
General M. Henri de Mitry 1918

Tenth Army
General Louis de Maud'huy 1914–15
General Victor d'Urbal 1915–16
General Joseph Micheler 1916
General Denis Duchène 1916–17
General Paul Maistre 1917–18
General Charles Mangin 1918

GERMANY

Commander-in-Chief
Field Marshal Helmuth, Count Moltke 1914
General Erich von Falkenhayn 1914–16
Field Marshal Paul von Beneckendorf und von Hindenburg 1916–18
Quartermaster General Erich Ludendorff 1916–18
General Wilhelm Groener 1918

Principal Army Commanders

First Army
General Alexander von Kluck 1914–15
General Max von Fabeck 1915–16
General Fritz von Below 1916–18

Second Army
Field Marshal Karl von Bülow 1914–15
General Fritz von Below 1915–16
General Max von Gallwitz 1916
General Georg von der Marwitz 1916–18

Third Army
General Max von Hausen 1914–15
General Karl von Einem 1915–18

Fourth Army
Field Marshal Albrecht, Duke of Württemberg 1914–17
General Friedrich Sixt von Armin 1917–18

Fifth Army
Crown Prince Wilhelm 1914–16
General Ewald von Lochow 1916
General Max von Gallwitz 1916–18

Sixth Army
Field Marshal Rupprecht, Crown Prince of Bavaria 1914–16
General Otto von Below 1917
General Ferdinand von Quast 1917–18

Seventh Army
General Josias von Heeringen 1914–15
General Richard von Schubert 1915–17
General Hans von Böhn 1917–18

Eighth Army
General Max von Prittwitz und Gaffron 1914
Field Marshal Paul von Beneckendorf und von Hindenburg 1914
General Erich Ludendorff 1914
General Richard von Schubert 1914–15
General Otto von Below 1915–17
General Oskar von Hutier 1917

Ninth Army
Field Marshal Paul von Beneckendorf und von Hindenburg 1914
General Erich Ludendorff 1914
Field Marshal August von Mackensen 1914–15
General Erich von Falkenhayn 1916–17

Tenth Army
Field Marshal Hermann von Eichhorn 1915
General Erich von Falkenhayn 1918

Eleventh Army
Field Marshal August von Mackensen 1915
General Max von Gallwitz 1915–16
General A. von Winckler 1916–17

Twelfth Army
General von Steuben 1917–18

Fourteenth Army
General Otto von Below 1917

Seventeenth Army
General Otto von Below 1918

Eighteenth Army
General Oskar von Hutier 1918

Nineteenth Army
General Felix, Count Bothmer 1918

ITALY

Commander-in-Chief
General Luigi, Count Cadorna 1915–17
General Armando Diaz 1917–18

Principal Army Commanders

First Army
General Roberto Brusati 1915–16
General Gugliemo, Count Pecori-Giraldi 1916–18

Second Army
General Pietro Frugoni 1915–16
General Settimio Piacentini 1916–17
General Luigi Capello 1917–18

Third Army
General The Duke of Aosta 1915–18

Fourth Army
Lt.-General Luigi Nava 1915–16
General Mario Nicolis di Robilant 1916–18
General Giardino 1918

Sixth Army
General Mabretti 1917–18
General L. Montuori 1918

Seventh Army
General G. Tassoni 1918

Eighth Army
Lt.-General E. Caviglia 1918

Ninth Army
General Paolo Morrone 1918

JAPAN

Principal Commander (Tsingtao Expedition)

Lt.-General Kamio	1914

OTTOMAN EMPIRE

Commander-in-Chief

Enver Pasha	1914–18
First Army	
General Otto Liman von Sanders	1914–15
Second Army	
General Vehip Pasha	1914–16
General Mustapha Kemal Pasha	1916–17
Third Army	
General Hasan Izzet Pasha	1914
General Mehmet Kamil Pasha	1914–16
General Vehip Pasha	1916–17
Fourth Army	
General Ahmed Djemal Pasha	1914–18
Fifth Army	
General Otto Liman von Sanders	1915–16
Sixth Army	
Field Marshal Colmar von der Goltz	1915
General Halil Pasha	1917
Seventh Army	
General Mustapha Kemal Pasha	1917
Eighth Army	
General Djevad Pasha	1918
Ninth Army	
General Yakup Sevki Pasha	1918

ROMANIA

Commander-in-Chief

King Ferdinand I	1916–18
Principal Army Commanders	
First Army	
General Culcer	1916–17
General Iliescu	1917
Second Army	
General Crainiceanu	1916
General A. Averescu	1916–17
Third Army	
General A. Averescu	1916
General Aslan	1916–17
Fourth Army	
General Presan	1916–17
Dobruja Army	
General Zayonchkovski	1916–17

RUSSIA

Commander-in-Chief

Grand Duke Nicholas	1914–15
Quartermaster General G.N. Danilov	1914–15
General Mikhail Alekseev	1915–16
Czar Nicholas II	1916–17
Principal Army Commanders	
First Army	
General Paul Rennenkampf	1914
General Litvinov	1915
Second Army	
General Alexander Samsonov	1914
General Scheidemann	1914–15
General Smirnov	1915
Third Army	
General Nikolai von Ruzsky	1914
General Radko-Dmitriev	1914–15
General Lyesh	1915–17
Fourth Army	
General Salza	1914
General Alexei Evert	1914–15
General Ragoza	1915–17
Fifth Army	
General Plehve	1914–15
Sixth Army	
General Churin	1915
General Tsurikov	1917
Seventh Army	
General Shcherbatchev	1916–17
Eighth Army	
General Alexei A. Brusilov	1914–15
General Alexei Kaledin	1916–17
Ninth Army	
General Platon A. Lechitsky	1914–17
Tenth Army	
General Pflug	1914–15
General Sievers	1915
General Radkevich	1915–16
Eleventh Army	
General Selivanov	1914–15
General Shcherbatchev	1915–16
General V.V. Sakharov	1916
General Balanin	1917
Twelfth Army	
General Plehve	1915
General Gorbatovsky	1915
General Klembovsky	1917

SERBIA

Commander-in-Chief

Field Marshal Rodomir Putnik	1914–16
Crown Prince Alexander	1916–18
Principal Army Commanders	
First Army	
General Zinojin Mišic	1914–15
Second Army	
Field Marshal Stepa Stepanovič	1914–15
Third Army	
General Paul Jurišić-Sturm	1914–15

UK OF GREAT BRITAIN AND IRELAND AND IMPERIAL FORCES

Commander-in-Chief

Field Marshal Sir John French	1914–15
Field Marshal Sir Douglas Haig	1915–18
Principal Army Commanders	
First Army	
Field Marshal Sir Douglas Haig	1914–15
General Sir Henry Rawlinson	1915–16
General Sir Charles Monro	1916
General Sir Henry, Lord Horne	1916–18
Second Army	
General Sir Horace Smith-Dorrien	1914–15
Field Marshal Sir Herbert Plumer	1915–17
General Sir Henry Rawlinson	1915–16
Third Army	
General Sir Charles Monro	1915
Field Marshal Sir Edmund Allenby	1915–17
General Sir Julian, Baron Byng	1917–18
Fourth Army	
General Sir Henry Rawlinson	1916–18
Fifth Army	
Lt.-General Sir Hubert de la Poer Gough	1916–18
General Sir Henry Rawlinson	1917–18
Gallipoli Army	
General Sir Ian Hamilton	1915
General Sir Charles Monro	1915
Salonika Army	
General Sir Charles Monro	1915
General Sir Bryan Mahon	1915–16
Lt.-General Sir George Milne	1916–18
Egypt/Palestine Army	
General Sir Julian, Baron Byng	1914
Lt.-General Sir John Maxwell	1914–15
General Sir Charles Monro	1915–16
General Sir Archibald Murray	1916–17
Field Marshal Sir Edmund Allenby	1917–18

UNITED STATES OF AMERICA

Commander-in-Chief

General John Pershing	1917–18
Principal Army Commanders	
First Army	
General John Pershing	1917–18
General Hunter Liggett	1918
Second Army	
Major-General Robert Bullard	1918

Admiralty
British government department for the Royal Navy and naval affairs, headed by the first lord.

ANZAC
Acronym for the Australian and New Zealand Army Corps, later used to denote any member of the Australian and New Zealand armed forces.

Attack in depth
Offensive strategy aimed at capturing objectives beyond the enemy's front system of trenches.

Attrition
Strategy of wearing out the enemy by continued offensives to exhaust his reserves of manpower.

"Bite and hold"
Offensive strategy of taking and consolidating the enemy's defensive positions, thereby forcing him to undertake costly counterattacks.

Breakthrough
The piercing of the enemy's defensive line to allow operations in the open country beyond.

British Expeditionary Force
The six divisions of the British regular army sent to France in August 1914. The term was thereafter applied to all British and imperial forces in France.

Cult of the offensive
Belief, prevalent in prewar European armies, that an offensive strategy is superior to one of defense in all circumstances.

Defense in depth
Defensive strategy of giving ground against an enemy attack, then retaking lost ground with strong counterattacks.

Devolved command
The passing of responsibility for the tactical conduct of a battle from the high command to the officers commanding in the field.

General headquarters
Department of the commander in chief responsible for the planning and conduct of military operations.

"Guerre à l'outrance"
(Fr.) All-out warfare ("to the bitter end"), to gain a military victory in preference to a negotiated peace.

Hindenburg Line
Prepared section of defensive line on the Western Front, to which the Germans withdrew in March 1917.

Infiltration tactics
Tactics, developed by the Germans for their 1918 offensive, and based on fast exploitation of successful assaults.

Landsturm
German second-line infantry formations, equivalent to Allied territorials.

Lines of communication
The network of roads and railways connecting a military formation with its base of logistic supply.

Logistics
The support services of an army, providing the men and materiel necessary for its effective operation.

Offensive
A carefully prepared, large-scale strategic attack.

Salient
A projection of forces into enemy-held territory.

Strategy
The planning and design of war; the "logic" of war.

Tactics
The small-scale conduct of war; the "grammar" of war.

Datafile

The first phase of the war was fought according to preordained plans. The French launched Plan XVII eastward toward Alsace, Lorraine and the Rhine, in part to achieve a lightning victory and invade Germany itself, and in part to aid their Russian allies, whose mobilization was bound to be a protracted affair. The Germans unfolded with clockwork precision the opening phases of the Schlieffen Plan, under which one million German troops invaded Belgium and Luxembourg, before wheeling south into France itself. The result was a bloodbath. Plan XVII played directly into German hands. The weight of French forces moved east, thereby exposing their forces to the north of Paris to the brunt of the German advance. Fortunately for the French, reinforcements moved west by railroad and north by any form of transport available, including the Parisian taxi fleet, and stopped the Germans on the River Marne. The failure of the Schlieffen Plan created a "race to the sea", the indecisive outcome of which fixed the military stalemate of the Western Front.

The parallel Russian advance into East Prussia resulted in a crushing German victory, on a scale similar to that inflicted on the French in 1870–71. Between 26 and 30 August a carefully executed redeployment of German troops took the Russians by surprise, at Tannenberg. The Russian Second Army under Samsonov was annihilated. Over 100,000 prisoners were taken, and Samsonov committed suicide. Two new heroes of German military history emerged: Erich Ludendorff and Paul von Hindenburg.

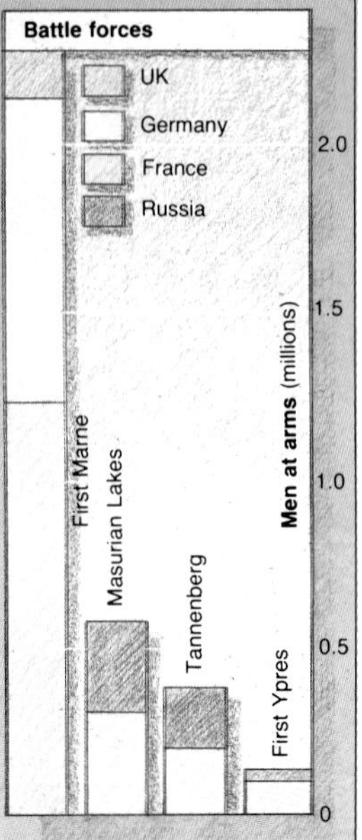

▲ **The Battle of the Marne dwarfed the other major encounters of the first year of the war. The weight of combat on the Western Front as a whole was greater still, in that it included the French thrust eastward in Plan XVII. At this stage, the British part in the war was minor. It grew rapidly, bolstered by significant imperial forces.**

Chronology

June 28
Assassination of Austro-Hungarian Archduke Franz Ferdinand in Sarajevo

July 23
(to Aug. 4) War crisis in Europe

August 1
FR: Mobilization of army with Joffre as commander in chief

August 2
GER: Moltke appointed chief of the general staff of German field armies

August 3
German invasion of Belgium begins

August 4
UK: Sir John French is appointed commander in chief of the British Expeditionary Force

August 11
Goeben and *Breslau* enter the Black Sea

August 21
GER: Ludendorff appointed chief of staff of the Eighth Army in East Prussia

August 22
GER: Hindenburg appointed commander of Eighth Army

August 24
Main German armies enter France

August 26–30
Battle of Tannenberg: German victory in East Prussia

August 29
RUSS: Commander of defeated Second Army, Samsonov, commits suicide

September 5–10
First Battle of the Marne: German advance halted

September 6–15
Battle of the Masurian Lakes: German victory in East Prussia

September 8–12
Battle of Lemberg: Russians capture Austria-Hungary's fourth-largest city

September 14
GER: Moltke resigns; succeeded by Falkenhayn

September 15
First trenches of the war are dug

September 17
(to Oct. 18) "Race to the Sea": front in the west is extended to the Channel coast

September 18
GER: Hindenburg appointed commander in chief of German armies in the eastern theater

October 12
(to Nov. 11) First Battle of Ypres: inconsequential conflict between Germans and Allies

November 1
Russia declares war on Turkey. Battle of Coronel: German Pacific Squadron defeats British naval force off coast of Chile

November 11
(to early Dec.) Germans force Eastern Front further to the east

December 2
Austro-Hungarians capture Belgrade (capital of Serbia)

December 8
Battle of the Falkland Islands: British fleet defeats the German Pacific Squadron

GER: Commander of German China Squadron, von Spee, perishes when his ship is sunk in the Battle of the Falkland Islands

December 11
Serbians recapture Belgrade

In warfare, according to the Prussian theorist Karl von Clausewitz (1780–1831), everything is simple, and the simplest things are infinitely complicated. The way World War I was fought in its first phase demonstrates the disturbing truth of these words. The vision of those who planned for war in 1914 was in some respects remarkable, but what they had not taken into account was another of Clausewitz's ideas. That is the concept of "friction", the tendency for plans to come unstuck, for things to go awry, for the unexpected to govern events.

Successful command in World War I was not the ability to execute great preconceived programs, to meet rigid timetables and to adhere to a set pattern of given objectives. It was rather the art of living with confusion and uncertainty, and accepting the limitations of even the best technology of the day. In this context the war fought by

Prewar Military Planning

Military planners before 1914 were set the task of finding ways to respond to potential threats to national interests. The instability of the international system provided many such threats. The existence of plans, however, increased political tension and contributed to the outbreak of war itself. In prewar Western Europe three plans caused problems. The first was for the enhancement of German naval strength, devised by Admiral Alfred von Tirpitz (see pp.30–31). The second was the French Plan XVII for the reversal of its humiliating defeat by Prussia in the war of 1870–71, which gave birth to the German Empire and stripped France of Alsace and Lorraine. The third was the German Schlieffen Plan, to break out of the "encirclement" of Germany, faced with the prospect of a two-front war against France and Russia. Each plan led Europe toward war, but when war came, each plan did not produce the anticipated outcome. The result was an unforeseen protracted and bloody war.

Count Alfred von Schlieffen 1833–1913

Schlieffen was a military strategist of genius. From his experience in the Franco-Prussian War (1870–71) and his interest in military theory and history he was able, as chief of the German imperial general staff (1891–1906), to conceive a daring plan for fighting a war on two fronts, the so-called Schlieffen Plan. Its aim was the annihilation of the French army before Russian mobilization was completed. Although he died before his plan could be tested in the field, he left his successor, Moltke, with a clear strategy wedded to an effective logistical support system. But Moltke weakened the crucial right wing and failed to take Paris in 1914. Whether or not Schlieffen's original plan could have succeeded is a controversial question.

1914 THE WAR OF ILLUSIONS

Improvisation was the key to military success

The Schlieffen Plan and Plan XVII fail

Reasons for the German failure

The Russians lose the Battle of Tannenberg

Austrian failures on the Eastern Front

Stalemate on both fronts

Initial naval skirmishes

the generals was littered with disasters, arising from limitations of imagination and materiel. Those who succeeded did so through improvisation, not planning.

From the Schlieffen Plan to the Marne

These points were epitomized by the first major campaign of the war, that of the German army in Belgium and France in August–September 1914. The war planned by the German general staff was in line with the strategic objective of knocking France out of the conflict before Russia would conquer Eastern Germany. It accepted the risks of an early Russian move westward and a French attack on Alsace and Lorraine, in order to unleash five armies – three-quarters of the entire German army in a gigantic westward sweep across Belgium and Luxembourg, followed by a wheel south into France. The whole operation was to take precisely 42 days. This was the "Schlieffen Plan", the German army's gamble to win the war in one fell swoop. It was devised between 1897 and 1905 by Alfred von Schlieffen, head of the German general staff (1891–1906), was modified in the next few years, and then finally put into operation by his successor, General Helmuth von Moltke, in August 1914.

German mobilization was underway by 1 August 1914. Between 1 and 3 August the German Fourth Army occupied Luxembourg; the following day, just as Schlieffen had planned, forward units advanced into Belgium. The forts surrounding Liège held up the progress of the Second Army, but the city surrendered on 16 August, after an 11-day siege.

The French army, under General Joffre, was unaware of its enemy's true intentions. In any event the French had their own preconceived set

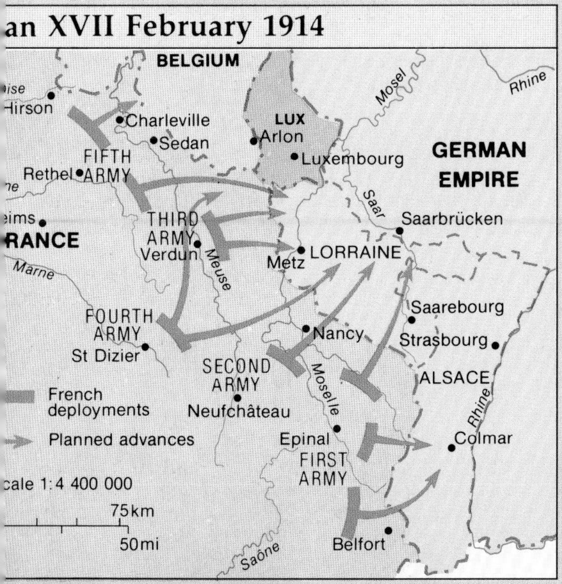

▲► French strategists knew of the Schlieffen Plan before 1914, but did not believe that Germany had sufficient numbers in the army to execute it. Plan XVII, implemented by Joffre in modified form in August 1914, played directly into the hands of the German army, and nearly cost France the war. Germany's Schlieffen Plan showed a better understanding of the enemy's strategy, but underestimated the difficulties of crossing northern France.

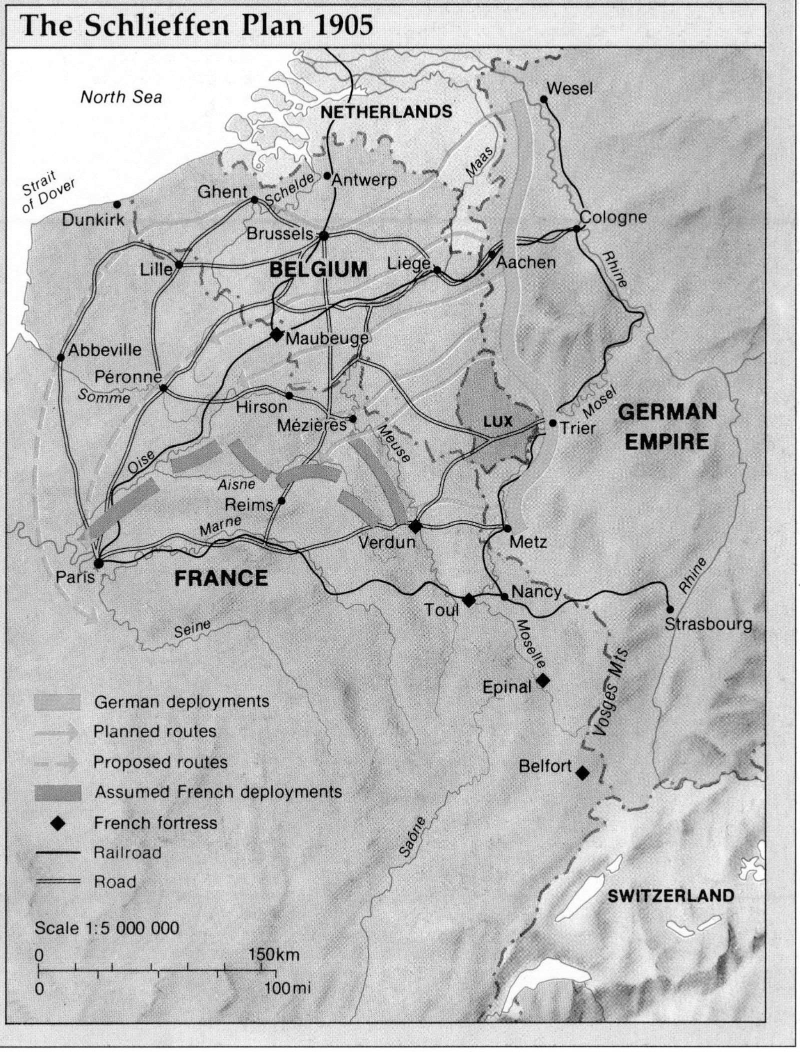

Helmuth von Moltke 1848–1916

Sixty-six years old in 1914 and in failing health, Moltke (chief of the imperial general staff since 1906) had to translate Schlieffen's plans into action. Faced with war on two fronts, he followed Schlieffen's principles of containing the Russian army with minimum forces in the east and outflanking the French in the west. Unfortunately he had modified Schlieffen's original plan by withdrawing six divisions from the west to strengthen the eastern forces. He was blamed for the German defeat at the First Battle of the Marne and relieved of his post.

Joseph Jacques Joffre 1852–1931

A veteran of the defense of Paris in 1870 and numerous colonial skirmishes, Joffre in the summer of 1914 was one of France's most experienced soldiers. At 63 he was commander in chief of the French army and led the resistance to the German invasion. He checked the German advance at the First Battle of the Marne. After the indecisive "race to the sea" and onset of trench warfare he became more a symbolic figure than a decisive leader. The Battle of Verdun gave the politicians the opportunity to ease him out. He played no further part in the war.

Sir John French 1852–1925

When Britain entered the war in August 1914 French was chosen to command the British Expeditionary Force, at the age of 66. A veteran cavalry officer, he retained command of the British army on the Western Front until the end of 1915. His departure was provoked by the fruitless struggles at Ypres and elsewhere, culminating in the Battle of Loos when British losses far outweighed those of the Germans for no gain. Like other cavalry men, he was puzzled by the nature of the war of 1914–15.

of operations to put into effect: Plan XVII. This was an eastward thrust into the provinces of Alsace and Lorraine (which had been occupied by Germany in the Franco-Prussian war of 1870). Such a move was precisely what the Germans wanted the French to do, since it weakened the French lines at the point at which they intended to strike, in the north. The implementation of Plan XVII (in an amended form) was a complete and bloody failure. The Germans repulsed repeated French attacks in the east between 10 and 28 August, while opening the key phase of their campaign in the west.

Five armies participated in the German invasion as a whole, but the most important was the First, under Alexander von Kluck. His forces (an army initially of 320,000 men) were on the outer edge of the German arc and would therefore cover the most ground of any unit. His men crossed into Belgium on 16 August, and entered Brussels four days later. The German armies then headed south, and by 29 August, in successful operations at Mons, Le Cateau and Charleroi, they had forced heavily outnumbered troops of the British Expeditionary Force (Britain's contribution to the defense of Belgium and France, commanded by Sir John French) and the French army to retreat southward.

Retreat is one of the most dangerous military maneuvers: the fact that it was accomplished at all was one of the wonders of the war. The new Allied line formed in early September just south of the Marne, and swept from the city of Meaux above Paris to Verdun on the River Meuse, 260km (160mi) away.

Along the River Marne, between 5 and 10 September, Allied counterattacks, known as the First Battle of the Marne, stopped the larger German armies, forced them to regroup north of the river, and destroyed the Schlieffen Plan. World War I was born.

▶ German reserve units and reinforcements assembling in the old market square of Mechelen (or Malines), about 25km (15mi) north of Brussels, in August 1914. Belgian armed resistance was unable to do more than slow down the Germans; the city of Liège fell only on 16 August after stiff resistance. The capital was taken on 20 August. German troops lived off the land and took severe measures against Belgians accused of resisting the German advance. The result was a panic among civilians, leading to an exodus of one million Belgian refugees.

The German Invasion of Belgium and France 1914

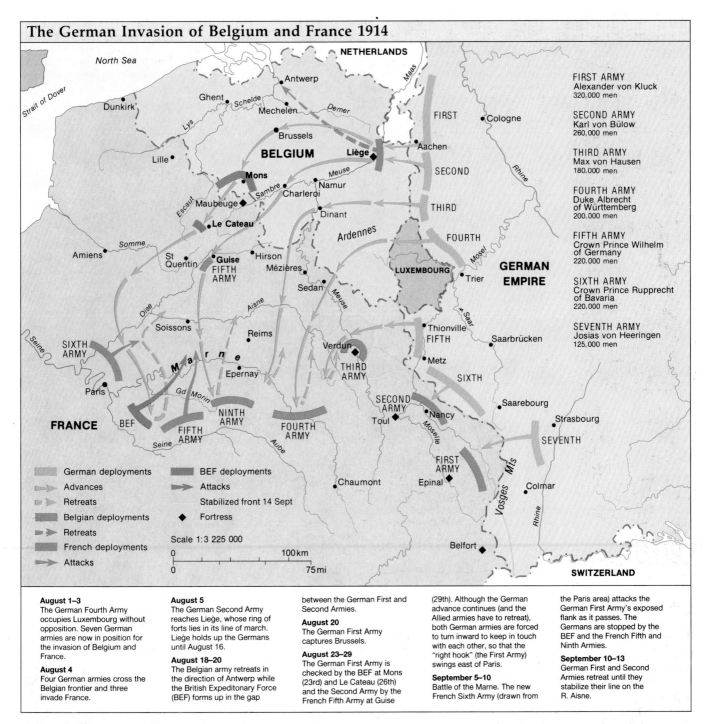

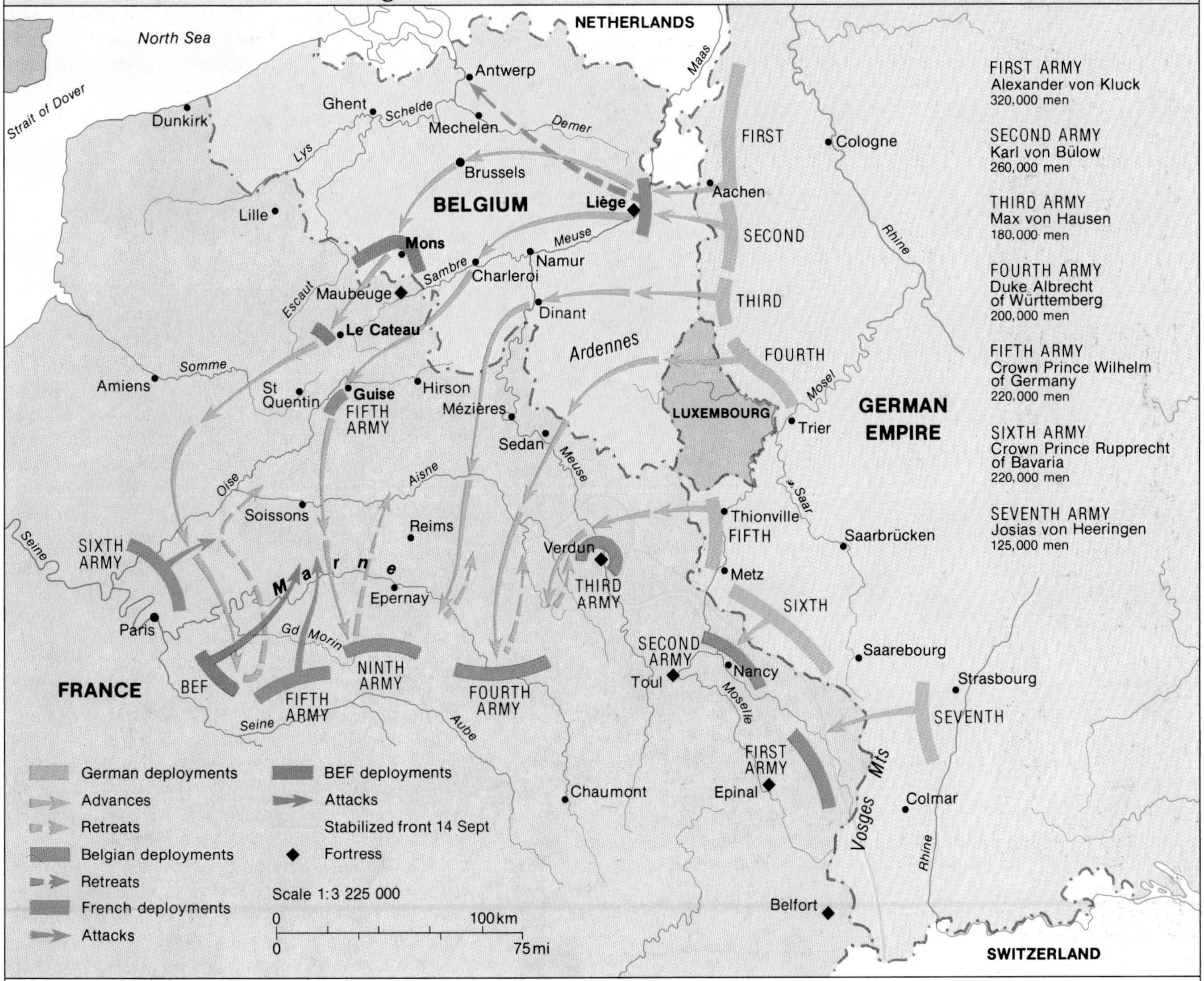

August 1–3
The German Fourth Army occupies Luxembourg without opposition. Seven German armies are now in position for the invasion of Belgium and France.

August 4
Four German armies cross the Belgian frontier and three invade France.

August 5
The German Second Army reaches Liège, whose ring of forts lies in its line of march. Liège holds up the Germans until August 16.

August 18–20
The Belgian army retreats in the direction of Antwerp while the British Expeditionary Force (BEF) forms up in the gap between the German First and Second Armies.

August 20
The German First Army captures Brussels.

August 23–29
The German First Army is checked by the BEF at Mons (23rd) and Le Cateau (26th) and the Second Army by the French Fifth Army at Guise (29th). Although the German advance continues (and the Allied armies have to retreat), both German armies are forced to turn inward to keep in touch with each other, so that the "right hook" (the First Army) swings east of Paris.

September 5–10
Battle of the Marne. The new French Sixth Army (drawn from the Paris area) attacks the German First Army's exposed flank as it passes. The Germans are stopped by the BEF and the French Fifth and Ninth Armies.

September 10–13
German First and Second Armies retreat until they stabilize their line on the R. Aisne.

Assessment of the Schlieffen Plan

Whether or not the Schlieffen Plan could have succeeded is one of the most hotly debated topics in military history. Critics of Moltke's tactics usually concentrate on the fact that his right wing (initially on the northern side) was not eight times stronger than his left wing, as stipulated by Schlieffen, but only three times stronger. They also question the wisdom of the decision to move north and east of Paris rather than south and west in an enveloping assault on the city, and point to the creation of a 48km (30mi) gap between the German First and Second Armies as a fatal mistake, leading to defeat on the Marne.

But these might-have-beens ignore three fundamental problems which doomed the Schlieffen Plan from the start. The first concerns human endurance; the second, logistical difficulties; the third, communications problems. The plan failed to take account of the limitations of the individual soldier and of the system which supplied and directed him.

First, the men of the German First Army had to cover 30–40km (20–25mi) per day. Is it a surprise that by early September many units were simply exhausted, and that others had been reduced to 50 percent of their original strength? Secondly, their lines of supply were so extended that, even had they won the Battle of the Marne, they almost certainly could have gone no further. Thirdly, the speed of the operation outpaced the communications system between the Front and the high command, situated in Luxembourg, 240km (150mi) away. Thus Moltke could not obtain

▲ Schlieffen's idea was that the sleeve of the last German soldier on the right flank would almost brush the English Channel in an arcing movement west and then south through Belgium and France. Moltke's reality (above) was only slightly less breathtaking. The First Army (under Alexander von Kluck) had to march, fight and march again in a 350km (220mi) line extending from Aachen to Brussels to Le Cateau to the River Marne. That it was stopped there is not surprising; the troops had reached the limits of human endurance.

▲ **German troops on the Eastern Front in 1914. "Eastern fronts" would be a more accurate description of the 1,000km (625mi) field of operations formed by the Germans and Austro-Hungarians on one side and the Russians and Serbians on the other. The Germans occupied the northern reaches of the "front" on the Baltic Sea near the present-day boundaries of Poland and Lithuania. The Austro-Hungarians were engaged in Eastern Galicia and in Serbia, in what is today Yugoslavia. This line included every conceivable kind of terrain, from marshland to forest to mountains, which gave to the Eastern Front its fluidity and varied character.**

enough information to direct the campaign. In fact the crucial decision of 9 September to withdraw the German right flank from its original route to the River Aisne was taken not by Moltke but by First and Second Army staff officers and Lt-Col. Richard Hentsch, sent by his commander to find out what was going on. The fog of war had simply obscured the battlefield from the people at the top who needed to know. More than just human error was involved in the collapse of the Germans' grand design of winning the war in its first months and repeating their spectacular successes of 1870–71. The German army had tried to do the impossible.

Tannenberg

An even more spectacular example of an offensive that went wrong was the initial Russian move west in August and September 1914. The calculated risk of the Schlieffen Plan was that it offered Russia the chance to attack Germany in the east. This challenge was accepted, and in the initial stages of the operation, between 17 and 22 August, two Russian armies advanced into East Prussia, one under Paul Rennenkampf in the north and the other under Alexander Samsonov further south. This led the commander of the German Eighth Army, Max von Prittwitz, to contemplate a general retreat to the River Vistula.

The thought of retreat convinced Moltke that Prittwitz had to go. He was sacked and replaced by the two men who later came to run the entire German war effort: Paul von Hindenburg, an elderly retired general (he was 67 years old), and Erich Ludendorff, a 49-year-old officer who had distinguished himself at the battle of Liège on 8 August, and who really directed military operations under Hindenburg's supervision. The reputation of these two men was made by the terrible defeat they inflicted on the Russian army at the end of August 1914 in the Battle of Tannenberg (southeast of Danzig). At Tannenberg a defensive force outwitted and outfought an offensive force superior to it in size. (It was therefore a closer parallel to the Battle of the Marne than the Germans were prepared to admit.)

It would be more accurate to give the credit for the victory not to Hindenburg and Ludendorff, but to a little-known staff officer, Max Hoffmann, who had already planned the master stroke well before Prittwitz's dismissal. This entailed negating the greater manpower of the combined Russian armies (totaling 21 infantry divisions as against 11 for the Germans) by withdrawing the forces facing the Russian first Army, under Rennenkampf, and sending them south to confront Samsonov's Second Army.

Alexander Samsonov 1859–1914

In 1914 Samsonov, a 55-year-old veteran of the Russo-Japanese War of 1904–05, was named as commander of the Second Army. It was ill-equipped and poorly trained and fell to the German Eighth Army in the Battle of Tannenberg. The German success was due in part to the failure of the Russian First Army to assist the Second, but no person was solely responsible for the debacle. However, after the defeat Samsonov shot himself, thereby providing an object of blame for Russian officials.

Paul von Hindenburg 1847–1934

In late August 1914 Hindenburg, a retired 66-year-old Prussian career soldier, was recalled to command the German Eighth Army. Success on the Eastern Front from 1914–16 made him a national hero and the natural choice in August 1916 to succeed Falkenhayn as chief of staff. He ended the war of attrition at Verdun and withdrew the army to the more defensive Hindenburg line. In 1918 he and Ludendorff launched a massive offensive on the Western Front. Its failure led to the Armistice. He was called again from retirement in 1926 to become president of Germany. One of his last acts was the appointment of Hitler as chancellor in 1933.

Erich Ludendorff 1856–1937

A brilliant tactician, Ludendorff was appointed quartermaster general of the German Second Army in the mobilization of July 1914. In the opening invasion of Belgium he played a decisive role in the taking of Liège. His reward was to be made chief of staff to Hindenburg. Their partnership continued to 1918. He was a key figure in the militarization of the German economy and the prosecution of unrestricted submarine warfare. After the war he became a leader of anti-Jewish, anticommunist and anti-Jesuit agitation.

▶ The early stages of the war on the Eastern Front went badly for the Central Powers. In August the Austro-Hungarian invasion of Serbia was repulsed. A few weeks later the Russians took Lemberg and forced the Austro-Hungarians to evacuate eastern Galicia. The German army also suffered similar reverses. The Russian First Army advanced into East Prussia and on 20 August defeated the German Eighth Army under Prittwitz in the Battle of Gumbinnen. This set the stage for the Battle of Tannenberg between 26 and 30 August, which resulted in the greatest German victory of the war.

In our new Headquarters at Allenstein I entered the church, close by the old castle of the Teutonic Knights, while divine service was being held. As the clergyman uttered his closing words all those present, young soldiers as well as elderly "Landsturm", sank to their knees under the overwhelming impression of their experiences. It was a worthy curtain to their heroic achievements.

PAUL VON HINDENBURG

East Prussian Battles 1914

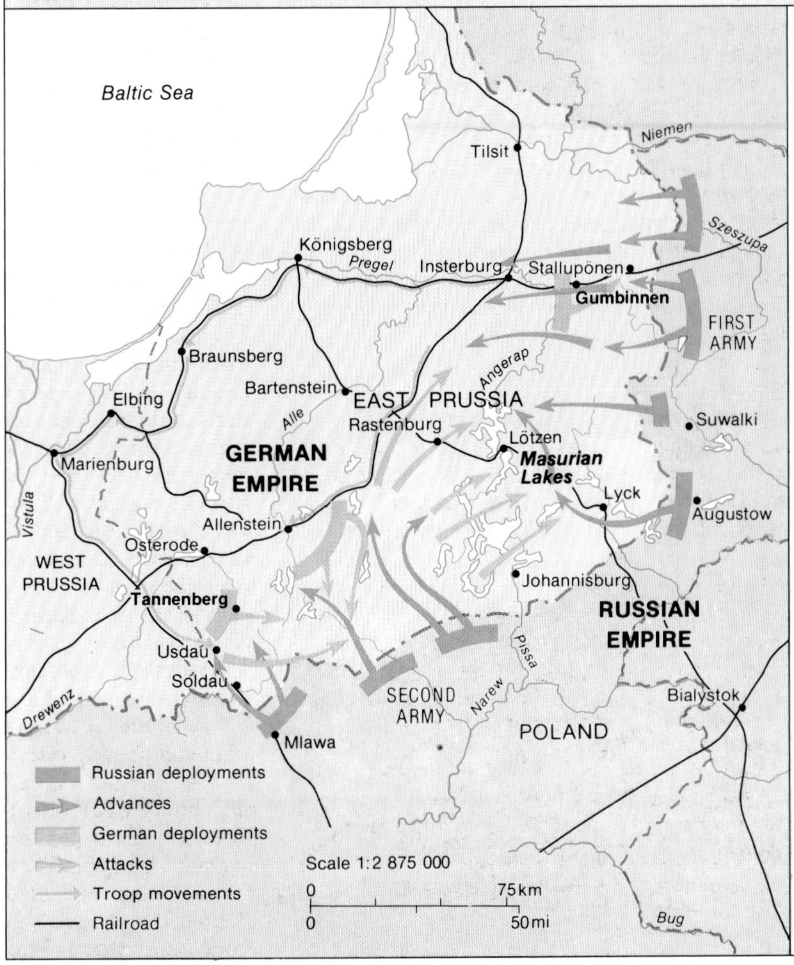

August 17
The Russian First Army advances into East Prussia.

August 20
Battle of Gumbinnen. Nine divisions from the German Eighth Army attack the advancing Russian First Army but are beaten off. The German commander, Max von Prittwitz, informed that the Russian Second Army has crossed the border in the south, decides to abandon the defense of East Prussia and is promptly sacked.

August 23
New German commanders, Hindenburg and Ludendorff, arrive at Marienburg (HQ of German Eighth Army) and endorse Max Hoffmann's plan to denude the Front opposite the Russian First Army and concentrate on the Russian Second Army. German troops are moved south by rail. The Russians assume that the Germans are retreating.

August 26–30
Battle of Tannenberg. The Russian Second Army, pushing forward on orders to cut off "retreating" Germans in East Prussia, is smashed by the German Eighth Army.

August 31
(to Sept. 4) The Germans rapidly move troops northeast to face the Russian First Army.

September 5–9
Battle of the Masurian Lakes. Advancing German forces cause rapid Russian retreat from German territory.

The War in the Balkans

The conflict which began as a Serbo-Austrian dispute in 1914 enveloped the entire Balkan region within two years. This brought to the surface all the rival ethnic, religious and national tensions which had existed for generations. The Allied and Central Powers tried desperately to manipulate these tensions in their favor. They shared the honors. Bulgaria entered the war in October 1915 on the German side; Romania, on the Allied side in August 1916. With Bulgaria as an enemy, the Allies landed two divisions at Salonika in Greece. They could hardly help the besieged Serbians, whose position deteriorated rapidly. The day after the Allied landing in Greece (5 Oct. 1915), General von Mackensen led a major Austro-German offensive against Serbia, which was totally defeated. The remnants of its army were forced on a long winter retreat through Albania to the sea. The survivors were shipped to Corfu, which had been specially occupied by the French. While none of the campaigns in this theater was decisive, they took a toll in lives proportionately greater than that on the Western Front.

◀ **Retreating Serbian cavalry cross the R. Drina.**

War in the Balkans 1914–18

1914

August 12–21
Austria-Hungary invades Serbia, expecting to crush the defenders easily. The invasion is a complete failure.

September 6–28
Both Austria-Hungary and Serbia launch attacks against the other. Neither can gain the upper hand and trench warfare begins.

November 6
(to Dec. 15) Austro-Hungarian forces capture Belgrade but are then beaten back.

1915

October 5
French and British troops begin disembarking at Salonika in neutral Greece to aid Serbia.

October 6
Bulgaria enters the war on the side of the Central Powers. Serbia now faces invasion from three sides.

October 7
(to Nov. 20) Stiffened by the presence of German troops a further Austro-Hungarian invasion of Serbia makes progress. The Serbian army is forced to retreat southwest while Bulgarian troops move to contain the Allied force at Salonika.

November 21
The Serbian army begins a fighting withdrawal to the sea through Albania.

1916

January 8–17
The Austro-Hungarians attack Montenegro and knock it out of the war. The Serbian army is evacuated by sea from Durazzo and Valona and taken to Corfu. After being reequipped it is despatched to Salonika.

August 17
(to Sept. 11) Aware that the Romanians wish to join the Allied side (Romania enters the war on August 27), the Bulgarians attempt to reduce the Salonika enclave.

September 12
(to Dec. 11) The French, British and Serbians counterattack from Salonika and retake some lost ground but cannot aid the hapless Romanians, who are crushed by a combined German, Austro-Hungarian and Bulgarian onslaught.

1917

April 24
(to May 22) Battle of Doiran. The Allies attack Salonika but suffer heavy casualties for few gains.

June 27
Greece enters the war on the side of the Allies.

1918

September 14–29
A renewed Allied offensive from Salonika causes the Bulgarian army to crumple. For the first time the Allies begin to make gains.

September 29
Bulgaria agrees to an armistice.

November 3
Austria-Hungary agrees to an armistice.

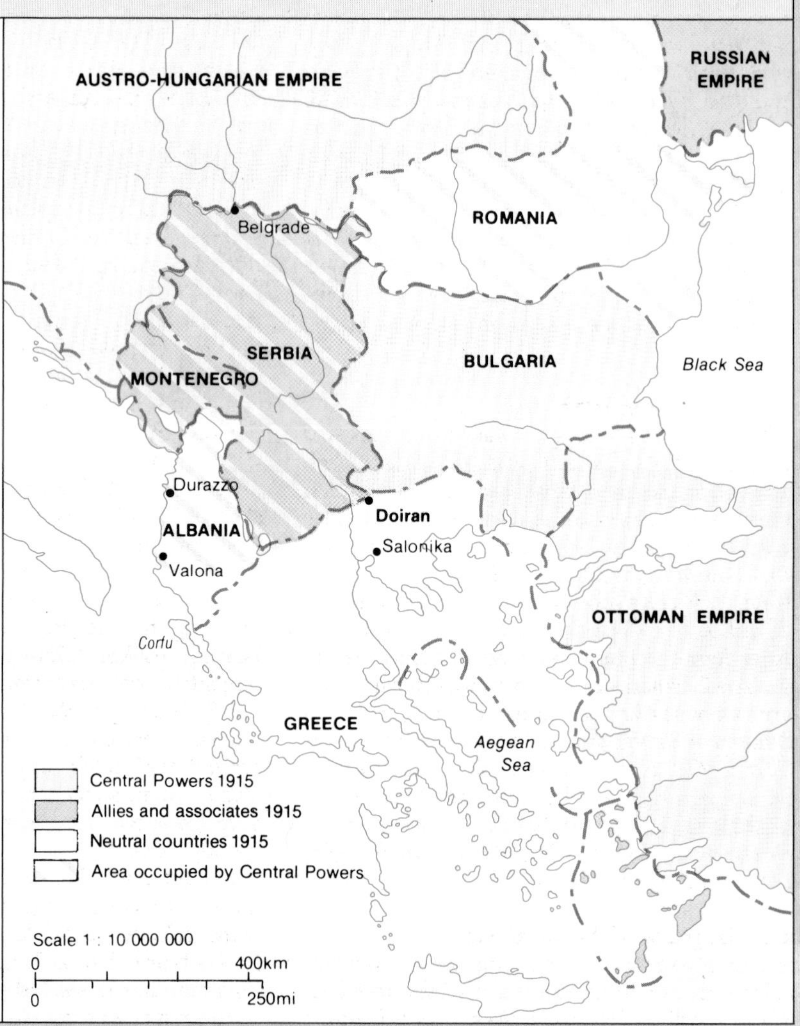

Between 26 and 30 August Ludendorff sprang his (and Hoffmann's) trap, into which Samsonov's army fell with ease. Everything went wrong for the Russians. Their supply system had collapsed, so the infantry were half-starved and also worn out by their long march. Because officers were unable to decode messages, the signals corps was reduced to sending uncoded signals which were easily intercepted by the Germans who thus knew both the intentions and position of their enemy.

In contrast the Russian high command had no idea what the Germans were up to until it was too late to prevent it. Samsonov believed that the Germans were retreating, and steadily advanced toward the whole German army. Rennenkampf was totally baffled by the elusiveness of the enemy, who seemed to have vanished in front of his eyes. Similarly Zhilinski, military commander of the entire northwestern sector of Russia, had at least six divisions of support troops, but never brought them into action.

The outcome was catastrophic for the Russians. Samsonov's army was destroyed and he committed suicide. The Germans captured over 100,000 men and 500 guns. Within two weeks, after a series of engagements known as the Battle of the Masurian Lakes, Rennenkampf's army was also forced back across the border.

The situation elsewhere in the east was more confused. Austrian forces went on a "punitive expedition" against Serbia in mid-August. They took Belgrade, but were pushed out again and suffered heavy losses, perhaps as many as 200,000 men. The Austrians also lost the Battle of Lemberg of 8–12 September to a group of Russian armies, which occupied large parts of Galicia (a Polish-Ukrainian-Jewish province of Austria-Hungary). Indecisive but bloody fighting between the Central Powers and Russia continued in Poland for the rest of the year, leaving the outcome of the war in the east as uncertain as that in the west.

The end of 1914 on land

By Christmas 1914 a rough balance of forces had formed in the west which was to last for years. After the Battle of the Marne, each side attempted to outflank the other to the north, but both sides lost the "race to the sea", and reached the coast without outflanking the other. Particularly bloody fighting took place around Ypres, which was held with difficulty by British and French forces.

After four months of war no decision was in sight. The German strategic plan was in ruins, but German armies had occupied most of Belgium and much of the most heavily industrialized parts of France. The costs of 1914's military operations were staggering. Casualty lists already stretched into millions, and all the armies could show for the losses was stalemate. The effort to break this is the story of the rest of the war.

The initial phase of the naval war

The early phases of the naval war were on a much smaller scale but covered a much wider area than the land conflicts. Still, the trajectory of the war at sea in 1914 paralleled the war on land: initial action followed by stalemate. Soon after the outbreak of the war, the German cruisers *Goeben* and *Breslau* escaped the Royal Navy in the Mediterranean and wound up in Turkey (3–11 August). Three weeks later, at Heligoland Bight in the North Sea, the British took revenge. A small squadron of British warships managed to sink four German ships and to inflict 1,200 casualties on the German navy. There were British losses too, and perhaps alarmingly, a British submarine had come within an ace of sinking the British light cruiser *Southampton.*

Soon thereafter German submarines began to pose a threat to Allied ships. On 22 September one U-boat managed to torpedo three British cruisers in the North Sea. This kind of warfare became increasingly important as the conflict dragged on. On 27 October a German mine accounted for the battleship HMS *Audacious* off the Irish coast, but both the British public and the German navy were unaware of the loss.

Further afield the fortunes of war were also shared. On 1 November 1914 Admiral von Spee's German "China Squadron" sank two British cruisers at Coronel, off the west coast of South America. But von Spee then made the mistake of deciding to raid Port Stanley in the Falkland Islands, 600km (375mi) off the east coast of Argentina, before returning to the North Atlantic. On 8 December 1914 the Germans ran into the battlecruisers *Inflexible* and *Invincible* which had arrived, with other support ships, the day before. The German squadron was destroyed; only one ship escaped, and that too was sunk a few months later.

In December 1914 the German navy shelled the northeast coast of England. A month later British ships inflicted serious losses on the German navy in the North Sea, at Dogger Bank. These events made the headlines, but the more significant part of the naval war lay elsewhere: in the crucial, if unspectacular, art of blockade.

▲ In 1914 the German East Asian fleet (above), under Admiral von Spee, stationed in Kiaochow in China, avoided an Anglo-Japanese naval force, and sailed across the Pacific to the Mariana Islands; to German Somoa; and to Easter Island. There the German squadron was joined by cruisers stationed off the West Indies and the California coast. They moved to Coronel off Chile, where two pursuing British ships were sunk. Proceeding to the Atlantic, von Spee decided to attack the Falkland Islands, a British base. There he met a superior force: four of his ships were sunk, and he and 1,800 of his men were killed.

Samsonov said repeatedly that the disgrace of such a defeat was more than he could bear. "The Emperor trusted me. How can I face him after such a disaster?" He went aside and his staff heard a shot. They searched for his body without success, but all are convinced that he shot himself. The Chief of Staff and other officers managed to reach Russian territory, having covered forty miles on foot...

SIR ALFRED KNOX

SURFACE NAVAL WARFARE

In the century before World War I naval warfare was revolutionized: the wooden sailing ship armed with broadside batteries of smoothbore cannon firing solid shot over relatively short ranges was replaced by the armored metal steamship, equipped with rifled guns capable of hurling large explosive projectiles over distances of 16km (10mi) or more. In the decade before the war all the major powers and most of their smaller imitators poured massive resources into the construction of modern "dreadnought" battleships (named for the first ship of this type, the United Kingdom's HMS *Dreadnought*).

After the opening few months of the war, during which there were small naval battles in distant waters, the focus of the surface naval war moved to European waters. In both the North Sea and the Mediterranean, larger Allied fleets maintained a distant blockade of enemy naval bases, while in both the Black Sea and the Baltic the Russian navy, still not fully recovered from its heavy losses in the Russo-Japanese war (1904–05), was easily contained by smaller German and Turkish forces.

The Battle of Jutland, fought at the end of May 1916, was the only full-scale fleet action of the war. Otherwise the huge European battlefleets fought only a handful of skirmishes and suffered few serious losses in the process. The generally low level of fighting was the product, first, of the numerical inferiority of the Central Powers and, second, of the disinclination of all combatants to risk the loss of irreplaceable capital ships.

Jutland itself proved a disappointment to both the British and the Germans. The Germans failed to isolate and destroy a small detachment of the British fleet, and in the end only extracted their own fleet from a disastrous engagement with a superior force by the narrowest of margins. The British not only failed to destroy the enemy which they had waited to catch away from his base for almost two years, but also suffered the more serious capital ship losses in the process. Overall, however, Jutland was a strategic victory for the British Royal Navy simply because it did not alter a situation already heavily balanced in its favor.

In the 1916–18 period the continuing preeminence of Allied shipbuilding programs and the eventual arrival of part of the US battlefleet in European waters accentuated the numerical inferiority of the Central Powers. Neither surface nor submarine action ever released the Central Powers from the constricting effects of Allied blockade. While historical debate still rages as to the impact of the blockade on the German war effort, the simple fact remains that Germany was unable to restore valuable economic links with the wider world that had been severed in 1914 by British naval supriority. The failure of German naval expansion was underlined with symbolic finality at the end of the war when the German fleet was first interned in the British naval base at Scapa Flow and then scuttled by its own crews to prevent its being divided among the victors.

▶ The British fleet entered the Battle of Jutland with a profound numerical superiority over Germany's high seas fleet. German pre-Dreadnought ships and Britain's armored cruisers were obsolete vessels of limited fighting power, but in the case of both major fleet units (Dreadnoughts and battlecruisers) and their ancillary screens (light cruisers and destroyers), the British enjoyed an advantage in numbers which allowed the Germans little hope of victory. German success could have resulted only from isolating part of the British fleet.

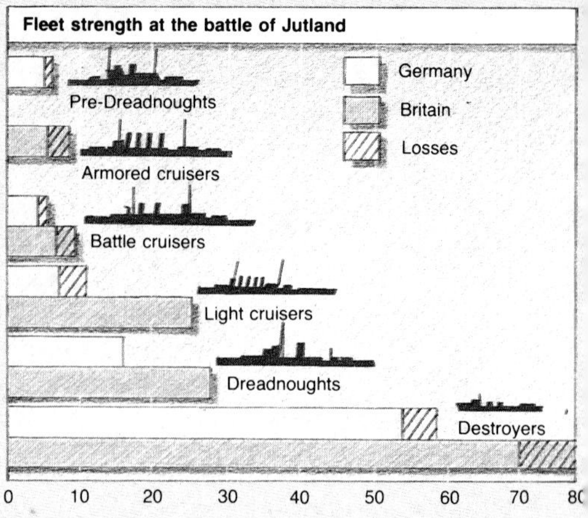

The Battle of Jutland 1916

▶ The Battle of Jutland was fought on 31 May and 1 June 1916, the British grand fleet having sailed to intercept a German sortie detected by radio intercepts. Poor communications and an imperfect grasp of the tactical situation on both sides resulted in a confused series of encounters beginning in the afternoon with a clash between the rival battlecruiser forces in which the outnumbered Germans destroyed two enemy vessels while drawing the remainder south toward their own main body. British forces then turned north in the face of superior numbers, bringing the Germans into contact with the full might of the grand fleet's Dreadnought squadrons. Although the British lost a third battlecruiser, they inflicted a severe mauling on leading elements of the German high seas fleet.

► The German Kaiser inspecting a naval dockyard. The German command placed a high priority on fleet construction, but failed to grasp the limitations and difficulties of their naval policy, and gradually lost faith in the battlefleet when it proved incapable of breaking British naval superiority in the North Sea.

▼ The sinking of the armored cruiser *Blücher* at the Battle of Dogger Bank on 23 January 1915. Her early loss pushed the German naval high command toward a policy of extreme caution.

▼ Repair work in progress to Q Turret of HMS *Lion* after Jutland. British battlecruisers proved vulnerable to shell damage to their lightly protected turrets and magazines. In this case only the gun crew was lost, but when a ship blew up about 1,000 men could be killed.

▼ Elements of the German fleet at sea in 1910. At this stage the naval-building race with Britain was beginning to gather momentum with the introduction of the new Dreadnought battleships and battlecruisers. Although Germany entered the war with a powerful and impressive fleet, its failure as an instrument of strategic policy was all but predetermined by Britain's superiority.

Datafile

Military action on the Western Front in the second year of the war left the stalemate intact. Attempts were made on both land and sea to find a way around the concentration of forces in France and Flanders. Both sides launched naval blockades, and the Allies tried to knock Turkey out of the war by an invasion of Gallipoli, launched in April 1915. Eight months later the Allies admitted defeat and withdrew from the Turkish coast.

▼ In late August 1914 German ships began to mine the English Channel. The British Royal Navy declared the entire North Sea to be a military area, and initiated a parallel blockade of Germany. Allied shipping losses were more spectacular, but the Allied blockade of Germany was more effective in the long run.

► Over one million troops were engaged in the Gallipoli campaign of 1915. At the same time as the Allies were being pinned down in untenable positions on the Turkish coast, a combined German/Austrian breakthrough took place at Gorlice, in Poland, where the Russian line was breached and most of Poland was lost.

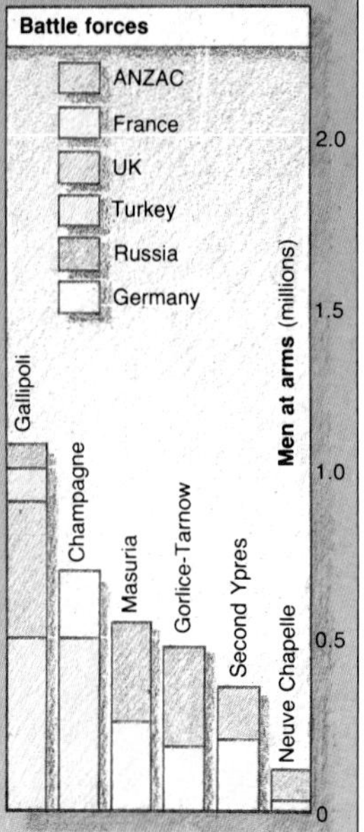

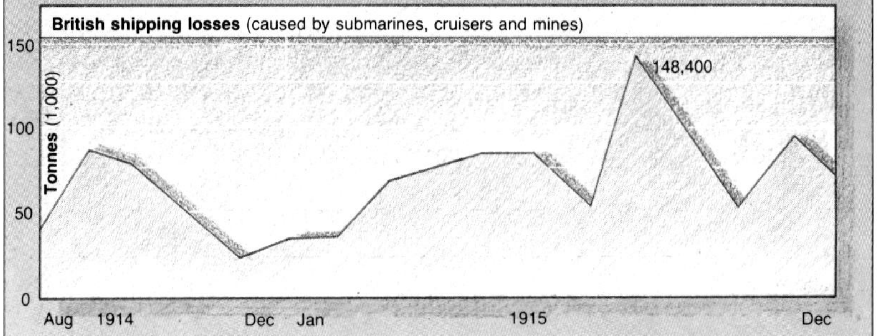

Chronology

February 8–22
Winter Battle of Masuria: Germans and Austro-Hungarians force Russians to retreat

March 10–13
Battle of Neuve Chapelle: British and Indian offensive on Western Front captures village of N.C.

March 12
UK: Sir Ian Hamilton appointed commander of Allied Dardanelles army

March 24
GER/TURK: Liman von Sanders is appointed commander of the Turkish Fifth Army in the Dardanelles

April 22
(to May 27) Second Battle of Ypres: German offensive on Western Front against Ypres fails to capture the town

April 24
(to Jan. 9, 1916) Allied land campaign against Turks on Gallipoli peninsula

May 2–4
Battle of Gorlice-Tarnow: Central Powers break Russian line and cause Russian retreat

May 4
(to June 18) Second Battle of Artois: French make small gain of land on Western Front from Germans

May 7
German submarine sinks passenger liner *Lusitania*

May 9–10
Battle of Aubers Ridge: unsuccessful British offensive on Western Front against Germans

May 15–25
Battle of Festubert: unsuccessful British and Canadian offensive on Western Front against Germans

May 23
Italy declares war on Austria-Hungary

IT: Cadorna appointed commander in chief of Italian armies

June 15
FR: Petain made commander of French armies

September 5
RUSS: Czar Nicholas II takes command of Russian armies from Grand Duke Nicholas (with General Alexelev as chief of staff)

September 25
(to Oct. 14) Third battle of Artois: French offensive on Western Front brings small gain of territory from the Germans

September 25
(to Oct. 6) French offensive in Champagne: small amount of territory gained from Germans

September 25
(to Nov. 4) Battle of Loos: British offensive on the Western Front captures the town of Loos

October 16
UK: commander at Gallipoli, Sir Ian Hamilton, is replaced by Sir Charles Monro

December 3
FR: Joffre becomes commander in chief of French armies

December 19
UK: Haig replaces French as commander in chief of British armies in France

December 23
UK: Robertson appointed to new post of chief of imperial general staff

THE SINKING OF THE *LUSITANIA*

▲ German medal commemorating the sinking.

On 7 May 1915 Commander Schweiger of the German navy was patrolling in the submarine *U-20* in the southern entrance to the Irish coast off the Old Head of Kinsale. Three months earlier Germany had declared all waters around the British Isles a "war zone".

At about 1.40 pm Schweiger suddenly saw the Cunard liner *Lusitania* in the submarine's sight, on the final stretch of the passage from New York to Liverpool. Half an hour later the submarine fired two torpedoes. The first caused a great explosion: the liner keeled over and sank within 20 minutes. About 2,000 passengers had been on board; of these 1,198 perished, including 291 women and 94 children. Among the dead were 128 American citizens. As their bodies drifted onto the beaches of Kinsale, a great outcry of protest was raised in neutral America. In Ireland (then part of the UK) the coroner's court found the Kaiser guilty of wilful murder. In Germany the authorities allowed commemorative medals to be struck.

Amidst the propaganda that followed the sinking several important facts were ignored. Germany had given clear warnings about the risks of traveling in the war zone. The ship was in fact carrying war materiel. The British first sea lord, Winston Churchill, admitted to the presence of a small quantity; in fact the quantity was substantial.

The sinking of the *Lusitania* brought home to both combatants and neutrals the ugly and deadly nature of modern war. At the same time the greatest neutral power, the United States of America, was inextricably drawn toward the Allied cause.

1915 STALEMATE AND STAGNATION

Britain imposes a naval blockade

Germany retaliates with unrestricted U-boat warfare

Britain seeks to knock out Turkey by landing at Gallipoli

Military failure leads to changes in the high commands

But the murderous cult of the offensive is maintained

In World War I there were two blockades: Germany's effort to cut the British lines of supply and Britain's attempt to cut the German ones. They developed together. Immediately on the outbreak of war, British ships began to patrol the North Sea, English Channel and Mediterranean, to prevent vessels reaching or leaving the ports of the Central Powers. In retaliation German Ships began to lay mines along the English coast. A major problem for both sides was posed by the presence of ships from neutral countries in blockaded waters. On 29 October 1914 a British order in council declared that neutral ships had to prove that their consignments were not destined for Germany. On 3 November the British declared the entire North Sea to be a military area. The Germans took this step to be a declaration of unrestricted economic warfare. They announced that from 4 February 1915 submarine warfare would begin against the UK. Three weeks later Britain issued a "reprisal order", authorizing the seizure of cargo heading to or from Germany.

The German action threatened traffic across the Atlantic, so the American response was crucial. President Wilson laid down the doctrine of "strict accountability", placing the responsibility for any loss of American lives on Germany. When the British liner *Lusitania* – a passenger liner sailing from New York to Liverpool that was almost certainly also carrying munitions – was sunk on 7 May 1915, with the loss of 1,198 people, including 128 Americans, this disaster put Germany in the dock. On 19 August three Americans perished in the sinking of the liner *Arabic* south of Ireland, thereby increasing hostility to the Central Powers. The Germans were forced to give assurances that henceforth no ships would be sunk without warning and without adequate provision for rescuing noncombatants. "Henceforth" lasted for about a year.

▼ Naval blockades. In the enforcement of blockades both sides broke the international regulations strictly determined by the London conference of 1909.

Naval Blockades 1914–19

1914

August 4
British ships establish patrols in the Mediterranean (in cooperation with the French), the North Sea and the English Channel to prevent the passage of shipping to or from the Central Powers.

1915

February 4
The Germans, unwilling to challenge Allied superiority on the surface, establish a submarine blockade and declare any vessel in the seas around the UK a legitimate target.

May 7
The German submarine *U-20* torpedoes the passenger liner *Lusitania* without warning. Among the victims are 128 Americans.

May 23
Italy enters the war on the side of the Allies and joins Allied Mediterranean patrols.

August 19
The German submarine *U-24* torpedoes the passenger liner *Arabic* without warning. Among the dead are three Americans.

August 30
In response to American protests the Germans prohibit the sinking of passenger vessels without warning.

September 18
To reduce further the danger to American shipping the Germans withdraw their U-boats from the English Channel and western approaches.

1916

March 13
Germany loosens its U-boat restrictions to allow captains to sink British vessels in home waters without warning, if they do not appear to be passenger ships.

March 24
German U-boat *UB-29* torpedoes the passenger ship *Sussex* without warning, causing the loss of more American lives.

April 20
The USA threatens to break off diplomatic relations with Germany.

April 24
German U-boats are instructed not to sink vessels without warning.

1917

February 1
Germany again declares unrestricted submarine warfare.

February 3
The USA severs relations with Germany.

April 6
The USA enters the war on the side of the Allies.

April 30
British prime minister Lloyd George insists that the British admiralty experiments with convoys for merchant shipping. They prove a great success and enable the Allies to survive the German blockade. The Allied blockade continues until 1919.

▲ An Anzac soldier at Gallipoli. The Australian Imperial Force was the product of Maj.-Gen. Sir W.T. Bridges, inspector-general of Australian forces in 1914. Bridges commanded the Australian contingent at Gallipoli, and died as a result of wounds received there. His major achievement was to retain the national distinctiveness of Australian units, whose sacrifices helped create Australian national identity. The AIF was trained in Australia and then sent not to England as planned, but to Egypt and then to Gallipoli. Anzac units later served with distinction in Palestine and in France. Out of a home population of about 5 million, 330,000 Australian troops served during the war; of these men, 59,000 were killed. New Zealand lost 17,000 men out of 220,000. Total Anzac casualties – 62 percent of those who served – were the highest of all units from the Anglo-Saxon world.

Gallipoli

Europe ends at Gallipoli, the Turkish peninsula at the tip of the Dardanelles straits which lead from the Aegean to the Sea of Marmara. This was the setting for one of the worst disasters suffered by the Allies in World War I.

The idea of knocking Turkey out of the war by naval action was first presented formally by the British first lord of the admiralty, Winston Churchill, to the British war council in late November 1914. In its initial form the plan was for a naval force to attack the straits to open a route to Constantinople. Despite reservations from several quarters, this was duly approved in January 1915.

The first stage of operations was a series of Allied naval bombardments beginning on 19 February. Minesweeping followed along the 60km (37mi) length of the straits, a stretch of water which narrowed from about 4km (2.5mi) across to a little over 1km (0.6mi). Had this been effective the campaign might have succeeded. But the hazard of mines was not eliminated. On 18 March the second phase of operations began. Allied ships again bombarded Turkish positions, but three battleships – two British and one French – were sunk by mines and three others were severely damaged. The effort to force the straits was suspended.

Instead, as a third phase of the operation, a land expedition was mounted. It put ashore, on 25 April, but by this time Turkish defenses had been strengthened. Some initial Allied gains were squandered, and the combined force of British, French, Australian and New Zealand troops found themselves pinned down between the sea and hills held by the Turks. Turkish defenses

Sir Ian Hamilton 1853–1947

Ian Hamilton enjoyed a long and successful military career before 1914. He had served in the Anglo-Boer War (1899–1902), and was appointed commander in chief of Mediterranean forces in 1910, aged 57. He was the obvious choice as commander for the Gallipoli campaign in 1915. It began inauspiciously: the British navy failed to force the Dardanelles straits. In the subsequent land campaign he failed to obtain his objectives, thanks to accomplished Turkish defense and poor Allied tactics. But in spite of appalling loss of life, Hamilton's communiques remained optimistic. His command ended after journalists leaked the truth about the scale of the Dardanelles disaster. Hamilton never again held a senior military position.

Otto Liman von Sanders 1855–1929

A Prussian career soldier, von Sanders was sent to Turkey in 1913 as leader of the German military mission. Its presence was a visible sign of Turkey's alignment with the Central Powers. Russian protests prevented von Sanders from taking command of the Turkish First Army, but he became "inspector" of Turkish forces and worked to increase the efficiency of Turkish military organization. In January 1914 von Sanders was made a commander of Turkish forces in the Caucasus. His real test came when appointed commander of the Turkish Fifth Army in Gallipoli in 1915. There he successfully opposed British, Anzac, and French attacks. Subsequently he saw action as Turkish commander in Palestine.

◀ **Turkish troops fought on fronts extending over 1000km (625mi) during the war. The campaign in which they inflicted the most serious defeat was at Gallipoli, where an Anglo-French invasion was blunted. The landings at Anzac Cove (left) on 25 April 1915 were poorly planned. The Anzacs were put ashore at the wrong place: on a narrow beachfront bordered by sheer cliffs. They secured a tenuous foothold, and were then told to dig in. The Turks held the high ground, and once more demonstrated the ascendency of the defensive. The date of the landing is marked in Australia as one of national heroism; in Turkey, as one of national pride.**

▶ **The idea of the Gallipoli campaign was to reestablish direct lines of supply and communication between Russia and its Western allies by taking Constantinople and knocking Turkey out of the war. But the underlying Allied motive was to find a way around the stalemate on the Western Front. The failure of the Gallipoli campaign ensured the continuation of the war of attrition in France and Flanders.**

Gallipoli 1915–16

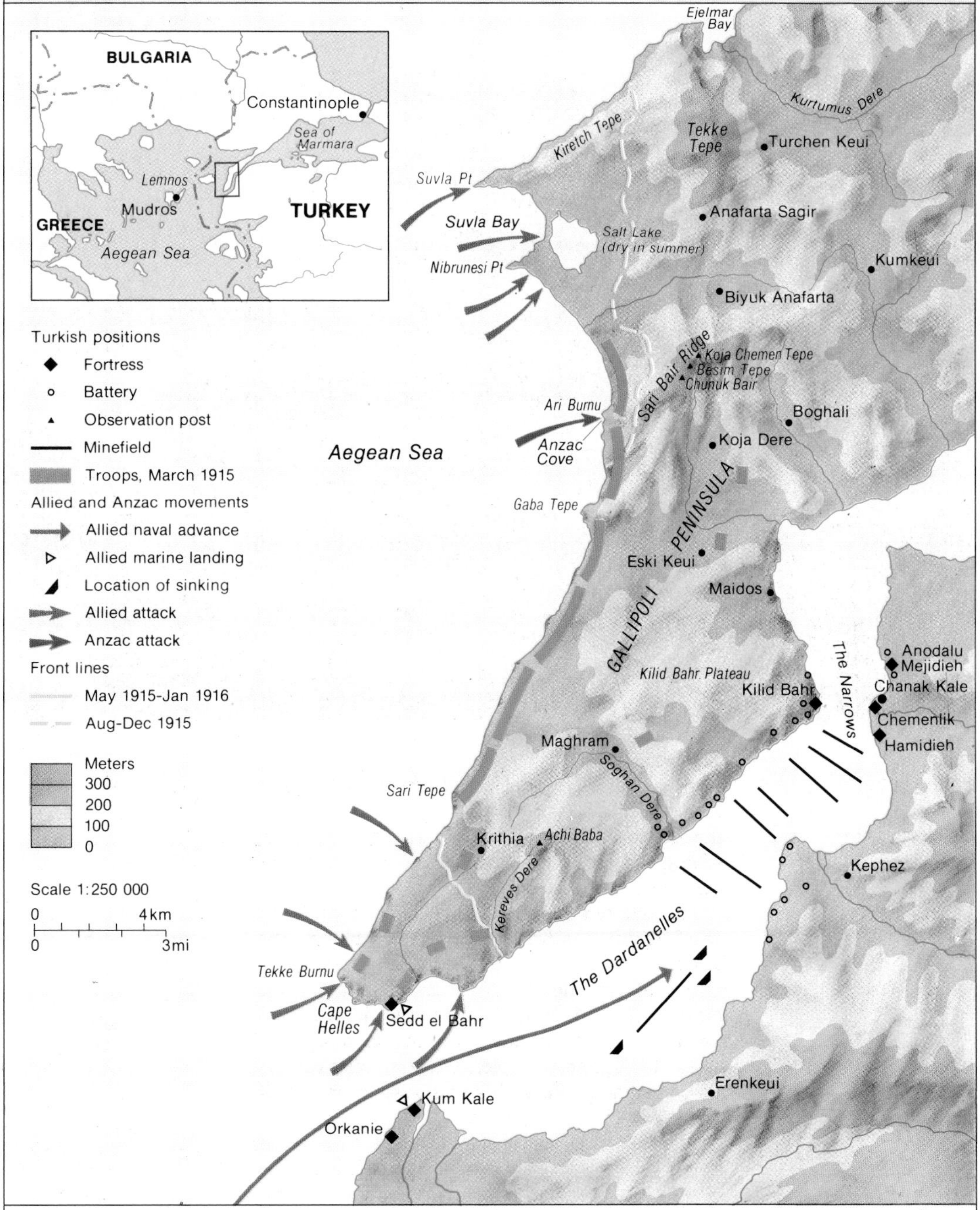

1914
November 3
British and French (Allied) forces make an ill-considered bombardment of Dardanelles forts, which focuses Turkish attention on the area

1915
February 19
Allied ships bombard Turkish forts at the entrance to the Dardanelles.

February 25
After a period of poor weather the Allied ships resume their bombardment. Small groups of marines land with impunity on the Turkish mainland on demolition missions, but Turkish strength is growing.

March 4
An attempt to repeat February's landings meets strong resistance and fails.

March 18
Attempts to push ships through the Dardanelles end in failure, with three capital ships sunk and a fourth crippled by mines. The Turks have practically no heavy ammunition left now, but unaware of this, the Allies conclude that a substantial invasion will be necessary to clear the straits.

March 24
The new commander of the Turkish Fifth Army, Liman von Sanders, deploys his six divisions to block any landings.

April 25
Allied troops land at Cape Helles and Australians and New Zealanders at Anzac Cove. Neither force pushes far inland.

May 1–8
Turkish attacks and Allied counterattacks result in minor gains for the Allies.

May 19
The Turks attack the Anzac forces but fail to dislodge the defenders.

June 21
(to July 5) French and British forces attack separately from the Helles front line, but cannot break out.

July 12–13
French and British forces attack jointly at the Helles front with no more success. The French are now finished as an offensive force.

August 6–7
The overall Allied commander, Sir Ian Hamilton, launches a new three-pronged assault. While the existing two enclaves renew their attacks, a third is created by landing fresh troops at Suvla Bay. The Helles and Anzac attacks fail to make any gains, and the Suvla force becomes bogged down just like the others.

August 10
Forces landed at Anzac and Suvla join in line but cannot push the front forward.

October 16
Sir Ian Hamilton is relieved of his post.

October 28
Hamilton's replacement, Sir Charles Monro, arrives from the Western Front.

October 31
Monro recommends evacuation as the best option.

December 8–20
Forces at Suvla and Anzac are quietly reduced in size. The Turks only become aware of this after the last parties have withdrawn safely.

December 28
(to Jan. 9 1916) The Helles force is withdrawn safely.

▲ Austrian staff officers studying maps in Galicia in 1915, during which the Central Powers pushed back the Russian army from virtually all of present-day Poland. On 2 May a joint German-Austrian advance was launched in Galicia, and made progress on a wide front. By the end of June 1915 Russia had lost all of Galicia and Bukovina. Worse was to come later in the summer. In July a second joint offensive was opened. Warsaw fell to the Germans on 4 August; Brest-Litovsk fell on 25 August, and the city of Vilna, in Lithuania, was captured in September.

Military Communications

With the massive increase in the size of armies in World War I, the problem of communication between the various headquarters and the front lines became acute. This was especially the case because orders had to go through several layers of command, and therefore time became a critical factor – it was not possible for a headquarters to issue orders and expect a divisional attack to take place the next day. Moreover, communication tended to flow in one direction: from headquarters to the front. This was often made worse by the reluctance of senior commanders to accept that events were not going the way they envisioned, and thus information from the front was frequently ignored or altered to fit preconceptions.

A final difficulty was the actual technical means of communication transmission. Thus, while telephone land line was readily available between higher headquarters, once the front line was approached, telephone lines were often cut by shell fire or run over by tanks. After an offensive commenced, it was extremely difficult to stay in touch with advancing units. In this case, resort had to be made to traditional methods of communication such as pigeons, runners, or flares. Later, methods were supplemented or replaced by technical means such as power buzzers and wireless, as well as by aerial observation.

As an example of how communications worked in an army, it will be useful to look at the British Expeditionary Force (BEF). Assuming that General Haig and his general headquarters (GHQ) were putting into action the strategies decided upon in London (which was sometimes not the case), then Haig would outline his ideas for operations to the army commander concerned, who would draw up plans. These would be criticized by Haig and his staff, but Haig's training led him to leave tactical conduct of operations up to the army commander.

Relevant orders would then be passed through many levels of command. Thus the army commander often left corps HQ to solve the tactical problems presented by GHQ, while Corps in turn would ask for ideas from their division and brigade staffs and attempt to coordinate them before sending them on to the battalion level, which then passed them on to lower levels, where their relevance was not always apparent. In addition, such was the length of the chain of command and the rigid centralization of the system that it was very hard to achieve changes from below, even at the level of division appealing to corps. This rigidity was partly due to the great difficulty of altering an exceedingly complex set of orders integrating different arms such as infantry, artillery, cavalry, air and the tank corps. Thus before the Somme offensive, one corps HQ issued a 76-page scheme for the attack, while there was a 365-page supplement for the divisional level.

Communication difficulties occurred therefore partly because of the huge size of armies, partly because technology was insufficient to the task and partly because prewar ideas were not appropriate to the needs of modern war.

► A German soldier with field-telephone equipment.

under the command of the German general Liman von Sanders, were ably manned, which greatly surprised the Allies. Among the men who distinguished themselves on the Turkish side was a young colonel, Mustapha Kemal, who was later to be president of Turkey and known as Atatürk.

A landing of fresh troops on 6 August made little difference, except to the casualty lists. These grew ominously in the summer heat. The conditions under which Allied soldiers were forced to operate were intolerable, but it took until November for the Allied high command to admit total failure. The survivors of the operation were evacuated in December 1915 and early January 1916. They left behind approximately 200,000 dead comrades.

Sir William Robertson 1860–1933

Robertson was the only man ever to enter the British army as a private and rise to the rank of field marshal. He joined in 1877 and gained a commission 11 years later. Service in the British Empire followed. After active service in the British Expeditionary Force in 1914–15 Robertson was recalled and at age 55 appointed chief of the imperial general staff. His central task was to act as middleman between the cabinet and the army. He maintained that the war would be won or lost on the Western Front and convinced the British cabinet to concentrate resources on France. Controversies over the management of manpower in 1917 made him enemies. He was removed from his post in February 1918.

The cult of the offensive

Gallipoli was but one in a series of disasters which marked the first year of World War I. It is remarkable that a catalog of defeats on both sides did not cause a change of heart about the way the war should be fought. It is true that some heads rolled on both sides. In Germany Moltke gave way to Erich von Falkenhayn as chief of the general staff. On the French side General Sarrail, a bit too popular for the comfort of his superiors, was sent to Salonika to command the French "Army of the East". In Britain Winston Churchill resigned as first lord of the admiralty after Gallipoli, and Kitchener's powers as minister of war were much reduced by the appointment of General Sir William Robertson as chief of the imperial general staff. He formed a powerful partnership with Sir Douglas Haig, who replaced Sir John French as commander in chief of the British Expeditionary Force in France.

The change in personnel on the Allied side obscured an underlying continuity in purpose. After a year of combat on many fronts, the cult of the offensive was still in the ascendant. The British and French high commands were still wedded to the idea that the war would be won by offensive operations in France. The entry of Italy on the Allied side on 23 May 1915 made no difference to these calculations. Reversals on the Eastern Front seemed to justify increased aggression in the west.

On the German side General Erich Falkenhayn also subscribed to the concept of what the French called *la guerre à l'outrance* – war to the bitter end. But on the Western Front he was prepared to wage this by attrition rather than annihilation.

His adversaries took the lead in launching attacks in 1915. In January and February the focus of French action was Champagne; in May and June, and again in September, Artois. The British made a successful attack on the village of Neuve Chapelle (10–13 March). They actually broke through the German lines, but could not capitalize on their gains. Similarly at Loos in late September, initial British gains turned into stalemate. As always happened, the attackers' losses were staggering; the defenders' less severe.

Falkenhayn was content to let the Allies destroy their men against his lines in the west. In the east he had to contend with his own side, in particular with Hindenburg and Ludendorff, whose aggressive posture certainly paid off against the Russians and the Serbs. On 2 May 1915 the Russian front line was broken at Gorlice in Galicia, and a combined Austro-Hungarian and German force advanced 130km (80mi). Galicia and indeed most of Poland were abandoned by Russia. An equally severe defeat was suffered by the Serbs, crushed in a combined autumn operation by German, Austro-Hungarian and Bulgarian troops. Still, such successes for the Central Powers did not bring the end of the war any closer. Victory was still to be won on the Western Front.

All those who criticize the dispositions of a general ought first to study military history, unless they have themselves taken part in a war in a position of command. I should like to see people compelled to conduct a battle themselves. They would be overwhelmed by the greatness of their task, and when they realized the obscurity of the position, and the exacting nature of the enormous demands made on them, they would doubtless be more modest. Only the Head of Government, the Statesman, who has decided for war, and that with a clear conscience, shoulders the same or a bigger burden of responsibility than that of the Commander-in-Chief. In his case it is a question of one great decision only, but the Commander of an army is faced with decisions daily and hourly. He is continuously responsible for the welfare of many hundred-thousands of persons, even of nations.

ERICH LUDENDORFF

SUBMARINE WARFARE

Few of the weapons used during World War I exercised a more profound effect on the conduct of hostilities than the submarine. In August 1914 all of the combatant navies possessed small submarine forces, but within two years major construction programs had brought hundreds of vessels into operational service. By this time the submarine was already forcing a complete revision of both conventional naval strategy and the protection or interruption of seaborne commerce.

The country most closely associated with the wartime development of the submarine was Germany. Other nations, most particularly Britain, did build up large submarine forces, but the quick disappearance of most enemy ocean-going surface vessels left submariners with few potential targets. Allied submarines spent most of the war on uneventful patrol duties.

The submarine war itself can be divided into two distinct campaigns: that waged against surface warships; that waged against merchant shipping. At the beginning of the war, naval planners were thinking almost exclusively in terms of the first, and several dramatic early German successes inspired a lasting fear of submarines in surface-fleet commanders, making them loath to risk their ships in enemy waters. In terms of actual losses, however, the submarine made little impact on major naval forces.

Submarine operations against merchant shipping were not widely envisaged in 1914, as conventions required the crew of an intercepted vessel to be placed in a safe positon before the vessel itself was destroyed. The practice of launching submerged torpedo attacks without giving prior warning emerged haltingly, and it was not really until the second half of the war that unrestricted submarine warfare became the general rule. Then the lead came from Germany's U-boat force.

Launched in February 1917 with a frontline force of over 100 vessels, the third German unrestricted submarine warfare campaign was a deliberate gamble aimed at bringing the United Kingdom to its knees. In its early stages it seemed that it might succeed: Allied merchant shipping losses averaged 630,000 tons per month and peaked at 866,000 tons in April 1917. In the second half of 1917, however, the introduction of the convoy system produced a sharp fall in losses while exposing the U-boats themselves to higher losses from escort forces. By early 1918 the Germans were clearly losing the submarine war and month by month the flow of military and nonmilitary supplies into Britain grew steadily in volume.

Despite the damage to the Allied merchant marine, the German campaign proved a strategic miscalculation. German planners underestimated the strength and resilience of a modern industrialized economy and overestimated the impact of even relatively high levels of shipping losses. For all its undoubted achievements, the U-boat could not reverse the course of the war, nor save Germany from defeat.

► A German UC44 class U-boat. Submarine design involved cramming as much as possible into a small space. The need to build in a petrol engine for surface use, a battery-powered motor for submerged sailing, torpedo tubes as well as steering, detection and depth-control machinery left little space for the crew.

◀▲ In 1916–17 individual U-boats (such as the highly successful U35, left) inflicted heavy losses on unescorted merchantmen, but unrestricted submarine warfare and the introduction of convoys and increased Allied shipbuilding efforts pulled Germany into a war of attrition which its U-boats could not win.

▶ Life aboard submarines was unpleasant and extremely hazardous. The cramped interior of a typical torpedo room (right) shows the conditions under which submariners lived. When submerged the interior of a submarine could be hot, fetid and claustrophobic. The moored contact mine (above) was only one of the weapons which could condemn an entire crew to a swift watery death without hope of escape.

▶ A German U-boat under air attack. Aircraft only became potent antisubmarine weapons in World War II. But in 1916–18 they increasingly harrassed U-boats.

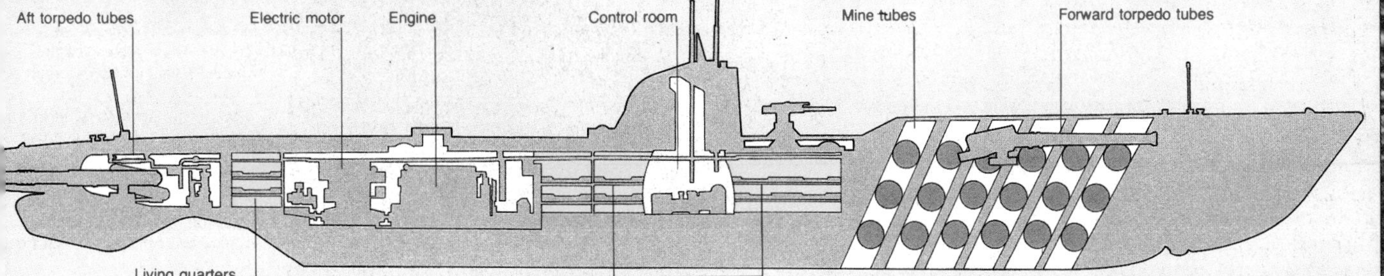

Datafile

The bloodiest battles of the war were fought in 1916–17. First, between February and November 1916, almost the entire French infantry fought to hold Verdun. In May 1917 the French army mutinied when a series of offensive operations pushed too far men whose bravery and patriotism had been demonstrated at Verdun. Second, the British army suffered the heaviest losses in its history at the Somme and Third Ypres.

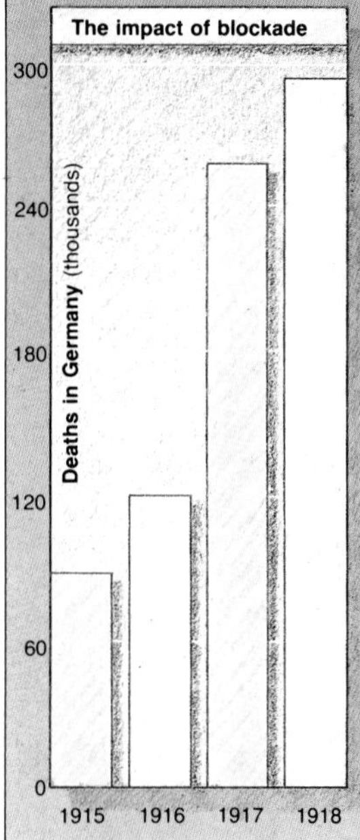

◄ **The effect of Allied blockade on nutritional levels in Germany may be gauged from figures on increased civilian mortality. The food situation worsened after 1916, when hunger became rife. The worst period of the war was the summer of 1918, when severe food shortages coincided with the retreat of the main German armies.**

► **Perhaps 5 million men took part in the great battles of 1916–17. The greatest was at Verdun, through which most of the French army passed. This was precisely the intention of Falkenhayn, who hoped to bleed the French army white. The shadow of Verdun may be seen in the failure of Nivelle's offensive of May 1917.**

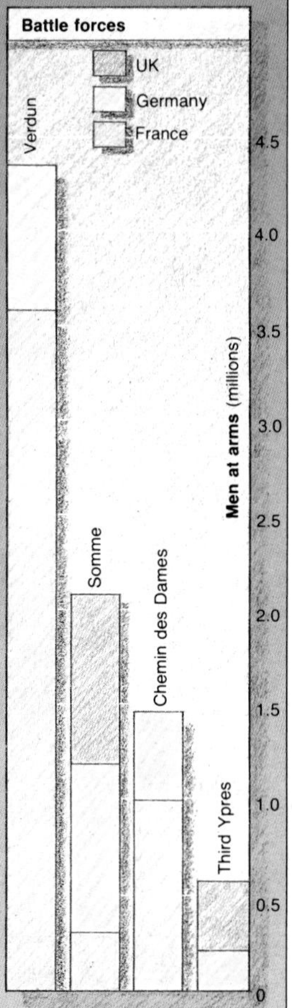

Chronology

1916
February 21
(to Dec. 18) Battle of Verdun: unsuccessful German attack on French city of Verdun

March 12
Allied military conference is held at Chantilly, France, to discuss summer offensive

April 4
RUSS: Brusilov is appointed commander of the Russian southern armies

April 24–29
Easter Rising of Irish Republican Brotherhood against the British in Dublin, Ireland

April 29
In Mesopotamia, Turks capture Kut and the remnants of the British invasion force

May 17
UK: Air board formed to coordinate air war

May 31
(to June 1) Battle of Jutland: major naval battle of war between UK and Germany

June 4
(to Oct. 10) Brusilov offensive: Russians push back the Austro-Hungarian line north of the Carpathians

June 6
Start of Arab revolt against the Turks in the Hejaz

July 1
(to Nov. 19) Battle of the Somme: unsuccessful Allied attack on German lines in the Somme Valley, France

August 29
GER: Hindenburg succeeds Falkenhayn as chief of general staff of German field armies (with Ludendorff as chief quartermaster general)

November 7
Woodrow Wilson is reelected president of the USA

December 12
FR: Nivelle becomes commander in chief of French northern and northeastern groups of armies

December 26
FR: Joffre is created Marshal of France

1917
March 15
Czar Nicholas II of Russia abdicates. Provisional government assumes power

April 6
The USA enters the war fighting on the side of the Allies

April 16–29
Chemin des Dames offensive: a large-scale French offensive on the Aisne fails to break the German line

April 29
FR: Pétain is appointed chief of French general staff

May 10
USA: Pershing is appointed to command American Expeditionary Forces

May 15
FR: Pétain succeeds Nivelle as commander in chief of the French northern and northeastern armies
FR: Foch succeeds Pétain as chief of general staff

June 4
RUSS: Brusilov becomes commander in chief of Russian armies

June 31
(to Nov. 10) Third Battle of Ypres: unsuccessful British offensive against the German forces in Flanders

In 1916 the chief of the German general staff, Erich von Falkenhayn, proposed to win the war in an indirect manner. By attacking the French salient at Verdun he intended not to make any major breakthrough, but rather to bleed the French army white. This was war of attrition with a vengeance, and it left a battlefield strewn with the corpses of over half a million men.

The clash at Verdun

Neither before nor since has there been such a bloody demonstration of the blindness of commanders, both political and military, as to the consequences of their actions. The French commander, Joffre, did not take very seriously the threat of a German assault on Verdun. Indeed, just before the attack was launched, its defenses were dismantled and reorganized. His response to those who worried about the depleted defenses was: "I ask only one thing, and this is that the Germans will attack me, and if they do attack me,

Erich von Falkenhayn 1861–1922

Fifty-three when war broke out, Falkenhayn was an experienced soldier who had been Prussian minister of war since 1913. After the German retreat in September 1914 he was chosen to replace the discredited Moltke. He rebuilt German strategy in the wake of the failure of the Schlieffen Plan. He believed that the war had to be won in the west, but after the failure of offensives at Ypres and elsewhere in 1915 he resorted to a policy of attrition to prevent the Allies from building up forces that could overwhelm his army. The high (or low) point of this policy was the massive German assault on Verdun in 1916. It succeeded in diverting French resources, but caused such losses of German troops that confidence in Falkenhayn faded. He was replaced by Hindenburg and Ludendorff.

Henri Philippe Pétain 1856–1951

Although he was a 58-year-old professional soldier in 1914, Pétain had never served outside France. Yet against the prevailing military consensus he had evolved his own views about the value of defensive strategy, a view that proved decisive once the war in France had become one of attrition. This strategy was tested to the limit at Verdun. In May 1917 he succeeded the discredited Nivelle as commander in chief of the French army and helped restore the morale of French troops. His "stinginess" with the lives of his men contrasted with earlier policy. He later earned the enmity of his country by presiding over France during the Nazi occupation. He was condemned to death in 1945, but the sentence was commuted by another veteran of Verdun, Charles de Gaulle.

1916–17 THE GREAT SLAUGHTER

Half a million men are sacrificed at Verdun

The Allies launch the Somme offensive

Rigidity of command persists

Eight kilometers gained 650,000 men lost

Heads roll but large-scale offensives continue

Over half a million die at Passchendaele

Campaigns are mounted in other theaters but cannot shift the balance of power

that it will be at Verdun." Falkenhayn obliged.

On the first day of the assault, 21 February 1916, more than a million shells fell on French positions, clustered around a series of forts on both sides of the River Meuse. Fort Douaumont fell on 25 February. The next day, the town's defense was entrusted to the commander of the Second Army, Philippe Pétain.

The defense of Verdun was to become an emblem of French military might. To hold it turned into a symbol of the will of the entire French nation; in this way a powerful national myth was born. The city itself was of no great strategic importance, but its loss would have been politically catastrophic. For this reason the French prime minister, Aristide Briand, insisted on holding the town. "If you surrender Verdun," he told Joffre and his staff, "you will be cowards, cowards! And you needn't wait till then to hand in your resignation. If you abandon Verdun, I sack you all on the spot."

▼ Fort Douaumont, which dominated the countryside northeast of Verdun, seen in a German aerial photograph of 1916. The fort was stormed by the Germans in February, retaken by the French eight months later.

The French did not abandon Verdun but defended it at all costs: with a total of 259 of the 330 infantry regiments in the French army. This is precisely what Falkenhayn had hoped for. But once it had been started, the battle took on a momentum of its own.

The more the French resisted, the greater the importance the Germans attached to taking Verdun, and the battle gradually turned into a slaughterhouse for the German army as well. Throughout the spring the assaults and bombardments intensified. Flamethrowers and phosgene gas were used. By late spring and early summer, thirst added to the misery of both sides, particularly of the entrenched French defenders. Another symbol of resistance, Fort Vaux, fell to the Germans on 7 June.

Stories of fantastic courage multiplied, most of them true. Others were the stuff of myth. One such was the "trench of bayonets", near Fort Thiaumont, northeast of Verdun. Here the 3rd

The Battle of Verdun 1916

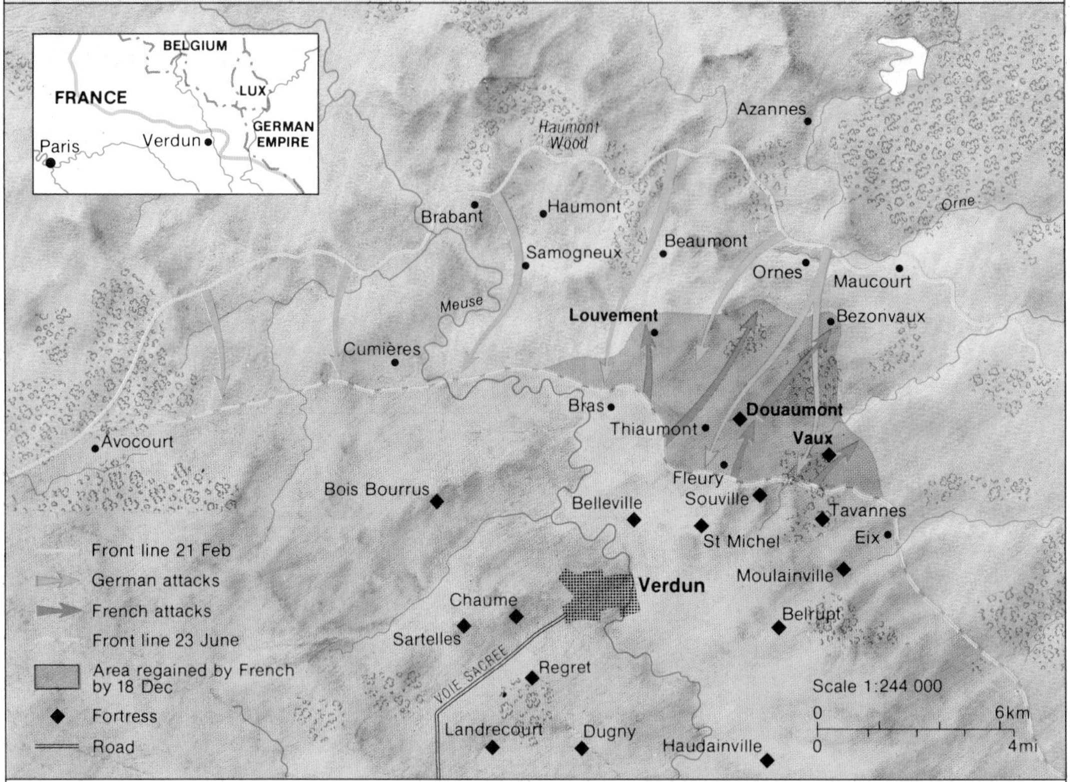

February 21
After mounting an artillery barrage, the Germans attack the French line in the area of Verdun.

February 22–29
The French fight fiercely to resist the German pressure, as Falkenhayn, chief of the German general staff had predicted. For him the Battle of Verdun is not about capturing ground but about killing Frenchmen. By maximizing artillery fire to keep his own losses down he will "bleed the French army white". His attack presses in the center of the salient surrounding Verdun, capturing one of the forts in the city's defense ring – Fort Douaumont – on February 25.

March 6
(to April 9) Fresh German pressure on the northern flank squeezes the salient tighter.

April 20
The French make a local counterattack in the north but it is completely checked by the Germans.

May 3
(to June 23) The Germans continue to grind forward and capture Fort Douaumont's neighbor on the right, Fort Vaux (June 7). By June 23 they hold a bulge stretching into the French defenses as far as Fleury. Because the French are constantly replacing chewed-up divisions with ones at full-strength, half the French army has now been affected by the fighting. But contrary to plan the German losses are also rising.

July 11
Following an unsuccessful attempt to absorb Fort Souville into the bulge, Falkenhayn orders his field commanders to hold their ground while he switches artillery to the Somme.

August 4
A French counterattack reduces the bulge and retakes Fleury.

October 24
(to Nov. 3) Nivelle's counteroffensive completely eliminates the German bulge and retakes Forts Douaumont (Oct. 24) and Vaux (Nov. 2).

December 15–18
Battle of Louvemont. The French force the Germans back further in the center, but the French abandon plans to regain more of the ground lost since February.

▲ From February to July 1916 the Germans moved south toward Verdun, first on the right bank of the River Meuse, then on the left. At its height, the German attack had passed forts Douaumont, Vaux and Fleury, and stood 5km (3mi) from the city itself. From July the Germans went on the defensive. The battle of attrition went on for another six months, until the French had retaken virtually all terrain previously lost in the battle.

► A German photograph of an assault in progress near Verdun in the spring of 1916. These men were at least spared the appalling conditions of combat in the heat of the summer or in the freezing weeks early and late in the battle.

▲ There were three fortified French garrison cities on the Western Front: Dunkirk, Belfort, and Verdun. The last was 200km (125mi) east of Paris, but only 65km (40mi) from the German fortress of Metz. Verdun was defended by two rings of forts, on the left and right banks of the River Meuse. After the German advance was checked, the French line stabilized 10km (6mi) north of Verdun. The population of the city had shrunk from 15,000 to 3,000. During 1916 the city was severely damaged by artillery (above), but was rebuilt after the war. This was not the case in the surrounding countryside, where many small villages simply vanished.

Thiaumont, northeast of Verdun. Here the 3rd company of the 137th French Infantry Regiment was wiped out in early June. After the battle, the trench they had occupied was found completely covered in. Protruding from the earth at regular intervals were 15 bayonets, beneath which were the remains of the men in this unit. The myth was that they had stayed at their posts until buried alive; common sense suggests that they were buried by the men who stormed their trench.

The Germans nearly broke the French lines on 23 June, but made no further progress thereafter. They spent the next six months on the defensive, repelling French counterattacks. In October and November the French eliminated the bulge in the center of the German line. Forts Douaumont and Vaux were retaken on 24 October and 2 November, respectively. Among those distinguished in combat at Verdun were Robert Nivelle, later to command the ill-starred offensive of 1917, and the young Charles de Gaulle. By mid-December the battle was over. The French had held Verdun.

◀ **For the French the key to defending Verdun was the problem of supply. Since the Germans had cut out the southern and western rail links to the city, an alternative had to be found. The only way to keep roughly 20 divisions provisioned was by motorized transport, organized in a constant stream of over 3,000 trucks per day on a minor road south of Verdun to Bar-le-Duc, 60km (38mi) to the south. This lifeline to Verdun took on the name of the *Voie sacrée* or the sacred path, the very name of which points to the elevation of the battle while it was still going on into a national myth.**

The Battle of the Somme

Just as the Battle of Verdun reached its climax, the Allies launched a major attack on the German lines further west, near the River Somme. On 1 July 1916, after a ferocious 5-day bombardment to level the German lines, 13 divisions of British troops and five of French assaulted German positions. But the bombardment had failed. The German positions were still intact, and no-man's-land, through which the British troops had to move, was a mass of craters and at points virtually impassable.

The combined infantry and artillery attack proceeded with clockwork precision. The artillery barrage, aimed at obstacles in front of the British troops, continued exactly as long as engineers believed was needed to destroy enemy emplacements, and then moved on to the next forward section of ground. Each infantry unit advanced in a straight line perpendicular to the Front.

Wave after wave of infantrymen left their trenches that brilliant, hot July morning, and were slaughtered by German machine-gunners. By the end of the first day, the British army had suffered 60,000 casualties, of whom one-third had been killed. This was the worst day of carnage suffered by any army during the war and the bloodiest day in the history of the British army.

The worst part of the story was that it continued in the same pattern, if not with the same intensity, for another six months. British and French casualties together exceeded 620,000; German casualties reached perhaps 450,000. Again the attackers suffered more than the defenders. The Somme was an Allied, and in particular a British, disaster.

The rigidity of the British plan was the source of its failure. Perhaps because Haig felt he could not trust an army of civilian volunteers to use their minds in battle, perhaps because he saw warfare as a large industrial operation, he presented his army with a plan which required no independent thought and tolerated no deviation from the timetable. Hence, when gains came unexpectedly, they were not followed up. This was warfare by the book; an attempt to control the uncertainties and confusions of battle by ignoring them. The results were meager enough:

▲ The meeting point of British and French forces on the Western Front was near the city of Amiens on the Somme. They faced a heavily defended German line which held the only high ground in a relatively flat terrain. The chalky subsoil presented ideal conditions for the construction of a honeycomb of deep trenches which protected German troops from artillery bombardment.

Sir Henry Seymour Rawlinson 1864–1925

Rawlinson's early military career was spent in India and South Africa. At the outbreak of war in 1914 he was 50 years old. As a field commander he fought at Antwerp, Ypres, Neuve Chapelle and Loos. He commanded the British Fourth Army at the Battle of the Somme, and operated within a rigid system of command largely responsible for the most disastrous failure in the history of the British army. The 18th and 30th Divisions, both under Rawlinson's command, did make progress at the beginning of the battle, but were forbidden to press ahead, since a further advance was not in the plan. Two years later his forces adopted different tactics and helped push the German army back from Amiens. In 1919 he directed the withdrawal of the British Expeditionary Force from Russia.

▲ The strategic aim of the Somme attack was to wear down the German reserves, which had frustrated any consolidation of Allied moves over the previous 18 months. This attrition, combined with the slaughter at Verdun, was (to Haig) the road to victory. The tactical aim of the battle was first to take the high ground between Albert and Bapaume, 20km (13mi) to the northeast, and then to drive north toward Arras, a further 25km (16mi) away.

► Plans for major offensives were made with meticulous care. Their effectiveness was compromised by poor communications, unreliable equipment, supply problems and clogged roads.

The Battle of the Somme 1916

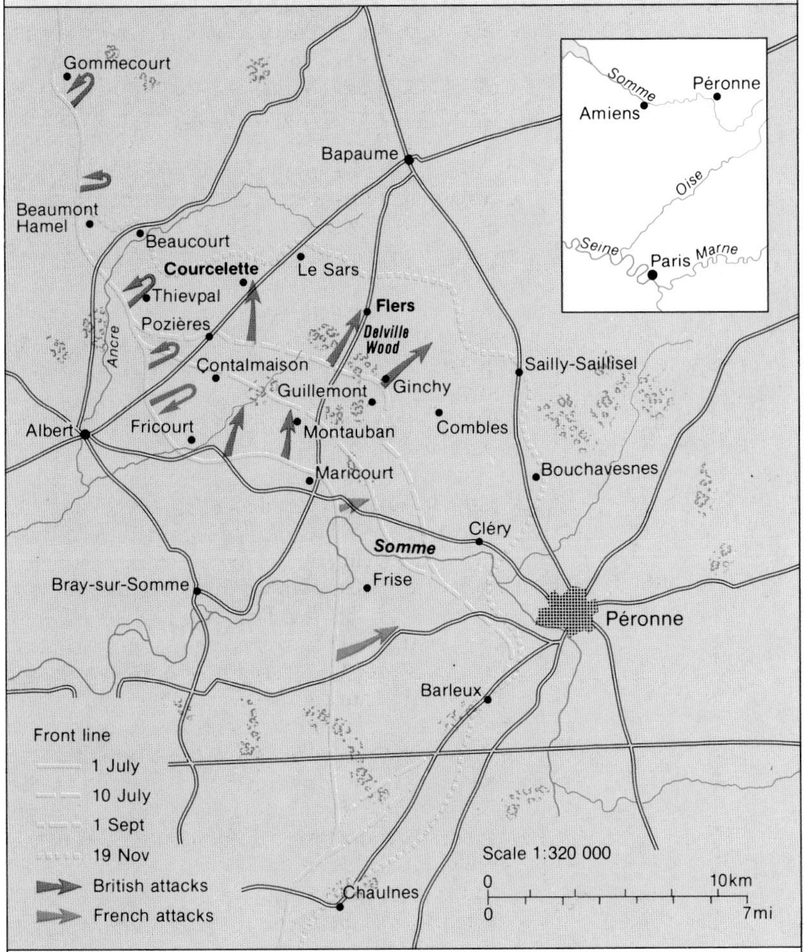

June 24
Allies begin large-scale artillery bombardment.

July 1
British and French infantry divisions begin an assault on the German front line.

July 2–10
The French and the right wing of the British make some progress, but the British center and left are held in check. Casualties are enormous on both sides, because Falkenhayn (chief of the German general staff) refuses to give up ground to save lives.

July 11
Falkenhayn orders the Verdun attacks to stop, and transfers artillery from Verdun to the Somme.

July 12
(to Aug. 27) The Allied attacks continue, but the Germans bitterly contest each trench and immediately counterattack if one is lost.

August 28
Falkenhayn is replaced by Hindenburg and Ludendorff.

September 15–22
Battle of Flers-Courcelette. Further Allied attacks attempt to enlarge the meager gains of July and August, but German resistance is too strong.

September 25
(to Nov. 19) Battle of the Ancre. A final Allied effort again fails to achieve a breakthrough.

Planning the Somme

The Somme offensive emerged from the Allies' conference at Chantilly in December 1915, which hoped that a series of "wearing-out" operations and major offensives would bring Germany to sue for peace by the end of 1916. The German offensive at Verdun, which started in February 1916, eliminated the need for wearing-out operations and reduced the potential contribution of the French. So the main responsibility for the major offensive lay with the British and was assigned to the Fourth Army, commanded by Rawlinson. At this point, there developed a difference of opinion between the commander in chief, Haig, and Rawlinson. Rawlinson wanted a "bite and hold" type of offensive: the Fourth Army would make heavy use of artillery and the infantry would seize part of the German lines. The infantry would then consolidate and destroy the inevitable German counterattacks. The process would then be repeated and three lines of German defenses would be captured in about two weeks. This would theoretically reduce British casualties while inflicting heavy losses on the Germans. Haig believed that the infantry could break through the German defenses and then cavalry would exploit the success. Thus Haig saw infantry rather than artillery as the breakthrough force, and relied partly on a panic occurring in the German lines, partly on the speed of the advance, and partly on a short preliminary bombardment.

However, when Rawlinson submitted his plans for the offensive to Haig in April 1916, there developed a certain confusion as to which conception of the offensive was going to predominate – Rawlinson's "bite and hold" proposal or Haig's breakthrough idea. What eventually emerged was a mixed plan. Rawlinson was permitted a lengthy artillery bombardment and, in the south of the offensive, limited objectives. In the center and north of the offensive, the objectives of the infantry assault were much deeper, and the cavalry would stand by for the exploitation.

This mixed plan was perhaps slightly closer to Rawlinson's beliefs, and he felt confident (on the basis of experience in 1915) that the infantry would at least be able to capture the first line of German trenches, despite certain problems with the artillery preparation. On the opening day the main problem would be infantry consolidation *after* the capture of German trenches, in order to beat off the anticipated German counterattacks. It was for this reason that when the British infantry went over the top early on 1 July 1916 they were heavily burdened with material and supplies for consolidation, and were not ordered to run forward.

Thus the hopeful plans of the Chantilly conference eventually led to the Somme offensive on the Western Front. Ironically, if Haig had insisted on his breakthrough idea, instead of permitting the mixed plan to go ahead, it is possible that the initial rush would have been much more successful on that fateful morning.

approximately an 8km (5mi) gain at most, in an operation that cut the heart out of the Kitchener volunteer armies.

Chemin des Dames to Passchendaele

By the end of 1916 there was indisputable evidence that the tactic of frontal assault on the Western Front had failed. But, tragically, more major attacks were in train. Again some men at the top vanished, but their attitude to the war lived on. In Britain Lloyd George replaced Kitchener as secretary for war, who drowned when his ship the *Hampshire*, en route to Russia, hit a German mine and sank on 5 June 1916. Lloyd George loathed General Haig, but thought he lacked the political support to get rid of him. In Germany Hindenburg replaced Falkenhayn as chief of the general staff, but adopted a similarly cautious policy, as shown in the German withdrawal to a new, more easily defended line (the Hindenburg line), east of Bapaume and north of Soissons, in March 1917. In France General Nivelle, the hero of Verdun, replaced Joffre as commander of the French army, but was even more fervently committed to *la guerre à l'outrance* (war to the bitter end).

This he demonstrated in his plans for a massive attack on well-fortified German positions in Champagne, north of Reims. The battle took the name of the "Chemin des Dames", after a road overlooking the River Aisne. It began on 21 April 1917, and soon turned into the Somme all over again: perhaps 40,000 men were lost on the first day alone, with more bloody and futile attacks in the next six weeks.

The battle's failure was undeniable. Pétain replaced Nivelle and resolved to protect his men from similar folly. But by then it was too late. The Nivelle offensive in Champagne broke the French army as a fighting force. Mutinies broke out in 68 of the French army's 112 divisions.

Robert George Nivelle 1856–1924

After successfully commanding the french counterattack at Verdun, the 60-year-old Nivelle was given charge of the armies of the north and northeast. In 1917 he promised to break through the enemy lines. The "Nivelle offensive" of April 1917 was simple in its concept – after an artillery bombardment immense numbers of men would overwhelm the enemy – but murderous in its execution. Nivelle failed; the army mutinied; France's war effort faltered. He was replaced by the other hero of Verdun, Pétain, whose sympathetic handling of the crisis saved the army. Moved sideways into the French North African command, Nivelle played no further part in the war on the Western Front. He died in 1924.

▼ Nivelle's plan for the Chemin des Dames offensive (inset) envisaged an artillery barrage and a decisive breakthrough. As on the Somme, the barrage failed; the defenders held the initial French advance to a mere 500m (1600ft). Repeated French attacks were futile and their repetition, inhuman. The French army lost over 270,000 men and the will to fight this kind of war.

The Chemin des Dames Offensive 1917

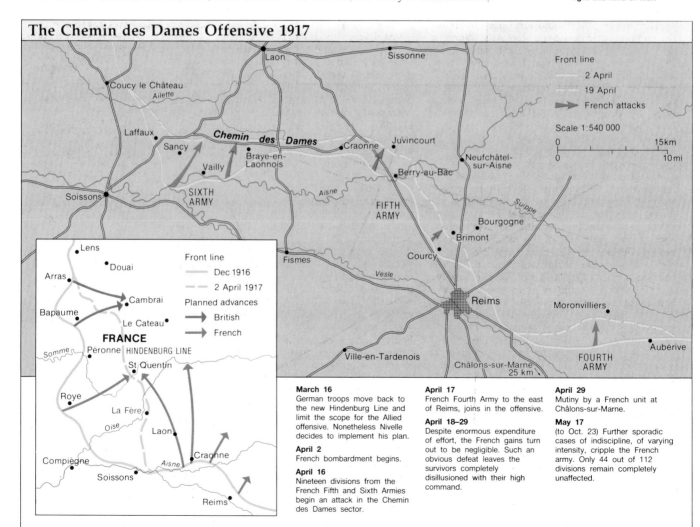

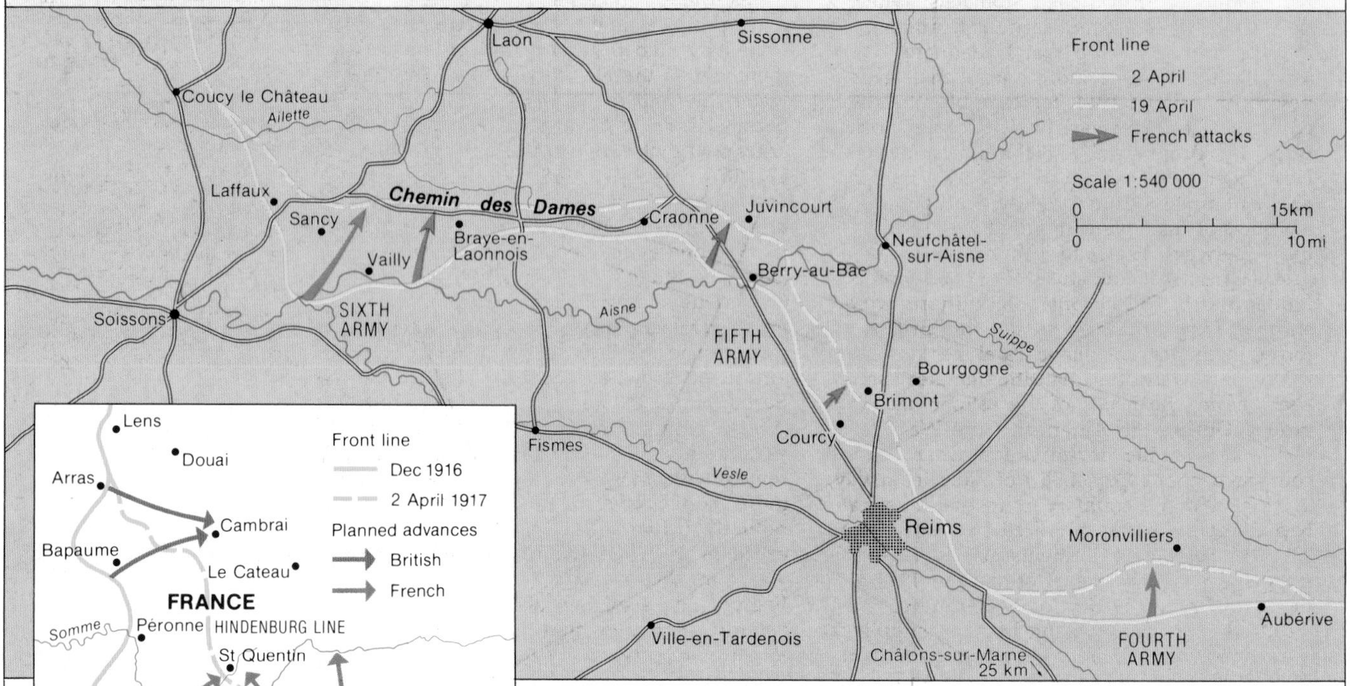

March 16
German troops move back to the new Hindenburg Line and limit the scope for the Allied offensive. Nonetheless Nivelle decides to implement his plan.

April 2
French bombardment begins.

April 16
Nineteen divisions from the French Fifth and Sixth Armies begin an attack in the Chemin des Dames sector.

April 17
French Fourth Army to the east of Reims, joins in the offensive.

April 18–29
Despite enormous expenditure of effort, the French gains turn out to be negligible. Such an obvious defeat leaves the survivors completely disillusioned with their high command.

April 29
Mutiny by a French unit at Châlons-sur-Marne.

May 17
(to Oct. 23) Further sporadic cases of indiscipline, of varying intensity, cripple the French army. Only 44 out of 112 divisions remain completely unaffected.

Provisioning Armies

▲ A mountain of stores destined for the British armies in France and Flanders piled up at Boulogne, one of the principal supply depots on the Channel coast. Large numbers of troops were required to handle supplies in such base areas while, from 1916 onward, the British army also employed some 193,500 native laborers drawn from China, India, South Africa, Egypt, the West Indies, Malta, Mauritius, Fiji and the Seychelles. There were similar native labor corps in Mesopotamia, East Africa, Egypt, Italy and at Salonika.

The French emperor Napoleon once remarked that armies march on their stomachs. When the European states put armies of millions into the field in World War I adequate provisioning became more crucial than ever before. In August 1914, for example, the ration strength of the (prewar) British regular army was 164,000 men and 27,500 animals: by November 1918 it stood at 5,363,352 men and 895,770 animals. Consequently prodigious amounts of food were required on a daily basis. Between 1914 and 1918 a total of 3,241,000 tons of foodstuffs, 5,438,602 tons of fodder and 5,253,538 tons of munitions were shipped from Britain to sustain the British forces in France and Flanders alone.

Not only were the quantities greater than ever before, the needs of the soldier had grown. During the American Civil War (1861–65) a soldier of the Union army consumed about 2kg (4.5lb) of supplies a day; his World War I counterpart in the American Expeditionary Forces required between 18 and 22kg (40–50lb). Requirements also increased irrespective of the size of armies: in 1914 a British infantry division of 17,000 men required 27 railroad wagon loads of supplies a day; the same division's daily requirements by 1916 filled 20 wagons with food and fodder and 30 wagons with other needs. Similarly a French division in 1918 was consuming more than a French army corps four years previously.

As a result the rear areas of armies came to resemble vast suburbs of depots. The British established major bases at locations such as Le Havre and Boulogne in France and Kantara in Egypt to receive foodstuffs requisitioned at home or purchased abroad. Fresh, frozen and preserved meat was imported from the United States, the Antipodes and Latin America; dairy products from the Netherlands; potatoes from Italy; and fish from Norway. Food was then sent to the Front by railway, internal waterways and motor transport. The latter became increasingly important – the British army's 80 motor vehicles of 1914 becoming 121,702 vehicles by 1918. At Verdun, too, it was motor transport that kept the French army supplied. During the defense of Verdun in 1916 one vehicle passed along the 60km (38mi) lifeline of the *Voie sacrée* between Bar-le-Duc and Verdun every 14 seconds. From advance depots, food would then be taken up to the Front on the backs of animals and men. Elsewhere methods might vary – in East Africa both sides used native porters.

Static trench warfare enabled armies to perfect lines of communication, but it must be remembered that difficulties could arise in more mobile warfare. Armies might be reduced to foraging crops from the fields much as in the past, as the Germany army was compelled to do during its advance in France and Belgium in 1914 when marching columns simply outstripped the horse-drawn and motor transport vehicles that were endeavoring to bring supplies forward from distant railheads. Indeed, the architect of the original German invasion plan, von Schlieffen, had failed to appreciate fully the logistic difficulties of the enterprise, merely remarking that the troops would have to make "very great exertions". Thereafter generals could not ignore logistic considerations and the British army was well served by the expertise of such men as Lt-General Sir Travers Clarke, the BEF quartermaster-general.

None of this deflected Haig from his chosen course of launching another massive attack on German lines, this time at Ypres in Belgium. There is some dispute as to his objective in this operation; he changed his own story several times in succeeding years. He might have been aiming at the German U-boat ports at Ostend, 50km (30mi) from Ypres; less ambitiously, he could have been trying to sever the rail link, roughly 15km (10mi) behind the Front, which supplied the German line; or attrition could have been the meaning of it all – the kind of attitude attributed, perhaps apocryphally, to the British commander Sir William Robertson, who is reported to have said that the war would end when there were two British soldiers and one German left in the field.

This last objective rings truest. Between 31 July and 10 November 1917 the British launched a series of attacks which are known as "Third Ypres", or more simply, Passchendaele, after an insignificant village 8km (5mi) east of Ypres which was finally taken in early November, and retaken by the Germans a few months later. The initial attack on German lines failed to achieve a breakthrough. In spite of this further attacks were ordered. Again casualties passed the 500,000 mark, for nothing. The British fought two battles: against the Germans and against the elements. The rain turned the battlefield into glutinous mud and destroyed any hope of a major advance. Again the only memorable feature of the operation was the resilience, the sheer persistence in the art of survival, of the men who fought.

Core and periphery: 1916–17

On one point Haig was right: the war would be won and lost on the Western Front. For this reason, even major military and naval operations in other theaters in 1916–17 were treated as of secondary significance. But it is wrong to draw a clear line between those generals who pressed for major campaigns on the Western Front and those who argued for initiatives elsewhere – so-called Westerners and Easterners. Both saw the war as a unity.

This was as true of Germany as it was of Britain and France. As perceived by its generals, the aims of Germany were to break the military threat to its vital interests posed in different ways by France, Russia and Britain. In 1914 this was to be done by a strategy of annihilation; later Falkenhayn adopted a strategy of attrition, to wear down enemy forces. But even when he was succeeded by Ludendorff and Hindenburg (in August 1916), and unrestricted submarine warfare was launched (in February 1917), the aim was the same: to defeat the more dangerous enemies in the west by military pressure in several theaters of operation.

Allied military leaders also accepted the need to see the war as a unity. Hence an attack in the east was both a way to outflank enemy strongpoints on the Western Front and to exploit British naval superiority. The argument was over how to distribute resources over many fronts. After the failure of the Gallipoli Campaign in 1915, though, a strategy of diverting men and materiel away

Sir Douglas Haig 1861–1928

When Haig sailed for France in August 1914 as head of the 1st army corps he was, at 53, one of the British army's most experienced generals. He returned in 1918 as a victor, but he was – and remains – one of the most controversial figures in British military history. In common with other leading soldiers in that conflict he failed to appreciate the changes that had occurred in military technology. His background was conventional enough: imperial and colonial wars culminating in the Anglo-Boer War of 1899–1902. His success in the field in 1914 and 1915 marked him out as the obvious successor to French as commander of the British Expeditionary Force. Yet as a cavalry man he had little knowledge of an infantry war and failed to see the passing of the cavalry into military history. His pursuit of impossible goals on the Somme and at Passchendaele cost the British dearly, and while he retained the affection of many, his name is still synonymous with an inhuman approach to command. Haig's answer to his critics was to say that he had fought one continuous battle in 1914–18 and had won it.

▶ The Third Battle of Ypres was a monumental exercise in futility. Just as on the Somme, overconfidence in artillery and underestimation of the difficulties imposed by the terrain yielded almost nothing for enormous costs. Ypres was a British salient overlooked by the German army on three sides. The prelude to the battle (known variously as Third Ypres or simply as Passchendaele) was the major British victory at Messines. On 7 June 1917, 19 mines were exploded under the German positions at Messines to the south of Ypres. This destroyed the German trenches, which were occupied and cleared by Irish, British and New Zealand troops. Six weeks later, the battle was joined.

Haigs aims (inset) are unclear: he may have intended to capture the railroad to Ostend or possibly to take Bruges and the U-boat base at Zeebrugge. On 16 July he launched a 10-day artillery bombardment, followed on 31 July by an advance on a 24km (15mi) front.

▼ Just as on the Somme, the very destruction unleashed during the battle ensured a British defeat. Heavy rains turned the battlefield into a quagmire, made worse by the obliteration of the Flemish drainage system. When the 2nd Canadian Division took the obliterated village of Passchendaele on 4 November, they reached an objective that had little military significance, but whose name has come to symbolize the appalling character of the war on the Western Front.

The Third Battle of Ypres 1917

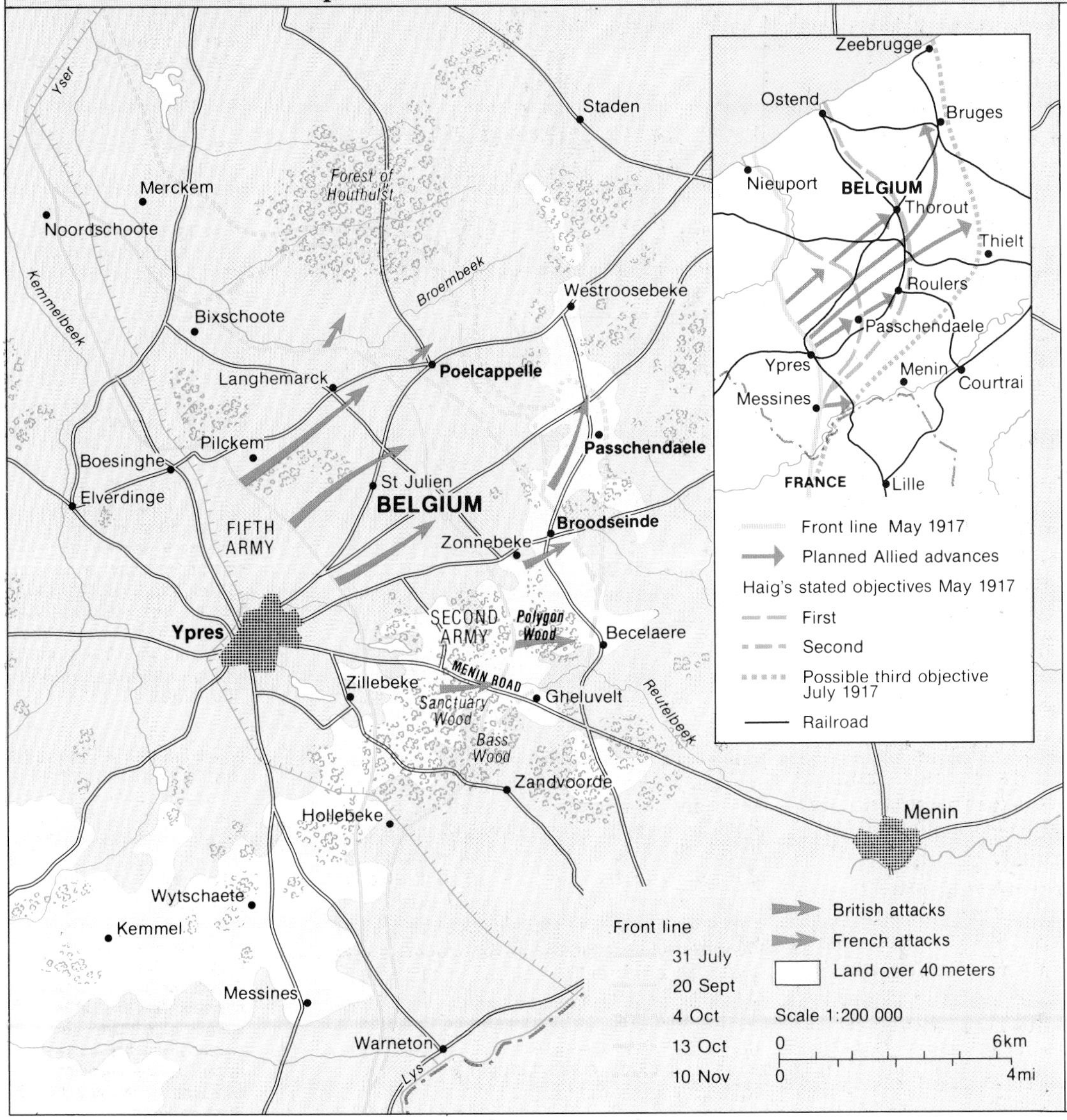

July 16
British artillery bombardment begins.

July 31
Despite poor conditions caused by bad weather, the British Second and Fifth Armies begin an infantry assault as planned.

August 1–18
The British find it impossible to achieve a breakthrough, but persist in their assaults.

September 20–25
Battle of the Menin Road. Haig, the British commander in chief, shifts the emphasis of the attack from General Sir Hubert Gough's Fifth Army, on the left, to General Sir Herbert Plumer's Second, on the right. Plumer adopts step-by-step tactics, and with the benefit of better weather achieves the objectives in this first step.

September 26
(to Oct. 3) Battle of Polygon Wood. Plumer's second step, is successful, so is his third, the Battle of Broodseinde (Oct. 4), but after that the weather begins to deteriorate again.

October 9
Battle of Poelcappelle. The main British attack and a subsidiary one to the north by the French gain little.

October 12
Battle of Passchendaele, which fails, and a halt is called until the conditions improve.

October 26
(to Nov. 10) Second Battle of Passchendaele. Spearheaded by the Canadians, the attack finally gains its objectives (including the village of Passchendaele). However, it comes nowhere near Haig's hope of a breakthrough.

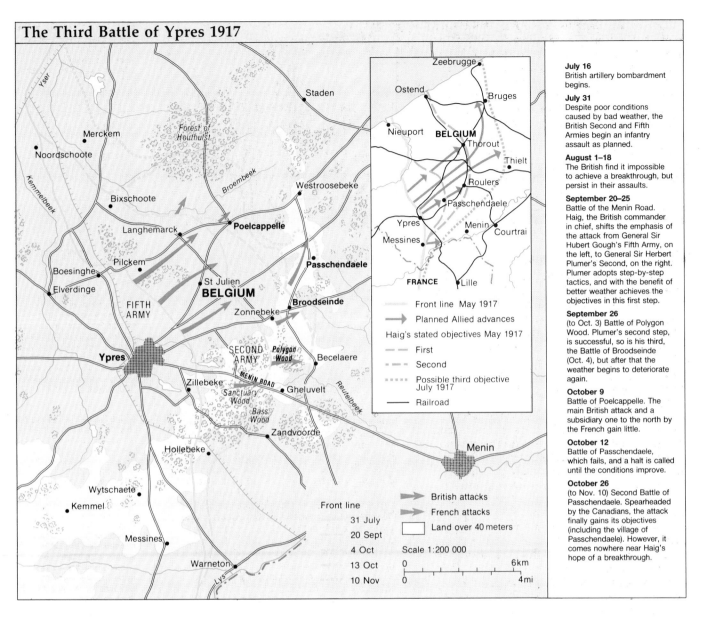

The War against the Turks

Anti-Turkish Campaigns 1914–18

1914

December 22
(to Jan. 18, 1915) The Turks seize the initiative in the Caucasus and attack Russia, but the attack costs them far more casualties than they can afford and the initiative in this area swings back to the Russians for the rest of the war.

1915

February 3
Small Turkish and British detachments spar for control of the Suez Canal and a British force begins to advance up the River Tigris in Mesopotamia.

April 25
(to Jan. 8, 1916) Allied troops are landed at Gallipoli, drawing in Turkish divisions badly needed elsewhere. The Allied attack, however, is a complete failure in face of stiff Turkish resistance.

November 22
(to Dec. 4) Battle of Ctesiphon. The advance up the Tigris finds itself over-extended and the British force is pushed back to Kut-al-Amara.

December 5
The Turks lay siege to Kut.

1916

January 8
The Allies complete their withdrawal from Gallipoli.

January 10
(to April 18) In the Caucasus the Turkish Third Army is rolled back by the Russians, losing Erzerum (Feb. 16) and Trabzon (April 18).

April 29
In Mesopotamia, however, the Turks wipe out the British invasion force by finally capturing Kut.

June 6
An Arab revolt in the Hejaz becomes an added distraction for the Turks.

August 4
(to Jan. 9, 1917) The British drive the Turks out of Egypt and back into Palestine.

1917

February 24
A new British force retakes Kut and then pushes on to Baghdad (March 11).

July 6
T.E. Lawrence and the Arabs capture Aquaba.

December 11
Jerusalem falls to the British as they drive up through Palestine.

1918

April 14
Turkish troops advance to occupy Batum. Only in the Caucasus, now Russia is out of the war, can the Turks make any gains. Everywhere else they are in retreat.

September 19
(to Oct. 25) Battle of Megiddo. Turkish forces in Palestine are routed by the British and Arabs. Damascus, Beirut and Aleppo are captured during the pursuit.

October 30
In Mesopotamia the Turkish Sixth Army surrenders to the British.

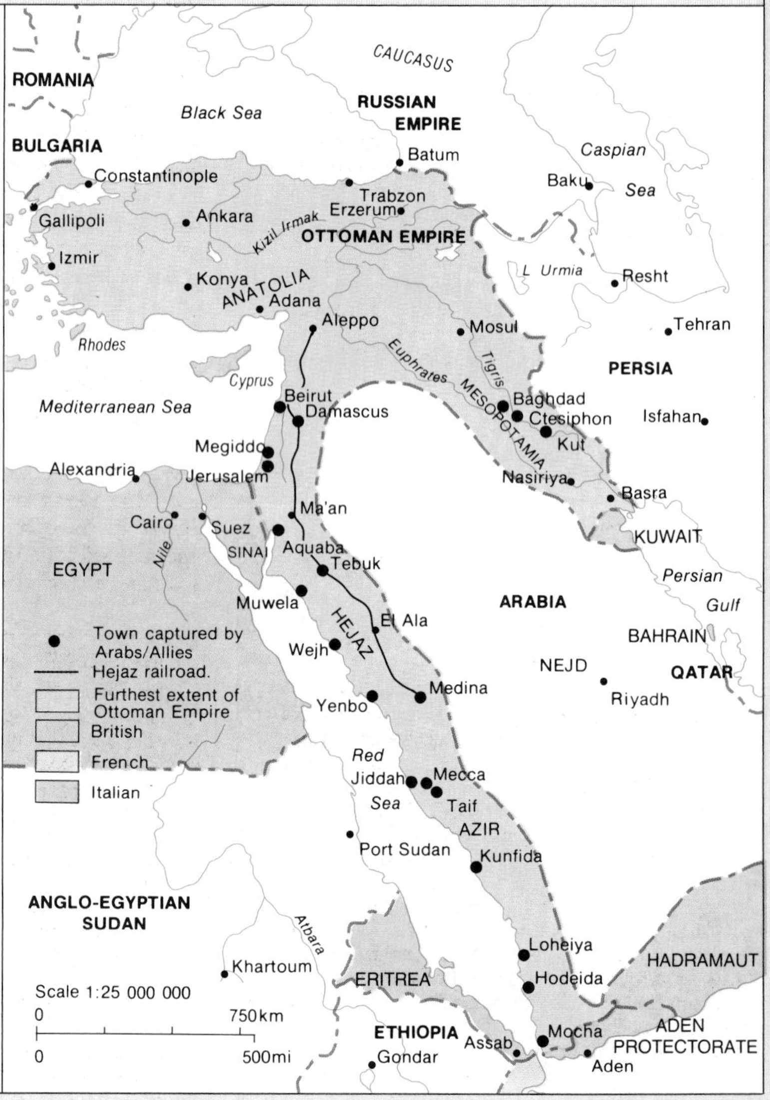

▲ T.E. Lawrence – "Lawrence of Arabia".

◀ Arab troops photographed by Lawrence.

The Allied campaign against Turkey took three forms. The first was the direct assault at Gallipoli (see pp. 82–83). The second was a series of loosely coordinated attacks involving British troops in Mesopotamia and Russian troops in Persia. The third was the revolt of Arab tribesmen against Turkish rule. The Mesopotamian campaign grew out of the British defense of the oil pipeline from Persia. From Basra near the Persian Gulf, British forces advanced toward Baghdad in early 1915. After initial successes, the British were forced back to Kut-al-Amara, where they were besieged and surrendered in April 1916.

A second campaign in 1917 was more successful. The Arab revolt arose out of Arab aspirations for independence from Turkey, recognized with some ambiguous qualifications by the British after long negotiations. Consequently, Hussein, the grand sharif of Mecca, led an attack on 5 June 1916 on the Turkish garrison at Medina. By December 1916 Hussein was recognized by the British government as king of Arabia. In association the British launched an offensive through the deserts of Egypt to Palestine, supported by guerrilla actions led and popularized by T.E. Lawrence, who has entered historical mythology as Lawrence of Arabia. He succeeded in capturing the tiny port of Aquaba on the Red Sea in July 1917, and later took an active part in the British advance through Palestine and Syria.

While recognizing Arab political aspirations, the British also stated in the Balfour Declaration of 2 November 1917 a commitment to "view with favour the establishment in Palestine of a national home for the Jewish people" without prejudice to "the existing non-Jewish communities in Palestine". Thus the present-day Arab–Israeli conflict was born out of subversion of the Turkish Empire in World War I.

from the Western Front was never given primary consideration. The emphasis in planning and priorities returned to France and Flanders, where the bulk of British, French and Allied troops were located.

The "core" of the war remained in northwest Europe. Events in the "periphery" were dramatic, but indecisive. Military action in this phase of the conflict seemed to lead only to new stalemates. For example, the Brusilov offensive against the Austrian Eastern Front in June–October 1916 was at first massively successful. A group of four Russian armies, commanded by the veteran general Alexei Brusilov, took over 400,000 Austro-Hungarian prisoners, and although the Central Powers quickly formed a new line, Brusilov had demonstrated sufficient military prowess to bring Romania into the war on Russia's side. This turned out to be a disaster for Romania, since Falkenhayn himself led a punitive expedition into that country, which in effect was knocked out of the war by December 1916.

Few clear-cut developments emerged from the fighting in other sectors in 1916–17. The Italian army had trouble holding the Austrians on the Trentino river, and on Austria-Hungary's southern border Sarrail advanced in Macedonia. In the Middle East, where the Allies were mounting a two-pronged attack on the Turkish Empire, British forces captured Beersheba (31 October 1917), Jerusalem (11 December) and Baghdad (11 March), which helped to weaken the Turkish Empire. None of these operations seriously shifted the balance of power in the conflict.

In the naval war, a similar stalemate followed the only major engagement of the war between the German and British high seas fleets. This took place at Jutland, off the Danish coast, on 31 May 1916. The British fleet lost more ships, but the German fleet clearly broke off the engagement to avoid being lured into an even bigger confrontation. On balance the battle secured British strategic supremacy, since German commanders would not again risk their fleet and kept it bottled up in the North Sea and the Baltic for the rest of the war. The Germans placed their hopes even more fervently on submarine warfare. Yet it also demonstrated to the British that another major confrontation might not end with a British victory.

After lunch with the Emperor [of Russia], the meeting began. Our Imperial President was even more absent-minded than he had been at the previous session. He was constantly yawning and took no part in the discussions. In spite of his self-confidence, Gurko, who was acting as Chief of Staff, had some difficulty in conducting the meeting, for although normally level-headed he had not sufficient authority. It came out that the problem of supplies for the troops was likely to increase in difficulty, for there were constant changes of Ministers, who were superseded before they could bring any proper organization into being. Most of them were appointed to offices of which they had no knowledge whatsoever, and had to begin by learning the duties they were supposed to perform. They really had no time to do anything, for they were kept constantly fighting with the Duma or with public opinion in order to keep their posts. It is not to be wondered at that in such circumstances the machine of government functioned less and less efficiently, and the Army suffered proportionately and directly.

GENERAL BRUSILOV

Alexei Alexeivich Brusilov 1853–1926

Brusilov had a long military career – he first saw action in the Russo-Turkish War of 1877–78. By 1914 he was a veteran soldier of 61 and commander of a Russian army. He gained some successes in East Prussia and in 1916 was appointed commander of four Russian armies south of the Pripet Marshes. The offensive he launched on 4 June 1916 and which bears his name brought relief to the hard-pressed Italians by compelling the Austrians to withdraw forces from the Italian Front to the Eastern Front. Lack of munitions caused the offensive to peter out with heavy losses. It was the last successful Russian offensive of the war. A year later the Russian army, to use Trotsky's phrase, voted with its feet for peace.

TANKS AND TANK WARFARE

The tank, an armored vehicle capable of crossing difficult terrain, was conceived by the British army journalist Lt-Col. Ernest Swinton as a means of breaking the state of siege that existed on the Western Front following the onset of trench warfare in late 1914. Trials with a variety of commercial tractors in Britain resulted, early in 1916, in the appearance of an effective machine. It had all-round caterpillar tracks which gave an excellent performance over rough ground and weapons mounted in sponsons at the sides. Two types were produced: "male" tanks, to tackle enemy strongpoints and machine gun positions, which mounted two 57mm guns; and "females", which carried four machine guns instead and were designed to deal with infantry. These original machines were slow, difficult to steer and foundered on soft ground but they could crush barbed wire and were impervious to small-arms fire and shrapnel.

The British employed tanks for the first time on 15 September 1916 on the Somme, but with inexperienced crews and impossible ground, their effect was minimal. Things hardly improved for 12 months but then, on 20 November 1917, at the Battle of Cambrai, everything changed. Over 400 of the new Mark IV machine were employed. After three days they had driven a salient 8km (5mi) deep into the Hindenburg Line for a fraction of the normal casualties. It was judged a striking, if short-lived, success.

Early French developments paralleled those of Britain but the need for good cross-country performance was underestimated. The French heavy Schneider and St Chamond machines were based on modified tractor chassis. In action they were inhibited by poor trench-crossing ability, and the Schneider was a death trap.

The initial German reaction to the Allied tanks was to denigrate them as a sign of martial weakness. This, in turn, created a state of mind at all levels which was resistant to the whole idea. Thus, German attempts to develop a tank were compromised by a late start – their only operational model, the A7V, did not enter service until March 1918.

As might be expected, the Americans adopted the tank idea with enthusiasm. They chose the French Renault and the British Mark V for their own tank corps. However, it took so long to get production under way that no American tanks were ready before the Armistice. Russia and Italy only managed to produce prototype tanks.

Early in 1918 the British Mark V entered service. It featured a more powerful engine than earlier models and was much more maneuverable. It was followed by the Mark V*, a stretched version capable of crossing wider trenches without artificial aids like fascines. Both types took part in the Battle of Amiens on 8 August 1918, in which the lessons of Cambrai were employed on a larger scale. It marked the start of a successful offensive which finally sealed the fate of the German Army. It would be wrong to claim that tanks won the war, but they did provide an answer to the stalemate of trench warfare.

▼ **British Mark IV tanks and infantry advance through the German line toward Cambrai, 20 November 1917. The attack was made across firm ground and produced the war's only major breakthrough on the Western Front. But it could not be exploited because of insufficient reserves.**

◀ **"Auld Reekie II", a Mark IV (female) tank of the 1st Battalion, British Tank Corps. Stowed above the cab is a fascine, which the tank would use as a stepping stone to cross wide trenches. The Mark IV was, numerically, the most important British tank of the war and fought in all the major actions from June 1917 until the end. It weighed 28 tons and had a top speed of about 6 km/hr (4 mi/hr). Its crew of eight (below) had to endure cramped, hot conditions.**

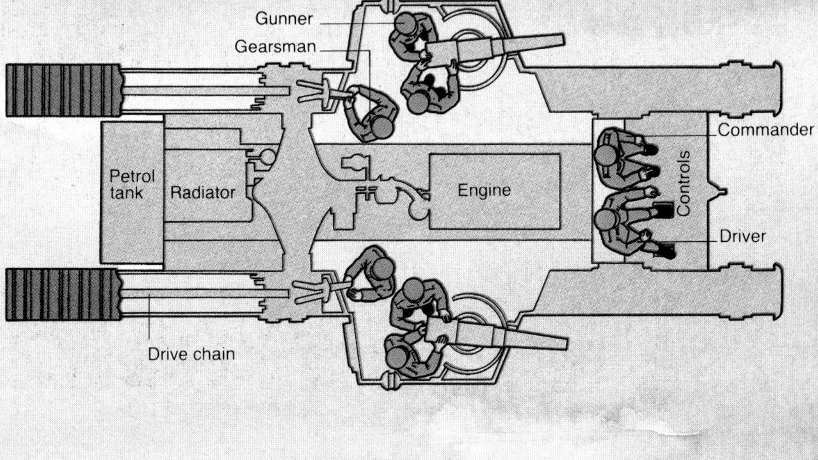

▲ The Hornsby caterpillar tractor of 1909 (top) was the first tracklaying vehicle to be purchased by the British army. It helped sow the seed for the concept of the tank. The Schneider (center) was one of three types of French tank to see service during the war. The Germans introduced their own tank, the A7V (above), in 1918. It proved to be cumbersome and unstable in action and required a crew of 18. Only 20 were completed by the end of the war. For the remainder of their tank force the Germans relied upon captured British machines, which were generally preferred.

◄ Conditions at the Third Battle of Ypres were more suited to naval than tank warfare. G46, commanded by Lieutenant D.G. Browne, stuck in this shell hole near Kitchener's Wood on 1 August 1917. The damage to the track occurred later.

Datafile

From November 1917 to November 1918 the character of the war changed dramatically. The Americans arrived; the Russians departed. The Italian line broke at Caporetto; the Germans made a massive breakthrough on the Western Front in March 1918, but then were pushed back inexorably through the late summer and fall. With the collapse of their Allies and chaos looming at home, German forces gave up their belief in victory.

▼ It is debatable whether the German U-boat campaign ever had the capacity to defeat the Allies. The peak of 545,000 tonnes lost due to enemy action in April 1917 alone certainly raised the specter of defeat, which admiralty officials admitted was a possibility. But by 1918 convoys drastically reduced Allied shipping losses.

▲ The crisis of the Italian army was the debacle of Caporetto in November 1917. A year later the Italian army had recovered, and helped seal the defeat of the Central Powers.

► American pressure increased substantially in 1918. Over 600,000 US troops took part in the Meuse-Argonne battle.

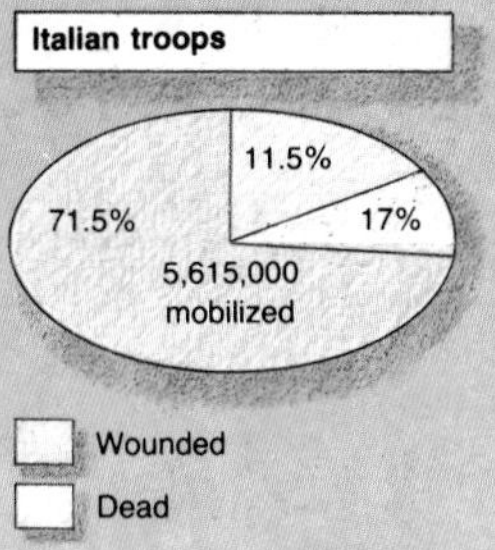

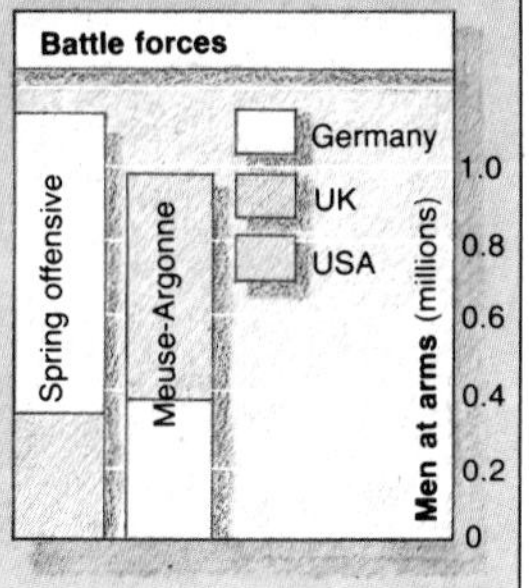

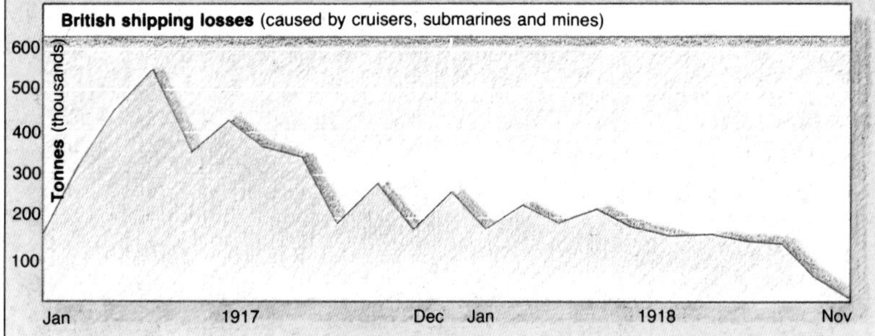

Chronology

1917
August 6
Kerensky is appointed prime minister of Russia

September 3
Germans capture Riga on the Baltic coast

November 7
Bolshevik socialists in Russia overthrow the provisional government

IT: Cadorna is relieved of command of the Italian armies and is succeeded by Armando Diaz

Allied conference at Rapallo: the Allies institute a supreme war council

December 3
The Bolshevik government in Russia signs an armistice with Germany

1918

January 2
UK: Air Ministry formed under secretary of state

January 8
US president Woodrow Wilson publishes his 14 points as a basis for peace

March 3
Russia signs the Treaty of Brest-Litovsk

March 21
The Germans launch their Spring Offensive on the Western Front and push back the Allied forces

March 26
UK/FR: Doullens Agreement: Foch appointed as commander to coordinate the British and French armies

April 1
UK: The Royal Air Force is formed

April 14
Foch is appointed commander in chief of Allied forces (except for Belgian army)

May 7
The Central Powers and Romania sign the Peace of Bucharest

May
(to Oct. 1919) Allied forces intervene in the Russian civil war

July 16
AH: Field Marshal Conrad von Hötzendorff is relieved of command of AH armies

July 18
(to Nov. 10) Allied counteroffensive on the Western Front: German forces are pushed back toward the border of Germany

September 30
The Allies and Bulgaria conclude an armistice

October 3–4
The German government offers peace based on President Wilson's 14 points

October 4
British and Arab forces occupy Damascus

October 27
GER: Ludendorff resigns as quartermaster general

October 28
German sailors mutiny at Kiel

November 3
Austria-Hungary sues for peace with the Allies

November 4–5
Antiwar and pro-Bolshevik risings in Germany

November 5
Foch is given responsibility for determining strategy of all Allied forces on all fronts

November 9
Kaiser Wilhelm II abdicates

November 11
The Allies and Germany sign the Armistice: fighting ends on the Western Front at 11 a.m.

On 10 November 1917 the British offensive around Passchendaele ended. At that point it would have been impossible to foresee that, a year and a day later, Germany would be defeated and the war would end. How did this happen?

In November 1917 the balance of military forces was distinctly favorable to Germany and its allies. Not only had the British offensive completely failed, but developments in Russia and Italy made it appear that the Allies and not the Central Powers should fear the future. First and foremost the war on the Russian Front was over. Lenin and the Bolsheviks seized power on 7 November, and were firmly committed to taking Russia out of the war. Within a month they opened peace negotiations at Brest-Litovsk. These came to an end on 3 March 1918, when Russia accepted the loss of Poland, Lithuania, the Ukraine, Finland and other territories (see p. 58). Secondly, the war on the Italian Front was going decidedly against the Allies. After combined German and Austrian attacks beginning on 24 October, General Cadorna's Italian army collapsed at Caporetto. The Italians tried to reform their line 65km (40mi) further east on the Tagliamento, but by 31 October they were forced into a second retreat. On 10 November they reached the River Piave, 130km (80mi) behind the line they had held two weeks before. There the Italians, massively supported by British and French troops, held the advancing Germans and Austrians.

Over the next 12 months three developments turned the tide the other way. The first was the entry of the United States into the war. The second was the failure of the final German gamble: the offensive of March 1918. The third was the combination of demoralization in the German army and unrest at home.

The United States at war

In a sense the United States was at war with Germany and its allies long before April 1917. The capital and materiel shipped across the Atlantic had helped make it possible for Britain to cope with the German blockade. By late 1916 the failure of German home agricultural production and distribution was so evident that more desperate measures were taken. Unrestricted submarine warfare began on 1 February 1917. Even though the German high command knew of its likely effects on American opinion and policy, they still hoped it would bring Britain to the conference table in a matter of months.

Like all the major German gambles of the war, this one *almost* succeeded. In April 1917 U-boats had destroyed over 850,000 tonnes of shipping, which exceeded their target of 600,000 tonnes, which they mistakenly thought would be sufficient to win the war. Some admiralty officials in

1917–18 REVOLUTION AND PEACE

In November 1917 the balance of military forces favors Germany

America's entry threatens to tip the balance

Germany launches a new offensive in spring 1918

Paris in danger

Allied troops halt the German advance

An Allied counteroffensive pushes back the German line

The Germans retreat and lose hope of victory

the UK began to contemplate defeat, a thought which had hardly crossed the minds of any British leader until then. But the success of the Allied convoy system (introduced in May 1917, whereby ocean-going merchant ships steamed in groups protected by warships), and the sheer capacity of the Allies' shipbuilding industries to replace lost tonnage, ultimately frustrated the German submarine effort.

It took some time for the American presence to make much of a difference in the war on the Western Front. A small contingent of troops arrived in the early summer of 1917, and received a weary reception when they were paraded in Paris, appropriately enough on 4 July 1917. But to provide additional manpower for the Allied cause, the United States brought in conscription on 18 May 1917. On Tuesday 5 June over 10 million men were registered for selective service. Initially two drafts of 500,000 men were chosen. From March 1918, 250,000 men were sent overseas per month. By the end of the war over 4 million men were in the army, and nearly 2 million in Europe. This was more than the sum of British forces then in action. In total 1124,000 Americans were killed in action or died on active service by the end of the war (including deaths from flu).

It was not so much what the American army did in 1918, but its potential if the war dragged on, that helped tip the balance in favor of the Allies. This is not to denigrate the contribution of American forces, under General John J. Pershing, to holding the Allied line in March 1918 and in pushing back the Germans in August–October. American units fought with distinction at Château-Thierry in early June 1918 and later at St Mihiel. Nine American divisions joined in the counterattack which ultimately defeated the German army. It is rather to suggest that the vast American potential – in materiel perhaps as much as in manpower – made it apparent to the German high command that to press on with the war was simply suicidal.

Germany's last gamble: March 1918

Just as American entry into the war was precipitated by unrestricted submarine warfare – the penultimate German gamble of the war – so the American presence helped bring about Germany's last major effort to grasp victory on the Western Front. This was the massive assault on the British and French lines between Arras and La Fère launched on 21 March 1918.

No preliminary barrage announced the attack well in advance. Artillery was vital, but it was now used on a different way. No frontal assault was planned, but rather 47 divisions were deployed in a vast attack along diagonals, which constituted a massive thrust to cut behind the British rear positions on the Somme, while holding off French units further south. This time new tactics of infiltration by small groups, rather than by massed ranks of infantrymen, were employed. A flexible system of command was put into effect. Headquarters made no firm attempt to control troop movements according to a rigid, preset plan. Commanders were instructed to leave their command posts and their telephones and get as close to the Front as possible. Liaison between artillery and infantry devolved to the divisional level. Close control from the top, in the style of General Haig, was out; independent movement within an overall plan was the order of the day.

Within half an hour of setting off, German stormtroopers had broken through the British

The Impact of Convoys

▲ The true value of Empire was demonstrated in World War I. Sea links provided the European Allies with access to a reservoir of men and materiel which the Germans could never match. By launching unrestricted submarine warfare, Germany tried to sever these links. This policy gave the Allies a considerable fright, but it never came close to winning the war. The convoy system helped limit the U-boat threat, the major achievement of which was (paradoxically) to help defeat Germany, by tipping the balance of American opinion toward the Allies. After 1917 Germany could not win the war.

A convoy is a group of merchant ships protected by warships. Although the United Kingdom depended on merchant ships for the import of foodstuffs and many raw materials, between 1914 and 1917 the British Navy resisted the idea of using convoys to guarantee imports. The admiralty was wedded to the 19th-century strategy of using the navy to protect sea lanes rather than ships.

While the navy maintained its opposition, British shipping losses mounted. Early in 1917 the first sea lord, Jellicoe, warned the new prime minister, Lloyd George, that Britain might lose the war at sea within six months. His fears were exaggerated but understandable. In April 1917, Lloyd George insisted that the navy should organize an experimental convoy. It was a success. By September convoys were in general use. In January 1917, before convoys were introduced, about 25 percent of ships that left UK ports were sunk. Between January and November 1918, 95,000 ships sailed in convoys and only 4 percent were sunk.

The War in Italy

The opening of hostilities on the Italian Front in May 1915 put at the disposal of the Allies an army of over one million trained troops, backed by a substantial naval force. Their efforts were directed first to blocking the threat of an Austrian advance into the Trentino in the west, which is the Italian region around Lake Garda. Secondly, they planned their own thrust toward Trieste in the east, along what became the Isonzo Front. In effect this replicated the geographical divide on the Western Front: a possible movement of the Central Powers from the north paralleled by a clear line of Allied attack due east. There the resemblance ended, for the Italian response to the Austrian threat in the west took place in countryside as remote as any from the flatlands of Flanders and northern France. In the west, the Stelvio pass, as 2,800m (9,000ft) and other high points were secured in the first few days of the war. Alpine warfare was necessarily limited to small raids and artillery bombardment, for the purpose of defending the Italian left. The more important sector was on the right. There, over the next two years, a dozen Italian campaigns achieved relatively little at enormous cost in men and morale. The effects of attrition and war weariness were dramatically exposed in late October 1917, when a German-Austrian offensive broke the Italian line at Caporetto in the Isonzo Valley. In the ensuing rout, 300,000 Italian prisoners and 3,000 heavy guns were taken. Reinforced by French and British troops, the Italians regrouped on the Piave river, 140km (90mi) to the west. It sensibly took up defensive positions for the next six months. In late October 1918, under the command of Diaz, who replaced Cardorna, the Italians defeated Austrian troops who knew the war was over.

The Italian Front 1915–18

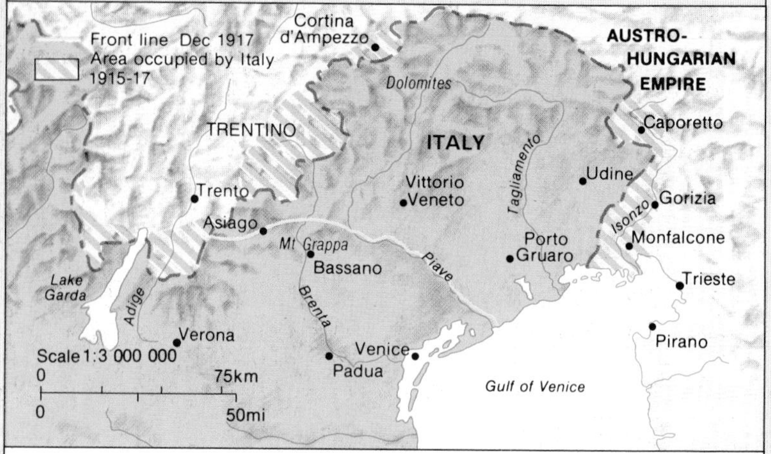

1915

May 23
Italy declares war on Austria-Hungary and seizes several strategically important points.

June 23
(to July 7) Battle of the Isonzo. The Italians attack toward Trieste but are stopped cold.

July 18
(to Aug. 30) Second Battle of the Isonzo.

21 October
(to Nov. 4) Third Battle of the Isonzo. The Italians make minor gains.

10 November
(to Dec. 2) Fourth Battle of the Isonzo. Little change.

1916

February 15
(to March 17) Fifth Battle of the Isonzo. The Italians make minor advances.

May 15
(to June 26) The Austro-Hungarians launch the Asiago offensive, but make few gains.

August 6–17
Sixth Battle of the Isonzo. The Italians make real progress and take Gorizia.

September 14–18
Seventh Battle of the Isonzo. The Italians make minor gains.

October 9–12
Eighth Battle of the Isonzo. Italians make minor gains.

October 31
(to Nov. 4) Ninth Battle of the Isonzo. Little change.

1917

May 12
(to June 8) Tenth Battle of the Isonzo. Italians advance.

June 10–26
Italians attack in the Trentino sector. Little gained

August 17
(to Sept. 12) Eleventh Battle of the Isonzo. Italians make minor gains.

October 24
(to Nov. 10) Battle of Caporetto. A German and Austro-Hungarian attack rips the Italian line open. Aided by six French and two British divisions, the Italians reform their broken front along the Piave river.

1918

June 15–23
Battle of the Piave. The Austro-Hungarians attack the new Italian defense line but are beaten back.

October 24
(to Nov. 2) Battle of Vittorio Veneto. In face of a determined Italian counteroffensive, the Austro-Hungarians collapse.

◀ Warfare in the Italian Alps required enormous efforts to move artillery pieces to mountain positions at a height at times over 3,000m (10,000ft). One observer marveled at the work of Italian Alpine troops who raised guns "with the same prodigious tenacity that is displayed by ants dragging a large grain of wheat".

Count Luigi Cadorna 1850–1928

Born into a distinguished Piedmontese family, Cadorna naturally joined the Italian army when he was 16. Steady progress took him to the post of chief of staff on 10 July 1914. He was then 64. He took over an inefficient army: the officer corps was of poor quality and general morale was low. In 10 months Cadorna transformed it. In May 1915 Italy was able to enter the war with a credible fighting force. It was worn down by problems of supply and inadequate command at all levels; the results were a dozen failed offensives on the Isonzo Front and signs of low morale. It was hardly surprising, therefore, that Cadorna's army suffered a stinging defeat at the Battle of Caporetto in October and November 1917: retreat and near collapse ensued. Cadorna was removed from his post and later retired. After the war Cadorna wrote accounts of Italy's war that (not surprisingly) defended his own role. His leadership of his army was no worse nor better than that of his allies or adversaries. They all underestimated problems of supply and failed to grasp the significance of war weariness on the home front. In 1917 this led to a disaster which Cadorna never lived down.

front lines. The British Fifth Army under Sir Hubert Gough virtually collapsed in the face of the initial onslaught of the German Eighteenth Army, which operated the new devolved command system effectively. Within a week the Germans had advanced 65km (40mi).

This initial phase of operations was followed by three subsequent attempts to break the Allied line. First between 9 and 11 April the "Georgette" offensive round and south of Ypres recaptured Passchendaele and much else that British troops had bled for over the previous four years. This was followed by an assault on the French Sixth Army on 27 May. By mid July it extended to and over the Marne. Once again Paris was under threat; the German front line was only 80km (50mi) from the city in early April 1918.

This led to the Second Battle of the Marne, and, although no one knew it at the time, the beginning of the end of the war. The Allied commander, Ferdinand Foch, initiated a counter-offensive in which French, Moroccan and American divisions, using hundreds of tanks, stopped the Germans and pushed them back over the Marne.

From this moment on, the Allies never lost the initiative. Further north and west the German line was broken on 8 August – the "black day of the German army" – when British, Australian and Canadian troops made an 8km (5mi) advance. Worse was still to come. On 12 September American troops, aided by French colonials and supported by a force of over 1,000 planes, destroyed the German salient of St Mihiel, southeast of Verdun. Successive offensives progressively rolled the Front north in September. The Allies successfully employed German tactical and command ideas against them. Positions that had been out of reach for four years were taken. Bruges and the Belgian coast fell in October. From mid July the Allies captured more than 400,000 German prisoners. The war was over.

The sources of German defeat

Why the German army finally surrendered in 1918 is a highly controversial subject. Adolf Hitler had his answer: the soldiers were betrayed by traitors at home. The key factors, though, lay elsewhere.

The German army's gamble of March 1918 was truly a desperate one. Even with the additional support of units released from the Russian Front,

▲ By 1918 the German army had developed an attack-in-depth system, which paralleled its successful defense-in-depth approach to war on the Western Front. Both avoided the overemphasis in Allied thinking on breaking or defending a rigid line. The new approach called for sudden gas and artillery barrages, to disrupt and demoralize the enemy, followed by the use of stormtroop infiltration tactics. In March 1918 the Germans revived mobile warfare: German columns again marched toward Paris. German innovation followed German recognition of the Allied advantage in materiel. The Allies paid the Germans the compliment of adopting some of these ideas in their successful riposte to the March 1918 offensive.

recently pacified if not peaceful, the army simply ran out of reserves when it reached the zenith of its advance in the summer of 1918. When the Allies proceeded to counterattack, the German troops they encountered were exhausted, poorly supplied and convinced that the promised victory had slipped through their fingers.

In this battle the Allies' overwhelming material advantage was finally demonstrated. The symbol of this gap between the two sides was the tank, first used in strength by the British in the Battle of Cambrai in November 1917. Six months later the Allies had learned to press home the advantage of armored warfare, curiously underdeveloped in the German army during the conflict. In the Allied counterattacks of July and August 1918 tanks were deployed in strength and used in coordination with infantry, artillery and air power, thereby keeping up unremitting pressure on the retreating German army. For the first time in four years the Front was moving, and no lull in the fighting gave the defenders a chance to rest, regroup and successfully counterattack.

The losses on both sides were heavy, but those of Germany could not be made up. It was this combination of fast-diminishing resources of men, materiel and morale which made the setbacks of 1918 so serious and the growing American presence so ominous.

Furthermore, by the time the German armies in the west were checked, the situation on the home front had become critical. In March 1918 the *Burgfrieden*, or political truce of 1914, was re-created, in anticipation of the impending victory on the Western Front: the deprivation and anxiety of the previous three years were eclipsed by a last surge of social solidarity and patriotism. But after the initial "victory" had turned into a massive and unmistakable retreat, the moods of Front and home front changed abruptly.

The line between the two should not be drawn too sharply. New drafts were constantly arriving at the Front, and the steady stream of wounded returning to Germany announced what most people knew but preferred not to admit: the war was going badly. Soldiers were not unaware of the food shortages, the black market and the profiteering that went on behind the lines. When advance in March turned into retreat from August to September, they and their families at home began to ask what positive reasons there were for going on with an unwinnable war.

▼ The German Spring offensive of 1918 was based on the same misconception as the Allied campaigns of 1916–17: that a successful military breakthrough on the Western Front would bring victory in the war. But even had the British and French armies crumbled in 1918, even had Paris itself been taken, Germany would still have had to face the enormous strength and resources of the non-European Allies. After 1917 there was no way that Germany could win this war of endurance. The German campaign of March 1918 was a remarkable feat of military skill, but in terms of influencing the course of the war, it was doomed from the start.

The German Spring Offensive and Allied Counteroffensive 1918

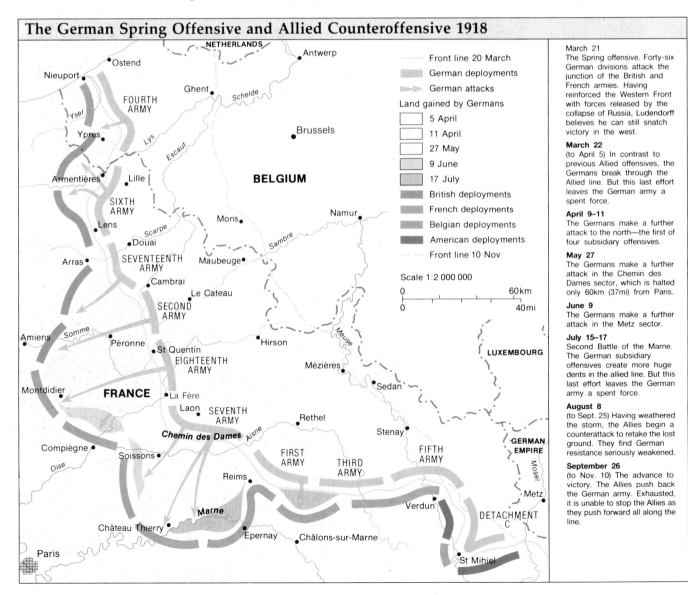

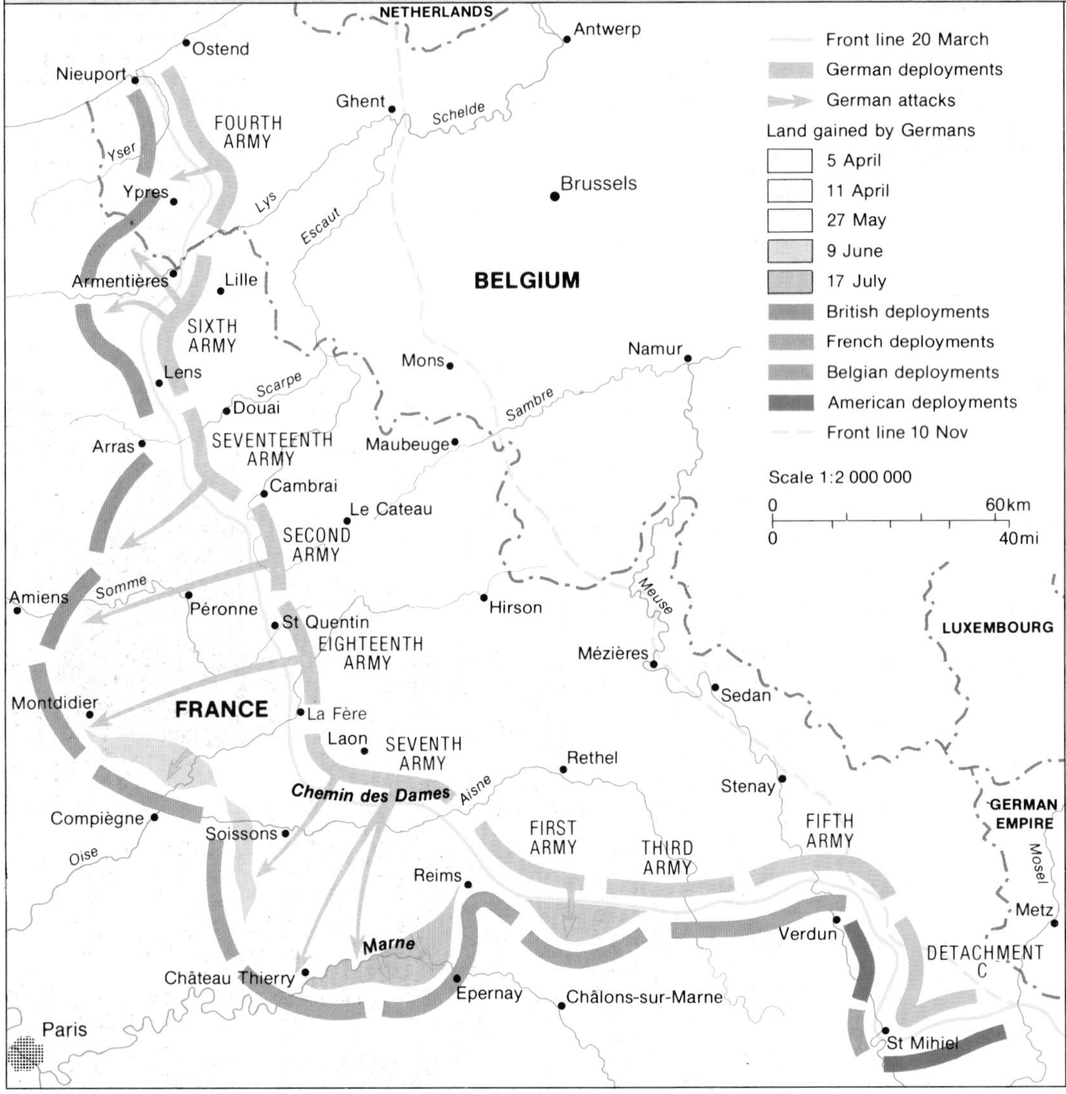

March 21
The Spring offensive. Forty-six German divisions attack the junction of the British and French armies. Having reinforced the Western Front with forces released by the collapse of Russia, Ludendorff believes he can still snatch victory in the west.

March 22
(to April 5) In contrast to previous Allied offensives, the Germans break through the Allied line. But this last effort leaves the German army a spent force.

April 9–11
The Germans make a further attack to the north—the first of four subsidiary offensives.

May 27
The Germans make a further attack in the Chemin des Dames sector, which is halted only 60km (37mi) from Paris.

June 9
The Germans make a further attack in the Metz sector.

July 15–17
Second Battle of the Marne. The German subsidiary offensives create more huge dents in the allied line. But this last effort leaves the German army a spent force.

August 8
(to Sept. 25) Having weathered the storm, the Allies begin a counterattack to retake the lost ground. They find German resistance seriously weakened.

September 26
(to Nov. 10) The advance to victory. The Allies push back the German army. Exhausted, it is unable to stop the Allies as they push forward all along the line.

Ferdinand Foch 1851–1929

Aged 63 when war broke out, Foch had behind him a brilliant career as a military teacher. He played a vital role in the opening phase of the war, at the First Battle of the Marne (1914), and later as general commanding the group of armies of the north. His star was eclipsed for a while after the failure of the Somme offensive. However, in March 1918 he was made, almost four years after the outbreak of war, the first commander in chief of the Allied armies in France. With Pétain, Haig and Pershing formally subordinate to Foch, grand strategy could at last begin to emerge. The failure of the German offensive in the summer of 1918 allowed the initiative to pass to Foch. He never lost it, until the Armistice was signed. After the war Foch was weighed down with honors.

John Joseph Pershing 1860–1948

When the USA entered the war early in 1917 President Woodrow Wilson appointed Pershing commander of the American Expeditionary Forces. Pershing was 57 years old and could look back on a distinguished military career in Cuba, the Philippines and in Mexico. In Europe he resisted requests from British and French commanders for American units to be dispersed among the hard-pressed Allied forces. The American army remained independent and under its own command, with the exception of the critical period after the German offensive of March 1918. His forces achieved some notable successes in the Allied counteroffensive, in particular with the capture of the Saint-Mihiel salient and in the Meuse-Argonne offensive at the end of the war.

On the 20th (July) I visited the commanders of our units engaged and found all roads west of the salient greatly congested. No one who has not been an eye-witness can visualise the confusion in traffic conditions that exists immediately behind the lines during the progress of a great modern battle. It is a most difficult problem to regulate circulation over the roads and keep them from becoming seriously blocked, especially at night, when vehicles must travel without lights and frequent halts are necessary due to accidents of various sorts.

GENERAL PERSHING

From August 1918 the German high command received increasingly serious reports of mass surrenders and a collapse in morale. They were confronted by what may be described as a soldiers' strike against the war – which was also reported on the home front. Thus military retreat fueled civilian hopelessness and anger at the regime that had got them into a cul-de-sac.

All this coincided with the surrender of Germany's allies. The Bulgarian, Turkish and Austrian armies all collapsed in September and October. By then Ludendorff had given up hope of an outright victory; his aim was to keep his army intact and the enemy off German soil. After all, the Germany army had not been broken; it had retreated, and could still inflict substantial casualties on the advancing Allies. Even as late as October 1918 Ludendorff played with the idea of fighting on, should peace negotiations break down. Such resistance would at least help to stop the spread of "Bolshevism" at home.

But such grandiose schemes of a final gesture – echoed in the German navy (see p.158) – were but pipe dreams. Everyone with eyes to see knew the war was over and that further bloodshed was pointless. Ludendorff resigned on 26 October. The Kaiser abdicated 14 days later. On 11 November 1918 hostilities ceased on the Western Front, where after all the war had come to an end.

▼ The mass surrender of German units near Amiens after the "black day" of 8 August 1918 signaled the beginning of the end of the war. But the German army itself remained intact until the Armistice, and could have gone on fighting, had the German people still believed in victory. But a disillusioned and hungry population had had enough. Both army and people knew that the war had to be brought to an end.

AIRCRAFT AND AERIAL WARFARE

In 1914 the aircraft was a new and almost entirely untested form of military technology. The first flight had been made only 11 years before. None of the great powers possessed more than a small number of flying machines, and the machines themselves were fragile, weak and unreliable. Military establishments saw little operational scope for aircraft beyond reconnaissance.

During the war itself, airpower made great steps forward. Aerial forces themselves expanded more than tenfold, while individual aircraft became both reliable enough to be used on an intensive and routine basis, and powerful enough to carry both air-to-air and air-to-ground weaponry. Military and naval establishments came to look on the aircraft as a valuable part of their arsenals, while generals and admirals alike began to depend on aerial support in all major operations. In many senses, it was World War I which witnessed the dawn of the air age.

Nonetheless, the aerial forces of 1914–18 never escaped from a subordinate role. Britain alone of the major combatant nations formed a separate and completely independent air force; elsewhere aerial forces remained under the control of navies and armies. While some attempts were made at strategic bombing operations, the overwhelming proportion of every country's air effort was devoted to the support of traditional forms of military and naval activity. This in turn was a reflection of the limits on the early aircraft's destructive capabilities. By any standards, the aircraft of were lightly armed – they could not do enough damage to major military or naval targets to be capable of affecting the course of battle or campaign in a major way.

The development of the aircraft as an ancillary weapon was most closely associated with the war on land. The static nature of trench warfare presented air services with a wide variety of challenges, ranging from long-range artillery observation, battlefield reconnaissance and infantry liaison to close ground attack and the bombing of communications and supply targets behind the lines. As these duties grew in importance so did efforts either to protect or to interfere with them through the use of fighter aircraft.

In the second half of the war in particular, the aerial campaign above the trenches rose sharply in intensity. Each air service attempted to carry out a growing daily program of army cooperation and tactical ground-attack duties, while rival fighter forces engaged in progressivly more costly attempts to suppress each other and disrupt reconnaissance and bombing missions.

By the end of the war over 50,000 airmen had been killed and the rival air forces together were deploying frontline strengths totaling over 10,000 machines. The industries behind them had had a proportional process of growth and were using up a substantial fraction of manufacturing and manpower resources. The aircraft itself, however, was still a weapon of limited potency with little capability to exercise a decisive influence on military operations. It had yet to threaten the place of other weapons in defense policy.

► The war saw a rapid development in the range, operating altitude and armament of both fighter and reconnaissance aircraft. The extent to which any one characteristic was developed was a function of the type of work for which the aircraft was intended, and higher altitude, for example, was only achieved at the cost of smaller fuel capacity and shorter range.

▼ British Sopwith Triplanes on Bailleul aerodrome, France, in 1917. Most early aircraft were biplanes, but both the monoplane with its lower wing drag and the triplane with its greater lift and maneuverability found favor. Designers searched for the best combination of power and airframe by practical experimentation rather than systematic enquiry into the science of aerodynamics.

◄▲ Eddie Rickenbacker (left) and Manfred von Richthofen (above), the leading air aces of the United States and Germany. Such pilots who accounted for a disproportionate number of enemy aircraft quickly became heroes, but for many, including von Richthofen, the cost of fame was prolonged exposure to combat and death in action.

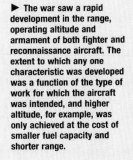

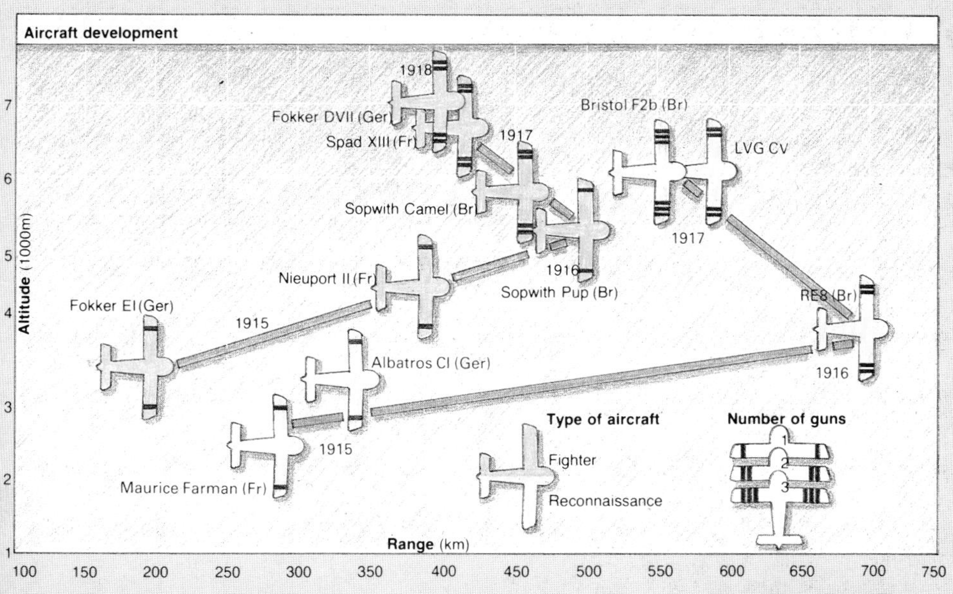

► Aerial photography was crucial to the conduct of military operations on the ground. The mapping and analysis of evidence brought back on film provided the best source of information on enemy emplacements.

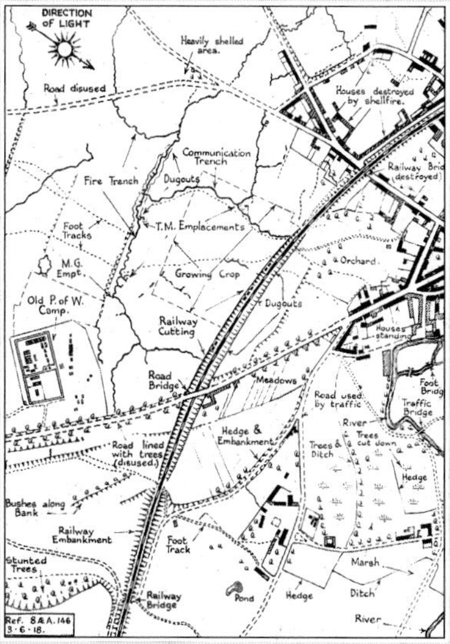

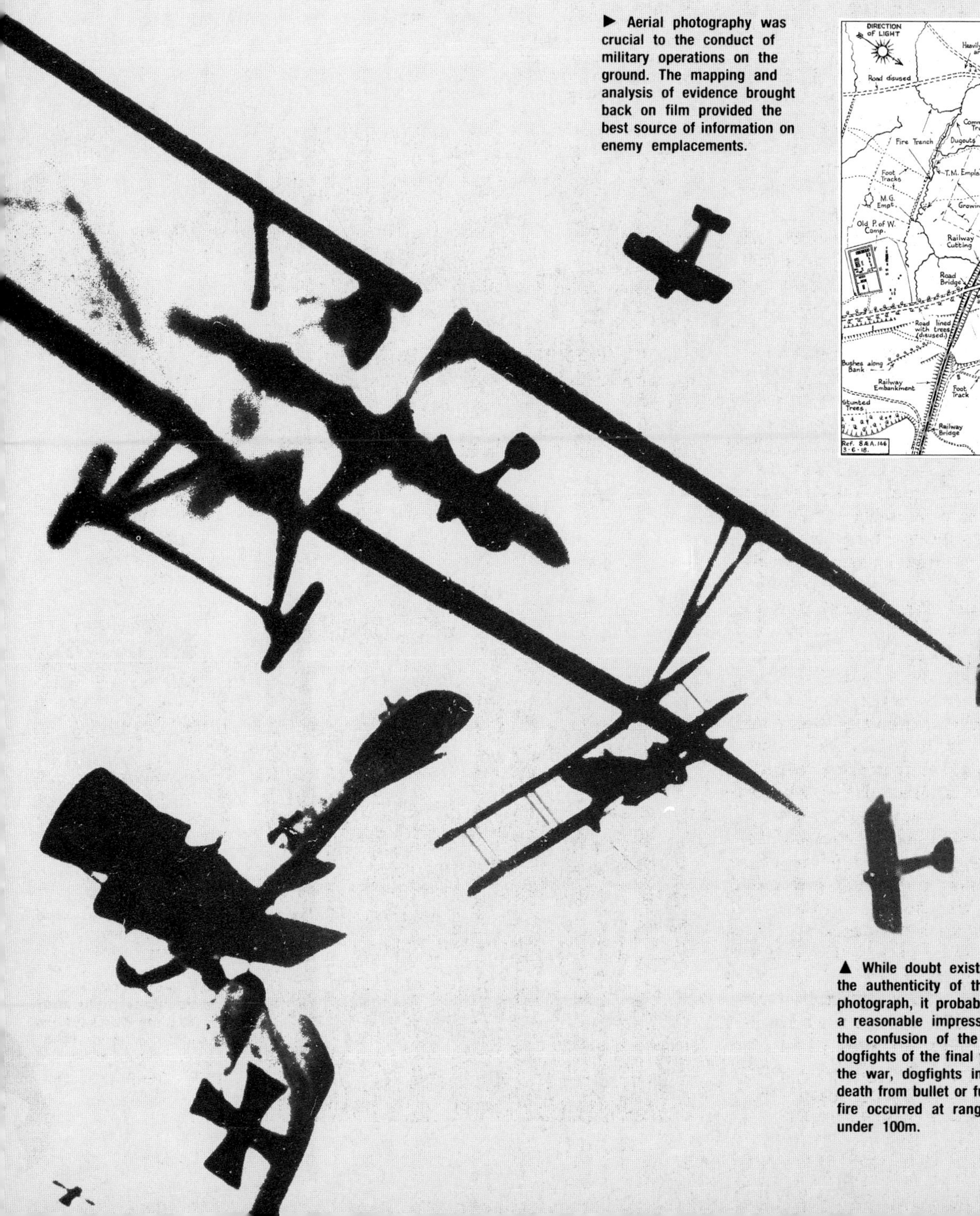

▲ While doubt exists as to the authenticity of this photograph, it probably gives a reasonable impression of the confusion of the large dogfights of the final years of the war, dogfights in which death from bullet or fuel-tank fire occurred at ranges well under 100m.

PART 3

THE SOLDIERS' WAR

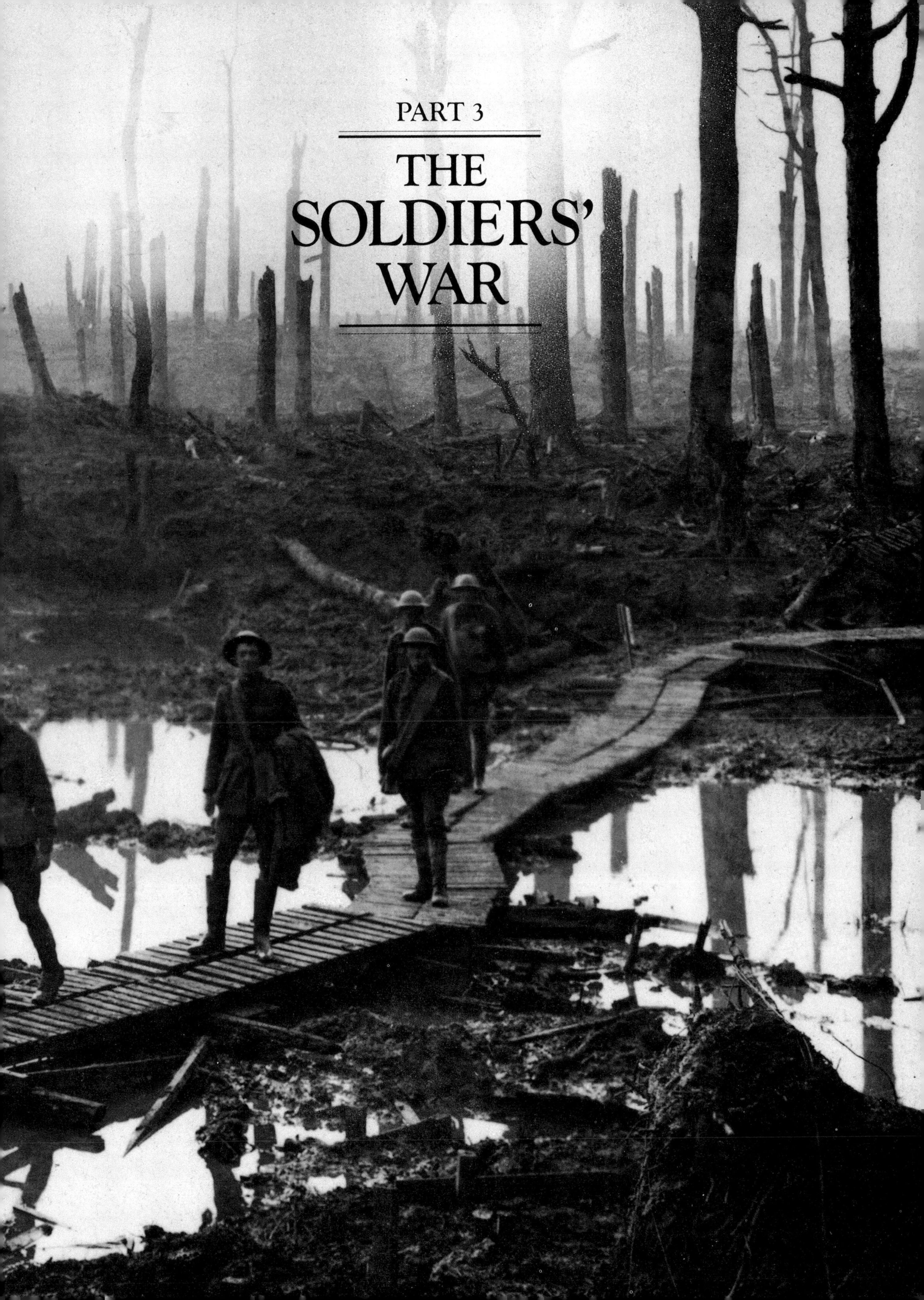

GLOSSARY

Active unit
Regular army unit maintained in a state of constant readiness for war.

Army corps
Military formation of two or more divisions and supporting units.

Artillery barrage
A coordinated program of artillery fire to devastate an area of ground.

Assault detatchment
(German: *Sturmtruppen*) An infantry unit specially armed and trained for attacking enemy defensive positions.

Auxiliary division
Military unit, usually of noncombatants, providing support services for the fighting formations.

Baptism of fire
A soldier's, or unit's, first engagement with the enemy.

Base hospital
Military hospital for the treatment of sick and wounded soldiers located well behind the front line.

Battalion
Infantry unit of three or four companies, numbering around 1,000 men.

Battery
A small artillery unit, usually of four to sixteen guns.

Billet
Accommodation for military forces while not currently in action, usually in requisitioned civilian buildings.

Box respirator
Breathing apparatus to protect soldiers and civilians against the effects of poison gas.

Brigade
Subunit of a division, comprising four to six battalions.

"Bull-ring"
Infantry training ground at British base camp at Etaples, notorious for bullying instructors and harsh discipline.

Camaraderie
Close bonds of friendship formed between soldiers as a result of their common experience and suffering.

Captain
Junior military officer, ranking below a major and above a lieutenant.

Casualty
A soldier killed or wounded by enemy action.

Casualty clearing station
Medical establishment behind the front line for the immediate treatment of wounded soldiers.

Chaplaincy
Clerical department of an army responsible for the spiritual welfare of troops.

Colonel
Military officer commanding a regiment (or sometimes a battalion).

"Combing out"
The drawing out of men from military service whose civilian skills are needed in the war economy. Also can be used to mean the withdrawal of men from support services for service in the front line.

Communications trench
Trench connecting the front line of trenches with the support line.

Company
Subunit of a battalion, numbering 150-250 men.

Conscript
Serviceman compelled by law to serve in the military forces.

Corporal
Junior noncommissioned officer in command of a section.

Court martial
Military tribunal established to try and sentence soldiers accused of breaches of martial (military) law.

Desertion
Deliberate absconding from a military unit or post.

Division
The smallest military unit comprising all arms and organized for independent action.

Drafts
Men brought up to replace casualties in a fighting unit.

Dugout
Underground shelter providing protection and living quarters for the troops while in the trenches.

Enlistment
Engagement to serve in the armed forces as a private soldier.

Entrenching company
Military unit responsible for digging and furnishing defensive lines of trenches.

Esprit de corps
(Fr.) Consciousness of, and identification with, the history and traditions of a military unit.

Field artillery
Light mobile artillery for the immediate support of the fighting troops.

Flamethrower
Device for projecting a jet of flaming liquid, to a range of about 34m (120ft).

Fraternization
Unauthorized friendly contact between troops of hostile armies, for example on Christmas Day 1914.

Front line
The first system of defensive trenches, immediately facing those of the enemy.

General staff
The department of the army responsible for the planning and preparation of operations.

Kit
A soldier's uniform, weapons, and military equipment.

Leave
Permitted temporary absence from the armed forces for home visits or recreation.

Lieutenant
Junior commissioned officer, normally in command of a platoon.

Logistics
The support services of an army providing the men and materiel necessary for its effective operation.

Loss of morale
Loss of the will to fight and belief in ultimate victory.

Major
Commissioned officer in command of a battalion.

Major-general
General officer in command of a brigade or division.

Manpower
The pool of able-bodied men available for military or associated duties.

Morale
The mental condition of the troops, which determines their will and ability to fight.

Mutiny
The refusal of disaffected soldiers to obey the orders of their officers.

No-man's-land
The unoccupied area of devastated ground between opposing trench lines.

Noncommissioned officer
Junior officer in a section or squad, exercising his authority through merit rather than the sovereign's commission.

Noria or shuttle system
French system of regular reliefs for troops in the front-line trenches.

Noncombatant
A civilian, or soldier, whose duties do not include fighting.

Officer
Military commander holding his authority by commission of the sovereign.

Officers' mess
Room where officers eat and take recreation separately from enlisted men.

Pals' battalions
Battalion whose members are recruited from the same community or workplace.

Pioneer company
Labor unit responsible for military works behind the lines and also trench-digging.

Plane defense
German defensive system of lightly defending the front line and retaking lost ground with strong counterattacks.

Platoon
Infantry unit commanded by a lieutenant and subdivided into sections.

Poilu
(Fr.) A French infantryman. The term, meaning "hairy", derives from his customary thick whiskers.

Rations
A soldier's daily allowance of food and drink.

Regiment
An infantry unit of three or four battalions, present in all but British divisions.

Regular army
The peacetime standing army of a nation.

Reliefs
Fresh troops to take over a portion of the defensive line from tired troops.

Rout
Unordered and undisciplined retreat in the face of an attack.

Second line
The system of trenches behind, and supporting, the front line.

Shrapnel
Shell fragments, particularly from shells designed to burst in the air to kill men.

Signal corps
Troops responsible for telephone communications on the battlefield.

Sniper
Rifle-armed sharpshooter who picks off individual enemy soldiers from a concealed position.

Squadron
Unit of cavalry numbering around 150 men.

"Square-bashing"
Rigorous military drill on the parade ground.

"Stand-to"
Order to take up firing positions.

Subaltern
Junior officer of the rank of lieutenant.

Support trench
Front-line trench behind the front trench and linked to it by the communication trench.

Tactics
Small-scale controlled battlefield maneuvers to achieve an objective.

Tank
Mechanized, heavily armed and armored, tracked fighting vehicle.

Territorial army
Nonregular military forces, originally responsible for home defense.

Trench newspaper
Newspaper produced by and for soldiers in the trenches.

Trench system
Defensive network of interconnected earthworks.

Tunneling company
Unit responsible for underground mining beneath the enemy defensive system.

Volunteer
One who enters military service when not compelled to do so by law.

War of movement
Warfare in open country in which military operations are not restricted by extensive defensive obstacles.

Datafile

The most important questions about the impact of the war on ordinary soldiers are how many served and what was their fate?

Surprisingly the answers to these questions have been wildly inaccurate and, on occasion, deliberately misleading. Manpower statistics were closely guarded secrets, and casualty figures were used as part of the propaganda war. To judge by some of the more extravagant claims of the press on both sides in 1914 (as well as later on in the war), the entire enemy army had been killed several times over. After the war military statistics were "adjusted" periodically to show that the other side suffered more, as if suffering can be reduced to a simple comparison of almost unimaginable totals of deaths. Consequently, we have no clear guide to the demography of the war. All we can do is provide a rough outline of the dimensions of the conflict.

If numbers alone defined power, then Russia – with a population of over 150 million, equal to that of France, Germany and the United Kingdom combined – was preeminent in Europe. But in terms of manpower trained for military service, Germany was the most powerful nation in Europe. France, Austria-Hungary and Russia had about 4 million men who had been in uniform, compared to 5 million in Germany. Again absolute numbers gave little indication of the true military strength of the Kaiser's army, demonstrated both in the sweep through Belgium and France and in the stunning victory at Tannenberg in 1914.

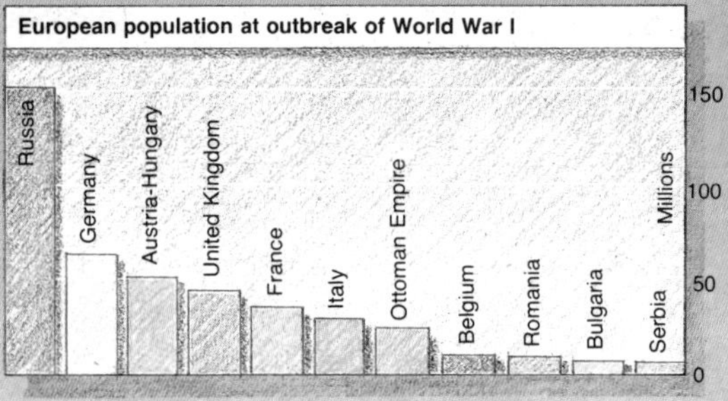

◄ The military implications of population growth in the 19th century were worrying to the French. From being the most populous nation in western and central Europe in the 18th century, France had fallen behind Germany, Austria-Hungary and Britain by 1914. Census information of declining fertility fed perceptions of waning political power.

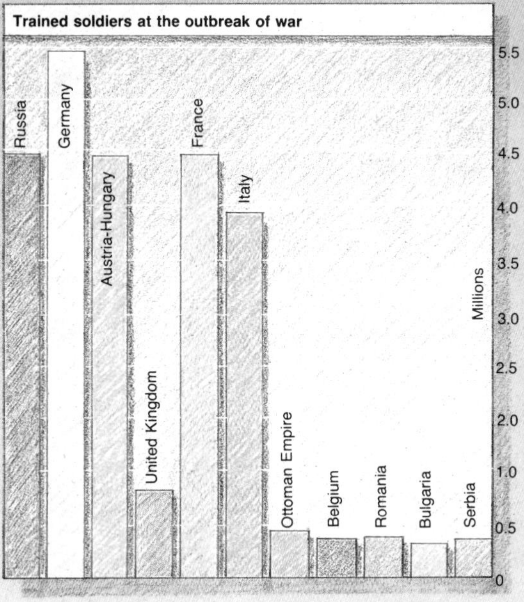

◄ Conscription provided the major powers with unprecedented large reserves of trained manpower in 1914. However, totals of men who had undergone military training were no sure guide to a country's military might. Germany's superiority as a military power was due to quality, not quantity. Its enemies lacked both Germany's sophisticated professional officer corps and the infrastructure of industrial supply and railway lines which enabled it to fight a two-front war. Manpower totals also understated British power. To note only the small size of Britain's volunteer army – equal to the forces of Romania and Bulgaria combined – leaves the Royal Navy out of the equation.

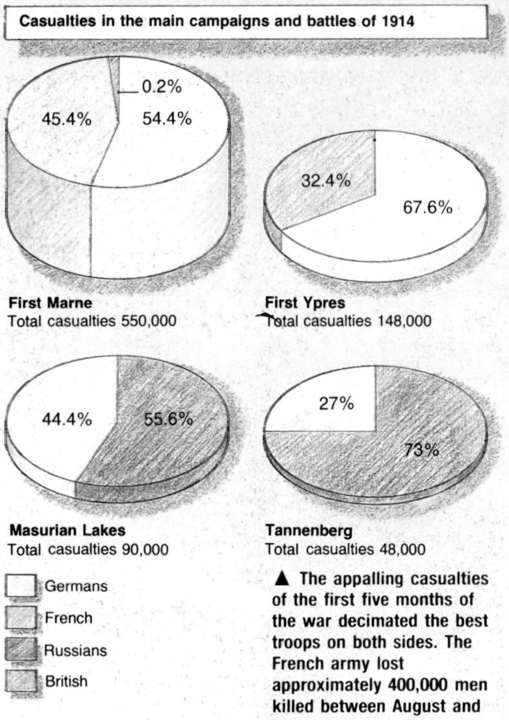

▲ **The appalling casualties of the first five months of the war decimated the best troops on both sides. The French army lost approximately 400,000 men killed between August and December 1914. German losses on the Western Front were lower, but it also lost approximately 140,000 men killled or missing in the east in the first year of the war. Russian losses were greater still.**

Chronology

June 28
Assassination of Austro-Hungarian Archduke Franz Ferdinand in Sarajevo

July 23
(to Aug. 4) War crisis in Europe

July 24
AH: Partial mobilization begins in Austria-Hungary

July 30
RUSS: General mobilization begins in Russia

July 31
FR: General mobilization begins in France

August 1
GER: General mobilization begins in Germany

August 3
German invasion of Belgium begins

August 7–16
British Expeditionary Force is landed in France

August 11
Goeben and *Breslau* enter the Black Sea

August 21
UK: Government issues orders for raising the first "New Army" of six divisions of volunteers

August 24
Main German armies enter France

August 26–30
Battle of Tannenberg: German victory in East Prussia

September 5–10
First Battle of the Marne: German advance halted

September 6–15
Battle of the Masurian Lakes: German victory in East Prussia

September 8–12
Battle of Lemberg: Russians capture Austria-Hungary's fourth-largest city

September 11
UK: Government issues orders for raising the second New Army of six divisions. Australian Expeditionary Force lands on the German Bismarck Archipelago

September 15
First trenches of the war are dug

September 17
(to Oct. 18) "Race to the Sea": front in the west is extended to the Channel coast

October 3
First units of Canadian and Newfoundland Expeditionary forces leave North America for UK

October 12
(to Nov. 11) First Battle of Ypres: inconsequential conflict between German and Allies

October 17
First units of Australian Expeditionary Force embark for France

November 1
Russia declares war on Turkey.

Battle of Coronel: German Pacific Squadron defeats British naval force off coast of Chile

November 11
(to early Dec.) Germans force Eastern Front further to the east

December 2
Austro-Hungarians capture Belgrade (capital of Serbia)

December 8
Battle of the Falkland Islands: British fleet defeats the German Pacific Squadron

December 11
Serbians recapture Belgrade

1914 THE WAR OF ILLUSIONS

The impact of prewar population patterns on military planning

In the British Empire the call to arms achieves impressive results

Why did men join up?

Different social groups had different rates of enlistment

In Britain particular groups of men went to war together

Everywhere men saw war as an adventure

Experience of battle changed their outlook

The most important consideration in military affairs in 1914 was how to get as many men as possible into uniform and into the field. This required a close scrutiny of three independent determinants of manpower: first, the size and age-structure of the male population; secondly, the propensity of men to join up, either as conscripts, as in most countries, or as volunteers, as in the cases of Australia and New Zealand throughout the war, in Canada until 1917 and in the British case from 1914 to 1916; thirdly, the physical fitness of recruits. Later a fourth factor would weigh heavily in discussions of manpower. This was the need to balance industrial and military requirements. In 1914, though, this point was not seriously considered, because the consensus was that the war would be over by Christmas.

Prewar population growth

The murderousness of World War I was made possible by rapid population growth in the prewar period. This made available to all warring countries the largest population of adult males in their history. But growth was not uniform before the war, and there was much discussion of manpower problems among writers and churchmen, as well as military and political commentators.

French strategists – generals and journalists alike – were particularly worried about the implications of differential population growth rates. The source of their anxieties was the fact that the French population of about 40 million was substantially smaller than the German, which was about 68 million.

The censuses of 1910 for Germany and 1911 for France made dolorous reading to the French. They revealed that while there were over 13 million Germans aged 20-49, there were only about 8 million Frenchmen in the military age range. To make matters worse, the French birth rate was substantially lower than that of Germany. Low fertility was a strategic threat and led many commentators to forecast the ultimate disappearance of the French race.

The implications were also serious for military planners. Conscription long antedated the war in both countries. In 1906 Germany had called up over 1.2 million men. In the same year France could muster only 368,000 new soldiers. Having about three times as many men available as their French counterparts, the German army could afford to select the fittest and send home over half of those who came forward, on the grounds that

▼ "Who hasn't seen Paris today and yesterday", exclaimed the poet Charles Péguy, "hasn't seen anything". He was referring to the send-off given to soldiers such as these. Six weeks later Péguy was dead; his romantic view of war took a little longer to die.

they were needed as wage earners by their families, or for a number of other reasons.

The true strength of the German army was its quality in command, logistics and *esprit de corps*. But it still had to face the prospect of a war on two fronts, which meant having to cope with Russian armies drawn from a population of 153 million, of whom 40 million were of draftable age. Even with the aid of the Austro-Hungarian armies, the Central Powers could not match the Russian potential. This is in part what lay behind the Schlieffen Plan. It aimed to defeat Germany's less populous (though militarily stronger) western enemy before its less dangerous (though more populous) eastern enemy had fully mobilized its massive armed forces and entered the war.

Germany's initial advantage compared with the French in command, materiel and in manpower was insufficient to bring it victory in 1914. Without a decisive and early outcome, all the combatant countries still had the manpower to fight a major war in 1914, and to continue to fight it for years.

Who went and why?

Of course this was true only if all the men required or eligible to join up actually did so. To the great surprise of some military men, they did. The French army had reckoned on over 10 percent not showing up; the actual figure was closer to 1 percent. In the case of a country facing invasion, this may not be surprising. But in Britain the

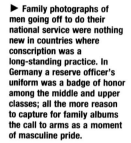

► Family photographs of men going off to do their national service were nothing new in countries where conscription was a long-standing practice. In Germany a reserve officer's uniform was a badge of honor among the middle and upper classes; all the more reason to capture for family albums the call to arms as a moment of masculine pride.

To my mind, the most typical and most moving case of such honest and at once insane ecstasy, was that of Ernst Lissauer... When the war broke out, his first act was to hurry to the barracks to enlist. I can well imagine the laughter of the sergeants and corporals when this fat body came puffing up the stairs. He was promptly rejected. Lissauer was in despair but, like the others, he at least wished to serve Germany with his muse. Everything that the newspapers and the German army communiqués published was gospel truth to him. His country had been attacked, and the worst criminal – as cast by Wilhelmstrasse – was that perfidious Sir Edward Grey, the British Foreign Minister. This feeling, that England was the arch-enemy of Germany and responsible for the war, found expression in his "Hymn of Hate"...

STEFAN ZWEIG

◀ In Russia, mobilization was greeted with the same outward display of national and imperial pride as in the West. These Russian troops are on their way to the central railway station in Petrograd (now Leningrad) with a marching band at their head. Ahead of them was a war far worse than anyone had imagined.

Recruitment in Australia

On 30 July 1914 the prime minister of Australia, Joseph Cook, said, "Remember that when the Empire is at war so is Australia at war". The next day he pledged that if the United Kingdom went to war, "Australians will stand beside our own to help and defend her to our last man and our last shilling".

Recruiting immediately began for an Australian Force. Enlisting stations were set up. The call to arms met a powerful response. Men left jobs, walked off farms, and risked their lives to tramp or ride hundreds of kilometers through outback drought to reach the enlistment centers in the cities. Many would-be recruits were rejected as unfit. Those accepted were exceptionally fit, which encouraged them to believe they were superior to recruits from other countries. Their motives for joining up were various. Younger men said they enlisted for adventure, older men out of duty. Some were attracted by the pay of 6 shillings a day. Many thought they had to prove themselves as men; others feared for the Empire. But all were united by a passion to halt barbarism and punish the Germans for a war that was happening far away. They were patriots of the empire.

The strong enlistment rates lasted until April 1915. Thereafter they only surged in times of crisis or when Australian soldiers were heavily committed in battle. When they fell the Federal government had to appeal for recruits. They resorted to films, advertisements and streetcorner orators.

By late 1915 the enlistment rate had fallen so low that the defense department could not make up numbers to replace casualties. In response the Federal government adopted two procedures. In September 1915 it took a census to identify by name men eligible and fit enough for military service. Men unwilling to serve had to explain why. At the end of 1915 Australia was divided into 36 recruiting areas and each area was given a quota-target for recruits. These measures prompted an increase in voluntary enlistment, but the rates fell below target in 1916, partly because of the high casualty rates that were sustained. Now the government concluded that voluntary enlistment had failed and had to be replaced by conscription.

Australia's recently appointed new prime minister, W.M. Hughes, already supported conscription for service in Australia. In mid-1916 (after a trip to the UK) he agreed to support conscription for service overseas. This was proposed in a public referendum in 1916 and rejected by electors. Hughes was expelled from the Labour Party. The government then again tried the most modern means of mass persuasion, and recruitment levels rallied again, but briefly. In late 1917 a second and milder proposal for conscription was put to electors, but fared worse than the first.

The referendum campaigns proved divisive and left a bitter legacy. Trade unionists and the country's large Irish Catholic population were accused of resisting conscription and thereby favoring the enemy and deserting the men at the Front.

But despite the hostility to conscription and the government's constant complaints about the shortages of soldiers, almost half of Australia's eligible men between the ages of 18 and 45 volunteered to serve in the war. Four-fifths of these fought overseas, of whom one-fifth died and half were wounded or maimed.

▲ An Australian recruiting poster by Norman Lindsay: a wounded bugler calls for help on the Western Front. The appeal to the British Dominions struck a powerful chord in Australia, where about 330,000 men voluntarily enlisted. Of these, about 59,000 were killed and 120,000 wounded.

response to the call to arms was equally impressive. In fact it was so great that many new British recruits had to train with umbrellas instead of guns, which were in short supply in the first months of the war.

If there was a limit on military manpower, it was not because of popular attitudes. Throughout Europe and in colonies and dependencies in every continent, ordinary people accepted military service simply as something they had to do – for a time. On the European continent they went because military service was required by law and because they believed their country was in the right. In the British Empire volunteers streamed into recruiting centers – from Canada to Australia – for the usual mix of reasons: the glamor of a uniform, the prospect of steady pay, escape from monotony, even, on occasion, altruism. In Britain, as much as in Germany, they joined up out of loyalty to their community, nation and Empire, probably in descending order of importance. The British way of expressing these commitments took the form of "protecting little Belgium", or "showing the Kaiser where to get off". Propaganda on both sides mobilized similarly oversimplified justifications for war.

But the key to mobilization in 1914 lies in one simple word: duty. Duty tempered, that is, by a sense of adventure. Millions of men were ready to join the ranks for an expedition into a totally imaginary war: one that armies would wage until a decisive breach in the enemy's lines was forced, leading to victory. If you asked how long this would take, the likely reply was a few months at most. The men of 1914 therefore thought of military service as a brief interlude in their lives. This was as true among the various national groups in the Austro-Hungarian Empire as among nationalists in Ireland.

In the same spirit, the white dominions of Australia and Canada answered the call to arms, as did India, Algeria and Senegal. Here again propaganda played a part, but the volunteers of 1914 must not be thought of as automata who simply responded to the mechanical appeals of their leaders. Some were fooled by recruiting slogans, but others joined up out of a real belief in the cause, or out of solidarity with their friends and acquaintances who had already joined up.

The sole problem in raising the volunteer armies from August 1914 onward was therefore neither men nor motivation. It was rather how to discover who could stand up to military life and who was physically unfit. To induct unfit men would cause trouble, since they were bound to break down either in training or at the Front. How many were likely to do so, no one knew, for there was no agreement as to the medical criteria for military fitness. Besides, few medical officers had the time to conduct rigorous medical examinations on the deluge of men who presented themselves at recruiting offices in 1914. The rule at the outset of war was: when in doubt, let him in. Of course many infirmities precluded front-line service – presenting the irony that ill health saved the lives of millions of men in Europe during the war. This was true throughout the conflict. Of the 2.4 million British men who were medically examined in 1917–18, over one million or 40 percent of those tested, were either totally unfit for army service, or capable of noncombtant duty only. They were the lucky ones.

Recruitment patterns among volunteers

In the British case, after the "August madness", the pattern of recruitment for the army revealed some important social variations. The highest rates of enlistment were among middle-class men employed in finance, commerce, the professions and the entertainment trades. About 40 percent of the men in these sectors volunteered between 1914 and 1916, compared to about 28 percent of men in industry.

In August 1914 a broad consensus stood behind the British declaration of war. A few months later strong support still existed, but those prepared to act rather than simply cheer were more likely to come from the better-off sections of the community. Why was it that men in middle-class or white-collar employment tended to join up in greater numbers earlier in the war than their working-class compatriots? The reasons were both cultural and material. Some were from families with military traditions; others had received the rudiments of military training at school or college; virtually all shared the culture of empire and national assertiveness, as well as the prevailing illusions, common to all classes, as to what war was all about.

Willingness to enlist was not the sole property of any one class in 1914 in Britain. But those among the less prosperous who were ready to show the Kaiser a thing or two still had to think twice before joining up. Who would look after their families? Would their jobs be there when they returned? These were very real questions in 1914 and caused more than a few working-class patriots to hesitate. In textile areas, enlistment was relatively low. This was probably related to the fact that the livelihood of families in these towns depended on both men's and women's work, which were threatened initially by the

▲▶ In the UK Lord Kitchener's index finger, immortalized in a famous war poster (shown here in its original version), pointed the way to the recruiting office; by December 1914, one million British and Irish men had joined up.

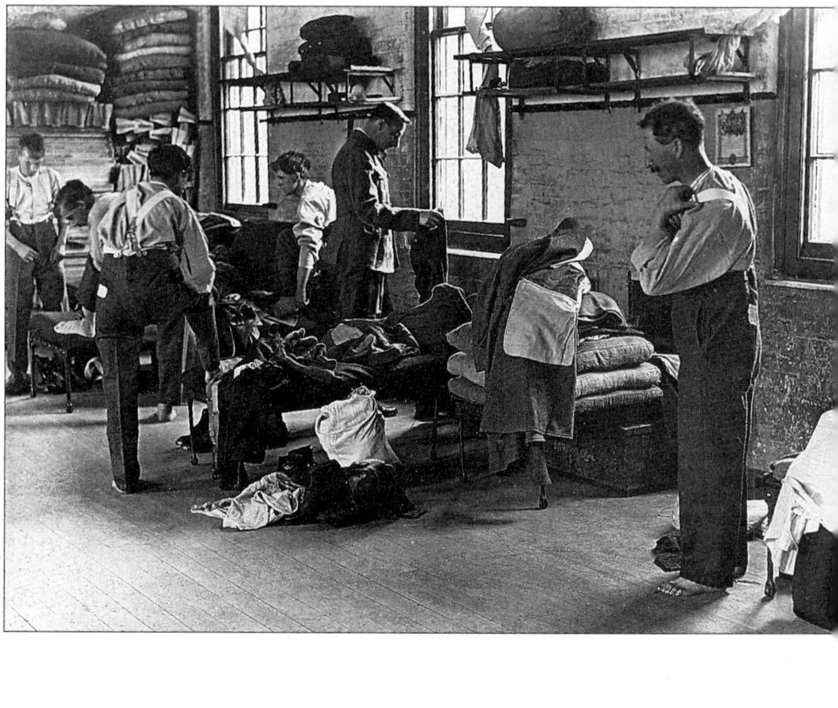

► No one knew how to measure medical fitness for military service during the 1914–18 war. In the British army, which did not have the experience of dealing with millions of recruits, a haphazard system was initially adopted. Medical examinations were cursory and inevitably incomplete. Later on, a more systematic approach was introduced, but medics still passed thousands of men with ailments which made them unfit for active service.

◄ The new uniform and kit contributed to the holiday spirit of the first phase of army service.

outbreak of war. Given the dislocation of international trade after August 1914, many people in the cotton and woolen industries were laid off. In some sectors of employment the direct substitution of wives for their husbands kept family incomes intact. But in the temporarily depressed textile trades this was out of the question. Men in these areas had every reason to ask, therefore, how their families would manage if they left for the army.

Some employers were prepared to help. Well before the British government passed legislation to provide separation allowances for soldiers' and sailors' dependents, individual entrepreneurs did the same on their own. Some were also prepared to band together with their trading associates to promise the men who went to war that their jobs would be waiting for them on their return. Employers even helped to provision new recruits in 1914, before the war office could house, clothe and feed them.

Special groups

This is the origin of that quintessential British institution of World War I, the "Pals' battalions". These were composed of men who joined up together and who shared an association at work or in their communities. Some were made up of middle-class men, like the Public School Battalions of the Middlesex Regiment and of the Royal Fusiliers, or the "Grimsby Chums", formed by some old boys at Wintringham Secondary School in the Lincolnshire port of Grimsby. Others were made up of working-class men who worked together, played football together, drank together and eventually fought together.

Another reason why working-class enlistment rates were lower than the national average was that some were told not to go. This was especially so in the case of railwaymen, but the need to keep others back to provide munitions was apparent from very early on. By 1916 these distinctions would be regularized by law; in 1914 they were established only informally, and in many cases were ignored. Witness the case of coal miners, among the most class-conscious, and also patriotic, of all British workers. By mid-1915, perhaps one-quarter of the workforce had enlisted. Later on miners had to be "combed out" of the army, so that coal production could be maintained.

The social structure of British enlistment

Given the different pressures on different parts of the community, it is not surprising that there was a social structure of voluntary enlistment in Britain between 1914 and 1916. The higher up a man was in the social scale, the more likely it was that he would join up early and serve throughout the conflict. This was bound to affect the social composition of casualty rates in British forces during the war – a point that will be discussed later. At this juncture what matters is that, whatever the propagandists said, the British army was not the nation in arms.

Roughly 6 million British men served during the war. Given that working-class enlistment rates early in the war were 10 percent below average for other classes, differential enlistment

The St Helens Pals

In 1914 the UK was faced with the need to expand its small standing army. Among those who took the initiative in recruiting were the leaders of local communities. Their efforts led to the formation of military units drawn exclusively from a particular place: so-called "Pals' battalions." A number of "Pals' battalions" were composed mainly of middle-class men, like the Public Schools Battalions of the Middlesex Regiment and the Royal Fusiliers. Many more were exclusively working class. The formation of these units provided a perfect occasion for the expression of civic culture. Municipalities vied with each other in their support of these units.

Prominent among landowners who led recruiting drives was the 17th Earl of Derby, who owned large parts of the English county of Lancashire. On 3 September 1914 he held a meeting in the Lancashire glass-making town of St Helens. Flanked by local religious and political leaders, Derby appealed for local men to volunteer and form a local battalion. At that meeting about 200 men volunteered. Another 800 men from St Helens and neighboring towns were then recruited. According to one of the last survivors of the battalion, Richard Heskith, the battalion consisted of coal miners, clerks, and workers from the St Helens glass factories, and a vast array of other young men from the town and its area. Lacking uniforms and weapons, they trained with broom handles instead of rifles, until the army was ready to equip them.

In November 1915 the St Helens Battalion of 1,000 men sailed for France and the Western Front. Though trained as infantry, they were also assigned to digging trenches. In three years they served in most of the major British campaigns. On 1 July 1916 on the Somme they were in the third wave of infantry that attacked the German lines. Twenty percent of the original members were killed or wounded in this battle. In 1917, 15 percent were killed or wounded in the Ypres salient and 10 percent in the Third Battle of Ypres. In the German offensive of spring 1918 the battalion met the full force of the German onslaught. The result was that effectively 50 percent of the (replenished) force became casualties.

The remnants of the battalion returned to St Helens at the end of 1918. They had gained 31 honors, including a Victoria Cross (the highest award for gallantry). At home they attempted to pick up the threads of their lives and put their war service into some kind of perspective. In the 1918 general election prime minister David Lloyd George spoke of making "a fit country for heroes to live in." In the 1920s and 1930s St Helens' registered unemployment rate was 25 percent. The town had both above-average infant mortality and below-average housing. The political rhetoric faded and the reality of deprivation returned.

▲ Lord Derby's initial success in raising men from the Northwest of England in 1914 gave him the job of Director General of Recruitment a year later. But by then the flood of volunteers had shrunk to a trickle. Conscription became law in January 1916.

▼ The men of St Helens Pals' Battalion in February 1915, on their way to war.

lowered the possible number of soldiers Britain could place in the field early on by 600,000. Another 10 percent were declared permanently unfit for service, which does not include those who should never have been in uniform in the first place. Another 600,000 men were spared due to temporary unfitness. Medical officers were unanimous that the bulk of them were working-men from the major towns and cities.

From 1916 restrictions were placed on the recruitment of workers in essential industries, thus further distorting the social composition of the army. But even if we discount this matter, which did not become a serious factor until later in the war, we are still able to conclude that British forces would have constituted a cross section of British society only had they contained over one million more working-class men.

However, because the majority of the male population were manual laborers, Britain's army in World War I was still preponderantly working class. Initially the officer corps was decidedly middle class, being staffed either from the old professional army, the territorial army, or the finishing schools of polite society – the public schools and the universities of Oxford and Cambridge. Later on, casualties forced a partial and grudging broadening of the social base of the officer corps. This was bound to affect the social composition of casualties. Initially elites suffered a disproportionate share of war losses, since officer casualty rates were significantly higher than casualty rates among the men in the ranks. Later in the war this differential casualty rate was reduced, but still persisted.

Other less urbanized combatant countries had armies largely composed of peasants and farm laborers. This group also suffered the most in numerical terms. But despite this difference between Britain and continental countries, some similarities can be seen. For instance, there had to be a "comb out" of French iron workers from Le Creusot: they were needed more on the home front. And as in Britain, there was a progressive infiltration of lower-middle-class and working-class men into the officer corps, as the bloodshed mounted. Again casualty rates among officers, also drawn from more privileged groups, were higher than among those they led. Within a few weeks of the outbreak of war, the entire 1914 graduating class of the French military academy at St-Cyr was dead. The slaughter of the professional armies and of the class from which they were recruited was a unifying feature of the war experience of all major combatant countries in World War I.

War as adventure: the end of a myth

It did not take long for soldiers to recognize the emptiness of the notions they had formed as to what the war would be like. Shrapnel and machine-gun fire put paid to the cavalry charges of August, and turned the varied and colorful European uniforms of 1914 to various shades of khaki and gray. Above all, the men were changed. All descriptions of the early part of the war speak of the great divide represented by the first day of action, the first exposure to the smell, the sound, and the chaos of battle. Consider this account of a French corporal, who saw service at Longwy near the Belgian-French border.

▲ **These German soldiers are on board "The Paris Express", direct from Leipzig to the French capital. Bedecked with flowers and graffiti proclaiming that the Germans were itching for a fight, these railroad cars poured millions of men into the 1914 offensives. By the end of the year, over 400,000 German soldiers had been killed.**

"August 22, 1914. A salvo bursts over the road. A horseman quits his stirrups, rolls off his mount, lies still. Quickly, going back from the effect to the cause, we become conscious of impending danger. This first victim, this hussar done away with in a second, disconcerts us. We knew there were some killed in every battle, and yet we were all in such a joyous state of unconcern that we were dumbfounded in the presence of this sudden misfortune. I see the smile congeal on the lips of my comrades. The bursts approach a hundred yards nearer. Now we look at these wicked little clouds less with curiosity than with apprehension....Suddenly shrill hisses which end in violent chuckles send us face against the ground, terrified. The salvo has just burst above us. Shot and splinters sail through the air, a big metal case comes whizzing and strikes the ground near my knee; instinctively, as if to ward off a blow, I had put up my arm to protect my face....More explosions. The balls rain, ricochet on the mess bowls, a canteen is pierced, squirts out its wine; a fuse hums for a long time in the air. With my head under my pack, I cast a glance at my neighbours; breathless, shaken by nervous tremblings, their mouths are contracted in a hideous grin, their teeth are chattering: their faces convulsed with terror recall the grotesque gargoyles of Notre-Dame: prostrate in this bizarre position, with arms crossed on their chests and heads down, they look like condemned men offering their necks to the executioner..."

As soon as the shelling ceased, this man's unit ran helter-skelter for a farmhouse 50 meters away, got over its wall any way they could, and then caught their breath and their nerve, after this, their baptism of fire.

INFANTRY WEAPONRY AND TACTICS

The stalemate on the Western Front grew out of the strength and tenacity of soldiers in the art of defense. The two essential weapons for this purpose were the shovel and the machine gun. The first dug trenches which protected troops from the effects of snipers or shrapnel, which showered jagged metal particles at ground level. The second made direct assault of an entrenched position an invitation to suicide.

All units equipped infantrymen with a small-bore (6.5–8.0mm) high-velocity bolt-action repeating rifle, which was capable of 15 shots a minute and had an effective range of 450m (500yd). But these were no match for the medium machine gun, which equaled the firepower of 60 riflemen. In 1915 the British army formed the Machine Gun Corps to coordinate its defensive deployment along whole sectors of the front. By 1918 the ration strength of the Machine Gun Corps was 120,000 men. Initially machine guns were heavy and unwieldy. Over time lighter weapons were introduced. The British had the 12kg (27lb) 47-shot Lewis gun; the Germans, the 18kg (40lb) 08/15 Maxim. By 1918 German and Italian troops were equipped with the first large-magazine capacity, pistol-caliber automatic weapons. These were the first sub-machine guns, variants of which were used by German stormtroopers in the 1918 Spring offensive.

Hand grenades sometimes provided an answer to machine-gun fire. German troops used both hand- and rifle-grenades. Some British soldiers improvised jam-tins packed with demolition explosive, but more used the standard No. 5 Mills bomb, last made in 1972. More effective still were tanks. The Germans developed an antitank rifle, with armor-piercing cartridges, but these arrived too late to affect the outcome of the war.

In 1915 gas warfare began in the Ypres salient on the Western Front (after first use on the Eastern Front), but even this hideous weapon was incapable of breaking the stalemate. At first the release of chlorine from cylinders induced panic among affected troops, but very rapidly soldiers learned how to live with it. This was for two reasons. First, they began to see that wind and damp seriously affected the direction and elevation of the gas cloud. Attackers could just as easily be devastated by gas as defenders. Secondly, they were supplied with moderately effective gas masks offering basic protection to troops who had only a moment's warning of a gas attack.

Most infantrymen carried bayonets, but casualty figures indicate that they had little value at the front. More effective were a vast array of fighting knives and home-made trench clubs used for raiding.

Whatever the nature of infantry weapons used on the Western Front, the men who carried them were trapped in a war of futility and monumental suffering, the sources of which lie not in guns but in the minds of the men who sent them there.

► This scene of the death of French troops attacking at Verdun was repeated countless times on the Western Front throughout the war. Soldiers moving forward over clear ground presented easy targets to machine-gunners. Even if the attacking force reached the enemy lines, they were frequently incapable of holding them or resisting counterattacks. This was true whatever the nature of the arms infantrymen carried. Gas weapons, smokescreens, shrapnel and high explosives made the battlefield, or at least the objective, virtually invisible, and separated the soldiers from their commanders and supporting lines. The main problem was not weaponry but outmoded tactics, which treated battle as if it were predictable. The only certainties of battle in the 1914–18 war were casualties and confusion.

▼► These photographs show four of the basic tools of the infantryman's war (top left to right). The first shows a German bombing post on the Western Front, with a soldier holding a primed hand grenade. The second is of a German light machine gun crew in 1916 near Fort Vaux on the vast battlefield of Verdun. The third is of a British front-line soldier at Ovillers on the Somme, in July 1916. The fourth demonstrates bayonet practice, this time by German soldiers kitted out with protective wear seemingly more suitable to fencing than to combat.

Datafile

The stalemate of 1915 produced casualty totals of staggering proportions: 300,000 German deaths, 400,000 Russian, 300,000 French, and on and on. In Asia and on the Eastern Front, disease – the time-honored companion of war – took its toll. On the Western Front, disease was controlled, but machine-gun fire, artillery bombardment, and for the first time, gas warfare accounted for the bulk of the losses suffered on both sides.

▼ The propensity for attacking troops to suffer higher casualties than defenders, and for little or no gain, was the hallmark of fighting until virtually the end of the war. In 1915, even when "break-throughs" occurred, the defensive forces were able to stem the enemy advance.

Casualties in the main campaigns and battles of 1915

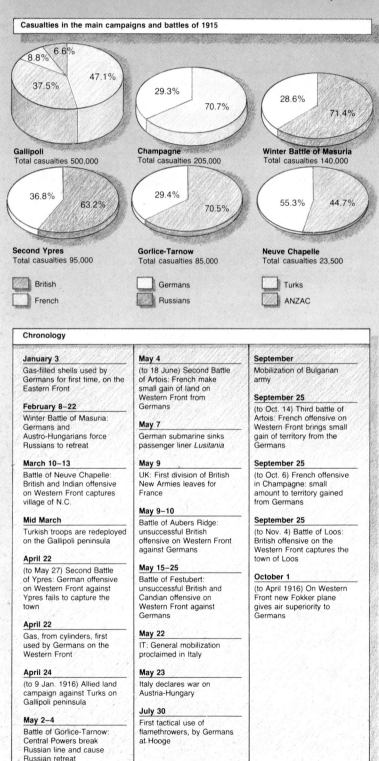

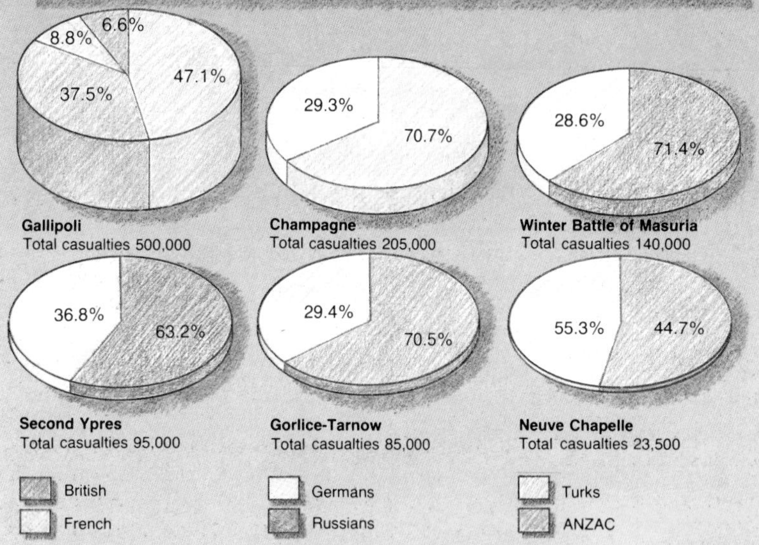

Chronology

January 3
Gas-filled shells used by Germans for first time, on the Eastern Front

February 8–22
Winter Battle of Masuria: Germans and Austro-Hungarians force Russians to retreat

March 10–13
Battle of Neuve Chapelle: British and Indian offensive on Western Front captures village of N.C.

Mid March
Turkish troops are redeployed on the Gallipoli peninsula

April 22
(to May 27) Second Battle of Ypres: German offensive on Western Front against Ypres fails to capture the town

April 22
Gas, from cylinders, first used by Germans on the Western Front

April 24
(to 9 Jan. 1916) Allied land campaign against Turks on Gallipoli peninsula

May 2–4
Battle of Gorlice-Tarnow: Central Powers break Russian line and cause Russian retreat

May 4
(to 18 June) Second Battle of Artois: French make small gain of land on Western Front from Germans

May 7
German submarine sinks passenger liner *Lusitania*

May 9
UK: First division of British New Armies leaves for France

May 9–10
Battle of Aubers Ridge: unsuccessful British offensive on Western Front against Germans

May 15–25
Battle of Festubert: unsuccessful British and Candian offensive on Western Front against Germans

May 22
IT: General mobilization proclaimed in Italy

May 23
Italy declares war on Austria-Hungary

July 30
First tactical use of flamethrowers, by Germans at Hooge

September
Mobilization of Bulgarian army

September 25
(to Oct. 14) Third battle of Artois: French offensive on Western Front brings small gain of territory from the Germans

September 25
(to Oct. 6) French offensive in Champagne: small amount to territory gained from Germans

September 25
(to Nov. 4) Battle of Loos: British offensive on the Western Front captures the town of Loos

October 1
(to April 1916) On Western Front new Fokker plane gives air superiority to Germans

The experience of ordinary soldiers in World War I was extremely varied. Indeed it makes little sense to talk about armies at all when surveying the conflict from the soldiers' point of view. Most men knew a lot about a very small sector of the front and virtually nothing about everything else. This was inevitable in a war of such an unprecedented scale.

The form and details of military organization varied substantially both between and within armies. But to appreciate the limits on the field of vision of the individual soldier, the organization and chain of command above him will be considered. The example to be used is that of the German army, but the basic point – that armies were enormously complicated and constantly shifting kaleidoscopes of forces – could be made equally well with any other combatant force.

The peace-time ration strength of the German army was 840,000 men. By December 1916 the German army had over 5.5 million men in active units. They were divided into 2,200 infantry battalions, 550 cavalry squadrons, 2,150 field artillery battalions, 1,950 foot artillery battalions, and 600 pioneer companies. Behind these units were the reserve, technical and auxiliary divisions. By the end of the war over 13 million men had served in the German army. The problem of organizing this force was staggering.

In peacetime the German army was divided into 25 corps. Each corps included two infantry divisions, with two cavalry brigades, one artillery regiment and one pioneer battalion in support. After 1914 the basic unit of tactical maneuver was the division. By February 1915 there were 51 active divisions in the field and 54 in reserve. By December 1916 a further 34 new divisions had been raised.

The size and structure of the component parts of infantry divisions varied considerably over time. Theoretically, the organization followed these lines. Each infantry division was divided into two brigades, led by major-generals. Divisions were made up of three regiments, each with approximately 80 officers, 3,200 other ranks, 200 horses and 60 vehicles. Regiments were commanded by a colonel, and were subdivided into three battalions, each commanded by a major and composed of approximately 25 officers and 1,000 men. Each battalion encompassed four companies, three infantry plus one machine gun company, led by a captain. Companies were broken up into three platoons, led by a lieutenant, and these in turn were divided into four sections led by a corporal. At the base of this gigantic pyramid was the squad – two to each section – made up of eight men and one lance-corporal.

This was the theory. In practice the situation was much more fluid. Units rarely maintained

1915 STALEMATE AND STAGNATION

The complexity of military organization

In 1915 military leaders still aimed to punch through the enemy lines

Men *en masse* turned into common soldiers

Different ways of coming to terms with army life

Trench systems and bunkers

Routine in the trenches

Housekeeping and kit

Entertainments

Trench newspapers

prescribed ration strength for any length of time. In addition, junior officers frequently took on command responsibilities for larger units. Thus during the war it was normal for a regiment to be commanded by a major, a battalion by a captain, and a company by a subaltern. In addition a noncommissioned officer – for instance, the company sergeant-major or *Feldwebel* – could be promoted to a temporary officer's rank if he had seen 12 years' service before the war. A sergeant-major could also be given the rank of "temporary officer" of a platoon. This gave him right of command in the field, but none of the privileges of permanently commissioned officers.

For the vast majority of men the war was fought and remembered at the level of the squad, the section, the platoon, or company. Superior units were simply too large to impinge directly on the soldier's day-to-day life. With long casualty lists and the constant stream of new recruits flowing into military units, it was inevitable that the soldier's field of personal vision and attachments remained close to the relatively small group of men with whom he served.

The British army probably relied less on the leadership skills of noncommissioned officers. Early in the war recruitment of officers from the ranks was infrequent in the British case, although the slaughter of 1916–17 led to a loosening of the criteria for promotion. Because the German army was a conscript force, it was natural that noncommissioned officers with previous training were given more responsibility than was the case in the all-volunteer British army of 1914–16. The result may have been a greater degree of flexibility in German units at group level, which may have operated with greater independence than could British platoons. It is possible as well that the British system, in which subalterns played a crucial role, was partly responsible for the exceptionally high casualty rates they suffered during the war. This is a speculative point, for casualty rates among German junior officers were also very high.

Supporting the front-line combat troops was a wide array of other forces. Particularly important was the artillery, in both the war of immobility of 1915 and the war of movement of 1918. The artillery of an active division in the German army was called a field artillery brigade. It was divided into two field artillery regiments, each of which was made up of two (and later in the war, three) detachments. In each detachment were three batteries. Thus each division was supported

▼ The first fully mechanized war still depended to a very substantial extent on horse power, as this photograph of an Austro-Hungarian supply column and pontoon bridge shows. For every taxi that brought supplies to the Marne, thousands of horse-drawn carriages connected railheads to every battle front.

by between 9 and 12 field batteries, each with its own array of vehicles and transport.

These supplies were in addition to those needed by the infantry regiment itself. Its transport consisted of 16 led horses, 58 two-horsed vehicles, and one four-horsed vehicle. They provided supplies from 12 small-arm ammunition wagons (one per company), 12 traveling kitchens (one per company), and three infantry medical store wagons (one per battalion). Further back stood the supply train, with each regiment drawing everything it needed from 16 baggage wagons, 12 supply wagons, three sutlers wagons and one tool wagon.

Specialist units also proliferated as trench warfare dragged on. Cyclist units and mountain units were formed. There were entrenching companies, tunneling companies, concrete construction squads, and labor companies. Men in these units were drawn from front-line companies, and returned to them when required.

By 1916 the German army developed new assault detachments or *Sturmtruppen.* Men of particular initiative were chosen for patrolling, trench raiding and other offensive operations. They were organized into assault companies of one officer and approximately 120 men, and were used first in 1916 at Verdun, and later extensively throughout the Western Front.

In addition to infantry units, front-line troops were supported by the machine-gun corps, detachments of which manned essential points in the front-line system. Attached to each infantry regiment were one or two machine-gun sections of 30–40 under an officer with three or four machine guns. By July 1916 approximately 11,000 machine guns were in use in the German army, irregularly scattered on both the Eastern and the Western Fronts.

Many books would be needed to describe the organization, function and deployment procedures of other major military units: cavalry, engineers, signal corps, communications troops, survey and map detachments, meteorological services, aircraft units and antiaircraft units, medical and veterinary units, and chaplaincies. The monumental scale of military operations made it inevitable that the different service arms knew very different wars. Furthermore, each soldier knew his own war, and could not have been expected to form an accurate or disinterested view of the whole.

Training and discipline

After the failure of the Schlieffen Plan and the inconclusive nature of the battles on the Eastern Front there was need for a drastic reappraisal of estimates of the probable duration of the war. Unfortunately it did not lead to a change in tactics, which still aimed at punching a hole in the enemy lines, to engage in the decisive war of movement required by strategical thought. This approach made no sense in the first three years of the war, and cost hundreds of thousands of lives.

Long after the men at the Front had learned the bitter truth about how static the conflict was, millions more were still being trained to fight a war of movement. All accounts of the 10-week course for converting citizens into soldiers in Britain emphasize three essential features: monotony, bullying, and the inculcation of what was known as "the aggressive spirit". Contemporaneous photographs show how new soldiers were kitted out, but not how they were treated.

The French army too had its advocates of the breakthrough by sheer bravura. How was this *élan*, this martial spirit, to be inculcated? In the British case, apparently by marching, humiliation and bayonet drill: in effect, breaking down recruits to the lowest common denominator. The putative aim was to take away the awkward individuality of civilians and replace it with the anonymity of the common soldier, ready to follow orders without delay. Training also aimed to provide a routine of behavior which would help still nerves and prevent the instinct for survival from taking over in battle.

The insufficiency of this approach to creating soldiers was demonstrated by the complete compatibility of noisy informality and military prowess in the Anzac troops (from Australia and New Zealand). No spit and polish here, and a completely different attitude to discipline. Australians were also notorious for a quite un-British approach to the question of how officers and men

► When one surveys the complexity of the German army – or that of any other major combatant power – it seems amazing that any order promulgated at the top of the chain of command actually reached the "poor bloody infantry" at the bottom, who had to carry it out. This diagram shows the bureaucratic "flow chart" of authority, and also suggests the profundity of Clausewitz's dictum that in war all things are simple and the simplest things are infinitely complicated. What is equally remarkable is that the edifice remained intact and functional, even when the war was lost. The German army never collapsed. In defeat in November 1918, it remained an army.

▲ Three veterinary officers were attached to each cavalry and field artillery regiment in the German army. Here a surgeon, with the aid of a complement of soldiers, operates on a horse.

◄ German units engaged in prewar drill. All armies suffered from a glaring gap between the war for which they had been trained and the war they had to fight.

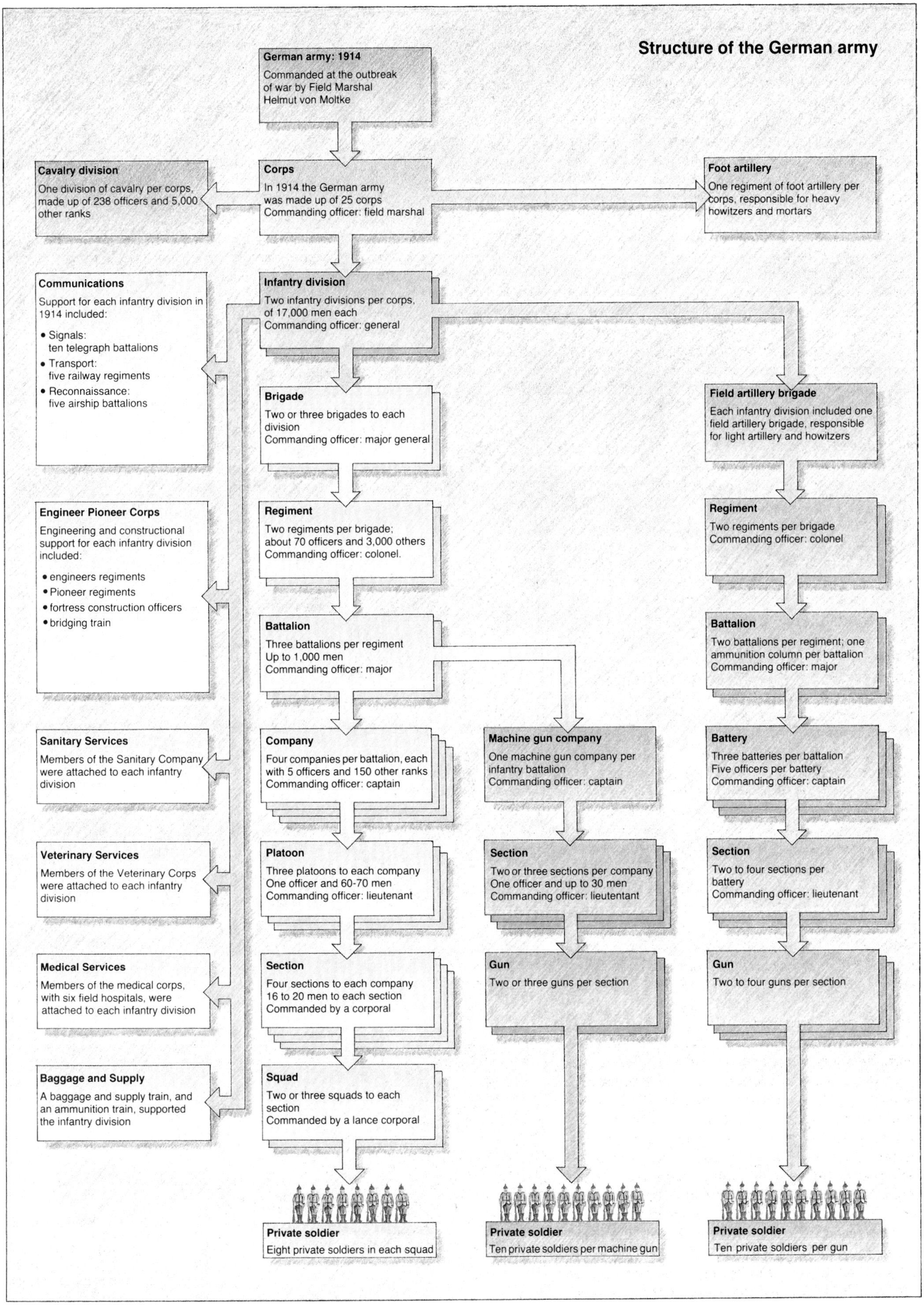
Structure of the German army
German army: 1914
Commanded at the outbreak of war by Field Marshal Helmut von Moltke
Corps
In 1914 the German army was made up of 25 corps
Commanding officer: field marshal
Cavalry division
One division of cavalry per corps, made up of 238 officers and 5,000 other ranks
Foot artillery
One regiment of foot artillery per corps, responsible for heavy howitzers and mortars
Infantry division
Two infantry divisions per corps, of 17,000 men each
Commanding officer: general
Communications
Support for each infantry division in 1914 included:
• Signals: ten telegraph battalions
• Transport: five railway regiments
• Reconnaissance: five airship battalions
Brigade
Two or three brigades to each division
Commanding officer: major general
Field artillery brigade
Each infantry division included one field artillery brigade, responsible for light artillery and howitzers
Engineer Pioneer Corps
Engineering and constructional support for each infantry division included:
• engineers regiments
• Pioneer regiments
• fortress construction officers
• bridging train
Regiment
Two regiments per brigade; about 70 officers and 3,000 others
Commanding officer: colonel.
Regiment
Two regiments per brigade
Commanding officer: colonel
Battalion
Three battalions per regiment
Up to 1,000 men
Commanding officer: major
Battalion
Two battalions per regiment; one ammunition column per battalion
Commanding officer: major
Sanitary Services
Members of the Sanitary Company were attached to each infantry division
Company
Four companies per battalion, each with 5 officers and 150 other ranks
Commanding officer: captain
Machine gun company
One machine gun company per infantry battalion
Commanding officer: captain
Battery
Three batteries per battalion
Five officers per battery
Commanding officer: captain
Veterinary Services
Members of the Veterinary Corps were attached to each infantry division
Platoon
Three platoons to each company
One officer and 60-70 men
Commanding officer: lieutenant
Section
Two or three sections per company
One officer and up to 30 men
Commanding officer: lieutentant
Section
Two to four sections per battery
Commanding officer: lieutenant
Medical Services
Members of the medical corps, with six field hospitals, were attached to each infantry division
Section
Four sections to each company
16 to 20 men to each section
Commanded by a corporal
Gun
Two or three guns per section
Gun
Two to four guns per section
Baggage and Supply
A baggage and supply train, and an ammunition train, supported the infantry division
Squad
Two or three squads to each section
Commanded by a lance corporal
Private soldier
Eight private soldiers in each squad
Private soldier
Ten private soldiers per machine gun
Private soldier
Ten private soldiers per gun

should treat each other. Master and servant was the essence of the British approach. Comrades in arms, with different levels of responsibility, was the Australian. This distinction was the point of a story (probably apocryphal) about an Australian officer telling his men how to behave before they were inspected by a British general: "Whatever you do, don't call me 'Alf'."

British soldiers managed to come to terms with their situation in many ways. Contemporary accounts repeatedly bring up three: the importance of regimental traditions, small-group loyalties and humor. The first gave men a sense of being part of history, of stepping into a formation that had been in battle before. Small-group loyalties gave them essential companionship. It usually involved two or three men in a platoon of a dozen, who went through it all together. This kind of camaraderie gave soldiers a powerful reason to stay the course: not to do so would be to

Songs of World War I

Soldiers traveling by train, on the march, drinking in bars, or idling in the trenches or behind the lines spent much time singing. Their songs came from various sources. France and Germany both had conscript armies with highly developed military musical styles. German songs, for example, often portrayed war as heroic and drew on traditional fears to encourage morale. Both aspects appear in the famous German song "The Watch on the Rhine" (below). In the British army, soldiers wrote songs to fit familiar tunes or simply sang old favorites. Some were humorous, often at the expense of high command. Others had more of a bite, such as the gallows humor expressed in the stanza from "The Old Barbed Wire" (right). The entry of the USA into the war in 1917 produced an outburst of patriotic songs. Songs written by professional songwriters usually did not find favor with soldiers, but an American exception to this was "Over There" by George M. Cohan. It was even recorded by the great Italian tenor Enrico Caruso.

From **The Watch on the Rhine**

There sounds a call like thunder's roar,
Like the crash of swords, like the surge of waves.
To the Rhine, the Rhine, the German Rhine!
Who will the stream's defender be?
  Dear Fatherland, rest quietly.
  Sure stands and true the Watch,
  The Watch on the Rhine.

To heaven he gazes.
Spirits of heroes look down.
He vows with proud battle-desire:
O Rhine! You will stay as German as my breast!
  Dear Fatherland, etc.

Even if my heart breaks in death,
You will never be French.
As you are rich in water
Germany is rich in hero's blood.
  Dear Fatherland, etc.

So long as a drop of blood still glows,
So long a hand the dagger can draw,
So long an arm the rifle can hold -
Never will an enemy touch your shore.
  Dear Fatherland, etc.

From **The Old Barbed Wire**

If you want to find the old battalion,
I know where they are,
I know where they are.
If you want to find a battalion,
I know where they are,
They're hanging on the old barbed wire.
I've seen 'em, I've seen 'em,
Hanging on the old barbed wire,
I've seen 'em,
Hanging on the old barbed wire.

Over There by George M. Cohan

Over There
Over There
Send the word
Send the word
Over There
That the boys are coming
The boys are coming
The drums rum-tuming everywhere.
Over There
Say a prayer
Send the word
Send the word
To Beware.
It will be over.
We're coming over
And we won't come back
Till it's over
Over There.

Johnnie get your gun
  get your gun
  get your gun
Back in town to run
Home to run Home to run
Hear them calling you and me
Every son of liberty
Hurry right away
Don't delay go today
Make your Daddy glad
To have had such a lad
Tell your sweetheart not to pine
To be proud their boy's in line.

◀ ***Morning in the Cattle Truck*** **(detail), by Harold Williamson, shows what became a familiar form of transport during the war. Rail journeys were always slow; provisions were scanty and occasionally nonexistent; and the end of the line was usually the beginning of a lengthy march.**

let down their mates. The third – humor – was a time-honored outlet for griping about the troubles and petty indignities of military life, and left in its wake some of the war's most popular songs.

In the line

Getting to the Front was certainly not half the fun. Most soldiers were transported by train: the rides were cramped and uncomfortable, and usually took a very long time to cover even short distances. It was said that on the Eastern Front a bicyclist would have done better. The problem was the sheer size of the units to be moved. A division of approximately 12,000 men, with its horses, stores and equipment, took up (according to some estimates) over 1,000 railway cars; getting it all on and off at appointed times were monumental tasks.

From the railhead followed the march: 50 minutes on, 10 minutes off every hour, with a 21–27 kg (50–60 lb) pack to carry. Fully disgorged from a train, a division took up fully 24km (15mi) of road, and it took about five hours for the whole parade to pass one spot. Fortunately northern France and Flanders are relatively flat, but those who served on the Italian and other Fronts frequently did a lot of climbing or desert marching. On the Western Front, for reasons of safety, the march up the line or to another section of the line, frequently took place at night. On the Western Front the destination could be anywhere from the English Channel to the Swiss frontier. In the east, the field of action covered a vast panorama from Poland to Palestine, not to mention the campaigns against German forces in Africa, and in Asia where the Japanese fought on the Allied side.

▼ **This British motorized column moving through northern France is accompanied by cyclists and mounted traffic. The potential for traffic jams, even on paved roads and in clear weather, was almost limitless.**

Trench systems and trench life

In France and Flanders the Front was not one line but many. The British system of trench warfare was fairly regular. Facing the enemy lines was the fire trench, built in a zigzag pattern to deaden explosions and prevent deadly fire from the flank from traversing the line. The trench was deep enough to eliminate the danger from shrapnel, though not entirely from snipers. Its floor was covered by wooden duckboards; a firestep (or ledge) brought the soldier to ground level.

At times the enemy front line was as close as 45m (50yd) away. Frequently "no-man's-land" was penetrated by what was known as a forward sap, or listening post, jutting out from the front line. In the British sector of the front the second line, built in the same way, was a support line, linked by a communication trench to reserve lines.

The disposition of forces in the French sectors was more irregular. Trenches with full components of men and equipment alternated with positions sparsely defended. No-man's-land was defined by two thick lines of barbed wire, punctuated by points of entry for patrols. Deeper dugouts lay beneath the support trenches, which were usually not backed up by a reserve line, as in the British case. Of course conditions varied enormously, and Verdun in particular was a special case.

The German trench system was more elaborate and, according to some reports, better built and maintained. This was due to the fact that for long periods the German army was on the defensive, and needed an environment which would enable their men to resist the massive bombardments and assaults of the Allies. German deep bunkers offered protection during the preliminary enemy bombardment that preceded most attacks, after which machine-gun crews and supporting soldiers could reemerge and annihilate the advancing lines of enemy troops.

The German line was much deeper than the British. At Neuve-Chapelle in northern France, for instance, the gap between the fully garrisoned front trench and the support trench was about 2,500m (8,200ft), with the same distance separating the support trench from the reserve trench behind it. In addition a chain of machine-gun emplacements, protected by concrete, was strung

▶ Boredom was a constant companion in the trenches. This, as much as the need for communication with one's family and friends, accounts for the volume of postal traffic from the Front during the war.

▼ An aerial view of one corner of the Western Front near Auchy-les-Labassée in France. The top right-hand quadrant of the photograph is German-held territory, marked by a clearly visible ribbon-like trench system. A three-line array of trenches, linked by communication trenches, can be seen just above no-man's-land, the devastated area in the center of the photograph. The round features dotting the center-right are mine craters. The left-hand side of the photograph shows the British trench line, which appears to be less extensive than the German line opposite it.

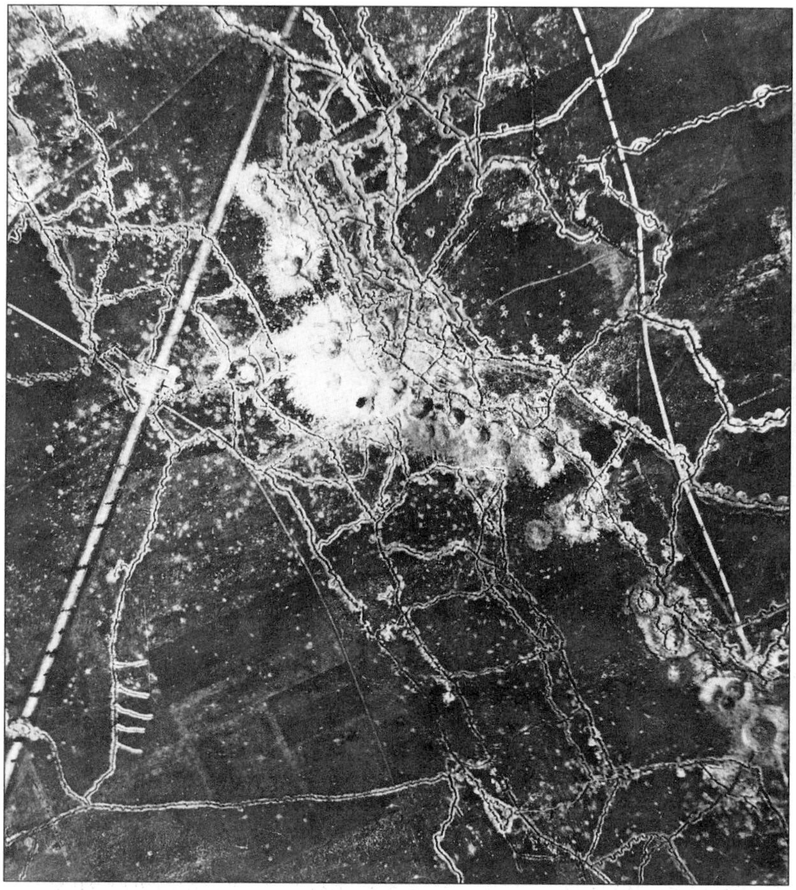

about 800m (2,600 ft) behind the front line. The interval between these lethal firing points varied, but could reach 600m (2,000ft).

By 1916 the Germans had developed a new approach, known as the system of "plane defense", which offered much greater flexibility to their men. In this the first line was lightly held, and easily evacuated in the event of an enemy attack. The second and third lines would then provide a massive counterattack, which would sweep back the exhausted enemy troops from their recently occupied, and expendable, positions. Ernst Jünger likened this system to a steel "sinew" or trap, flexible at first, but ready to spring shut after the initial pressure had been absorbed. But even Jünger – who wrote tactical manuals for the German army (and war memoirs after the Armistice) – admitted that this description provides too mathematical or architectural a view of the trenches. There was much greater variety in troop emplacement and liaison than is suggested in linear descriptions of the Front. Jünger preferred the image of a net, in which advancing soldiers were trapped at various points and depths.

The irregularity of a net suggests something of the vast and varied system of fortifications and trenches built by the French at Verdun. In 1916 these were involved in what was for soldiers the most difficult and murderous campaign of the war. Over the 10 months of the battle huge concrete blockhouses, such as Fort Douaumont and Fort Vaux, were defended by their own contingents, at times linked to other units, at times isolated and surrounded. This clustering of

▼ The key to German resistance to the massive artillery bombardments which preceded the attack on the River Somme in 1916 was the construction of bunkers. Built to a depth of 3–9m (10–30ft), they could house up to a dozen men, who could withstand any barrage and still emerge rapidly to man machine-gun emplacements.

strong points was not unusual on the Western Front. What made warfare at Verdun unique was its absolutely monumental scale. By 15 July, five months after the Germans launched their initial attacks, fully 70 divisions of the total of 95 in the French army had passed through Verdun. They served on a front of less than 30km (48mi), on which were deposited the remains of over 650,000 men of both armies.

The average period in the line at this sector of the Front was eight days: soldiers could not take more. In the cold of February or the heat of July conditions were appalling, intolerable, perhaps unimaginable. A huge system of relief and reinforcement was therefore absolutely essential. This created what was dubbed – according to North African slang – the *noria* or the shuttle system. It meant that every unit in the French army had to take its turn, and that consequently new units knew very little about the terrain, conditions, or other minutiae of the battle. In effect the French army came to resemble a gigantic chain which passed through Verdun in a seemingly never-ending circle. Verdun was an extreme case of trench warfare at its most intense and horrifying. Fortunately few sectors had to endure anything like it for any length of time.

Let us consider some facets of life on relatively quieter sectors of the Front. One of the persistent myths of the war is that soldiers were in the front line all the time. This is simply untrue. In the British army, as a rule of thumb, out of every month an infantryman spent about one week in the two front lines, split equally between the fire trench and the support trench, one week in the

In due course the prisoners arrived at Headquarters... The first was a great big ox of a 2nd Lieutenant who could have been hardly twenty... At his side stood a "Gefreite", a lance-corporal, small, stocky, with his hair close-shaven, a low forehead, and a shy look... He then told his story in passable French, continually putting on and taking off his leather gloves. Our front line, which had been the German second- or third-line trench, was naturally connected to the new German first line (their former third or fourth line) by old communication trenches choked up with sandbags and "chevaux de frise" – wooden frames covered with barbed wire. As it was night they had got lost and had finished up in our lines. "I haff come to the army," said the 2nd Lieutenant, " two veeks ago. I did not know the gutters" [the German Graben means both gutter and trench] "and I expected the Gefreite to guide me." As to the Gefreite, who was interrogated in German by the battalion sergeant-major, he winked and said, "Not my fault! the Offizier!" suggesting that he, as a simple soldier, was not responsible, that his job was to follow his officer. We felt that he had known only too well that the Lieutenant was going in the wrong direction, but he had held his tongue in the hope that in this way he would soon be finished with the war.

RENE ARNAUD

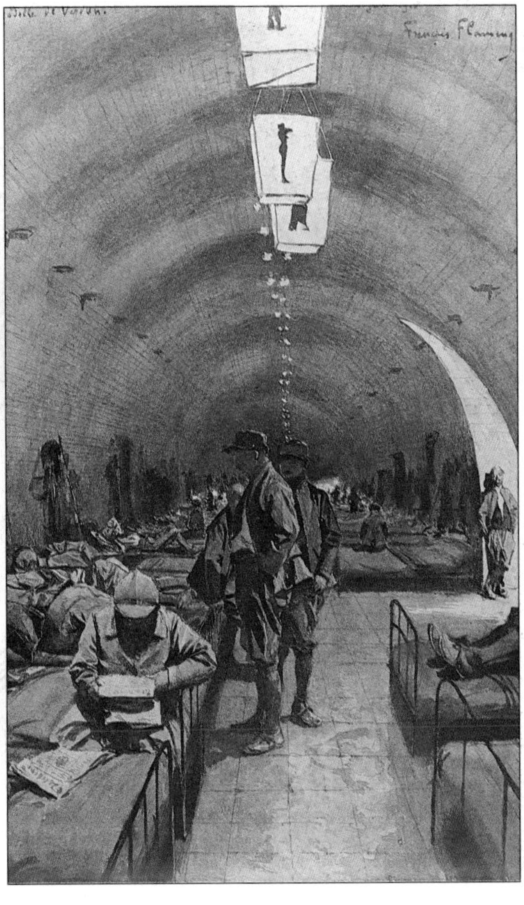

◀ This painting by F. Flameng shows French troops housed within the Citadel of Verdun on 6 June 1916. By then the German attack, begun in February, had reached its apogee. Forts Douaumont, Vaux, and Thiaumont were in German hands. There, outside the city of Verdun, they were held, at a cost of approximately 300,000 German casualties. French losses were higher still. Soldiers encased in concrete forts faced appalling conditions; the French defenders of Fort Vaux surrendered due to lack of water. This was siege warfare on a monumental scale.

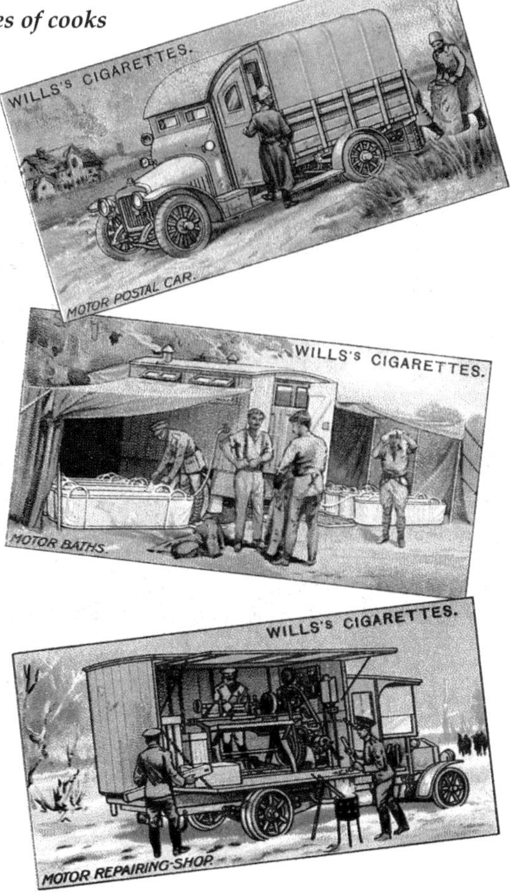

▶ These three cigarette cards, inserted in cigarette packs, show wartime British lorries. The top picture is of a revamped British postal van which was used in Russia; the center picture is of a portable bath; the third is of a mobile repair shop, also as used in Russia. The illustrations are striking in that they acknowledge some of the basic (and irregularly supplied) supports of morale: letters, hot baths, efficient maintenance of equipment. Even though the pictures are idealized, they spoke in a language soldiers understood. No doubt most were more interested in a smoke.

reserve lines. The rest of the time was spent behind the line.

Daily routine in the trenches was fairly predictable. The day began half an hour before sunrise, with the order to "stand-to". This would bring the whole platoon to the firestep, just in case an attack was in store. If it was not, sentries were posted and breakfast was taken. The next order of business was inspection, followed by more sentry duty and other mundane tasks, which usually involved repair work on the trench system. Rations arrived after a second "stand-to" of the day at dusk. Then the rotation of sentry duty continued.

This is the war most frontline soldiers knew most of the time. It was dreary, lice-ridden and very frequently wet and extremely muddy or dry and exceedingly dusty. But most of the time it was spent waging defensive rather than offensive warfare. It is true that raiding parties were organized to gather intelligence and cause trouble to the other side, and snipers were at work at all times. But these were inter- ruptions in a war of endurance more than of bravado.

At some points a "live and let live system" evolved – a means of existence involving tacit co-operation between the sides, recognizing a rough parity of forces. Since neither was likely to dislodge the other, there were ways of minimizing

▲ A Bulgarian transport column passing through a Serbian town. The primitiveness of conditions on the Eastern Front made horse power (and other animal power) more reliable than motorized transport.

▶ It is best to leave to the imagination the cuisine dished out to soldiers from this French traveling field kitchen, shown at the front in 1916.

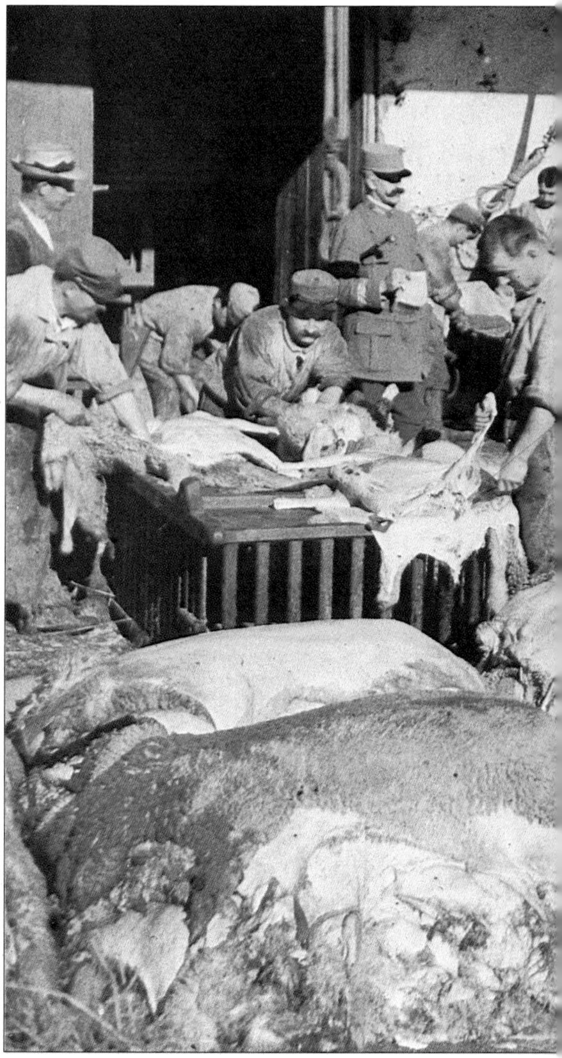

▲ One of the most time-consuming enterprises in a soldier's life was the repair, cleaning and replacement of his kit. Inevitable wear and tear, matched by endemic petty pilfering, made it almost impossible for a soldier to have all his regulation gear in order at any one time. Inspection required ingenuity and tolerance when items disappeared and reappeared before and after roll call. In addition to the equipment soldiers were supposed to have, most added all sorts of items to make their lives easier. The French *poilu* (literally "hairy one") shown right was notorious for carrying on his back the equivalent of a corner shop. Belgian troops (above left) fought as an independent force virtually throughout the war.

◀ A French military abattoir showing the slaughter of sheep, preparation of skins, and collection of meat and remains for food. The massive and never-ending task of provisioning armies began here and ended in the mobile kitchen opposite.

The Treatment of Prisoners

The most striking contrast between the two world wars was in terms of the treatment of prisoners of war. Atrocities were committed in both conflicts, but the systematic inhumanity of the 1939–45 war was by and large unknown in World War I. Prisoners' conditions varied considerably. Some did agricultural work, but most faced inadequate nutrition, miserable sanitary conditions, and boredom, rather than the degradation and extermination of camps on the Eastern Front in Hitler's war.

As the 1914–18 war dragged on, the numbers taken prisoner grew substantially. By June 1916 the Germans held 300,000 French prisoners, while the French held 95,000 Germans; 160,000 British soldiers became prisoners of war during the conflict. Of the total of 500,000 French prisoners held in Germany between 1914 and 1918, 40,000 died there.

Partly to defray the costs of their upkeep, prisoners were put to work in industry, agriculture and public works. An agreement reached at Berne in December 1917, and ratified three months later, led to the exchange of prisoners aged over 48 who had been in captivity at least 18 months.

On both sides civilians were interned and treated as prisoners of war. Germans were held at Wakefield, Yorkshire, and a British community of 4,000 men were confined for the duration to the racetrack of Ruhleben, near Berlin. The treatment of Armenian civilians by the Turks, in contrast, descended to bestiality; about 600,000 Armenians were massacred.

▼ All prisoners were alike, and yet each had his own story. This massive column of Russian soldiers taken prisoner in the Battle of Tannenberg in 1914 was full of soldiers with the same fatigue, fatalism, haunted eyes and fear masked by determination seen in the faces of all nationalities during the war.

◀ This German prisoner holding his food containers was among thousands who lived a life of boredom, disease, and occasional dreams of escape and reunion with family and friends. The ranks were frequently thinned by outbreaks of epidemics including the terrible visitation of influenza in 1918.

the risk and discomfort of trench warfare. One was to have an unspoken agreement (worked out through trial and error) not to shell latrines nor to open fire during breakfast. Another was to make as much noise as possible before a minor raid, so that the other side could withdraw to their protected bunkers.

This limitation on hostilities did not exist everywhere and was stamped on by command when it came to light. But even such informal arrangements as survived could be quickly buried, along with men killed by snipers, by the odd shell, or gas. The fraternization that did go on briefly between the lines on Christmas Day 1914 did not characterize the way the war was fought in the trenches. Violence was always below the surface, ready to explode.

After sentry-duty was completed, any spare time that trench soldiers had was spent in a rough-and-ready kind of personal housekeeping, either of the delousing variety or patching and mending the poor-quality kit with which they were provided. This often became the art of finding essential uses for the most unlikely implements. Regulation equipment rarely sufficed for the running repairs that had to be done time and again. For this reason standard gear formed only the core of a soldier's personal effects.

In addition to a rifle, ammunition and a gas mask, French soldiers carried on their backs "their trunk and even their cupboard", as the French author Henri Barbusse put it. Their knapsacks – weighing up to 27kg (60lb) – contained the regulation "two tins of pressed beef, a dozen biscuits, two tablets of coffee and two packets of dried soup, a bag of sugar, fatigue smock and spare boots" as well as jam, tobacco, chocolate, candles, soft shoes, soap, a spirit lamp, a blanket, a waterproof sheet, some cooking utensils, a trenching tool and a water bottle.

In addition all sorts of odds and ends were carried around. In Barbusse's unit one man had 18 pockets stuffed with personal effects. In one pocket he had writing paper, an army squad book, maps, newspaper clippings, a folder of photographs from home; in another, mirrors, flasks of mineral oil, scissors, tubes of aspirin or opium tablets; elsewhere, he had his purse, pipe, pocket pipe-lighter, pack of cards and set of drafts, with a paper board and sealing wax pieces. Others in the same platoon had a German pay book, some phials of iodine, several knives, a revolver, string, nails, and a drinking cup. Clearly, provisioning was a very individual art in the trenches, entailing the storage for later use of items purchased, stolen, looted from enemy trenches, or taken from the dead.

Behind the line

When men were withdrawn from the front lines, they faced different problems. Since the war was originally supposed to end by Christmas 1914, members of the French army had been given little leave until 1915. It is therefore not surprising that French popular artists celebrated such moments of leave as there were with particular fervor. British enlisted troops were only occasionally given leave to return to Britain, but officers were

▲▶ After the search for food, the search for shelter preoccupied most soldiers behind the lines. Billeting was a difficult and delicate operation, involving soldiers – at times resembling (and more than resembling) an armed band of thugs – entering the domestic world of peasants and townspeople. There was the universal language of children to mediate between hosts and guests, as shown above, but when household space was scarce, any available shelter had to do. These Canadian soldiers (right) had to make the best of a barn. Others were housed in overturned water towers.

permitted to return home more often. Otherwise British soldiers were sent to the coastal enclave of Etaples, which housed a training camp to toughen up new drafts and keep older soldiers fit to return to the Front. This was the location of the notorious "bull-ring", where, for rest and recreation soldiers were treated to "square-bashing" (marching endlessly in squares), all sorts of onerous drills, and some of the nastiest sergeant-majors and military police in the army. For others the problem of billeting became crucial. Tact was needed to convince the local populace to offer shelter to what often appeared to be a band of brigands. Domestic scenes went on roughly as before, despite the presence of a large number of onlookers. Where houses were unavailable, other accommodation had to suffice. Once shelter and food were found there was still the minor problem of language, and enterprising business- men supplied pocket dictionaries and phrase books to the troops. One Belgian shipping company produced a guide to *The Language of Three Allies*, telling the British soldier all he needed to know about the Flemish and French equivalents and pronunciations of key phrases.

Life behind the lines was an important part of the soldiers' war and troops naturally looked to peace-time entertainments to occupy their time when away from the Front. The chief licensed recreations of British soldiers were sport, theatrical events and cinema. There was a vast proliferation of football leagues, and later on even baseball leagues for Americans. Countless plays were performed, by visiting entertainers or by the troops themselves, who often dressed up in drag to entertain their fellow soldiers.

Another wartime adaptation was humorous magazines, modeled among British troops on some of the more tasteless forms of schoolboy publication. But this gives them too little credit, for trench journalism was an extraordinary phenomenon in the British army, and had its equivalents in other forces as well. Virtually every brigade had its amateur journalists, who found ways to mimeograph and distribute several

▶ This rare photograph shows the production of a German trench newspaper. The soldier in the center is typesetting one of the hundreds of ephemeral journals produced by soldiers themselves in all major combatant armies. The mix of stories included humor, bad poetry, and swipes at those in authority, at home or at the Front.

hundred copies of an eight- or ten-page paper for a few weeks or months. The most famous was the *Wipers Times* ("Wipers" being the English slang name for Ypres), which was produced by a number of men of the Sherwood Foresters in a ramshackle office near the Menin Gate. It was printed on an abandoned machine salvaged by a sergeant who had been a printer before the war. Its first issue was 12 February 1916, and under different names it continued to appear for the rest of the war. The names of most of its contributors have faded away, but one, Gilbert Frankau, was a best-selling author in the 1920s. The tone of this paper, and of the many that tried to follow its success, was unabashedly rude in a public-school sort of way. On 31 July 1916 the paper (now rechristened the *SommeTimes*), printed an advertisement for a sure cure for optimism (an artillery barrage). Other articles sent up the absurdity of civilian attitudes toward and the reporting of the war. Chauvinistic nonsense of the kind produced by the journalists Hilaire Belloc and Horatio Bottomley was parodied under the by-line of Belary Helloc or Cockles Tumley. The peace camp also came in for a barracking. Such well-known Labour politicians as Ramsay MacDonald, Victor Grayson, and Arthur Henderson were caricatured as "Flamsey MacMonald", "Grictor Vrayson", and "A. Tenderson." They were portrayed as innocents who knew nothing about the war.

Staff officers came in for persistent ribbing. The *B.E.F. Times* of 8 September 1917 defined "a few more military terms." Among them was: "DUDS – These are of two kinds. A shell on impact failing to explode is called a dud. They are unhappily not as plentiful as the other kind, which often draws a big salary and explodes for no reason. These are plentiful away from the fighting areas."

Other issues had articles of a satirical kind which raised the delicate question of the faithfulness of girlfriends or wives back home. In one Biblical parody, the Book of Kings is rewritten: the plan of King David to kill Uriah the Hittite in order to get his wife, Bathsheba, goes seriously awry. On the whole, though, the subject of sex was very rarely broached.

These papers were successful largely because they showed that even in the exposed Ypres salient, some British soldiers managed to keep a sense of humor. This kind of insouciance was highly valued. But trench magazines had a wide appeal for other reasons. Partly, it was because of their tone of irreverence for authority; partly because soldiers had little to do and these papers helped to pass the time. The same sense of the ridiculous within the grimness of the war made Charlie Chaplin the most popular screen performer with the soldiers. His ability to survive against all odds in a storm not of his own making, and even occasionally to plant a boot on the seat of authority, translated easily to the landscape of war. His short film *Shoulder Arms*, made in 1918, was a masterpiece of this kind of soldiers' humor. It was this mixture of the sentimental, the frivolous and the mildly indecent which soldiers' songs also captured and which underlay the variety of soldiers' entertainments produced during World War I.

ARTILLERY WEAPONS AND TACTICS

In 1914 the main artillery weapon was the light field gun, designed for mobile offensive warfare. All major combatant armies were equipped with field guns based on the French 75mm gun. These could fire up to 20 shells a minute with relatively high accuracy, and played an important role in the mobile warfare of 1914, but after the "race to the sea" stalemate set in along a 750km (475mi) front and, in effect, siege warfare took over.

One response was the development of heavier ordnance, to produce gaps in the enemy's barbed-wire entanglements and destroy enemy guns. In this the German army was at an advantage. Its general staff had learned from the Russo-Japanese War (1904–05) and had retained an emphasis on firepower. Each corps was provided with at least 12 150mm heavy howitzers – known for their noise and black smoke explosions as "Jack Johnsons" after the black world heavyweight boxing champion of 1908 to 1915.

As heavier howitzers and guns of longer range became available, all sides attempted to adjust to the new siege warfare. Trench mortars were devised to fire virtually straight into the air. The number of heavy guns grew exponentially. In 1914 the French had 300 heavy guns; in 1918 about 7,000, of which 400 were mounted on railway carriages. Of the 20,000 artillery pieces in the German army in 1918, about 8,000 were heavy guns. The biggest of them all, "Big Bertha" delivered a 108kg (238lb) shell to a target 148km (90mi) away. That destination was Paris.

Vast quantities of ammunition were spent on counterbattery work, the destruction of strong points, and wire-cutting operations. But heavy intensive bombardments before attacks sacrificed the element of surprise. The bombardments also blotted out not only the enemy defenses but also roads and identifying features and restricted the movement of infantry, guns and subsequently tanks alike. As tactics developed barrages were devised to protect infantry during their attacks. Guns were initially trained on enemy front lines and then lifted and moved on to support trenches. Later the more successful "creeping" or "rolling" barrage was introduced which moved in advance of infantry on a timed basis. But the absence of radio communications for control made these arrangements inflexible if the infantry were delayed or diverted.

The increased importance of artillery led to an enormous expansion of artillery forces. At its peak the British army's artillery men numbered 526,000 – a quarter of its total ration strength. The other side of the coin was that artillery and mortars caused the most casualties. In the British army artillery caused 58 percent of casualties, machine-gun and rifle bullets 39 percent.

Artillery did not win the war, but the noise and the surreal landscape it produced defined war on the Western Front. Nothing like it had ever occurred before.

▶ **Artillery came in every conceivable size during the war. Guns on the Eastern Front (top right) were occasionally of Crimean vintage; newer models included a 6in 13-ton howitzer (second right, being dragged through the mud), and a 9.45in trench mortar (third right). The most compact French version of a trench mortar could be carried on a man's back. It was called *Le Crapouillot*, which was also the title of a celebrated trench newspaper. The biggest guns, like the German "Big Bertha" or the American 14in railway gun (fourth right), had a range of 50km (30mi) or more.**

▼ **Devised in mid-1916 for supporting infantry attack, the creeping barrage entailed a bombardment lifting forward short distances at fixed times, with the assault troops creeping forward as close as possible behind it. This was most effective when infantry stayed close to the shell bursts, no more than 100m (330ft) behind the point of impact. On the first day of the Somme (1 July 1916), this sheet of fire worked well with 7 and 18 Division of the British XV Corps; other units were not so successful. Of course, coordination between artillery and infantry was frequently difficult, and gas could disrupt the most meticulous planning. On its own, artillery was incapable of breaking the stalemate on the Western Front.**

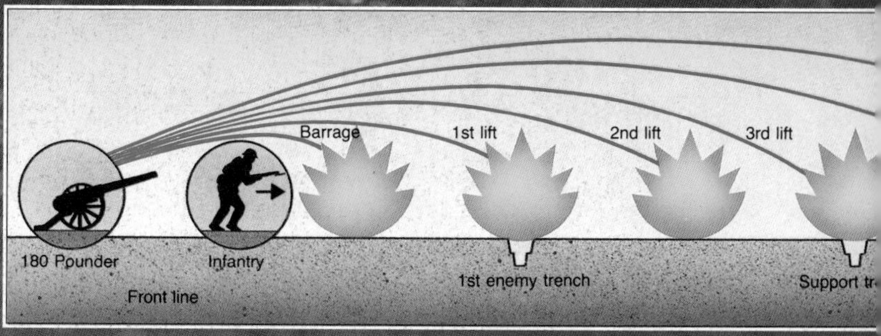

5th lift
Reserve trench

Datafile

Each of the great campaigns of 1916–17, Verdun, the Somme, Chemin des Dames and Passchendaele (Third Ypres), symbolizes the futility of the war. Taken together they present a catalog of offensive operations which went on for weeks or months after their initial failures, and succeeded only in cutting the heart out of the citizen armies which went to war in 1914. Total casualties in these offensives exceeded two million men.

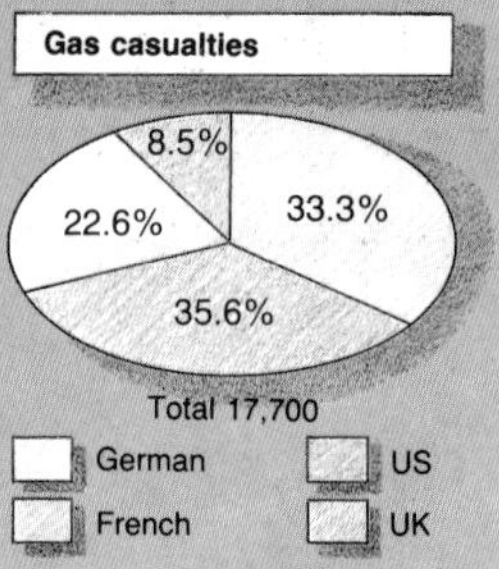

▲ **Deaths from chemical warfare are understated in this chart. Thousands of men who survived the war suffered from respiratory complaints for years after the Armistice. Their deaths, which numbered in the tens of thousands, must be added to the above official totals to give a full picture of the damage caused by gas warfare.**

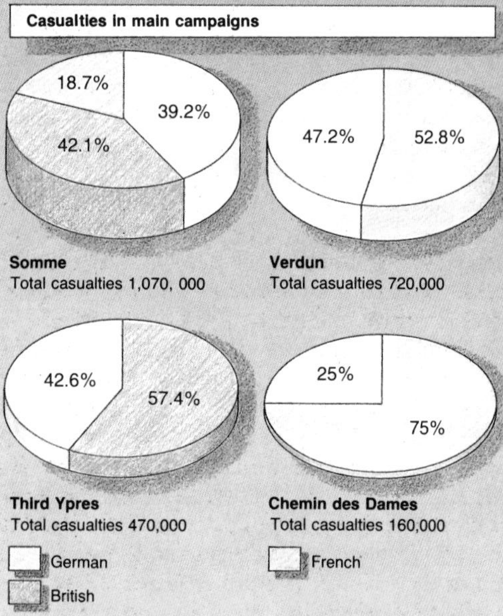

◀ **Statistical skirmishes continued long after the war to prove that one side or the other suffered greater casualties in particular encounters. These charts can only indicate the rough parity of the slaughter at Verdun and on the Somme in 1916, and the futility of French and British attacks of 1917 in Champagne and Flanders.**

Chronology

1916

January 24
UK: First military service bill passed by House of Commons

February 21
(to Dec. 18) Battle of Verdun: unsuccessful German attack on French city of Verdun

April 24–29
Easter Rising of Irish Republican Brotherhood against the British in Dublin, Ireland

April 25
UK: Second Military Service Act passed: compulsory military service extended to married men

April 26
In Berlin agreement is signed for transfer of wounded and sick prisoners of war to Switzerland (signed in UK on May 13)

April 29
In Mesopotamia, Turks capture Kut and the remnants of the British invasion force

May 31
(to June 1) Battle of Jutland: major naval battle of war between UK and Germany

June 4
(to Oct. 10) Brusilov offensive: Russians push back the Austro-Hungarian line north of the Carpathians

June 5
Start of Arab revolt against the Turks in the Hejaz

July 1
(to Nov. 19) Battle of the Somme: unsuccessful Allied attack on German lines in the Somme Valley, France

November 7
Woodrow Wilson is reelected president of the USA

November 25
GER: German army establishes air forces as separate military division

1917

March 15
Czar Nicholas II of Russia abdicates. Provisional Government assumes power

April 6
The USA enters the war fighting on the side of the Allies

April 16–29
Chemin des Dames offensive; a large-scale French offensive on the Aisne fails to break the German line

April 28
USA: Congress passes bill to raise 500,000 men for US armed forces

April 29
FR: First mutiny by unit in French army

June 17
Portuguese troops in action on Western Front for first time

July 6
Canadian Parliament passes conscription bill

July 31
(to Nov. 10) Third Battle of Ypres: unsuccessful British offensive against the German forces in Flanders

August 3
GER: Mutiny among sailors at Wilhelmshaven

September 11
UK: Return to England of first party of repatriated prisoners of war

November 1
UK: Formation of Ministry of National Service

Verdun, the Somme, Passchendaele: these are the names of some of the major encounters of 1916–17, the third phase of World War I; they have come to symbolize the war as a whole. This is for two reasons. The first is the scale of the casualties in these huge battles. The second is that these operations, in effect, led nowhere.

Two questions immediately arise about this phase of the war, which have preoccupied historians and commentators ever since 1918. What was combat like for the men who fought in these fantastic and futile encounters? And, given the odds against survival, why did ordinary men, under no illusion as to what they were being asked to do, continue to fight in this kind of war? With respect to 1914, the historian asks: why did men go to war? By 1916, the question is really: why did they stay?

As if these questions were not hard enough to answer, the temperature of discussion has been raised by a few commentators who have set them in the context of the even more appalling carnage of World War II – slaughter not of soldiers but of civilians. To some observers the trenches were the concentration camps of World War I, in which a whole generation was slaughtered. This is an

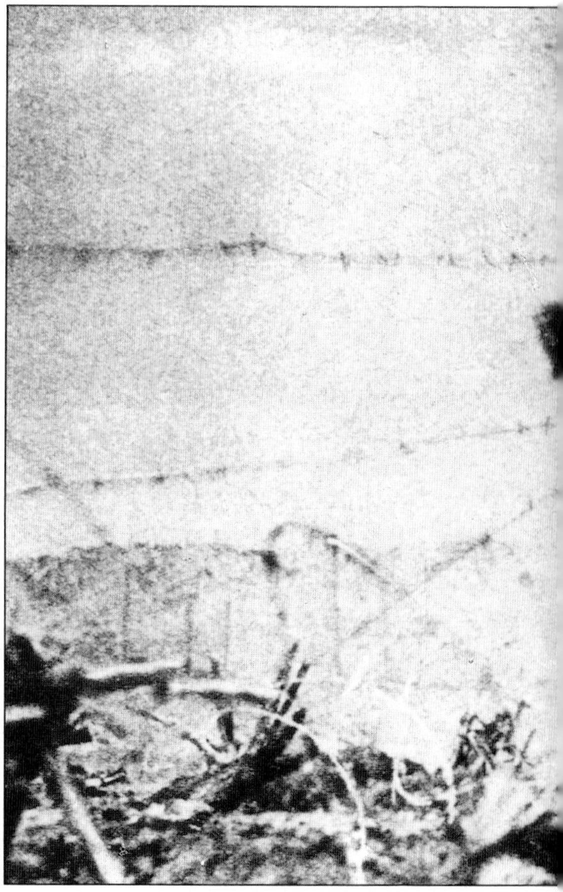

1916–17 THE GREAT SLAUGHTER

The major campaigns of 1916–17 symbolize World War I

What was combat like?

How did men cope with the conditions?

The fog of war was made worse by gas attacks

Men had to live in a landscape of destruction for years

With the risk of being blown to pieces

Often in the company of the dead

Men were bound by group loyalties and humor

extreme position, hard to accept in the light of the fact that millions chose to fight in 1914–18. However abused were their initial faith and commitments, they both killed and suffered; hence their status as victims is highly questionable. The noted French scholar Antoine Prost has found a better way to put the point. His remarks refer to Verdun, but have a bearing on many other facets of the war. "Like Auschwitz in World War II," he has written, "Verdun was a transgression of the limits of the human condition."

Prost's statement is profoundly true. This section will attempt to explore some of these claims by presenting three kinds of evidence. The first deals with the infantryman's landscape of battle. The second concerns his motivation. The third (in the next chapter) relates to the varied pattern of loss of morale, disaffection and mutiny, which was visible by mid-1917 and which grew irregularly over the following 18 months until it put an end to the war itself.

The fog of war

A persistent fog of confusion hung over the battlefields of World War I. Men in combat rarely knew what was happening or on occasion even where they were. The front line was well enough marked, but as soon as an attacking force entered no-man's-land, which was usually an irregular terrain pockmarked with craters, the combination of terror, noise, bombardment, machine-gun fire, barbed wire, casualties and natural human error made it inevitable that men frequently lost their bearings and went forward, if at all, largely out of inertia.

All attempts must be abandoned to picture battle as a series of moves on a giant chess board – which is what military maps did, both at headquarters and in civilian newspapers. In battle, soldiers tended to move in every conceivable direction, and only occasionally in the one intended in the plan of attack. This was not a new feature of combat: witness the French writer Stendhal's accounts of the fog of war in *The Charterhouse of Parma* (1839) and Tolstoy's in *War and Peace* (1869). As in other wars, combat was a haphazard set of encounters, only some of which were planned. But the soldiers of 1914–18 did live through a war very different from those of Waterloo or the Crimea. In particular, three features of combat were unanticipated and very difficult to locate within any familiar frame of reference.

▼ French troops advancing through barbed wire entanglements on the Western Front. A direct hit by high explosives could completely obliterate all traces of a man; those hit by shrapnel risked being maimed or dismembered.

I wish those people who write so glibly about this being a holy war could see a case of mustard gas... could see the poor things burnt and blistered all over with great mustard- coloured suppurating blisters with blind eyes all sticky... and stuck together, and always fighting for breath, with voices a mere whisper, saying that their throats are closing and they know they will choke.

VERA BRITTAIN

The deadly cloud

The first feature is related to new weapons introduced in the course of the conflict. Most commentators describe the great battles of 1916–17 as wars of men against machines, with the men inevitably coming out on the losing end. This suggests that technical changes in weaponry prior to 1914 had transformed battle out of all recognition. To some extent this was true. The war in the west (but not in the east) saw the end of the cavalry as a key attacking force. It initiated soldiers into the use of camouflage, tank warfare, and aerial combat and reconnaissance. It produced artillery barrages on a scale never before known. And it presented a new and hideous kind of weapon: poison gas.

The onset of chemical warfare on the Western Front transformed the landscape of battle in a most bizarre and spectacular way. The first use of poison gas there was at Langemark near Ypres on 22 April 1915. German troops opened 6,000 cylinders of chlorine along an 8km (5mi) front. The French and Algerian troops subjected to this attack either suffocated or fled. Two days later it was the Canadians' turn to be gassed. This attack was less successful, since the gas hardly rose above ground level, but the psychological effect was considerable, and the Canadians also retreated. On 1, 6, and 10 May 1915 British troops were gassed, but, due to a change in the direction of the wind, both sides suffered casualties.

This raises the key limitation of this innovation in warfare. It could cripple attacker as well as defender, and frequently did so. It also eliminated the possibility of a surprise attack. Hence it was rare for gas, or that other chemical device, the flamethrower, to do anything other than *stabilize* the lines. By 1915 the advantage in warfare had

▲▶ After their first appearance on the Western Front in 1915, gas attacks became a regular feature of the war (above). Box respirators or other antigas devices became standard field equipment, alongside impromptu means of defense against gas, such as that used by this Russian infantryman fighting near Baranovici in western Russia in 1917 (right). With luck, rain or damp would keep the gas below knee level; high winds would disperse it, or drive it back toward enemy lines. Gas shells were a greater menace.

► A makeshift gas factory. With the aid of a soldier, a German chemist is preparing a brew to be placed in bottles and laid near enemy lines for activation by sniper fire. Multiply this example by thousands, and it provides a rough idea of the demand for chemicals during the war. To meet it, huge industrial complexes were set up or expanded with government funds. These units provided a significant boost for the companies that became the industrial giants of the postwar years: ICI in Britain (formed by mergers in 1926), DuPont in America and I.G. Farben in Germany.

shifted in favor of the defensive. Relatively effective countermeasures were soon developed, in particular the box respirator, a device which kept soldiers alive at the minor price of making them look like invaders from another planet.

By 1918 roughly one shell in four fired by both sides on the Western Front was a gas shell. By then chlorine had been joined by the more lethal phosgene and by mustard gas, the antecedent of napalm, which blistered the skin in hideous ways. A gas alarm at any point on the Western Front would bring about a feverish transformation of faces into elephantine masks. After a time they became part of the scene. Soldiers drilled in them, read through them, fought in them, and on occasion kitted out their horses with them. Because of the range of German artillery, French schoolchildren were given gas masks too, but fortunately, few were needed.

▲ A German soldier carrying food to a dugout during a gas attack on the Western Front.

◄ These British soldiers were victims of a gas attack near Bois de l'Abbé in France in May 1918. The lucky ones would recover their sight within a few hours; the unlucky ones would have been blinded for life, or have had their lungs so badly damaged that recovery was extremely painful and very uncertain. Mustard gas accounted for some of the most severely wounded: blistering the skin as well as asphyxiating the men who inhaled it. Compassion rather than a cure was all that medical science could offer these men.

◀ Troops of the Canadian 4th Division holding the "line" at Passchendaele on 14 November 1917, at the end of Third Ypres. The water-logged landscape defined the conditions of combat and ensured the failure of Haig's attempt to break through German positions. In the March 1918 offensive, the Germans retook these craters, but gave them up again in the retreat of summer 1918.

Destruction

A second feature of the war on the Western Front was the extraterrestrial landscape of destruction produced by artillery fire, barbed wire and mud. The soldiers lived in a world where everything had been torn up and twisted, and where men could drown in mud. To the infantryman of 1914–18, Henri Barbusse remarked, hell was water. None of this was new in 1914. Many examples could be cited as precedents for the devastation of 1914–18: the destruction of Carthage in 698, the Dutch revolt of the 16th century and aspects of the Napoleonic wars (1800–15), among others. Closer still were the terrible battles of the American Civil War. The cornfields at Shiloh were said to have been yellow before the battle there; blood red after. But what made the landscape of destruction in World War I such an enduring feature in popular memory was that millions of men were forced to live in it, at times under it, for years. The paintings of the British war artist Paul Nash bring home the eerie unfamiliarity of the world the soldiers knew.

Of course, parts of the Front escaped the worst of the fighting. And even on the Somme or at Passchendaele wild flowers insistently returned, providing an enduring symbol of the war: the poppy, indigenous to northern France and Flanders, and liberally sprinkled, blood-red, across the battlefields of the war.

The company of the dead

The front-line soldiers of 1914–18 saw things that people should not see. Among them were hideously wounded men. Medical reports on the wounded make particularly harrowing reading, despite the language doctors used to distance themselves from suffering. But at least they had anesthetics to use, unlike surgeons in earlier wars. The butchery of battle was worsened by the

▲ British stretcher-bearers bring a wounded man back to a casualty clearing station through the mud of the Ypres salient on 1 August 1917. This man was a casualty of fighting near Boesinghe, a set of encounters dignified with the name of the Battle of Pilckem Ridge. For the wounded, the battle against infection was frequently hopeless.

▶ Detail of *Hell* by Georges Leroux. This painting suggests the truth of Henri Barbusse's assertion that for the front soldier, hell was water. As one trench newspaper put it, "This simple word, rain, which means next to nothing to the civilian, with a roof over his head, this word encapsulates the horror of the soldier in the field." (*L'Horizon*, July 1918.)

development of artillery, which could literally tear a man to pieces, even at times without leaving a single trace of his existence. On the other hand, medical advances meant that the ravages of disease were less severe in this war than in 19th-century conflicts. Appallingly wounded men were to be found on all fronts in World War I. Some were beyond help: others, whose minds had gone, were beyond communication. The wounded were evacuated to base hospitals and, when possible, back home.

Many veterans of 1914–18 spoke of their memories of the wounded. But what made at least as deep an impression was another and more unusual aspect of the conflict: the persistent presence of the dead. In previous wars battles had lasted a few days at most. They had had a beginning and an end, after which the dead of both sides, usually as complete bodies, were buried. But this war was different: combat went on for months; artillery fire dismembered men in a flash; and the front line hardly moved at all. Consequently, the line of trenches stretching from Switzerland to the English Channel was littered with the remains of perhaps one million men. Soldiers ate with the dead, made jokes about them, and rifled their possessions.

After the war attempts were made to provide the dead with dignified resting places. Remains were gathered and reburied with proper ceremony. Round Ypres, for instance, about 200,000 British soldiers killed in the war lie in well cared-for cemeteries. During the war no such measures were possible. Soldiers had to carry on in the presence of countless bodies of dead men, some familiar, most anonymous. Those buried would reappear during bombardments, and be reinterred, at times to help support, quite literally, the trenches in which they had fought. Many soldiers recalled the stench of decomposition, and the swarms of flies on corpses, especially during the summer months. Everyone execrated the rats. It is difficult to imagine the nature of this ghastly environment. Human bones can still be found round Verdun to this day.

◀ ***"And have we done with War at last?***
Well, we've been lucky devils, both,
And there's no need of pledge or oath
To bind our lovely friendship fast,
By firmer stuff close bound enough".

***Two Fusiliers* by Robert Graves**

Coping with combat

It would seem to be the most natural thing in the world for men forced to live in this way to drop their guns and go home. This is no idle suggestion, and there was a steady trickle of deserters throughout the war. But aside from the desire to avoid being shot by your own side for cowardice,

▶ Only those who had been through battle could really know how human beings could be squashed like ants or rearranged like "ghastly dolls", as the British writer Siegfried Sassoon put it. Many soldiers developed a defensive callousness after having seen dismembered corpses time and again. What ex-soldiers recalled in later years varied substantially. In R.H. Mottram's *Spanish Farm Trilogy* (1924–27), it was not a legless man but a headless man who continued to haunt the central character. Others blotted such images out of their conscious minds for ever.

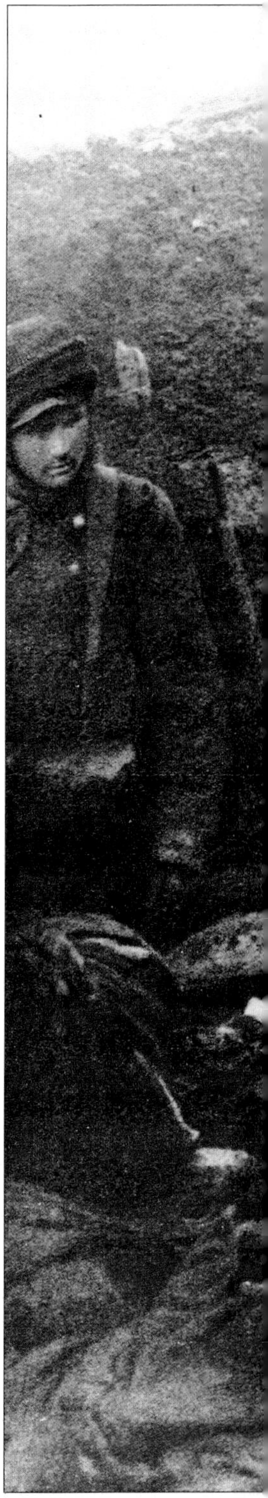

there were other ways in which men came to terms with the stress of trench warfare.

The first was the human tendency to direct one's primary loyalty to very small groups. Such camaraderie made the war a very private affair indeed, focused on the survival chances of two or three men. These bonds, at times forged before the war, were reinforced by the isolation of platoons under conditions of bombardment or combat. To cut and run meant first and foremost to violate the trust of a handful of friends.

It also meant breaking faith with junior officers who shared the risks and whose casualty rates were even higher than those of the men they led. The English writer Robert Graves estimated that a subaltern's life expectancy at the front was about two weeks. Other evidence points to the greater risks officers faced: perhaps 20 percent of the men who held commissions and who served at the Front were killed, compared to a 10–12 percent death rate among enlisted men in combat units. There is evidence that many privates felt a bond of shared experience with officers with whom they served in the trenches, and whom they followed whatever the dangers.

There were other supports for the front-line

▼ **This photograph captures the immediate aftermath of hand-to-hand combat between French and German troops in the Meuse region of the Western Front. This trench was taken by the French only an hour earlier. Under these conditions, the dead were left where they fell, or were simply added to the fortifications.**

▶ **Mass or Holy Communion was said in the field of all armies. Here the Russian rite is observed in a forest in what is now Poland. The czar and czarina encouraged mystical religious fervor during the war. To what extent their sentiments were shared by ordinary Russian soldiers – overwhelmingly peasants – is difficult to say. All armies had their own version of the American saying that there are no atheists in a foxhole.**

▼ **The incongruous geometry of the steeple of Albert Cathedral was a landmark for British soldiers stationed on the Somme Front. Speculation was rife as to a supernatural reason for the suspension of Madonna and child.**

The harmonium has arrived... It has been wonderful to have it for Easter Day. Colonel Hooper allows me to have an ambulance to take it and me as near the line as possible... My barrel-organ, as it is called, causes great amusement. "Now, Padre," they say "all you want is a monkey." To which the obvious reply is, "well are you looking for a job?" At the South Wales Borderers headquarters, the Adjutant had got hold of some flowers, and had hung blankets round the shattered walls. We had four celebrations of Holy Communion, and after that a long round of services until late in the evening, but I have a very comfortable bed to come back to every day.

REVD H.W. BLACKBURNE
BRITISH ARMY CHAPLAIN

soldier. For those who wanted it, religious communion was available. On both sides chaplains went up the line with the rest of the army. Among them Catholic priests had a particularly strong reputation for bravery, and were seen frequently at the Front giving final absolution. Some clergy of other denominations also earned respect by sharing trench conditions.

Some soldiers lived in a different kind of supernatural world – a world of superstitious beliefs, which, like most prerational modes of thought, moved in two contrary directions. On the one hand superstitions arose out of the fatalistic belief that all was preordained, that a soldier was hit when the bullet "with his name on it" was fired. On the other hand they emerged out of the sense that the individual could change his fate by a carefully prescribed set of actions, or by touching a magical talisman. Superstition described a world in which men were both powerless and all-powerful: in which they could do nothing to alter their destiny, and could survive by touching a rabbit's foot.

Closely allied to this kind of mentality was the sense that supernatural forces were not far from the battlefield. There was the famous instance of the Angels of Mons, who appeared above and protected retreating British soldiers in August 1914. This idea probably derived from a short story published early in the war describing the return from the dead of the men of the medieval Battle of Agincourt, appearing luminously between the two armies. There was the Madonna of Albert – a statue of Mary and Child on top of a church near the British front line on the Somme. A direct hit had bent the statue to a right angle to the church's spire. British soldiers who passed this gravity-defying statue conjured up the idea that the war would end the day the Madonna fell. Potshots tried to hurry the day along, but without success. She fell under British bombardment after the Germans captured Albert in 1918.

Combat out of the trenches

The experience of the trench soldier in World War I has been emphasized primarily for two reasons. First his war was that of the majority of fighting men in the major combatant countries. Secondly the outcome of the series of skirmishes, standoffs, and battles in which he and his comrades were engaged on the Western Front determined the outcome of the war.

▼ Chaplain T.R. White conducts a burial service over the common grave of 12 men who died in January 1918 at the American Red Cross Evacuation Hospital at Fleury-sur-Aire, in the Meuse region of France.

The Provision of Chaplains

All armies in World War I recognized the value of spiritual support for ordinary soldiers, but the provision and position of chaplains varied between armies according to national attitudes to religion. In 1914 there were no chaplains in the French army. They had been withdrawn in 1880 for fear of clerical opposition to the French republican constitution. The American army also omitted a corps of chaplains, as a consequence of the strict separation of church and state stipulated by the constitution of the USA. At the other end of the spectrum, the established churches of Britain (Anglican in England and Wales, Presbyterian in Scotland) dominated the British army chaplaincy department even though nonconformist churches were strong within Britain.

Because the French were fighting on their own soil they could draw on French clergy in the towns behind their front line. Army officers were happy to welcome clergy when they would consolidate discipline, but feared men who might undermine it. The American army allowed private supporters to pay chaplains and provide chapels. About 2,300 ministers served in France and were given the rank of first lieutenant, but to minister to troops required the goodwill of unit commanders and force of personality. The British army adapted to wartime needs by recognizing the "fancy religious sects" and providing chaplains for members of them. The proportion of Anglican clergy fell from 76 to 57 percent. Although the British army supported chaplains they remained adjuncts of the military machine. The British padres were shocked by the magnitude of religious ignorance in the army but saw that circumstances were inappropriate for attempting a religious revival.

◀ Military life was full of ritual, some sanctioned, some not. This was as true of peasant armies in the east as of industrial armies in the west. Here a Serbian priest blesses a cake handed to officers and enlisted men, in the presence of priests and a choir in June 1916. By then most of Serbia had been overrun.

► This British/Indian convoy, drawing water from the River Tigris, faced extremely harsh conditions in the Iraqi desert. Water was always in short supply, and mechanical difficulties reduced many units to older forms of desert transport. These problems were at the heart of the failure of British troops to relieve the siege of Kut-al-Amara. Townshend's British garrison surrendered on 29 April 1916, and was forced to walk across the Iraqi and Syrian deserts.

A large percentage of the (British) men were quite done for and could not possibly march another inch. They were lying on the ground (at Mosul, Mesopotamia) suffering from high fever and dysentery, and, needless to say, were smothered from head to foot in filth and covered with flies, the latter helping to make the sight, if possible, more sickening. Day after day we had seen men fall out of the columns on the line of the march, and after the escort had stripped the unlucky man of any clothing fit to sell, he had been given a final thrashing and left on the roadside to the mercy of the Arabs and Kurdish tribesmen. It had been a sickening sight, and one never knew when one might be the next one to fall out.

PRIVATE D. HUGHES

► Australian units served in Egypt, Palestine and Syria throughout Allenby's succesful campaign against the Turks. Conditions were harsh, particularly when camping in the Sinai, the Negev or Judean deserts. The temperature could plummet 30°C in a few hours. Water was always scarce: Allenby's troops and animals consumed 400,000 gallons per day. Disease was a greater threat than the Turks.

Other wars were fought by units scattered throughout the world. Here four of the "myriad faces of war" (in the words of the English novelist F.E. Manning) will be considered, to provide a greater sense of the variety of combat in World War I. The first is the doomed British expeditionary force in Iraq. After initial successes in 1915 against the Turks along the River Tigris, a combined British and Indian force under General Charles Townshend was forced to retreat to the fortress of Kut-al-Amara, where it was besieged. After 143 days the British and Indians surrendered. Over half of the men in the ranks then perished of disease and ill-treatment on a forced march over the desert to Aleppo in Syria.

Equally remote from the world of the trenches were the mixed African and German forces who led British, South African and Indian troops on a futile chase through East Africa between 1914 and 1918. The Germans were skillfully led by Colonel Paul von Lettow-Vorbeck, who managed to pin down Allied troops and keep them away from the European fronts for the duration of the war.

At sea it was inaction rather than action that caused most comment. Long periods of routine and drill were interspersed with rare moments of battle. After the anticipated major duels at sea had failed to materialize, other tasks awaited the navies. Among the Allies, protecting convoys was a hazardous and tense exercise. Similarly, running the Allied blockade of Germany or fighting the submarine war took skill, training, stamina and strong nerves.

The war in the air drew dare-devils to it and created instant heroes, like Baron Manfred von Richthofen, "the Red Baron", or the British aces Alfred Ball and Edward Mannock, all killed in

▼ This Indian soldier became a Turkish prisoner of war after the siege of Kut in April 1916. Men who were in this condition probably did not survive the desert march to captivity in Syria.

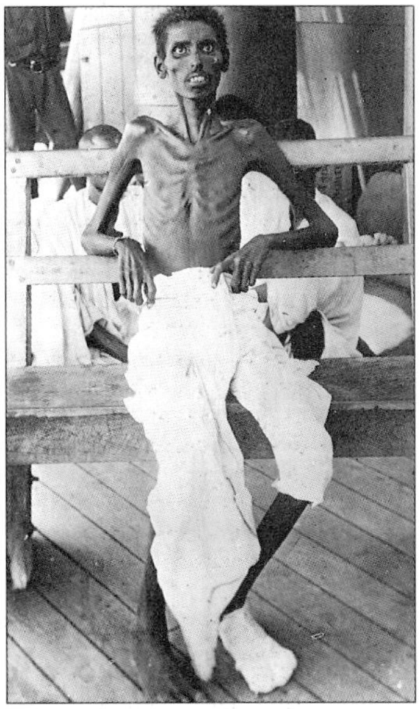

▲ This German column of Askaris in East Africa passed through another desolate landscape of the 1914–18 war. Some jungle fighting took place, but combat in Africa stretched over arid plains and vast territories and involved relatively small units, mostly of African natives.

combat. What is less well-remembered is the huge backup that was required to keep these flyers in the air. The war of the mechanics was absolutely vital, although unlikely to produce decorations or headlines.

All the men engaged in these theaters of operations knew stress in many forms. Many suffered appalling privations: little need be added to the image of Townshend's defeated army struggling through the Iraqi desert. But their war (and their imprisonment) was in a way very traditional, as indeed was that of the bush warriors of Lettow-Vorbeck or the seamen patrolling the North Sea or the Atlantic. Even when the world of technical warfare is considered in the case of the war in the air, there was a curiously feudal flavor to combat, as if the most advanced form of aggression resurrected ancient and decorous codes of conduct. In contrast the war in the trenches was terrifyingly new. Not only were there the innovations in weaponry but also the unprecedented degree of stress faced by hundreds of thousands of men. The British historian John Keegan has put it this way. To cope with fear a soldier in the Battle of Agincourt (1415) could ride or run to the safety of the next hill; his descendant at Waterloo (1815) could arrive a day late or take a wrong turn. But where could a soldier go when he had reached the limits of his endurance at Verdun or Passchendaele? It is true that most soldiers saw limited and intermittent duty in the trenches, but eight days could last a lifetime. And the fact of prior experience may not have made it any easier for a man to go back up the line, or to maintain morale during a retreat, as the German army did in late 1918. The world they knew was indeed unique. What is most remarkable is not that some broke under the strain, but that so many did not. Their resilience is one of the mysteries of the war.

MEDICAL SERVICES AND MEDICINE

The size of the armies mobilized and the huge casualty figures in World War I presented military medical services with unprecedented problems. Wounded men had to be evacuated from the firing lines at nightfall or using barrage techniques – stretcher parties venturing out under covering fire. Regimental medical officers gave first aid in improvised shelters but new methods were developed for transporting casualties, in successive stages, to increasingly sophisticated medical posts further from the front. On the Western Front motorized ambulances soon replaced horsedrawn vehicles and new ambulance corps were created. One British development proved to be pivotal and was subsequently adopted by other nations: the casualty clearing station. This was a mobile hospital stationed a few kilometers behind the lines, out of range of all but the heaviest artillery. Surgical teams worked in relays in theaters designed to handle four or more simultaneous opeations. Their essential functions were to identify and retain the 10 percent of casualties that required immediate surgery, together with those too sick to be moved and redirect all others to base hospitals as rapidly as possible—often by train.

For the surgeons on the Western Front, the incidence of wound infection was an unpleasant surprise. Shells caused extensive tissue damage and the well-manured fields of France were laden with organisms that caused gas gangrene (infection of tissue with gas-forming organisms) and tetanus (causing muscle spasm). Military surgeons also had to contend with the poorly-understood problem of surgical shock, and with "trench-foot," recognized by 1916 as a form of near-frostbite. Many soldiers were affected by war gases which intensely irritated the eyes and throat, burnt the skin and in some cases killed by asphyxiation. The horrors of trench warfare also combined to produce a debilitating illness that had not previously been described. Called shell shock, it was only gradually accepted as a psychological condition. Sufferers became hysterical, disorientated, were paralyzed, or ceased to obey orders and had to be hospitalized away from the Front.

Contagious disease further depleted the armies. Body lice were more than a minor discomfort. During the war they were identified as carrying typhus fever and were implicated in the spread of a new disease, trench fever.

The requirements and experience of the war stimulated notable medical advances. New clinical techniques were tested. Blood transfusion was successfully employed under battle conditions, in some instances using stored blood rather than blood from immediate donors. X-ray equipment was routinely supplied to casualty-clearing stations to locate bullets and shrapnel. The controversial concept of medical specialization itself gained ground, as did that of trained, women nurses working at the Front.

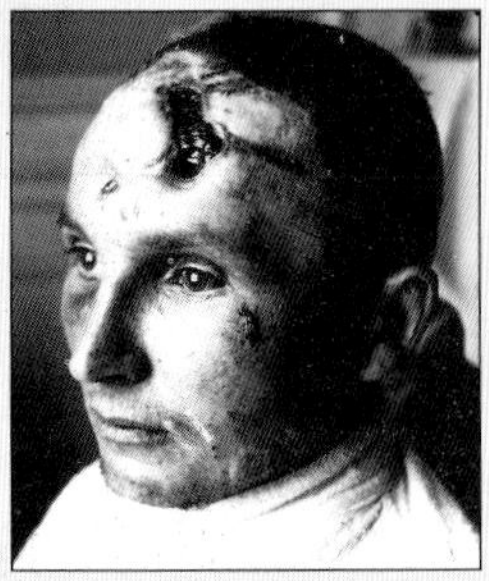

▲ Shells blew away bone and muscle, leaving wounds which were hard to close.

◀ German wounded receiving mail. Some base hospitals had 20,000 beds.

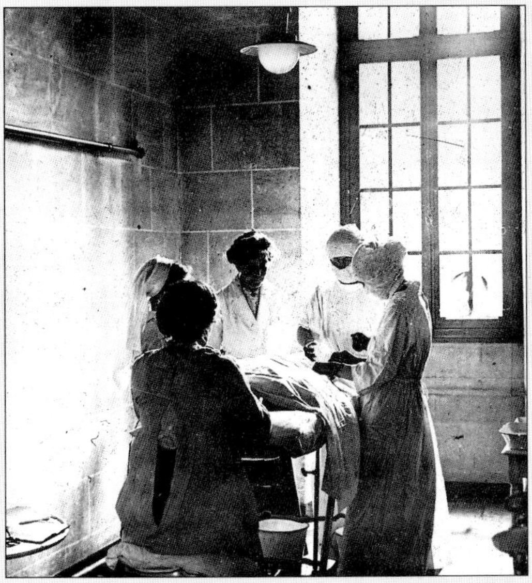

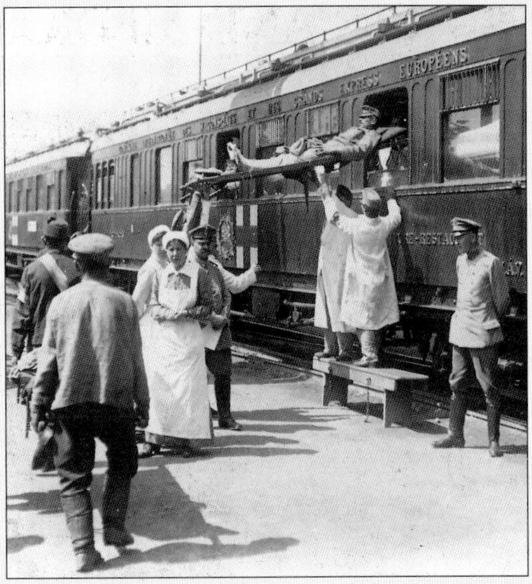

◀ Despite makeshift conditions (far left), surgeons attached to field hospitals gained unrivaled experience and established safe techniques for head, chest and abdominal operations. Ambulance trains (left), with 500 or more casualties, covered the long distances to base hospitals.

▼ Detail of ***An Advanced Dressing Station at the Front***, by Henry Tonks, a British artist who had been a qualified surgeon. In 1917 he was sent to the Somme to paint this scene. He peopled it with casualties sketched throughout his wartime experience. Medical officers are seen classifying the wounded, and the absolute dependence on stretcher bearers is apparent.

Datafile

Despite the fact that the war on the Russian Front ended with the Bolshevik revolution of November 1917, casualties in the last year of the war equalled or surpassed those of the previous three years. Partly this was due to the gigantic struggle which followed the German offensive of March 1918. Heavy fighting also continued in Italy, the Middle East and the Balkans. There was also the fact that an entire new Expeditionary Force entered the field – the Americans – who brought with them a formidable arsenal of weaponry. And we must not ignore the appearance of the "Spanish flu", a viral infection which struck down soldiers by the tens of thousands (and civilians by the millions) on both sides.

► It is one of the mysteries of the war how the German army remained unaware of the scale of disaffection which underlay the French mutinies of 1917 following the doomed Chemin des Dames offensive. Over one-quarter of the French army in the field was described as "seriously" or "profoundly" affected by mutiny. Equally surprising is the relatively light treatment of the mutineers: "collective disorder" occurred in 68 divisions; perhaps 61 mutineers were executed.

French mutinies

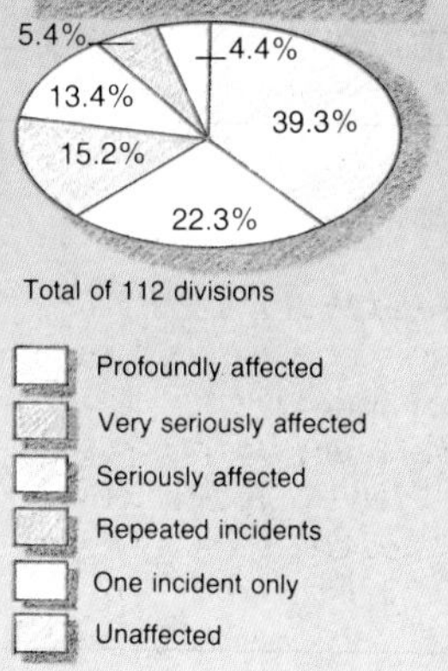

Total of 112 divisions

Mutineers' sentences

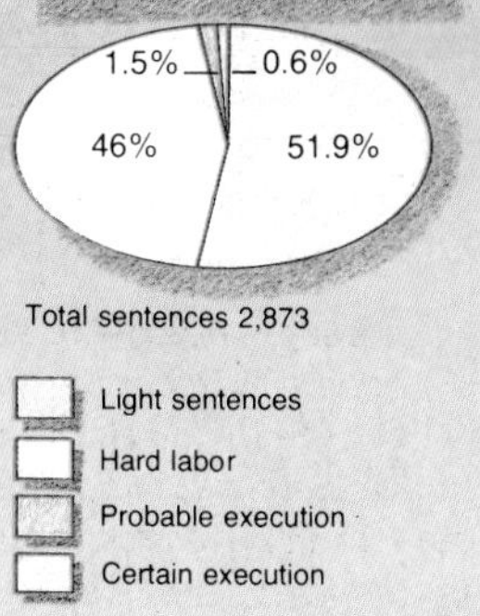

Total sentences 2,873

Russian losses

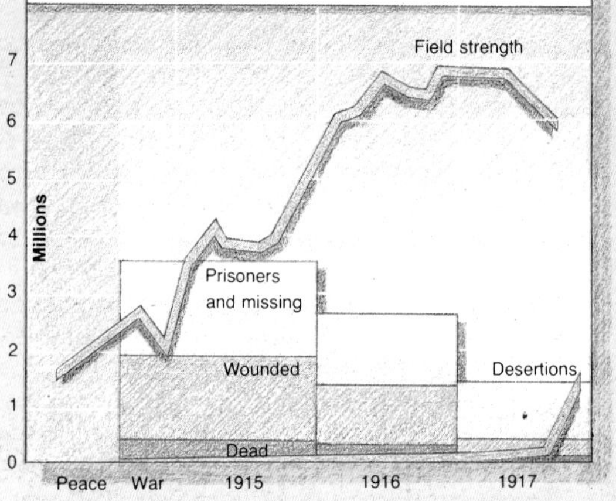

◄ Casualty statictics for the Russian army are even more unreliable than those available for Western armies. Estimates of total killed between 1914 and 1917 vary from 500,000 to 800,000. Less controversial is the steady rise in Russian prisoners of war. In 1914, on average 11,000 Russian soldiers were captured each month; in 1915 the figure had risen to 82,000; in 1916 it had reached 125,000. The desertion rate in 1917 describes the Army's final disintegration, which weakened the provisional government and led to the Bolshevik revolution.

Casualties in main campaigns

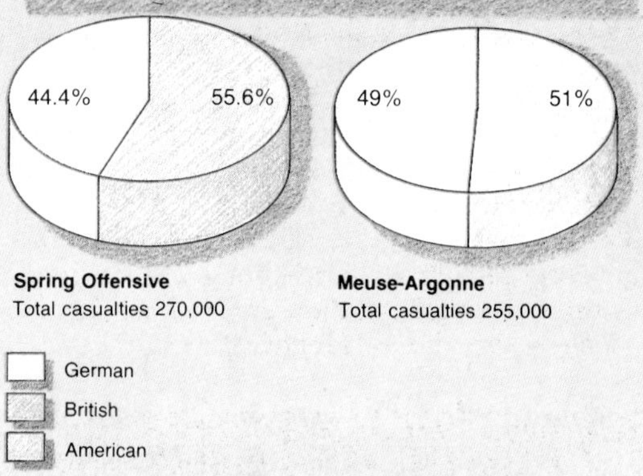

▲ The success of the March 1918 offensive in its initial phases is shown by the fact that defenders' losses, in this case the British, were greater than those of the attacking force. The fact that the Germany army remained an effective fighting force to the end of the war is shown by the losses inflicted on American troops in the Meuse-Argonne campaign.

▼ The American Expeditionary Forces had to deal with three obstacles in 1917–18: inexperience, the German army, and influenza. Substantial logistical and organizational problems had to be surmounted. Fighting was difficult until the Armistice was agreed, and by then, approximately 60,000 American service men had died of the "Spanish flu".

American troops

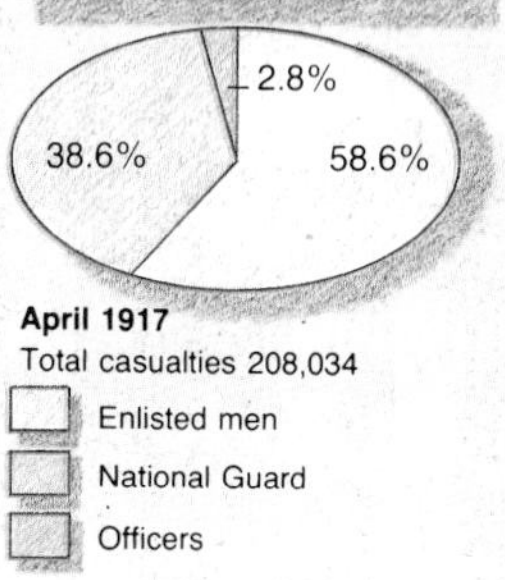

American casualties

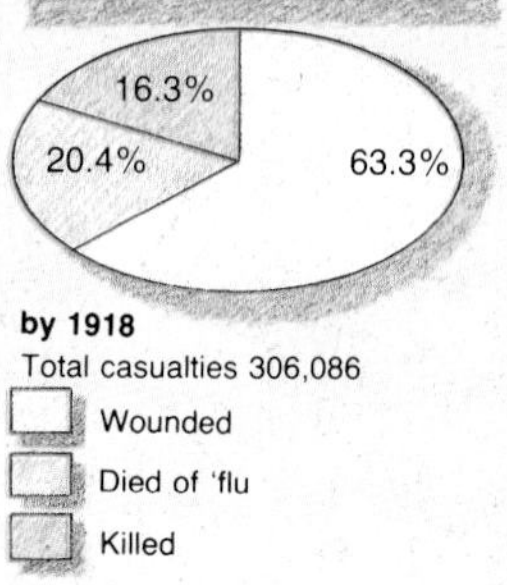

Chronology

1917

August 6
Kerensky appointed prime minister of Russia

September 3
Germans capture Riga on the Baltic coast

September 9–16
UK: Unrest in British army at Etaples training base

November 7
Bolshevik socialists in Russia overthrow the provisional government

December 3
The Bolshevik government in Russia signs an armistice with Germany

1918

January 8
US president Woodrow Wilson publishes his 14 points as a basis for peace

January 28
RUSS: Bolsheviks found the Red Army

March 3
Russia signs the Treaty of Brest-Litovsk

March 21
The Germans launch their Spring Offensive on the Western Front and push back the Allied forces

April 1
British Royal Air Force established

April 2
US: American forces fight on the Western Front for the first time

April 10
UK: Parliament passes third Military Conscription Bill (upper age limit extended to 50; conscription extended to Ireland)

April 14
Foch appointed commander in chief of Allied forces (except for Belgian army)

April 21
German air "ace" Manfred von Richthofen shot down

May
(to Oct. 1919) Allied forces intervene in the Russian civil war

May 7
The Central Powers and Romania sign the Peace of Bucharest

July
(to Nov. 10) Allied counteroffensive on the Western Front: German forces are pushed back toward the border of Germany

September 30
The Allies and Bulgaria conclude an armistice

October 3–4
The German government offers peace based on President Wilson's 14 points

October 4
British and Arab forces occupy Damascus

October 28
German sailors begin mutiny at Kiel

November 3
Austria-Hungary sues for peace with the Allies

November 4–5
Antiwar and pro-Bolshevik risings in Germany

November 9
Kaiser Wilhelm II abdicates from throne of German Empire

November 11
The Allies and Germany sign the Armistice: fighting ends on the Western Front at 11 a.m.

1917–18 REVOLUTION AND PEACE

After three years of war morale begins to falter

Serious mutinies in the French army

In July 1917 the Russian army dissolves

A crisis in morale hits German forces in 1918

A naval mutiny in October 1918 spreads to the army and industry

The British army is free of similar mutiny

But in September 1917 a giant brawl occurs at Etaples

In the last 18 months of World War I, in 1917–18, the bonds of commitment among both soldiers and civilians began to loosen, and in certain cases completely unraveled. In 1917 there was a crisis of morale in several combatant forces. In one sense, it is remarkable that it did not come earlier. But those who saw the way in which men wore out in battle like old clothes, as Lord Moran put it, knew that it was bound to come. When it did, it took different forms ranging from lethargy to brawls in base camps to mutiny. All arose out of a lowering of morale, and took on the distinctive features of armies made up of very different communities of men.

Morale has been defined in many ways, but in the memoirs of World War I three stand out. They are the maintenance of a belief in victory; the perpetuation of a will to fight; and the acceptance of duty and discipline. Morale broke down when men lost their belief that the war could be won in the way it was being fought.

▼ The "grumblers" shown here had much to complain about in 1917. It was simply too much to ask the men of Verdun to face another bloodbath a few months later in the Chemin des Dames offensive. The outcome was mutiny.

French, Russian and Italian mutinies

The first case in point was the French mutinies of 1917. They were precipitated by the Nivelle Offensive, a disastrous series of attacks on heavily fortified German positions in Champagne, east of Reims. The mutineers were drawn from units which had already fought well and suffered heavily in these operations. This was no minor incident. Between April and June 1917 250 separate acts of collective indiscipline were recorded. They occurred in 68 divisions or two-thirds of the French army. The mutineers had no formal organization and no clear-cut political objectives. They came from every walk of life and every part of France. Given the nature of French society, the majority were farmers or agricultural laborers. They were rarely violent. They had simply had enough: the most common form of mutiny was refusal to go back up the line.

Despite the attempts of military authorities to portray the mutineers as men led astray by

radicals and revolutionaries, they were non-political. Only one division of the 68 in turmoil had it in mind to march on Paris. The rest had more immediate demands: better leave arrangements, and an end to the murderous offensive. Some of these demands were met. Nivelle was replaced by Pétain on 16 May 1917, and the new commander made it his business to reduce casualties. Leave arrangements were improved, as were provisions behind the lines. Even the food got better, according to some reports.

Under the circumstances, repression was relatively mild. Military tribunals found 3,427 soldiers guilty of various acts of mutiny. The death penalty was set for 554 men, of whom all but 49 were reprieved. Those convicted of lesser crimes were imprisoned, half under conditions of hard labor, half under less severe conditions.

Mutiny of similar kinds happened in every other major army (bar those of Britain and the United States) between 1917 and the end of the war. On occasion it happened earlier, as in the mass defection of the Austro-Hungarian 29th Infantry from Prague in April 1915. In the Brusilov offensive of 1916 some Czech and Ruthenian units surrendered *en masse*. But the trouble got much worse in the third year of the conflict, when war weariness set in both at home and at the front. On 1 July 1917 the Russian army of the new Provisional government launched a

All the companies are in a state of turmoil; the men are receiving letters from friends informing them of the present spirit and urging them not to march; the ringleaders are becoming insolent; others are trying to influence their comrades.

HENRI DESAGNEAUX

American Troops in Europe

When the USA entered the war in April 1917 its army was small and unprepared for warfare on the Western Front. Within 18 months, however, conscription and a remarkable mushrooming of military organization had increased its size over 30 times, to about 4 million men, of whom 3.7 million served in France.

In the process of conscription some quintessentially American problems emerged. About 8 percent of conscripts were unable to speak or understand English. Many had no idea of what Germany and the Kaiser were. Then there were problems raised by American racism and the participation of blacks. The peace-time standing army contained 10,000 black soldiers and officers in segregated regiments. Whites feared that expansion would bring trouble, but nevertheless blacks were recruited and some 200,000 sent to France. They remained segregated and most worked as laborers, some as stevedores in the docks. But the black soldier did gain from his experience of the war: the French treated him for the first time as an equal and in Europe the racism of the USA seemed largely to fade away. The black regiments also brought their own music: jazz. Europeans were drawn to it, and the band of the 15th New Yorkers, led by Lieutenant Jim Europe, caused a particular sensation.

The American Expeditionary Forces entered the Western Front in October 1917. At the insistence of its commander, General John J. Pershing, they remained an independent fighting force and played a key role in the successful Allied counteroffensive in July and August 1918. By the Armistice they occupied 21 percent of the length of the Western Front. Over 50,000 American soldiers were killed in the war. A new generation of commanders emerged, including George Patton and Douglas MacArthur. The latter led American troops at the battle of St Mihiel.

In some ways the American forces of 1917 resembled the idealistic European armies of 1914. The arrival of millions of well-fed, confident young men at a time of crisis on the Western Front substantially bolstered the war-weary Allied armies. American optimism was well personified in a remark made by a marine sergeant. When told by a French officer to retreat in the face of a German attack, the American apparently responded: "Hell no. We just got here."

▶ **Black American recruits at Camp Meade, Maryland, 1918.**

► Whatever they said about the political sources of the 1917 mutiny, the French general staff knew that their men had simply been pushed too far. The reputation of Pétain (shown right) rested on the belief that he was miserly with the lives of his men and that he was responsible for improved conditions, both in and behind the lines.

major offensive and aimed to capture the city of Lemberg in Galicia (Austro-Hungarian Poland). Within a fortnight the attack had petered out. In the ensuing German counterattack the Russian army dissolved, its troops voting against the war with their feet, to use Trotsky's phrase. On 24 October 1917 the Austro–Hungarian army launched a surprise attack on Italian positions in the Isonzo Valley. The Austrians broke through the Italian line, and the subsequent Italian retreat from Caporetto turned into a rout. Three hundred thousand Italian prisoners were taken in the next 15 days. Many of these men were poorly fed and poorly led.

The resilience and defeat of German forces

One argument has it that mutiny was a function of attrition. When the ration strength of an army (the number in uniform) was reduced in number to the total number of losses it had suffered, it was likely to break. This happened in most armies in 1917. There were two exceptions. The first is the German army, which endured combat until very late in the war, well after its casualties exceeded its ration strength. The German army was one of the most remarkable military organizations ever created. The disturbances of 1917 in other forces did not affect it, although serious trouble broke out in the German navy during the summer.

But by August 1918 it was clear to many German fighting men that they could not win the war. High command was bombarded with reports of men refusing to go on, and of mass surrenders. These soldiers had lived for years with a belief in their invincibility, inculcated by a steady stream of propaganda. When the line began to move back in the summer of 1918 they finally lost the will to fight on.

The fact that the German army withstood the stress of war for more than four years was a remarkable achievement, placed in proper perspective by a brief glance at the history of wartime mutinies in the German navy. In July 1917 the first major set of disturbances broke out in the fleet. The sources of trouble were manifold. The fleet was bottled up in the Baltic, and the sheer drudgery and monotony of life on ship were made worse by the propensity of inexperienced officers (the good ones were in the U-boat fleet) to enforce every petty regulation.

This was bad enough, but it would not have led to a breakdown of morale had the sailors' food been anything other than appalling. The contrast with the officers' mess was both evident and a source of increasing irritation. To defuse the situation, the navy ordered the formation of food supervisory committees on all ships. Some captains blatantly ignored this, and hunger strikes and other forms of action were organized to force them to do so.

No one could ignore the political context in which all this took place. The sailors were fully aware of the role their comrades had played in the Russian revolution, and openly discussed the Stockholm conference of socialist parties to be held (or so they believed) in a few weeks' time. Their representatives visited the offices of the radical Independent socialist party in Berlin, and so provided the navy with the evidence they sought to blame outsiders for trouble in the fleet.

But as in almost all mutinies in World War I, military grievances, rather than political agitation, were at the heart of the breakdown of discipline. On 31 July 1917 the recreation and cinema program of stokers on board the *Prinzregent Luitpold* were canceled, and the men were ordered to report for infantry drill. About 50 refused to do so, and left the ship, on which trouble had been brewing for months. When they returned 11 were arrested and imprisoned. A sympathetic strike by other sailors on their behalf did no good at all. Many were jailed and five were convicted of "treasonable incitement to rebellion", with the sentence of death. Admiral Scheer, chief of the high seas fleet, commuted the death sentences of three men, and confirmed execution orders on two others. They were shot on 5 September 1917.

A year later, repression of this kind was a thing of the past. On 27 October 1918 the German fleet at Wilhelmshaven and other ports received orders to put to sea for a final confrontation with the British. It never took place. Some sailors refused to weigh anchor; others extinguished their boilers at sea. The ships that had left harbor sailed back.

The reasons for the trouble were, as usual, complex. Partly it arose out of the same suspicion among ordinary sailors of the motives of the officer corps that had surfaced in July 1917. The sailors were in daily contact with disaffected workers in the major port cities. They all knew the war was lost. All the more reason to resist any desperate, last-minute attempt by the command of the high seas fleet to demonstrate their "honor" – and to do so against the will of the new government. Not only would peace negotiations be placed in jeopardy; so would the lives of thousands of sailors.

In the aftermath of the mutiny 47 sailors were arrested. But this time, peremptory courts-martial did not settle the issue. The changed political environment precluded that. A delegation of

▲ These sailors in Kiel are listening to an address by Gustav Noske, an emissary of the social democratic party about to take power in November 1918. Noske had come to Kiel to quiet the situation after 8 sailors had been shot by a naval patrol, in the wake of a successful mass mutiny against the high command's decision to fight one last (and hopeless) battle at sea.

My God – why did we have such criminal conscienceless officers? It was they who deprived us of all our love for the fatherland, our joy in our German existence, and our pride for our incomparable institutions. Even now my blood boils with anger whenever I think of the many injustices I suffered in the navy... on the Thüringen, *the former model ship of the fleet, the mutiny was at its worst. The crew simply locked up the petty officers and refused to weigh anchor. The men told the captain that they would only fight against the English if their fleet appeared in German waters. They no longer wanted to risk their lives uselessly.*

RICHARD STUMPF

sailors went to Berlin to explain their demands to the government. The demands were remarkably moderate: no reprisals; an end to meaningless discipline; recognition of the right of assembly; and an improvement in conditions on board ship. In effect this was the normal list of grievances found in most industrial conflicts. What turned such men to mutiny was the fear – not without foundation – that their officers were going to take advantage of their patriotism and launch a senseless attack on the British just to make up for the lackluster record of the high seas fleet in the war. "What price glory?" was a real question in the last weeks of the war.

This last hopeless battle never took place, and the mutineers who prevented it were finally released in the general chaos of the last week of the war. But the trouble was not over yet. On 3 November eight sailors were killed by a naval patrol. To quieten the situation, two political emissaries were sent to Kiel by the government. Sailors' councils joined workers' councils in taking over Kiel and other port cities. The revolt in the navy quickly spread to the home army and to the industrial working class, putting an end to both the monarchy and the war.

British loyal indiscipline and riot

The second exceptional case was the British army, which was the only European fighting force to avoid a major mutiny in World war I. But the absence of mutiny should not be taken to mean the absence of chronic and widespread indiscipline; on the contrary. Throughout the war the British army, like every other, had trouble keeping order among the troops. Regulations were so numerous that all soldiers were likely to break some of them; some soldiers insisted on breaking them all the time. The "good soldier Schweik" – that bulwark of the Austro-Hungarian army, who got away with breaking rules by feigned incompetence – populated all armies during World War I. Examples of failure to comply with orders could be found in every army and at all ranks. More

Naval Conditions

Life below ship decks has always been cramped and claustrophobic, with bunks shared by men on different watches and privacy absent. The German seaman diarist Richard Stumpf called his ship in World War I an "iron prison".

Consideration of wartime naval conditions must differentiate between submarine and surface fleets and between the surface fleets of Germany and the United Kingdom.

Submariners led a miserable existence. Enforcing the blockades required long tours of duty. The need to maintain radio silence resulted in isolation. Submarines were also exposed to the antisubmarine warfare of their opponents: over half of the 307 German submarines actively employed in the war succumbed to enemy action.

Examination of life in the surface fleets of the major belligerents reveals important social differences. The British navy went to war with a long tradition and volunteer ratings. Although there was the usual hierarchical divide between officers and men, both groups were provided for and they experienced the same dangers and engagements.

Stumpf's diary reveals how in the German navy, in the long periods of inactivity, tensions between officers and conscript crews grew into conflict. In the "turnip winter" of 1917–18 Junker naval officers dined on good food with fine wine while the ratings starved. To maintain some kind of discipline the officers imposed mindbending, brutal and, meaningless tasks. In July 1917 there was a naval mutiny. It should have been a warning to German authorities, but was not heeded. In late October 1918 German admirals attempted to mount a last-ditch attack on the British fleet: the response was another mutiny, which inflamed civilian discontent.

Stumpf shows that a key to maintaining an impressive naval force was the provision of good living conditions. Without these the best crews were ineffectual. Germany's failure to understand this cost it dearly.

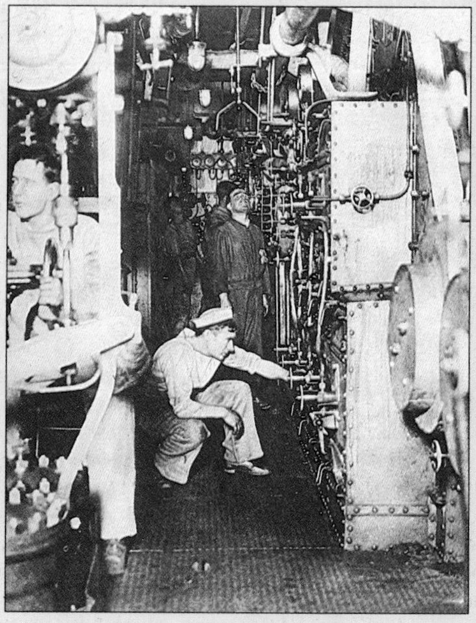

▲ The boiler room of a British man of war, 1917.

than this was necessary for mutiny, which in this context is best defined as a collective challenge to the chain of command, entailing a widespread and persistent refusal to fight the war the generals had ordered. While the British army was frequently beset by disorder and indiscipline of varying degrees of seriousness, at no time before the Armistice was it confronted by large groups of men who would not go back up the line.

The one incident that has been described as a mutiny was nothing of the sort. The trouble started at the base camp at Etaples – notorious for the harshness of its regime. On 9 September 1917 a New Zealander was arrested by police. Crowds demanding his release (which it appears, had already taken place) included Australians and Scots. They got into a brawl with some military police, one of whom panicked and fired his pistol. Two men were wounded, and one Scots corporal, an innocent bystander, was killed. Afterward men streamed out of the camp and into the town of Etaples. Some hours later, and somewhat the worse for drink, they returned to base. One regular soldier – who apparently urged the men to throw an officer, bound hand and foot into the river – was court-martialled and shot. Disturbances, apparently more unruly than violent, continued on 11 and 12 September. Men milled around the local towns; but there were no further shootings. The next day a contingent of 400 men from the Honourable Artillery Company arrived. By then the trouble was largely over.

In the context of 1917, it is stretching the term considerably to call this set of events a mutiny at all. These disturbances showed clearly that many of the British men in the camp had been abused long enough by the canaries (instructors) and redcaps (military police) – men whose jobs kept them away from the front. When one totally innocent man was killed, they took out their anger and resentment not on the officer corps or the army or the war, but rather on the military police.

This kind of violent protest against the appalling conditions in Etaples was a case of loyal indiscipline rather than mutiny. The men who rioted came from units which had seen considerable military action, and would do so again. But the men at Etaples did not refuse to face the enemy or to relieve front-line troops. They did not reject the way Haig was fighting the war. Rather they behaved as many other workingmen have done in the course of industrial disputes. They simply conducted their own private war with the military police.

The roots of British discipline

The question remains as to why the British army was able to avoid the more serious disturbances which at one time or another disrupted all other European armies. It is possible that there were differences in the speed and perceived impartiality of military justice among combatant forces in the war, but as yet no systematic evidence has been presented that this was so. Perhaps a more likely answer to the question "why did the British army avoid mutiny in World War I?" may lie in the social composition of the different forces. The French and German armies and, even more so, the Italian and Russian armies, were made up of peasants. The British army was largely manned by what was probably the most highly disciplined industrial labor force in the world. Just as in civilian life, men were prepared to defend themselves when they considered that they were being unfairly treated, or just pushed around. This is precisely what the protesters did at the Etaples camp in 1917. Afterward they went back to the war.

In surveying all these incidents, it is apparent that a much more disturbing question than why mutinies occurred is why so few took place between 1914 and 1918. Some reasons why soldiers carried on fighting after years of combat have been suggested, but it is important to note that the vast majority of the men who served simply did what they were told to do. It was their duty, because the state said so; and thus the bloodbath continued for four years.

▲ The base camps at Étaples on the French coast near Boulogne housed over 100,000 men in 1917, both new drafts from England and units recently returned from the front. The Ypres salient was a mere 80km (50mi) away, and in the closing months of 1917 the Third Battle of Ypres was still under way. The camp was infamous for the brutality of its military police (redcaps) and instructors (called canaries, for their yellow armbands) who pushed men around over a ten-day course in the "Bull Ring" or training ground. The violent incidents which took place at this base in September 1917 showed how morale could be undermined by a mindless regime behind the lines.

PART 4

THE CIVILIANS' WAR

GLOSSARY

Atrocities
Crimes of violence committed against civilians or prisoners of war.

"August madness"
The rush to volunteer for the British army on the outbreak of war (August 1914).

Belligerents
Countries or individual people involved in war.

Birth rate
The number of babies born alive, usually expressed as the number of live births per thousand population per year.

Black market
Illegal clandestine economy dealing in goods not generally available because of wartime shortages and rationing.

Blockade
Cutting, especially by naval means, of the enemy's overseas communications to disrupt the domestic economy.

Burgfriede
(Ger.) "Truce of the fortress" – cessation of hostility between social groups in the interest of a common purpose.

Call to arms
Appeal for volunteers to join an army.

Censorship
Official restriction on the freedom of the press to publish war news or on the inclusion of military information in private letters from soldiers on active service.

Class consciousness
An awareness of, and pride in, belonging to, a particular social class.

Commercial propaganda
The use of material related to the war effort to promote commercial products; the items so produced.

Consumables
Goods required to sustain life, especially food and energy supplies, eg coal.

Conspiracy of silence
Collusion by the press to keep bad war news from the civilian population.

Cultural assimilation
Identification by particular groups with national interests and ambitions.

Czarist Russia
The absolutist Russian Empire ruled by czars of the Romanov dynasty before the first revolution of 1917.

Defeatism
The belief that defeat in war is inevitable in the long run.

Dilution of labor
Easing or abandonment of trade-union restrictive practices, to allow quick introduction of newcomers to established work forces.

Food control
Government control of the supply of food to the civilian population.

Food ration
Daily or weekly governmental allowance of food for a civilian, usually controlled by means of ration books supplied to each household.

Food riot
Violent popular disturbance in protest at the shortage of food.

Germanica
Female personification of Germany and German culture.

Home front
The domestic civilian population and economy supporting the war effort.

Industrial concentration
Concentration of industrial production into increasingly fewer manufacturing firms.

Inflation
Rise in prices, usually accompanied by a decline in personal spending power.

Internationalism
Identification of common international class interests by national socialist organizations.

Labor corps
Units of civilian or colonial subjects employed as manual labor behind the battle lines.

Marianne
Female figure personifying the French republic and the French people.

Militancy
Vigorous and aggressive protest against a government's or employer's policies.

Misinformation
The publication of false or incomplete information to mislead an enemy, or to prevent the unintentional supply of correct information to the enemy.

Munitionettes
Popular term for women employees of munitions factories.

Munitions
Military equipment, particularly bullets, shells and explosives but also including transport, clothing, etc.

Neutral
A nonbelligerent state unaligned with either of the opposing alliances.

Noncombatant
A civilian or soldier whose duties do not include fighting.

Old order
The prevailing European political and social structure before the war.

Pacifism
The belief that war is morally wrong and unjustifiable under any circumstances, resulting in a refusal to fight.

Passport
Identification document used to assist passage from one country to another, commonly introduced as a result of the war.

Paternalism
The provision of welfare for the poorer classes by the state, or by members of the privileged classes to those they considered deserving.

Patriotic league
An association of nationalistic supporters of the war effort.

Patriotism
A deep-rooted devotion to one's country and a belief in the justice of its cause.

Peace resolution
Decision by a national assembly to seek a peace by negotiation to end hostilities.

Profiteering
The making of an excessive profit from participation in the war economy.

Polonaise
(Fr.) French and German word play describing as a dance queues of women waiting to buy scarce commodities.

Propaganda
Organized selective publication of information in order to influence public opinion at home or abroad.

Public opinion
The attitude to political issues of the voting population.

Real wages
The actual value of earnings, assessed according to their purchasing power in relation to current commodity prices.

Refugees
Civilians who have fled from their homes to escape the war.

Relief organizations
Charitable organizations to aid refugees or the civilian populations of occupied countries.

Restrictive practices
Limitations upon freedom of employment or use of labor imposed by organized labor.

Separation allowance
Governmental allowance paid to the wife or family of a serving man to compensate for the loss of his civilian earnings.

Social truce
The cooperation between normally hostile social classes in time of war.

Spanish flu
Influenza epidemic of 1918–19 which caused more deaths than four years of war.

Volunteer movement
Nineteenth-century British organization for home defense, replaced by the Territorial Army in 1907.

Wilhelmine Germany
The German Empire under Kaiser Wilhelm II (1890–1917).

Xenophobia
Fear and hatred of foreigners and their society.

Datafile

Fear, enthusiasm and resignation or apathy marked civilian reactions to the outbreak of war. The first can be seen on the faces of the millions of refugees who streamed away from advancing armies in Belgium and France or in Serbia and East Prussia. The second was seen in cities where students paraded and recruits were sent off to war. The third dominated reactions in the vast rural areas of Europe where most people still lived.

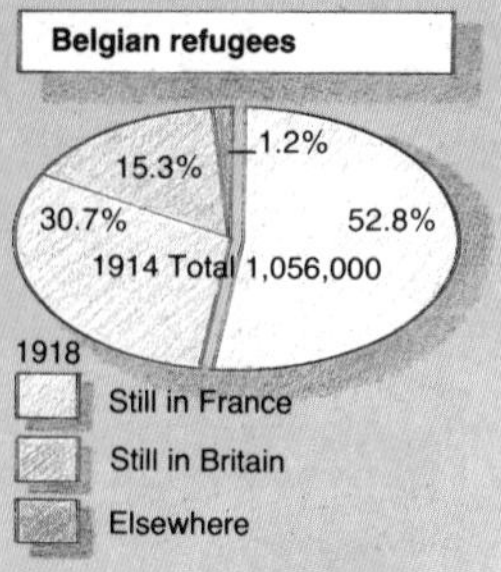

▲ **The flight of civilians from the front lines occurred on both the Eastern and Western Fronts. In the more densely populated regions of Belgium, the German army cut a path through urban and rural areas, from which over 1 million people fled. Most moved north to Holland, but many fled southward to France.**

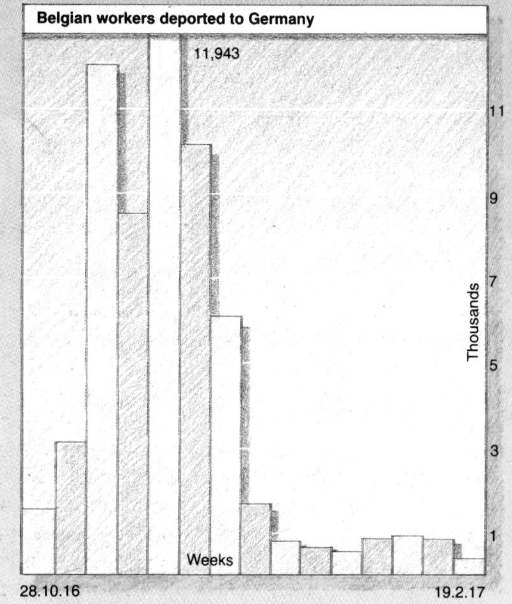

◀ **The status of civilians living in occupied territories has always been unclear in wartime. All occupations have incidents such as occurred in Belgium, where those who resisted the Germans were shot. But more sinister was the forcible deportation of 60,000 Belgians to work in German arms factories in 1916–17.**

Chronology

1914

June 28
Assassination of Austro-Hungarian Archduke Franz Ferdinand in Sarajevo

July 23
(to Aug. 4) War crisis in Europe

July 31
UK: London stock market is closed

August–September
BELG: One million Belgians leave their country

August 13
German invasion of Belgium begins

August 11
Goeben and *Breslau* enter the Black Sea

August 24
Main German armies enter France

August 26–30
Battle of Tannenberg: German victory in East Prussia

August 30
FR: First German aeroplane raid on Paris

September 5–10
First Battle of the Marne: German advance halted

September 6–15
Battle of the Masurian Lakes: German victory in East Prussia

September 8–12
Battle of Lemberg: Russians capture Austria-Hungary's fourth-largest city

September 15
First trenches of the war are dug

September 17
(to Oct. 18) "Race to the Sea": front in the west is extended to the Channel coast

October 12
(to Nov. 11) First Battle of Ypres: inconsequential conflict between Germans and Allies

November 1
Russia declares war on Turkey. Battle of Coronel: German Pacific Squadron defeats British naval force off coast of Chile

November 11
(to early Dec.) Germans force Eastern Front further to the east

December 2
Austro-Hungarians capture Belgrade (capital of Serbia)

December 8
Battle of the Falkland Islands: British fleet defeats the German Pacific Squadron

December 11
Serbians recapture Belgrade

December 16
UK: East coast towns of Scarborough and Hartlepool bombarded by German battle cruiser squadron

December 21
UK: South coast towns bombed in first German air raid on country

December 26
GER: Government places food supplies and allocations under its control

In 1914 popular support for the war effort was not universal, but the relatively few voices raised against the war were drowned by a chorus of approval in the popular press, in the churches, and even among organized labor. What the rest of the population thought is not so clear, but the masses in the towns and in the countryside took the war in their stride, thereby enabling the major belligerents to mobilize without the fear of internal popular opposition. Of course, the war they all supported was not the war they were to fight, but few had the prescience to realize what they were getting themselves into by rallying round the flag in 1914.

From peace to war

No one in 1914 had thought it would be so comparatively easy to shift from peace to war. But the transition to a war footing in the space of a few weeks went so smoothly throughout Europe that fears for the social stability of the combatant countries seemed to have been misplaced. Perhaps all the prewar talk of class fighting against class, of subject peoples unprepared to fight for their imperial rulers, was so much sound and fury, signifying nothing when a real or perceived threat to the nation appeared.

The faults in such a rosy analysis were exposed later in the war. But in 1914 this assertion could not be so easily dismissed. In effect, it posed three questions. First, why did socialists throughout Europe choose country over class? Secondly, why did intellectuals choose nation over reason? Thirdly, why did peasants and workers assimilate war into their normal routine of life? Each question will be examined in turn.

The fundamental reason why the socialist organization the Second International could not stop the war was that it failed to recognize the compatibility of patriotism with class consciousness. In 1914 one French pacifist trade union leader is reputed to have said: "French workers would not have permitted French soldiers to shoot anti-war activists; they would have shot us themselves." In the French case there was a long tradition of popular patriotism, drawing on the image of the citizen-in-arms of the French revolution and the defiance of the Parisian communards of 1871, surrounded by enemies on all sides. In the British case, patriotism was not so well grounded in working-class traditions, but it still commanded respect, especially among the better-off workingmen who flocked to the volunteer movement, the "Home Guard" (or civil defense organization) of its day, from the 1890s. The virtues of the British Empire and the monarchy were not anathema to the bulk of the working-class movement; on the contrary, loyalty to nation and loyalty to class went hand in hand.

1914 THE WAR OF ILLUSIONS

Why did support for war transcend sectional interests?

Enthusiasm for the war was real but transient

Flag-waving was a phenomenon of capital cities

Less enthusiasm in town and country

The press supports the war effort by self-censorship

And the spreading of atrocity stories

The churches face a dilemma

In Germany such a solution was specifically rejected by the most powerful socialist party in the world, the German social democratic party. This party was committed to an existence separate from the state which it would take over when conditions had ripened sufficiently to ensure the withering away of the old order. The central problem was that, although German socialists claimed to be untainted by the values and practices of the Wilhelmine state, they were in reality as German as their class enemies. They claimed to live in a separate society, a state within a state, with its own newspapers, social clubs, and welfare programs. But the very elaboration of functions and hierarchy which accompanied its growth helped to deepen the gap between theory and practice. In effect, their party had become a machine which in some ways replicated the bureaucratic features of German society. Ideologically, they remained apart; effectively, they were more assimilated – and patriotic – than they dared to admit.

This fundamental fact could be covered up in different ways. Marx himself had taken up the idea of socialists supporting their own nations in defensive wars, and there was very little sympathy for a czarist victory in the east. A party which stood out against the war also risked separating itself from the mass of its members, who believed that the conflict had been forced on Germany. However they tried to rationalize it, though, when their party voted in the Reichstag for war credits on 4 August 1914, German socialists stripped away the rhetorical veil of their prewar assertions that they would stop an act of fratricide among the European working class.

The psychology of war enthusiasm

The war showed that the culture of assimilation was deeper than the ideology of internationalism. This also helps to unravel our second question, about intellectual bellicosity in the autumn of 1914. The need to embrace (and perhaps more importantly to be embraced by) the community in arms at a moment of national danger accounts for much of the rash of war enthusiasm which spread in intellectual circles at this time. The novelist Thomas Mann asserted that "only the enemies of the spirit opposed the war which would leave Germany stronger, prouder, freer, happier." The composer Alexander Scriabin said "My Russian ecstasy is fulfilled." The dancer Isadora Duncan noted of her Parisian friends, "We were all flame and fire."

What many felt was an end to the isolation, the alienation from the masses that had been virtually an indispensable feature of intellectual life. Some accepted war as a great adventure; others saw it as a liberation from the decadence of a corrupt, commercial civilization. Still others believed it would cause a spiritual revolution, and some simply succumbed to the mystique of violence. Charles Péguy wrote a poem which expressed the emotional charge of the moment as well as its intellectual bankruptcy:

> Happy are they who die for they return
> Into the primeval clay and the primeval earth.
> Happy are they who die in a just war,
> Happy as the ripe corn and the harvested grain.

In effect, these writers were proclaiming their allegiance to a romantic war, the seductive force of which intellectuals were unable to resist.

In Britain some of these notions had wide appeal at the outset of the war; otherwise, it would be hard to explain the deluge of recruits who responded voluntarily to Kitchener's call to arms. On the continent, where conscription antedated the war, men joined their units out of a mixture of duty and conformity to the law. It may be useful to borrow an analogy of the philosopher Bertrand Russell which he used to describe the ambience of the early days of the war. Perhaps the trajectory of the "August madness" was a collective manifestation of a very familiar form of individual behavior, namely a love affair. In the first stages there is exhilaration and elation. Then comes a sense of contentment and identification with the loved one, followed by a return to normalcy. Next come inevitable tensions and attendant grumbling, followed in a few cases by separation, in others by resignation, quiet despair

These students in Berlin were the enthusiasts of August 1914. Here they are shown marching off to join up. Their romantic bravado was matched in Paris, London, Vienna and Prague. Many of them left accounts of that fateful moment, which have colored our understanding of the outbreak of war. Consider these words of Stefan Zweig, an Austrian writer whose hatred of war did not blind him to the depth of feeling the war released: " I must acknowledge that there was a majestic, rapturous, and even seductive something" in the air, and "in spite of all my hatred and aversion for war, I should not like to have missed the memory of those first days".

or cynicism, in some, even by contentment, depending on circumstances and temperament. It may not be too fanciful to suggest that something like this happened all over Europe in 1914.

But in some areas there was little war enthusiasm at all. The most famous instances of flag-waving occurred in capital cities. This is unsurprising since these were also centers of rail traffic, and therefore staging points for mobilized soldiers, who were indeed given a noisy and emotional send-off when they went to fight.

But what about the villages and country towns where the bulk of Europe's population lived? There seems to have been much less to-do about the outbreak of war in such places. In France and Germany, Russia and Austria conscription was a "normal" experience; men who left were just doing what had been done many times before.

In addition, expectations of a short war directed anxieties to the need to bring in the harvest of 1914. Women, old men and boys did the job, as did unoccupied soldiers. Taken together with early measures in a number of countries to provide separation allowances for the families of conscripted men, the smooth gathering of the 1914 harvest ensured that the war would not bring severe economic hardship initially.

There were two institutions which helped to mold public opinion in the early days of the war: the press and the churches. Both journalists and clergymen helped bridge the gap between war and peace and allay whatever doubts surfaced as to the merits of each nation's cause.

The press

For the duration of the war most editors and their staffs were prepared to forgo the critical function of the press. This was true in all the major combatant countries and affected the style and character of journalism, both high and low. For instance, in 1914 the German satirical magazine *Simplicissimus* shelved its traditionally acerbic wit and adopted a patriotic line. This lasted well into the war. On a more popular level, the *Hamburger Fremdenblatt*, for example, previously a left-liberal paper, became the defender of the military high command and an opponent of defeatism, criticizing, for example, the Reichstag peace resolution of 1917. Such changes of attitude were common, and were not at all surprising in a country where the press was traditionally responsible not to the public but to a particular interest group or party. When the parties accepted the *Burgfrieden*, or truce of the fortress, so did the press.

Circulation figures in wartime Germany rose in a spectacular fashion, which is understandable at a time when so many lives were at stake. But what was printed was rarely reliable; and the effect of "a state of siege on truth" was ultimately to undermine the credibility of the press.

One difficulty in handling the evidence of the wartime press is that it was censored virtually from the first day of hostilities. Military authorities of course made efforts to stop the publication of information likely to be of use to the enemy, but a kind of self-censorship was also evident early on in the war. This took four forms. The first was simply not to report bad news. Very few people knew of the scale of the carnage of the battles of 1914, when over 400,000 French soldiers were killed. In the British press a similar veil of silence was drawn over the loss of the battleship *Audacious* in October 1914.

Secondly, the press encouraged its readers to believe that victory was within easy reach. "Berlin anxious. Vienna in a panic" read one headline on 2 September 1914 in the Parisian paper *Le Matin* and the same kind of thing appeared repeatedly on the other side too.

Thirdly, newspapers made light of the dangers facing the men at the Front, turning them into happy-go-lucky daredevils. One correspondent assured readers of *Le Petit Parisien* that "our troops laugh at machine guns now... Nobody pays the slightest attention to them". The same journal printed what purported to be a letter from a soldier who wanted to assure the readers that "The German shells are not nearly as bad as they appear to be." This seemed to be the sentiment of one wounded soldier, whose story appeared in *Echo de Paris* on 15 August 1914: "My wound? It doesn't matter... But make sure you tell them that all Germans are cowards and that the only problem is how to get at them. In the skirmish where I got hit, we had to shout insults at them

▲ This scene of an anti-German riot in High Street, Poplar, in the East End of London describes the release of xenophobia in the early days of the war. Russian and Polish families suffered from the indiscriminate hostility of crowds too ignorant or inebriated to distinguish between foreigners on "our" side and enemy aliens. All "strange-sounding" names were suspect in war. This was as true of the elite as it was of the masses; witness the conversion of one part of the British royal family from Battenburg to Mountbatten.

The Occupation of Belgium

On 20 August 1914 German troops entered Brussels. The king of Belgium and his government fled, as did one million other Belgians (out of a total population of 7.5 million). All of Belgium, except the Flanders region (behind the Allied line), was placed under the rule of a German military governor-general, who ruled by decree. Belgian provincial councils were suppressed; many burgomasters were deported; and in 1917 the indigenous judiciary was removed. The Germans also levied a tax to pay for the maintenance of the occupying army.

From the start the Belgian economy was shattered. The industrial base was deprived of raw materials and markets, and contracted. By July 1918 the occupying power had confiscated or destroyed 167 factories and what could not be shipped to Germany was systematically looted. The remaining industrial installations, including 26 blast furnaces, were razed. By the end of hostilities over 800,000 men were unemployed and one-third of the population was on public assistance.

By early 1915, the country faced famine. Aid was provided by a semiofficial "Comité Nationale de Secours et d'Alimentation". It had been formed to distribute supplies shipped to Belgium by the "Commission for Relief in Belgium". These relief organizations operated with the acquiescence of Britain and Germany, although in 1917 alone 12 ships bringing supplies were torpedoed by German U-boats. However nothing they did could fill the gap between prewar and wartime import levels. Total imports between 1915 and the end of hostilities in 1918 equaled the total of imports for 1913 alone.

The Comité did however succeed in establishing an effective distribution chain via soup kitchens and public assistance institutions and hospitals. But it was quite unable to prevent a flourishing black market, based on domestic produce. By the end of the war, black market prices were estimated to be 1,200 percent above 1914 prices.

The result for the Belgian population was that people did without basic necessities. They reverted to preindustrial diets of bread and potatoes and were deprived of meat and dariy products. Wartime mortality rates were more than double those of peacetime. The birthrate fell by 75 percent, in part on account of severe malnutrition. The war, for Belgians, was a total disaster.

◄ The German treatment of Belgian civilians was the subject of much controversy during the war. Atrocity stories abounded from the outset; virtually all were pure fantasy. But what was true was bad enough. There were numerous accurate accounts of harsh German punishment and reprisals for Belgian harassment of their troops during the August 1914 offensive. Thereafter the specter of espionage made German soldiers, like the one in this photograph, suspicious of every civilian. But this image captures a wider truth: there were no noncombatants in the war. The conflict obliterated the distinction between civilian and military targets in wartime, a distinction which has never been effectively revived.

▼ The first economic crisis of the war arose at its outbreak. But once the harvest of 1914 was gathered in, it became clear that the war could become part of everyday life. Here we see two kinds of activity going on side by side in the Belgian countryside. Women carried on the fieldwork, while the civil guard and army dug trenches in the very same fields.

▲ **To many Poles, and even more to Jews, the arrival of German troops in Russian Poland in 1914 was initially greeted with enthusiasm. This German band is playing on the streets of occupied Lodz in December 1914.**

▼ **The Bishop of London, Dr Winnington-Ingram, in uniform. His bellicosity was matched by churchmen in every combatant country.**

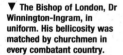

to make them come out and fight." The fourth kind of propaganda journalists spread without any order to do so was most sinister. This was the portrayal of the enemy as a monster. Here the art of the caricaturist, used to feeding off the physical idiosyncracies of leading politicians, came into its own. The hideous German, more ape than man, was a constant preoccupation of Allied journalists; similar instances of an appeal to hatred appeared on the other side too.

In Britain and France, such images fed on atrocity stories about German "crimes" in Belgium which Allied propagandists were happy to perpetuate, whatever the truth of the claim. A good example of this is the famous case of the "martyred" clergymen of Antwerp, cited by Robert Graves to show how lies could grow.

Stage 1: A Cologne newspaper reports that after the fall of Antwerp in August 1914, bells were rung in churches throughout Germany.

Stage 2: The Parisian paper *Le Matin* reports that the clergy of Antwerp were compelled by victorious German troops to ring their churches' bells.

Stage 3: In London *The Times* reports that Belgian clergymen who had refused to ring their bells after the fall of Antwerp had been arrested.

Stage 4: The Milanese newspaper *Corriere della Sera* reports that recalcitrant Belgian priests had been sentenced to hard labor for refusing to ring their bells to celebrate the Germans' victory.

Stage 5: *Le Matin* reports that Belgian clergymen who had refused to ring their bells after the fall of Antwerp were tied to the bells upside down and used as human clappers.

A stream of Belgian refugees both to France and to Britain brought home to all who wanted to know the true horrors of warfare in their native land. But as if the reality of warfare was not enough to stir the imagination, journalists let their fantasies run wild in an effort to galvanize support for the war.

The churches

One might have expected clergymen to resist these tendencies to demonize the enemy. The fact that many did not was perhaps inevitable, for two reasons. The first was that most clergymen spoke for established churches. As such they were part of the moral and (in a broad sense) political leadership of their countries, and shared the educational and ideological background of those who had taken the decision to go to war. The second was that there was a fundamental conflict faced by the wartime churches in all combatant nations between their theological mission and their pastoral mission. Essentially their theological role pointed toward the reconciliation of enemies, the search for a road to peace, and the reassertion, especially in time of war, of the humanity of all people. This was repeatedly affirmed by Pope Benedict XV, who thereby incurred the wrath of sections of the French Catholic Church.

The problem was not just one of the blind patriotism of the clergy. It was also that in their pastoral work in wartime, clergymen faced a different set of tasks. More and more they were engaged in the consolation of the bereaved, the fortification of the anguished, the care of the widow and the orphan. After all, how were they supposed to react when they visited a family which had lost a son, and were asked whether

◀ The war made the use of passports a commonplace affair. But in occupied territory passes were obligatory. Here German soldiers are photographing French civilians in the occupied north of the country. The photographs were taken in groups, apparently to save time and money. Individuals were identified by a number in the group portrait in which they were placed.

▼ Twice in this century French roads have been clogged with grim families trying to escape from the battle lines by traveling south. These families from the Pas de Calais are on their way to a safer home. Belgian refugees traveled north to Holland, south to France, thus swelling the migratory tide, which also reached England.

their son had died for a just cause, or what kind of person could have torn their son from them?

Perhaps their upholding of the patriotic cause was simply a reflection of the dilemma of all national churches espousing an international creed. But some clergymen went further, and contributed to what can only be termed the moral pollution of the war. One such was the Bishop of London, Arthur Winnington-Ingram, who in 1915 let loose this sermon of hate: "And first we see Belgium stabbed in the back and ravaged, then Poland, and then Serbia, and then the Armenian nation wiped out – five hundred thousand at a moderate estimate being actually killed: and then as a necessary consequence, to save the freedom of the world, to save Liberty's own self, to save the honour of women and the innocence of children, everything that is noblest in Europe, everything that loves freedom and honour, everyone that puts principle above ease, and life itself beyond mere living, are banded in a great crusade – we cannot deny it – to kill Germans: to kill them not for the sake of killing, but to save the world; to kill the good as well as the bad, to kill the young men as well as the old, to kill those who have shown kindness to our wounded as well as those fiends who crucified the Canadian sergeant, who superintended the Armenian massacres, who sank the *Lusitania*, and who turned the machine-guns on the civilians of Aerschott and Louvain – and to kill them lest the civilisation of the world should itself be killed." The effect of such rhetoric may have been as minimal as that of clerical pleas for forgiveness. But the wartime bellicosity of some churchmen helped discredit them in later years.

WARTIME LIFE IN PARIS

To live in Paris during World War I was to live virtually at the front line. In 1914 the city became the embarkation point for millions of soldiers proceeding from the Gare du Nord to stem the German invasion. The early threat to Paris was contained on the River Marne in September 1914, but the city was so close to the fighting – at times only 80km (50mi) away – that inevitably a mass exodus of civilians followed. This still left approximately 1.8 million civilian inhabitants, plus an undisclosed number of soldiers and a sizable number of French and Belgian refugees who had fled south to Paris to avoid the German invaders.

The welfare of this population was in the hands of the city's military governor, General Gallieni, and the prefect of police. As the time passed and the war continued the municipal authorities provided essential supplies for those unable to pay for them: soldiers' wives, widows, orphans, and refugees. They received subsidized food and coal, shortages of which became chronic in 1916–17. Municipal soup kitchens were particularly popular and effective in maintaining civilian well-being and morale, under conditions which initially had raised unemployment to sky-high levels. Perhaps 44 percent of the Parisian work force was laid off in the fall of 1914. This hit women workers particularly hard, that is, until they began to staff munitions factories.

During the war, Paris was a dangerous place in which to live. The main problem was enemy bombardment. The first bombs were dropped by zeppelins on 30 August 1914, killing one old woman. Thereafter bombing was sporadic. A second danger was the presence in the city of armaments of workshops and factories. Accidents here turned whole blocks of flats into rubble. On 20 October 1915 48 people were killed and 100 wounded when a grenade factory blew up in the south of the city. An explosion at the Billancourt Renault factory in 1917 killed 25.

On the whole, life in Paris was gray and monotonous during the war. The use of public and private lighting was restricted, and coal for domestic heating was in such short supply that shivering through cold winters left an enduring impression. On 6 February 1917 the temperature fell to -14degrees centigrade. It was not even possible to resort to the traditional means of keeping spirits high: the scale and production of one drink, absinthe, were outlawed; later in the war, the sale of other alcoholic beverages was restricted to mealtimes.

The one commodity which was not rationed was entertainment. After an initial blackout in 1914 cinemas and theaters gradually reopened. The Moulin Rouge, the famous cabaret in the Montmartre district, reopened on 28 November 1914, with a range of patriotic acts. In 1917 Paris was entertained by the Allies. The city was visited by The Diaghilev's *Ballet Russe,* which provided inspiration for Pablo Picasso and Jean Cocteau. Their cubist ballet *Parade* shocked conventional Parisians on 18 May 1917, as did jazz, which was introduced by American soldiers.

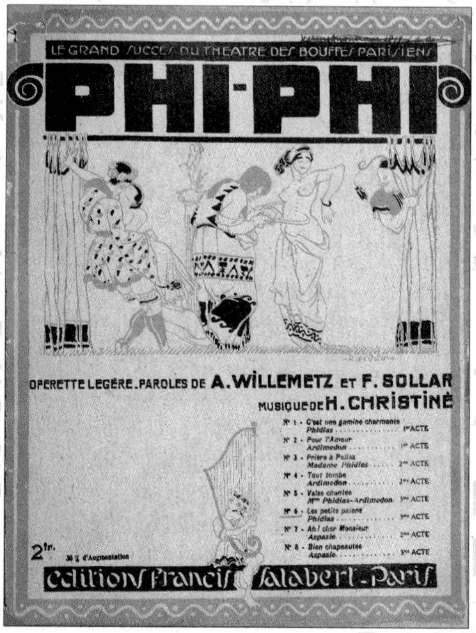

◄ **After the threat of defeat receded in 1914, Parisian theater life flourished. Public entertainments reopened on 23 November 1914, and both the classical *Comédie Française* and the worldly *Moulin Rouge* produced patriotic acts throughout the war. The prefecture of police kept a careful eye on the contents of popular entertainments (and no doubt on some of the performers).**

▶ Paris was littered with bomb craters, such as this one on the Blvd de Belleville in the east of the city. The wartime civilian death toll included 88 people killed in the church of St Gervais on Good Friday 1918.

▶ Queues in front of the Paris opera formed not for tickets but for coal rations. By 1917 tolerance for shortages and price rises had worn thin; a wave of strikes expressed the new mood of the last year of the war.

◀▶ A wine cellar transformed into a shelter during the aerial and artillery bombardment of Paris (left). These Parisians had an easier time than did the thousands of Belgian refugees who streamed south in the first months of the war (right), and for whom Paris was but the first stop on a long and uneasy journey. The sheer diversity of the Parisian population in wartime was partly a reflection of its refugee population, and partly because the Bois de Boulogne in the west of the city had become a huge armed camp replete with provisioners of goods and services, licit and otherwise.

Datafile

War meant hard work for most civilians. Women traded jobs in textiles or domestic service for munitions work or substituted for men in nonessential jobs. In the countryside, women took over the management and cultivation of farms. After work, married women had to cope with looking after families on their own, with eternal queues and shortages, and with the fear of the loss of husbands, sons, relatives and friends, or the problems of wounded veterans. Millions of families were separated. Those on the battle fronts scattered as refugees. Adolescent men and women migrated to towns and cities, as did foreign workers. This pattern of movement and upheaval led many to fear for the future of the family. Their anxieties were misplaced. Women did their share in the war for the duration only. Afterward they went back to their former lives and their subordinate positions at work and at home.

Living standards fell for most people on the continent. Inflation wiped out savings and canceled out wage increases in Germany and Austria-Hungary. In occupied Belgium, severe shortages of food led to malnutrition. Economic difficulties in Italy were worsened by a drop in income repatriated from Italians in America. Civilians in Britain and France fared better. After a period of dislocation in 1914, war industries grew rapidly. Unemployment vanished, and social subsidies in the form of rent control and separation allowances helped protect families from the full effect of rising prices and military mobilization.

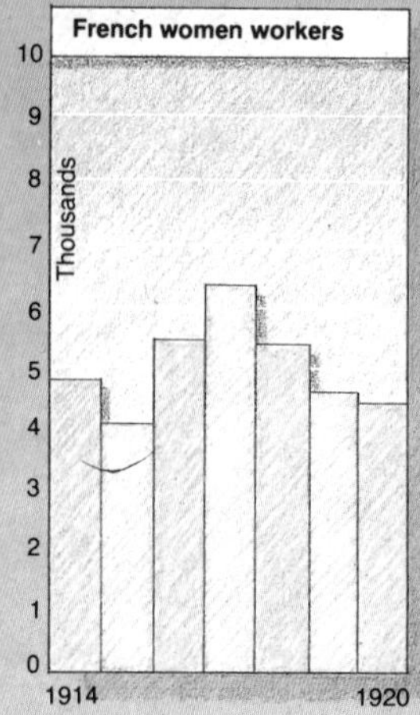

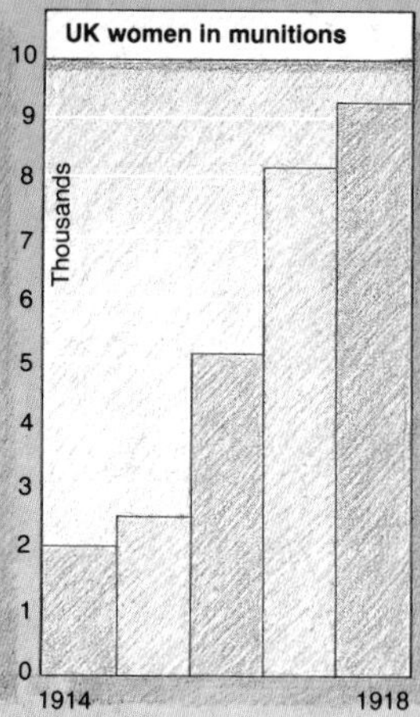

◀ The majority of women-workers in the 1914–18 war had had paid employment before the war. The female labor force was redistributed, to substitute for male workers in uniform and to staff the expanding munitions sector. In France (far left), perhaps 40 percent of the workforce was female during the war. Roughly similar figures were registered for female labor in the west, while in the east agricultural labor became preponderantly female. After 1918 women left industrial work, but remained in the clerical and service sectors.

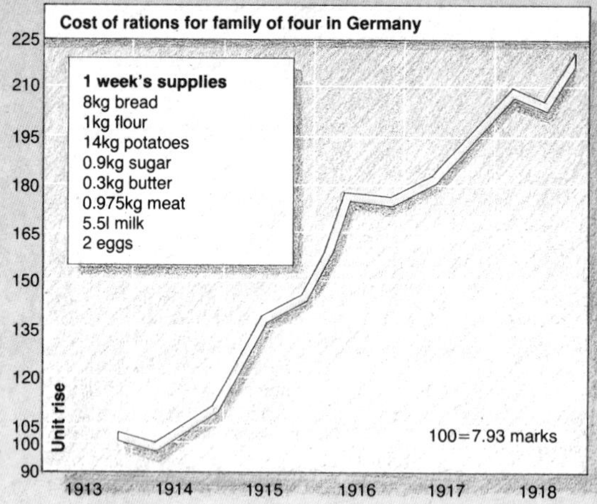

◀ The official statistics describing the rise in the cost of living, on which this graph is based, underestimated drastically the difficulties ordinary Germans faced in feeding their families. Official rations supplied only about half the minimal needs of the population. This meant that everyone had to find food on the black market, where prices dwarfed official maximum prices.

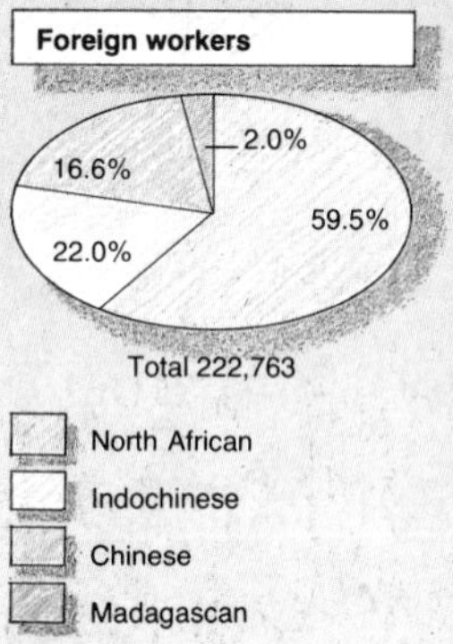

◀ During the war immigrant labor in france made up for the gaps created by both mobilization and low prewar birth rates. Roughly 500,000 foreign workers entered France during the war. One-third came from Spain; the rest (left) mainly from the French North African colonies of Tunisia, Algeria, Morocco and Madagascar, Indo-China and China. This influx of immigrant labor was not new; it merely constituted an accentuation of prewar trends.

Chronology

1915

January 4
UK: London stock exchange is reopened

January 19
UK: First German airship raid on England

February 8–22
Winter Battle of Masuria: Germans and Austro-Hungarians force Russians to retreat

March 10–13
Battle of Neuve-Chapelle: British and Indian offensive on Western Front captures village of Neuve Chapelle

March 21
FR: First German airship raid on Paris

April 8
Turkey begins massacres and deportations of Armenians

April 22
(to May 27) Second Battle of Ypres: German offensive on Western Front against Ypres fails to capture the town

April 24
(to Jan. 9 1916) Allied land campaign against Turks on Gallipoli peninsula

May 2–4
Battle of Gorlice-Tarnow: Central Powers break Russian line and cause Russian retreat

May 4
(to 18 June) Second Battle of Artois: French make small gain of land on Western Front from Germans

May 7
German submarine sinks passenger liner *Lusitania*

May 9–10
Battle of Aubers Ridge: unsuccessful British offensive on Western Front against Germans

May 15–25
Battle of Festubert: unsuccessful British and Canadian offensive on Western Front against Germans

May 23
Italy declares war on Austria-Hungary

May 31
UK: First German airship raid on London area

July 16
UK: National Registration Act requires registration of men eligible for military service

September 25
(to Oct. 14) Third Battle of Artois: French offensive on Western Front brings small gain of territory from the Germans

September 25
(to Oct. 6) French offensive in Champagne: small amount of territory gained from Germans

September 25
(to Nov. 4) Battle of Loos: British offensive on the Western Front captures the town of Loos

October 12
In Belgium Germans execute British nurse Edith Cavell for aiding the escape of Allied prisoners

1915 STALEMATE AND STAGNATION

A long war of mass armies needs the support of a large work force

Women take over their husbands' jobs and move into new areas of employment

But the proportion of women in the labor force rises only marginally

In France some soldiers are conscripted for factory work

In Britain unskilled workers move into "skilled" jobs

Living standards vary considerably

In 1915, when the military lines stabilized, it became apparent that all belligerents faced a monumental task of clothing, feeding, housing and arming millions of men. If domestic industry were not to grind to a halt, the men who had joined up had to be replaced; if munitions orders were to be met, new workers had to be found, trained and set to work. This inevitably led to a change in the size and composition of the labor force in all warring nations. Of course these developments were uneven, and certainly not restricted to 1915; the process of recruiting new labor in industry, commerce and agriculture which began in the second phase of the war continued unabated until the Armistice.

The mobilization of a new labor force entailed four parallel sets of changes. First, the feminization of the labor force; secondly, a reduction in the average age of industrial laborers; thirdly, the tapping of new sources of labor supply; fourthly, dilution, or a change in the skill composition of the labor force.

The wartime employment of women

The feminization of the work force was the most important development and elicited much comment during the war itself. During the war women took on a myriad of tasks. Some took over their husbands' jobs, and became blacksmiths, paper-hangers and grave-diggers. Others were drawn into nonmanual trades where women rarely worked: witness women dentists, ambulance drivers, and switch-pillar inspectors. In addition, banks and offices employed women tellers and clerks to do jobs traditionally reserved for men. These were instances of substitution in the domestic economy. But women were also required to help out in munitions production. It must be remembered that munitions meant more than guns and bullets; the term came to encompass virtually everything the armies needed.

Some of the pride in the work of these new "munitionettes" is attested to by the displays that were made of the first shells produced by "lady operators" in one war factory. Photographs recapture the world of women's work in trades as diverse as the manufacture of army tropical helmets and airplane propellers, as well as in caustic soda works, coke works and the numerous filling factories which sprang up throughout Europe. These changes elicited much anxious comment at the time. Employing women on jobs

▼ In addition to traditional tasks in farming and textiles, women's war work included munitions production, clerical work, transport and all kinds of manual labor. This photograph of local women in a British ammunition dump in Italy may have suggested that women who should have been cradling babies were cradling bombs.

traditionally done by men presented a challenge to traditional sex roles. Some concerned voices were raised about the moral dangers of industrial work, the physical risks to the health of women, and the prospect of child neglect presented by the full-time labor of mothers.

These (usually male) commentators were right in pointing to the fact that the war efforts required the mobilization of women in the labor force. But they both understated the degree of women's industrial work in the prewar period and overstated the change caused by the war. The French case illustrates this point. Early German successes required a major revamping of French industry. Women were drawn into new French factories, first by private employers and then by the state. They were concentrated especially in the chemical, wood and transport sectors, where they performed handling tasks of all kinds. Many specialized in running all sorts of machines: presses, furnaces, saws, cranes, paste grinders and lathes. In some areas, such as in metallurgy, fully a quarter of the labor force was female in 1918, compared to a twentieth in 1914. But this was the exception, not the rule. Elsewhere the proportion of women in the labor force did not go up much. Roughly 35 percent of the labor force was female in 1914; during the war, the figure rose to about 40 percent.

The same can be said of Germany. Women workers were recruited not from those previously unoccupied, but rather from those who had already been in paid labor elsewhere in the economy. Thus it is best to regard with considerable skepticism the numerous statements made during the war about its "revolutionary" effects on women's work.

After the Armistice, older patterns were restored in industry. In contrast, lasting gains in opportunities were registered in the clerical and commercial sectors. In Britain the female labor force in commerce rose by 400,000 during the war, and stayed high in the postwar years.

It is much more difficult to be precise about what war work meant to these women. Many recall the sociability of the job, and the satisfaction of learning new skills. But others recall the long hours and the double burden of paid work and unpaid child-minding and housework, which meant queuing up for scarce supplies either before or after working hours. German women ironically called these queues "polonaises", snaking their way slowly into a shoemaker's shop, a bakery or a butcher's shop.

Patriotism may have carried many along initially, but the glamor of war work faded very rapidly, as the second set of workers recruited to war industry – adolescents – also found. Here too we must be wary of attributing to the war what had long been a fact of industrial life. Whatever the law said about compulsory education, boys and girls were employed in marginal tasks before the war in both agriculture and industry. The war simply brought out into the open and tacitly legitimated what had long gone on in the shadows. The education of these adolescents clearly mattered less than providing the men at the Front with the tools of war.

◀ The war brought about a change in the distribution of the female labor force. Women replaced men who had enlisted in all kinds of labor, like this bill poster in Thetford in East Anglia, England (top), or the mechanic on the Parisian metro (center). Much of the work was dreary and unending. The working week for many war workers extended to more than 70 hours. The weight on the back of the woman coke worker (bottom) should help dispel any lingering romantic illusions about women's work during the war.

▲ These women workers in a German state munitions factory performed a variety of tasks. These are turners and lathe operators in a shell factory, doing the kind of skilled work denied to women before the war. Between 1913 and 1917 the total female labor force employed in metal works rose from 606 to 11,816, or from 5 percent to fully 28 percent of the labor force. The rise in women's wages was substantial. Before the war the average take-home pay for female metalworkers was about 2 marks per day; by 1917 they took home between 5 and 6 marks per day. A year later the figure rose to about 7 marks for a 10-hour day, an unprecedented wage for women's manual labor.

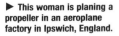

► This woman is planing a propeller in an aeroplane factory in Ipswich, England.

Women's Attitudes to the War

Many wartime propaganda images suggest that women stood firmly behind the war effort. Women's attitudes, however, were as varied as their lives. Certainly there were patriotic bigots – among them England's Mrs Pankhurst. Behind extreme patriotism often lay fear or anger. As one propagandist reported, of her visit to a munitions factory in England: "I speak to two High School Mistresses from a town that has several times been visited by Zeppelins. 'We just felt that we must come and help kill Germans', they say quietly ..." At the other end of the spectrum were the pacifists, who like the ardent patriots were in a minority. The views of most women lay between the two. Many realized that their labor would "release" men from their jobs to serve in the army, or that their work would help maintain the war. Some middle-class women soon gave up their new jobs, not wanting to support the conflict in any way; they could afford to do so. Working-class women had to work on, even though as one woman wrote: "Only the fact that I am using my lifes (sic) energy to destroy human souls, gets on my nerves. Yet on the other hand, I am doing what I can to bring this horrible affair to an end." The idea of women "doing their bit" has become a cliché, yet many women did feel they must do something to help the men.

Surprising as it may seem, there were also women who were left almost untouched by the war. Many very young or older women had no husbands or brothers in the trenches. They recognized the horror of the conflict but were personally unaffected. They threw themselves into war work – they were enthusiastic about the new jobs, new wages and new freedom. For them it was the twenties and thirties which brought poverty and misery.

► **A pre-revolutionary Russian war worker.**

Industrial recruitment and dilution

The third group of recruits to the war industries came from outside traditional channels. In France, foreigners, especially from the Mediterranean countries, and residents in French colonies were put to work. So were prisoners-of-war and disabled soldiers. In addition, in France (but not in Britain), soldiers were conscripted and then directed to work in factories, and did so under military discipline.

The need to intensify production and maximize output led to a series of changes that were summarized under the heading of "dilution". Essentially this meant the end of the demarcation of some jobs as skilled and others as unskilled. This divide had been the subject of long and bitter conflicts, waged over many years, to establish the right of artisans to a decent wage, protected by restricting entry into a trade and requiring newcomers to go through a period of apprenticeship. In Britain after 1915 skilled men gave up these privileges very reluctantly and only for the duration of the war. The result was to give the new recruits to labor – especially to women – access to relatively well-paid jobs denied to them before the war. Given the additional earnings available for overtime and under piece-work conditions, where output determines pay, it should not be surprising that some munitions workers were substantially better off than they had been before the war.

Living standards in wartime

Early in the war most of these gains were wiped out by rapid price inflation. Some workers, for example the notoriously independent South Wales miners, were prepared to take industrial action as early as 1915 to defend their living standards. Most other workers at this time were very remote from this kind of militancy. But as we shall see, a substantial part of this new labor force was to show its discontent in very alarming ways, later in the war. One source of these disturbances was visible from early on. This was the phenomenon of "profiteering". The term "profiteer" itself had been coined to denote those who had made a fortune out of the Napoleonic wars (1800–15). A century later, rumors spread about similar practices in several European countries. We have only sketchy evidence to back up these claims, but

► **These men of the Egyptian Labor Corps, stationed at Boulogne, formed part of a huge multinational and multiracial labor force backing up Allied units. By 1918 over 250,000 men from China, Vietnam, Egypt, India, the West Indies, South Africa and elsewhere were employed in all kinds of construction, maintenance and repair work. Given the endemic racial prejudice of the time, it is not surprising that they were segregated in special camps, and when they complained about conditions of wages, treated with the utmost severity. In September 1917, 23 Egyptian workers were shot after a strike at Boulogne. In the following months, 9 Chinese workers were killed in a similar disturbance. Such actions would have provoked a storms of protest had the victims been white; but no one in or outside the army spoke out against these brutal measures.**

they did describe one feature of the wartime scene. In Germany the *declared* profits and dividends in joint stock-companies in 1915–16 were at the same level as in 1913. It will never be known whether or not this represented the normal sleight-of-hand tricks of accountancy, but there are many other indicators that show that profit margins rose in those sectors of industry supplying the war effort. Some firms in iron and steel did particularly well, as might be expected. As a rule, the larger the firm, the better were its chances of increasing its return on capital, whatever the inflation rate. Government agents appreciated the economies of scale to be gained by dealing with large units of production. Consequently, industrial concentration intensified during the war.

The benefits reaped by this well-to-do section of the population were not hidden at the time. Holiday resorts and spas still did a thriving business, and the luxuries some of the rich took for granted remained available, albeit at vastly inflated prices. The rest of the home population had a much harder time dealing with war conditions. The old, the retired, and those living on fixed incomes were impoverished by war inflation. Similarly affected were white-collar workers, particularly those in the lower grades. The position of manual workers varied according to the distance of their jobs from the war economy: the closer they were to the heart of the war effort, the better off they were. This may explain why so many women who had worked in the textile trades before the war moved into munitions work; they simply could not afford to stay put while the purchasing power of their wages diminished day by day.

Overall there was substantial variation in standards of living in wartime. In Germany average real wages for all employees dropped by ten percent in each wartime year. This covered a range of experience. Some munitions workers found that their pay kept up with prices; most did not. In France and Britain real wages were eroded early in the war, and picked up later. In occupied Belgium destitution was the fate of a substantial part of the population throughout the war.

Food supply

The food situation also varied considerably. Here we confront one of the fundamental errors of the German war effort. When it came to food supply the German high command was adamant in giving the army priority over civilians. This may seem common sense, but in a long war it was an invitation to disaster. By failing to organize civilian food distribution properly, the German leadership not only ensured chronic disaffection, it also undermined the efficiency of the munitions effort itself.

Making matters worse for the Central Powers was the combination of the Allied blockade and the run of poor and disastrous harvests in the middle years of the war in Germany and Austria-Hungary, leading to the infamous "turnip winter" of 1916–17. But bad management made a poor situation a critical one. Alongside absurd mistakes in pricing policies, which created a glut one month and a dearth the next, there was the shortage of men, horses and oxen needed to till the land. The result was an increasingly inadequate food supply, and eventually malnutrition. Some parts of Europe reverted to a kind of

▶ This photograph of the ruins of Termonde in Belgium gives some idea of the landscape of civilian life near the front lines. The widespread destruction of houses and utilities increased the risk of accidents to children and the spread of water-borne infectious diseases. From 1916 mortality rates throughout Belgium increased, reflecting falling conditions of housing, heating and nutrition. The average birth-weight of babies born in Antwerp during the war was about 750 grams (1.6lb) lower than in the prewar period.

We can get no potatoes again at present... The reason is this – a fortnight ago, the municipality idiotically announced that till the 1st of August potatoes were to cost 10 pfennig a lb – then each week a pfennig less, till they came down to 6 pf a lb. So to get that extra 1/8 of a penny, the growers before the 1st of August have pulled up masses of winter potatoes, which are not nearly ripe yet. They have put masses of these on to the market, and of course in a fortnight they went bad.

ETHEL COOPER, LEIPZIG

Food Shortages in Germany

About 19 percent of the average German's diet was provided by imported food inthe prewar period; in addition, 27 percent of protein and 42 percent of fats came from abroad. These simple statistics show how vulnerable Germany was to the Allied blockade. The response of German administrators to this problem was inadequate. Most items of daily consumption including bread, were rationed by separate local authorities. Some set price ceilings, but dealers easily evaded them by sending their food to adjacent and uncontrolled areas. A war food office was set up on 1 June 1916 to rationalize controls, but chronic shortages persisted, leading to periodic food riots. Then came the disastrous harvest of 1916, which made potatoes scarce and established the turnip as a staple food.

Official wartime rations provided about half the calorific requirements of the population. The rest came from the thriving black market, which – at dizzying prices – prevented hunger from turning into starvation. From mid-1917 food supplies improved, but real scarcity returned again in June and July 1918, coinciding with the turn of the tide on the Western front.

▶ German housewives queue for potato peels, 1917.

economy unknown for a century, with city dwellers foraging in harvested fields for whatever they could find. Of course, these difficulties still paled in comparison withwhat faced the men at the front, which may explain why so many civilians put up with them.

Conditions on the Allied side were not nearly so bad. This was partly because, despite submarine warfare, the lines of naval supply were kept open. It was also due to a much more successful effort at increasing or maintaining home agricultural production in the UK and France. But the success of Allied food policy was ultimately grounded in the fact that, slowly and in an entirely unplanned manner, the Allies came to see that the only way to win the war was to defend *civilian* living standards, and to ensure that the distribution system did not break down. One of the keys to the Allied victory, therefore, was that they were able to mobilize and equip mass armies effectively without impoverishing the home population.

◀ This family portrait of 1916 was idealized in French graphic art in the style of the *Image d'Epinal*, reiterating the bond between Front and home front. In fact the joys of leave for the French soldier were few and far between. Better leave arrangements were among the first reforms introduced after the mutinies of 1917.

ONE FAMILY'S WAR

Captain John Francis Mott, of the York and Lancaster Regiment in the British army, came from a family with a strong military tradition. He was brought up in the Edwardian country-house elegance of Kilvington Hall, Yorkshire, and was educated at Wellington College and Sandhurst. In 1907 he met Muriel Backhouse, and they married the same year. Their eldest son was born shortly afterward.

By 1914 two further sons had been born. By this time his relations with his mother had become strained, and financial problems were beginning to press. On the outbreak of war the regiment remained in England, and trained at Grantham, Lincolnshire, then at Witley, Surrey.

At the end of June 1915, the regiment got wind of a posting to the Eastern Mediterranean, as part of the expeditionary force at Gallipoli. It left England on 1 July, and arrived ten days later at Mudros, the base for the Gallipoli forces in the eastern Mediterranean for acclimatization and training. Meanwhile Mrs Mott struggled with a new pregnancy, and the demands of various creditors.

Capt Mott paid a visit to the Gallipoli front at the end of July. A week later, on 6 August 1915, the regiment disembarked at Suvla Bay, and the next morning advanced across Salt Lake. During this advance, less than 24 hours after his active service began, Capt Mott was wounded in the leg while trying to help a wounded fellow officer. Mott died during the night.

Muriel gave birth to their fourth son two months later. She never remarried. The family was housed in north London by the Housing Association for Officers' Families. Money to bring up the boys came from her widow's pension, family allowances, and a small grant from Capt Mott's mother.

The short, uncomfortable and sad active service of Capt Mott, and the longer struggle of his wife to maintain family life at home, epitomize the reality of the experience of war for millions of families in each combatant country. The human experience of World War I was made up of a tapestry of countless such individual stories.

PASSED BY
№2745
CENSOR

24 Sept 1914
Grantham

My darling Childie
How about you coming down? I shall finish parade at 12.30 on Saturday, but there is night work at 8pm. I shall be able to sleep with you Saturday night, and motor you home on Sunday after church. I am longing to be with you for a night, for reasons you know of…It will be quite funny being away from this beastly camp, having meals in a house and sleeping in a room again. I don't suppose we shall go to sleep at once, either? do you.
No more now

Your loving husband
John F. Mott

30 June
TELEGRAM
WITLEY CAMP

Orders just arrived start early day after tomorrow. My kit from stores not arrived. If cannot be sent in time bring down with you tomorrow. Will write again later. Jack.

1 July

My darling Childie
I hope you got home safely. I have been promised that I shall know the ship we go on tomorrow. But it will be no good writing to Gibraltar as we should get there before the letter. Try Malta as that goes over land. If you get overdrawn go and see Cox. Goodbye Darling. Don't worry I shall come back alright. Your devoted husband

John F. Mott

9 Ju
HMS Aquitan
High sea off Cr

My darling Childie
I am sending you this by one of the ship's officers, as it is the only uncensored letter I shall be able to send you…It appears that at about 5am on the 4th our destroyer escort left us; at 20 minutes past five we were fired at by a submarine. The torpedo only missed us by 3 feet. We never knew where it was fired from…Of course the alarm went up and we all stood ready to launch the boats till 11pm when we were dismissed.

The most extraordinary thing about it was that our torpedo escort left us just off the Scilly Islands, where five ships had already been torpedoed. Everyone including the ship's captain was furious with the Admiralty. Here was the biggest ship in th world with 9,000 men on board being left helpless in the most dangerous part of the whole sea. Anyhow we got safely through it which is something, but on of the stewards who had been on the Lusitania when she was sunk got such a shock that he had to go sick from nerves. . . .

13 July
Mediterranean field force Mudros
My darling Childie
…This island is very hot indeed but beastly windy. We have absolutely no news from the Front. Troops are pouring out now and I expect we shall be in it next week.

We have all gone through our little bout of diarrhea. I was not too bad and only had pains in my stomach otherwise I am very well indeed.

Everyone is standing the heat very well. The Brigadier has a tent but everybody else is out in the blazing sun.

3 July
y Darling Childie
have just written to Cox & Co about the allowance
nd my pay, as my pay should be at 14/6 a day now
nd allowances 3/– = 17/6 a day or £26-5-0 a
month. As soon as you get this write to him about
it. 91 days at 3/– a day should have been paid to
Cox from the date of sailing, and I expect it will
have by now. I am most awfully sorry about the
money, Childie; I can't make out how it got to be
such an enormous overdraft. I was a fool on the
ship as I lost money at cards there. Have you
consulted a solicitor about the writs? I am sure they
can't do anything without serving them personally
on me. I wish to goodness I was at home to try and
worry the thing out. I feel an awful beast being
away with all this money trouble...

31 July

My darling Childie
I got more letters from you today dated 5th, 6th 7th. I had no idea till I read the letter that they could do all that about writs. I would never have left things in such a muddle, I only hope you can get straight...

Yesterday I left here at 5.30am to go to the trenches with the Brigadier. We had an awful day, and I am not at all keen to go into that lot at all events. We sailed over in a trawler and had a long walk in the open under shrapnel fire. It was not very pleasant. Then we got to the communications trenches and had a mile and a half of them to go up. When we got to the fire trenches the stink was awful. Arms and legs of Turks sticking out of the trench parapets and lying dead all round. In one place the bottom of the trench was made up by dead Turks, but this has been abandoned as the place was too poisonous. One poor youngster in the Lincolns was shot just before we arrived and they were burying him just behind the trench., He was only a 2nd Lieutenant.

Our battle ships have been shelling very heavily so there may be an attack on. I must write to my mother tonight. All my love and kisses for ever

Your loving husband
John F Mott

▲ **Mrs Mott with her family during and after the war.**

▼ **Mrs Mott in mourning.**

◄ **Captain and Mrs Mott (center) at a regimental sports day a few years before the outbreak of war.**

1 Aug

arling
blowing a gale and the dust is awful. I was
red this morning when I woke up. My stomach
ost annoying. I get violent gripes about three
es a day. I have to make tracks for our little
een; once there nobody can hurry as the seat is
y ricoty but it is better than squatting. I wish
is beastly show was over. We are simply doing
dinary training now just as we were at Witley
nly under more uncomfortable circumstances. Send
e out something to read, also socks.
How are you and the kids, Childie? If no 4 is a girl it will have to have Muriel for one of its names. I have been thinking about Kilvington Hall. The only advantage I can see is that you will save money and might be able to get out to Alexandria late this year for a bit. One or two officers' wives are there, and if any leave is granted that is the place I should be able to get to easiest. One chap in the summer had awfully bad luck. He was killed the day his wife got to Alexandria.

Let me know if mother is doing you well, Childie. I dare say it is very good of her having you but I know you loathe the place and it is my fault you are there. I wish I had gone and seen a solicitor before I left, I meant to but kept putting it off. I have had three letters from mother now all saying I am not to worry and that she will do everything for you.

Bye Childie, I am just off to the little canvas screen again. I have taken to carrying spare sheets of Army form "Blank" in my pocket. My ration amounts to 1 3/4 sheets a day but I got a roll on the Aquitania so am well supplied.

6 August

My darling Childie
I most certainly have not borrowed money from anybody. The last loan was £250 from Cox on my mother depositing Bonds to the value of £450. It was either early last year or the year before.

We are off today just as we stand up, with four days rations. I can't say where we are going but we shall see spots. I shall not get a chance to write again for a bit as we shall be on the move. I expect you have got a map of the place by now and perhaps you will hear where we have gone.
Very good to get away.
All my love and kisses for ever
Your loving husband

John F Mott
Best love to all kids and baby

Pte A Thompson
6 Batt Y & L Red Cross Hospital
Thirsk Yorks

To Mrs J Mott
We landed on the 6th of Aug and took 2 hills and at daybreak on the 7th advanced across an open plain to the left of Salt Lake and got an awful shelling. We came to a small hill which was flat on top and it was about 2 hundred yards further on where the Capt was hit. They gave us it worse than ever when we got on there and I might have been happen 50 yds away when I saw the Capt and about 5 men fall badly hit. I could not say whether it was shrapnel or common shell but I think it was most probably shrapnel as they use that mostly. It was that thick that no one could get to the Capt at the time and I don't think he lived very long, well he could not the way they were hit and was afterwards buried when things had quietened down in the evening and a cross was put on his grave with an inscription and he got as good a burial as could be given out there. Well I think I have told you all I know about Capt Mott. I only wish I could have given you better news, so I will close with
Kind Regards

Yours Obediently
Pte Thompson

Datafile

Propaganda helped lengthen the war by steadying morale, silencing dissent, and bringing in wavering neutrals. Official agencies produced books, pamphlets, posters and films by the thousand to proclaim the virtues of the cause. Unofficial campaigns were waged through the press, which managed news in the interest of the war effort. Atrocity stories proliferated, as if the war's true bestiality was not enough.

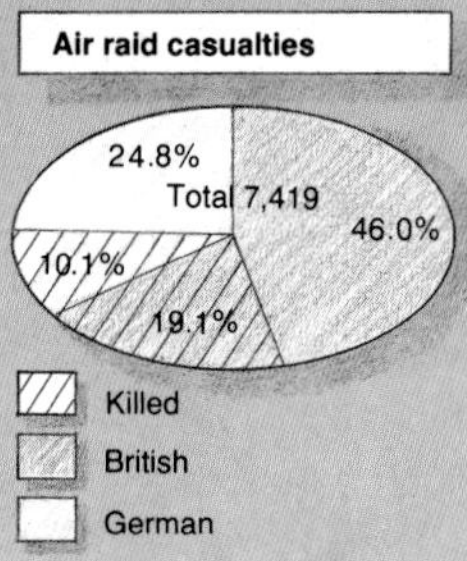

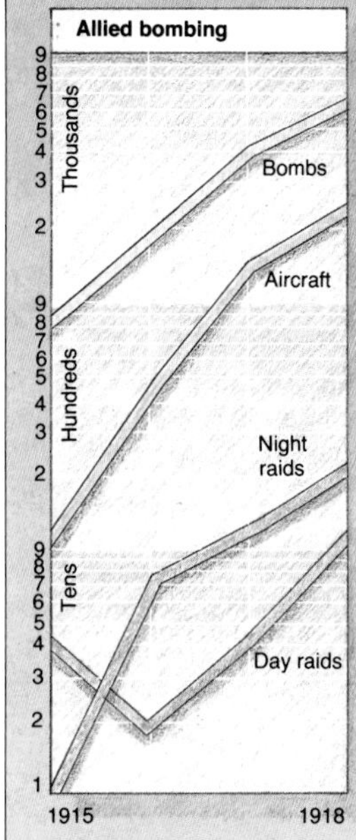

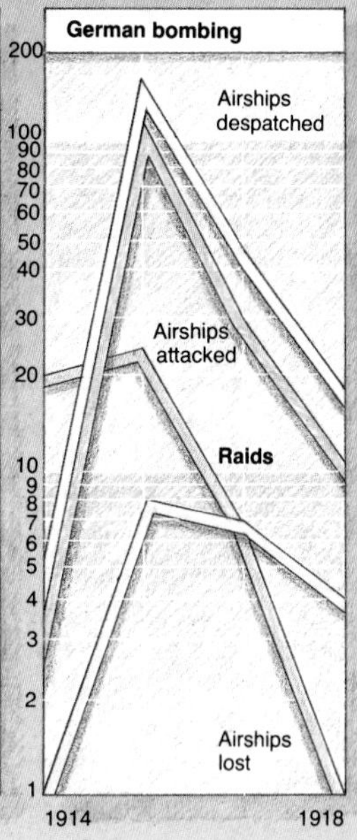

◀ Like military occupation, air raids obliterated the distinction between civilian and military targets in wartime. Approximately 1,400 people were killed and 3,400 injured by German air attacks on British cities and towns (left). The material damage these raids caused was substantial.

◀ Allied retaliatory air raids (far left) killed approximately 700 and wounded 1,800 German civilians. As German air raids diminished, Allied raids intensified. By 1917 the majority of attacks were night raids. In the last year of the war, 350 Allied air raids involving 2,319 aircraft dropped over 7,000 bombs on Germany.

Chronology

1916

January 24
UK: House of Commons passes first Military Service Bill

January 29
FR: Last German airship raid on Paris

February 21
(to Dec. 18) Battle of Verdun: unsuccessful German attack on French city of Verdun

April 24–29
Easter Rising of Irish Republican Brotherhood against the British in Dublin, Ireland

April 29
In Mesopotamia, Turks capture Kut and the remnants of the British invasion force

May 31
(to June 1) Battle of Jutland: major naval battle of war between UK and Germany

June 4
(to Oct. 10) Brusilov offensive: Russians push back the Austro-Hungarian line north of the Carpathians

June 6
Start of Arab revolt against the Turks in the Hejaz

July 1
(to Nov. 19) Battle of the Somme: unsuccessful Allied attack on German lines in the Somme Valley, France

September 2
UK: 14 German airships simultaneously attack locations in England

September 24
GER: British aeroplanes bomb Krupp works at Essen

October 28
(to 10 Feb.1917) BELG: Germans forcibly deport over 60,000 Belgian workers to Germany

November 7
Woodrow Wilson is reelected president of the USA

1917

February
In Central Europe the "Turnip Winter" reaches its depth with large losses of life

February 2
UK: Government introduces rationing of bread

March 16
Czar Nicholas II of Russia abdicates. Provisional Government assumes power

April 6
The USA enters the war fighting on the side of the Allies

April 16–29
Chemin des Dames offensive: a large-scale French offensive on the Aisne fails to break the German line

April 24
USA: Liberty Loan Act authorizes issue of war bonds

April 25
USA/UK: USA makes first loan, of 200 million dollars, to UK

July 31
(to Nov. 10) Third Battle of Ypres: unsuccessful British offensive against the German forces in Flanders

In 1916–17, as the great battles of Verdun, the Somme and Passchendaele proceeded to their bloody and inconclusive ends, a massive campaign of propaganda was launched on both sides to broadcast the virtues of the cause. By this period of the war it involved the presentation, by both private parties and government agencies, of four kinds of appeal, aimed primarily at, first, home civilians, to keep up their morale; secondly, enemy civilians, to undermine their morale; thirdly, enemy soldiers, for the same purpose; fourthly, neutrals, to bring them into the war. There is almost no way of telling how effective campaigns were in influencing opinion about the war, especially when most people, in and out of uniform, developed a kind of immunity to what was called in Britain the "eyewash" presented to them in the press. Until the very end of the war, propaganda probably had little effect on the commitment of civilians on either side. Ironically it may have made it harder for both soldiers and civilians in the Central Powers to accept the reality of defeat when it came in 1918.

A stronger case can be made with respect to propaganda aimed at neutrals, and in particular at the United States. It would be foolish to reduce American entry into the war to a response to the officially sponsored campaign to convince Ameicans of the virtues of the Allied cause. But the British appeal, much more skillfully managed than the German campaign in the United States, did strike an increasingly loud chord, especially after the propaganda disaster of the Zimmermann telegram (see p. 165) and the intensification of German submarine warfare in 1917.

French propaganda was under the control of the foreign office, the army and the navy. Press reports abroad were distributed through the Maison de la Presse liaison officer in foreign consulates. A useful and effective argument used in the USA by France was that the Frenchman Lafayette's contribution to the American Revolution should be repaid.

Many patriotic leagues and associations joined in the effort to win the war of words. The difficulties in France were less severe than in the case of Britain or Germany, for France had been invaded and could simply present its case as one of national defense. The variety of French propaganda was its hallmark. Some effort was made to organize French artistic propaganda under the aegis of the minister of education and fine arts. But of much greater importance was propaganda aimed at Germany, Alsace and Lorraine, and the occupied northeast of France and Belgium. A key figure here was the artist Hansi (see p. 229). He was a French patriot who escaped from Alsace in 1914 and helped broadcast anti-German messages to those who lived under occupation.

1916–17 THE GREAT SLAUGHTER

In 1916–17 the propaganda effort is stepped up

The purposes of propaganda

Allied home propaganda preaches to the converted

German propaganda faces a more difficult task

In Britain a conspiracy of silence suppresses bad news

Murdoch and Gallipoli

Disinformation

Patriotism mixed with ribaldry

British and German propaganda

After the war at least one prominent ex-soldier was convinced that British propaganda had undermined the morale of the German fighting man in the war. This was Adolf Hitler. But for once in his life he probably paid his adversaries an unjustified compliment. The morale of the German army faded when it saw it could win, not when it read Allied fly-sheets dropped on its lines. The despondency of German soldiers, for example at the battle of Amiens on 8 August 1918, was not induced by propaganda but by tanks. Still, it is significant that Hitler believed in the effectiveness of British propaganda, since this belief helped to establish the stab-in-the-back legend about why Germany lost the war: Germany's defeat was not due to material factors but to the subtle erosion of the soldiers' minds by enemies at home and abroad.

This situation Hitler would not allow to happen again. He consequently decided to use in Nazi propaganda what he took to be British methods of persuasion. This is how he put the point in *Mein Kampf* ("My Struggle"), published in 1925:

"The great majority of a nation is so femine in its character and outlook that its thought and conduct are ruled by sentiment rather than by sober reasoning. This sentiment, however, is not complex, but simple and consistent. It is not highly differentiated, but has only the negative and positive notions of love and hatred, right and wrong, truth and falsehood. Its notions are never partly this and partly that. English propaganda especially understood this in a marvelous way and put what they understood into practice."

What Hitler could not understand was that the success or failure of propaganda is primarily a function of the willingness of people to listen to it and to believe what it has to say. British propaganda proclaimed the virtues of the war effort to a fundamentally unified society. It worked because of the already existing consensus about the legitimacy of the regime and the justness of the Allied cause. Similarly, few people in France needed to be convinced about the

▼ War loans were a device to which all combatants resorted in order to soak up excess purchasing power and thereby keep inflation under control. They were advertised by many striking posters. Among them was this cartoon, by the French artist Abel Faivre, showing the Kaiser humbled.

Are YOU in this?

Gott strafe England

◀ The use of allegory and mythical figures in wartime propaganda was universal. The German poster "God punish England" shows Germanica defending her shores against the marauding British Royal Navy. The French female equivalent was Marianne, usually portrayed in neoclassical garb, striding bare-breasted into battle. One can appreciate the power of myth in wartime propaganda when such images are set against the more mundane portrait of the British nation at war, produced for the Parliamentary Recruiting Committee in 1915 by Lord Robert Baden-Powell.

Photography in World War I

World War I ushered in a new era in the control of information for publication at home and abroad by all combatants and in the formal organization of propaganda. Systems of official reporting, including photography, were set up. Professional photographers were appointed, given commissioned status and allowed privileged access to the battlefronts. The numbers employed varied considerably. Germany, anxious to present its efforts in the best possible light and generally speaking the technical leader in photography, maintained an average of about 50 official operators in the most important and controlled theater of war on the Western Front; France, concerned to sustain the national effort against the invader, had approximately 35; but Britain, less directly affected and chary of condescension to either the home or foreign press, maintained only an average of four.

Outside the Western Front in theaters such as the Eastern Front, control was less organized and there was considerably more scope for the professional reporter if his newspaper was prepared to finance him. Even so, although hard to assess accurately, the numbers of professionals engaged in war photography for any length of time remained small, probably no more than a few hundred altogether, including the official photographers. There were many incidents, particularly in naval warfare, where there was no room and no welcome for supernumeraries in actions, which were recorded by amateurs. A Kodak camera was frequently part of the equipment taken to war by the troops. Not only did these ordinary soldiers offer an occasional source of supply to the press but they were also to contribute an important part of the full historical record.

As far as can be established, the professional and official photographers were guided as much if not more by the publishing standards of the day as by the military censors. They were concerned to reflect the fighting effort and its successes and treated the human cost of war with discretion because patriotism and contemporary standards of decency did not allow full disclosure.

▼ Despite considerable risks and technical difficulties, official photographers (like the Australian H. Baldwin seen here in France in 1917) provided invaluable evidence about the nature of the war. So did countless amateurs, who carried a Kodak camera as part of their equipment, and left a pictorial legacy which still exists in family albums and attics worldwide.

▲ **The visual dimension of wartime propaganda took many forms, from stirring films of front-line troops (advertised on a Paris billboard, top) to posters, postcards and commercial ephemera. All combatants explored each of these media, and produced a vast array of designs and products. Some were aimed at an educated public. Witness the poster "In Deo Gratia", by the Frankfurt-based artist Fritz Böhle. It was clearly derived from the famous medieval woodcut *St George on Horseback* by Albrecht Dürer (1471–1528). In contrast, the message of Frank Brangwyn's British war poster "Put strength in the final blow" was more populist, realistic and accessible to a general audience.**

need to throw the German army off French soil. In effect, Allied propagandists preached to the converted.

There is much more controversy about the character and persuasiveness of German propaganda. To judge by poster art, film and newsreel propaganda, as well as by pamphlet literature, the German campaign to influence opinion about the nature of the war differed little from that of its enemies. But some scholars disagree. The founder of the study of wartime propaganda, Harold Lasswell, showed that conflicts between civilian and military authorities hampered efforts to develop a smooth propaganda campaign during the war. No ministry of propaganda was established, despite repeated requests by the military authorities. Instead they set up their own press service, the *Deutsche Kriegsnachrichten* ("German War News") and broadcast patriotic appeals, with the blessing of Ludendorff himself.

Lack of coordination also marked German efforts to inform opinion abroad. Private groups proliferated, but little could be expected from brochures produced by phalanxes of patriotic professors. Some of them mixed a defense of German culture with advocacy of racial prejudice, as in the letter signed by 94 prominent German intellectuals that countered Allied claims of German barbarity in Belgium in 1914 by pointing out that it was not Germany that let loose a black army on the white people of Europe. Signatories to this document included some of the most prominent figures in German intellectual life. The heavy-handedness of these and similar efforts has led other scholars to claim that in general German propaganda was elitist, condescending, unsubtle, and worked through coercion, rather than by characteristic British means of cooptation. In Germany public opinion was distrusted (especially in some army circles) as was the press. Consequently, propaganda was never geared to the language of the population: it spoke in the all-too-familiar tones of a Prussian officer or schoolmaster. It is claimed as well that this too reflected much deeper strains within the Central Powers. Propaganda simply could not recreate

Allied and German Propaganda in the USA

The declaration of US neutrality by President Woodrow Wilson in August 1914 accurately reflected the views of most Americans. Few knew or understood the causes of the war in Europe and in 1914 hardly anyone in America contemplated US involvement. But as soon as the guns began to fire across France and Belgium the major belligerents began to woo the greatest neutral power.

Germany spent over 100 million dollars in direct propaganda in newspapers and other publications. German-American groups were sponsored in many cities. Latent anti-British sentiment, specially among Irish Americans, was cultivated. Germany, however, could never overcome the taint of being the aggressor in Belgium.

The British propaganda effort, headed by Sir Gilbert Parker from the propaganda center at Wellington House, London, succeeded in building up a regular and remarkable correspondence with influential figures and institutions in the USA. By means of pamphlets, books and other tracts, Parker ensured that, for example, editors of American local newspapers received the Entente versions of news and opinion. This personal approach paid dividends in terms of forging trans-Atlantic ties with ordinary Americans. When added to the sinking of the *Lusitania* in 1915 and the USA's investment in the Allied war economy, it helped tilt the balance for war. When war came in April 1917, Parker could rightly claim the credit in helping to form the opinions and attitudes that underlay America's entry into the war. However, the Entente powers' greatest advantage was the ineptness of German propaganda, diplomacy and naval action against the USA.

◄ **Rousing support: an American Liberty Loan choir.**

Nothing strikes me so much to-day as the difficulty in arriving at the truth; there are so many statements and counter-statements from able people; but in all the propaganda, and in the German propaganda, and in the great "ouptut" of war documents which they are flooding the world with, in those I have seen there seems to me a great lack of candour... As for the propaganda here it has failed where they most desired it, doubtless, to produce an effect. The German-American, I suppose, the Fatherland counts to be loyal, but the American whom they have tried to convince, remains coldly unmoved by their every appeal in their pamphlets, their books, and their newspaper.

SARA NORTON DEC. 1914

social unity when much that was being done to the home population was divisive.

In effect, the argument is that deepening class divisions within wartime Germany made the working class more and more impervious to appeals designed by their class enemies. Similarly the hard-pressed middle class, squeezed by rampant inflation and chronic shortages of essential goods, had a difficult time squaring what they could see with what they were told about the war. The appeal of 1914 to take up arms in defense of their country was one thing; the call to carry on in a war enriching the few and impoverishing the many was another. Propaganda clearly failed to impress the increasing number of workers prepared to go on strike from 1916 on. High-sounding phrases simply could not compensate for a cut in the bread ration. Hungry families needed food, not more patriotic appeals.

Those who point to the difference between the propaganda efforts of Britain and Germany also emphasize the contrast in the nature of the press in the two countries. A strategy of cooptation required an already existing free and largely independent press fully prepared to lie for victory. This Britain had in abundance, since prominent newspapermen and proprietors were well integrated into the social and political scene, and exercised real power in making and breaking coalitions and governments. Such newspaper proprietors as Lord Northcliffe and Lord Beaverbrook were prepared to put all their talents and resources at the disposal of the government. So were German newspapermen, but in Germany high politics were conducted in very different ways. The close association of German papers with particular interest groups and parties has already been pointed out. The press reflected but did not shape political events. In addition, German newspaper proprietors, many of whom were Jewish, were kept at an arm's distance by the men who ran the German war effort. Yet again social divisions that originated long before the war hampered the capacity of the belligerents to mobilize public opinion effectively.

The British conspiracy of silence

The techniques by which the British press early in the war either failed to report bad news or broadcast atrocity stories were developed later in the war into an art form. Reports from "our own correspondent" at the front were littered with euphemisms designed to obscure the reality of battles. Thus a retreat was called a rectification of the line; deaths became wastage; and heavy casualties were a baptism of fire. The conspiracy

◀ The British royal family distanced itself from many of its German associations during the war. King George V was, after all, first cousin of the Kaiser. In 1914 the first sea lord was Prince Louis of Battenburg, a descendant of German nobility. In 1917 the English members of the House of Battenburg renounced their German titles and anglicized their name to Mountbatten. Other members of the royal family were tireless in their efforts to encourage national unity during the war. They visited munitions factories and hospitals, and in 1917 King George V and Queen Mary visited the troops in France. Here the queen places flowers on a roll of honor for fallen servicemen in a working-class district of London's East End.

▲ General Hindenburg, the hero of Tannenberg, became a symbol of the immovable power of Germany during the war. His square features were instantly recognizable, and were reproduced in numerous posters and statues during the war. The graphic artist Louis Oppenheim created a widely disseminated war-loan poster of Hindenburg, and other artists and craftsmen did their bit to deepen the Hindenburg legend. There is no evidence that Hindenburg himself objected to such glorification, although it presented a clear challenge to the authority and prestige of the Kaiser.

of silence about bad news was usually maintained. Not surprisingly, a major effort was made in 1915 to keep the story of the Gallipoli disaster off the front pages. This would have succeeded, had it not been for the ingenuity of one young Australian reporter, Keith Murdoch (father of the current newspaper tycoon, Rupert Murdoch) who spilled the beans. British journalists would not have behaved in such an uncouth manner.

The story is an interesting one, since it shows that important and disturbing news got out only when it suited politicians to let it out. It was apparent from early on in the Gallipoli campaign that the enterprise was a disaster (see p. 82). But military censorship simply blocked the reports of the journalists who were there. One of them, Ellis Ashmead-Bartlett of the *Daily Telegraph*, passed to Murdoch some evidence of what was going on, in the hope that he could smuggle it back to Britain. Murdoch got as far as Marseilles, before another correspondent at Gallipoli, who was not going to let the *Telegraph* get the scoop, told the British authorities. Murdoch was arrested, and handed over all his papers. But on his arrival in London, he wrote down all he knew in a letter to the Australian prime minister, who duly notified Lloyd George, then minister of munitions, about what he had heard. Lloyd George was known as a man who had no love for the military leaders and saw that the story would help him get rid of the men responsible for the debacle. He passed the letter to Asquith, who put it on record in the parliamentary debate over the Dardanelles campaign. The upshot was the dismissal of the commander, Sir Ian Hamilton. This episode was, therefore, less an example of free reporting than a case of the use of a "leak" of military information as part of an ongoing battle between politicians and generals over who ran the war.

Misinformation

Misinformation, some of it calculated, was the stock in trade of many journalists. Some times they reported impossible casualty statistics. On other occasions they added yet another atrocity story to the existing stockpile.

One such invention is the famous story of the German "corpse factory", initiated in a report in London in the *The Times* on 16 April 1917. This noted that "One of the United States consuls, on leaving Germany in February, stated in Switzerland that the Germans were distilling glycerine from the bodies of the dead." This was followed later by a report from a German correspondent about a "Corpse Exploitation Establishment." This seemed to establish the validity of the story, which was repeated in cartoon form at home and in British propaganda around the world.

The author of this malicious lie was probably Brigadier-General Sir John Charteris, head of British military intelligence. Some years after the war he half-admitted that he had produced the story, simply by switching the captions of two photographs: one showing Germans removing their dead for burial; the other showing horses' cadavers on their way to a soap factory.

It is one of the ironies of history that the invention of this kind of lie prevented many from believing reports about the real "soap factories" constructed by the Nazis in the course of World War II. In this case, history appears to have happened twice: first as a farce, and then as a tragedy, which World War I helped indirectly to bring about.

Commercial propaganda

Journalists were not alone in presenting stylized views about the war. Commercial artists also moved into the propaganda game. There was a veritable flowering of kitsch, or sentimental art, in all combatant countries. In Britain, this took the form of advertisements for "Lifebuoy Soap: the Royal Disinfectant", or for the kitchen agent "Vim" set up like a motorized gun, or for Gibbs Dentifrice, apparently used by one airman who found it (so the advertisement claims) as "fragrant as the lofty air". In Germany too, the trade in patriotic mementos boomed.

In France some propaganda took on an earthier aspect. Lithographs, for example, showed the potential for mildly licentious propaganda in portraying French women seducing the enemy, apparently to keep them occupied while a French soldier slips away to carry on the fight. The caption of one card is so bold as to suggest in so many words that German artillery looks fine, but it never delivers the goods.

► The picture postcard industry boomed during the war. The French were particularly good at mixing patriotism with a commercial pitch on cards which soldiers and their families used for easy and cheap communication. Many of the images they bore were banal and full of simple sentimentality. The brotherhood of the Alliance, pictured right, inspired many such maudlin designs, clearly aimed at an international market.

▼ The Michelin company made sure that everyone knew that through their products they did their bit for the war effort too. The readers of the *Illustrated London News* of 2 May 1915 were told that the Michelin tyre, desperately needed by an ambulance or red cross vehicle, was a "rib of life" for the men waiting for medical help to arrive.

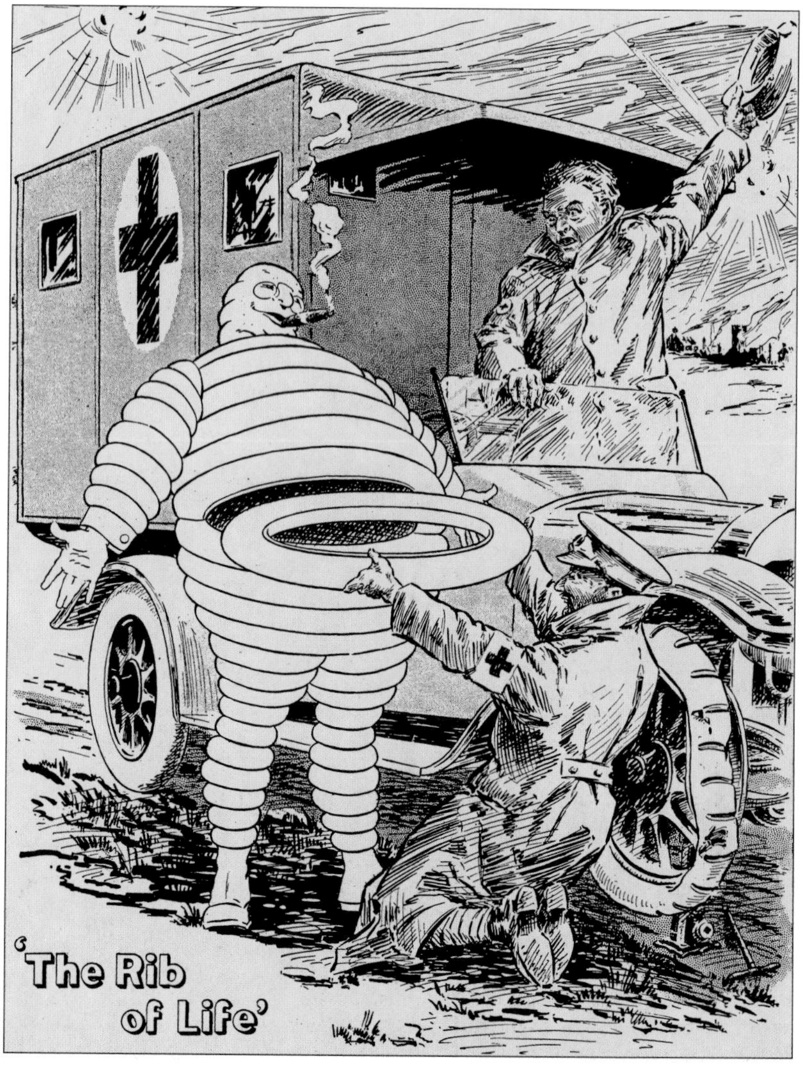

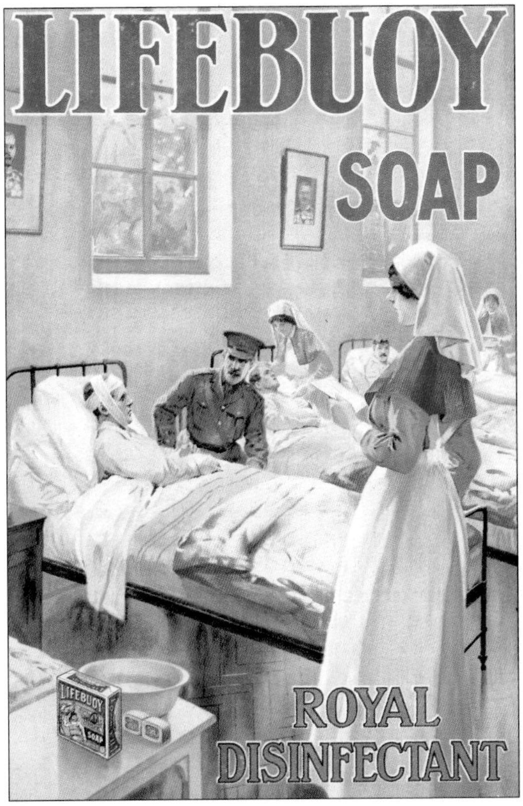

▲◀▼ Commercial artists domesticated the war in many ways. Septimus E. Scott sold Lifebuoy Soap as a "Royal Disinfectant" against the backdrop of a British military hospital (above). Other artists drew on stereotypes of women for their central imagery. In a typical German postcard (left), the loyal wife or girlfriend is daydreaming of her man at the Front. The returning soldier is spending "an exquisite hour which he will always remember" in bed with his girlfriend (below). The woman shown as the *"repos du guerrier"* (soldier's comfort) is found time and time again in this genre of wartime art.

The more respectable forms of French commercial art addressed themselves to the campaign to raise the French birth rate. The characteristic form was seen on one side of the postcards many soldiers used for sending messages home from the Front. Some show two French babies confronting five German ones, or have little boys emerging from cabbages and little girls, from roses, saying to a newly-married couple: "On your honeymoon, do not forget about us". Thus the producers of these postcards could do their bit for the war by selling a product which enabled people to indulge in a mixture of patriotism and light-hearted ribaldry. In Germany and elsewhere postcards expressed a mixture of uplifting messages of a patriotic and religious kind. Many highlighted the comfort women offered the men who fought for the Fatherland, but did so in a more discreet format than did some of their French counterparts.

THE EMERGENCE OF STRATEGIC BOMBING

World War I witnessed the first attempts at using air power against strategic targets to affect the course of hostilities. Attacks were launched on factories, transportation networks and even civilian residential areas far away from the theaters of military and naval operations. Generally speaking, however, such attempts were fitful, attracting only a small fraction of available aerial resources, and did little damage to the targets attacked. In no way did they change either the course of World War I or overall war strategies.

Two problems were at the root of air power's failure to emerge as a viable strategic option until after 1918. First, the available technology was imperfectly suited to the task. Large machines were too expensive to build in large numbers, could not carry a bombload commensurate with their size, and were hindered by mechanical unreliability. Secondly, neither political leaders nor senior military and naval officers were sufficiently air-minded to conceive of aerial operations as anything other than useful supplements to land and sea warfare.

This said, all the major powers did develop a strategic air weapon. Paradoxically, the two countries which made the most rapid early progress possessed the weakest war economies. The Russian *Ilya Muromets* bomber was the first viable multiengined aircraft of the war. The Italians produced an early range of similar aircraft and waged a long, if intermittent, campaign against Austrian cities. In the long term, however, the most significant strategic bombing campaigns were waged by the Germans and British.

In the giant airships designed by Zeppelin, Germany possessed an aerial weapon of much greater range and bomb-carrying capacity than any early aircraft. Operated largely by the navy, German zeppelins began to launch night attacks on British cities in 1915, doing little material damage but causing considerable concern among the civilian population. By the end of 1916 the development of incendiary bullets and effective night-fighting techniques had made the hydrogen-filled zeppelin a greater danger to its own crew than to its potential victims on the ground, but in 1917 the German army took up the campaign with the two-engined Gotha aircraft. Several successful daylight raids on London caused a reassessment of British air policy. Britain created an independent air service (the Royal Air Force) with the partial object of pursuing a retaliatory bombing campaign against Germany.

British strategic bombing began in autumn 1916 with attacks on industrial targets in the Saar basin. After six months, military opposition to the diversion of aerial resources from the Western Front brought this campaign to an end, but the subsequent Gotha raids produced irresistable public pressure for a resumption of attacks. The resulting bombing campaign, however, proved to be as ineffective as the German attacks which had called it into being.

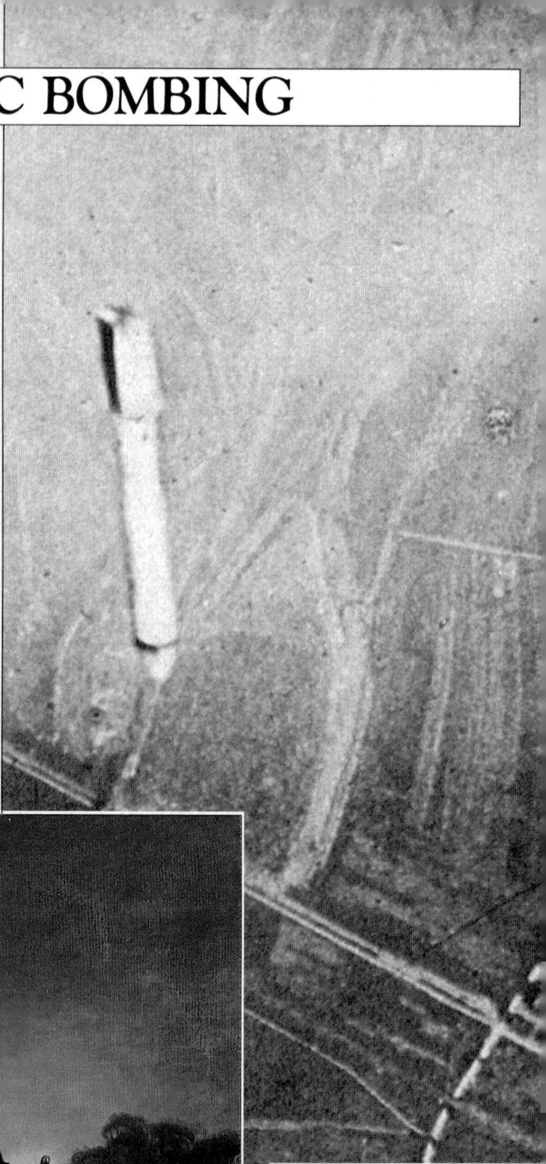

▼ **Bombing campaigns were more of a nuisance than a major component of the war effort. In early months, small, hand-dropped devices (below right) caused little panic. Larger bombs, dropped later in the war, were more accurate and destructive, but usually caused only superficial damage to residential or industrial objectives (such as the German factory, seen right, under British attack in 1918). The bombing aircraft themselves were a major limiting factor: airships (such as the zeppelin L33, bottom, brought down over Essex, England, in September 1916) were too vulnerable to defensive countermeasures, including the ever-increasing number of antiaircraft guns (below left), while multiengined aircraft (such as the German machine seen below right, being "bombed up") were unreliable.**

► Bomb damage to a residential area of East London caused by a zeppelin raid in October 1915. Civilian casualties in such attacks were usually light, but occasionally circumstances could lead to hundreds of deaths.

Datafile

Working-class patriotism was undeniable in the 1914–18 war. But by 1917 the strains of material shortages, overwork and lengthening casualty lists led many workers to question whether the sacrifices of war were shared equally and whether the war had to go forever. The conflation of these questions in Russia led to revolution; in the west, it led to a wave of strikes, and the reemergence of class conflict in a new and heightened form.

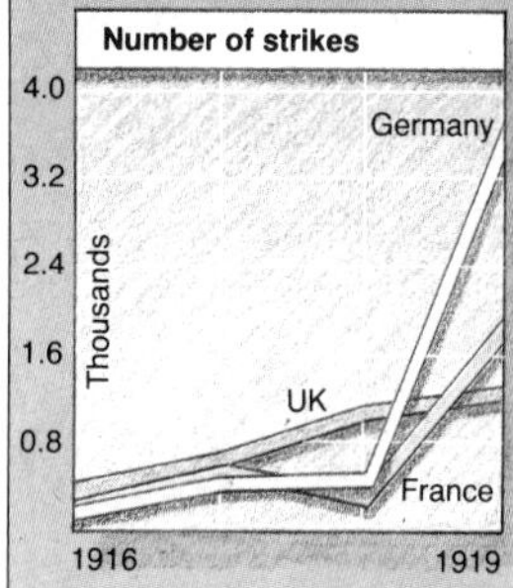

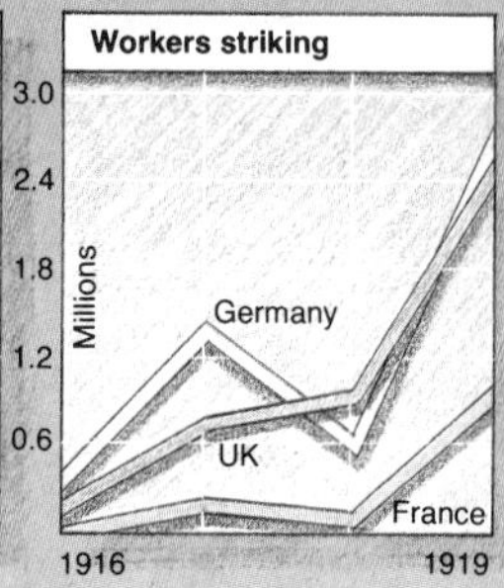

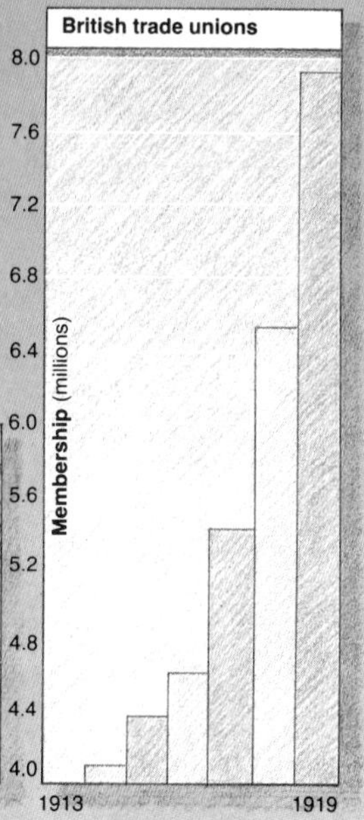

▲▶ Strike statistics in wartime underestimate labor militancy. This is because they leave out many unofficial strikes. But even official figures show that 1917 was a year of industrial conflict in Britain, France and Germany. Strikes exposed the pent-up anger and frustrations of the wartime labor force. The *Union sacrée* was over.

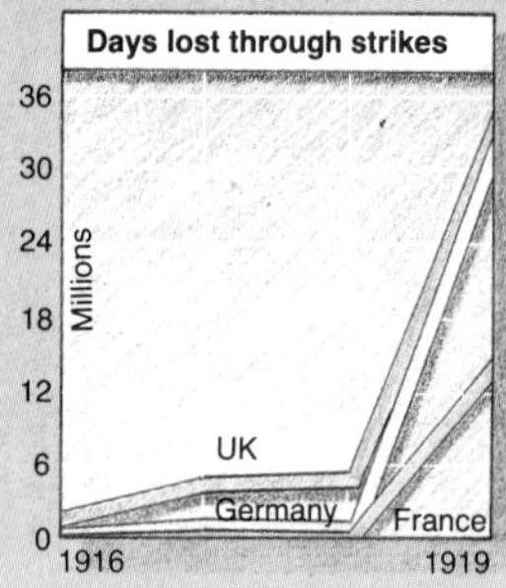

▲ British trade union membership mushroomed during the war. This reflected both full employment and official recognition of unions through the Treasury Agreement of 1915. The better pay and conditions in the state-controlled munitions industries helped deepen support for state socialism.

Chronology

1917

August 6
Kerensky appointed prime minister of Russia

September 3
Germans capture Riga on the Baltic coast

September 29
(to Oct. 1) UK: German aircraft make night raids on London

November 7
Bolshevik socialists in Russia overthrow the provisional government

December 3
The Bolshevik government in Russia signs an armistice with Germany

1918

January 1
UK: Government introduces rationing of sugar

January 8
US president Woodrow Wilson publishes his 14 points as a basis for peace

March 3
Russia signs the Treaty of Brest-Litovsk

March 21
The Germans launch their Spring Offensive on the Western Front and push back for Allied forces

March 23
(to 15 Aug.) FR: Shelling of Paris by German long-range gun

April 14
Foch appointed commander in chief of Allied forces (except for Belgian army)

May
(to Oct. 1919) Allied forces intervene in the Russian civil war

May 7
The Central Powers and Romania sign the Peace of Bucharest

May 18
GER: First British air raid on Germany; towns bombed

June 17
AH: Strikes and food riots occur in Vienna

July 1
USA: Government introduces rationing (sugar)

July 18
(to Nov. 10) Allied counteroffensive on the Western Front: German forces are pushed back toward the border of Germany

August 5
UK: Last German attack on England with airships

September 30
The Allies and Bulgaria conclude an armistice

October 3–4
The German government offers peace based on President Wilson's 14 points

October 4
British and Arab forces occupy Damascus

October 28
Mutiny of Germany sailors breaks out in Kiel

November 2
AH: Riots occur in Vienna and Budapest

November 3
Austria-Hungary sues for peace with the Allies

November 4–5
Antiwar and pro-Bolshevik risings in Germany

November 9
Kaiser Wilhelm II abdicates

November 11
The Allies and Germany sign the Armistice: fighting ends on the Western Front at 11 a.m.

A justly celebrated cartoon of World War I by Jean-Louis Forain shows two trench soldiers in conversation. One says, "Let's hope they hold out." The other asks, "Who?" "The civilians" is the tart reply. There was more than a grain of truth in this oft-repeated soldiers' jest, for the strain of the war began to tell on the home front at about the same time as it did in the armies. From the spring of 1917 the armies and noncombatants of most combatant countries became restless, war-weary and, on occasion, even rebellious. Here it is necessary to consider, first, the sources of popular discontent with the war and, secondly, what prevented it from spilling over into revolt until almost the end of the war.

Sources of disaffection

The first reason for disaffection with the war was material deprivation, which became critical from

1917–18 REVOLUTION AND PEACE

In spring 1917 the strain of war brings restlessness on the home front

Price increases and low wages provoke strikes and disturbances

Early 1918, more disturbances

Which now have a political content

Other sources of strike action in 1918

Methods of containing turbulence

The war ends just in time

early 1917. This was apparent to all observers of the Russian economy, and was a crucial factor in the collapse of the Russian monarchy. After three years of war, the turbulence of the Russian scene spread west, and for similar reasons. In the summer of 1917 there were bread riots in Turin, which left 41 people dead. The outcry heard in Italy over the yawning gap between deprivation and privilege, between the lot of industrial workers and the luxuries of the *pescecani* (sharks), was echoed virtually all over the Continent.

Between March and May 1917 prices of vegetables, coal and rice doubled in France. This was the single most spectacular increase in the cost of a basket of consumables at any time during the war. The outcome was the largest and angriest May Day demonstration of the war in Paris, followed by a series of bitter strikes, which started in the clothing industry but spread to bank employees, telegraph messengers and finally to munitions workers, especially in the aircraft industry. Similar disturbances broke out in Toulouse. As in Paris, women workers were prominent among the strikers.

Most of the evidence about these conflicts suggests that they concerned wages and were settled once increases were granted. The same motives may be detected in strikes which brought out 300,000 Berlin workers in April 1917. The trouble here started when, a few days after the Kaiser had made some vague promises about future political reform, it was announced that the bread ration would be cut. Strikers went back to work only on receiving assurances that their food ration – already at or below subsistence level – would be increased. Similar disturbances followed in Leipzig, Halle, Braunschweig and Magdeburg. A series of unofficial strikes broke out in British

▼ Parisian seamstresses on strike in May 1917. Their militancy in January 1917 touched off the most serious wartime French strike wave.

▲ **The arrest of a striker near a German munitions factory. Most wartime disputes were about wages and hours, but by 1918 strikes in Germany had a clear political content.**

▼ **Mass demonstrations were commonplace in Petrograd in 1917. This one in June called for "All power to the social revolutionaries".**

industrial districts at about the same time, prompting a commission of inquiry into industrial unrest. Again prices and wages headed the list of complaints. By the summer of 1917 the Kerensky regime was swamped by strikes. It is apparent that workers all over Europe were reaching the end of their patience with appeals for sacrifices on behalf of the war.

Even more ominous was the industrial unrest of early 1918. By then the food situation had deteriorated still further. In January, when the flour ration in Austria was reduced from 200 to 165 grams (7–6oz) per day, strikes broke out among munitions workers in Wiener Neustadt and spread to Vienna and Budapest. At the same time, Berlin again became a magnet for discontent. In all perhaps one million workers downed tools in many German cities in what was the biggest single protest of the war. New outbreaks of labor unrest were also registered in France, this time in towns unaffected by the 1917 troubles. What distinguished this second wave of militancy from the first was that by 1918 most strikes had an undeniable political content.

This is, not surprising in the light of the two major political events of 1917: American entry into the war and the Russian Revolution. The first brought the question of war aims to center stage. It was no accident that both the US declaration of war and the strikes of spring 1917 were soon followed by the passage of a resolution in the Reichstag in favor of peace.

Russian events presented the European working class with a new vision of the future, at a time when the old order was patently failing to deliver the goods: food and victory. This lay behind the long overdue split within the German social democratic party, and the appearance, in the form of the independent socialists, of the first real opposition force of the war.

Sources of militancy

By 1918 it had become impossible to separate the political from the economic threads of industrial unrest. But there were other sources of strike action which account in part for the turbulence of the last year of the war. Five specifically war-related developments which affected each of the major European combatants help to explain the explosion of militancy in the last year of the war. They are: first, the changed character of the labor force; secondly, the leveling effects of the war; thirdly, the displacement onto the state of traditional hostility to the employer; fourthly, the release of bottled-up tension, contained too long by the constraints of the wartime social truce; fifthly, the creation of new aspirations and expectations.

As the war went on, the proportion of women and adolescents at work in war factories and workshops increased. In German heavy industry in 1913, 13 percent of the labor force consisted of women and boys under 16 years of age; in 1918, this group comprised 34 percent of the workforce

The "Spanish flu"

In the autumn of 1918, as the Allies were pushing back the German line, a further disaster occurred in most parts of the world: a virulent outbreak of influenza of pandemic proportions. The flu had first emerged in the spring of 1918. Its place of origin is unknown, but one widespread theory about its origin was reflected in its popular name. A first wave of the epidemic peaked in June and July 1918 and was followed by a more deadly wave which peaked in October and November and only abated in spring 1919.

Epidemic mortality was enormous. In France 166,000 died; in Germany 225,330; in Britain 228,900; in the USA 550,000. Worst hit was India, where perhaps 16 million people were killed. The flu had a particularly heavy impact on children and young adults. About 25 percent of its victims were 15 or under and about 45 percent between 15 and 35. Overall at least 20 million people died - more than were killed by the war itself.

Explanations for the flu abounded, but at the time its causal agent was not isolated. It had the character of a plague, so it was seen by some as divine punishment for the terrible man-made slaughter on the Western Front. Others pointed to circumstances that they believed (mistakenly) had been favorable to the virus: on the home front, poor health caused by rationing, food shortages, and the impact of blockade; on the military Front, insanitary, lice-ridden trenches and barracks.

Treatment of the flu was ineffectual and ignorance of its aetiology meant that a vaccine could not be prepared. The viral cause of the flu was not discovered until as late as 1933 and by then the mutant virus had largely disappeared.

► **A totally useless antiflu spray for London buses.**

in this key sector. This growth was eventually reflected in the prominence of women and young workers in strikes. These were people who had not been "tamed" by the disciplines of union membership and shopfloor routine. It was therefore impossible for the old guard to control incipient outbreaks of trouble, or to predict them.

The second arose out of the fact that wage differentials between well-paid and poorly-paid, industrial and agricultural, male and female workers were reduced during the war. This was in part a function of the need to draw as many workers as possible into the labor market. It was also an outcome of inflation, rent control and rationing, which tended to level social conditions, downward in Germany and Austria, upward in parts of Britain and France. This meant that workers in different trades faced similar problems and expressed in industrial action a widely-shared sense of resentment about their lot compared to that of their richer countrymen.

The third derived from the very prominence of the state in industrial life during the war. One consequence of the creation of wartime controls was that the paternalism of the state could rebound against itself. Once the state took upon itself responsibility for feeding as well as employing workers in essential industry, it was bound to attract to itself the anger inevitably generated by the mistakes, the mismanagement and the arbitrary action of the petty tyrants and bureaucrats who proliferated during the war.

The fourth concerned the costs of the abrogation of the right to strike during the war. Normal outlets for letting off steam, so to speak, were blocked, and for three years no one had provided an alternative. Such mechanical metaphors are never very helpful in accounting for labor disputes, but there is considerable evidence that after three years of war, exasperation had simply reached breaking point. There is a wealth of comment on the part of observers of the industrial scene as to the irritability and progressively more assertive mood of industrial workers in the last phase of the war.

The fifth relates to the effects of the vast movement of populations during the war upon workers' attitudes toward what constituted an acceptable standard of living. People uprooted in this way tended to give up traditional ideas of what is a decent wage. They were less likely – especially under conditions of rapid inflation – to accept what their fathers or mothers had taken for granted or to act deferentially to anyone in authority. In a more general sense, too, the geographical mobility of the war changed the

For revolutionary propaganda the metalworkers' union was in the front line in Berlin. The first workers' rebellion, which bore an undercurrent of revolutionary grumbling, was the single general strike on the day that a war tribunal was dealing with Karl Liebknecht. 55,000 workers, both men and women, are said to have laid down their tools. In April 1917 200,000 workers allegedly went on strike in protest against the military conscription of one of their foremen, Richard Müller... One day after the outbreak of the strike, Müller was released from military service. The January strike of 1918 can be seen as symptomatic of the revolutionary feeling then current in Germany.

GUSTAVE NOSKE

▲ On the whole urban workers were worse fed than were farmers or soldiers. In the last two years of the war, soup was dispensed on street corners to hungry urban crowds throughout central and eastern Europe. This scene took place in Russia in May 1916.

► The volume of Allied food purchases in the United States forced up the price of bread and led to shortages. In February 1917 riots broke out on the Lower East Side of New York when stores ran out of bread. This photograph shows an American food queue in 1918.

► In the last year of the war urban populations in Germany and Austria-Hungary were reduced to foraging for food, even, as this photograph shows, in refuse. Hunger forced people into the countryside, where they bartered whatever they had for food and kindling wood.

views many people had about whether they had to accept the world as they had found it. At least for a time, fatalism and passive resignation seem to have become two of the unintended casualties of the war.

Wartime militancy in the long perspective

These were the decisive features of the outburst of industrial unrest in the critical last year of the war. We must not lose sight, though, of some longer-term developments which underlay the wave of militancy which began in 1917 and lasted until well after the war. Let us consider just two. The first is related to the fact that in the late 19th and early 20th centuries strike waves appear in roughly regular intervals. They tend to follow periods in which previously unorganized workers join unions. This had happened in the late 1880s and seems also to have been the case after the growth of trade unionism in the early years of World War I. Secondly, the tendency for workers to demand political rights and to use political means to better the material conditions of their lives was certainly not created by the war. What the war did was to open a new phase in that struggle. This was largely because workers had come to see that in wartime all wage questions are political questions. By 1918 strikes had become a very effective political weapon in the wider campaign for political equality and a decent standard of living.

Restraints on militancy

It is therefore clear that new and powerful forces had appeared during the war which threatened to end it and topple the regimes engaged in it. What held this movement back? First, it must be reiterated that class consciousness and patriotism are not contradictory, but rather are compatible commitments. Most workers did want their country to win the war, and faced years of anxiety over the fate of loved ones in uniform. This helps to account for the lull in industrial action during the German offensive that began in March 1918. It also explains why workers waited so long before giving vent to their anger in strike action. It is also important to note that trade unionism still represented a minority of workers in all European countries. And even though joining a union in wartime was positively encouraged, many of those who did so had no interest whatsoever in disturbing the war effort. Furthermore, the growth of trade unionism during the war acted at times as a brake on militancy. Newly-organized workers may not have been well-disciplined, but they were loyal to their own unions, at least until conditions worsened to the point that any action was better than silence. Shop stewards, who were both union men and represented workers of different grades on the shop floor, usually took action on their own. But this was the exception rather than the rule in wartime.

Furthermore, in countries where living standards were maintained, trade unionism had achieved a recognition and an unprecedented degree of respectability. Workingmen had been brought into councils of state, and intended to stay there. The key roles played by Albert Thomas in France and Arthur Henderson in the UK were a pointer to the future.

The new situation was also recognized by the more far-sighted employers in both the winning and the losing camps. The way forward, in their view, was to perpetuate alliances between business and labor which had brought gains at least to the bigger battalions. This was the motive behind the famous Stinnes-Legien agreement, drawn up a few days after the Armistice, on 15 November 1918, whereby German employers and trade unions entered into a social partnership necessary for the transition to peace. In Britain similar intentions took the form of "Joint Industrial Councils", through which an ongoing dialog could be maintained. Such flexibility in the stance of big business helped stabilize its position in the uncertain conditions of 1918 and after.

For all these reasons the substantial turbulence of the last year of the war was contained. But only just. Had the war carried on for another year – which was indeed possible, had Ludendorff delayed or canceled his decision to win the war on the Western Front by just one more gamble — the outcome might have been very different, regardless of how many Americans were thrown into the fray. The ordinary people of Europe on both sides had been stretched to breaking point by 1918, and however great their patriotic commitments, many people, both high and low, heaved a sigh of relief when the German army at last accepted defeat.

◀ How far removed from the cheering crowds of 1914. Starving and malnourished children were a common sight in central and eastern Europe, both before the Armistice and in the following period up to July 1919 when the Allies continued their blockade of food supplies to the Central Powers.

▼ The numbers of losses – killed, wounded, missing and prisoners of war – were so huge that it was virtually impossible for the combatant nations to keep an accurate count of the human cost of the war. These women are shown in 1915 trying to account for German prisoners captured on the Russian and French Fronts. Each card told the story of World War I in its own way. It was a story of suffering, multiplied by many millions, which taken as a whole is comprehensible not in statistics but perhaps only in art.

PART 5

THE SHADOW OF WAR

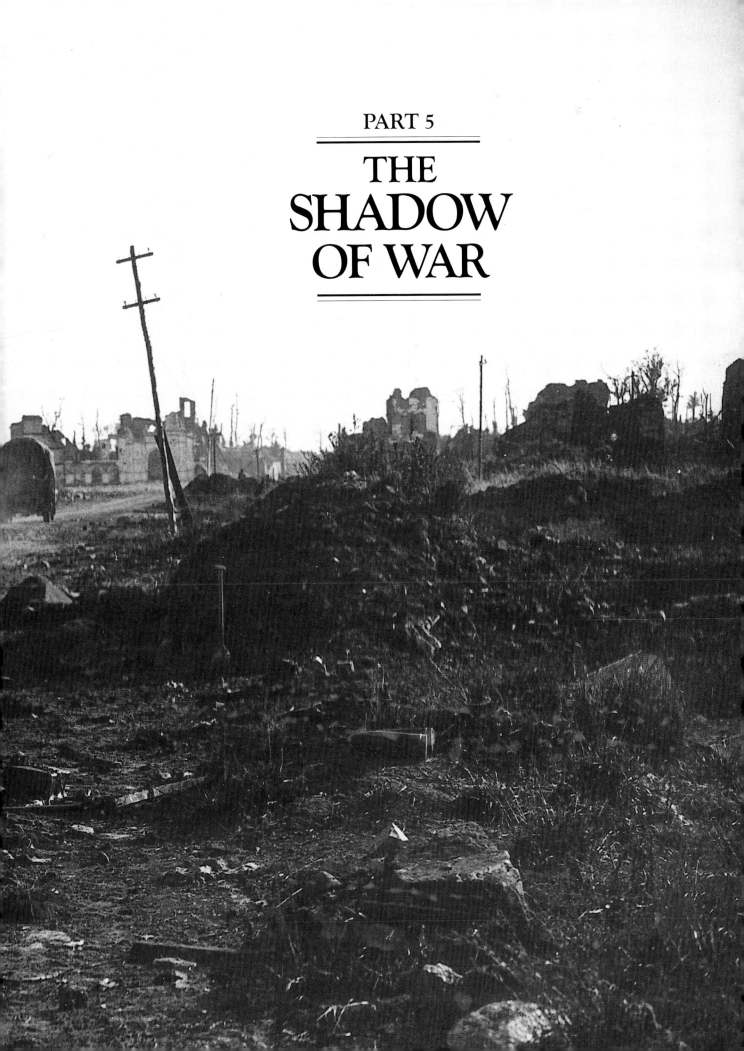

BIOGRAPHIES AND GLOSSARY

Balfour, Arthur, J. 1848–1930
Scottish-born British prime minister (Conservative, 1902–06), first lord of the admiralty (1915–16) and foreign secretary. He played a prominent part in the shaping of a new Europe after the war and was second plenipotentiary at the Paris Peace Conference. As foreign secretary he issued the "Balfour Declaration" (1917) which pledged British support for the establishment of a Jewish national home in Palestine and formed the basis for the League of Nations mandate for Palestine. He represented the UK at the League of Nations in 1920.

Churchill, Winston 1874–1965
British politician who was first lord of the admiralty at the start of World War I. Before the war he had supported the modernization of the British Royal Navy. He resigned after the disastrous Allied invasion of Gallipoli and became a commander of the Royal Scots Fusiliers. He returned to government as minister of munitions (1917–18) and served as minister for air and war (1919–20). He held a number of influential posts in postwar Conservative governments but was out of office in the 1930s. He became prime minister after the start of World War II (1940–45) and served again from 1951 to 1954.

D'Annunzio, Gabriele 1863–1938
Italian poet, war hero and political adventurer, D'Annunzio used his literary talents to popularize nationalist views. In 1914–15 he advocated Italian entry into the war, against Austria-Hungary. During the war he served in the Italian air force. Dissatisfied with the 1919 peace talks he organized the seizure of the port and city of Fiume. He was forced to surrender them in 1921.

Ebert, Friedrich 1871–1925
German social democrat politician, who became chancellor of Germany after the abdication of the Kaiser in November 1918. He ordered the signing of the Armistice with the Allies. He played a prominent part in the formulation of the postwar Weimar constitution and served as the republic's president until his death.

Hitler, Adolf 1889–1945
Austrian-born dictator. In the early stages of World War I Hitler served in the Bavarian infantry. He fought at Ypres, the Somme and Arras. He was twice awarded the Iron Cross: in December 1914 (2nd class) and in August 1918 (1st class). He was also temporarily blinded by British gas in an attack in Flanders. After the war he became leader of the national socialist German workers' party (Nazis) and made an unsuccessful attempt to seize power in a *Putsch* in Munich in 1923. He gained power in Germany in 1933 and became Führer (leader) of Germany after President Hindenburg's death.

Hoover, Herbert 1874–1964
The 31st president of the United States of America, Hoover was noted during World War I for his contribution to relief work in Belgium, central Europe and Russia, which continued during the chaotic period after the Armistice. From 1921 to 1928 he served as US secretary of commerce under presidents Harding and Coolidge and was then elected to the presidency. He served one term, until 1933, when he was defeated by his democrat opponent, F.D. Roosevelt.

Keynes, John Maynard 1883–1946
British economist. Keynes's major achievement was the development of an economic policy whereby governments could combat depression by state-spending policies. He served as a representative of the British treasury at the Paris Peace Conference but resigned because he could not support central features of the Treaty. He published his criticisms in *The Economic Consequences of the Peace* (1919).

Liebknecht, Karl 1871–1919
German socialist and a passionate and outspoken pacifist. In 1912 he was elected to the German Reichstag as a social democrat. On the outbreak of war he denounced his party's support for the war effort and continued to oppose the war throughout, earning imprisonment for his views. In 1916 he and Rosa Luxemburg founded the Spartacus League. After the Armistice, in January 1919, they attempted to overthrow the new republican regime, but were captured and murdered.

Luxemburg, Rosa 1871–1919
Born in Poland, Luxemburg took German citizenship on her marriage in 1898. She was strongly opposed to World War I and was imprisoned for most of the period between February 1915 and November 1918. During her imprisonment she smuggled out letters calling for mass revolutionary action against war. Together with Karl Liebknecht she founded the Spartacus League. Along with Liebknecht she was captured in January 1919 and murdered.

Morgan, J.P. 1867–1943
US financier and industrial organizer, and one of the world's major financial figures. During the war he acted as agent for the Allies in raising American loans for the war effort and also organized the purchase of munitions. After the war he floated securities for loans to European states.

Mosley, Oswald 1896–1980
British politician who fought in World War I, first as an infantryman, later as a member of the Royal Flying Corps. After the war he entered the House of Commons as a Conservative, but later became a member of the Labour Party (1924–30), of the New Party (socialist, 1931–32) and was then leader of the British Union of Fascists, which attempted (unsuccessfully) to emulate the fascist parties of Italy and Germany.

Mussolini, Benito 1883–1945
Italian politician, who was a leading socialist before World War I. He became an ardent nationalist in the early months of World War I, and (with French subsidies) founded a newspaper, *Il Popolo d'Italia*, to work for Italian entry into the war. After Italy joined the Allies, Mussolini served in the Italian army. After the war he organized the *Fasci di combattimento*, a right-wing organization of war veterans, who helped him win power in 1922 with their "March on Rome". He served as Italian premier until 1943.

Noske, Gustav 1868–1946
German socialist politician who is remembered largely for his ruthless suppression of the Spartacus rising in Berlin in 1919. He had strongly supported Germany's participation in World War I, and became the social democrats' military expert. In December 1918 he was elected to the six-member interim government; in the Weimar republic he was defense minister but resigned after being implicated in the Kapp *Putsch* of 1920.

Röhm, Ernst 1887–1934
German politician. Rohm was wounded three times in World War I, but emerged with the new rank of major. After the war he helped to found the national socialist German workers' party (Nazis) and helped Hitler to power. He was murdered on Hitler's instructions in 1934.

Rothschild, Lord 1868–1939
British politician who was also a zoologist. A strong supporter of Zionist aspirations, he was able to take advantage of wartime conditions to extract from the British foreign secretary, A.J. Balfour, the so-called Balfour Declaration promising British support for the establishment of a Jewish national home in Palestine (1917).

Scheidemann, Philip 1865–1939
German social democratic politician who, without mandate from either party or government, declared the establishment of the German republic from the balcony of the German chancellery in Berlin on 9 November 1918. From November 1918 to February 1919 he was a member of the six-man council that formed an interim government of Germany and served as chancellor. He resigned in protest at the Treaty of Versailles.

Sokolow, Nahum 1861–1936
Polish Jewish writer and Zionist leader. In 1906 he became secretary general of the Zionist Organization. On the outbreak of war he went to England where he played an important role in the meetings that led to the issue of the Balfour Declaration promising British support for the establishment of a Jewish national home in Palestine. He was president of the World Zionist Organization from 1931 to 1935.

Victor Emmanuel III 1869–1947
Italian monarch – the last king of Italy. He was responsible for appointing Mussolini as premier in 1922 after Mussolini's March on Rome of 1922. Following his long association with Mussolini he was forced to abdicate in 1946. He died in exile in Egypt.

Weizmann, Chaim 1874–1952
Polish Jewish politician and chemist. Born in Russian Poland, Weizmann was to become the first president of Israel, in 1948. He had become a British subject in 1910 and was director of the admiralty laboratories (1916–19). He played a major part in securing the grant of the Balfour Declaration in 1917. After the war he was president of the World Zionist Organization.

Abdication
Formal renunciation of the throne by a monarch.

Abrogation
The official revocation of a previous treaty or agreement.

Antisemitism
Hatred, persecution and discrimination directed toward Jewish people.

Army of occupation
Military forces of a victorious nation occupying part or all of the territory of its defeated enemy, for example as security for a war indemnity or reparations.

Capital
Material wealth, or knowledge.

Communist
Socialist believing in a classless society and communal rights to all wealth and property; supporter of the Bolshevik revolution.

Counterrevolution
Reactionary movement to restore a pre-revolutionary situation after a revolution.

Council movement
Organization of local committees of soldiers, workers and peasants in Germany, loosely modeled on the Russian soviets.

Decolonization
The voluntary or forced granting of independence to overseas colonies.

Demilitarization
The voluntary or forced removal of a military presence from a particular territory; the reduction in strength of the postwar German army.

Demobilization
The disbanding of military formations.

Democratization
The establishment of a democratic form of government.

Disenfranchise
To remove a previously recognized right to vote.

Dismemberment
The breaking up of an empire or state into independent nations.

Ethnic minority
Minority population of a different racial group from the majority population of a state.

Fascism
Right-wing Italian political movement, inspired by Benito Mussolini, combining nationalism, antisocialism and corporatist autocratic government policies; fascists – European allies of Hitler and Mussolini.

Free trade
Trade between nations without restrictive customs duties on foreign imports.

Freikorps
German paramilitary organizations of ex-servicemen.

Genocide
The systematic extermination of a racial group.

Great Depression
Worldwide economic slump, beginning in 1929 and lasting until the mid-1930s.

Import substitution
The replacing of imported manufactured goods by those produced at home.

Indemnity
Financial payment exacted from a defeated nation as punishment and compensation for the war.

Inflationary spiral
Successsive and irreversible price rises, caused by shortages, rising profits, or rising wages.

League of Nations
Interwar international organization with the objective of preserving peace by settling international disputes by arbitration rather than war.

Mandate
Territory administered under the authorization of the League of Nations by one of its member states.

March on Rome
Seizure of power by Mussolini's Fascist party in Italy in 1922.

Militarization
Dependence upon the use of armed force, particularly as a means of political control.

National Socialists (Nazis)
German fascist party led by Adolf Hitler, which came to power in 1933.

Paramilitary
Ordered, trained political or social groups, and sometimes armed along military lines.

Protectorate
Territory administered by, but not part of, another state.

Public/private domain
The relative spheres of action of state and individual authority.

Putsch
(Ger.) Attempted seizure of power.

Reconstruction
The rebuilding of the economy and society after war.

Red Army
The army of the Bolshevik state in Russia, organized by Trotsky.

Reichswehr
The postwar German army, restricted to 100,000 men by the Treaty of Versailles.

Reparations
Financial indemnity exacted from a defeated nation by the victors as compensation for the cost of a war.

Revisionism
Movement, particularly in Germany, to revise or annul the terms of the Treaty of Versailles.

Self-determination
The right of a nation or people to determine its own form of government without interference from outside.

Spartacus League/Spartacists
Militant German socialist movement, led by Karl Liebknecht and Rosa Luxemburg, smashed when it attempted an abortive coup in 1919.

Tariffs
Customs duties placed on foreign imports to protect the domestic economy.

Treaty of Versailles
Peace treaty, signed at Versailles on 28 June 1919, which brought the war between the Allies and Germany to an end.

Veterans associations
Organizations of ex-soldiers, often united by common political interests.

Weimar Republic
German democratic regime established after the war, whose national assembly initially sat in the town of Weimar in Thuringia.

White Armies/Russians
The armies of the czarists and their supporters opposing the Bolshevik regime in Russia.

Zionism
Political movement for the establishment of a Jewish national homeland in Palestine.

Datafile

The Armistice of 11 November 1918 was not the end of the war. Peace treaties were negotiated over the following two years, and armed conflict continued in Russia between the Bolshevik government and a mixture of White armies supported by Western troops and supplies. But the war in the west *was* over, leaving behind a trail of material and, more importantly, human devastation. Over 9 million soldiers died in World War I. The war created an international army of disabled veterans. After 1918 men continued to succumb to their war wounds or complications of war-related conditions. Ex-soldiers themselves spoke of a "burnt-out" generation, including all survivors of the war.

Pensioners' disabilities

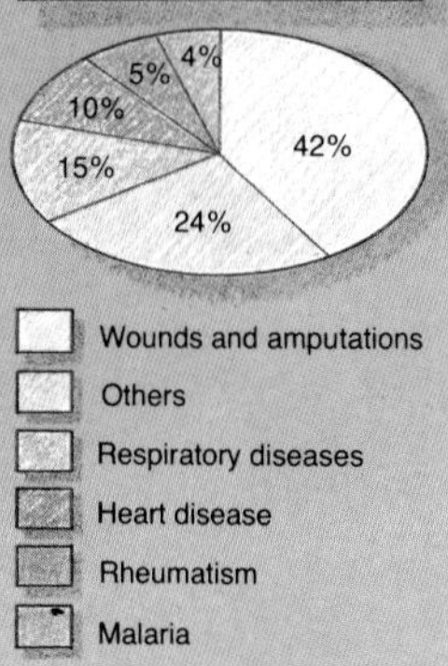

Chronology of the peace treaties

11 November 1918 Armistice between Germany and the Allies	**June 28** Treaty of Versailles is signed with Germany
December 13 The Armistice is prolonged to January 17, 1919	**September 10** Treaty of Saint-Germain is signed with Austria
16 January 1919 The Armistice is prolonged to 17 February 1919	**November 27** Treaty of Neuilly is signed with Bulgaria
February 16 The Armistice is prolonged again	**4 June 1920** Treaty of Trianon is signed with Hungary
May 7 Allied peace terms are handed to Germany	**August 10** Treaty of Sèvres is signed with Turkey
June 2 Allied peace terms are handed to Austria	**24 July 1923** Treaty of Lausanne signed with Turkey

Pensioners' injuries

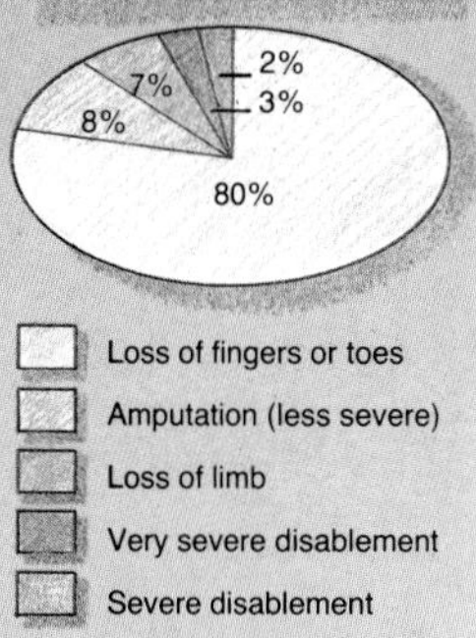

Amputation (less severe)
Partial amputation of arm or leg (less severe)

Loss of limb
Partial amputation of arm or leg

Severe disablement
Amputation of arm or leg; facial disfigurement; loss of speech

Very severe disablement
Loss of two limbs; leg and eye; both feet; total paralysis; lunacy; permanent confinement to bed; severe disfigurement; incurable disease

▲ The Treaty of Versailles, signed 28 June 1919, ended the state of war between Germany and the Allies. Over the next two years, Austria, Hungary, Bulgaria and Turkey signed separate peace treaties. In all cases, defeated countries were to pay reparations, limit their armies, and cede territory to one of the Allied powers or successor states.

► Most of the soldiers who died during the war were victims of enemy action. But the range of disabilities from which survivors suffered covered every kind of illness. Less than half of British war pensioners suffered from the effects of wounds and amputations. The majority had to cope with the effects of war-related disease.

British casualties

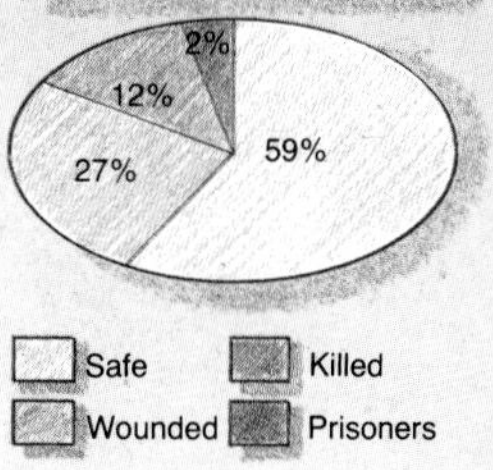

French casualties

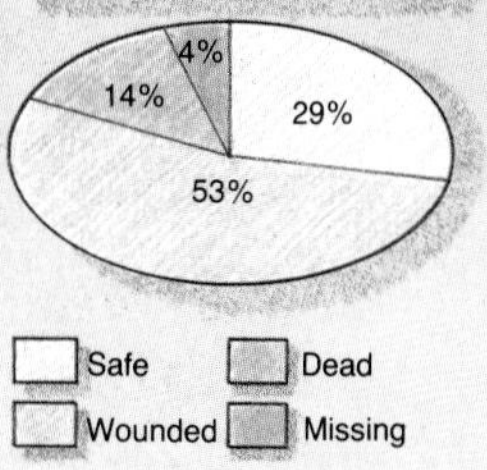

◄▼ The scale of French casualties was much greater than that of Britain. Less than 30 percent of all French soldiers survived the war unscathed; roughly 60 percent of British soldiers did so. Over 1 million Frenchmen died in action, compared to 722,000 British soldiers. German losses were higher still: perhaps 2 million men died in the war.

British army

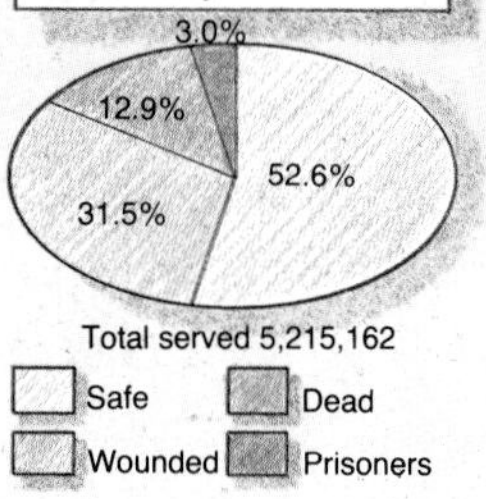

British navy

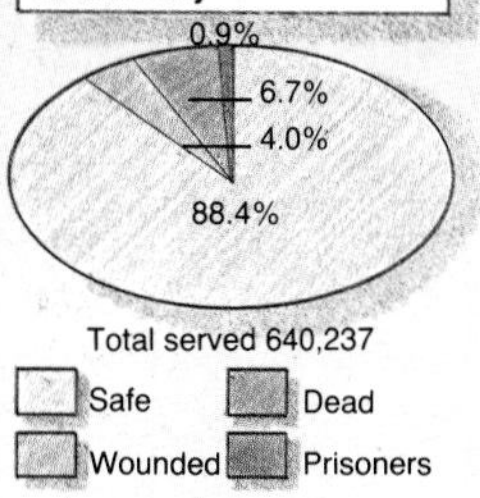

British air force

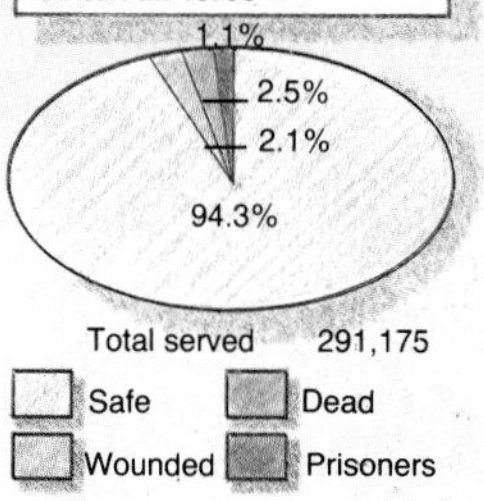

In Western Europe and outside the continent the eleventh hour of the eleventh day of the eleventh month of 1918 was the moment when the war ended. Soldiers and their families rejoiced. But did the war really end that morning?

On one level the answer is obviously yes, since the political struggle which had been carried out in military form had been effectively decided. There was the business of diplomacy and peacemaking to attend to, which meant that military pressure had to be kept up at least until Germany had accepted the Allies' peace terms. This they did at Versailles on 28 June 1919. The other losers accepted defeat in five separate treaties signed over the subsequent 14 months. Ink dried on the last document officially ending hostilities on 20 August 1920, when Turkey and the Allies signed the Treaty of Sèvres.

Such precision in defining the end of a war is necessary under international law. But to accept legalism as reality is to court historical myopia, for what lawyers and diplomats say rarely describes the world in which ordinary people live. On this basis, a number of reasons will be suggested for why it is necessary to see World War I as an upheaval which continued well beyond the formal, temporal end of the conflict.

THE IMMEDIATE AFTERMATH

Fighting ended on 11 November 1918

Did the war end then?

The final peace treaty was signed almost two years later

The economic blockade continued until 1919

Hostilities in Russia continued until 1921

Did the war solve the German problem?

War, civil war and revolution, 1918–21

One reason for doubting that the war ended in 1918 is that hostile action against the Central Powers continued until the diplomats had concluded their work. The Armistice was, after all, only a truce, rather than a formal end to hostilities. To prevent Germany from using this breathing space to reconstitute its armies – a hopeless enterprise in any event – the Allied blockade of central Europe continued until July 1919. This meant that food and other essential goods were in short supply during the difficult winter of 1918–19 throughout Central Europe, just as they had been in the later years of the war. It would have been hard to convince many in Vienna or Prague who had to survive one more winter under extremely difficult conditions that the war was over and that they could therefore resume their normal lives.

It was even more difficult to discern a straightforward division between war and peace in eastern Europe. Bolshevik Russia had left the war on 3 March 1918, when, under the Treaty of Brest Litovsk, it ceded to Germany all of Russian Poland, the Ukraine, and other border areas. The defeat of Germany six months later ensured the abrogation of this settlement, but also left a vacuum of power in what had been the westernmost regions of the old Russian Empire.

What made the situation explosive was, of course, the intersection of war and revolution. This left a cloud of uncertainty not only over the future of Russia, but also over the political disposition of Germany and of the dismembered parts of the Austro-Hungarian Empire, deemed states by the Treaties of St Germain (with Austria, signed on 10 September 1919) and the Trianon (with Hungary, signed on 4 June 1920).

After the Russian Revolutions of 1917 the European revolutionary movement, which had been buried at the outbreak of war, reemerged and threatened to fill the political vacuum left by the defeat of the Central Powers. Consequently, armed disturbances, insurrection and counterrevolution followed the Armistice throughout central and eastern Europe.

In Russia hostilities that had begun before the end of the war continued until 1921. Allied military intervention against the revolutionary regime was launched before the Armistice and merged with the efforts of the polyglot collection of "White Armies" to unseat the Bolsheviks. Not only did this campaign fail completely in Russia, but by summer 1920 the Red Army had pushed

▼ Wilson and Trotsky represented the two paths that led out of the upheaval of World War I. Wilson, seen addressing the US Congress in April 1917 (below left), spoke for democracy; Trotsky (below right in 1921) spoke for revolution. Both failed to govern the course of European politics, dominated by nondemocratic and counterrevolutionary movements which emerged out the 1914–18 war.

as far west as Warsaw. The "Red Bridge" which Trotsky, creator of the Red Army, had promised to build across Europe seemed to be near completion. The Bolsheviks were pushed back, but the fact that they were there at all, three years after the supposed end of the war, shows the difficulty of accepting the conventional date of 11 November 1918 or some arbitrary moment in diplomatic life as the conflict's terminal date.

The German problem

It has been argued above that the war was fought in part because no one had worked out a stable answer to the problem of the growth of German political and economic power in the late 19th and early 20th century. Did World War I provide such an answer? Certainly not. Just a glance at the fundamental political problems left unresolved or exacerbated by the war will suffice to make the point. First Germany acquiesced, through the unchallengeable dominance of the Allies in the peace settlement of 1919, but it never accepted it. There was a consensus from left to right that the peace terms were unjust and therefore had to be changed. How this was to be done was a matter of dispute, but few doubted the need for a revision of the Treaty of Versailles. Secondly, even though Germany's western borders were secured by the Locarno Treaty of 16 October 1925, there was no such agreement over its eastern boundary; nor was there a consensus about the political fate of those ethnic Germans who lived outside Germany, but shared common hopes and aspirations with their kinsmen in the new Weimar Republic. The explosive material for the next round of hostilities was not defused by the war; it was simply rearranged, and was at hand for someone who wanted to ignite it.

Economic disorder

In economic terms the disturbances of the war emphatically did not end in 1918. The apparatus of controls and agencies of war production erected in each combatant country could not simply be brushed aside at the Armistice. Both the ostensible winners and the losers went through a difficult period of adjustment to peacetime conditions, requiring careful economic management. Since capital and labor were mobilized on an unprecedented scale between 1914 and 1918, demobilization was both monumental and dangerous.

This was as true in financial as in industrial affairs. Forcing Germany to pay reparations was an economic disaster. The uncertainties of the immediate postwar years meant that Britain risked a return to the pre-1914 financial system only in 1925, and even then it was impossible for it to regain, in international economic terms, the ground lost during the war to those, like the USA and Japan, further removed from the epicenter of the struggle.

In Europe inflation wiped out savings and transformed the relation between debtor and creditor. The inflationary spiral which began in wartime went completely out of control in Germany in the following five years. Prices had risen by a factor of four in Germany between 1914 and 1918; by 1921 the price level was 20 times that registered in the last prewar year. In Britain and France the price level doubled over the war period. Less extreme but equally palpable signs of economic instability marred the fortunes of other major European combatants. Only the USA seemed to reap unqualified gains from the war; in this sense it may not be too farfetched to argue that only the United States won the war.

▲ Everyone in wartime Germany broke the law to stay alive. The black market supplemented rations which were insufficient for minimal needs. After the Armistice, hyperinflation made normal trading arrangements impossible. Savings evaporated overnight, and the occasional police roundup of black-market traders (as seen here) did little to regularize commercial life.

If we aim deliberately at the impoverishment of Central Europe, vengeance, I dare predict, will not limp. Nothing can then delay for very long that final civil war between the forces of Reaction and the despairing convulsions of Revolution, before which the horrors of the late German war will fade into nothing, and which will destroy, whoever is victor, the civilisation and the progress of our generation.

J.M. KEYNES, 1919

"War guilt" and Reparations

Under the terms of the Armistice signed on 11 November 1918 Germany was to hand over goods, materiel and valuables looted from occupied countries. Germany also had to make good the damage done to those countries during occupation. The idea of reparations to be paid to countries that had suffered at the hands of Germany during the war grew between the Armistice and the Versailles Conference, fueled by a clamor to make Germany "pay until the pips squeak", as one British newspaper put it. After all, France had been forced to pay Germany a substantial sum after defeat in the Franco-Prussian War of 1870–71.

Reparations were an annual indemnity, payable over a period of 30 years, both as international atonement of "war guilt" and as a deterrent to prevent a future military buildup in Germany. The principle of reparations was established at the peace conference of Versailles. A schedule of payments was set at a later date.

As the demand for punishing Germany economically grew early in 1919, entirely unrealistic figures were proposed. It was seriously suggested that 120 billion gold marks (30 billion US dollars) could be extracted from Germany, half in gold and half in currency. This figure contrasts starkly with the gross national product of Germany in 1929: 84 billion gold marks.

A few voices spoke out against such punitive reparations. Most influential was the British economist J.M. Keynes, who in 1919 published *The Economic Consequences of the Peace*, in which he argued that restoration of the shattered world economy was the first priority, and that reparations could only obstruct that goal. But governments wanted revenge, short-term security and economic advantage. In January 1921 the Reparations Commission set the sum to be paid: 6.6 billion pounds plus interest. Germany funded some payments by international loans from Britain and the USA, and others by exports of coal and manufactured goods following the collapse of the Germany currency in 1921. In 1923 France occupied the Ruhr industrial region to force compliance with reparations in the form of coal deliveries. The Dawes Plan (1924) finally regularized payments.

In the end, reparations failed in their aim of making Germany pay for the war, and they acted as an unnecessary wound in the world economy at a critical moment. The German people were disgruntled at being forced to accept "war guilt" and a massive debt to the victors. In the long run, the only beneficiaries of reparations were the National Socialists in Germany, who exploited this dissatisfaction by repudiating the Treaty of Versailles, reparations and all.

▲ The Versailles Treaty specified that the armed forces of Germany must not include military or naval air forces, that no zeppelins could be kept, that all air force personnel were to be demobilized within two months of the Treaty's coming into force, and that (with minor exceptions) all stores and equipment of military aircraft were to be handed over to the Allies. Given the German bombardment of French and British cities, these terms are hardly surprising. By 1920 much of this military materiel was scrapped, as is shown in this photograph of propellers being destroyed for kindling.

◀ Allied military intervention in Russia – initially a response to the Bolshevik decision to sue for peace and an attempt to reconstitute the Eastern Front – was both foolish and inept. The dispatch in 1918 of 8,500 troops to Archangel (of whom 4,800 were American, 2,400 British, 900 French and 350 Serbian), the skirmishing of freed Czech prisoners of war in the Volga area, and the entry of some 70,000 Japanese troops into eastern Siberia in September 1918 did not affect the course of the war, but only rallied Russian opinion to the Bolsheviks. In 1919 French, Greek and Romanian forces landed in Odessa, but could do little other than postpone the demise of the Western-backed White armies. These American sailors on board the US cruiser *Des Moines* on route to Archangel in 1919, were part of this doomed expedition.

THE HUMAN COST OF THE WAR

No one will ever know how many men perished while on military or naval duty in World War I. An estimate of about 9 million – the total population of New York City – may give some idea of the magnitude of the catastrophe. Over 70 million men were mobilized; thus over one in eight of those who served was killed or died on active service.

A statistical presentation of estimates of the losses in World War I hints at the sheer scale of the slaughter, but it is difficult to grasp the full meaning of such statistics: two million German dead, 1.3 million French dead, and so on; but anyone who wants to know what World War I brought about has to start at this point.

Some further inferences can be drawn from these appalling statistics. Although more Russians died than members of any other nationality, the greatest proportional losses were suffered by Serbians, Romanians, Bulgarians and Turks. The Western Front was where the war was won and lost, but the Eastern Front was, if anything, an even bloodier field of combat. American losses were relatively low.

What did casualties on this scale mean to those who survived the war? The answer to this question may never be known, but we can appreciate the poverty of accounts which fail to pose it. It is true, of course, that for those who fell the war was over. But when did it end for their parents, widows, children, relatives and friends? It is likely that by 1918 every household in most combatant countries had lost a relative or friend.

In the interwar years, special commemorative services for the fallen were begun. In Germany the Nazis used them to glorify the dead. But there was nothing intrinsically sinister about the belief that the living owed a debt to the dead, which could be acknowledged, if never discharged, in public ceremonies. A vast monument to the fallen of Verdun was erected in the interwar years; literally thousands of others dot the countryside of France, Flanders, Italy, Turkey and Palestine. Collective exercises in mourning and remembrance continue to this day – Armistice Day in France, Anzac Day in Australia and New Zealand, Remembrance Sunday in Britain, Memorial Day in the USA.

What did the war mean to the millions of men wounded on active service? Here diffidence must be adopted. For some, pensions helped compensate for injury, and they eventually recovered. For others, for example victims of shell shock, little could be done. After a while polite society shunned their company, but as the art of Georg Grosz and Otto Dix suggests, they were a familiar sight nonetheless. Similarly, the millions of widows and orphans produced by the war received some help from public authorities, but no one pretended this made up for their loss. And when consideration is given to the stories contemporaries themselves told of broken lives and marriages, lost careers and opportunities, we again confront the fact that the war lasted much, much longer than the conflict itself.

▼ The Cenotaph in London's Horse Guards Parade became the focus for British ceremonies of remembrance. Other monuments drew those who knew private grief, and who, like this Munich woman (bottom), sought a name on the list of the fallen. To touch a name engraved in stone was for many a necessary act of mourning. In France war memorials were placed in market squares, rather than in churchyards, to testify to the civic virtues of the 1.3 million men who fell.

▼ Over 240,000 British soldiers suffered total or partial leg or arm amputations as a result of war wounds (below right). Artificial limbs helped them try to resume "normal life". Less could be done for blind veterans, gas victims or tubercular men. Psychiatric wounds were untreatable. But in the UK and elsewhere, most disabled veterans suffered from less visible ailments. In postwar Aachen, in Germany, about half of the disabled veterans had orthopedic trouble.

▼▶ The "Lost Generation" numbered over 9 million soldiers who died in the war. About one in eight of those who served was killed. Turkey, Romania, Serbia, France and Germany suffered higher than average rates of loss. But those who mourned did so for people, not proportions. The great majority of the men who fell were under age 30. Most were ordinary workingmen: agricultural laborers on the Continent; industrial workers in England and Scotland.

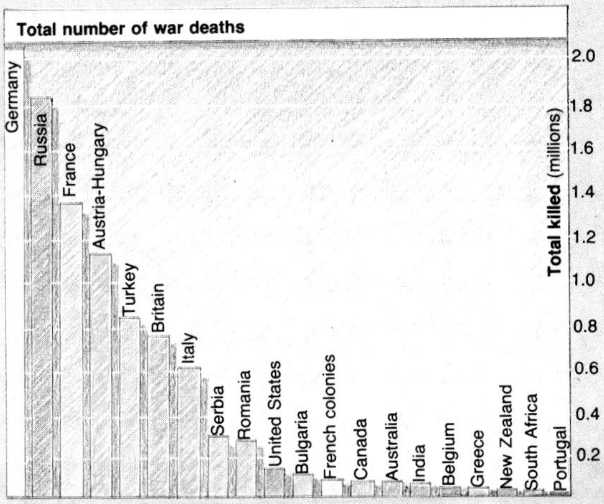

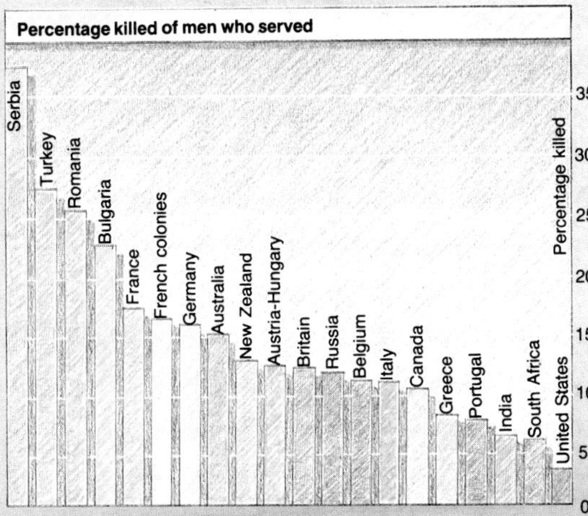

VERSAILLES AND THE NEW MAP OF EUROPE

The postwar settlement was produced by a conference of the victorious powers. It convened in Paris on 18 January 1919. Thirty-two states were represented but France, the USA, the UK and its Dominions were the most influential. The victors had four major objectives. The first was moral: to force Germany to accept guilt for the war. The second was economic: to exact reparations from Germany and its allies for the material damage caused by the war, and to distribute among the Allied nations control of the colonies and dependencies of the Central Powers. The third was political: to set up a League of Nations and to establish recognized boundaries in both east and western Europe. The fourth was ideological: to stem the tide of Bolshevism. Sole responsibility for the war was assigned to Germany, in Clause 231. This provided moral justification for the establishment of a war crimes tribunal, which was to try the Kaiser and other alleged war criminals, and for the imposition on Germany of the economic costs of the war. It agreed to "devote economic resources directly to the physical restoration of the invaded areas". This entailed coal and coal-derivative shipments to Belgium, France and Italy, as well as transfers of farm animals to Belgium and France. Punitive reparations payments of astronomical sums were to be divided among the Allies thus: 52 percent to France; 22 percent to Britain; 10 percent to Italy; 8 percent to Belgium.

The political structure set up under the Treaty had two parts: geographical and administrative. The first set Germany's boundaries; transferred authority for German colonies and interests and areas formerly under Turkish control to the Allies, and abrogated the Treaty of Brest-Litovsk. The second entailed the establishment of a League of Nations, under whose covenant signatories abjured recourse to war.

In Part XIII of the Treaty, an International Labor Organization was established, based in Geneva, which was empowered to ground international peace in principles of social justice. Unjust conditions of labor were deemed a threat to peace, and had to be remedied through international action. This was clearly a reply to the Bolshevik challenge.

The Treaty was signed at Versailles on 28 June 1919, five years to the day since the assassination of Franz Ferdinand. The Germans had no option but to sign the humiliating provisions of the treaty. The German army had disbanded, and the Allied blockade was still in force. By using hunger as a political weapon after the war, and by exacting particularly harsh penalties in the Treaty, the Allies effectively lost the moral argument about which side had fought for justice. Justice vanished at Versailles.

The Peace Treaty, supposedly based on Wilson's 14 points, did not create the new start in international affairs. Instead the old order reasserted its will, distributed the spoils of war, and left unresolved the problems which had led to one war in 1914 and which would lead to another conflict in 1939.

▼▶ World War I was a test of international power. The imperial and informal links that Britain and France had with extra-European nations and peoples gave the Allies an insurmountable advantage over the Central Powers. Consequently, the contribution of the non-European allies and associated powers was recognized, and their leaders joined Wilson and Clemenceau (right) in formulating the peace treaty which was signed at Versailles in 1919 (below).

One injustice of Versailles was the failure to grant Arab lands taken from the Ottoman Empire their political freedom. These were placed under the rule of the British and French as mandated territories of the League of Nations (below).

▼ In spite of the Treaty, military activity soon flared again. French tanks and troops (below) occupied the Ruhr industrial area from 1923–25, after Germany defaulted on reparation.

Europe 1919 and Middle East Mandates

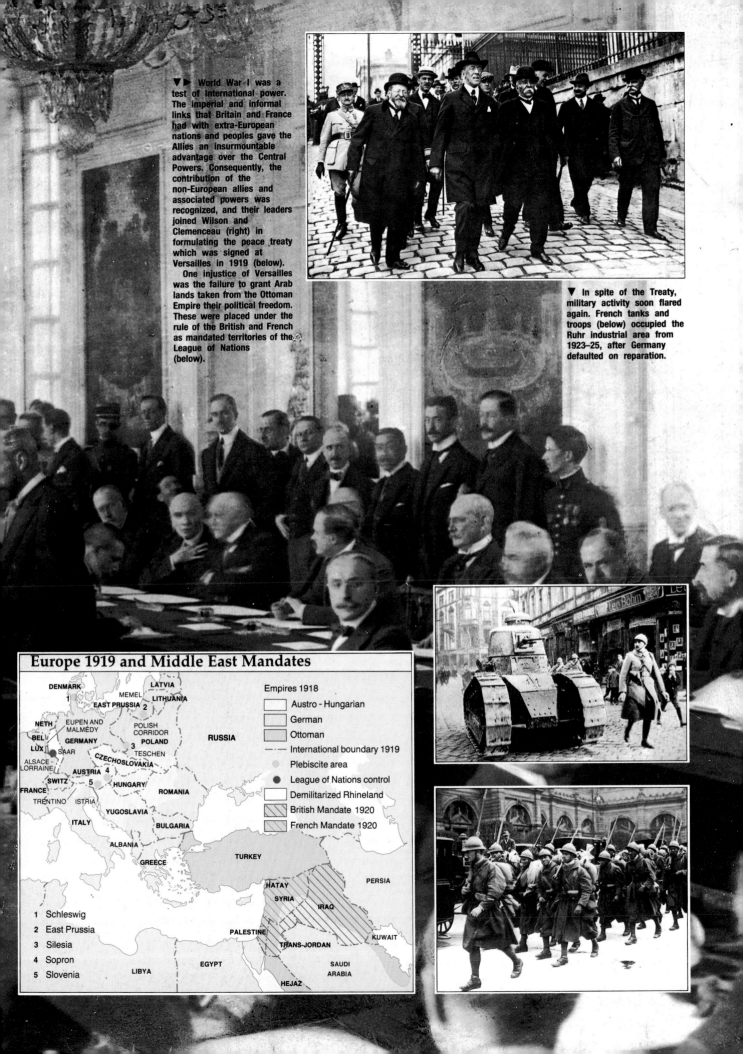

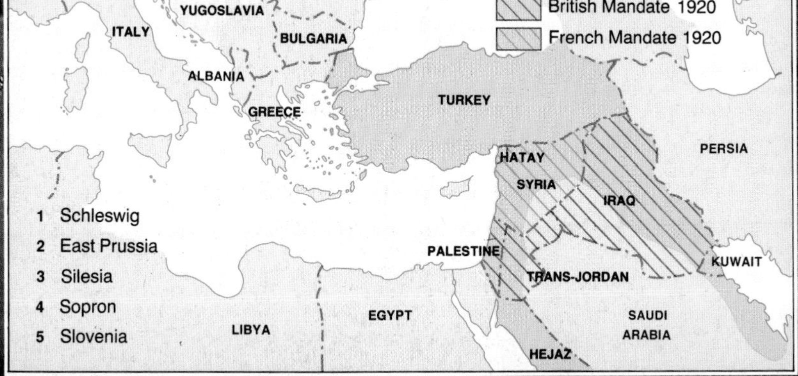

Datafile

Revolutions in Russia and Germany were the most important political consequences of the war. The first took Russia out of the conflict in December 1917; the second led to the Armistice of November 1918. By 1920 the Bolshevik regime had survived counter-revolution and Western intervention, but remained isolated, beleaguered and poor. The reaction to socialism was the most powerful political current of the interwar years. The turbulent birth of the German republic was accompanied by the suppression of the revolutionary left and the restoration of the forces of order, prepared for the time being to work with a moderate socialist government. Other revolutions were short-lived. Bela Kun's Bolshevik regime in Budapest lasted from March to August 1922. In 1920 workers occupied factories in Turin and other Italian towns. But workers' militancy was crushed by more powerful counterrevolutionary forces. The dark age of totalitarianism of the European right had begun.

▼ In Britain and France the war initially boosted the electoral fortunes of conservative parties. In Italy the traditional right could not contain the challenge of the fascist movement, which came to power in 1922. Everywhere liberals were squeezed by militants to the right and the left. In Germany and elsewhere in Europe, the socialist movement split into revolutionary and reformist camps. Communist parties were formed, and tried to emulate the principles and practice of the Bolsheviks. Moderate socialists came to power in Germany and stabilized their position temporarily by the suppression of the revolutionary left.

British, French Italian and German postwar elections

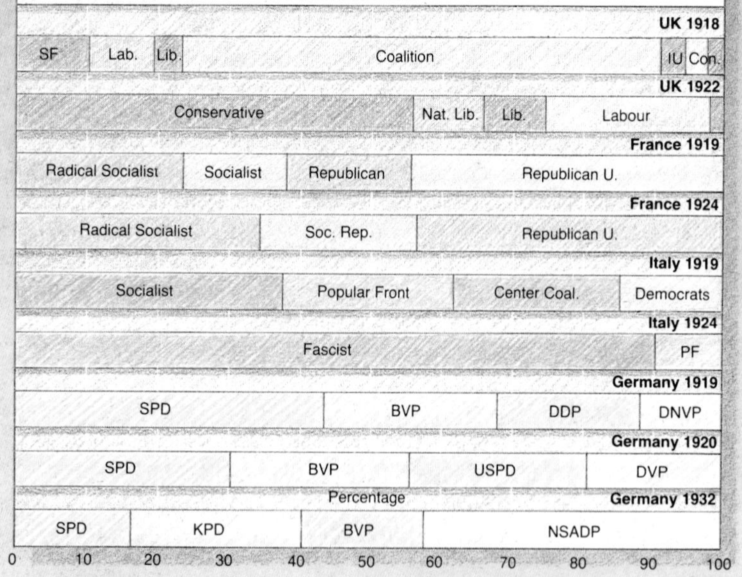

Chronology of the German revolution

March–July 1918
German Spring offensive fails to bring about a military breakthrough

July
Collapse of the German army in the field

August 8
Allied tank offensive at Amiens: "The black day of the Germany Army"

August 14
Supreme command advise the Kaiser that there is no prospect of a German victory

September
The Germany army pulls back to the Hindenburg line. Hindenburg and Ludendorff call for an immediate armistice

October 3
Prince Max von Baden is appointed Chancellor of Germany

October 3–4
German government offers President Wilson an armistice based on the 14 points

October 29
Mutiny on the German fleet in Wilhelmshaven. Soviets of workers and soldiers are formed

November 7
Revolution breaks out in Munich

November 9
Revolution in Berlin. Kaiser Wilhelm II and Crown Prince abdicate. Proclamation of a Republic. Provisional government formed by SPD chairman Friedrich Ebert

November 10
Kaiser Wilhelm goes into exile. "Executive council of the workers and soldiers deputies" form a parallel government

November 11
Armistice signed, based on the 14 points

January 1919
Ebert, with the support from the military, overturns the Sparticist uprising. The Sparticus leadership Rosa Luxemburg and Karl Liebknecht are murdered by *Freikorps* military police

February
Opening of the first Weimar Assembly. Friedrich Ebert is elected president. Philip Scheidermann becomes the first chancellor

August 11
The Weimar constitution comes into force.

The history of the early days of the German Revolution of 1918–19 shows much about the political consequences of the war. In effect the conflict created conditions which both led to the formation of a socialist government in Germany and ensured its ultimate demise. This story has wider implications as well. The failure of revolutionaries to make an imprint on the new order in Germany effectively sealed the fate of socialism in Russia, which became socialism in one country rather than part of a wider socialist system. In Germany the events of late 1918 and 1919 poisoned the political atmosphere of the succeeding decade and beyond.

The German republic and its opponents

The German revolution of November 1918 was the replacement of the Wilhelmine monarchy by a provisional government which oversaw the construction of a parliamentary democracy. The abdication of the Kaiser and the formation of a more popular form of government in Germany were conditions set by the Allies before they would agree to an armistice. Reluctantly the Kaiser accepted the inevitable and abdicated; a republic was proclaimed on 9 November 1918.

The revolution was in no sense the work of an organized political movement. It began spontaneously, as the revolt of a disillusioned population – fed on four years of propaganda about inevitable victory – which had just digested the news of imminent defeat. On 10 November 1918 a joint Commissariat of "Independent Socialists" (on the left wing of the socialist movement) and "Majority Socialists" (on the right) took power in Berlin. Its authority was endorsed on the same day by the workers' and soldiers' councils of Berlin. But this show of unity was an illusion, because the constituent parts of the new provisional government and its supporters had very different views on the future of Germany.

The history of the German revolution is really the history first, of an attempt by the left wing of the German labor movement to seize the moment of defeat to create the conditions for a socialist revolution, and secondly, of the stubborn and successful resistance to this aim by the right wing of the labor movement, the army, big business, and the political center and right. The stated aims of the new regime were democratization, demilitarization, and nationalization. Nothing less could have been expected from a government formed by what had been before 1914 the largest and most important socialist party in the world. But to secure a version of the first objective, the second and the third were shelved and quietly buried. Moderate socialists like Philip Scheidemann, who had proclaimed the republic, and Friedrich Ebert, later its first president, saw their

THE POLITICAL EFFECTS OF THE WAR

task as the reestablishment of order, rather than as the construction of a socialist society. To this end they were prepared to come to terms with both the army and with German industrialists, in order to prevent what they saw as chaos overtaking their country.

The price they were prepared to pay was the suppression of the radical wing of their own party. In a famous telephone conversation (never reported to his colleagues), Ebert assured General Groener (who had organized the logistics of Germany's mobilization of 1914 and later played a prominent part in running the war economy) that in return for the support of the army, the provisional government was prepared to combat Bolshevism.

They did so in a number of ways. The first was to assert the writ of the new executive by destroying what was known as the council movement. This was a very loose conglomeration of committees which had been set up throughout Germany spontaneously by workers, soldiers, and (in Bavaria) even by peasants in the turbulent last weeks of the war. They took the glorified name of "workers' and soldiers' councils" from the Soviet model, but the resemblance stopped at the name. Radicals rarely formed the majority of these groups. In some places, such as in Munich, councils temporarily seized power at the end of the war; in other areas they were caretaker committees, looking to hand over power whenever a fully constituted government was formed. To Ebert the councils were an obstacle to the creation of stable government, as they appeared to push aside and thereby disenfranchise the middle and upper classes, whose tacit support was, in his view, indispensable. A few councils also had links with the Spartacus League, a group of militant socialists (known as Spartacists) led by Rosa Luxemburg and Karl Liebknecht, who had opposed the war from the outset and who wanted to push the revoluton to the left.

A clash between the government and the radicals was inevitable. On 6 December soldiers acting on behalf of the government shot dead 16 Spartacists. On 23 December 1918 revolutionary sailors who were camping in the royal palace in Berlin refused to evacuate their new quarters. Indeed, they were so incensed by the attempt to evict them that they marched to the chancellery to try to arrest Ebert. He telephoned the army for help, and the next morning about 30 sailors were killed by shellfire. This forced the departure of the independent socialists from the government five days later. With his hands freed, Ebert was thus able to reestablish a kind of order.

The lessons of the German Revolution of 1918–19

The Kaiser abdicates and a republic is proclaimed

In Berlin socialists seize power

Elsewhere workers' and soldiers' councils are set up

Sparticist radicals and revolutionary sailors agitate for change

President Ebert's government suppresses a Spartacist rising

And the councils

▼ In January 1919 revolutionary socialists took to the streets of Berlin to overthrow the provisional government of moderate socialists, which had come to terms with business and the army. Street fighting – such as this incident in the newspaper quarter of Berlin – was vicious and bloody, but the outcome was never in doubt. The war was over and few workers supported the uprising.

▲ There was not one revolution in Germany in 1918–19 but many revolutions. Uprisings of various kinds took place in Berlin, Düsseldorf, Munich and other German cities. They were crushed one at a time by troops assembled by the social democratic minister of order, Gustav Noske, who is reported to have said, "Someone must play the bloodhound; I am not afraid of the responsibility." After the Berlin uprising had been suppressed, and Rosa Luxemburg and Karl Liebknecht murdered, other measures were taken by government troops to restore order. The most serious challenge to the new regime was the establishment of a Soviet republic in Bavaria on 4 April 1919 (destroyed by May Day 1919). The price of the restoration of order was the final and irreversible schism of the German socialist movement.

Rosa Luxemburg 1870–1919

Rosa Luxemburg was the equal of Marx and Lenin as a revolutionary theorist and political figure. She dominated the left wing of the German social democratic party by the sheer power of her mind and her unshakable dedication to revolutionary socialism. She was born in Russian Poland in 1870, and migrated to Germany in 1895. Her early work in the socialist movement was as a journalist, but she also established a powerful reputation as a scholar and theorist. She was an advocate of the mass strike, and an opponent of the desiccated bureaucracy of the German social democratic party. The party's decision to vote for war credits in 1914 led her into a struggle against both the war and the supine acceptance of it by the workers' movement. She spent most of the war either in prison or anticipating the knock at the door. The letters she wrote in prison describe a humanist, whose socialism grew out of her moral indignation at the bestialities of the economic system which produced exploitation and war. She was freed in the turbulent last days of the war, and resumed her revolutionary activity, as editor of the *Rote Fahne* (Red Flag), and as central figure with Karl Liebknecht in the Spartacus League. She openly criticized Lenin's policies on land, nationalities, and democracy, and helped found the German communist party. Her attitude to the Spartacist uprising of 1919 was ambiguous. She was aware of its futility, but saw little of value in remaining a socialist thinker who stood aside when workers manned the barricades. She was arrested, beaten and shot on 15 January 1919.

Karl Liebknecht 1871–1919

The son of Wilhelm Liebknecht, one of the founders of the German social democratic party, Karl Liebknecht was born in 1871, at the end of the victorious Franco-Prussian War which his father had had the courage to condemn. In this respect Karl was his father's son, and will be remembered as the most uncompromising socialist opponent of the 1914–18 war. By 1914 he was a leader of the left-wing faction of the social democratic party and a deputy in the Reichstag. His refusal to vote for war credits made him an outcast within his own party, which initially was deluded enough to believe that Germany was fighting a defensive war. His defiant public stand against the war made him the target of repeated vilification and prosecution. He shouted "Down with the War!" to passersby (including soldiers) in Berlin in 1916, an act of defiance that earned him a lengthy jail sentence. His imprisonment led to a series of strikes organized by militant workers in the Spartacus League, which he had founded with Rosa Luxemburg. On his release from prison in late October 1918, he placed himself at the vanguard of the militant left and opposed the decision of the independent socialists to join in the creation of a provisional socialist government in November 1918. His aim was to force the revolution to the left, and his support for an insurrection in January 1919 must be seen in this light. He was captured on 15 January 1919, beaten and shot. Liebknecht was a romantic revolutionary with unlimited courage, but without the intellectual brilliance or political acumen of Luxemburg or Lenin.

While I was raising troops in Dahlem, there were negotiations for days in the imperial chancellery with representatives of the opponents of the people's spokesmen. I opposed any compromise most emphatically... An influx of reliable soldiers arrived from Potsdam. On Saturday 11 January [1919], I moved at the head of 3,000 well-armed, strictly disciplined soldiers to Berlin. During the course of the week the greater part of Berlin was occupied by the troops.... The national elections followed on Sunday 19 January 1919, without any serious disturbance. In Berlin, as throughout the empire, an unending and wearisome task of reconstruction and cleansing began. The government's authority had to be created almost step by step, partly through bloody struggles.

GUSTAV NOSKE

The suppression of the left

Between 5 and 15 January 1919 the Spartacists took to the streets and declared the Ebert government deposed. But the rising was suppressed by soldiers turned paramilitary police, the notorious *Freikorps*, working ironically under the authority of the socialist minister of order, Gustav Noske. The street fighting that ensued was bloody, but the result was inevitable. The Spartacists never stood a chance against a better armed and better trained adversary. Rosa Luxemburg and Karl Liebknecht were captured, beaten up and murdered (15 January 1919). The brutal suppression of the Spartacists helped to establish the legitimacy of the new regime in the eyes of the center and the right. Indeed, it is difficult to avoid the conclusion that the radicals had played directly into the hands of their enemies.

The unpopularity of the revolutionary action of January 1919 was underlined just four days after the end of the uprising. In elections to the national assembly, the moderate socialists received 38 percent of the vote, the independents received under 8 percent, and a narrow but real majority voted for the nonsocialist parties. This balance of forces was reflected in the provisions of the new "Weimar constitution". Parliamentary government, with cabinet responsibility to the legislature, was established, putting an end to both the old Wilhelmine system and the hopes (or dreams) of workers' power or participatory democracy along the lines laid down by many within the council movement at the end of the war. Gone too was the possibility of effectively challenging the political influence of the army and big business, which was also on the agenda of the November revolution.

But this clear political triumph of the right-wing socialists was a Pyrrhic victory. The suppression of the left permanently crippled the socialist movement as a whole. On the one hand, embittered radicals now saw communism and a complete transformation of society as the only answers, and developed a fanatical hatred for socialists (later dubbed "social fascists") which made a common front against counterrevolution a political impossibility. On the other hand, the moderate socialists in power lost much rank-and-file support and further alienated themselves from part of their natural constituency within the working class. And this occurred precisely when the new government had to take the responsibility for the economic difficulties of postwar adjustment and, in particular, for signing the Treaty of Versailles, thus accepting its humiliating provisions and guilt for having started the war. Over time the new constitution earned the contempt of the right as well as of the left, and when the time came, both abandoned it.

It may not be too far-fetched to describe the Weimar Republic as a candle burning at both ends, with the left end burning more rapidly than the right, in effect consuming itself in internecine warfare. This was the immediate political legacy of World War I in Germany, one which had ominous implications for the history of socialism, for Germany's own future and for that of the rest of the world.

The militarization of politics

The suppression of the Spartacist uprising by paramilitary groups of the right in January 1919 demonstrated one of the most disturbing legacies of the war: the tendency in many European countries for the camaraderie of arms to be resurrected and used as a weapon in internal political conflict. One example was Britain's "black and tans", recently demobilized soldiers, still in their khaki, modified by the black leather insignia of the police, who served as special police officers in Ireland between 1920 and 1922. Their reputation for brutality in the "dirty war" between Irish nationalists and the British was well-deserved. More prominent still were Mussolini's *fascisti* in Italy, a mixed group of idealists, adventurers, poets and thugs. They took from the war two essential lessons: first, that parliamentary institutions did not matter; and secondly, that a population inured by war to violence would not resist an armed insurrection by a determined and ruthless minority.

What Mussolini and his fellow arch-patriot, the poet Gabriele D'Annunzio, had learned during the war about the efficacy of the theatrical politics of the streets they applied in the immediate postwar years. Building on popular resentment of the supposedly shabby treatment Italy had received at Versailles, D'Annunzio decided to demonstrate Italy's unrecognized claim to the city of Fiume, on the Yugoslav border, by force of arms. He led a motley army of followers into the city on 12 September 1919. In response the Italian government under Francesco Nitt, disavowed his action, but did absolutely nothing to unseat him. Three years later Mussolini repeated virtually the same performance: his fascist gangs took over the cities of Bologna and Milan in the late spring and summer of 1922 and the government did nothing. Within a few months he led his famous "March on Rome" (a glorified train journey), after which he was invited by King Victor Emmanuel III to take power.

The line linking 1915 with 1919 and later with Mussolini's seizure of power in 1922 is clear. In all three, parliamentary or constitutional considerations were simply brushed aside by the nationalist vanguard. In all three the resort to force was successful, because no one in authority was prepared to call the bluff of these operatic mountebanks and respond to force with force. And in all three, the ranks of rightist radicals were swollen by ex-soldiers, whose presence gave to these movements a degree of prestige and popular legitimacy.

Furthermore, the mystique of the ex-soldier was in itself a useful ideology. It provided the nascent fascist movement with its uniforms, its marches, its eternal flames, its ceremonies, and its contempt for the flabby politicians who had schemed in safety while soldiers like Mussolini – according to his own account – suffered on the field of battle. It resurrected the camaraderie of the trenches as a principal of political action, rekindled the cult of the leader, and dressed up domestic violence as the continuation of the war that Italy had won, but the fruits of which it had never been allowed to enjoy.

▲▼ **Two faces of fascism: above, Oswald Mosley, leader of the British Union of Fascists in 1938; below, Adolf Hitler and Ernst Röhm in Braunschweig in 1931. Three years later, Hitler ordered the murder of Röhm and many of his followers.**

Politics in Germany and France

If we turn from disgruntled victor to disgruntled vanquished, from Italy to Germany, the same pattern is seen of the "politics of the streets", emerging out of the war to plague postwar society. Germany had had veterans' organizations before 1914, but after World War I they achieved an unprecedented degree of political prominence. These groups spanned the political spectrum. On the left were the *Reichsbanner* (republican combat league), linked to the social democratic party, and the *Rote Frontkämpferbund* (red soldiers' league) and *Rote Marine* (red navy) loosely allied to the German Communist Party. On the right there were various groups, the most prominent of which was the *Stahlhelm*, founded on the 13 November 1918 to promote comradeship, defend ex-soldiers' interests, and stop the "*Schweinerei*" (rabble) of revolution.

Alongside them stood the men of the *Freikorps*, numbering over 500,000 in 1919. This was not a veterans' organization, but rather a volunteer army, collected and paid by the social democratic government, and entrusted with the harsh and frequently brutal restoration of order in the immediate postwar period. It attracted regular soldiers, freebooters and anticommunist adventurers, the men who formed the nuclei of the embryonic national socialist movement.

On 6 March 1919 a provisional *Reichswehr* (imperial army) was set up, incorporating the *Freikorps*, former army officers and men, and other volunteers. Within a few weeks 300,000 men had joined up. However, the Treaty of Versailles, signed a few months later, limited this force to 100,000 men and placed severe restrictions on its weaponry, its command structure and its sphere of operations. These provisions were bitterly resented, but had to be endured, at least for the moment. Thousands were demobilized and formed the core of radical right-wing groups that grew ominously in the early postwar period. There is no doubt that Versailles helped turn many men who had served in the war against the new republic, and paved the way for the Kapp *Putsch* of March 1920, an abortive attempt to seize power by disgruntled army officers and ex-soldiers in volunteer organizations.

Not all those who joined these groups or supported the Kapp *Putsch* later became Nazis. Some did; others faded into apathy. But what they shared in common with their Italian brethren was, first, a hatred of communism; secondly, deep resentment about the immediate postwar settlement; and thirdly, a belief in the decadence of a discredited political system. These beliefs helped create the Nazi movement and make it a major political force.

In France the fascist leagues which emerged at this time were also a product of war and the ex-soldiers' mystique. Men of the *Croix de feu* (cross of fire) wore blue shirts and berets, gray trousers and military boots, which announced their affinity with German and Italian fascism. They too hated parliamentary democracy, and saw it as a corrupt weed to be uprooted at any cost. They too saw Bolshevism as an enemy to be fought on the streets. They too attempted a *Putsch*, on 6 February 1935, which was suppressed leaving 15 dead and hundreds injured.

It is true that left-wing and moderate veterans' groups were also formed at this time. The most famous was Henri Barbusse's Republican Association of War Veterans (*ARAC*), which he funded from the proceeds of his best-selling war novel *Under Fire*, published in 1916. But by 1923 this organization and others like it were politically marginalized by becoming little more than the veterans' wing of the communist movement.

What gave ex-soldiers' organizations a place on the political map of interwar Europe was widespread disillusionment with the postwar settlements and unease over the chronic economic difficulties of the time. The more traditional political parties were discredited by the war, the more successful were ex-soldiers' organizations in proclaiming a purer, more manly, more defiant alternative. This helps account for the strength of these movements in Germany, France and Italy, for example, and their relative weakness in Britain, where conservatism benefited from the war. This is a fact which Oswald Mosley, the one British politician who tried to build an analogous political movement (his New Party, with its uniforms and street confrontations) failed to see. The result was well-deserved political failure. But his noisy effort to mobilize the masses against the "communist and Jewish menace" in the 1930s testifies to the lingering effects of the conflict on the political culture of the postwar world.

Total War

▲ Tension between Turks and Armenians living in the Turkish Empire was not new in 1914: massacres of Armenians had taken place in 1894, 1896 and 1909. This left a legacy of hatred and mutual suspicion which underlay the Turkish decision of 27 May 1915 to deport the entire Armenian population of Turkey to Syria and Mesopotamia. Of a population of about 1.8 million, one-third was deported, one-third evaded the order, and about one-third was massacred. The slaughter of innocent civilians, among them the children pictured above, in World War I, set a terrible precedent for World War II.

World War I both expanded the public domain at the expense of the private, and raised the level of tolerance of "civilized people" toward political violence and brutality. First, propaganda prepared the ground for the suppression of dissent and the vicious vilification of the enemy. Propaganda became a synonym for government-sponsored lies, propagated to stop people from thinking in wartime. Hatred was preferable to thought. One of the worst repercussions of this kind of thought control was that in World War II, when accurate stories of German atrocities in concentration camps appeared, they were consistently and tragically disbelieved. After all, it was said, governments always make up such stories. But not always; just from 1914 onward.

Secondly, the war created conditions which made internal subversion and its suppression key aspects of the waging of war. Undermining the war effort of the enemy by means of subversion was not invented in 1914; witness the guerrilla warfare waged in Spain during the Napoleonic era. A century later wartime subversion – or the undermining of the enemy from within – took on a new form, appropriate to the imperialist age. Each side tried to pry the other's colonies away from the mother country by covert means. Minorities became potential enemies, and were treated as such.

Thirdly, whatever the pious words of the combatants, all civilians became legitimate targets of hostilities. One conspicuous example is the case of the German submarine campaign, the purpose of which was to cut off essential supplies from the UK and bring about a negotiated settlement. A second example is the perpetuation of the Allied blockade of German ports after November 1918. This was intended to keep pressure on Germany to sign a formal peace treaty rather than simply regather its forces and fight on. But its primary result was to increase death rates among noncombatants, infants, the elderly and the infirm. Here is a classic example of how, after four years of war and staggering losses, a kind of numbing of sensibilities occurred among political leaders and the populations they led, so that they were able to convince themselves that killing civilians by starvation was a legitimate tactic of warfare.

It may well be that this blockade was a war crime. But even this act pales in comparison with the policy of genocide which the Turks carried out upon defenseless Armenians. With little or no military justification, and under the cover of war, the Turks forcibly deported from their traditional homes over one million Armenians, of whom perhaps 500,000 died of torture or disease. In numerical terms, these actions dwarfed atrocities committed in China during the Boxer rebellion of 1900 and in Macedonia in 1902–03, where an estimated 30,000 Bulgarians were killed. Turkish war crimes in World War I were original, therefore, not in conception, but in their sheer scale.

The Nazis took a special interest in the Armenian massacres. Whatever were the sources of Hitler's policy of exterminating the Jewish people during World War II, his mad project was not the first of its kind, but, like so many other abominable features of 20th-century life, was prefigured a generation earlier during World War I.

Datafile

European dominance of world political and economic affairs ended in 1914, or more accurately, in 1917, when the USA entered the war. Colonies increased their demands for self-government and independence. States dependent on European goods developed domestic manufacturing sectors. Overseas assets were liquidated; markets lost to America and Japan, and New York displaced London as the financial capital of the world.

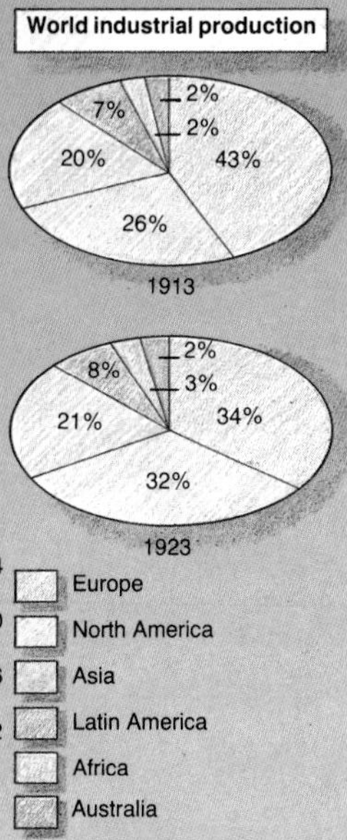

▲ The decentralization of the world economy is illustrated by the decline in Europe's share of industrial production from 43 percent in 1913 to 34 percent a decade later. The chief beneficiaries of European decline were the USA and Canada, but industry in Japan, India, South Africa and Brazil made major strides in this decade.

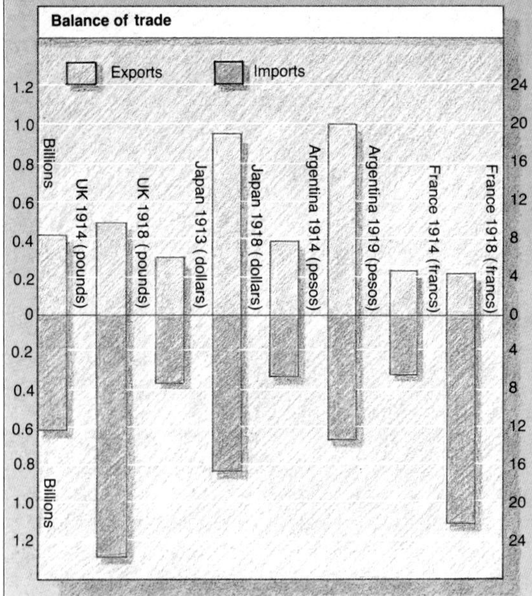

► The prewar pattern of international trade was torn up during the 1914–18 war, and could not be restored. The USA and Japan became net exporters for the first time Argentina increased its export surplus. In contrast both the UK and France incurred huge trade deficits. By 1918 France imported four times the value of its exports.

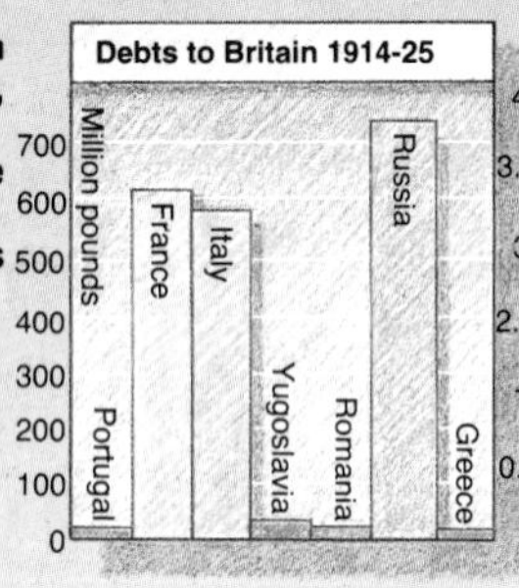

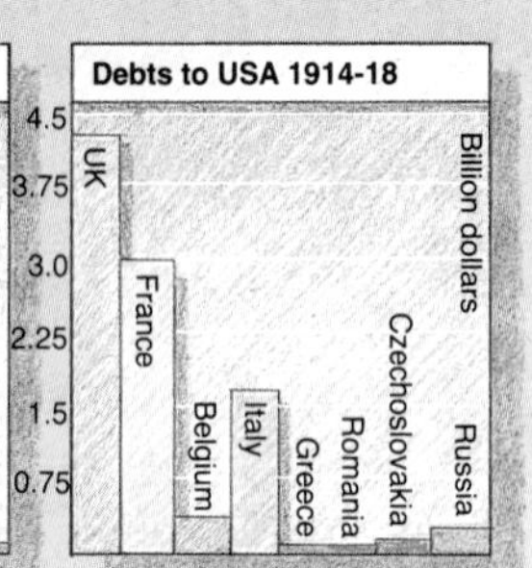

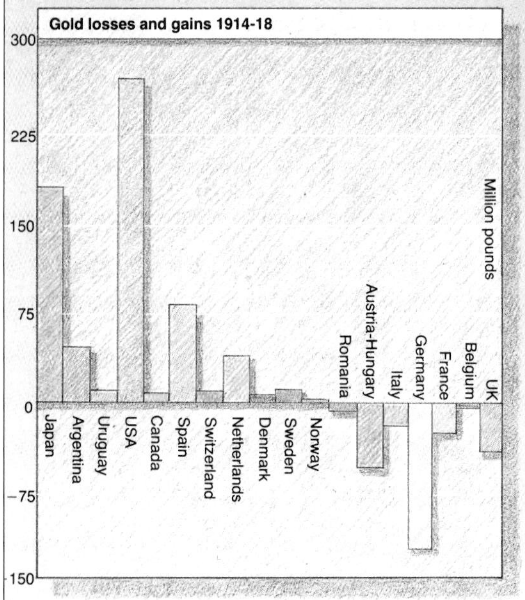

▲ The war created a triangle of indebtedness. A series of countries incurred debts to the UK, which in turn was heavily indebted to the USA. A group of seven European countries owed the UK over 2 billion pounds after the war; British indebtedness to the United States stood at 4.2 billion dollars. The major European combatants lost markets, the income from financial services and assets. Their liquidation can be estimated from a rough balance sheet of gains and losses of gold reserves. Nine European countries reduced their gold reserves by about 280 million pounds; this is almost identical to American gains.

One key area in which we can see the clear impact of war is in the field of imperial politics. On the one hand the war demonstrated the economic value of imperialism, in the palpable form of human and material capital. On the other it undermined the ability of the major imperial powers to command their far-flung dependencies and set in motion forces which eventually would tear apart the imperial fabric.

Imperial gains and losses

The best evidence for the strength of imperial sentiments in 1914, not only among rulers but also among the ruled, is in wartime military recruitment statistics. To the French war effort Indochina contributed some 150,000 men. Algeria and French West Africa added half a million more. For a country obsessed by the numerical superiority

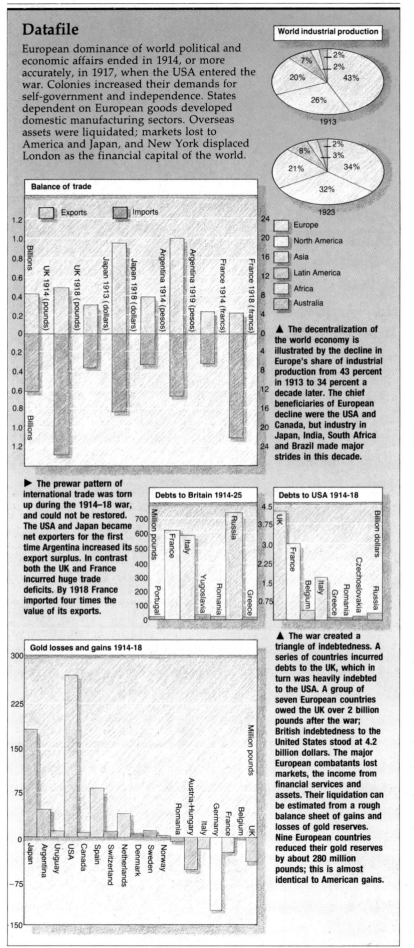

THE WAR AND GLOBAL POWER

of its neighbor across the Rhine, this was a vital transfusion during the war.

The contribution of India to the war effort of the British Empire dwarfed that of all French dependencies put together. India provided 1.3 million soldiers and laborers for the Allied cause. About the same number of fighting men came from Australia, New Zealand, South Africa and Canada to serve alongside British forces. If the Irish contingents are added – both Protestant and Catholic – then the British Empire added over 40 percent to the manpower Britain was able to put into the field in World War I.

When the peace settlement is considered a further reason is seen for regarding World War I as the apogee of empire. German holdings and colonies were transferred as mandates and protectorates to a variety of powers: in east and southwest Africa, to Britain; in the Cameroons and Togo, to France; and in the Far East to Japan, Australia and New Zealand. The Ottoman Empire was similarly dismembered: what are today Syria and Lebanon became French mandates while Palestine, Transjordan and Iraq became British mandates.

Imperial dependencies made vital contributions to the war effort

The war contributed to decolonization

It also accelerated decentralization of the world economy

American economic strength grew at the expense of Britain

Japan also made economic gains

In general the war was an economic disaster for Europe

▼▶ "Imperial" manpower: W. Indian troops in Kingston, Jamaica (below), and Indian soldiers in France (right).

This was the positive side of the story, at least for the winners of the war, and it was certainly not negligible. But like so much else about the war it was a mixed blessing, for several reasons. The first was economic. Given the cost of the war, Britain, for example, could not afford to defend the Empire as it existed in 1914, let alone provide troops to look after any new trouble spots. Postwar budgetary constraints militated against the maintenance of imperial power, let alone its extension. Secondly, the war had uprooted substantial rural populations in imperial lands, and by bringing them to the cities had exposed them to nationalist sentiments and movements. Then, there was what may be described as the ideological boomerang of wartime propaganda. The Allies themselves had announced their faith in the principle of self-determination; what applied to the Austro-Hungarian Empire could be applied to all the others too. Furthermore, colonial reforms made in the interests of wartime recruitment had the paradoxical effect of increasing rather than allaying the colonies' discontent with the occupying powers. There was also the slow and uneven spread of communist ideas in the postwar decades. Finally, nationalist aspirations rose at a time when inflation and economic instability provided material reasons for ordinary people to express their discontent in political movements dedicated to the struggle for independence. For all these reasons, the true impact of the war was to accelerate, rather than retard, the process of decolonization.

Changes in the world economy

Outside the framework of empire, other centrifugal forces were released by the war. The most fundamental of these was the decentralization of the world economy, a shift of strength from its older European core to the extra-European periphery. The origins of this trend antedated the 1914–18 conflict. But the war turned a trickle into a flood, and marked the beginning of the end of the period in which European economic and political power dominated world affairs.

The benefits of this shift in the balance of power were shared among many nations, but the main beneficiary was the United States, which entered the war at a relatively late stage. The war brought an export boom to the USA. By 1918 fully 10 percent of its national product was sold abroad; this was the highest rate ever recorded to that date. Much of this new business went straight along the North Atlantic routes to help the Allies, who could not afford to use more distant sources of essential supplies, like New Zealand, Australia and Argentina. The cost of waging war also altered fundamentally the debtor–creditor relationship between the United States and Europe. The United Kingdom in particular was forced to liquidate its American assets. First through the offices of J.P. Morgan, and after 1917 through the US Treasury, the UK secured over 4 billion dollars in loans to help cover war expenditure. By the end of the war the UK had become an economic satellite of the USA. Subsequent generations have learned that dependent economies rarely have independent foreign policies. Overall, US investment abroad rose from 3.5 billion dollars in 1914 to 7 billion dollars in 1919, and foreign holdings in the USA correspondingly plummeted from 7.2 billion dollars in 1914 to 4 billion dollars in 1919.

But this was not the end of the story. In addition American merchants and shippers occupied trade routes and provided insurance, brokerage and other services, traditionally the domain of the City of London. The UK's loss of "invisible income" from these services was largely America's gain. Furthermore, New York displaced London as the world's premier financial center. This change might have happened anyway, but the protracted European war made it an urgent business necessity.

Similarly spectacular economic gains were made during the war by Japan. Huge shipping contracts (including some for America) were awarded to Japan. A substantial degree of diversification occurred in Japanese home production, which enabled it to attain a creditor position for the first time in its history. This led to a Japanese investment drive into China, whose domestic economy also benefited from European economic preoccupations during the war.

Other smaller powers also began to cut the umbilical cord which had tied their economies to that of Europe. This was largely the result of wartime "import substitution", whereby the old cycle of selling domestic raw materials for European finished goods was broken. This occurred in Argentina and Brazil, South Africa and India, to name but a few countries thus affected by the

The Roots of the Palestine Tragedy

◀▲ In 1914–18 Jews fought on both sides as patriotic citizens. British Jews answered Lord Rothschild's call to serve (left). German Jews were equally patriotic, but their military service did little to stem the tide of antisemitism, leading in the 1930s to the expulsion (above) or murder of many of those who had served with distinction in the war.

◀▼ In 1917 Chaim Weizmann (left), the British chemist and Zionist leader, persuaded A.J. Balfour, Britain's foreign secretary, to issue a declaration of support for the establishment of a Jewish homeland in Palestine. In the 1920s many new settlements (including Nahalal, below) were established as the vanguard of a state in the making.

World War I was a decisive period for both Jewish and Arab nationalist movements. Before 1914 the population of Palestine was overwhelmingly Arab. There were about 90,000 Jews in Palestine, living in Jerusalem, Haifa and the newly-born city of Tel Aviv, as well as in 43 agricultural settlements. They were supported by an international Zionist movement, centered in Germany, Austria and Russia. The outbreak of war shifted the center of gravity of the Zionist movement westward. Zionist leaders living in England, such as Chaim Weizmann and Nahum Sokolow, exploited the new political situation created by the war between Britain and Turkey, the legal authority in Palestine. On 2 November 1917 the British foreign secretary, A.J. Balfour addressed a letter to Lord Rothschild stating that Britain viewed "with favour the establishment in Palestine of a national homeland for the Jewish people" without prejudice to the "civil and religious rights of the non-Jewish communities". This doctrine was ratified at the Treaty of San Remo in 1920 as official British policy. In 1922 the League of Nations conferred on Britain a mandate to rule Palestine, which the then colonial secretary, Winston Churchill, saw as entailing increased Jewish immigration without the "disappearance or the subordination of the Arabic poulation, language, or culture in Palestine."

This even-handed policy was bound to fail, since the war gave as great an impetus to Arab nationalism as it had done to jewish nationalism. British promises to respect Arab independence were ultimately inconsistent with the commitment to help build a Jewish homeland. The acquisition of land in Palestine by the Jewish Agency and other groups and the creation of the infrastructure of a state in the interwar years was accompanied by Arab protests, which led to bloody riots in 1929 and 1936–39.

After the Nazis' extermination of six million Jews, Palestine became a haven for the survivors. Their suffering increased international support for the creation of a Jewish state, recognized by the United Nations on 29 November 1947. Since then several increasingly bloody wars have failed to resolve the tragic clash of national aspirations between Palestinian Arabs and Jews.

war. What was good for their development was bad (in the short term) for the health of Europe's staple export trade.

Four other war-related developments further exacerbated European economic difficulties in the aftermath of the conflict. The first was the loss of assets invested in czarist Russia, primarily but not only by France. The second was the self-defeating policy of reparations. Payment for damages were first made to Belgium and then to France. In 1921 other schedules of reparations were set. These did not even begin to pay for the war, and they conspired to form a dangerous triangle of indebtedness – from Germany to Britain, and then from Britain to the USA.

The third was the imposition of tariffs and other restrictive trade practices in the United States and elsewhere. This made free trade, so dear to the British liberal temperament, hopelessly outmoded. The fourth was the end of free immigration to the United States, which had brought opportunities to refugees and income to the families they left behind. In Italy in particular, this loss of capital was a very serious matter.

In sum, the war was an economic disaster for Europe. The conflict had undermined stable currencies and had torn up the entire fabric of prewar economic affairs. The war put an end to the free movement of capital; the United States put an end to the free movement of labor; and sooner or later virtually everybody put an end to the free movement of goods. This hit the UK particularly hard, since it had imported three-quarters of its food supply before 1914, and paid for it by export earnings. The damage suffered by other European countries was more tangible, though less enduring. The job of rebuilding farms and factories and rehousing populations displaced by fighting had to be done in Belgium, France, Poland, Italy and Russia – where fighting continued well after the Armistice. Elsewhere, thanks to human ingenuity, the task of reconstruction had largely been accomplished by 1924, when European production regained the prewar level. But by then the USA was far ahead.

The Great War and the Great Depression

In 1924 there were many in the West who thought that the disturbances of the war and the postwar years were over, but their optimism was somewhat misplaced. Five years later the New York stockmarket crashed and drew the rest of the world into the Great Depression. Scholars have yet to agree on the exact source of this debacle, but the economic instability induced by the war was partly to blame. The problem was that structural changes caused by the war had been insufficiently appreciated. Some had seen them as temporary aberrations, which would vanish in an always imminent postwar boom. This is the most likely explanation for the blinkered attempt by the Bank of England in 1925 to bring the British currency back to its prewar level of parity with the dollar. The results were disastrous.

To some the war itself had demonstrated the remarkable flexibility of capitalism to expand and adapt to new requirements. No one could have believed before 1914 that economies could cope with total war, but they did. Surely, the postwar argument went, they could cope with the lesser problems of peace. Such delusions helped prepare the ground for the crisis. But of much greater importance was the fact that the war had given an irreversible westward shift to the center of gravity of the world economic system. From 1918 on, what happened in the American economy largely determined what happened in the European economy, not the other way round. When the American economy went into a tailspin in 1929, the rest of the world was bound to follow, thereby creating the worst economic crisis in the history of capitalism.

Would this have happened without the war? No one will ever know, but this much can be stated: the war undermined a dynamic and relatively stable set of economic relationships which could not be rebuilt in the same form after 1918. Attempts to do so, or to deny on isolationist grounds the interconnectedness of American and European developments, only made matters worse. In this context it may be fair to describe the Great Depression as a child of World War I. The shock of the Depression brought home how deep an economic divide separated the prewar from the postwar world.

▶ In the United States the depression hit the farming population with particular force. Between 1929 and 1932 the price of wheat, corn, cotton, and tobacco fell by two-thirds. The result was to bankrupt small farmers, and impoverish tenant farmers and agricultural laborers. In the midwest and southwest, unused land, swept by winds in the West Texas plain, turned into a "dust bowl", out of which millions migrated west. Among them was the poet and songwriter Woody Guthrie, who sang of their plight in ballads such as "So long, it's been good to know you" (1936) and "I ain't got no home in this world any more" (1938).

◀ In the midst of the depression, men and women from all walks of life joined the bread line. Unemployment reached unprecedented levels: 80 percent in Toledo, Ohio; 50 percent in Cleveland. In Donora, Pennsylvania, less than 300 people had a job out of a workforce of 14,000.

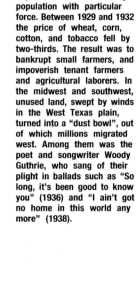

HOOVER'S
POOR FARM
TOBACCO
HARD TIMES ARE STILL
"HOOVER"ING OVER US

▼ A "bonus army" of about 15,000 out-of-work American veterans and their families marched on Washington in the spring of 1932. After President Hoover and the Congress failed to help them, the protestors' camp was violently dispersed by the army, led by General Douglas MacArthur.

PART 6

THE MEMORY OF WAR

BIOGRAPHIES AND GLOSSARY

Arnoux, Guy died 1951
French artist, a member of the Salon des Humoristes and remarkable for his military and maritime scenes. His most famous work was the illustrations produced for *The Battle* by Claude Farrere. Arnoux helped to create a new popular art by drawing posters or illustrations in archaic character, mixing ancient and contemporary forms.

Attenborough, Richard 1923-
British actor and film director, who served with the Royal Air Force film unit during World War II. After the war he was associated with the move to greater realism in British film. He directed the antiwar fantasia *Oh! What a Lovely War* in 1969, based on the play by Joan Littlewood.

Barbusse, Henri 1874-1935
French novelist, the author of *Le Feu (Under Fire* (1916), which portrays in starkly vivid terms the experience of the common soldier during World War I.

Beckmann, Max 1884-1950
German painter who worked in Berlin and Frankfurt until 1938, when political intimidation drove him to Amsterdam. His experiences during World War I led him to an art which was often allegorical, concerned with symbolic rather than pictorial truths. His most important works, such as *The Departure* (1932–35), were large allegorical figure compositions, sometimes brutal in treatment.

Bone, Muirhead 1876-1953
Scottish architect and draughtsman who was also an accomplished etcher and excelled in drypoint and drawings of intricate detail. He was one of the most prolific official British war artists in World War I, and also served as a war artist in World War II.

Borzage, Frank 1983-62
American film director, who began his career as an actor. By the mid 1920s he had become one of Hollywood's most successful directors. He directed the film adaptation of Hemingway's *A Farewell to Arms* in 1932. His style was full of imagery. *The Mortal Storm* (1940) was a frightening and perceptive study of fascism.

Brecht, Bertold 1898-1956
German dramatist and poet. In the early 1920s Brecht created the experimental theater characteristic of the interwar period. A committed Marxist, he left Germany in 1933, and returned to East Berlin after World War II. His works include *The Threepenny Opera* (1928) and *Mother Courage and her Children* (1941).

Brittain, Vera 1896-1970
British writer, whose experiences as a nurse in World War I are movingly documented in her autobiographical novel *The Testament of Youth* (1933). She published sequels, *Testament of Friendship* (1940) and *Testament of Experience* (1957).

Brooke, Rupert 1887-1915
British poet, who, on the outbreak of war, took up a commission in the Royal Naval Division. His early death, at Skiros while on the Dardanelles expedition, made him a symbol of patriotism and the waste of war, although he died of sunstroke and bloodpoisoning rather than in battle. His poetry of the early part of the war, published in *1914 and Other Poems* (1915) presents a romantic view: he had not then experienced the horror and disillusion of the war.

Cannan, May Wedderburn 1893-1973
British poet, who served in the war as a nurse in the Voluntary Aid Detachment, and later worked for the press. She wrote three volumes of war poetry, *In War Time* (1917), *The Splendid Days* (1919), *The House of Hope* (1923).

Chaplin, Charlie 1889-1977
British comedian and film director, who became the first international film star with his persona of the woefully endearing tramp. In 1910 he went to the United States to work with the Keystone Company. His film *Shoulder Arms* (1918) satirized the absurdities of military life.

Cocteau, Jean 1891-1963
French writer and artist, best known as an avant-garde playwright but exploring with many forms of art. He was the leading French playwright between the wars, with *Orphée* (1926) and the novel *Les Enfants Terribles* (1929). In 1940 he became a member of the French Academy.

Daryrush, Elizabeth 1887-1976
British poet, the daughter of British poet laureate Robert Bridges. She was concerned as much with the form of the poem as with its subject matter.

Dix, Otto 1891-
German painter, who fought in the army during World War I and in the early 1920s, like Grosz, turned to an aggressively realistic and political conception of art known as *Neue Sachlichkeit* (new realism). He had a preference for subjects drawn from working-class life. His paintings involve passionate social comment. His work was suppressed by the Nazis during World War II, but he became active again after 1945.

Dufy, Raoul 1877-1953
French painter and textile designer. He first experimented with Impressionism and then converted to Fauvism in 1905. During the 1920s he developed a witty calligraphic style, drawing on brightly colored background washes.

Eisenstein, Sergei Mikhailovich 1898-1948
Russian film director, who came to film through working as a theatrical scene painter. In his work he substituted the individual hero with a group or crowd. His skills lay chiefly in cutting and recutting to achieve a mounting impressionistic effect. His best known works include *Strike* (1924), *Battleship Potemkin* (1925) and *October* (1927), dealing with the Bolshevik Revolution.

Gance, Abel 1889-1981
French actor, screenwriter and playwright. Gance directed his first film in 1911, and was a brilliant technical innovator. He was highly acclaimed for his sensational epic *J'accuse* (1919)

Graves, Robert 1895-1985
British writer and poet, best known for his historical writings. In 1929 he published *Goodbye to All That*, an autobiography that reacreated his experiences in the trenches as a member of the Welch Fusiliers. Graves's poems concerning the war do not deal directly with the brutal reality of war, but after the war was over he dealt with such themes as the blasting apart of societal norms, the guilt of the survivors, and the desperation of men deprived of their usual cultural and institutional edifices.

Griffiths, D.W. 1875-1948
American film director, responsible for inventing many film techniques such as fade-outs, long-shots and close-ups. In 1914 he directed *The Birth of a Nation*, a successful film on the aftermath of civil war. Although a technical triumph, it was censored in many cities because of its racist message. He also made the epic *Intolerance* (1916).

Grosz, Georg 1893-1959
German painter, illustrator, caricaturist and writer. Grosz was an antibourgeois illustrator before the war and a leading member of the Berlin Dada group after 1918. He was fiercely antimilitarist and anticapitalist, and his drawings frequently criticized Berlin society. In 1932 he settled in New York, and after 1945 produced nightmarish, surrealist work.

Hansi 1873–1951
Nom de plume of Jakob Warz, an Alsatian caricaturist working during the war. He served with the French army in 1914-15 and was sentenced to a year's imprisonment for his illustrations in a children's book which offended the Germans. He was never caught, however, and did not serve his term.

Hasek, Jaroslav 1883-1923
Czech writer whose experiences during the war led him to produce the popular satire on military bureaucracy and the business of war, *The Good Soldier Schweik* 1920-23.

Hawks, Howard 1896-1977
American film director, who made his first film in 1926. During his long and respected career, his films were distinguished for their incisive dialog, visual clarity and absence of clever effects. He directed *The Road to Glory* (1936) about a French regiment in World War I.

Hemingway, Ernest 1898-1961
American writer who developed a wholly individual style of writing. During World War I he served as an ambulance driver, and later as an infantryman in the Italian army. His works, which include the novel (later filmed) *A Farewell to Arms* (1929), deal broadly with how violation and trauma can be healed.

Hughes, Howard 1905-76
American film director, who was a successful tycoon before directing his first film, *Hell's Angels*, in 1930. This was the most expensive film made to date, and dealt with the air war of World War I. Hughes was an excessively private man and withdrew from public attention in the 1950s.

Ingram, Rex 1893-1950
An Irish film director, who moved to the United States in 1911, and became a successful director of spectacles and supernatural and horror films. His film *The Four Horsemen of the Apocalypse* (1921), about a young man fighting for France in World War I, starred Rudolf Valentino.

Kafka, Franz 1883-1924
German author, born in Prague. Although little known during his life, as a highly individual novelist Kafka has had great influence on writers of the Surrealist school. His works, which include *The Trial* 1925 and *The Castle* (1926), are allegorical and speak of the isolation of modern life.

Kollwitz, Käthe 1867-1945
German graphic illustrator and sculptor. She lived for most of her life in the poorest part of Berlin, and her work is suffused with sympathy for and understanding of the working class. She declared herself a communist. Among her most famous sculptures was the war memorial at Dixmuiden in Flanders, which was completed in 1932.

Kubrick, Stanley 1928-
American film director, who made his first feature film in 1953. *Paths of Glory* (1957), dealing with military injustice in the trenches of Flanders, was his first critical success. He has made several other outstanding antiwar films.

Lawrence, Thomas Edward 1888-1935
British soldier and writer. An archeologist in the Middle East before 1914, Lawrence joined British Intelligence in Egypt, and joined the Arab revolt against the Turks, helping to capture Damascus. After the war he supported Arab independence, and joined the Royal Air Force in 1922. His *Seven Pillars of Wisdom* (1926), abridged as *Revolt in the Desert* (1927), described his Arabian adventures.

Lean, David 1908-
British film director, who began as a film editor. His later films were expensive international extravaganzas, but his work, which includes *Lawrence of Arabia* (1962), about the exploits of T.E. Lawrence, has been highly acclaimed.

Lewis, P. Wyndham 1884-1957
British painter and novelist, who formed the Rebel Art Centre in 1913 and was one of the founders of the Vorticist movement, editing its magazine *Blast* from 1914 to 1915. He was an official war artist and worked in a semiabstract style.

Marc, Franz 1880-1916
German painter, one of the leaders of the Blaue Reiter group. After 1908 he tried to express his love of nature through expressionistic animal paintings. One of his most famous works, *Animal Destinies (Tierschicksale)* (1913) is an apocalyptic vision of catastrophe. He died in the Battle of Verdun.

Marinetti, Emilio 1876-1944
Italian writer, one of the guiding spirits of Futurism. He condemned all traditional forms in literature and art. In his writings he glorified war, the machine age and nationalism. He was one of the earliest followers of Mussolini.

Milestone, Lewis 1895-
Ukrainian-born film director, who moved to the USA in 1917, having served in World War I. His reputation was established by his film version of Remarque's *All Quiet on the Western Front* (1930). During World War II his films reflected the glamor of battle and the glorification of war.

Monroe, Harriet 1860-1936
American poet and editor, most renowned for her work in establishing *Poetry: a Magazine of Verse* in 1912. The magazine ran for many years and became a forum for creative writing in the war years.

Nash, Paul 1889-1940
British artist and designer, an official war artist in both world wars. He enlisted in the Artists Rifles in 1914 and, after having seen active service, been wounded and sent home, he returned to the Front as a war artist in 1916. His paintings deal directly with the immedicay of terror and death; he also painted the landscapes of war with desolation and horror, combining elements of the English pastoral tradition with abstract forms.

Nevinson, Christopher 1889-1946
British painter, associated with Wyndham Lewis in the formation of the Vorticist movement. His exhibition at the Leicester Gallery in 1916 was one of the first exhibitions of war paintings and led to other war artists being appointed.

Owen, Wilfred 1893-1918
British poet, who served in the Artists Rifles and Manchester Regiment in the war. In his letters home he gave a uniquely realistic account of the realities of trench warfare. Before his death in France, only a week before the Armistice of November 1918, he was awarded the Military Cross. His poems demonstrate technical originality and intense compassion; they were published posthumously in 1920.

Pabst, Georg Wilhelm 1885-1967
Bohemian-born film director, who worked in Germany in the 1920s. In 1925, he directed *Streets of Sorrow*, a social comment on human misery, and in 1928 he made *Westfront 1918*, about the war. In the 1930s he was associated with pacificsm, and in 1933 he moved to France. He returned to Germany in 1939 and made several films during World War II. His film *The Trial*, concerning antisemitism, won acclaim in 1948.

Pasternak, Boris 1890-1960
Russian poet and novelist, who published several volumes of poetry between 1914 and 1917, but is perhaps best known for his novel of the Russian Revolution *Dr Zhivago* (1958). The book was banned in the Soviet Union until 1988.

Picasso, Pablo 1881-1973
Spanish painter and sculptor, who settled in Paris in 1903. Together with Georges Braque he created Cubism from 1909, and continued to develop the style through the war years. Perhaps his best known painting is the mural *Guernica* (1937), expressing his loathing for fascism and the horrors of war and painted after the bombing of a Basque town during the Spanish civil war.

Remarque, Erich Maria 1897-1970
German novelist, who was severely wounded on active service in World War I. His celebrated war novel *All Quiet on the Western Front* (1929) is an outstanding account of the horrors of warfare as seen by the men in the trenches. He became a naturalized American.

Renoir, Jean 1894-1979
French film director, the son of painter Pierre Auguste Renoir. His films, which include *The Grand Illusion* (1937), are notable for their slow pace, soft focus and compassionate characterizations. During World War II he fled to the United States, where he directed several films before his death.

Rosenberg, Isaac 1890-1918
British poet, who fought as a private soldier during the war and was killed in action in France. In his writing he developed unique symbols for war, without any moral judgement as though the war was a medium through which to explore his interests and ideas. His *Collected Works* were published in 1937.

Sassoon, Siegfried 1886-1967
British poet and novelist, who was awarded the Military Cross for his bravery during the war. In 1918 he published a series of bitter antiwar poems, *Counterattack*, one of the first published expressions of the horrors of war to tbe written by a soldier. He ultimately declared himself a pacifist. His wartime experience is recounted in his semifictional autobiographical works *Memoirs of a Fox-Hunting Man* (1928) and *Memoirs of an Infantry Officer* (1930).

Wellman, William 1896-1975
American World War I flying ace and film director, who is said to have got his break into films by landing a small aircraft on the polo field of actor Douglas Fairbanks. He made his directorial debut in 1923, and in 1929 directed *Wings*, which won the first Academy Award as being the best film of the year.

Williamson, Harold Sandys 1892-
British painter and poster designer. He was a member of the London Group in 1933. His work as an official war artist was in a realistic style.

Avant-garde
Experimental, or in advance of generally accepted artistic techniques.

Cubism
Artistic school, of whom the most celebrated member was Pablo Picasso, using geometric shapes to represent natural forms.

Camaraderie
Close bonds of friendship formed between soldiers as a result of their common experience and suffering.

Estaminet
French bar serving alcoholic drinks for troops.

Futurism
Italian intellectual and artistic movement devoted to progress and the cult of the machine.

Image d'Epinal/imagistes
French historical and traditional image conveying a patriotic message; creators of such images (see p.230).

Jingoism
Patriotic and belligerent nationalism.

Pacifism
The belief that war is morally wrong and unjustifiable under any circumstances, resulting in a refusal to fight.

Patriotism
Deep-rooted devotion to one's country producing belief in the justice of its cause.

Poilu
A French infantryman. The term, meaning "hairy", derives from his customary thick whiskers.

Propaganda
Organized selective publication of information to influence public opinion at home or abroad.

Union sacrée
The bond between all elements of the French nation at war.

Vaudeville
American theatrical genre consisting of variety acts, equivalent to the British music hall.

War artist
Artist paid by a government to make a graphic or pictorial record of the war.

War art program/commission
Governmental patronage of artists to produce an official message and visual record of the war.

Datafile

The 1914–18 war occasioned a vast outpouring of literature. Most was conventional and evanescent, but some was challenging, experimental and enduring. What has lasted includes soldiers' poetry, some by men killed in the war, like Isaac Rosenberg and Wilfred Owen. The most powerful wartime novel by a serving soldier was Henri Barbusse's *Under Fire*, which is infused with the moral outrage of the poets. They both worked to recapture language from the corruption of propaganda and to shake the indifference of those in power to the sufferings of ordinary soldiers. In the first postwar decade, much mediocre prose was published by veterans, but through the haze of clichés a few important novels reminded readers of the war's tragedies and absurdities. Between 1928 and 1935 a new wave of war works appeared. Remarque's *All Quiet on the Western Front* was the first of a many books which spoke of the waste of the war, and which have introduced later generations to it.

▼ There were three phases in the history of literary responses to World War I. The first was during the war itself, when much poetry and fiction appeared in all the major countries. The second period extended for about a decade after the Armistice, during which much pulp literature and a few enduring novels and memoirs appeared. During the third period, from 1928 to 1935, some of the most widely-read and controversial novels about the war appeared (such as Remarque's *All Quiet on the Western Front*, 1929, and Graves's *Goodbye to All That*, 1930). This body of memoirs, fiction and poetry is one of the enduring legacies of the war.

Major literary works of World War I

1915
When Blood is their Argument
United States
Ford Madox Ford
(1873–1979)

1916
Path to Sacrifice
Germany
Fritz von Unruh (1885–1970)

Under Fire
France
Henri Barbusse (1873–1935)

Letters from America
United Kingdom
Rupert Brooke (1887–1915)

1917
The Old Front Line
United Kingdom
John Masefield (1878–1967)

1918
Collected Poems
United Kingdom
Rupert Brooke (1887–1915)

Calligrammes
France
Guillaume Apollinaire
(1880-1918)

1919
The Wooden Crosses
France
Roland Dorgelès (1886–1973)

The Change
Germany
Ernst Toller (1893–1939)

Poems and Stories
Germany
Alfred Lichtenstein
(1889–1914)

1920
Collected Poems
United Kingdom
Wilfred Owen (1893–1918)

The Good Soldier Schweik
Czechoslovakia
Jaroslav Hašek (1883–1923)

Collected Works
Germany
August Stramm (1874–1915)

The Storm of Steel (German edition)
Ernst Jünger (b. 1895)

1922
The Wasteland
United States/ United Kingdom
T.S. Eliot (1888–1965)

No More Parades
United Kingdom
Ford Madox Ford
(1873–1979)

1927
The Case of Sergeant Grischa
Germany
Arnold Zweig (1887–1968)

Karl and Anna
Germany
Leonhard Frank (1882–1961)

The Spanish Farm Trilogy, 1914–1918
United Kingdom
R.H. Mottram (1883–1971)

Revolt in the Desert
United Kingdom
T.E. Lawrence (1888–1935)

1929
Goodbye to All That
United Kingdom
Robert Graves (1895–1986)

Memoirs of a Foxhunting Man
United Kingdom
Siegfried Sassoon
(1886-1967)

All Quiet on the Western Front
Germany
Erich Remarque (1898–1970)

A Farewell to Arms
United States
Ernest Hemingway
(1898–1929)

1930
Fire from the Boilers
Germany
Ernst Toller (1893–1939)

1932
The Men of Good Will
France
Jules Romains (1885–1986)

1933
A Testament of Youth
United Kingdom
Vera Brittain (1893–1970)

1958 (UK publication date)
Dr Zhivago
Soviet Union
Boris Pasternak (1890–1960)

1971
August 1914
Soviet Union
Alexander Solzhenitsyn (b. 1918)

One of the most extraordinary features of World War I was the extent to which it gave birth to a special literature of commemoration: a body of soldiers' and ex-soldiers' memoirs and fiction which has come to be termed "war literature". We must beware, here as elsewhere, of exaggerating the innovative effect of military service in the 1914–18 war. The true pioneers of this kind of military meditation were American veterans of the Civil War. But what the men of "14–18" wrote was unique in at least two respects. First, it became vastly popular, and produced bestsellers like Erich Maria Remarque's *All Quiet on the Western Front*, the English edition of which went through 24 printings in its first year of publication in 1929 and remains in print. Other ex-soldiers, seeing what happened to Remarque's book, decided to quarry this literary gold mine, and wrote similarly successful bestsellers, for example Robert Graves's *Goodbye to All That*, which appeared in 1929 and is still in print in paperback over half a century later. We are, therefore, dealing with literature that emphatically and repeatedly touched a chord in public taste and popular memory.

A new kind of literature?

The enduring character of the literature of World War I is a function of the broad appeal of both its subject matter and its style. This has led Paul Fussell, in *The Great War and Modern Memory*, to claim that the generation of soldier writers created more than just a testament to their military careers. He suggests that they created a language – on occasion, bitter, wistful, sad and deeply ironic – which is that of much subsequent fiction. Indeed, he goes so far as to suggest that war literature established a new kind of literature, which has come to characterize 20th-century writing in general.

This is a bold claim, and deserves scrutiny. Let us consider the nature of Fussell's argument. He takes from literary criticism a three-stage model of narrative forms, which divides imaginative literature into the epic, realistic and ironic modes. In the epic mode the hero's freedom of action is greater than our own. Such is clearly the case in the ancient Greek epic *The Iliad*, where Achilles, for example, stands above us, half-way to the gods. What characterizes the realistic mode is that the hero's freedom of action is about the same as ours. As in the case of Dickens's characters, we can (as it were) look them straight in the eye as equals. Our hopes and aspirations are theirs. In contrast, the ironic mode is one in which the hero's freedom of action is decidedly less than ours. His life is bounded by the grotesque, the absurd, and the imminence of death. This is the landscape of Kafka, although, as it happened, he

THE WAR AND LITERATURE

World War I produced an extensive "war literature"

Was this just a continuation of old traditions or did ex-soldiers create a new kind of language?

Paul Fussell claims that war literature lies on the boundary between the realistic and the ironic

That it embodies different kinds of irony

But this appreciation fails to consider the range of sensibilities in French and German literature

did not fight in the war. It is also, according to Fussell, the landscape of the trenches, as recreated by the men who were there. In effect Fussell claims that World War I soldiers' literature is on a knife-edge between the realistic and ironic modes. Hence a book like *Goodbye to All That*, Graves's account of his life as a soldier with the Royal Welch Fusiliers, is both fictional and autobiographical, both untrue to the events of the war and a profoundly accurate account of the mentality of the trench soldiers. Anyone who reads this book – or dozens like it – as a way of finding out the historical facts is looking for the wrong message. These are imaginative rather than historical documents, and above all, Fussell says, deeply ironic statements.

Here irony is taken to mean three separate but overlapping sensibilities: the first is the sense of a jarring contrast between expectation and reality, between intention and outcome, between the innocent illusions of 1914 and the harsh reality of Verdun, the Somme and Passchendaele. In this sense the writings of nearly all those who joined up early in the war were profoundly ironic. In addition these works are ironic on another level. Here irony describes the author's shifting viewpoint about the war itself. For most ex-soldiers turned writers the war was at once fascinating and horrifying; both the apogee and the end of their youth; both a catastrophe and the occasion for the expression of some of the noblest human sentiments: loyalty, compassion, humor, and the sheer resilience of men who managed to survive and retain their dignity under intolerable conditions. Their writings are ironic because they were under no illusions as to the murderous

▼ The funeral of Henri Barbusse, who was laid to rest in the Père Lachaise cemetery in Paris in 1935.

character of the war, but they did not adopt a straightforward attitude to it. To ask what Graves, or Siegfried Sassoon, author of *Memoirs of an Infantry Officer*, thought about the war is to explore indirection, contradiction and ambiguity; in sum, according to Fussell, it is to enter an ironic environment. That landscape of irony may be understood on a third level: it is the creation of a language to describe the indescribable, to communicate what many soldier-writers felt could never be known. This is what Fussell means when he says that literature of World War I created "modern memory". It is the wresting to new uses and new forms of traditional images and metaphors, which can approach – but never reach – the full horror of having lived through World War I as a front-line soldier. The new language, created by soldier-poets like Isaac Rosenberg and Wilfred Owen, both of whom were killed in the war, and by survivors like Graves and Sassoon, is (according to Fussell) one of the most important legacies of the war itself, for it has provided the basis for literary attempts to convey the meaning of later disasters of this century. Here we find the origins of Norman Mailer's *The Naked and the Dead* (1948) and Joseph Heller's black comedy *Catch 22* (1961), both about World War II, and more recent fiction, such as Thomas Pynchon's *Gravity's Rainbow* (1973). They all build on the literary legacy of 1914–18, in an effort to convey the ghastly character of 20th-century warfare.

Qualifications to Fussell's argument

This discussion of the creative literary experiments of the men of 1914–18 raises essential features of the cultural aftermath of World War I. But Fussell's claim must be qualified in a number of ways. First, it is too exclusively Anglo-Saxon to do justice to the full range of war writing. One of the greatest war novels, *Under Fire* by Henri Barbusse, published in 1917, bears little of what

◄► Among the most prominent soldier writers of the 1914–18 war were Siegfried Sassoon (far left), Rupert Brooke (left), Robert Graves (below, writing), Wilfred Owen (with cap), and Erich Maria Remarque (seated). Brooke and Owen were killed in the war. The others produced haunted memoirs, which describe the mentality and conditions (for example, right) of the front-line soldier and the terrible difficulty many survivors had in living with the memory of the war.

Women's Poetry of World War I

The vast quantity of poetry and verse published during the war is now regarded as a phenomenon in the history of English literature. A bibliographical study of English poetry of World War I revealed that some 2,225 individuals had published verse on the theme of the war, and of these at least 532 were women. The study covered only printed books, taking no account of the many thousands of poems that appeared in newspapers and magazines.

The poetry written by women during the early months of war generally reflected the sense of patriotism, honor and duty in the United Kingdom. As the death toll mounted after the first trench battles, the appalling casualty lists made those at home well aware of the reality and grand scale of the slaughter. As the war went on the topics of the poems became many and varied – war shortages, nurses, hospitals, wounded soldiers, troop trains, canteens, knitting socks. Humor is often present and jingoism abounds but, overwhelmingly, the poems mourn for the dead. The note of grief is both personal and general, demonstrating abhorrence of war, and anger, despair, bitterness and endurance. There is a desperate longing for the fighting to stop and for peace to return, with often a backward look at the halcyon prewar days. The generally received view of "women at home" as ignorant and idealistic is quite false; women were writing their own protest poetry long before Wilfred Owen and Siegfried Sassoon. Many of the poems show honest responses of indignation and pity from women who had witnessed the consequences of war in human suffering and were deeply moved. Others captured the anguish of separation and the inequality of sacrifice ordained by the "shibboleth" of gender.

Eminent British women poets include: Vera Brittain and May Wedderburn Cannan, both Red Cross nurses; Edith Nesbit, author of children's stories; Margaret Cole, a fabian socialist; and Elizabeth Daryush, daughter of Robert Bridges. American poets include Amy Lowell, Harriet Monroe and Sara Teasdale.

So dreadfully safe! O, damn
the shibboleth
of sex! God knows we've
equal personality.
Why should men face the dark
while women stay
To live and laugh and meet
the sun each day.

Nora Bomford, *Drafts*

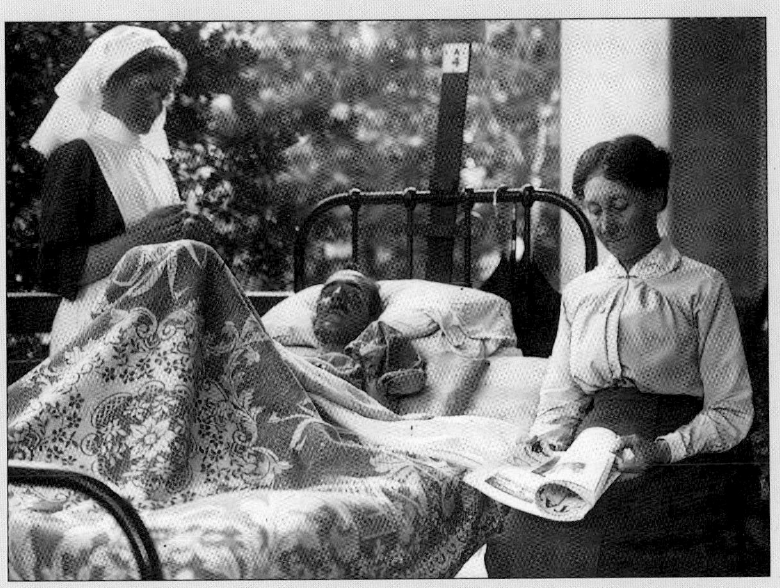

Fussell describes as irony. It is a shocking naturalistic account of French troops in Artois. One of its most memorable sections is a description of one *poilu* (French infantryman) unwrapping his pack, which seemed to contain an entire household's worth of useful items. Here we are clearly in the realistic mode. But at the end of the novel Barbusse enters a surrealistic world, in which mud-encrusted soldiers on both sides of the line declare their commitment to pacifism.

Again the language and form of Remarque's novel are ironic in only the first sense of the word, of innocence betrayed. The key dramatic scenes are purely Gothic, such as the occasion when the hero, Paul, spends an appalling night in a shell hole in a cemetery, his sole companion being a French soldier whom he, Paul, had bayoneted, and who dies in his arms. The unremitting gloom of *All Quiet* and the descriptive writing of Barbusse – who was dubbed the Zola of the trenches – seem so far from the world of Fussell's soldier-writers, that we are justified in suggesting that each combatant nation developed its own literary forms, within which soldiers' memories were conveyed both to their comrades and to those who were not there.

This raises the second point on which Fussell's interpretation must be qualified. The emphasis on what is new in this body of writing obscures what is old in it: that is, that war literature was written *by* soldiers and *for* soldiers, primarily with two purposes in mind. The first was to create a *literature of separation* and thereby to recall the extent to which the men in uniform formed what they called a race apart, indelibly imprinted with an experience that those who had not been there could never really know. Of course, on one level this attitude was inevitable: there was a gulf between the experience of men who saw combat and those who did not. But on another level, this viewpoint reiterated much of what soldiers took as the profound ignorance of civilians about the war and the need to fight it to the bitter end. The second was to create a *literature of bereavement* through which soldiers could commemorate the men who failed to return from the war. The soldier-authors of the war address the difficult question of how is it possible to commemorate those who die in war without glorifying war itself? This was at the heart of much of the writings of the men of "14–18", and far from being original, adds little to what Tolstoy, for example, had to say on the subject. The third qualification of the claim that war literature was the harbinger of "modern memory" relates to the work of those who did not fight, but whose prose and poetry are enduring features of our culture. From T.S. Eliot's *The Wasteland* (1922) to Pasternak's *Dr Zhivago* (1958) works of great literature have appeared, which recreate the awful years of the war and its aftermath. But these masterpieces were not written by ex-soldiers, and it would be rash to claim that they are in a sense less valuable or less influential for that reason. It is probably safer to suggest that the authors of the war literature of "14–18" created not "modern memory" but rather a memorial to their youth, their comrades and the men they left behind.

Datafile

Just as in prose and poetry, the visual arts produced both highly conventional and highly experimental paintings, sculpture and films during the war. Some of the avant-garde artists joined up early in the war; some, like Franz Marc and Umberto Boccioni, joined the lists of the fallen. Others survived and carried their nightmares with them in later years.

All the major combatants mobilized war artists to record the war effort and help rally the nation to the cause. Some artists responded to the war in cliches; others with skepticism; still others by turning their back entirely on convention and by creating an art of the absurd – Dada.

▼ The celebration of Frenchness in wartime French art was a patriotic act organized in numerous public exhibitions. Often the emphasis was on classicism rather than experimentation. During the critical early months of the Battle of Verdun in 1916, 40 public exhibitions were held in Paris alone. In the first six months of 1917, 75 were held; and a similar number from September 1917 to March 1918. A virtual rash of exhibitions accompanied the Armistice.

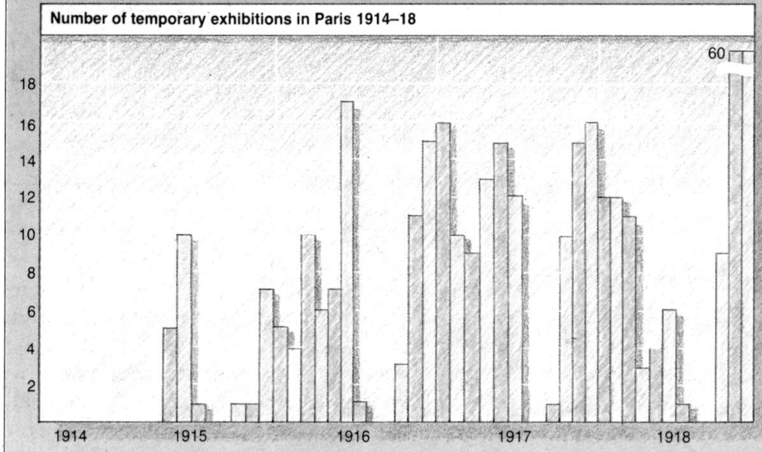

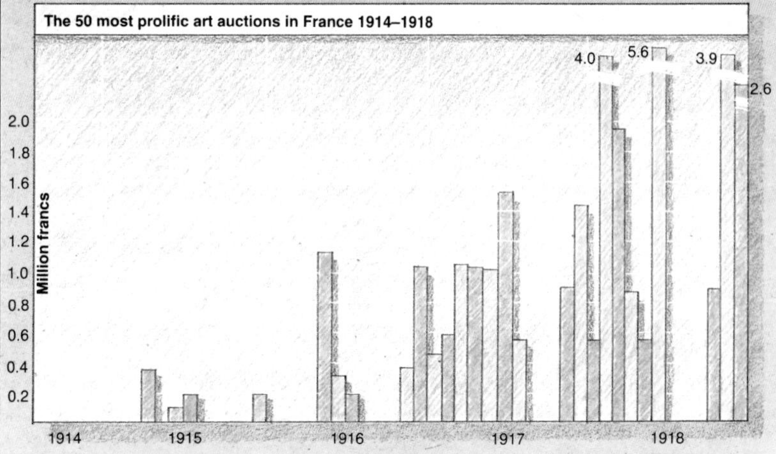

▲ In the early days of the war, the market for artwork almost disappeared. This impoverished those artists, like Picasso, who were not in uniform. But by 1917–18 the appearance of British and American buyers in Paris led to a boom in sales. Many of the major collections of French art which adorn the museums and galleries of the world were assembled at this time. The most extraordinary month was June 1918, when a record 5.6 billion French francs exchanged hands in the world of art dealers.

▶ As measured by the number of paintings accepted under the British patronage scheme for war artists, Muirhead Bone was the most successful British war artist. He was sent to the Western Front on a six-month contract in August 1916, on condition that all his paintings were the copyright of the War Office. What made Bone's work attractive to officials was its competence and conventionality. As usual, official recognition and experimentation were mutually exclusive events.

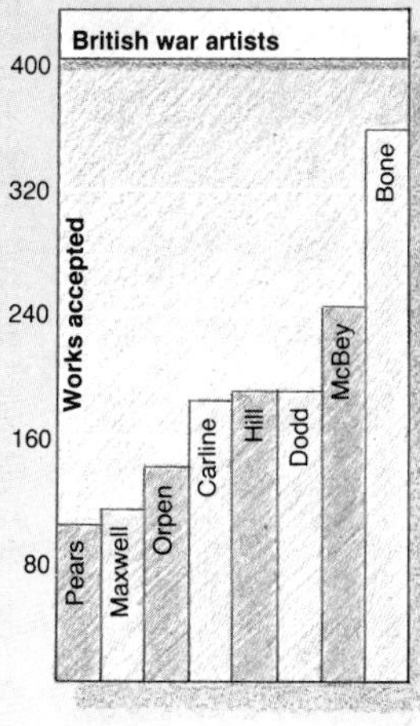

Many generations since World War I have been introduced to the war through the art it provoked or occasioned. In this area, as in literature, there was a mixture of the old and new. Indeed, one way to see these developments is as a dialectic between, on the one hand, experimentation in form and content, and, on the other hand, a retreat into and reiteration of profoundly traditional themes and images.

French art of World War I

The best way of illustrating this mixture of backward-looking and forward-looking developments is in terms of an extraordinarily beautiful and popular art form of World War I. This is the French *image d'Epinal*, a kind of artistic iconography of the French nation at war. *Images d'Epinal*

THE WAR AND GRAPHIC ARTS

Art provoked by World War I looked both backward and forward

In France the traditional *image d' Epinal*

carried sentiments of all kinds

Cocteau strove to purify French art

Violent images tended to surface in German art

At this end of the spectrum stands the savage work of Georg Grosz.

emerged in the 1830s as part of the cult of Napoleon and later became folk art, first in woodcut form, then in lithograph, which described the virtues of the people of France. Children's primers were illustrated in this fashion, to teach the young the values of toil and decent labor, and the evils of the idle rich.

During World War I this left-wing republican art form was, as it were, hijacked by the right to bring home to the civilian population the enduring features of eternal France. This was done in a number of ways. One was by placing the war in the long-term perspective of French history in general and of the French martial spirit in particular. Thus in a poster by Guy Arnoux the sleeping sentry in the trenches is rescued from dishonor by none other than Napoleon himself, who stands guard over the exhausted and neglectful soldier. Another of the same kind is entitled *Old-timers to the Rescue* and aligns the men of battles past with the front-line soldiers of 1914. A constant preoccupation of this art is the need to place a war that threatened to destroy all that was familiar within a wider historical sweep. A good example of this genre is a popular drawing of 1915 by Raoul Dufy. Entitled *The End of the War*, it is a collage of past and present with a message for everyone. Surrounding the Gallic cock are easily identifiable sketches of Joan of Arc, Reims cathedral set ablaze by German shelling in 1914, and General Joffre himself.

► *The Sleeping Sentry*

▼ *Old-timers to the Rescue*

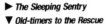

"Papa" Joffre was a popular and reassuring figure in much of this popular art work. A poster entitled *The Victory of the Marne* shows a spirited "Marianne" – the traditional female symbol of France – striding forward to battle, with her dress high on her legs, and row upon row of French soldiers below and in the background, following the lead of Joffre, their general.

The second preoccupation of this form of propaganda was the unity of the nation at war. Here we can see the way artists helped civilians to believe that they too were contributing to the war. One *image d'Epinal* shows two women doing their bit for the war, one by darning socks, the other by writing letters to a soldier, who will soon receive the parcel on the table. Another depicts a triumvirate of soldier, priest and worker and announces the true character of the *"union sacreé"*. One of the most beautiful of all *images d'Epinal* is of a theater party in which an elegant actress enthrals the serried ranks of soldiers before her. This could have been a reference to the appearance of Sarah Bernhardt before French troops in 1916. The third major emphasis in this genre was on the joys of military leave. This was a privilege hard to come by early in the war. Childlike images of reunion and delight touch on both a frequent refrain of soldiers' complaints and a constant preoccupation of their loved ones. A fourth theme is more specific, and refers to the

▲ Dante joins the Allies, according to this 1915 cartoon in Cocteau's *Le Mot*.

◀ *Les Marraines* (self-appointed godmothers) offer support to the men at the Front.

▶ The joys of the family man home on leave.

▼ Hansi's postwar vision of a French lesson for the children of Alsace, who had been forced to learn German for 48 years.

origins of this remarkable art form. The city of Epinal is in Lorraine, and its recovery from German occupation was one of the clear aims of the French war effort. It is therefore not surprising that some *imagistes* would return to the source of their inspiration. Two good examples are by a French war artist named Hansi, whose upbringing in German Alsace did not dampen his Gallic enthusiasm. Both of these posters present *images d'Epinal* at their best. The first is of a French soldier giving a French lesson to the children of a village in Alsace. The second is of a miraculous event. Following the Armistice, as legend had it, the graveyards of Alsace flowered unnaturally in November, and tricolors or ribbons of red, white and blue spontaneously appeared on the graves, announcing to the dead that Lorraine was once again free, happy and French.

Here we see all the components of this form of art: a childlike innocence; an appeal to a heroic, martial past; a comic-strip simplification of war to the level of eternal verities. But this preference for the allegorical and the naive should not delude us into thinking that this work is in any way unsophisticated or unthinking. On the contrary, it is an attempt to return to a stylized past at a time when the present was perhaps too unpalatable to face directly.

The extent to which World War I occasioned a return to the past may be seen clearly in the work of the artist, poet and playwright Jean Cocteau. After the outbreak of war in 1914 Cocteau led a crusade against the exotic, dangerous, and (what he took to be) Germanic influences in modern art. In his journal *Le Mot*, he presented many illustrations of the virtues of the Mediterranean versus the Nordic, the Gallic versus the Teutonic, the poetic versus the prosaic, or in other words, the French cause versus the German. Somehow he got it into his head that cubism was a German development, until an encounter with Picasso convinced him he was wrong. The art of *Le Mot* had much in common with *images d'Epinal*, including the search for an historical context in which to place the war. After Italy had joined the Allies in 1915, Cocteau celebrated the event by elaborating on the traditional profile cameo of Dante, and announcing to the world that "Dante is with us."

The same mixture of childlike art with patriotism may be seen in another avant-garde journal, *L'Elan* ("*The Spirit*"), to which Picasso himself was a contributor. The fact that wartime currents in art moved both backward and forward in time and form may perhaps be illustrated by references to one of the most remarkable collaborations of the war, between Cocteau and Picasso on the ballet *Parade*. This work, first performed in 1917, was a remarkable reworking of the language of French folk art – slapstick, the circus, the music hall. But in this ballet, the dancers wore masks – "ambulent pieces of cubist art" – designed by Picasso. In effect here cubism met the childlike art of the *images d'Epinal*. What *Parade* expressed to the avant-garde, *images d'Epinal* expressed to the masses. It captured a graphic language of patriotic longing for a simpler and more peaceful world.

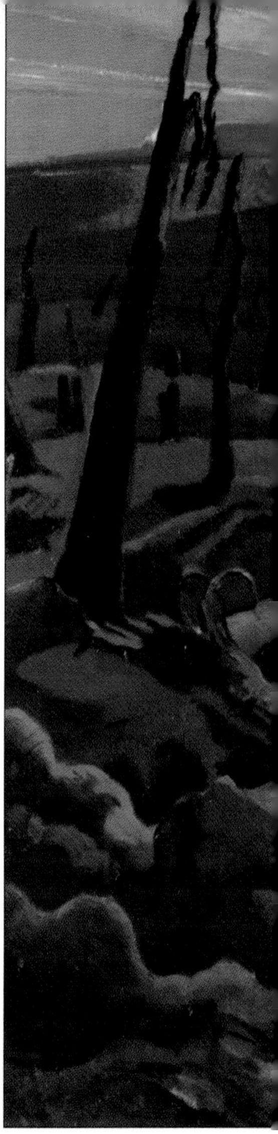

Toward a harsh sensibility

"Avant garde" was originally a military term. It was therefore entirely appropriate that artists who served in the armed forces of a number of combatant countries also illustrated the dialectic between tradition and experimentation during and after the conflict. The French army even formed a unit of camouflage artists, the *Camoufleurs*. Their work emphasized portraiture, perhaps to catch the images of individual men lost in the vastness of war. But some artists in these units, such as Luc-Albert Moreau, began to break up classical forms and flirt with cubist ideas. This kind of nonrepresentational art was also produced by British war artists. Such men were commissioned to produce visual propaganda for the Department (later Ministry) of Information, or commemorative art for the Canadian and British War Memorials Funds. Whatever their official status, many adopted unconventional styles and came to see the war in a harshly critical light.

One such artist was C.R.W. Nevinson, who had studied in Paris before the war, and had shared a studio with Amedeo Modigliani. He absorbed the tenets of Cubism, and became an enthusiast for the Futurist movement in art, extolling in a pamphlet written with the Italian Futurist Emilio Marinetti the view that art had to express force and motion. The war gave them the chance to show what this meant. Soon fascination gave way to horror. Many of Nevinson's paintings describe his experiences as an ambulance driver for the Belgian Red Cross, which he joined after being rejected as unfit by the British army. In 1917 he was invited to paint war scenes as an official British war artist. His work took on a

▲ ***We Are Making a New World.*** **Paul Nash's evocation of the ravaged landscape around Ypres drew on the English pastoral tradition, to which many soldier poets and writers referred ironically in their work. No celebration of war here: only a vivid memory of its destructive force.**

◀▶ C.R.W Nevinson's *La Mitrailleuse* (the machine gun) shows one facet of abstraction and experimentation in British war art.

◀▲ *A German Attack on a Wet Morning (April 1918)* by Harold Sandys Williamson, later head of Chelsea School of Art.

◀ *A Battery Shelled* by Percy Wyndham Lewis. The artillery was the natural home for Lewis, whose prewar theory of "vorticism" celebrated abstract art and the use of mechanical forms.

somber realism, in contrast to the Futurist composition in his most famous painting *La Mitrailleuse* (the machine gun).

Two other prominent British war artists were Paul Nash and Wyndham Lewis. Nash held a commission in the Hampshire Regiment, and was posted to the British garrison at Ypres. His paintings of the landscape around Passchendaele (for example, *We are Making a New World*), or some of his sketches of the wounded, caught the unearthly and barbaric quality of the conflict. The quiet tone of his work is matched by Wyndham Lewis's series of paintings of an artillery unit (for example, *A Battery Shelled*). Lewis held a commission in a battery near Bailleul, but was taken out of the line as a war artist for the Canadian War Memorials Fund. Later he produced for the equivalent British fund a series of paintings of the gunners' life, and caught some of the onlooker's stance of their war. The work of these three men demonstrates clearly that many British war artists were witnesses rather than propagandists during the war. They created works of art that defied traditional rules of composition or portraiture. But alongside them worked men like Muirhead Bone, a very traditional Scottish landscape artist, who was attached to the intelligence branch of general headquarters in France, and whose work was dismissed by George Bernard Shaw as simply "too good to be true".

Patronage of War Artists

The large-scale commissioning of war art, for both propaganda and historic record, was essentially an invention of World War I. Between 1914 and 1918 war art programs of significant size were administered by countries on each side. Projects tended to adopt similar administrative outlines regardless of which government was organizing them. Artists considered to have the requisite technical and interpretative skills were given honorary rank and attached to active units. In Britain and Canada artists were also assigned to record home-front activities. Those sent to accompany fighting units were sometimes over military age or physically unfit for combat. This was usually the case in Austria-Hungary, for example. More often the artists would be exempted from military duty for the duration of their contracts.

The first British war artists were appointed in 1916 but the British organization did not become extensive until Lord Beaverbrook was made minister of information in 1917. He replaced the earlier emphasis on propaganda in art with his own interest in the compilation of historic records. He modeled the scheme on the one he had established to create a record of Canadian wartime activity: the Canadian War Memorials Fund (founded in 1916). The Canadian and British projects came to share a concentration on historic record, and consequently exploited portraiture and home-front subjects to an extent unmatched by the other, propaganda-oriented war art projects.

A substantial proportion of French war art was unofficial, being the uncommissioned work of soldiers and especially, of camouflage specialists. By 1916 the Mission des Beaux-Arts had two artists attached to army units. By early 1917 artists were assigned to specific war zones or subjects.

In Germany young artists were frequently released from the army as being physically unfit for combat, while many Munich artists received special protection as the result of pressure from Bavaria following the tragic death of Franz Marc in 1916. But of the rich constellation of German artists active during the second decade of the 20th century, only a few became war artists. They included Max Slevogt, who used his influence to obtain appointment, but who worked for only two weeks before being sickened by the carnage that he had been sent to Belgium to record. In Austria-Hungary the war ministry created the independent *Kunstgruppe* in the early days of hostilities. But as the war dragged on, entry into it became increasingly difficult for artists whose services were needed elsewhere.

Whatever the specific contractual arrangements and official expectations about the uses to which the work of the artists was to be put, the pattern of official art patronage established during World War I proved successful enough to persist throughout the wars of the subsequent decades.

▼ **The viciousness underlying the polite respectability of the bourgeoisie is the subject of a series of drawings and paintings by Georg Grosz (1893–1949). He specialized in teeming, Hogarthian scenes, in which the conventions of Weimar society are stripped away to reveal the true face of the *Pillars of Society* (1926). More an anarchist than a communist, Grosz presented the same indictment of capitalism that Bertold Brecht and Kurt Weill expressed on the stage.**

Liberation of the bestial

In contrast to Muirhead Bone, some German war artists chose characteristically expressive and visually violent ways to convey their feelings about the war. There is none of the sensibility of Cocteau and Dufy in Otto Dix's *Self-portrait as a Soldier* of 1914. Dix was 25 in 1914 and served in the ranks on the Western Front and in Russia. The fact that he was prepared to admit visually his own horrifying fascination with the war gave to his later work an additional element of disgust with and reaction against the soldiers' world. In the 1920s his paintings of cripples, staggering on under the uncaring gaze of passers-by, reiterated this savage and poignant message.

This shocking sense of the liberation of the bestial in wartime became a preoccupation of many other artists, both those who served and those who did not. One case in point was Georg Grosz. He was aged 21 in 1914, and already kitted out as a bohemian dandy. He joined up in 1914, simply to be able to choose his own division, but was soon invalided out after, of all things, a sinus operation. By 1917, when he was conscripted, his hatred of German society had grown apace. He has left an artistic memento of his reentry into the

▲ Otto Dix served on both the Eastern and Western Fronts. His oil painting *Flanders* (1934–35) recalls some of the nightmares of Hieronymus Bosch. The soldiers are like rotting tree stumps, a theme reiterated in his postwar sketches of war cripples.

◀▲ Otto Dix's *Self-portrait as a Soldier* of 1914 captures the fascination with violence and the release of brutality within the generation of 1914.

◀ Georg Grosz's vicious caricature of the suppression of the Spartacist uprising of January 1919, directed by the socialist minister of order, Gustav Noske. The sketch is entitled *Cheers Noske! The Young Revolution is Dead!*

army, in the form of a sketch of his medical examination. To his shock he was passed fit for service, but soon entered an army sanatorium. When a medical student suggested he should get out of bed, an altercation ensued, which Grosz never forgot. After more time in an army hospital for the mentally disabled, he was finally discharged from service.

From there he migrated to the fringes of the German revolutionary movement, which gave him an ideological justification of his personal hatred of the ugliness and flabbiness of the German state. This attitude was immortalized in a set of Grosz's sketches prompted by the turmoil of the immediate postwar period. There can be few better instances of disgust and outrage in artistic form than his drawings of the bloody suppression of the so-called Spartacist uprising of January 1919. The aftermath of this abortive insurrection, during which a small and hopelessly outnumbered revolutionary group took to the streets of Berlin eight weeks after the end of the war, is well known. The revolutionaries were hunted down by ex-soldiers in paramilitary groups, the notorious *Freikorps*, and when caught, their leaders were brutally murdered. All this was done in the name of the minister of order in the new socialist government of the Weimar Republic. Hence Grosz's sketches "celebrating" the minister responsible: *Cheers Noske*. And as if the first, filled with bodies littering the streets, were too mild, Grosz presents a second version, this time with a pig-like baby skewered on the sword of a victorious and tipsy soldier.

How far have we come from the gentle themes and warm colors of *images d'Epinal*. If anything captures the opposite pole of artistic comment on the war, it is the work of Grosz. There were of course other influential European artists, in Weimar and elsewhere, whose war experiences marked much of their subsequent work. The work of Max Beckmann and Käthe Kollwitz captured some of the ways in which the nightmare of the war lingered long after 1918. But in the confines of this brief survey, suffice it to say that there was a vast spectrum of artistic reactions to the 1914–18 conflict. At one pole stood defiant illusion and naive celebration of military virtues; at the other, there are images of nightmare and savage denunciation of military crimes. The spectrum between formed an important part of the cultural legacy of World War I.

Datafile

Film produced popular images of World War I which have endured to this day. Much larger audiences were introduced to the war through film than through prose, poetry, or painting. In film the ugliness of war largely faded. Instead the film industry humanized the conflict, by placing it within the context of very familiar and mundane stories, full of romance, adventure, heroism, treachery. But it also mythologized the war, as an enormous epic struggle, in which the great themes of death, resurrection, love and loyalty unfolded.

Most films about the war were incapable of touching the subtlety and profundity of war prose and poetry. Irony, which marks much of war fiction, was out of the reach of all but the greatest film directors. The exception that proves the rule is the French director Jean Renoir whose film *The Grand Illusion*, (released in 1937) is a work of genius and one of the enduring cultural legacies of the war.

▼ The commercial success of war films began before the Armistice. Chaplain's *Shoulder Arms* was the first of many films set in the war which drew postwar audiences to film theaters by the millions. In addition to the classics listed here, many other major films traversed the war in the pursuit of other themes.

► The dominance of the international film industry by American products began during the war. Some 2,500 films were released in America between 1915 and 1918. Second came Germany, where 500 films appeared in these years. Details of films produced in France during this period are not available.

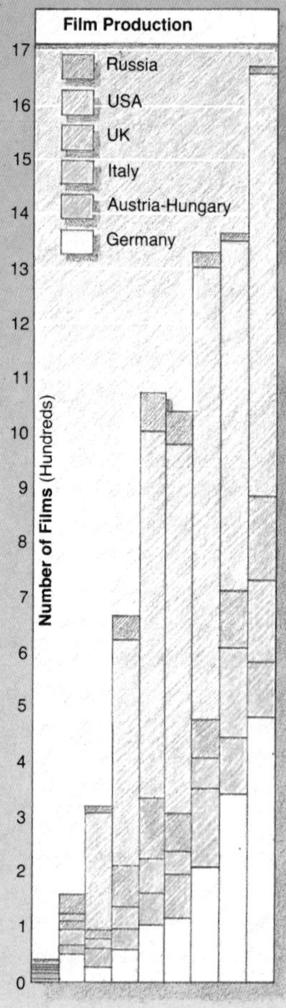

Major films about World War I

1918
Shoulder Arms
United Kingdom
Charlie Chaplin (1889–1977)

1919
J'Accuse (remake 1937)
France
Abel Gance (1889–1981)

1921
The Four Horsemen of the Apocalypse
United States
Rex Ingram (1893–1950)

1923
The White Sister
United States
Henry King (1888–1982)

1925
The Big Parade
United States
King Vidor (1894–1982)

1927
Wings
United States
William Wellman (1896–1975)

Verdun – Visions d'Histoire
France
Léon Poirier (1884–1968)

1930
Westfront 1918
Germany
G.W. Pabst (1885–1967)

Hell's Angels
United States
Howard Hughes (1905–1976)

All Quiet on the Western Front
United States
Lewis Milestone (1895–1980)

Journey's End
United Kingdom
James Whale (1889–1957)

1931
Mata Hari
United States
George Fitzmaurice (1895–1940)

1932
A Farewell to Arms
United States
Frank Borzage (1893–1961)

Pack Up Your Troubles
United States
Stan Laurel (1890–1965) and Oliver Hardy (1892–1957)

1933
I Was a Spy
United Kingdom
Victor Saville (1897–1979)

Duck Soup
United States
Marx Brothers

1935
Dark Angel
United States
Sidney Franklin (1893–1972)

1936
The Road to Glory
United States
Howard Hawks (1896–1977)

1937
The Grand Illusion
France
Jean Renoir (1894–1979)

1938
Nurse Edith Cavell
United Kingdom
Herbert Wilcox (1892–1977)

1941
Sergeant York
United States
Howard Hawks (1896–1977)

1957
Paths of Glory
United States
Stanley Kubrick (b. 1928)

1969
Oh! What a Lovely War
United Kingdom
Richard Attenborough (b. 1923)

1971
Johnny Got His Gun
United States
Dalton Trumbo (1905–1976)

1982
Gallipoli
Australia
Peter Weir (b. 1944)

Of all the arts there was one which arguably reached a much wider audience than all others and which had a much greater effect on the way the war has been imagined in the decades since the Armistice: the world of film. It happened that the cinema came into its own as the centerpiece of mass entertainment precisely in the period of World War I.

War films

The 1914–18 conflict has formed the setting for hundreds of films, and is likely to continue to do so in the foreseeable future. The reasons why that war has been such a popular theme in cinema are obvious: the conflict formed a splendid setting for adventure stories, melodramas, love stories, and the like. Whenever a director needed a handy separation or tearful reunion, the war could provide it; if the virtues of heroism and loyalty were to be the vehicle for the celluloid star of the moment, why not use the war?

But if we leave aside the sheer entertainment value of war as good box-office business, there is another level on which to interpret the way in which cinema, in both the interwar years and after 1945, has contributed to popular memories of the 1914–18 conflict. By locating the war within identifiable and mundane themes, such as romance, adventure and comedy, cinema humanized the war. By suggesting the sheer monumental scale of the conflict, in a way few novels and paintings can, cinema mythologized the war. It was repeatedly visualized as a vast earthquake against the backdrop of which the petty conflicts of ordinary mortals were played out.

The framework used by Paul Fussell in his analysis of war fiction can also be employed to highlight the character of war films. If war novels stood on a knife-edge between the realistic and the ironic modes of narrative, war films oscillated between the realistic and the epic. This is precisely what the early commercial film industry was good at and what the mass audience wanted. Consequently war films showed wonderfully the surface of events, and did so often in very moving ways. This was frequently in the form of a love story, a comedy, a melodrama or a simple action film. But whatever the setting, they all share one feature: the capacity to mythologize the war, to recreate it in a form which was much more palatable to live with than was the event itself. Hence many war films, in particular those of the interwar years, served (and still serve) an essential purpose: to bury the past and help people recreate it in a form they can accept.

Before the films themselves are considered, it is important to point to a number of difficulties in the use of this kind of evidence about the memory of war. First, there is the problem of

FILMS OF THE WAR

At the time of World War I film became the centerpiece of mass entertainment

Film has served to mythologize the war

Six categories of war films

Mythologies of war

Landscapes of battle

The camaraderie of arms

Romantic themes

Noble warriors

Pacifism and the pity of war

selection. Many films describe wartime events, but are only marginally war films. Eisenstein's *Oktober* or *Ten Days that Shook the World* (1927), Truffaut's *Jules et Jim* (1961) and David Lean's *Lawrence of Arabia* (1962) are all set in the period of the war, but focus on themes which transcend it. We have chosen instead to concentrate on films which deal directly with the war and the war experience. Thus we shall omit reference to many films which are obliquely about the war, but which are best analyzed in other ways.

Secondly, there is the problem of presentation. Here, photographs are reproduced from stills. This is unavoidable, but it does distance us from the real effect of film, which is in its dynamic (rather than static) quality, its fluidity, its dream-like quality, its movement.

Thirdly, there is the problem of the audience. There is some evidence about the effects of films on the viewing population, but it is too patchy to enable us to draw any firm conclusions about the direct effects of cinema on popular attitudes. The most that can be said is that many films reached millions; fiction and the visual arts, at the best of times, touched a much smaller population. It must be recognized that film spoke in its own distinctive terms about the war, and its language must be distinguished from the more profound, but less widely disseminated, discourse about the war to be found in prose and poetry.

In addition, many of the films described here were made in Hollywood, but they were so widely distributed in Europe between the wars and after 1945 that it would be futile to draw a line between European and American filmic reactions to the war. Of course, the trauma of the war was much greater in Europe than in the USA; hence film probably had a greater role in shaping and reshaping European rather than American memories of the conflict.

With these considerations in mind, it may be useful to suggest that the kinds of films which have been made about the 1914–18 war and which have been important sources of popular images of the conflict can be roughly divided into six general categories.

▼ D.W. Griffiths went to France in 1917 to film *Hearts of the World*, a story full of evil Huns mistreating Lillian Gish and other civilians living under German occupation. Despite its realistic scenes of the horrors of war, the film boosted military recruitment in America.

▲ In Abel Gance's *J'Accuse* of 1919 (above) dead soldiers rise from the grave to haunt the living, who are unworthy of their sacrifices. In his remake of 1937, dead soldiers rise again, this time to prevent another war. Both versions show the power of film to touch the nightmares of an age.

▲ Paul Baumer, the central figure in Lewis Milestone's film version of Remarque's *All Quiet on the Western Front*, was the quintessential victim of the war. The casting of American actors as German soldiers reinforced the antinationalist appeal of the film, which, after Nazi riots, could not be shown in Germany on its release in 1930.

Mythologies of war

The first category is composed of films concerned with mythical themes and in particular with the idea of the return of the dead from the field of battle. Myth here can be taken as a narrative, usually oral, but also literary or filmic, which touches life, death, love, friendship, resurrection – enduring themes in all cultures.

The very title of one famous film helps us locate it within this tradition. It was one of the earliest war films, *The Four Horsemen of the Apocalypse*, an American venture directed by Rex Ingram which appeared in 1921. It starred Alice Terry and Rudolf Valentino in a predictable but poignant love story which shifts from Argentina to Paris. Valentino seduces the wife of a French senator in a Parisian flat, above which lives a strange Russian philosopher named Tchernoff. On the eve of war in 1914, this modern Jeremiah tells Valentino that "in a few hours the world will behold the Four Horsemen – enemies of mankind." The doom foretold in the book of Revelations was about to come to pass.

And indeed, just as Tchernoff foretold, the horrors of battle descend on mankind. The German army sweeps forward and arrives on the Marne. There they act like beasts and brutally humiliate Valentino's father, who is saved by the arrival of the French army. For the next four years, Conquest, War, Pestilence, and Death sweep all before them, including Valentino, who dies in a military encounter with a German cousin. But his soul is ennobled by his heroic death. He appears in a vision to his lover, and instructs her to return to her husband, who was blinded in combat, and needs her help.

Similarly timeless is the theme of the resurrection of the dead in another early film classic, *J'Accuse*, by the French filmmaker Abel Gance. It appeared in 1919, and was remade by Gance in 1937. Both versions were extraordinary melodramas, rescued from bathos at the very end by Gance's exploration of the mythical realm.

The first version of *J'Accuse* – which had nothing to do with the Dreyfus Affair and Zola's famous letter of the same title accusing the French army of corruption – was made during the war itself, and for it Gance was able to use soldiers on leave as his actors and extras. After setting up a mundane love triangle, Gance had the idea of giving his hero a mission, which was to return from the Front and tell the villagers of a dream he had. In it the dead rose from their battlefield graves and returned home to see if their sacrifice had been in vain. What they saw was the pettiness of civilian life, the advantage being taken of soldiers' wives and businesses. This reverie – transformed to film by Gance – was so powerful that the civilians mended their ways and the dead returned to their graves. The film seems more poignant when it is remembered that of the soldiers on leave used by Gance to play the dead most returned to the Front and were killed. In the 1937 version the dead are raised from their graves, return to terrify the living, and put an end to war forever.

The return of the dead was used in other war films, most notably in the American film, *All Quiet on the Western Front* (1930), directed by Lewis Milestone. But as powerful as this visual image was, it avoided Gance's flights of fancy into Christian iconography.

◀ The retreat of the Italian army from Caporetto was portrayed in Frank Borzage's film version (1932) of Hemingway's *A Farewell to Arms*. The gray, misty quality of the sequence helped convey some of the confusion of military defeat, but even scenes of destruction retained a curious beauty. Perhaps film could never recapture the hideousness, the noise or the chaos of battle. Instead dozens of films captured the monumental scale of operations, and moved rapidly from epic to melodrama. In *A Farewell to Arms*, Helen Hayes dies just as Gary Cooper, an American volunteer and deserter from the Italian army, reaches her bedside.

▼ William Wellman's 1927 film *Wings* created a sensation by announcing the epic proportions of aerial warfare in a daring manner. The small rectangular screen suddenly expanded to create a huge field of vision in which biplanes and zeppelins fought to the death.

Landscapes of battle

The balance of epic and realistic elements in war films can be seen most clearly when the portrayal of landscapes of battle is examined. These took many forms, but the most popular and enduring concerned silhouettes of soldiers on battlefields, trench explosions at night, and scenes of the surrealistic chaos of battlefields. All these may be observed in stills from *All Quiet*, as well as in the fine 1931 film of the German director Pabst, *Westfront 1918,* as well as in the 1932 film version of Hemingway's *A Farewell to Arms*, directed by Frank Borzage.

It was probably the intention of these film-makers to show us the ugly side of combat. But one of the features of film itself is that even when the director wanted to present unremitting gloom, the very gloss of film sometimes took over. Visual beauty must often have softened the image of destruction with which the audience was left. The battle scenes in Pabst's *Westfront 1918,* staged and lit with great ingenuity and power, illustrate the ambiguous quality of war films, even when it is clear that the director intended to produce an indictment of the waste of war.

Visual beauty also marked another side of the filmic landscape of the war, namely the presentation of the war in the air. Many films celebrated this dashing side of the war. Among them was *Wings* (1927), an American film directed by William Wellman, starring Richard Arlen, Buddy Rogers and Clara Bow, with the young Gary Cooper in a supporting role. The most memorable aspect of this film is the footage of aerial combat. The same is true of another early film of the war in the air, *Hell's Angels*, directed by

Howard Hughes. This 1930 venture was planned as a silent film, replete with flaming zeppelins and soaring biplanes, and then turned into the first "talky" extravaganza.

The camaraderie of arms

A third major theme in the cinematic recreation of the war is the camaraderie of arms. Here too we are on the border between epic and realistic, for the notion of comradely affection and loyalty has occupied literature at least since the *Iliad.* The bonds formed by small groups of front soldiers were the most powerful supports of military morale. It is not surprising, therefore, that many films reflect this facet of the war.

A characteristic scene of many war films is exemplified by the 1936 film *The Road to Glory*, directed by Howard Hawks and starring Frederic March and Lionel Barrymore. It shows a group of soldiers in a bar or *estaminet*, cheerily drowning their fears in alcohol. In Gance's 1937 version of *J'Accuse* the same scene recurs, and this time the absence of women is temporarily compensated for by a doll, with whom one soldier dances.

This same theme of male companionship as the antidote to fear and despair is at the heart of perhaps the greatest film to be made about the war, Jean Renoir's masterpiece, *The Grand Illusion*, which appeared in 1937. There are many cinematic portraits of the community of the men of '14–18, but none of the stature of this remarkable film. Partly this was due to immaculate performances by some of the finest actors in the world, and partly to the subtlety of Renoir's direction, which was able to say so much about the war without showing us a single moment of combat or a single field of battle. It is not too rash to suggest that when all other World War I films fade away, *The Grand Illusion* will still remain as a masterpiece of the art of the cinema.

Romantic themes

If films recounting the camaraderie of arms raised enduring and timeless issues of how men retain their humanity in wartime, other films dealt with the equally universal subject of romance. Indeed, a dazzling array of leading ladies on the Continent or in the United States were obliged to make a film set during World War I. The casual encounters, the heart-rending separations, the shock of unrequited or lost love in wartime provided the elements of dozens of films.

One early example was *The White Sister* (1923), directed by Henry King and starring Lillian Gish and Ronald Colman. The flavor of many similar films may be savored by a brief review of the plot. Gish is a sheltered Italian aristocrat and Colman her fiancé. He is captured by Bedouin (!), and in a fit of bereavement, Gish gives up this world and becomes a nun. Imagine her surprise when Colman escapes from his captors and returns. The lovers struggle with the conflict between her vows and her heart. Finally her vows win, and she returns to the convent. Fortunately Colman too has a happy end: he dies bravely trying to rescue people threatened by an eruption of Mount Vesuvius.

This film, remade twice in the next decade, had all the elements of melodrama which seemed to thrive in a wartime setting. Alongside it may be placed the similar, though more somber, melodrama the *Dark Angel*. This film appeared in 1935, was directed by Sidney Franklin from a script by Lillian Hellman. The stars, Herbert Marshall and Merle Oberon, are lovers in Britain on the eve of war. Before Marshall goes over to France to do his bit, the lovers go to Dover and look for a priest to marry them. None is available, but they spend the night together in sin anyway. Some time later Marshall is blinded in combat, and while recovering, he conjures up the fear that on his return Oberon will marry him out of pity. So he first lets her think he is dead, then encourages her to believe he no longer loves her. But since films of this kind need a happy ending, her perseverance pays off, and they walk off together. Incidentally, the book from which the film was made left the lovers unreconciled. The screenplay was presumably given its happy ending in the interest of box office appeal.

There was also the *femme fatale* in the form of irresistible spy. The greatest of these was *Mata Hari* (1932), directed by George Fitzmaurice, and starring Lionel Barrymore and Roman Navarro with the incomparable Garbo. Among others of the same genre was *I Was A Spy*, a British film released in 1933, directed by Victor Saville for Conrad Veidt and Madeleine Carroll. This may have been intended to remind British audiences of the Nurse Cavell affair, which received a suitably noble cinematic treatment with Dame Anna Neagle as the doomed nurse (executed by Germans in Belgium in October 1915) in Herbert Wilcox's 1938 film *Nurse Edith Cavell.*

◀ *The White Sister* is the tale of a tragic love affair. Lovers are parted by war, and a false report of death on the field of battle leads the heroine to turn her back on this world and join a convent. The return of her lover from the dead presents her with a terrible choice. Her anguish and the outcome were so popular that the film, originally made in 1915, was remade not only in the version pictured here, showing Ronald Colman and Lillian Gish as the lovers, but also in 1933 with Helen Hayes and Clark Gable and in 1957 with Rock Hudson and Jennifer Jones.

▼ Howard Hawks's film *The Road to Glory* (1936) centered on the tragedy of a group of French soldiers ordered to hold their positions despite the certainty of death if they did so. It placed the French "lost generation" alongside that of Lewis Milestone's Germans in *All Quiet on the Western Front* as common victims of the war. As in the case of Renoir's *The Grand Illusion* (1937), the camaraderie of arms is a dominant theme, readily grasped in scenes where doomed men share wine, bread and good humor.

▲▶ The attractions of romantic melodrama mixed with a defense of patriotism marked many films about *femmes fatales* at war. Victor Saville's British film *I Was a Spy* (1933) presented (right) one doomed adventuress turned spy, played by Madeleine Carroll. But the role was given its most elegant performance by Greta Garbo in *Mata Hari* (1932). Garbo (above) seduces both Lionel Barrymore and Roman Navarro before paying with her life for being caught at the "game" of espionage.

The Growth of Cinema

In the period 1914–29 the film industry became the centerpiece of mass entertainment and a social force in its own right. Prewar cinema accompanied vaudeville acts, and many of the early stars, like Chaplin, emerged from the popular stage and music hall. While European cinema was set back by the war, the American motion-picture industry thrived. The allure of patriotic service through propaganda, added to substantial profits, drew talent and money to the industry. After the Armistice, American film imports to Europe were so numerous that we can speak of the birth of a transatlantic film culture. The introduction of sound films in 1927, with *The Jazz Singer,* starring Al Jolson, further reinforced the vogue of cinema-going, so evident in the immediate aftermath of the war.

In the 1920s in France and Germany there was a boom in cinema-theater construction, creating large and elegant halls for both the well-to-do and the masses. In 1919 the lavishly decorated Gaumont Palace in the Place Clichy in Paris had room for 5,000 viewers and an orchestra of 80. In the 1920s the theater entertained 4 million people each year. Small towns echoed this growth in their own way; the French village of Tulle (pop. 17,000) had two cinemas in the 1920s. The same exponential growth occurred in Germany and throughout Europe. Film making was a very profitable but high-risk business, with as many bankruptcies as successful enterprises.

▲ Gary Cooper immortalized the life of Alvin York, a Tennessee man who won a Congressional Medal of Honor by capturing single-handed over 100 Germans in the Argonne forests in 1918. York himself was reluctant to collaborate in making the film, but agreed when he heard that Cooper was to be given the lead. The film, directed by Howard Hawks, appeared five months before Pearl Harbor was attacked in 1941, and was a major critical and box office success.

▶ Released just four weeks before the Armistice, Chaplin's *Shoulder Arms* remains the most brilliant comic portrayal of the 1914–18 war. Chaplin's blend of slapstick and sentimentality uniquely caught the mood of veterans and civilians alike. During the war he made several short comedies and propaganda films, including a pitch for British War Loans with the veteran music hall star Harry Lauder. In *Shoulder Arms*, he had the assistance of his half-brother Sydney Chaplin, who played both the Kaiser and an American sergeant. What made the film so popular was Charlie's ability to poke fun at the absurdities of military life.

▼ Lewis Milestone's image of the hand of Paul Baumer, the central figure in Remarque's *All Quiet on the Western Front*, reaching out for a butterfly just as he is shot by a sniper, is perhaps the most famous image to emerge from the recreation of the 1914–18 war in film. Baumer was played by Lew Ayres, then an unknown actor, whose very anonymity helped Milestone direct the viewers' attention away from individuals to the tragedy of the war itself.

▲ Richard Attenborough's film *Oh! What a Lovely War* (1969) used the songs of the war to contrast the lyricism of popular culture with the horror and madness of trench warfare. In one scene, Sir Douglas Haig, played by John Mills (above), leapfrogs over a colleague to the tune of the contemporary ditty, "The First Staff Officer Jumped Right Over Another Staff Officer's Back". The good works he left behind him are shown in an endless field of crosses.

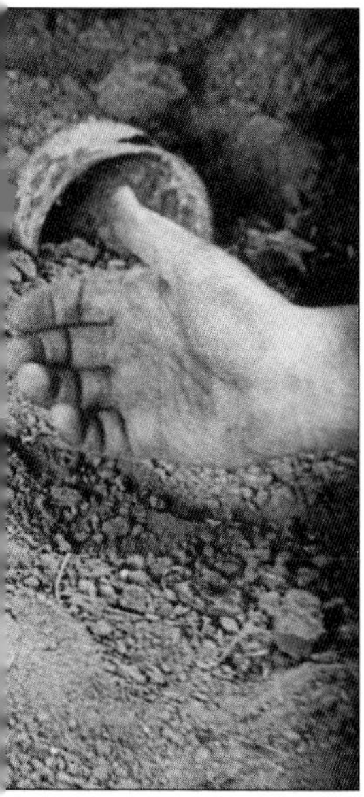

Noble warriors: comic and otherwise

In a sense, romantic films either humanized or trivialized the war, turning it from tragedy to melodrama. A similar transmutation took place with respect to comedy. For all who felt the need to escape into laughter, Charlie Chaplin was there at the ready. All accounts agree that he was the most popular film entertainer of the war and post-war periods. One of the greatest successes, particularly among ex-soldiers, was his short film fantasy *Shoulder Arms* (1918), in which he dreams of capturing the Kaiser, and engages in some extraordinary military mayhem. The genius of Chaplin was simply unique, but we should not underestimate how close to real life his acting was. In addition, in this wartime spoof – as in so many of his other films – Chaplin touched everybody's sympathy as the man struggling against a machine far more powerful than he is, and every kick he planted on the seat of authority was cheered by millions who knew what military life was all about.

By the 1930s Laurel and Hardy got into another fine World War I mess in *Pack Up Your Troubles* (1932), and the Marx brothers had made the war film to end all war films, *Duck Soup* (1937). Other lesser works followed, but it still remains the case that the center of the comic stage in the cinema of World War I is occupied by Chaplin.

There were of course other, more somber, noble warriors. German films about submarine warfare attested to the bravery of the men who almost won the war. The stoical acceptance of duty was reiterated in the British film *Journey's End* (1930), directed by James Whale, and starring Colin Clive in the tragic role of Lt Stanhope. A powerful American gloss was given to this theme in *Sergeant York* (1941), directed by Howard Hawks. It portrays Gary Cooper as a pacifist country boy turned military hero, and clearly must be set in the context of the campaign to bring the United States into World War II. Noble warriors abound in virtually all countries' filmic recreation of the conflict.

Pacifism and the pity of war

From myth to landscape to camaraderie to romance to comedy: this interpretation of the ways in which film recreated World War I suggests a very rough and nonchronological descent in war films from the rarefied air of the mythical return of the dead, to the vast panoramas of battle, to the moving portraits of military companionship, and then to the perhaps more readily identifiable reaches of romance and comedy. This approach tends to ignore the one genre not yet discussed: the overtly political interpretation of the war. It is important, though, to recognize that, with one major exception, this kind of film was not central to the cinematic recapitulation of the war in the interwar years and after. The exception is the original version of *All Quiet on the Western Front*, which was so powerful that the Nazi party rioted and successfully prevented it being shown in Germany on its arrival in 1930. This film was considered an intolerable assault on Nazi views about the glories of the war.

Stanley Kubrick's 1957 film *Paths of Glory* is another rare example of a pacifist film. Set in the French sector of the Western Front, it tells the story of a plot by evil and twisted generals to cover up their insane strategy of frontal assault by shooting three ordinary soldiers for cowardice after an abortive attack on an impregnable German position. Far from being cowards, these men were ordinary people chosen to stand trial for arbitrary or malicious reasons. Kirk Douglas plays an officer who defends the three men on trial for their lives, but even his stirring rhetoric fails and the men are shot. Given the nature of the film, we should perhaps not be too surprised to learn that it took decades before it was licensed for commercial distribution in France.

Two more recent examples of this genre are the British music hall satire *Oh! What a Lovely War* (1969), directed by Richard Attenborough and adapted from Joan Littlewood's play, and *Gallipoli*, an Australian film made in 1982 by Peter Weir. Both have a clear vision of the war as a catastrophe in which men's lives were thrown away for nothing, and appear to be statements as much about Vietnam as World War I.

But whatever the contemporary echoes, it is understandable that the message of the futility of war, the truth of which some war poets knew well before the Armistice in 1918, was not particularly prominent in earlier filmic recreations of World War I. Instead films – especially those of the interwar years – tended to sanitize the war, to remove some of its harsher features, and thereby to enable both those who went through it and those born long after 1918 to create in their mind a different war, a filmic war which could be remembered in a heroic or romantic haze.

Of course some filmmakers tried to do the opposite and make an equally unreal one-dimensional view of the war as unmitigated horror and waste. Here too myth displaced reality, and gave those who wanted it a cinematic reinforcement of their political beliefs.

With rare exceptions, therefore, the real effect of the extraordinarily popular medium of film has been not to record but to recreate the war in an imaginary form. This is one (but surely not the only) way that World War I has turned into a legendary event. After all, a legend is simply a narrative of events, which may have happened, but which are recreated to suit the purposes of the author and his audience.

Naturally, the war has been remembered in many other ways too. In public ceremonies, like Armistice Day, and in the erection of countless war memorials in tiny hamlets and obscure village churchyards, ordinary people continue to meditate on the earth-shattering events of their times, or of their fathers' time. But the accident that World War I ended just as the cinema came into its own as a medium of popular entertainment and popular culture inevitably gave it a central role in the redefinition of precisely what happened in 1914–18. Perhaps the war of 1914–18 was too terrible to remember; if so, the cinema has been one of the most important agencies of what the Czech writer Milan Kundera has called the necessary arts of laughter and forgetting.

THE GRAND ILLUSION: FILM AS ELEGY

Perhaps the greatest film to be made about the war is Jean Renoir's masterpiece, *The Grand Illusion*, which appeared in 1937.

The company directed by Renoir played a group of French prisoners of war, all officers and airmen shot down over German lines, who represented a cross-section of French society. Among them are the central figures of de Bœldieu, the aristocrat and career officer, played by Pierre Fresnay; the rich Jew, Rosenthal, played by Marcel Dalio; and the ordinary Parisian worker, Maréchal, played by Jean Gabin.

The first part of the film presents these men as they fight boredom and think about escape. To wile away the time the Frenchmen in captivity are given costumes for a vaudeville performance in drag. As they receive the clothes, the youngest-looking soldier among them, Maisonneuve, puts on a woman's dress, and to the unnerved astonishment of the others who had not seen a woman for years, becomes femininity itself. The performance is a comic success, until reality intervenes.

Gabin interrupts the show to bring to the French soldiers and their German captors the news that the French have retaken the fort of Douaumont at Verdun. They burst into *La Marseillaise*, (the French national anthem), forcing the German officers to leave and to throw Gabin into solitary confinement.

After repeated and unsuccessful attempts at escape, the prisoners wind up in a fortress prison commanded by none other than von Rauffenstein, played by Erich von Stroheim, who had shot down Maréchal and de Bœldieu in the first scenes of the film. The social bond between the two career officers draws them together, but the national bond and the bonds of camaraderie prove stronger still.

De Bœldieu devises an ingenious diversionary plan to play a pipe on the roof of the castle – and thereby really becomes, as his name suggests, the "god of the forest" – and to draw his captors' attention away from his escaping comrades. This succeeds precisely as planned, but at the cost of de Bœldieu's life, mortally wounded by his brother-in-arms, Rauffenstein. Maréchal and Rosenthal, aided by a German war widow, who takes pity on them, finally reach Switzerland and safety.

These brief references to the plot only give a hint of the brilliance and humanity of this film in recreating the world of the soldiers of 1914–18, which Renoir knew of, having served in the French air force. He later said that the story was a true one, but whatever its source, his film provides the most moving tribute to the men who fought on both sides of the conflict.

▲ French officers (top), from all social levels, watch a military parade from their prison window in Germany.

▲ Preparations for a prison show stop when one soldier dresses up as a woman, and awakens dormant memories.

► Bœldieu on the prison roof, courting death to cover the escape of his fellow officers, Rosenthal and Maréchal.

► Bœldieu to Rauffenstein: "For a man of the people, it's terrible to die in the war. For you and me, it is a good solution."

FURTHER READING

Introduction

On Germany's military gambles: M. Kitchen, *A Military History of Germany* (London, 1970).

The Politicians' War

On German responsibility for war: V. Berghahn, *Germany and the Approach of War in 1914* (London, 1973); H. Mommsen, "The topos of inevitable war in Germany in the decade before 1914", in V. Berghahn and M. Kitchen (eds.), *Germany in the Age of Total War* (London, 1980).

On miscalculations and illusions: J. Joll, *1914: The Unspoken Assumptions* (London, 1968).

On war as redemption: R. Stromberg, *Redemption by War: the Intellectuals and 1914* (Lawrence, Kansas, 1982).

On war as escape: M. Ferro (trans. N. Stone), *The Great War 1914–1918* (London, 1973).

On Italian intervention: D. Mack Smith, *Mussolini* (London, 1982); J. Whittam, "War and Italian society 1914–16", in B. Bond and I. Roy (eds.), *War and Society: a Yearbook of Military History* (London, 1975).

On French civil–military relations: J.C. King, *Politicians and Generals* (New York, 1951).

On the German war economy: G. Feldman, *Army, Industry and Labor in Germany, 1914–1918* (Princeton, N.J., 1966); J. Lee, "Administrators and agriculture: some aspects of German agricultural policy in the First World War", in J.M. Winter (ed.), *War and Economic Development* (Cambridge, 1975).

On the French war economy: J. Godfrey, *Capitalism at War: Industrial Policy and Bureaucracy in France 1914–1918* (Leamington Spa, 1987).

On the British war economy: K. Burk (ed.), *War and the State* (London, 1984).

On German dissent: F. Carsten, *War against War: British and German Radical Movements in the First World War* (London, 1982).

On the U-boat campaign: M. Kitchen, *The Silent Dictatorship: the Politics of the German High Command under Hindenburg and Ludendorff, 1916–18* (London, 1976).

On the Russian peace campaign of 1917: R. Wade, *The Russian Search for Peace* (Stanford, Calif., 1969).

On Allied intervention in Russia: R.H. Ullman, *Intervention and the War* (Princeton, N.J., 1961)

On the sources of Germany's defeat: W. Diest, *Militär und Innenpolitik im Weltkrieg 1914–18* (Düsseldorf, 1970).

The Generals' War

On command: M. van Creveld, *Command in War* (Cambridge, Mass., 1985); T. Wilson, *The Myriad Faces of War* (Oxford, 1986).

On the Schlieffen Plan: M. van Creveld, *Supplying War* (Cambridge, 1978); G. Ritter, *The Schlieffen Plan* (London, 1968).

On Tannenberg and on Russia, 1914–17: N. Stone, *The Eastern Front, 1914–1917* (London, 1975).

On the war at sea: R. Hough, *The Great War at Sea, 1914–18* (Oxford, 1983).

On the naval blockades: C.P. Vincent, *The Politics of Hunger: the Allied Blockade of Germany, 1915–1919* (Athens, Ohio, 1985).

On Gallipoli: R.R. James, *Gallipoli* (London, 1965).

On Verdun: A. Horne, *The Price of Glory: Verdun, 1916* (London, 1962); J.-J. Becker, *La Première Guerre mondiale* (Paris, 1985).

On the Somme: J. Keegan, *The Face of Battle* (London, 1975).

On the Chemin des Dames: A. Ducasse, J. Meyer, G. Perreux, *Vie et mort des Français 1914–1918* (Paris, 1959); J.-J. Becker, *La Première Guerre mondiale* (Paris, 1985).

On Passchendaele: T. Wilson, *The Myriad Faces of War* (Oxford, 1986).

On the American entry into the war: A.J. Link, *Woodrow Wilson* (Princeton, N.J., 1970).

On the March 1918 offensive: M. van Creveld, *Command in War* (Cambridge, Mass., 1985); M. Middlebrook, *The Kaiser's Battle* (London, 1980).

The Soldiers' War

On recruitment in Britain: J.M. Winter, *The Great War and the British People* (London, 1985).

On the baptism of fire: J.N. Cru, *War Books* (Santa Barbara, Calif., 1980).

On the structure of the German army: *Handbook of the German Army in War: January, 1917* (Wakefield, Yorkshire, 1973).

On military discipline: D. Winter, *Death's Men: Soldiers of the Great War* (London, 1978).

On the trench system: J. Meyer, *La Vie quotidienne des soldats pendant la grande guerre* (Paris, 1966); T. Ashworth, *Trench Warfare 1914–1918: the Live and Let Live System* (London, 1980).

On soldiers' songs: J. Brophy and E. Partridge, *The Long Trail* (London, 1967).

On the live and let live system: T. Ashworth, *Trench Warfare 1914–1918: the Live and Let Live System* (London, 1980).

On the contents of a *poilu*'s knapsack: H. Barbusse, *Under Fire* (London, 1917).

On gas warfare: L.F. Haber, *The Poisonous Cloud: Chemical Warfare in the First World War* (Oxford, 1985).

On casualty rates: B. Urlanis, *Wars and Population* (Moscow, 1971); J.M. Winter, *The Great War and the British People* (London, 1985).

On morale: E. Leed, *No Man's Land: Combat and Identity in World War I* (Cambridge, 1979); S. Audoin-Rouzeau, *14–18: Les Combattants des tranchées* (Paris, 1987); C. Moran, *The Anatomy of Courage* (London, 1945); J. Keegan, *The Face of Battle* (London, 1975).

On the French mutiny: G. Pedroncini, *Les Mutineries de 1917* (Paris, 1967); J.-J. Becker, *La Première Guerre mondiale* (Paris, 1985); S. Audoin-Rouzeau, *14–18: Les Combattants des tranchées* (Paris, 1987); D. Englander, "The French soldier, 1914–18", *French History* (1987).

On the German naval mutiny: D. Horn, *Mutiny on the High Seas: the Imperial German Naval Mutinies of World War I* (London, 1973); A. Rosenberg, *Imperial Germany: the Birth of the German Republic* (New York, 1970).

On Étaples: D. Gill and G. Dallas, *The Unknown Army* (London, 1985).

The Civilians' War

On public opinion in 1914: J.-J. Becker, *The Great War and the French People* (Leamington Spa, 1985).

On the collapse of socialist internationalism: G. Haupt, *Socialism and the Great War* (Oxford, 1972); J.P. Nettl, "The German Social Democratic party as a political model", *Past and Present* (1965).

On intellectuals and war: R. Stromberg, *Redemption by War: the Intellectuals and 1914* (Lawrence, Kansas, 1982); R. Wohl, *The Generation of 1914* (Cambridge, Mass., 1979); J.M. Winter, *Socialism and the Challenge of War* (London, 1974).

On the press: P. Knightley, *The First Casualty* (London, 1975); C. Bellanger *et al.* (eds.), *Histoire générale de la presse française* (Paris, 1980), vol. 3.

On the bishop of London: S. Mews, "Spiritual mobilization in the First World War", *Theology*, vol. lxxiv (1971).

On pacifism: M. Ceadel, *Pacifism in Britain 1914–1945* (Oxford, 1980); J.D. Shand, "Doves among eagles: German pacifists and their government during World War I", *Journal of Contemporary History* (1975).

On wartime labor and on women's work: J.M. Winter and R.M. Wall (eds.), *The Upheaval of War: Family, Work and Welfare in Europe 1914–1918* (Cambridge, 1988).

On women, sex and gender: M.R. Higgonet *et. al.* (eds.), *Behind the Lines: Gender and the Two World Wars* (New Haven, Conn., 1987); J.M. Winter and R.M. Wall (eds.), *The Upheaval of War* (Cambridge, 1988); F. Thébaud, *La Femme au temps de la guerre de 14* (Paris, 1986).

On living standards: J. Kocka, *Facing Total War: German Society 1914–1918* (Leamington Spa, 1984); L. Burchardt, "The impact of the war economy on the civilian population of Germany during the First and Second World Wars", in W. Deist (ed.), *The German Military in the Age of Total War* (Leamington Spa, 1985); J.M. Winter, *The Great War and the British People* (London, 1985); J.M. Winter and R.M. Wall (eds.), *The Upheaval of War* (Cambridge, 1988).

On labor unrest and class conflict: J.-J. Becker, *The Great War and the French People* (Leamington Spa, 1985); P. Fridenson (ed.), *1914–1918: L'Autre Front* (Paris, 1977); B. Moore, *Injustice* (London, 1982); J. Hinton, *The First Shop Stewards' Movement* (London, 1974); J. Cronin, "Labor insurgency and class formation", *Social Science History* (1980); J. Kocka, *Facing Total War* (Leamington Spa, 1984); B. Waites, *A Class Society at War* (Leamington Spa, 1987).

On propaganda: H.G. Marquis, "Words as weapons: propaganda in Britain and Germany during the First World War", *Journal of Contemporary History*, vol. xii (1978); and H.D. Lasswell, *Propaganda Technique in World War I* (London, 1927); G.D. Bruntz, *Allied Propaganda and the Collapse of the German Empire in 1918* (Palo Alto, Calif., 1938).

On Paris in wartime: E. Hausser, *Paris au jour de jour: Les Évènements vus par la presse 1906–1919* (Paris, n.d.); H. Sellier, *Paris pendant la guerre* (Paris, 1926).

On the Russian Revolution: J.P. Nettl, *The Soviet Achievement* (London, 1967); L. Trotsky, *The History of the Russian Revolution* (London, 1965); E.H. Carr, *A History of Soviet Russia* (London, 1950–).

The Shadow of War

On peacemaking: A. Mayer, *The Politics and Diplomacy of Peacemaking: Containment and Counter-revolution at Versailles 1918–1919* (New York, 1967).

On colonialism: R. von Albertini, "The impact of two world wars on the decline of colonialism", *Journal of Contemporary History* (1969).

On the economic consequences of the war: J.M. Keynes, *The Economic Consequences of the Peace* (London, 1919); G. Hardach, *The First World War* (London, 1976).

On the demographic consequences of the war: J.M. Winter, *The Great War and the British People* (London, 1985); B. Urlanis, *Wars and Population* (Moscow, 1971); J.M. Winter and R.M. Wall (eds.), *The Upheaval of War* (Cambridge, 1988).

On disabled veterans: R.H. Whalen, *Bitter Wounds: German Victims of the Great War* (Ithaca, N.Y., 1984).

On remembrance ceremonies: D. Cannadine, "War and death, grief and mourning in modern Britain", in D. Whaley (ed.), *Mirrors of Mortality* (London, 1981); A. Prost, *Anciens combattants et la société française 1914–1939* (Paris, 1970); A. Prost, "Monuments aux morts", in P. Nora (ed.), *Les Lieux de mémoire* (Paris, 1985); G. Mosse, *The Myth of the War Experience* (New York, 1988).

On the German revolution: J.P. Nettl, *Rosa Luxemburg* (London, 1966); A.J. Ryder, *The German Revolution of 1918* (Cambridge, 1967); R. Rurup, "Problems of the German revolution", *Journal of Contemporary History* (1968).

On ex-soldiers' politics: D. Mack Smith, *Mussolini* (London, 1981); S. Ward (ed.), *The War Generation* (Port Washington, N.Y., 1975); A. Prost, *Anciens combattants et la société française 1914–1939* (Paris, 1970).

The Memory of War

On war literature: P. Fussell, *The Great War and Modern Memory* (London, 1975); J.M. Winter, *The Great War and the British People* (London, 1985); H. Klein (ed.), *The First World War in Fiction* (London, 1976); C. Reilly (ed.), *Scars Upon My Heart. Women's Poetry and Verse of the First World War* (London, 1981); F. Field, *Three French Writers and the Great War* (Cambridge, 1970); E.M. Remarque and Sir I. Hamilton, "The end of war?", *Life and Letters*, vol. iii (1929); M. Howard, "Military experience in literature", *Essays by Divers Hands: Transactions of the Royal Society of Literature* (1980).

On war artists: K. Silver, *Esprit de Corps* (New Haven, Conn., 1989); E. Kahn, *The Neglected Majority* (Lanham, Maryland, 1984); M. Eberle, *World War I and the Weimar Artists* (New Haven, Conn., 1984).

On war film: K. Brownlow, *The War, the West and the Wilderness* (London, 1979); M. Eksteins, "*All Quiet on the Western Front* and the fate of a war", *Journal of Contemporary History*, vol. xiv (1980); J. Daniel, *Guerre et cinéma: grandes illusions et petits soldats 1895–1971* (Paris, 1972); J. Renoir (trans. M. Alexandre and A. Sinclair), *La Grande Illusion* (London, 1968).

Sources of quotations

34 **Norman Angell** *The Great Illusion* (1910)
55 Wilhelm Groener *Lebenserinnerungen* (1957)
65 Woodrow Wilson *War and Peace: Presidential Messages, Addresses, and Public Papers 1917–1924* (1927)
75 Paul von Hindenburg *Out of My Life* (1920)
77 Sir Alfred Knox *With the Russian Army, 1914–17* (1921)
85 Erich Ludendorff *My War Memories 1914–18* (1919)
96 *Sir Douglas Haig's Despatches* (1919)
99 A.A. Brussilov *A Soldier's Notebook* (1930)
107 J.J. Pershing *My Experiences in the World War* (1931)
116 Stefan Zweig *The World of Yesterday* (1943)
131 René Arnaud *Tragédie Buffe* (1966)
142 Vera Brittain *Testament of Youth* (1933)
148 Harry W. Blackburne *This Also Happened on the Western Front* (1932)
150 D.L. Neave *Remembering Kut* (1937)
156 Henri Desagneaux *A Soldier's War Diary 1914–1918* (1975)
158 D. Horn (ed. and trans.) *War, Mutiny and Revolution in the German Navy* (1967)
178 Decie Denholm (ed.) *Behind the Lines* (1982)
186 Morton Price (ed.) *Sixty American Opinions on the War* (1915)
195 Gustav Noske *Erlebtes aus Aufstieg und Niedergang einer Demokratie* (1947)
204 J.M. Keynes *The Economic Consequences of the Peace* (1919)
213 Gustav Noske *Erlebtes aus Aufstieg und Niedergang einer Demokratie* (1947)

ACKNOWLEDGMENTS

Picture credits

1 British soldier and cross: IWM
2–3 Russian prisoners after the Battle of Tannenberg: Robert Hunt Library, London
4 German prisoners, 1918: IWM
6 Arras Cathedral: IWM
22 Czar Nicholas II (Russia) and President Poincaré (France): HPL
66 General Fritz von Below and staff (Germany): IWM
110 Australian troops at Château Wood near Ypres, 1917: IWM
160 Belgian refugees: NAW
198 Ruins of the Cloth Hall, Ypres: IWM
222 Battle scene from *All Quiet on the Western Front*: National Film Archive, London

11 RV **12–13** IWM **15** Historisches Archiv F. Krupp, Essen **21t** RV **21c** IWM **21 bl** IWM **21br** BDIC **27** EPA **28** Edimedia, Paris **29t** HPL **29b** HPL **30t** PNL **30–31t** BSV **30c** HPL **30–31b** ADNZ **30b** EPA **31** HPL **32–33** BSV **33** Musée Royal de l'Armée et d'Histoire Militaire, Brussels **34** ADNZ **35t** HPL **35c** RV **35b** RV **36** Popperfoto **36–37** HPL **38t** HPL **38–39** HPL **38b** HPL **39** EPA **40–41** IWM **40** HPL **44t** BSV **44b** HPL **44–45** UB **45** HPL **46–47** IWM **46** HPL **47** RV **48** *Punch* **49t** HPL **49b** HPL **50–51** IWM **53l** IWM **53r** NAW **54t** UB **54c** Popperfoto **54b** ADNZ **55** Institut für Marxismus–Leninismus, Berlin **56t** RV **56b** HPL **57** National Museum of Ireland, Dublin **59** Popperfoto **60** EPA **60–61** HPL **61t** HPL **61ct** Novosti Press Agency, London **61cb** Robert Hunt Library, London **61b** BSV **62** BDIC **62–63** BSV **63** HPL **64** RV **64–65** Popperfoto **65** EPA **71** HPL **72tl** HPL **72cl** ADNZ **72bl** ADNZ **72br** BSV **74–75** HPL **74** Popperfoto **75** UB **76** IWM **77** ADNZ **78–79** BSV **79t** UB **79c** Popperfoto **79b** IWM **80** HPL **82t** HPL **82b** EPA **83t** HPL **83b** EPA **84** UB **85t** HPL **85b** RV **86–87** ADNZ **87l** BSV **87t** ADNZ **87c** IWM **87b** IWM **89tl** HPL **89bl** ADNZ **89r** BSV **90** UB **90–91** Librairie Larousse, Paris **91** Jean-Loup Charmet, Paris **92t** EPA **92b** ADNZ **93** IWM **94** HPL **95** IWM **96** IWM **96–97** IWM **98** IWM **99t** IWM **99b** EPA **100** TM **101tr** TM **101tc** TM **101br** NAW **101l** IWM **103** IWM **104l** EPA **104r** EPA **105** BSV **107t** HPL **107b** IWM **108–109** UB **108tl** IWM **108bl** NAW **108r** IWM **109t** IWM **109b** IWM **113** IWM **115** Librairie Larousse, Paris **116** EPA **117t** Popperfoto **117b** EPA **118–119** IWM **118** IWM **119l** IWM **119r** IWM **120t** EPA **120b** St Helens Public Library, St Helens, UK **121** PNL **122–123** BSV **122t** IWM **122b** BSV **123l** IWM **123r** ADNZ **125** PNL **126t** Popperfoto **126b** Popperfoto **128** IWM **128–129** IWM **130t** IWM **130b** IWM **131** Jean-Loup Charmet, Paris **132t** (cards) PNL **132c** Popperfoto **132b** HPL **132–133** Elsevier Séquoia, Brussels **133l** IWM **133r** Jean-Loup Charmet, Paris **134–135** Robert Hunt Library, London **135** IWM **136t** IWM **136b** EPA **136–137** IWM **138–139** BSV **139tr** HPL **139cr** IWM **139br** IWM **139b** NAW **140–141** HPL **142t** PNL **142b** Novosti Press Agency, London **142–143** IWM **143t** Popperfoto **143b** ADNZ **144** IWM **145t** **IWM** **145b** IWM **146t** IWM **146b** RV **146–147** RV **148l** IWM **148r** HPL **149t** NAW **149b** HPL **150–151** IWM **150** IWM **151t** IWM **151b** Bundesarchiv, Koblenz **152l** BSV **152r** RV **152–153** IWM **153l** HPL **153r** UB **155** BDIC **156–157** NAW **157** Bibliothèque Nationale, Paris **158t** UB **158b** IWM **159** IWM **162–163** IWM **165** RV **166** HPL **167t** BSV **167b** EPA **168t** Popperfoto **168b** *Illustrated London News*, London **168–169** EPA **169** RV **170–171** Harris Collection, Bampton, UK **170** Jean-Loup Charmet, Paris **171l** Edimedia, Paris **171tr** RV **171cr** Edimedia, Paris **171br** RV **173** IWM **174t** IWM **174c** EPA **174b** IWM **174–175** UB **175** IWM **176** IWM **177** IWM **178** UB **179t** Popperfoto **179b** RV **180–181** (all) Reginald Mott, Cobham, UK **183** Phaidon Press Picture Archive, Oxford, UK **184tl** IWM **184tr** PNL **184b** IWM **185tl** BDIC **185bl** IWM **185r** IWM **186** NAW **187l** EPA **187r** EPA **188** EPA **189l** PNL **189tr** IWM **189cr** BDIC **189br** BDIC **190–191** EPA **190tl** IWM **190tr** Robert Hunt Library, London **190b** BSV **191t** IWM **191b** BSV **192–193** Edimedia, Paris **194t** Popperfoto **194b** Novosti Press Agency **195** HPL **196t** HPL **196c** BDIC **196b** IWM **197t** EPA **197b** EPA **202–203** NAW **203** HPL **204** UB **205t** HPL **205b** HPL **206–207** UB **206t** HPL **206b** ADNZ **207** IWM **208–209** Popperfoto **209t** Popperfoto **209c** Weimar Archive, Telford, UK **209b** Popperfoto **211** BSV **212** Keystone Collection, London **213t** HPL **213b** Institut für Marxismus–Leninismus, Berlin **214t** Keystone Collection, London **214b** UB **215** HPL **216–217** IWM **217** IWM **218** HPL **218–219** HPL **219t** HPL **219b** Mansell Collection, London **220t** HPL **220b** HPL **221** HPL **227** RV **227** (inset) RV **228tl** HPL **228tr** Robert Hunt Library, London **228bl** HPL **228cr** HPL **228br** IWM **229t** IWM **229b** IWM **230–231** IWM **231** IWM **232** IWM **233tl** BDIC **233tr** IWM **233b** IWM **234t** Tate Gallery, London **234c** IWM **234b** IWM **234–235** IWM **236l** Nationalgalerie, Berlin (West) **236tr** Galerie der Stadt, Stuttgart **236br** EPA **237** Nationalgalerie, Berlin (West) **239** NAW **240–247** (all photos) National Film Archive, London

ADNZ	Allgemeiner Deutscher Nachrichtendienst, Zentralbild, Berlin (East)
BDIC	Bibliothèque de Documentation Internationale Contemporaine, Paris
BSV	Bilderdienst Süddeutscher Verlag, Munich
EPA	Equinox Picture Archive, Oxford, UK
HPL	Hulton Picture Library, London
IWM	Trustees of the Imperial War Museum, London
NAW	National Archives, Washington
PNL	Pictorial Nostalgia Library, West Wickham, UK
Popperfoto	Popperfoto, London
RV	Roger-Viollet, Paris
TM	The Tank Museum, Bovington Camp, Wareham, UK
UB	Ullstein Bilderdienst, Berlin (West)

Abbreviations

t = top, tl = top left, tr = top right, c = center, b = bottom, etc.

Author's acknowledgments
I am grateful to the following people and institutions who have helped me in the course of the preparation of this book: the staff of the British Film Institute, the Imperial War Museum, the British Library, the Cambridge University Library, the Musée de Cinéma et Cinémathèque Française and the Bibliothèque de Documentation Internationale Contemporaine (BDIC) in Paris. Special thanks are due to Cécile Couttin, whose kindness was especially welcome on my visits to her remarkable collection of French graphic art in the BDIC archive in the Hôtel des Invalides. For advice and guidance on points particular and general, I would like to thank my teacher and friend, Fritz Stern, and Mary Bernard, Volker Berghahn, Marion Berghahn, Heather Glen, Jacqueline Hecht, Peter Martland, Kenneth Silver, as well as scores of students at Cambridge who listened, criticized and unwittingly helped me to write this book. Thanks are also due to the historians who contributed Special Features and Ancillary Features based on their specialist interests. A congenial environment in which to finish this study was provided by colleagues and staff of the Institute for Advanced Studies of the Hebrew University of Jerusalem.

Equinox acknowledgments
Equinox (Oxford) Ltd wishes to thank the following people and institutions for their help in making this book: Shirley Jamieson, Claire Jones, Andrew Lawson, Reginald Mott, William Philpott, Dave Smith, Graham Speake, Del Tolton; Bodleian Library, Oxford; Imperial War Museum, London; London Library.

Artists
Robert and Rhoda Burns, Chris Forsey, Alan Hollingbery, Colin Salmon

Maps drawn and originated by Alan Mais, Hornchurch; Lovell Johns, Oxford.

Index
Ann Barrett

INDEX

Page numbers in *italics* refer to illustrations or their captions and to datafile captions. **Bold** page numbers refer to the subjects of special or ancillary text features.